Theatrical Design and Production

An Introduction to Scene Design and Construction, Lighting, Sound, Costume, and Makeup

J. MICHAEL GILLETTE

University of Arizona

Mayfield Publishing Company
Palo Alto, California

For Joyce Ann, who knows why.

Library of Congress Catalog Card Number: 86-061128
International Standard Book Number: 0-87484-578-5

Manufactured in the United States of America
10   9   8   7   6   5   4   3

Mayfield Publishing Company
1240 Villa Street
Mountain View, CA 94041

Sponsoring editor: C. Lansing Hays
Developmental editor: Janet M. Beatty
Production coordinator: Nancy Sjöberg/Del Mar Associates
Manuscript editor: William Waller
Designer: John Odam
Art director: Cynthia Bassett
Managing editor: Pat Herbst
Production manager: Cathy Willkie
Compositor: Allservice Phototypesetting
Printer and binder: Maple-Vail Book Manufacturing Group

Cover:
Sunday in the Park
Photo: © Martha Swope
Costume design: Tricia Zipprodt and Ann Hould-Ward
Scenic design: Tony Straiges
Lighting design: Richard Nelson
Theatre: The Booth Theatre, New York

First courses in the world of theatrical design and production, like the art they introduce, come in a bewildering array of shapes, sizes, textures, and colors. Some students receive their introduction to this subject area in a general overview course that covers the design and production elements of scenery, costumes, lighting, and sound in a single semester. Other students may enjoy the luxury of an entire year in which to discuss the same material. Still others may take individual courses that specialize in the theory and craft of the separate areas that comprise the field of theatrical design and technical production. The course content is very flexible indeed.

To create a text that will serve the needs of all these courses is a distinct challenge. I've tried to rise to that challenge by organizing the material in two ways. The chapters appear in a logical sequence, but each chapter is also an island of information that can stand alone. My hope is that this organization will enable each instructor to pick and choose the type and amount of material that is appropriate for his or her particular course. This type of organization also makes the text a useful reference work for students to keep throughout their design and technical production careers.

Organization and Content

Just as a play wouldn't start without the scenery being in place, this book doesn't delve into technical procedures without first setting the stage. Chapters 1 through 4, *Production Organization and Management, The Design Process, Theatre Architecture,* and *The Stage and Its Equipment,* provide a grounding in real world issues and are appropriate for use in almost any type of technical production class.

Of special significance is Chapter 2, *The Design Process.* It contains material new to beginning technical theatre texts. It is a problem-solving and conceptual-thinking model created specifically for theatrical practice. Its purpose is to increase each student's creative capacity by reducing the effects of two prime ingredients of creative dysfunction—fear and frustration. The mechanism used to effect this change is a seven-step procedure that enables students to make logical, rational, and considered decisions when making the myriad choices involved in creating a design or solving a technical challenge in any area of theatrical production.

Chapter 3, *Theatre Architecture,* provides a concise chronology, both pictorially and textually, of the history of theatre architecture. I've included this information for two reasons: the functional design of the environment in which a play is produced has always been a major factor in determining the type, style, and design of technical elements used in a production, and all too frequently student designers are not required to take courses in theatre history.

Chapter 13, *Electrical Theory and Practice,* provides a concise explanation of the nature and function of electricity and electronics, the practical use of the power formula, as well as information on wiring practices and standards.

The last three chapters in the book, *Mechanical Drafting, Perspective,* and *Rendering,* contain specific how-to information on the drawing and rendering techniques most commonly used in theatrical production. Chapter 18, *Mechanical Drafting,* provides information about the materials and types of drafting used in the theatre and helpful hints on the process of drafting. Chapter 19, *Perspective,* offers a step-by-step procedure *with exercises* for drawing in accurate scale mechanical perspective. Chapter 20, *Rendering,* provides an overview of the types of paints, pastels, markers, and papers commonly used in theatrical rendering as well as information on basic application techniques used with these media.

The remainder of the text provides an overview of the function and responsibilities of the scenic, lighting, costume, and sound designers. It also contains primary information about the tools and basic techniques that are used to bring each designer's concepts to the stage.

As with any art form, the basic element necessary for creating a successful design in theatre is an understanding of design principles and chosen medium. I hope that this text not only provides those basics, but also offers encouragement and inspiration to create.

Features

In many ways, *Theatrical Design and Production* is a traditional introductory text for the various design and craft areas of theatrical production. A number of features, however, strive to set this text apart.

PHILOSOPHY The underlying spirit of this text is firmly rooted in my belief that learning and creating in the various fields of theatrical design and production can be, and should be, fun. With that thought in mind I've tried to make this text not only informative and practical but also motivating and inspirational.

COLOR SECTION The sixteen-page color section presents a discussion of the practical applications of color theory by analyzing the interactive effects of the color selections for the scenery, costumes, and lighting for two productions—one with a very narrow, muted palette and the other with a full spectrum, heavily saturated color style.

SAFETY TIPS Safety tips are discussed throughout the text. They have been placed in special boxes adjacent to the relevant text to help readers integrate learning about a tool, material, or process with its safe use.

RUNNING GLOSSARY To help students learn and remember the vocabulary of the theatre, new terms are defined in the margin on the page where they first appear.

BOXED MATERIAL Additional material that provides further depth and practical information has been placed in boxes outside the mainstream text. This added material is included to enhance student understanding by providing insights into and solutions to real theatrical problems.

ILLUSTRATION PROGRAM An extensive photo and illustration program provides a very strong adjunct to the textual information. Photos from professional theatre productions are used to provide a model that students can strive to emulate.

Acknowledgments

There are a great number of people whose contributions, encouragement, and counsel have helped to shape this text. I'd like to thank them all, but I especially want to express my sincere appreciation to Peggy Kellner for her designs, drawings, counsel, and enthusiasm; Shari Warburton for her help and research on the costume chapter; Tom Benson for his designs, scene painting work, and dedication to quality theatre; Peter Wexler for the generous donation of his designs and advice; Susan Lesnik for her review of the material for the design process; Paul Reinhardt for his design work, encouragement, and friendship; and Pam Rank for the innumerable excellent suggestions that she made in her review of the manuscript for this text.

I am especially indebted to my father, A. S. Gillette, who gave me a love for theatre, drew the majority of the line drawings for this book, offered many outstanding suggestions, and remained unfailingly enthusiastic throughout the book's gestation.

This book would never have come to fruition without the continuous support, encouragement, and friendship of Lansing Hays. His faith in the project was of paramount importance to me. I also owe a special debt of gratitude to Jan Beatty, the developmental editor for this text. The book wouldn't have been the same without her insightful, professional, helpful, friendly, and positive encouragement. In addition I'd like to thank Fred Duer for his wonderfully descriptive illustrations in Chapter 3; Bill Waller for his help and cooperation in editing; and Nancy Sjöberg for her tireless work on the production of this book.

Finally I'd like to acknowledge my appreciation to the following reviewers of text for their many excellent suggestions: Odis Ball, Los Angeles Pierce College; C. Lance Brockman, University of Minnesota; Donald T. Cate, City College of San Francisco; Kenneth R. Dorst, San Jose University; D. Andrew Gibbs, University of Arkansas; Russell T. Hastings, Ohio State University; Richard C. Huggins, Ohio State University; Douglas R. Maddox, Pennsylvania State University; Thrim B. Paulsen, University of Colorado at Boulder; Arpad E. Petrass, Loyola Marymount University; Pam Rank, University of Southern California; Chuck Sheffield, Richland College (Dallas, Texas); Bernard J. Skalka, California State University at Long Beach; W. Joseph Stell, University of Georgia.

BRIEF CONTENTS

CONTENTS

1

Production Organization and Management

"Great art conceals art." That statement has been attributed to Konstantin Stanislavski, founder of the Moscow Art Theatre and developer of Method acting. He was referring to the phenomenon that occurs when actors create brilliantly believable roles. Great actors don't seem to be working. They make us believe that they *are* the characters they are playing and that everything they say or do is happening spontaneously, without thought or effort. Stanislavski meant by his aphorism that a seemingly effortless job of acting is the end result of years of training, dedication, and just plain hard work.

Great art *does* conceal art, but not just the art of the actor. Imagine, if you will, a male actor, wrapped in a heavy fur cape, standing in the middle of the stage and delivering a soliloquy. The stage resembles a craggy mountain peak, with an angular platform surrounded by an immense expanse of solemn purple and blue sky. The actor strides to a rocky outcropping. Under his weight the platform slowly starts to tip. The actor scrambles backward to save himself and catches the hem of his cape on another "rock." The cape comes off, and the **followspot** reveals the actor standing in his BVDs with his cape around his ankles. The spotlight operator, horrified, tries to turn off her light. But she doesn't hit the right lever and, instead of turning it off, changes its color from deep blue to brilliant white.

Followspot: A lighting instrument with a high-intensity, narrow beam; mounted in a stand that allows it to tilt and swivel so the beam can "follow" an actor.

This unlikely scenario illustrates the fact that less-than-great art conceals little. It also demonstrates that Stanislavski's injunction can be just as true for the design and technical elements of the production as it is for the actors. Together, they can create the delicate illusionary reality that we call theatre. The illusion that the spectators see is just that. A great performance doesn't simply happen; it is the product of a great deal of organization, teamwork, talent, and dedication.

Theatre folk have always delighted in surrounding the process of putting on plays with an aura of mystery. This tradition stems from the probably accurate belief that a play's entertainment value increases if the audience thinks that the production just spontaneously happens. The Mickey Rooney and Judy Garland movies of the 1930s are perfect examples. Mickey, Judy, or one of their friends says, "Let's put on a show!" Someone chimes in that her uncle owns a barn. Amazingly, the barn happens to have a highly polished linoleum floor that is perfect for tap dancing, and the barn is equipped with a full orchestra, sets, lights, and spectacular costumes. The show is an astounding success.

The real world of theatrical production isn't like that. Getting a play from the written word to the stage requires a great deal of challenging work. The result of all this effort, the **production team** hopes, will be artistic and artful, but the business of making a script come alive on the stage is a process that isn't really all that mysterious.

Production team: Everyone working, in any capacity, on the production of the play.

Production design team: The producer, director, and scenic, costume, lighting, and sound designers who develop the visual and aural concept for the production.

Production concept: The creative interpretation of the script, which will unify the artistic vision of producer, director, and designers.

THE PRODUCTION SEQUENCE

How does a play happen? What sequence of events must occur for it to move from the pages of a script to a live performance before an audience? Every play goes through several stages of development.

Script

Most productions begin with a script. This is not true, however, for every theatrical performance. The production of some plays begins with just an idea. That idea may be developed by the performing group in a variety of interesting and creative ways. Some of these concepts may evolve into written scripts, and others may remain as conceptual cores that the actors use as guides when they improvise dialogue during the actual performance.

The producing group frequently modifies scripts to suit its particular needs. New scripts are often "developed" (a euphemism for changed, rewritten, or otherwise modified) by the producer, director, and playwright to suit the needs and desires of the producing group.

Design and Construction

We will assume that our hypothetical production begins with a traditional script. After the script has been selected, the producer options it, or secures the legal rights to produce it, and hires the director, designers, and actors. The members of the **production design team** read the script and then develop the **production concept.**

After the production concept is agreed on, the sets, props, lights, costumes, and sound are designed. Then the various diagrams, sketches, and other plans are sent to shops for construction, fabrication, or acquisition of the production elements (see Figure 1.1).

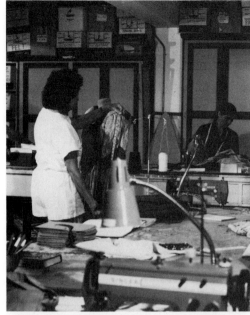

Figure 1.1 A great deal of backstage activity occurs before the production reaches the stage.

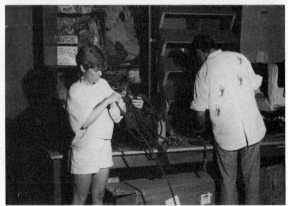

Figure 1.2 The
director discusses
a scene with the
actors.

While the various visual elements are being built, the director and actors
are busy rehearsing (see Figure 1.2). After the rehearsal and construction
period, which usually lasts three to seven weeks, the play moves into the
theatre, and the technical and dress rehearsals begin.

Rehearsals

Technical rehearsals are devoted to integrating the sets, props, lighting, and
sound with the actors into the action of the play. During this rather hectic
period the patterns and timing for shifting the scenery and props are established. The movements of any scenic or property elements (see Figure 1.3),
regardless of whether those movements happen in front of the audience or
behind a curtain, have to be choreographed or blocked just as are the movements of the actors. This ensures that each shift will be consistent in timing
and efficiency for every performance. The shifts may be numerous or complex enough to warrant holding a separate **shift rehearsal,** in which the
director, scene designer, technical director, and stage manager work with the
scenery and prop crews to perfect the choreography and timing of all scenic
and prop shifts.

Technical rehearsals: Run throughs in
which the sets, lights, props, and sound are
introduced into the action of the play.

Shift rehearsal: A run through without
actors to practice changing the scenery
and props.

Figure 1.3 Scene
shifting must be
carefully organized
and choreo-
graphed.

CHAPTER 1: PRODUCTION ORGANIZATION AND MANAGEMENT

Figure 1.4 Sound operator at work.

Figure 1.5 Costumes must be adjusted to fit properly.

The basic timing and intensity of the light **cues** will have been established during the **lighting rehearsal** (which precedes the first technical rehearsal). But during the tech rehearsals almost all of the light cues have to be adjusted in some way, since it is the rule rather than the exception that new lighting cues are added and old ones deleted or modified during this time. The lighting designer meets with the director and stage manager in the theatre to discuss the modifications and have a look at them. The intensity, timing, and nature of the sound cues are subjected to similar changes during the technical rehearsals (see Figure 1.4). Depending on the production schedule and the complexity of the show, there are generally one to three tech rehearsals over the course of a week or so.

The **dress rehearsals** begin toward the end of "tech week." During these rehearsals, which are a natural extension of the tech rehearsals, any adjustments to costumes and makeup are noted and corrected by the next rehearsal time (see Figure 1.5). Adjustments to the various sound, lighting, and shifting cues continue to be made during the dress rehearsals. Depending on the complexity of the production and the number of costumes and costume changes, there may be one to three dress rehearsals.

After the last dress rehearsal there are frequently one to four preview performances (with an invited audience and/or reduced ticket prices) before the production officially opens.

Cue: A directive for action, for example, a change in the lighting.

Lighting rehearsal: A run through without the actors to look at the intensity, timing, and placement of the various lighting cues.

Dress rehearsal: A runthrough in which the actors wear costumes and makeup for the first time.

Production meeting: A conference of appropriate production personnel to share information.

THEATRE ORGANIZATION

More than anything else good theatre requires good organization. Every successful production has a strong organizational structure that follows a fairly standard pattern. Figure 1.6 depicts the organization of a hypothetical, but typical, theatrical production company. Each company's structure is unique to its own needs, and it is doubtful that any two companies would be set up exactly the same. The functions of the various members of the company will be taken up in the next section.

The **production meeting** is probably the single most important device for ensuring smooth communication among the various production departments. The initial production conferences are attended by members of the production design team. Their purpose is to develop the production concept. After the designers begin to produce their drawings, sketches, and plans, the production meeting is used as a forum to keep other members of the team informed about the progress in all design areas. At this time the stage manager normally joins in the discussions.

When the designs are approved and construction begins, the production

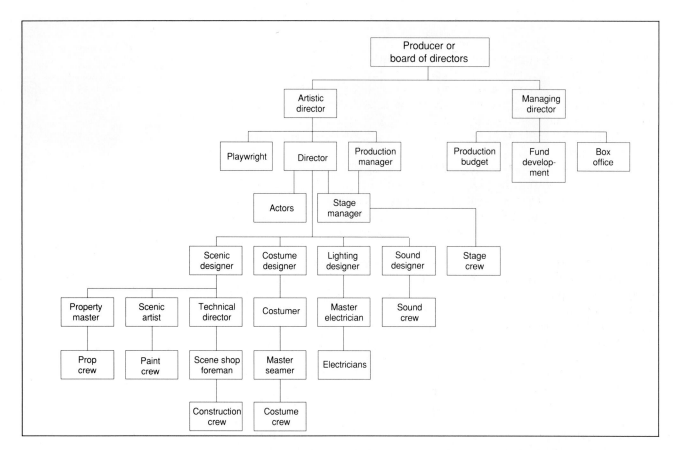

Figure 1.6 The organizational structure chart of a typical theatrical production company.

meeting expands to include the technical director and appropriate crew heads. As construction starts, the director becomes heavily involved in rehearsals. At this time a few adjustments are almost inevitably necessary in one or more of the design elements. These changes should be discussed and resolved at the production meeting, so that all departments are aware of the progress and evolution of the production concept.

While the production concept is being developed, the production meetings are frequently held daily. As the meetings become less developmental and more informational, their frequency decreases to about once a week. The last meeting is usually held just before the opening of the production.

Who participates in production meetings depends, to a great extent, on the nature of the producing organization. A single-run, Broadway-type professional conference usually includes only the members of the production design team and their assistants. A production conference at a regional professional theatre includes the production design team and some of the other members of the permanent production staff, such as the production manager and technical director. For a professionally oriented educational theatre, the staffing of the production meeting is generally the same as for the regional professional production group, with the addition of faculty supervisors overseeing the work of student designers, technical directors, and crew heads.

PRODUCTION JOB DESCRIPTIONS

Although the organization of any company will fit its own needs, the duties of those holding the various positions will be much the same.

Producer

The producer is the ultimate authority in the organizational structure of a theatrical production. He or she is, arguably, the most influential member of the team. The producer secures the rights to perform the play; hires the director, designers, actors, and crews; leases the theatre; and secures financial backing for the play. The specific functions of the producer can vary considerably. In the New York professional theatre most productions are set up as individual entities. As a consequence the producer and his or her staff are able to concentrate their efforts on each production. They will sometimes be working on the preliminary phases of a second or third production while another show is in production or in the final stages of rehearsal, but in general they concentrate on one show at a time.

Regional professional theatres such as the Guthrie Theatre in Minneapolis, the American Conservatory Theatre (ACT) in San Francisco, the Arizona Theatre Company in Tucson, the Asolo Theatre in Sarasota, Florida, and others have been set up in every section of the country over the past twenty years. Generally, these theatres produce a full seven- or eight-month season of limited-run productions. Some of them have active summer programs. Because of the sweeping responsibilities imposed on the producer within these organizations, the functions of the position are generally divided between two persons, the *managing director* and the *artistic director*. The business functions of the producer—contracts, fund raising, ticket sales, box office management— are handled by the managing director, and any artistic decisions—selection of directors, actors, and designers, for example—are made by the artistic director. The managing and artistic directors are hired by the theatre's board of directors, which is responsible for determining the long-range artistic and fiscal goals of the theatre.

In educational theatre the department chair and administrative staff frequently function in the same capacity as the managing director. The duties of the artistic director are often assigned to a production committee, which selects the plays and is responsible for their artistic quality.

In other nonprofit theatres, such as community or church groups, the functions of the producer are usually carried out by a production committee or board of directors, which functions as previously described.

Playwright

The playwright is obviously an essential link in the production chain. The playwright creates and develops the ideas that ultimately evolve into the written script. In the initial public performance of the play he or she may be involved in the actual production process. The playwright frequently helps the director by explaining his or her interpretation of various plot and character developments. During this developmental process the playwright often needs to rewrite portions of some scenes or even whole scenes or acts. If the playwright is not available for conferences or meetings, the production design team proceeds with the development and interpretation of the script on its own.

Director

The director is the artistic manager and inspirational leader of the production team. He or she coordinates the work of the actors, designers, and crews so that the production accurately expresses the production concept. Any complex activity such as the production of a play must have someone with the vision, energy, and ability to focus everyone else's efforts on the common goal. The

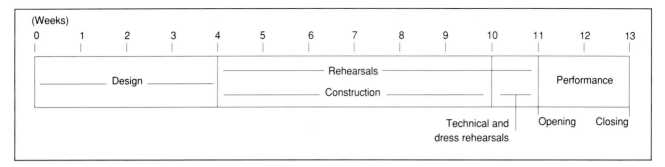

director is this leader. He or she works closely with the other members of the production design team to develop the production concept and also works with the actors to develop their roles in a way that is consistent with the production concept. The director is ultimately responsible for the creative interpretation of the play as it is expressed in production.

Production Manager

The production manager must be an adept mental gymnast, because this important position has the responsibility for coordinating the complex activities associated with a multishow season. The necessity for a production manager has evolved with the development of regional professional theatres. Each production within the theatre's season requires its own logistical structure to bring it from concept to the stage. Figure 1.7 illustrates a typical period needed to develop a play from production concept to reality. Since most regional professional theatres or professionally oriented educational theatres produce eight to twelve plays a season, frequently on several different stages, they must develop rehearsal and performance schedules for all of them simultaneously.

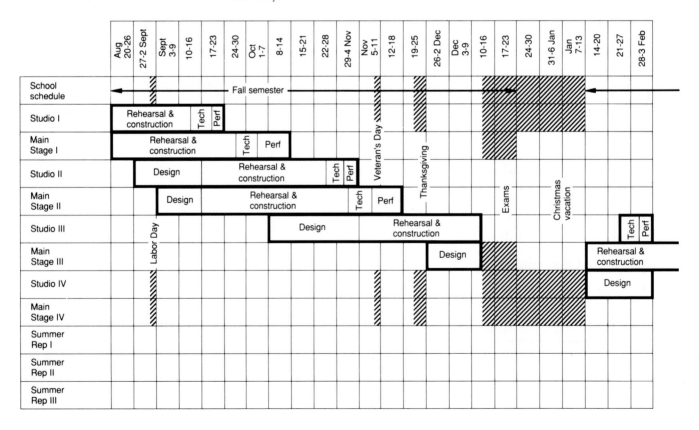

CHAPTER 1: PRODUCTION ORGANIZATION AND MANAGEMENT

The production calendar shown in Figure 1.8 is used by the production manager to help keep track of the various stages of development for each play in the season. This master calendar contains all pertinent information regarding tryouts, rehearsals, design and construction deadlines, technical and dress rehearsals, and performances. From the production calendar the production manager gleans the information necessary to coordinate the assignment of personnel and rehearsal space as well as the scheduling of the various production meetings and other necessary activities.

Stage Manager

The stage manager can be compared to a slightly eccentric master mechanic who keeps a cantankerous, highly complex machine running at top efficiency by talking to it, soothing it, and lovingly fixing whatever is broken. The specific duties of the stage manager can be broken down into two primary categories: (1) assisting the director during rehearsals and (2) being responsible for all backstage activity after the show opens.

The stage manager is hired or assigned to the production at just about the same time as the director. In the professional theatre the stage manager must be a member of Actor's Equity, the actors' union, because he or she may be called on to understudy one or more of the roles in the production. The stage manager is sometimes in an awkward position, because he or she not only assists the director but also, if elected the Equity deputy by the union actors, functions as the enforcer of the Equity rules during rehearsals and performances. Since the Equity deputy can be viewed as enforcing the union rules to save money for the producer, some stage managers decline to serve as deputy because of the potential conflict of interest. Other stage managers elect to serve as deputy since they are already in a leadership position and do not see these activities as a conflict of interest.

Figure 1.8 A sample production calendar.

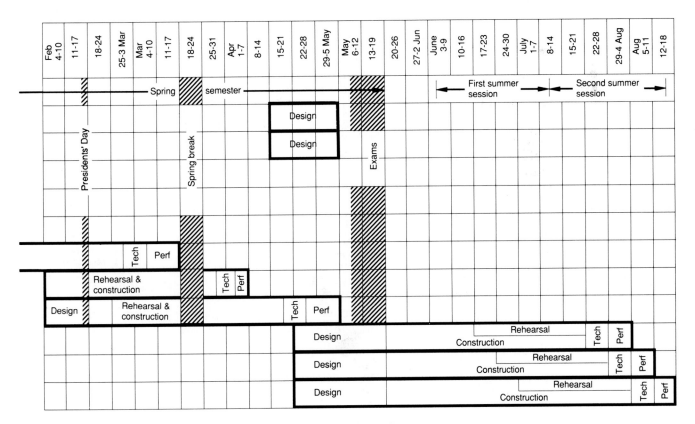

Although every production company has specific rules that relate to its own production circumstances, some general rules of backstage etiquette are universal.

1. Don't talk to other crew members backstage during rehearsals or performances unless it is about the business of the production. Then talk only in a low whisper.

2. Don't talk to the actors backstage during rehearsals or performances unless it is about the business of the production. Their job—acting—takes a great deal of concentration, and they shouldn't be distracted.

3. Wear dark clothes, preferably dark blue or black, to minimize the distraction to the audience if you are seen. Wear sturdy rubber-soled shoes (no tennis shoes, cowboy boots, sandals, or flip-flops). Sturdy shoes will protect your feet and the rubber soles will minimize noise.

4. Be sure to show up on time for your crew call (the time you are scheduled to arrive at the theatre ready for work). Sign the sign-in sheet, and check in with your crew head for work.

5. Don't smoke, eat, or drink backstage.

Prompt book: A copy of the script with details about each actor's blocking as well as the location of all sets, props, lights, and sound cues.

Stage business: A specific action, also known as a "bit," performed by an actor during the play.

Call: To tell specific crew members when to perform their cues.

The stage manager helps the director by taking responsibility for the majority of administrative details. They include such diverse duties as making sure that the ground plan of the set is taped or chalked on the floor of the rehearsal hall, arranging for rehearsal furniture (substitute furniture for the set) as well as tables and chairs for the director and other production personnel, and writing the blocking (actor movements) in the stage manager's **prompt book.**

The stage manager also assists the director by keeping information flowing among the director, the designers, and the various technical shops. During the rehearsal process the director may decide to introduce a piece of **stage business** that requires the modification of some technical element. If the director decides that an actor should bounce a ball against one of the set walls, the stage manager needs to tell the set designer that this section of the wall must be sturdy.

Until the production moves into the theatre—or until the beginning of technical rehearsals, if the play has already been rehearsing in the theatre—the stage manager usually sits beside the director to facilitate communication. When technical rehearsals begin, the stage manager moves to the location from which he or she will **call** the show. The crew members will have previously recorded what to do on their cue sheets, but they don't start the action until they receive their "go" cue from the stage manager. Stage managers have traditionally called the show from backstage, because this location kept them in close contact with the cast and crew. However, the development of new theatre conventions, environments, and equipment enables the cast to make entrances through the auditorium and allows the lighting and sound operators to be in the optimal positions for seeing and hearing the stage action. This dispersion of the actors and crew from the backstage space has freed the stage manager to call the show from whatever position provides the best overall view of the action.

CHAPTER 1: PRODUCTION ORGANIZATION AND MANAGEMENT

STAGE MANAGER'S PROMPT BOOK

The stage manager's prompt book is the bible of the production. The stage manager details all pertinent information about the production in a loose-leaf notebook as shown. Each page of the prompt book contains one page of the script. The blocking is usually indicated in the wide margins of the pages with arrows showing the movement of each actor. The nature, location, and duration of each technical cue (lights, sound, shifting) is also written in the margins.

Warning cues (to prepare the appropriate personnel for any forthcoming cue) are normally placed in the prompt book about half a page before the actual cue location.

The prompt book also contains a ground plan of the set(s), a prop schedule detailing the placement and condition of props ("a half-full glass of milk on the coffee table"), and a "contact sheet" listing the phone numbers and addresses of all cast members, crew members, and other production personnel.

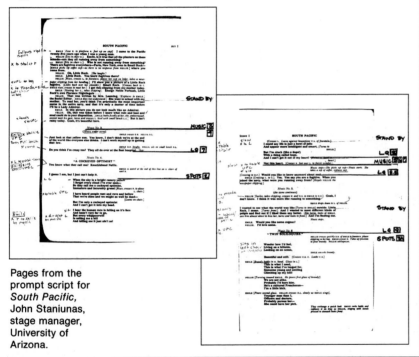

Pages from the prompt script for *South Pacific*, John Staniunas, stage manager, University of Arizona.

When the stage manager begins to call the show, the primary focus of his or her responsibility changes from administrative support for the director to technical coordination of all production activities. The director and various designers determine the nature and timing of the cues, but it is the stage manager who is responsible for seeing that those instructions are carried out. Figure 1.9 illustrates the change in organization that takes place when the play goes into technical and dress rehearsals and performances.

The stage manager calls the show from notes written in the prompt book. Preliminary locations for many of the cues will have been noted in the book during the rehearsal period. During the tech and dress rehearsals the location, timing, and character of these cues are adjusted. When the last dress rehearsal or preview performance is finished, the prompt book will contain a complete and accurate set of instructions for running every cue in the production.

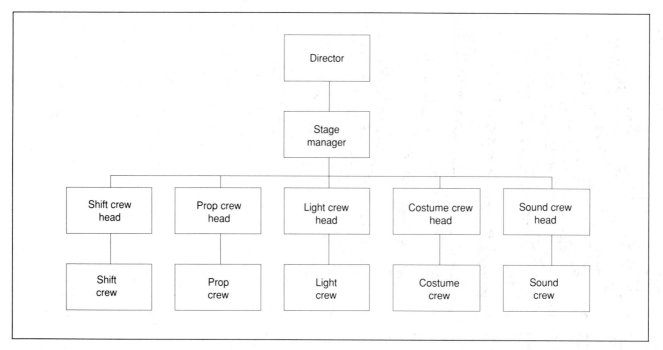

Figure 1.9 The
organizational
structure changes
as a play goes
from regular
rehearsals into
the tech/dress
rehearsals and
performances.

Scenic and Property Personnel

Those who work with the scenery and props in a production are the scenic
designer, the scenic artist, the paint crew, the property master and crew, the
technical director, the scene shop foreman, the construction crew, and the
stage crew.

SCENIC DESIGNER The scenic designer is responsible for the visual appearance and function of the scenic and property elements used in the production.
To translate the scenic design from concept to the stage, the designer produces
colored sketches or renderings of the sets and properties, scale models of the
various sets, and scale mechanical drawings that fully describe the settings (see
Figure 1.10). The scenic designer's job will be explored in depth in Chapter 7,
Scenic Design.

SCENIC ARTIST The scenic artist, under the supervision of the scenic designer, is responsible for the painting of the scenery. He or she needs to be an
excellent artist capable of working in a variety of media and styles. Although
the scenic artist does a great deal of the actual scenic painting, he or she is also
responsible for supervising the work of the paint crew.

PAINT CREW The paint crew, under the supervision of the scenic artist,
paints the sets and sometimes the **properties.** This challenging job involves
painting the set (walls, floor, background, properties) to make it reflect the
character of the design. Rarely do playwrights set their plays in freshly
painted environments. More frequently than not the paint crew must make
the set look old, tired, abused, and worn. Techniques for achieving these
results are detailed in Chapter 10, *Scene Painting.*

PROPERTY MASTER The property master is a unique artisan in the theatre.
He or she must be adept at a variety of skills ranging from design to painting,
sculpting, furniture construction and upholstery, welding, and electronics.
The property master is responsible for the design and construction of the

Properties: Elements such as furniture,
lamps, pictures, table linens, bric-a-brac, and
window drapes that provide the finished set
with visual character.

(A)

Figure 1.10 (A) *Look Back in Anger,* scenic design by A. S. Gillette, University of Iowa. (B) *The Petrified Forest,* scenic design by Peggy Kellner, University of Arizona.

(B)

various decorative and functional props that are used in a production. He or she generally works under the artistic supervision of the scenic designer and works closely with the technical director and scene shop foreman. Chapter 11, *Stage Properties,* contains information about stage prop construction techniques.

PROPERTY CREW The property crew, under the supervision of the property master, constructs or acquires all the props used in a production. During rehearsals and performances the supervision of the prop crew shifts to the stage manager, who oversees its work involving the placement, shifting, and storage of the props.

TECHNICAL DIRECTOR The technical director, under the artistic supervision of the scenic designer, is responsible for building the scenery and properties, mounting them on the stage, and overseeing the work of the scenic and property crews during rehearsals and performances. The primary activity of the technical director, also known as the TD, is supervising the construction of all scenery and properties. To accomplish this task the TD uses scale plans from the scenic designer. These drawings may have to be supplemented with **plates,** drawn by the technical director, showing the construction details and techniques that will be used to build the scenery. The TD also supervises the transporting of the scenery from the shop to the stage as well as the mounting, rigging, and maintenance of the scenery while it is in the theatre. An introduction to scenic and property production (the organization, tools, and construction techniques) is contained in Chapters 8 (*Tools and Materials*) and 9 (*Scenic Production Techniques*) as well as Chapter 11 (*Stage Properties*).

SCENE SHOP FOREMAN The scene shop foreman, under the supervision of the technical director, is responsible for the construction, mounting, and rigging of the scenery. He or she usually supervises a crew of carpenters in the actual construction. The foreman is also normally responsible for the maintenance of the scene shop equipment and supplies.

CONSTRUCTION CREW The construction crew is composed of the people who actually build the various pieces of scenery and properties for the production. After the set has been built and painted, they move the sets from the shop to the theatre and assemble the sets on the stage.

STAGE CREW The stage crew **shifts** the set during technical and dress rehearsals and during the performances. This work is accomplished under the direct supervision of the stage manager.

Lighting Personnel

The lighting staff is made up of the lighting designer, the master electrician, and other electricians.

LIGHTING DESIGNER The lighting designer is responsible for the design, installation, and operation of the lighting and special electrical effects used in the production. Because light is a nontactile sculptural medium, it is all but impossible to build a model or draw a sketch of what the lighting will look like. To show where the lighting equipment will be placed, the lighting designer produces a light plot, which is a scale drawing that details the placement of the lighting instruments relative to the physical structure of the theatre and the location of the set. The techniques and materials that the lighting designer uses are discussed in Chapters 12 (*Lighting Design*), 13 (*Electrical Theory and Practice*), 14 (*Lighting Production*), and 15 (*Projections*).

MASTER ELECTRICIAN The master electrician, under the supervision of the lighting designer, implements the lighting design. He or she is directly responsible for the acquisition, installation, and maintenance of all lighting equipment and the supervision of the crews who hang, focus, and run the lighting equipment.

ELECTRICIANS The work of the electricians can be divided into three areas: **hanging, focusing,** and **running.** The *hanging crew* places the lighting instruments and associated equipment in the positions designated by the light plot. They also **circuit** and **patch** the instruments. The circuit and dimmer for each instrument are indicated on the light plot or **hookup sheet;** or the master electrician designates the appropriate circuit and dimmer during the

Plate: A sheet of mechanical drawings, drawn to scale.

Shift: To change the position of the scenery, props, or stage equipment.

Hanging: Placing lighting instruments and equipment in the designated positions on the light plot.

Focusing: Directing light from the lighting instruments to a specific area.

Running: Controlling or operating some aspect of production.

Circuit: To connect a lighting instrument to a stage circuit.

Patch: To connect a stage circuit to a dimmer circuit.

Hookup sheet: A sheet containing pertinent information (hanging position, circuit, dimmer, color, lamp wattage, focusing notes) about every lighting instrument used in the production. Also known as an instrument schedule.

hanging session. The hanging crew also puts the **color media** on the lighting instruments and, under the supervision of the lighting designer, focuses the instruments.

The *running crew* is responsible for the operation of the lighting equipment during the rehearsals and performances. Depending on the complexity of the production, as few as one or as many as five or more electricians are needed to run the lights.

Costume Personnel

Those staff members who are responsible for the production's costumes include the costume designer, costumer, master seamer, and costume construction crew.

COSTUME DESIGNER The costume designer is responsible for the visual appearance of the actors. This area includes the design of the clothes, accessories (shoes, hats, purses, canes, parasols), jewelry, wigs, and makeup worn by the actors during the performance. Designs for theatrical costumes consist of colored sketches depicting the clothing and accessories that will be worn by the actor. In the case of complex costume designs, sketches that show more than one view may be needed. In either case the sketches normally have appropriate construction notes jotted in the margins, and small swatches of the fabrics from which the costumes will be made are usually attached to the sketches. Additional information about costume and makeup design as well as costume production is found in Chapter 16, *Costume Design and Production.*

COSTUMER The costumer is the costume technician who, under the artistic supervision of the costume designer, actually builds or supervises the building of the costumes. The costumer must be a skilled pattern drafter, fabric cutter, and stitcher. In addition, he or she must be well acquainted with a variety of special clothing, millinery, and wig-making techniques.

MASTER SEAMER The master seamer is in charge of costume construction and supervises the costume crew. Also known as the wardrobe mistress or costume shop supervisor, this person must be adept at all phases of costume construction from pattern drafting through cutting, draping, fitting, tailoring, and the various techniques (and machines) used in sewing costume materials.

COSTUME CONSTRUCTION CREW The costume construction crew can be subdivided into several specialty areas. The *pattern maker* translates the costume design, as visualized in the costume sketch, into a workable pattern. Pattern making is vital to the appearance of the finished costume, because the shape of the pattern will determine the hang and fit. The *cutter* actually pins the pattern to the fabric and cuts out the pieces for the costume. The skill of the cutter greatly affects the finished appearance of the costume, because the placement of the pattern in relationship to the **warp and weft** of the fabric determines how the fabric will hang when it is sewn into a finished garment. The *stitcher* actually sews the costumes together.

Hats are an important accessory for most period costumes. They are frequently made in the costume shop by the *milliner.* Wigs, like hats, are an important part of costuming. The *wigmaker* not only styles and arranges wigs but also makes them.

A *cobbler* is a person who makes shoes. Although many theatres adapt modern footwear through the use of appliqués that disguise the period of the footwear being worn, a complete costume shop frequently has the necessary

Color media: The colored plastic, gel, or glass filters used in lighting instruments.

Warp and weft: The vertical and horizontal threads in a fabric.

equipment and expertise required to construct period footwear, or it has access to a company that produces this specialized work.

Sound Personnel

Those who create the sound for a production include the sound designer and the sound crew.

SOUND DESIGNER The sound designer is responsible for the design, recording, equipment setup, and playback of any sound used in the play. The sound design can vary in complexity from simple recorded music used during intermissions to a meticulously designed special-effects tape used to underscore the entire production. This newest design field in theatre is very challenging; it will be discussed in greater depth in Chapter 17, *Sound Design and Technology.*

Sound reinforcement system: The amplification of sound coming from the stage.

SOUND CREW Under the supervision of the sound designer the sound crew does the actual recording, editing of tapes, and the playback during rehearsals and performances. The sound crew is also responsible for the running of any **sound reinforcement systems** during the production.

The Design Process

It may come as a rude shock, but design is more a process than an art. It is a series of steps through which we pursue the goal of creating what we hope will be a work of art—a scenic design, costume design, lighting design, or audio design—or the artistry of an efficiently coordinated production. The design process is a method for finding answers to questions. Although the examples and terms used in this chapter will direct your thinking toward theatrical design and production, the principles of the design process can be applied with equally productive results to acting, directing, and, for that matter, life in general. These principles and techniques can help you discover an appropriate and creative solution to almost any design problem. A problem-solving model for theatrical design and production consists of seven distinct phases: (1) commitment, (2) analysis, (3) research, (4) incubation, (5) selection, (6) implementation, and (7) evaluation.

Unfortunately, the design process isn't a simple, linear progression. As you move from step to step, you must check back on your previous steps to make sure that you are headed in the right direction with your proposed solution. Figure 2.1 shows the back-and-forth movement that occurs as you move through the various stages of the design process. Although Satchel Paige, the wise old pitcher, once advised, "Don't look back; something may be gaining on you," you would do well to look back during your progression through the design process, because the thing that might be gaining on you could be a new thought, a better mousetrap.

COMMITMENT

Commitment is probably the most important step in the whole design process. If you wholeheartedly *commit* your energies to an assignment, you are

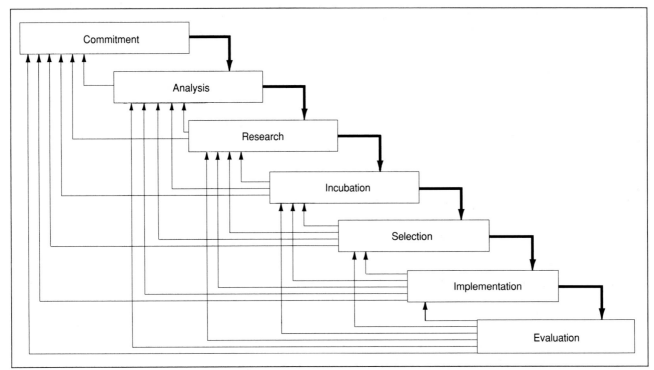

The boxes, top to bottom: Commitment, Analysis, Research, Incubation, Selection, Implementation, Evaluation.

Figure 2.1 The design process is not simply a linear progression. As you move through the steps of the design process, you monitor your progress by continually checking back to see where you have been.

promising yourself that you will do the best work you can possibly do.

A very simple semantic game may help you commit yourself to an assignment. Use the word *problem* as infrequently as possible—it has a negative connotation—and substitute the word *challenge*. Everybody likes a challenge: the word itself hints at fun, games, and competition. When your problem has been transformed into a challenge, it automatically becomes more interesting and manageable.

ANALYSIS

The analysis step in the design process has two objectives: (1) gathering information that will help clarify and refine the definition of the challenge you are facing and (2) identifying areas that will require further research. Analysis in theatrical production is primarily a search for information and an objective evaluation of the data you discover. Prime sources of this information are members of the production design team—the producer, director, and your fellow designers. In your discussions with them you need to examine everything—production style, concepts, budgets, schedules—that is relevant to your design project. "*Who* is producing the play? *What* is the production budget? *Where* is the play being produced? *When* is the design due? *Why* are we doing this play? *How* is the scenery being moved from the shop to the theatre?" The answers to these questions will provide you with information that will further define and clarify your challenge. Each answer should also raise another question or two in your mind. Ask them. This **stream-of-consciousness questioning** can provide you with invaluable information about your challenge.

At some point in your information gathering you will read the script. Some designers prefer to read the script before they talk to other members of the production design team; others wait until later. Either way is fine. There

Stream-of-consciousness questioning: Asking whatever relevant questions pop into your mind in the course of a discussion.

really isn't any rule about when you should read the script. Just make sure that you discuss it and share your ideas with the other members of the production design team.

Analyzing the Script

Although it is not at all unusual for designers to read scripts many times, they undertake the first three readings of the script with specific objectives in mind.

FIRST READING The first time you sit down with the script, just read it for fun. Discover the flavor of the play. Learn its general story line, the nature of its characters, their socioeconomic status, and their interrelationships. One of the first things you see when you open the script is the description of the physical environment of the play. Usually written in italics just before the opening lines, it describes the set and, occasionally, the costumes, sound, and lights. Unless you are working from an original script, these descriptions are usually taken from the stage manager's prompt book for the first major professional production of the play and explain the specific designs for that particular production. These descriptions shouldn't be thought of as the correct design solutions for the play; they are just one way that the show can be designed. Your production is entitled to a fresh design treatment that will be appropriate to its personnel, time, place, and budget. To believe that you have to, or should, copy the original design is an insult to your creative ability. Use the descriptive information in the script along with the other information you gather to synthesize an original design concept.

SECOND READING During the second reading of the script you should be looking for specific moments and incidents within the play that stimulate your imagination and provide you with strong visual and textural images and feelings. These inspirations are random, often disconnected, thoughts and impressions about the appearance of the various design elements. Jot them down. If they are more visual than verbal, sketch them. Carry a small notebook with you. Whenever a thought or idea pops into your mind, regardless of how inconsequential it seems, put it into your notebook. These thoughts can be anything relevant to the design challenge. A thought about a character's texture—"He is rough like burlap"—is an idea that should be noted. An impression that the atmosphere of the play is hot, heavy, and sticky is important. Your sense that the play is soft and curved, not sharp and hard, should also be noted.

As you continue to reread the play you will get more ideas. Ideas will also appear when you are not reading the script. They can materialize when you are talking to the director, discussing the play with another designer, eating breakfast, or walking to class. Don't judge the ideas at this point. Gather information now, and weed later.

THIRD READING In the third reading you are looking for specific mechanical information rather than broadly based concepts. For example, set designers look for such things as the number of sets, whether the scene changes are going to happen in front of the audience or behind the curtain, and specific requirements such as a closet door that needs to be hinged on the upstage side. Information that affects the budgets (time and fiscal) should also be noted at this time. Such notes include any special properties, construction, costumes, or effects that will require extra time or money.

Information from the third reading is gathered not only from reading the script but also from conferences with other members of the production design team. As with the first and second readings, all of this information needs to be put in your notebook.

The Questioning Process

Questioning is one of the keys to creativity. Your drive to create is based, to a great extent, on your perceived need for change, or your creative discontent with the status quo. If you are satisfied with everything in your world, you will see no need to change, modify, or create anything.

To analyze effectively it is necessary to shed fear—fear of criticism, fear of making mistakes, fear of seeming less than brilliant, fear of being thought a fool or somehow different. Fear inhibits thinking and makes us afraid to ask

---

TALK IT OVER

The most unified production concepts are developed as a result of talking. In a production of *Cabaret* at the University of Arizona, the production design team began preliminary concept discussions in early January for a production that was to open on April 25.

The director indicated at the first meeting that he wanted to stress the decadence of Berlin society. Our initial informal discussions centered on what this decadence should look like. Someone said that the cabaret should appear to be below ground level (to subliminally support the idea of descending into the hell that was about to engulf Germany). Another person mentioned that it could be useful to have four towers onstage with followspots on top, because the audience might make a connection between them and the guard towers in a concentration camp. The director said he wanted to have the cabaret audience watching the onstage action (cabaret and noncabaret scenes) at all times. He thought that this device would add an appropriately voyeuristic quality. Ideas just seemed to pop up as we all became more excited about the project.

Within a month we developed the production concept through our discussions at these once-a-week meetings. We all brought rough sketches, photos, and ideas to every meeting. We discussed everything—acting style, acting areas, color, visual motifs, atmosphere, history. When the deadline for final designs arrived, we all knew what everyone else was thinking and doing.

This example shows what can happen when the production design team, under the leadership and coordination of the director, works together to evolve the production concept. For a variety of reasons, however, it frequently isn't possible for the director and designers to sit around a table and work together to develop the production concept. When this happens, a good director usually adopts a more authoritarian posture in the development of the production concept. He or she develops a primary production concept and discusses it in individual meetings with the designers. The designers then work toward this concept.

The two methods work equally well. Quality productions can be achieved with either method. The common denominator is communication. A good production concept can evolve only if the director and designers talk to one another and share their ideas, thoughts, and imagination.

CHAPTER 2: THE DESIGN PROCESS

questions. All too frequently I hear students in my classes say, "I don't want to ask a dumb question, but . . ." As far as I am concerned, the only dumb question is one that isn't asked.

Analyze the script, question the director, question the other members of the production design team, and question the producer. Learn what they are thinking, feeling, and planning for the production. Analyze what they say. See how it fits in with your reactions and plans. The more information you receive, the more source material you will have to draw on when you finally begin to design.

RESEARCH

As you gather information, you will discover small pockets of knowledge in which your personal experience and background are weak. List them in your notebook as the areas in which research is necessary. You will be doing both background research and conceptual research.

Background Research

Designers have to study the historical background of each production they design. This type of research involves searching the library for books, catalogs, paintings, periodicals, and other sources of information about the era.

Your historical research should include reading about previous productions of the play and looking at photos, sketches, and models of those prior productions. Don't fall prey, however, to the temptation to simply duplicate someone else's design. That practice squelches your creativity, and, more pragmatically, it is illegal in most states.

Additional background research in the field of color will also be necessary for all designers. A thorough understanding of this extremely important area will enable the designer to match and blend colors in pigment and light. Additionally, by studying the psychology of color, you will be able to design color keys that help the audience understand the primary character motivations and relationships in the play. Color is discussed in Chapter 6.

HOW DID IT LOOK?

A number of references are helpful in any search for visual information. Photo magazines such as *Life* and *National Geographic* contain excellent pictures of costumes, furniture, props, and decoration for plays set in the twentieth century. Department store catalogs can provide additional visual information for the turn of the century and earlier. Visual information about earlier eras must usually be gleaned from paintings, sculpture, and engravings. Art-history books have photographs of these items.

The ultimate use of these visual references is up to the individual designer. Some designers faithfully reproduce a costume or piece of furniture so that they can be sure the "look" they have achieved is authentic for the desired period. Other designers study a variety of sources and then design something new that reflects the general style of the period.

HISTORICAL RELEVANCE FOR DESIGN

Although each designer must look at visual material relevant to his or her design area, all designers should also study the history of the period. As an example, the costume designer needs to know the history and style of dress of the era of the play. This study could begin with a look at a text on costume history to get a general understanding of the style of the time. More detailed study will also be necessary. You can look at paintings, photos, museum displays, catalogs, and any other sources that illustrate the fashion of dress for the period.

An understanding of the socio-economic background of the play's environment is also useful, because clothing styles are usually a reflection of the morals and economics of the time. Throughout the major periods of fashion there have been subtle, and sometimes not so subtle, shifts of style based on the socio-economic status of the individual. Servants have rarely dressed like their employers, and it has usually been fairly easy to differentiate between classes based on the cut and quality of their clothes.

Additional research into the arts (painting, sculpture, literature, music) and history of the playwright's era can provide information on the world that shaped the author's thinking. Essays and critical reviews of the playwright's work are another good source of background information.

Conceptual Research

Conceptual research involves devising multiple solutions to specific design challenges. In reading a script, for example, you may discover that the heroine leaves the stage at the end of Act I in a beautiful gown and reappears at the start of Act II with the same dress in tatters. Your conceptual research would be to figure out as many ways as possible that this challenge could be solved.

A snag frequently encountered during conceptual research is our apparently natural inability to conceive of any more than two or three possible solutions to any given challenge. Too often our brains go numb and refuse to dream up new ideas. In psychology this type of nonthinking state is referred to as a perceptual block. If the perceptual block can be eliminated, our ability to devise, or create, additional solutions to any given problem is greatly improved. In other words, the removal of perceptual blocks significantly increases our personal creative ability.

INCUBATION

How many times, having left the room after finishing an exam, have you suddenly remembered the answer to a question that eluded you while you were writing the test? How many times have you come up with the solution to a problem after having "slept on it"? In both these cases the information necessary to answer the questions was locked in your subconscious and only needed time and a little stress reduction to allow the answer to float into your conscious mind.

Incubation provides you with time to let ideas hatch. During this time you should basically forget about the project. Your subconscious mind will use the time to sort through the information you've gathered in the previous steps and may actually construct a solution to the design challenge or at least point you in a valid direction.

Give yourself enough time to let your subconscious mind mull over the data that you have absorbed. It simply isn't possible to do your best work if you wait for a deadline and then rush through an assignment. Quality work happens more easily if you allow time for incubation.

UNBLOCKING YOUR THINKING

How can we get rid of our perceptual blocks? By eliminating the cause, we can usually eliminate the block. Proper identification of the real challenge is extremely important. Many times challenges are not what they first seem to be. If a play requires three sets, one of the design challenges would be to devise ways to shift among them. To most of us that would mean finding ways to move the sets. We see sets shifted in this way all the time. It's normal. But couldn't the challenge be solved just as well by putting all three locales on a unit set and shifting the audience's attention by lighting only the part of the set that we want it to see? or by using three separate theatres, each with its own set, and having the audience move? or by having two of the sets hidden behind the upstage wall of the third set and moving sections of the wall to reveal the appropriate set? These additional solutions to the challenge are the result of nothing more than a very careful examination of the specific question being posed in the challenge.

DEFINE YOUR CHALLENGE MORE BROADLY

If you thought about the traditional ways of shifting between sets in the previous problem, you were actually defining the challenge too closely. By unconsciously limiting your quest for possible solutions to the traditionally accepted methods,

you were shutting off a whole realm of new, effective solutions to the challenge. Think creatively about the elements of the challenge, and don't accept only the commonplace answers to the questions posed in the challenge.

OVERCOME TUNNEL VISION

When working on a design it is very easy, and egocentrically convenient, to fall into the trap of not seeing your assignment from the viewpoint of others involved in the challenge. When designing scenery it is very easy to put a ceiling on the set without worrying about how this is going to affect the lighting design. Similarly, when determining the width of doors to be used on your set, it is quite easy to forget that the costume designer is planning to use hoop skirts that measure four feet in diameter at the hem.

Tunnel vision can be avoided if members of the production design team discuss their ideas in production meetings. By conferring on a regular basis the director and designers can remain aware of everyone else's work as it progresses from conception to completion.

AVOID VISUAL STEREOTYPING

Visual stereotyping refers to seeing what you expect to see rather than what is actually in front of you. It limits your ability to conceive of existing elements in new combinations. If you expect to see casters attached to the bottom of a stage

wagon, it may be difficult for you to envision turning the casters upside down and attaching them to the stage floor. But that inverted thinking may provide a really effective solution to the problem of shifting scenery for a complex show when you don't have enough casters to accomplish the task in the more conventional manner.

REMEMBER DETAILS SELECTIVELY

People remember things selectively. If we decide that something doesn't have great personal significance, we tend to forget it. To demonstrate this principle try to draw, from memory, a detailed sketch of the front door of your house, apartment, or dorm room. Most people can't do it. We see and use the door several times every day, but most of us never really look at it very closely.

All of us remember details that we have determined will be important for us to recall. Albert Einstein was reputed not to have known his own telephone number. When asked why, he reportedly said that he didn't want to clutter up his mind with information he could look up.

Although it is very important for a designer or technician to have a thorough knowledge of the various subjects that make up his or her field of expertise, it is equally important to follow Einstein's dictum and not clutter up your mind with details that can be found fairly easily in a reference work.

Figure 2.2 Thumbnail sketches for the University of Arizona Department of Drama's production of *Nicholas Nickleby,* scenic design by Tom Benson, directed by Harold Dixon and Dianne Winslow. The first sketch (A) shows a basically symmetrical platform arrangement flowing from the upstage center high point down toward the edges of the proscenium. The set has an elaborate gridwork behind the platforms and a planked wooden floor. (B) The directors and designer made notes and sketches on a copy of the design as they discussed modifications to the set. (C) The stage right platforms were then opened to make the space underneath more usable, and the downstage left staircase was curled further onto the stage, making the set asymmetrical and more dynamic. The background gridwork was also abstracted, and the planked floor was eliminated to make the central floor more visually useful. In the final sketch (D) some of the background gridwork was angled to create a more dynamic line, and the lighting instruments were included as a scenic element.

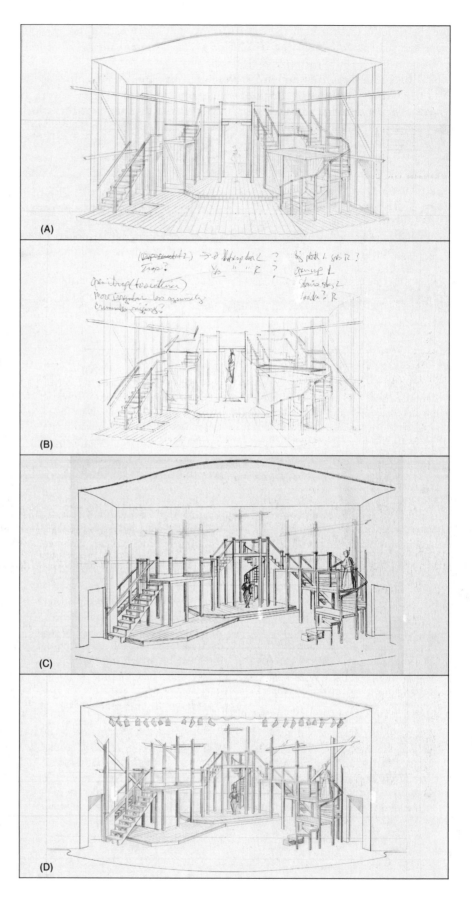

CHAPTER 2: THE DESIGN PROCESS

SELECTION

Selection is the step in the design process in which you sift through all of the data you've accumulated and decide on your specific design concept. Because the choices of each designer affect the work of all members of the production design team, everyone's designs need to be discussed in another production meeting.

The scenic designer draws as many **thumbnail sketches** as necessary to explain the scenic concepts for the production (see Figure 2.2). If the sets for the play are rather complex or the sketches do not fully explain the concepts, then a **functional model** of each set idea must be constructed. The scenic designer also provides an indication of the intended color scheme with the thumbnail sketches. This can be done by coloring on them or by accompanying them with color sample cards (paint chips). The method of presentation of the color palette doesn't really matter so long as the other members of the production design team understand the plan.

The costume designer provides pencil sketches or pictures of the intended costumes. Although the costume designer attaches fabric swatches to the final costume renderings, these preliminary sketches require only an indication of the color and type of fabric that will be used (see Figure 2.3).

The lighting designer submits sketches showing the general characteristics of the concept for the lighting design, if such sketches are appropriate. At the least, he or she presents the intended palette and a verbal description of the atmospheric effect of the lighting during the production meeting. The sound

Thumbnail sketch: A small, quick, rough drawing, usually done in pencil, that shows the major outline, character, and feeling of the object but does not have much detail.

Functional model: A three-dimensional thumbnail sketch of the scenic design; normally built on a scale of one-half or one-quarter inch to one foot; usually made from file folders or similar cardboard; also known as a white model.

Figure 2.3 The costume designer uses preliminary pencil sketches as a visual notebook to record ideas that may ultimately find their way into a finished costume design. Preliminary costume designs by Peggy Kellner for *MacBeth,* produced at the Old Globe Theatre, San Diego, California.

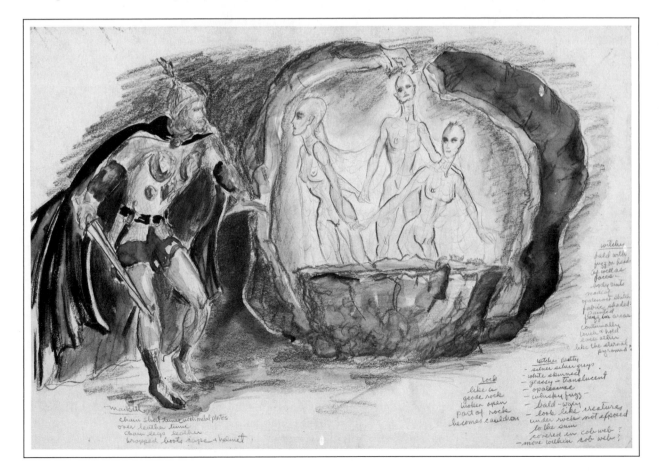

A lot of art is the result of happy accident. When designing the lights for some forgotten production I noticed that one area of the stage seemed to have a rough texture. I went up on stage and looked more closely. The floor didn't have any texture; it was painted a smooth, flat color. Then I looked up at the lights. One of the instruments had a gobo (a thin metal template that creates a shadow pattern) left in it from a previous pro-duction. That instrument was creating the texture. Although I took the gobo out of the instrument, I remembered the effect. Now whenever I want to create a textured atmosphere I put gobos in the instruments.

The moral? Always evaluate what you've done, even if you think it's a "mistake." Just because something isn't right for one situation doesn't mean it won't be right for another.

designer discusses the types of background and specific sound and musical effects as well as the location and function of the various speakers' setups.

The selection phase of the design process is finished when the director feels satisfied that all design areas support the production design concept.

IMPLEMENTATION

Production model: A scale model, similar to the functional model but fully painted and complete with all furniture and decorative props.

Sound plot: A list describing each sound cue in the production.

Quite simply, the implementation phase begins when you stop planning and start doing. At this time you produce all drawings, models, plans, and instructions necessary to construct the scenic, lighting, costume, and light designs.

The scenic designer makes the final color renderings for each set of the production and, if necessary, constructs **production models** of the sets. He or she also drafts the plans that describe, to scale, all the details of how the set should look (see Figure 2.4). After completing the paperwork for the design, the scenic designer monitors the progress of the construction and painting of the set(s) and properties to make sure that they are completed according to plan, on time, and within budget.

The lighting designer draws the light plot as well as the other paperwork associated with the lighting design (see Figure 2.5). He or she then supervises the hanging and focusing of the lights and determines the intensity levels and timing for all lighting cues.

The costume designer produces colored renderings for each costume, complete with notes and sketches that fully describe the accessories as well as the general style, period, and feeling of the costume (see Figure 2.6). Fabric samples are attached to each sketch to indicate the various materials from which the costume is to be made. These designs are turned over to the costume shop. The costume designer maintains close contact with the shop to determine that the costumes are being built as planned and will be completed on time and within budget.

The sound designer completes the **sound plot** and begins gathering and recording the various musical and effects cues, as well as assembling the necessary playback equipment and speaker systems. During the technical and dress rehearsals the sound designer determines the appropriate loudness

DESIGN PROCESS CHECKLIST

The following checklist provides a short review that will help you use each step of the design process.

COMMITMENT
A. Make a commitment to yourself to do your best work on the project.
B. Overcome any negative feelings toward the project.

ANALYSIS
A. Gather information to clarify and refine the definition of the challenge.
B. Identify areas needing further research.
C. Read the play.
D. Talk to other members of the production design team.

RESEARCH
A. Background research
  1. Study the social and artistic history of the period of the play.
  2. Study the trends and styles of the costumes, architecture, furniture, and the like (as appropriate) for the period and the economic status of the characters in the play.
B. Conceptual research
  1. Be a mental pack rat. Think up as many potential solutions to the challenge as possible.

  2. Don't judge or discard any idea. Save them all.

INCUBATION
A. Just forget about the project. Do something else.
B. Allow enough time for your subconscious mind to work on the challenge.

SELECTION
A. Develop your solution to the challenge.
B. Don't be afraid to take a piece of one idea and a piece of another to create the most effective solution.

IMPLEMENTATION
A. Stop thinking and start doing.
B. Produce all necessary drawings, sketches, models, and plans to facilitate construction of the design.

EVALUATION
A. Reflect on the challenge. Did you do everything you could to make it succeed?
B. Review your use of the design process. Did you fully analyze the question? Did you do sufficient background and conceptual research?
C. Did you effectively communicate your ideas and thoughts to the other members of the design team?

---

levels for each sound cue and does any necessary rerecording or reediting of the sound tapes.

At this time the technical director completes the production calendar, makes any necessary construction drawings, orders the materials for construction of all sets and props, organizes the crews, and begins construction. During rehearsals the director's view of the production concept will probably change or evolve as the actors become involved in the production. Minor changes should be expected as part of the process of putting a production together. Production meetings during the implementation phase help to ensure that the information keeps flowing.

Figure 2.4 Finished scenic design for *Nicholas Nickleby.* (A) The production model, (B) the ground plan, (C) (on page 30) some construction drawings.

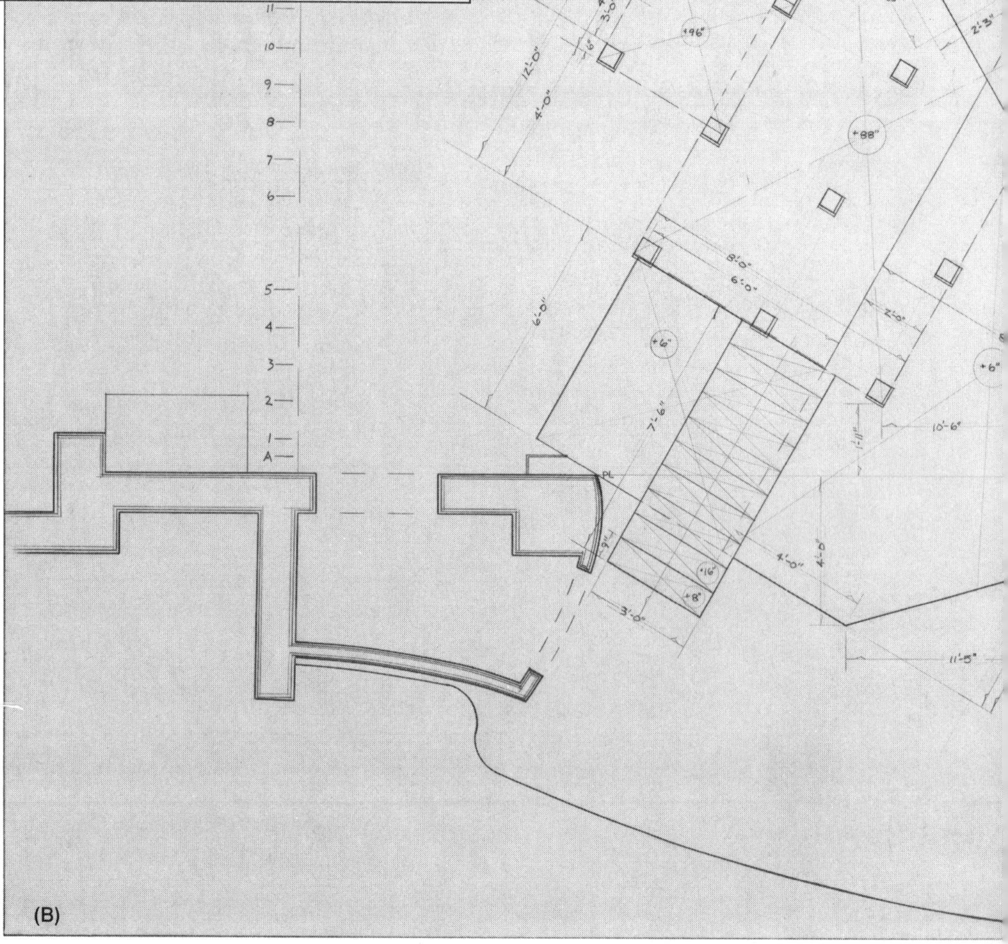

(A)

(B)

CHAPTER 2: THE DESIGN PROCESS

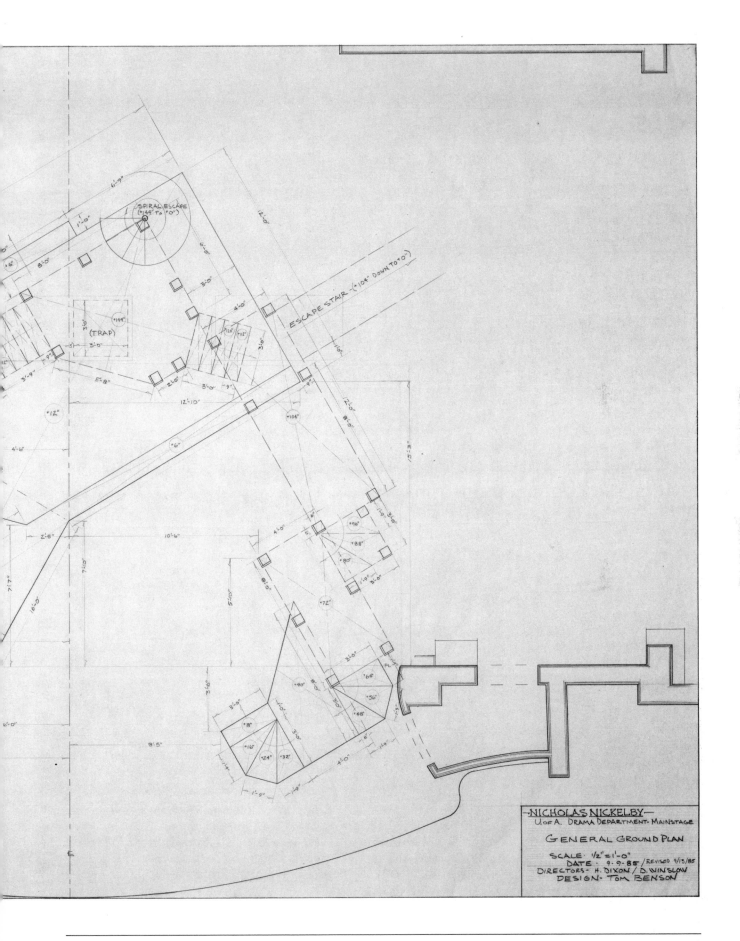

SPIRAL ESCAPE
(+144" TO +0")

ESCAPE STAIR - (+104" DOWN TO +0")

(TRAP)

NICHOLAS NICKELBY
U. OF A. DRAMA DEPARTMENT - MAINSTAGE

GENERAL GROUND PLAN

SCALE · 1/2"=1'-0"
DATE · 9·9·85 / REVISED 9/13/85
DIRECTORS - H. DIXON / D. WINSLOW
DESIGN - TOM BENSON

Figure 2.4 (C)

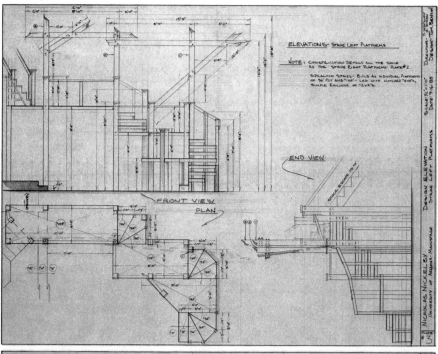

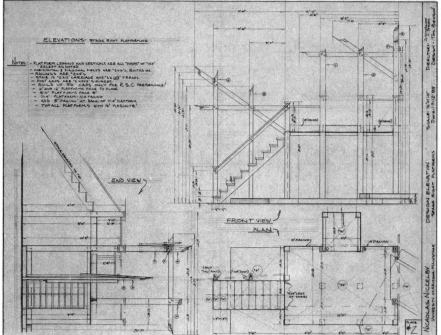

EVALUATION

Evaluation takes place within each step of the design process, and it also occurs when the project is completed. This final evaluation, or review, is not so much a back-patting session as an examination of the methods and materials used to reach the final design goal. All designers evaluate their selections to see if they were really appropriate and to determine if they could be used in the future in another context.

CHAPTER 2: THE DESIGN PROCESS

Figure 2.5 The light plot for *Nicholas Nickleby.* The lighting designer uses the light plot to codify his or her design.

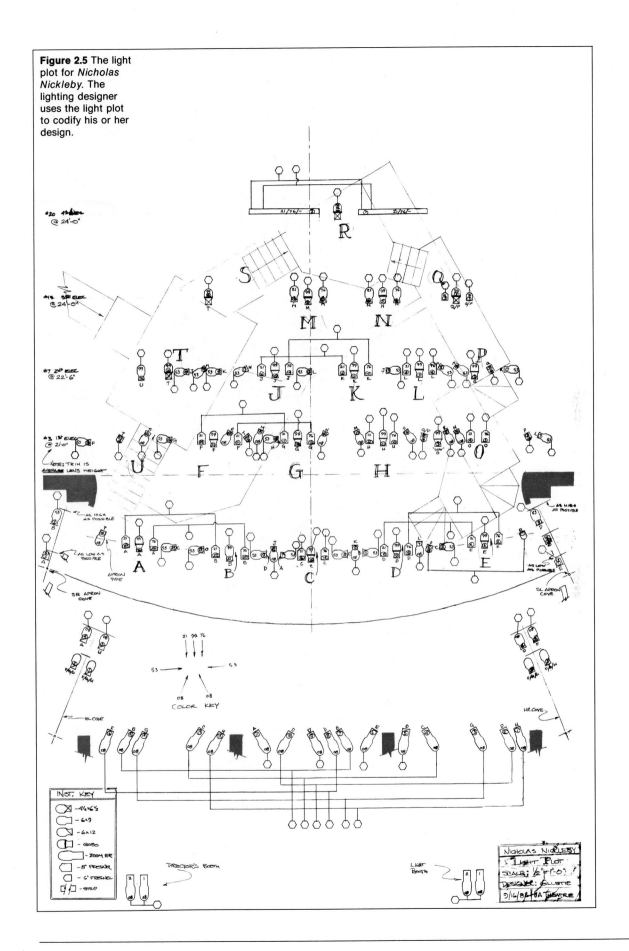

Figure 2.6 The costume designer provides annotated colored sketches of the costumes, complete with samples of the fabrics to be used, to the costume shop for construction of the costumes. Costume design for *Two Gentlemen of Verona* by Peggy Kellner, Old Globe Theatre, San Diego, California.

All members of the production design team look objectively at the communication process that took place inside and outside the various production conferences. They examine the various interchanges between the director, producer, and other designers to see if they can improve the communication the next time around. The designers also evaluate the judgments they made to see if anything that might have helped was left out, ignored, or rejected.

As you become more familiar with the design process, you will discover that your own work is more creative and that you can produce it faster and more easily. The design process is a valuable, efficient, time-saving, and frustration-reducing tool. Use it and enjoy.

3

Theatre Architecture

"Last night the curtain rose at the . . ." could have begun almost any theatrical critic's review during the 1940s or 1950s. Interestingly, the curtain rises on few productions these days, not for a lack of productions but because two of the three current styles of stage configuration don't use a front curtain. Of the three types of theatrical space used in the modern theatre—**proscenium, thrust,** and **arena** (see Figure 3.1)—only one, the proscenium, has a front curtain. Each of these spaces has its own set of design and staging requirements, but they have all evolved from the same common heritage—the theatres of ancient Greece.

GREEK THEATRE

Our knowledge of Greek or Roman theatres is based almost exclusively on archaeological studies and educated guessing. No one can say with authority that "this is the way it was." My summary offers the same disclaimers.

In practical reality there was no single style or type of Greek theatre. A number of elements, however, seem to have been common to almost all the ones we know. The typical Greek amphitheatre illustrated in Figure 3.2 is a composite reconstruction based on a number of theatres dating from the fifth century B.C.

The steeply raked seating area for the audience, called the auditorium, or *theatron,* surrounded on three sides the circular playing area, known as the *orchestra.* Immediately in back of the orchestra was the *skene* (skee'-nee), or stage house. The front wall of the skene probably had several doors or arches through which actors made their entrances. The exact purpose of the skene isn't known, but since it hid the actors from the audience's view and contained a number of rooms, it is assumed that it served various functional

Proscenium: A stage configuration in which the spectators watch the action through a rectangular opening (the proscenium arch) that resembles a picture frame.

Thrust stage: A stage projecting into, and surrounded on three sides by, the audience.

Arena stage: A stage completely surrounded by the audience.

Figure 3.1
Examples of (A)
proscenium, (B)
thrust, and (C)
arena theatres.

(A)

(B)

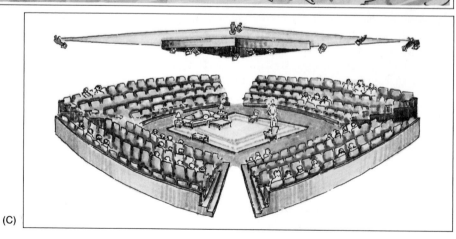

(C)

CHAPTER 3: THEATRE ARCHITECTURE

Figure 3.2 A typical
Greek theatre.

purposes such as housing for stage machinery, storage for props, and possibly space for dressing rooms. The *paraskenia* were long, high walls that extended on either side of and parallel with the skene. It is believed that a low platform, about a foot high, extended across the front of the *paraskenia.* On later Greek theatres they did not extend directly from the skene but were placed closer to the audience. A natural byproduct of this relocation was to extend the low platform across the front of the skene to create a platformed stage. A columned arch, the *proskenium,* was located at the rear of this stage and just in front of the skene. It served to support a porchlike projection from the second story of the skene.

ROMAN THEATRE

Roman architects tinkered with Greek designs, but most of their theatres were simply modifications of the basic Greek form. The most conspicuous Roman development was the compression of the three separate parts of the traditional Greek theatre (orchestra, auditorium, and skene) into one structure. The integration of these elements caused some interesting developments in the structure of the Roman theatre, as shown in Figure 3.3. The auditorium (called a *cavea*), was limited to a semicircular configuration. In many of the theatres the *cavea* was separated from the orchestra by a short wall. The orchestra became a semicircle extending outward from the stage area, which was framed by the proscenium. The skene was transformed into an elaborately decorated single facade called the *scaenae frons.* Its height generally matched the height of the *cavea.*

A number of subtle changes were also brought about by the development of the consolidated Roman theatre structure. The theatres were usually built on level ground instead of the hillside sites favored by the Greeks. In addition, a roofing system was developed for a number of the theatres. The roof extended from the *scaenae frons* to the edge of the proscenium. Some of the theatres even had an awning, known as a *velum,* covering the entire seating area.

With the fall of the Roman Empire in A.D. 364 these grand theatres, which were also the sites of circuses, gladiatorial fights, and lion feedings (Christians and slaves being the primary food), were essentially abandoned, silent relics of a lost era. For approximately five hundred years after the empire fell, the formal theatre was virtually dead. Yet the theatrical tradition

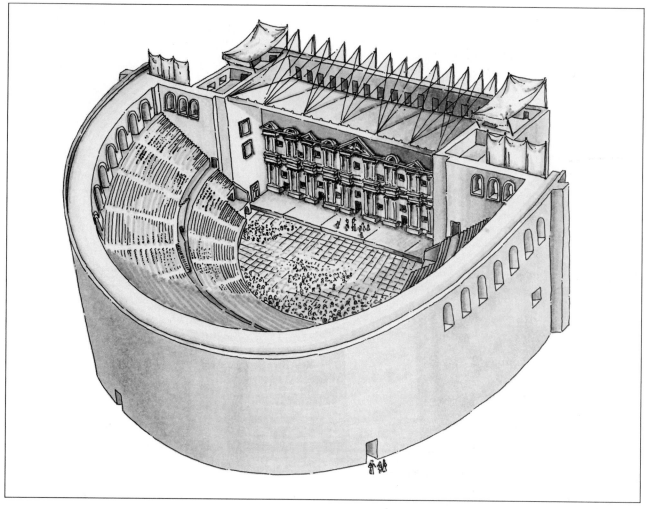

Figure 3.3 A typical Roman theatre.

was kept alive by bands of traveling entertainers, primarily actors and jugglers. These vagabonds surreptitiously performed wherever they could find an audience—in courtyards, village squares, and other temporary stage locations.

MEDIEVAL THEATRE

During the Middle Ages the suppression of theatrical activities was a direct result of the church's opposition to secular drama. Yet the same church that denied the sacraments to actors was also responsible for the revival of the theatre. Sometime during the tenth century, clerics began to use dramatized scenes to help convey their lessons and church doctrine to congregations. During the thirteenth century many of these interludes became too complex to be staged inside the churches, so they were moved outdoors. Staging techniques naturally varied from church to church and location to location. Platform stages were generally constructed adjacent to the church, and the audience stood in the town square (see Figure 3.4). In some cases the platforms were mounted on wagons, appropriately called *pageant wagons* (Figure 3.5), which were pulled from town to town to perform the plays.

All these productions shared some common characteristics. The sets were identical, in concept if not detail, and followed the conventions that had been developed by the clergy for the church productions. The sets were composed

CHAPTER 3: THEATRE ARCHITECTURE

Figure 3.4 A
platform stage.

Figure 3.5 A
pageant wagon.

Although most of the scenes in Greek plays were set outdoors, the Greeks used several devices to move or change scenery. The *eccyclema,* a wheeled platform, was apparently used in a variety of ways. If a scene called for a throne, the central doors in the skene were opened and the *eccyclema,* with a throne on top, was rolled forward. One of the Greeks' theatrical conventions dictated that violent deaths take place offstage, but the bodies were later revealed onstage. The *eccyclema,* this time piled with corpses, was again rolled onto the stage.

Periaktoi, which probably date from the fourth century B.C., were tall, three-sided forms that rotated on a central pivot. Each side was painted with a different scene. Although their exact use isn't known, they were probably placed in the background, and when a change of scene was desired, the *periaktoi* were rotated to reveal another face.

Possibly the most interesting machine was the *machina* (ma-kee´-na). This was a basket or platform that was lowered to the orchestra level from the second story of the skene. Many plays called for intervention by the gods, and the *machina* was used to help the gods descend to, or rise from, the earth.

of small buildings called *mansions,* or stations, that depicted locations appropriate to the biblical stories dramatized in the productions (see Figure 3.6).

The mansions for heaven and hell were on opposite ends of the stage, with the other mansions sandwiched between them. There was a common playing area, called a *platea,* located in front of the mansions, where most of the play's action took place.

One interesting by-product of the medieval theatre was the development of a large number of relatively realistic special effects. Stage machinery, appropriately called *secrets,* included trap doors and a wide variety of rigging that was used to move people and objects about the stages. In one account of "a play staged at Mons [a city in southwestern Belgium] in 1501, technicians were hired to construct the secrets, and seventeen people were needed to operate the hell machinery alone; five men were paid to paint the scenery, and four actor-prompters were employed both to act and to help with the staging."[1]

1. Oscar G. Brockett, *The Theatre: An Introduction,* 4th ed. (New York: Holt, Rinehart and Winston, 1979), p. 106.

Figure 3.6 A typical medieval mansion stage.

RENAISSANCE THEATRE

With the Renaissance the theatre became a central part of the cultural reawakening that quickly spread throughout Europe. Although church-sanctioned pageants continued, secular drama reemerged and became the dominant theatrical form. Theatres, which hadn't been permitted or constructed for over a thousand years, sprang up all over Europe. Because of the strong interest in classical forms and structures the basic shape of almost all these theatres corresponded with the description of Greek and Roman theatres contained in the architectural writings of Vitruvius. Although the theatres were patterned after the classical forms, their designers made many interesting, and clever, adaptations.

The Teatro Olympico in Vicenza, Italy, was one of these theatres (see Figure 3.7). Built between 1580 and 1585, it was designed in the style of the ancient Roman theatres. Probably the most significant change was that the theatre finally moved indoors, with the entire structure enclosed in a building. The *cavea,* or auditorium, was designed not as an exact semicircle but as an ellipse, and this minor change dramatically improved the sight lines in the theatre. The *scaenae frons* was no longer a single decorated wall but was broken by several arches; elaborate permanent sets of street scenes were built, in **forced perspective,** on a **raked stage** floor in back of the arches. In many Renaissance theatres the stage floors were raked to improve the visual effects of the scenery. The actors normally performed on a flat playing space in front of the raked stage.

A second major Renaissance innovation in southern Europe was the introduction of elaborately painted scenery. The use of **stock sets**—usually

Forced perspective: A visual distortion technique that increases the apparent depth of an object.

Raked stage: A stage floor that is higher at the back than the front.

Stock set: Scenery designed to visually support a generalized location (garden, city street, palace, interior) rather than a specific one; commonly used from the Renaissance through the early twentieth century and still in use today in some theatres.

Figure 3.7 The Teatro Olympico.

Drop: A large expanse of cloth, usually muslin or canvas, on which something (a landscape, sky, street, room) is painted.

painted **drops** of the "comic scene," the "tragic scene," the "satyric scene," and so on—necessitated the evolution of the proscenium, or picture frame, stage. Drops were usually hung at the upstage edge of the stage.

ELIZABETHAN THEATRE

At approximately the same time, drama in England was being produced in a different type of structure. A number of theatres had been constructed just outside London by 1600. Probably the most famous was the Globe (1599–1632), the home theatre of William Shakespeare (see Figure 3.8). Although these theatres differed in detail, their basic shape was quite similar.

Figure 3.8 The Globe Theatre.

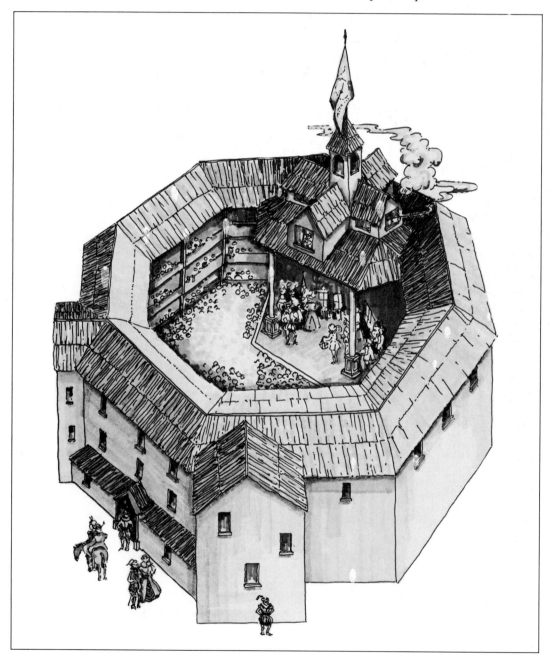

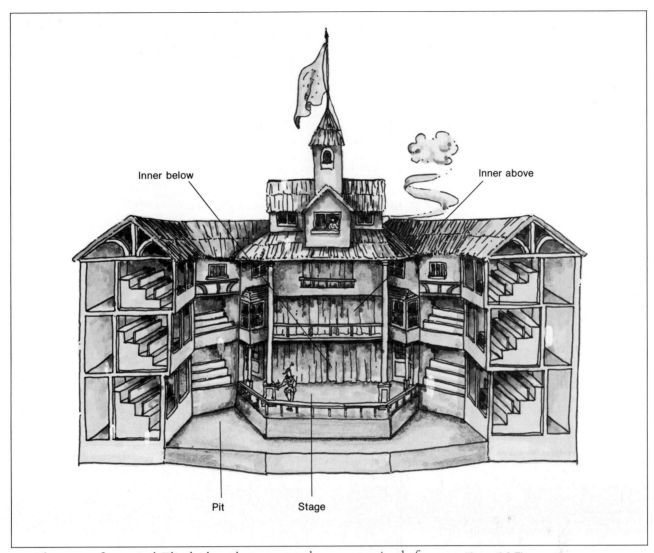

Inner below

Inner above

Pit

Stage

Figure 3.9 The stage of the Globe Theatre.

The stage of a typical Elizabethan theatre was a large, open-air platform generally raised from four to six feet off the ground (see Figure 3.9). The platform was surrounded by a yard, or *pit,* which served as the space for the lower-class audience—the groundlings—to stand. At the upstage end of the stage platform was the area that formed the *inner below.* There is some dispute about the shape of this structure. One theory maintains that it was a curtained alcove recessed into the upstage wall. Another hypothesis holds that it was a roofed structure, curtained on three sides, that projected a little way onto the stage platform. A final theory contends that there was no inner below at all. Depending on the theory to which you subscribe the *inner above* was either an area above the inner below on the back wall, the acting area provided by the roof of the structure that projected onto the stage, or an area that didn't exist as a playing space. In any case, separate entrances apparently flanked either side of the inner below to provide access to the stage.

The stage, the pit, and the wall behind the stage were surrounded by the outside of the building, a three-story structure that housed the galleries and private boxes for the wealthier patrons and nobles.

Little scenery seems to have been associated with Elizabethan productions, although contemporary records do indicate that a number of props—rocks, trees, and the like—were associated with the theatres.

Figure 3.10 A typical Restoration theatre.

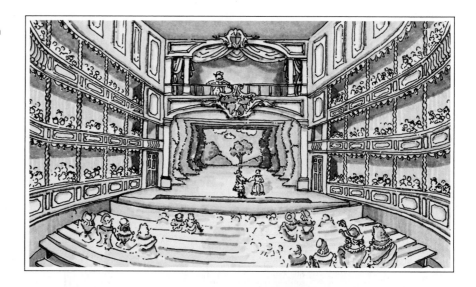

Apron: The flat extension of the stage floor that projects from the proscenium arch toward the audience.

Wings: In scenic terms, either tall, cloth-covered frames or narrow, unframed drops placed on either side of the stage, parallel with the proscenium arch, to prevent the audience from seeing backstage; were usually painted to match the scene on the upstage drop.

Borders: Wide, short, framed or unframed cloth drops suspended to prevent the audience from seeing above the stage; normally match the decorative treatment of the wings and drops in wing and drop sets.

RESTORATION THEATRE

The interest in spectacle and visual effects that began in Italy in the mid-1500s moved rapidly northward across Europe during the next one hundred years. By about 1660 the architectural style of theatre buildings and the types of scenery used in them were fairly standardized throughout England and the rest of Europe.

The theatres were primarily rectangular, with the stage set at one end of the building, as shown in Figure 3.10. The raked stage was framed by the proscenium arch, and the **apron** thrust toward the auditorium. Like its historical antecedents, the forestage of the Elizabethan stage and the *platea* of the medieval theatre, the apron was the site of the majority of the action of the play.

Although the scenery had become more elaborate by this time, with more locations depicted, it still followed the tradition of providing a visual background for the play rather than an environment in which the action of the play could happen. It was painted in perspective on movable drops, **wings,** and **borders** and was placed on the raked stage, where the inclined floor greatly added to the sense of depth created by the perspective painting of the scenery. Most of the plays took place in one of the generalized locations

FUNCTION FOLLOWS FORM

The structure and equipment of theatres has affected theatrical conventions through history. The funeral marches so prominent in Shakespearean tragedies were simply expedient methods to clear bodies from the stage. The Elizabethan theatres didn't have a curtain to hide the stage, and the plays were held in the daytime, so the stage was always lit. This pre-cluded any artful, or semibelievable, method for getting rid of the bodies. Hence the funeral marches.

In the Restoration and eighteenth-century theatres entrances were made from doors on either side of the apron, because the raked stage was cluttered with scenery and the actors' intrusion there would have distorted the illusion of depth carefully designed into the forced-perspective scenery.

CHAPTER 3: THEATRE ARCHITECTURE

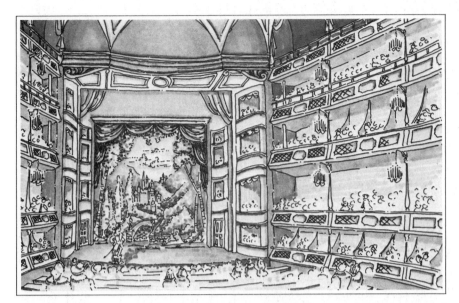

(drawing room, courtyard, palace, garden, and so on), so each theatre owned stock sets that depicted these various scenes. When the action of the play took place in a library, the library set was used. If the theatre didn't happen to have a library set, another stock interior set, such as the drawing room, was substituted.

The auditoriums of these theatres also followed a traditional arrangement (see Figure 3.11): multitiered boxes (for dignitaries and other notables), galleries (for those who could afford the extra charge), and the pit (for those who wanted to see the play but couldn't afford, or weren't permitted, a better seat). This style of proscenium theatre was essentially modern. Some theatres continued to install raked stages, but more and more new structures were built with flat stages. Theatres were constructed in this style until the late nineteenth century.

MODERN THEATRE STRUCTURES

A revolution in the style of theatre began in the late 1800s and continued into the early twentieth century. The work of a number of theatre artists was taking a decidedly different turn from the declamatory style of earlier theatre. The new theatre was devoted to a more realistic and naturalistic type of drama and stressed the previously unheard-of concepts of unity of style for all elements of the production. The Théâtre Libre, founded by André Antoine in Paris, and the Moscow Art Theatre, founded by Konstantin Stanislavski and Vladimir Nemerovich-Danchenko, were but two of the leading groups in this movement toward a more naturalistic and unified style.

As the productions became more realistic, it was natural for the shape of the theatres to change to support this new form. The new plays required that the settings become environments for the action of the drama rather than backgrounds. Consequently, as the action of the play moved onto the stage from the apron, the depth of the apron shrank. When this happened, it became difficult to see all of the action from the boxes and gallery seats adjacent to the proscenium, so the shape of the auditorium began to evolve. The side seats were eliminated, and the remaining seats faced the stage.

Everything speeded up in the twentieth century. Almost as quickly as the realistic movement became the dominant mode of theatre, splinter groups broke off from it to create a number of antirealistic movements. These move-

Throughout history the various shapes of theatre have been determined, to a large extent, by the mores of the sponsoring society. In ancient Greece everyone (except the slaves) was considered of equal rank, so the seating was similarly democratic and unsegregated. In the southern Renaissance and in Europe for the ensuing two hundred years, the majority of theatres were built by the aristocracy for their own amusement. The visual illusions of forced-perspective scenery were best seen from a single point in the center of the auditorium.

This ideal location, subsequently known as "the Duke's seat," was usually found in the second-level box at the back of the auditorium.

The theatres of Elizabethan England, such as the Globe, also had elevated boxes surrounding the stage. The aristocracy and those others who could afford the higher ticket prices sat in the boxes. The common people stood in the pit. About the time of the French Revolution seats began to appear in the pit throughout European theatres as the various societies became more democratic.

ments rose, fell, and evolved so rapidly that most of them didn't have a chance to develop distinctive types of theatre structures. Actually, most of these movements didn't need to change the basic shape of the proscenium theatre or its machinery, because the existing theatres provided a workable environment for their divergent styles.

In the United States the Little Theatre movement of the 1920s and 1930s was an effort to establish quality productions outside of New York City. It also gave new playwrights a chance to improve their craft and have their works produced in an environment that was less critical than the supercharged atmosphere of Broadway. This movement grew and expanded throughout the country. Its crowning glory has been the establishment of a number of excellent contemporary regional professional theatre companies in such cities as San Francisco, Dallas, Denver, Minneapolis, Tucson, and Sarasota.

A ripple effect of the Little Theatre movement was that fledgling companies, funded more by inspiration and lofty intentions than money, began to produce theatre in "found" spaces. Existing barns, churches, feed stores, grocery stores, libraries, old movie houses, and other large, relatively open buildings were all candidates for takeover. Many of these groups relished the enforced intimacy between the actors and audience that shoehorning theatres into these cramped spaces provided. Whether by accident or design, many of these converted theatre spaces didn't have the room to erect a proscenium stage and auditorium. For whatever reasons, thrust and arena stages sprang up all over the country.

The form and structure of the physical theatre have gone through a great many developments. Any number of people have attempted to "improve" the spacial relationship between the stage and auditorium. It is doubtful, however, that anyone will ever devise any genuinely new developments in this relationship, simply because the theatrical experience is based on the premise that the actors need a space in which to perform and the audience must be in a position to see and hear them. When the form of the physical theatre is thought of in this context, it becomes apparent that there really are no different types of theatre, only variations on a basic theme.

4

The Stage and Its Equipment

Theatrical performing spaces have undergone an interesting evolution since about 1960. Influenced by a number of experimental theatre movements as well as economic pressure to make theatres usable for dance groups, symphony concerts, and esoterica such as car, home, and boat shows, companies are changing the shapes of theatres and playing spaces.

Probably the most dominate trend in this evolution is the reduction of the physical and psychological barriers that separate the audience from the production. The New York production of *Cats* was indicative of this change. The set, a stylized representation of an incredibly cluttered junkyard, did not just sedately sit behind the proscenium arch. It negated the concept of the **picture frame stage** by placing elements of the set not only on the stage and apron but also in and on the **orchestra pit,** up the walls of the auditorium, around the balcony rail, and actually up into the ceiling of the auditorium (see Figure 4.1). The actors made entrances through the house, touched members of the audience and talked directly to them. This exciting new style of theatre doesn't let the audience simply sit and observe but directly involves them in the production.

Innovative productions like *Cats* have been happening with increasing regularity throughout the country, and the theatre spaces being designed today are reflecting these production trends. Although an ingenious production concept and large budget can radically alter the appearance of almost any stage-auditorium relationship, it is still true that there are three primary stage configurations—*proscenium, thrust,* and *arena*—that dominate the world of theatre.

Picture frame stage: A configuration in which the spectators watch the action of the play through a rectangular opening; synonym for proscenium arch stage.

Orchestra pit: The space between the stage and the auditorium, usually below stage level, that holds the orchestra.

Figure 4.1 *Cats,* New York production, produced by Cameron Mackintosh, The Really Useful Company Limited, David Geffen, and the Shubert Organization. Photo by Martha Swope.

Figure 4.2 Proscenium stage, Gammage Auditorium, Arizona State University, Tempe.

CHAPTER 4: THE STAGE AND ITS EQUIPMENT

As we have seen, the proscenium stage is also known as the picture frame stage, because the spectators observe the action of the play through the frame of the proscenium arch (Figure 4.2). Although there is debate among theatre artists regarding the appropriateness of using this aloof stage, which forcefully separates the audience from the action, the fact remains that the proscenium stage and its machinery have, for three hundred years, been the dominant mode of presentation. The reason is simple. Like the alligator and the shark, which have survived virtually unchanged through the eons, designs that work needn't be tinkered with.

Proscenium Arch

The proscenium arch, which gives this type of stage its name, is a direct descendant of the *proskenium* and skene of the Greek theatres (see Figure 4.3). This arch, which separates the stage from the auditorium, can vary greatly in both height and width. The average theatre (with three hundred to five hundred seats), generally has a proscenium arch that is eighteen to twenty-two feet high and thirty-six to forty feet wide.

Stage

The playing area behind, or upstage, of the proscenium arch is referred to as the stage (see Figure 4.4). A stage floor is a working surface that serves a

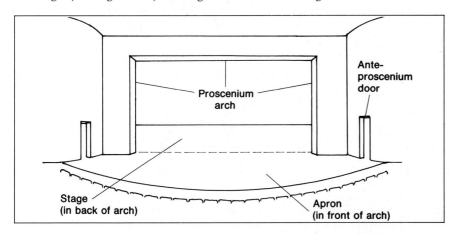

Figure 4.3 The parts of a proscenium stage.

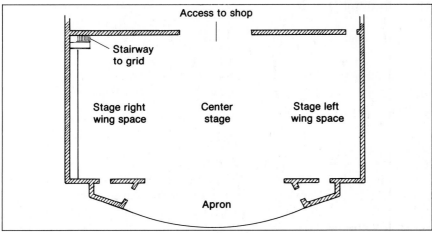

Figure 4.4 The proscenium stage and wings.

STAGE FLOORS

A good stage floor is actually composed of several layers. The subfloor should be made of soft wood such as pine or plywood. These materials are resilient and tough and will hold nails and other fasteners. Traditionally, a heavy, canvas groundcloth covered the subfloor. But a groundcloth can wrinkle or tear when heavy scenery is moved over it, can be painted only a few times before it starts to deteriorate, and is lousy for tap dancing. Quarter-inch tempered Masonite has all of the qualities needed for a good stage floor surface. It has the added advantage of being relatively inexpensive, and individual sections of the floor can be replaced as needed. The one drawback to this fiberboard floor is that it has a tendency to warp when first painted. This problem can be significantly reduced if the sheets are painted *on both sides* before being nailed to the subfloor. (Stand the fiberboard on edge, and paint both sides simultaneously.)

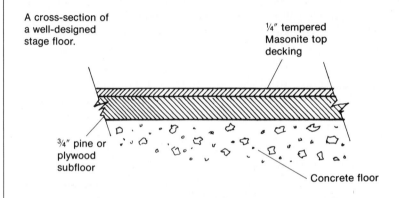

A cross-section of a well-designed stage floor.

¼" tempered Masonite top decking

¾" pine or plywood subfloor

Concrete floor

number of diverse functions. For the actors it must provide a firm, resilient, nonskid (but not too sticky) surface that facilitates movement. For scenic purposes a stage floor needs to be paintable. It should also be reasonably resistant to splintering and gouging caused by heavy stage wagons and other scenic pieces, and it should slightly muffle the sound of footfalls and shifting scenery.

Although many directors choose to move the action of their productions forward onto the apron to bring the play closer to the audience, the primary playing area for most proscenium productions still remains the stage.

Wings

The spaces on either side of the stage are called the wings. Wings are primarily used for storage. During a multiscene production all sorts of scenic elements, props, and other equipment are stored in the wings until they are needed on stage.

Apron

The apron, or forestage, is an extension of the stage from the proscenium arch toward the audience. It stretches across the proscenium arch to the walls of the auditorium and can vary in depth from a narrow sliver only three or four feet deep to as much as ten or fifteen feet. It generally extends for five to fifteen feet beyond either end of the proscenium arch.

Orchestra Pit

Many proscenium theatres have an orchestra pit, which is almost always placed between the apron and the audience. It is used to hold the pit band, or orchestra, during those performances that need live music. To hold an orchestra the pit obviously needs to be fairly large. Most pits extend the full width of the proscenium and are roughly eight to twelve feet across. The depth of the pit varies, but a good pit is deep enough so that the orchestra won't interfere with the spectators' view of the stage.

Obviously, the size of the orchestra pit imposes a rather formidable gulf between the audience and stage when it is not in use. Various solutions have been adopted to remedy this situation (see Figure 4.5). In some theatres the orchestra pit is hidden beneath removable floor panels under the apron; when the pit is needed for a production, the floor panels are removed. In other theatres the pit is placed beneath the auditorium floor. When not in use it is covered with removable panels, and auditorium seats are placed on top. This method has the obvious advantage that additional tickets can be sold when the pit isn't being used.

In some theatres the entire forestage area (apron, orchestra pit, front of the auditorium) is composed of one or more hydraulic lifts. With their great lifting power it is possible to raise or lower whole sections of the stage. When more than one lift is used, they are able to shape the forestage into a variety of configurations, as shown in Figure 4.6.

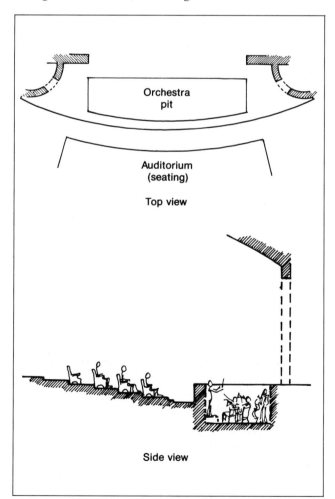

Figure 4.5 The orchestra pit usually occupies part of the apron.

Top view

Side view

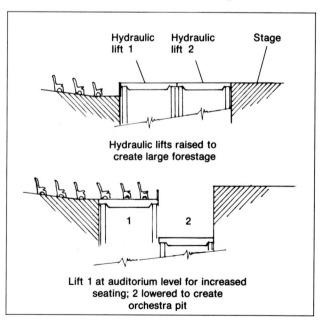

Figure 4.6 Hydraulic lifts can provide a variety of interesting auditorium/stage arrangements.

Hydraulic lift 1   Hydraulic lift 2   Stage

Hydraulic lifts raised to create large forestage

Lift 1 at auditorium level for increased seating; 2 lowered to create orchestra pit

Mike: To place one or more microphones in proximity to a sound source (instrument, voice).

Mix: To blend the electronic signals created by several sound sources.

Balance: To adjust the loudness levels of individual signals while mixing, to achieve an appropriate blend.

The MGM Grand Hotel in Las Vegas has created what may be the ultimate answer to the orchestra pit: there isn't any. The orchestra plays in a room in the basement of the hotel while watching the production on closed-circuit television. Each section of the orchestra is **miked,** and the sound is **mixed** and **balanced** with that of the singers before it is amplified and sent into the auditorium. Although this solution works well in the high-tech atmosphere of Las Vegas, it is doubtful that every musical director would feel comfortable working in this remote and seemingly disconnected manner.

Auditorium

The shape of the typical proscenium theatre auditorium, or house, is roughly rectangular, with the proscenium arch located on one of the narrow ends of the rectangle (see Figure 4.7). Normally, each seat is approximately perpendicular to the proscenium arch. To reduce the reflection of sound waves in an auditorium none of its finished surfaces (walls, ceiling, floor) should be parallel with any others. Thus, the side walls of most auditoriums angle out from the proscenium arch in the shape of a slightly opened fan. The rear wall of the auditorium is almost always curved, and the ceiling generally slopes down toward the rear of the house.

Figure 4.7 Types of seating configurations.

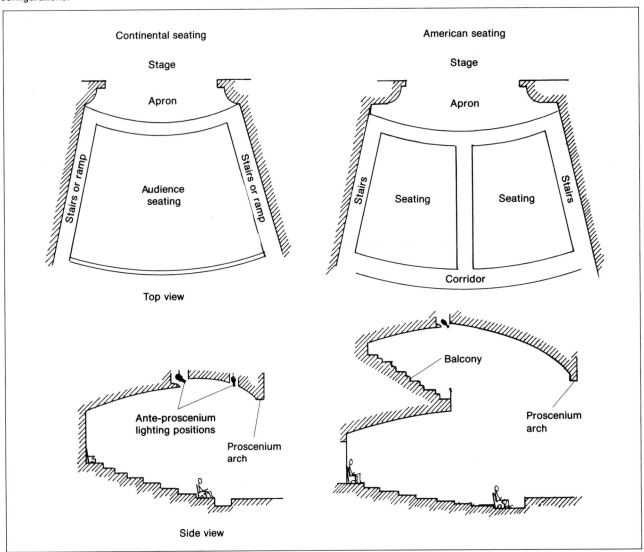

Many contemporary performance spaces have been designed to house productions of dramas, musicals, operas, and orchestral music. A significant challenge in the design of these multipurpose theatres is the differing acoustical requirements of their various tenants. Orchestral music requires a relatively long reverberation time (the amount of time it takes a sound to fade to in-

audibility). A much shorter reverberation time is needed for spoken words to be heard and understood. To solve this challenge many theatres designed in the past twenty-five years have adjustable acoustical panels on the walls and ceilings of the auditoriums. The reverberation time of the auditorium can be changed by adjusting the angle and the reflective quality of these panels.

The floor of the auditorium is raked, or inclined, from the stage to the rear of the house. Angling of the house floor improves not only the acoustics of the theatre but also the spectators' view of the stage, by elevating each successive row.

The lighting control booth is generally located at the back of the auditorium. It normally has one or more large windows to provide the light board operator(s) with an unobstructed view of the stage. Although a sound booth with a large window (which can be opened) is usually located in a similar back-of-house location, the sound operator frequently runs the **sound mixer** from a position actually in the auditorium so he or she can hear what the audience is hearing and balance all the sound sources accordingly. The resulting sound "picture" has a focal point, usually the voice of the actor or singer.

Sound mixer: An electronic device used to adjust the loudness and tone levels of several sources, such as microphones and tape decks.

Proscenium Stage Equipment

Several interesting pieces of permanent stage equipment are frequently associated with proscenium theatres.

TRAPS Many theatres have traps cut into the stage floor. These removable sections provide access to the space beneath the stage (see Figure 4.8). This hole in the middle of the stage can be filled with stairs, an elevator, or a slide,

Figure 4.8 Stage traps provide access to the area beneath the stage.

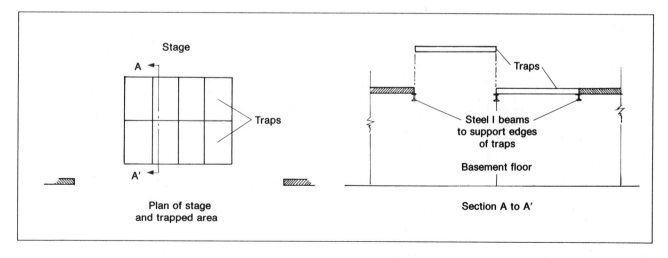

Stage

A

Traps

A'

Plan of stage and trapped area

Traps

Steel I beams to support edges of traps

Basement floor

Section A to A'

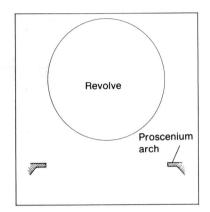

Figure 4.9 A revolving stage is sometimes built into the stage floor.

or can just be left open, depending on the desired visual and physical effect. Ideally, the majority of a stage floor is trapped. If only a few traps have been installed, Murphy's Law indicates that they will almost always be in the wrong places. Although traps are more frequently found in proscenium theatres, there is nothing preventing this very useful piece of equipment from being installed on either thrust or arena stages.

REVOLVE The *revolve,* also called a turntable or revolving stage, provides a visually interesting and efficient manner of shifting scenery (see Figure 4.9). Some theatres have revolves built into the stage floor. Depending on the size of the revolve, part or all of a multiset design can be fit onto it and rotated to bring other scenic elements into view.

SLIPSTAGE The slipstage is a huge stage wagon large enough to cover the full width of the proscenium arch (see Figure 4.10). When not in use the slipstage is stored in one of the wings. Entire sets can be mounted on the slipstage. When needed, it is simply rolled into place on stage.

Revolves and slipstages are permanent features of a theatre's stage. Smaller, temporary versions can be constructed to meet the needs of individual productions. Construction techniques for making these smaller versions are discussed in Chapter 9, *Scenic Production Techniques.*

Figure 4.10 A slipstage is designed to hold an entire set.

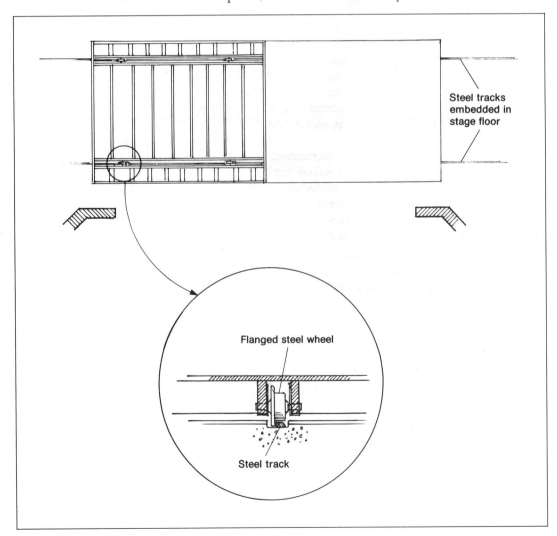

Fly Loft

The area directly over the stage is called the fly loft (see Figure 4.11). The fly loft, also referred to as "the flies," is usually quite tall, minimally two and a half times the height of the proscenium arch, to allow the scenery to be raised out of sight of the audience. The **grid,** or gridiron, is located just below the roof of the fly loft. It serves as a platform to hold some of the equipment used to **fly** scenery, as well as providing the primary support for the weight of the scenery and curtains being flown.

Several systems are used to fly scenery. The two primary methods, rope set and counterweight, work on the same operating principle—counterbalancing.

ROPE SET The oldest method of flying is with rope and pulley. The pulley is attached to the grid, and the rope is fed through it and tied to the scenery. A stagehand pulls on the free end of the rope and raises the scenery. If the load is too heavy, a sandbag is tied to the free end of the rope as a counterbalance.

Grid: A network of steel I beams supporting elements of the system used to raise and lower scenery.

Fly: To raise an object or person above the stage floor with ropes or cables.

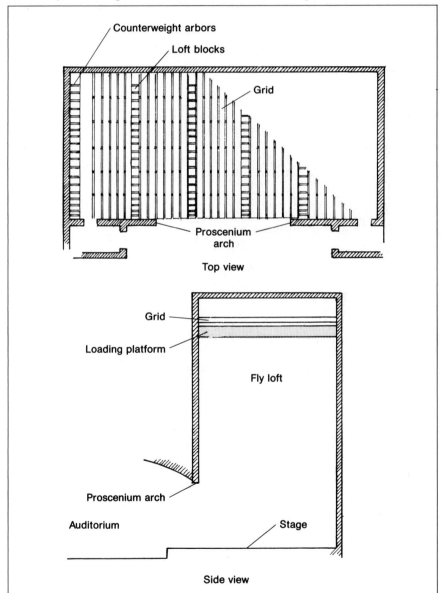

Top view

Side view

Figure 4.11 The fly loft and grid are integral parts of any flying system. Scenery and equipment can be flown for storage in the fly loft, while the grid supports the loft blocks.

Figure 4.12 A rope set.

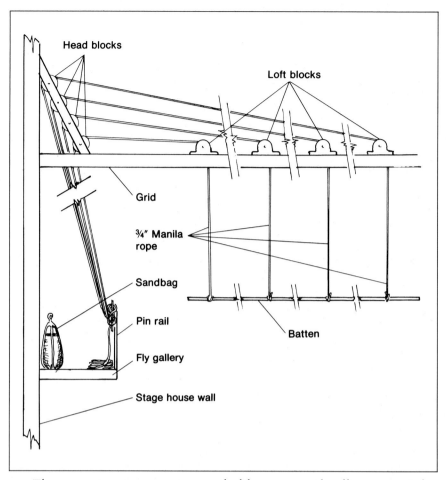

Batten: A thick wooden dowel or metal pipe (generally 1¼ to 1½ inches in diameter) from which are suspended scenery and lighting instruments.

Loft block: A grooved pulley, mounted on top of the grid, used to change the direction in which a rope or cable travels.

Stage house: The physical structure enclosing the area above the stage and wings.

Head block: A multisheave block (one with two or more pulley wheels), used to change the direction of all the ropes or cables that support the batten.

Fly gallery: The elevated walkway where the pin rail is located.

Pin rail: A horizontal pipe or rail studded with belaying pins; the ropes of the rope set system are wrapped around the belaying pins to hold the batten at a specific height.

The rope set system operates exactly like a rope and pulley, except it has three or more lines instead of one (see Figure 4.12). The ropes, usually three-quarter-inch manila, support a **batten.** From the batten they run to the grid, where they pass over **loft blocks,** which direct them toward the side of the **stage house.** At the edge of the grid the lines pass over the **head block** and then down to the **fly gallery,** where they are tied off on the **pin rail.** The fly gallery is generally located fifteen to twenty feet above the stage floor to give the flypersons, or operators of the flying system, a relatively clear view of the stage.

SAFETY TIP

Rope Set Systems

Although the rope set system is relatively simple, it is not particularly safe. The ropes, which are made from manila fiber, and sandbags, which are made of heavyweight canvas, are subject to constant—and all but impossible to detect—stress and deterioration. They must be continually inspected for cuts, nicks, and other indications of wear. The ropes should be replaced as soon as any abrasions or cuts are noticed. Even if no deterioration is noted, they should be replaced at least once a year if the system is used with any frequency and more frequently if it is used heavily. The sandbags should also be replaced at least once every five years or immediately if any damage is noticed.

The scenery must be raised to its high trim mark (the height at which it will be stored) before the counterweight sandbag can be attached to the free end of the rope. Finally, the system must always be batten heavy (the scenery must always be heavier than the counterweight), so the scenery can be lowered without having to attach special ropes to pull it down.

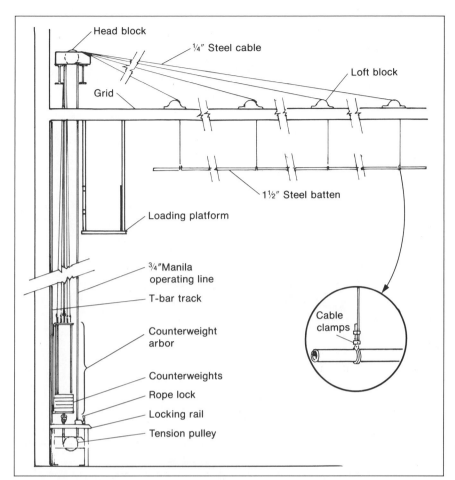

Figure 4.13 A counterweight system.

Head block

¼″ Steel cable

Loft block

Grid

1½″ Steel batten

Loading platform

¾″Manila operating line

T-bar track

Counterweight arbor

Cable clamps

Counterweights

Rope lock

Locking rail

Tension pulley

COUNTERWEIGHT SYSTEM The counterweight system works on the same principle as the rope set system and is much safer. As shown in Figure 4.13 the support ropes for the battens have been replaced with steel cables. The cables are attached to the batten, and they run up to the loft blocks and over to the head block. But instead of being tied off at the pin rail, they are secured to the top of a **counterweight arbor,** or carriage. The counterweights in the arbor balance the weight of the scenery that is attached to the batten. When the batten is lowered to the stage level, the arbor automatically moves upward to the level of the **loading platform** just below the grid. This allows the counterweights to be loaded onto the arbor while the scenery is still resting safely on the stage.

The system is controlled by an operating line of three-quarter-inch manila rope. The operating line is attached to the top of the arbor, runs over a head block, down through a rope lock to a tension pulley, and then back to the bottom of the counterweight arbor. To lower the batten you pull down on the part of the line that is closest to you. To raise the batten you pull down on the offstage part of the line. The **locking rail** is located on the stage floor against the stage house wall. Although this arrangement is convenient, it does take up floor space that could be used for other purposes.

In theatres with limited offstage space the use of a multiple-speed counterweight system solves the problem by raising the locking rail off the stage floor. This type of system, shown in Figure 4.14, creates a mechanical advantage (2:1) that allows the batten to move twice as far as the counterweight arbor. The drawback to this system is that twice as much weight must be loaded onto the arbor to balance the weight of the scenery.

Counterweight arbor: A metal cradle that holds the counterbalancing weights used to fly scenery.

Loading platform: A walkway, suspended just below the grid, where counterweights are loaded onto the arbor.

Locking rail: A rail that holds the rope locks for each counterweight set.

Figure 4.14 A multispeed counterweight system.

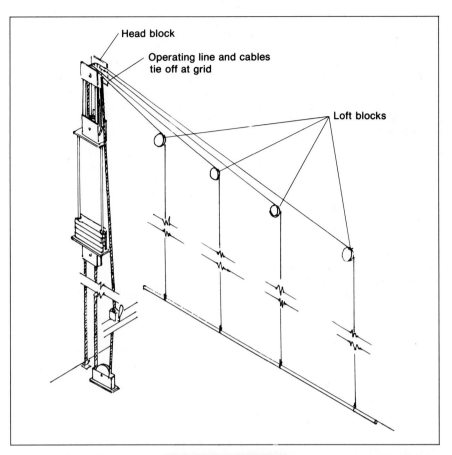

Head block

Operating line and cables
tie off at grid

Loft blocks

S A F E T Y   T I P

Counterweight Systems

It isn't very difficult to make a counterweight system safe to operate. A few basic rules need to be observed.

1. Make sure that everybody clears the stage area under the loading platform when counterweights are being loaded on the arbor.
2. Don't stack counterweights above the lip of the loading platform or anywhere where they might be knocked off of the platform.
3. When working on the grid, loading platform, or pin rail, don't carry anything in your pockets other than the tools you are going to use. Extra tools, pencils, or keys might fall on someone, causing serious injury.
4. Inspect all flying hardware, and repair or replace *any* defective equipment.
5. Bolt in place the hardware supporting all flown units. Nails or screws can pull out of the wood.
6. Always attach the scenery to the batten first, then load the counterweights.
7. When removing (striking) flown scenery, always unload the counterweights first, then remove the scenery from the batten.
8. Any unit other than a very light flat should be flown under compression. This means that the lines supporting the piece are attached to the bottom of the unit rather than the top.

The three-quarter-inch manila operating line should be inspected for abuse or unusual wear at least once a year. If any nicks or abrasions are noticed, replace the rope at once. Routinely replace the rope every five years. The cable clamps securing the cable to the batten and arbor should be inspected and tightened at least every six months. Any bent or otherwise broken or abused batten pipes should be replaced immediately. The entire rigging system should be inspected by a reputable professional rigger at least once every five years.

CHAPTER 4: THE STAGE AND ITS EQUIPMENT

Certain mechanical systems can provide a power-multiplying effect known as mechanical advantage. A 2:1 mechanical advantage means that you can move twice the weight, with the same amount of force, that you can with a system providing no mechanical advantage.

The single whip illustrated in the first figure doesn't create any mechanical advantage, because it is just changing the direction of pull on the operating line. If, however, we attached one end of the rope to a strong beam in the ceiling, as shown in the second figure, attached the pulley to the weight we were trying to raise, and then pulled *up* on the rope, we would create a 2:1 mechanical advantage. This system is called a running block.

It is relatively easy to determine the mechanical advantage of any tackle-rigging configuration. Simply count the number of lines that pass through the block. Don't count the operating line if it is hanging down from the last pass through the block (the housing for the pulley wheels). The total number of lines will be equal to the mechanical advantage for that particular block and tackle system. Friction reduces the actual efficiency of any block and tackle arrangement by 10 percent for each pulley sheave in the system.

With block and tackle you create increased lifting power, but you do so by losing speed. For example, with a double whip (2:1 mechanical advantage) the load moves half the distance that the operating line travels, while the watch tackle (3:1 mechanical advantage) moves the load one-third the distance that the operating line travels.

Four common tackle rigs.

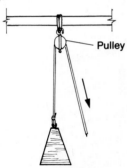

**Single whip
(no mechanical advantage)**

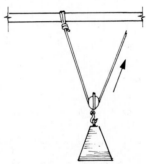

**Running block
(2 to 1 mechanical advantage)**

**Double whip
(2 to 1 mechanical advantage)**

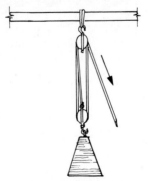

**Watch tackle
(3 to 1 mechanical advantage)**

Motorized systems are also used to fly scenery. These vary from simple systems that drive the operating line of a regular counterweight set to complex designs of great electronic sophistication, as shown in Figure 4.15.

Stage Drapes

The proscenium stage uses more types of stage drapery than either the thrust or arena stage. Although they have relatively specific functions, all stage drapes are designed to **mask** backstage areas from the spectators. Stage drapes are usually made of black, light-absorbing material such as heavyweight velour or similar material (commando cloth, duvetyn, rep). Typical hanging positions for the various types of stage drape are shown in Figure 4.16.

GRAND DRAPE The purpose of the grand drape (also known as the main curtain, main drape, or grand rag) is to cover the proscenium opening. In theatres that have a fly loft the grand drape, which is usually made from heavyweight velour, can normally be flown or **traveled.**

GRAND VALANCE The grand valance is located just downstage (or upstage, in some theatres) of the grand drape. It is made of the same material as the grand drape but is much shorter, usually only eight to twelve feet high. It is used to mask the equipment and scenery that are flown immediately upstage of the proscenium.

Figure 4.15 A motorized winch system. The winch drives cables over standard loft blocks positioned on the grid. Illustration courtesy of the Peter Albrecht Corporation.

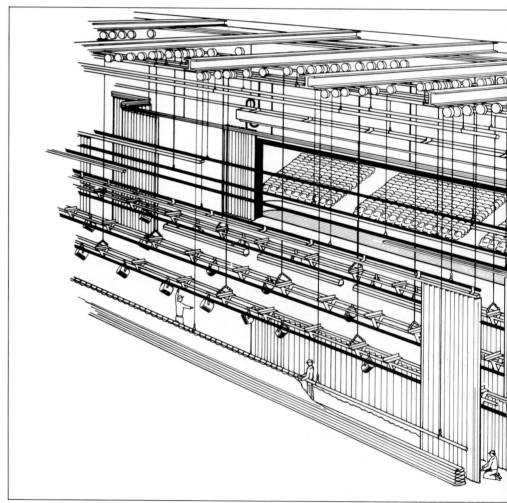

CHAPTER 4: THE STAGE AND ITS EQUIPMENT

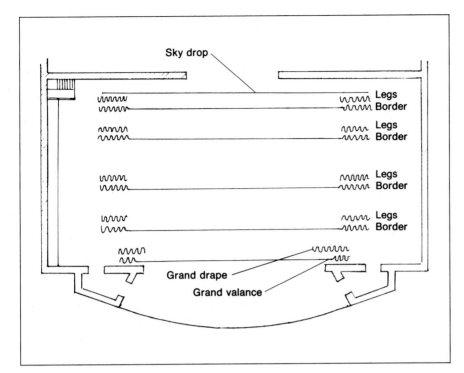

Figure 4.16 Standard hanging positions for stage draperies.

Sky drop

Legs
Border

Legs
Border

Legs
Border

Legs
Border

Grand drape

Grand valance

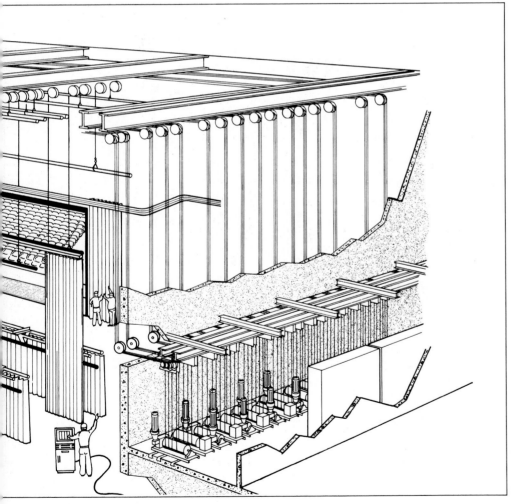

Flat: A framework, normally made of wood or metal; usually covered with fabric, although a variety of other covering materials may be used.

Hard teaser: The horizontal element of the false proscenium; usually hung from a counterweighted batten so its height can easily be adjusted.

Tormentor: The vertical flats that form the side elements of the false proscenium.

Show portal: A false proscenium that visually supports the style and color palette of a particular production.

Figure 4.17 A false proscenium.

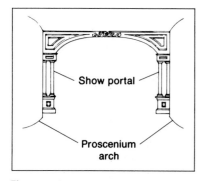

Figure 4.18 A show portal.

FALSE PROSCENIUM The false proscenium (Figure 4.17) is located immediately upstage of the grand drape and grand valance. It is normally mounted on a rigid framework. The **flat** structures of both the **hard teaser** and **tormentors** are usually covered with black velour or some similar type of black, light-absorbing material. The primary purpose of the false "pro" is to provide masking. The tormentors mask the sides of the stage, and the hard teaser provides primary masking for the flies. Since both the tormentors and hard teaser are movable, they can also be used to shrink the apparent size of the proscenium opening.

A **show portal** (Figure 4.18) is a false proscenium designed for a specific production. It not only masks the stage but also provides a picture frame for the set.

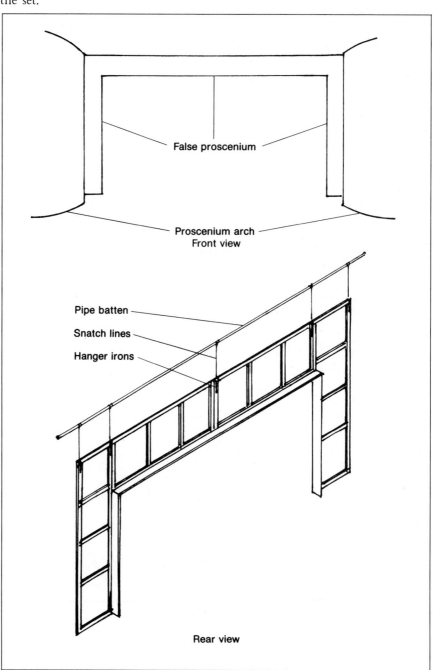

LEGS AND TEASERS Legs are narrow, vertical stage drapes that are used to mask the sides of the stage upstage of the proscenium arch. They are generally made of the same light-absorbing material as other stage drapes. Teasers are short horizontal draperies, normally four to ten feet tall, used to mask the flies. Legs and teasers usually have long strings, called ties, either sewn to the jute tape at the top of the drape or slipped through brass **grommets,** which are fixed to the jute tape so they can be tied to a supporting batten. Ties are usually made from thirty-six-inch pieces of half-inch-wide cotton tape, although thirty-six-inch shoestrings work very well.

Teasers are normally used in conjunction with a set of legs (two legs) to provide a complete framework of masking for the stage, as shown in Figure 4.19. If the theatre is equipped with a counterweight system, teasers and legs are rarely hung on the same batten, because the trim height of the teaser needs to be variable, whereas the legs should be trimmed so that the lower hem barely brushes the stage floor. Teasers are generally hung on the batten immediately downstage of the one holding the legs. If the theatre doesn't have a counterweight or adjustable height rigging system, the legs and teasers are normally hung on the same batten.

Grommet: A circular metal eyelet used to reinforce holes in fabric.

Figure 4.19 Hanging positions for legs and teasers.

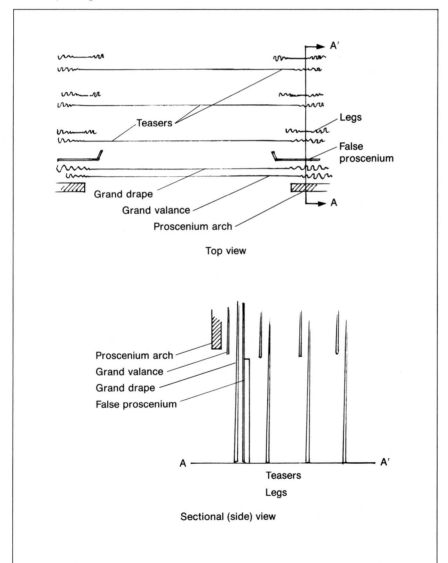

Top view

Sectional (side) view

SKY DROP The sky drop (Figure 4.20), also known as a sky tab, is, as its name implies, used to simulate the sky. It is a large, flat curtain, without fullness, normally made of muslin or scenic canvas. It is usually hung on a batten as far upstage as possible.

The sky drop has traditionally been dyed a uniform blue to help simulate the color of the sky. Current practice suggests that the sky drop should be made of unbleached fabric, which is off-white. This neutral color allows the lighting designer to create a sky color that is appropriate to the mood and concept of the production.

Figure 4.20 A sky drop.

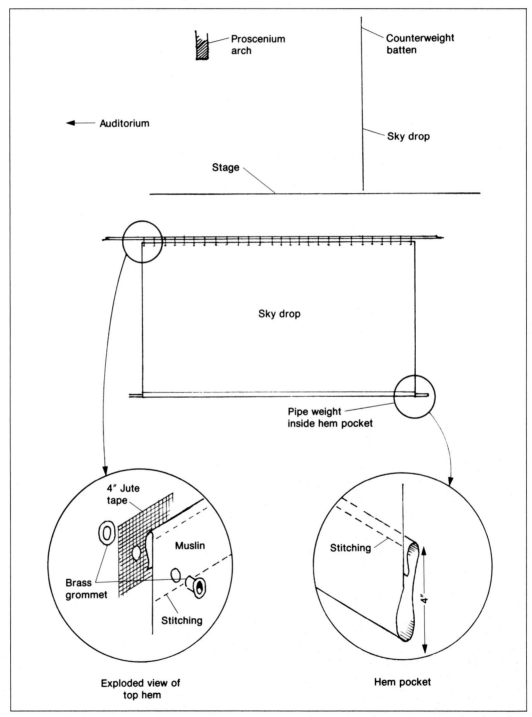

CHAPTER 4: THE STAGE AND ITS EQUIPMENT

Cyclorama The cyclorama, or "cyc" (Figure 4.21), is an expansion on the concept of the sky drop. Although the sky drop works very well for productions that require only a small patch of sky, it doesn't surround the set with the illusion of vast expanses of open sky. Historically, when plays began making this type of scenic demand, technicians responded by hanging two more sky drops at almost right angles to the original curtain to provide a wraparound expanse of sky, as shown in Figure 4.21B. Where the drops met, they were overlapped to prevent gaps in the smooth expanse of simulated sky.

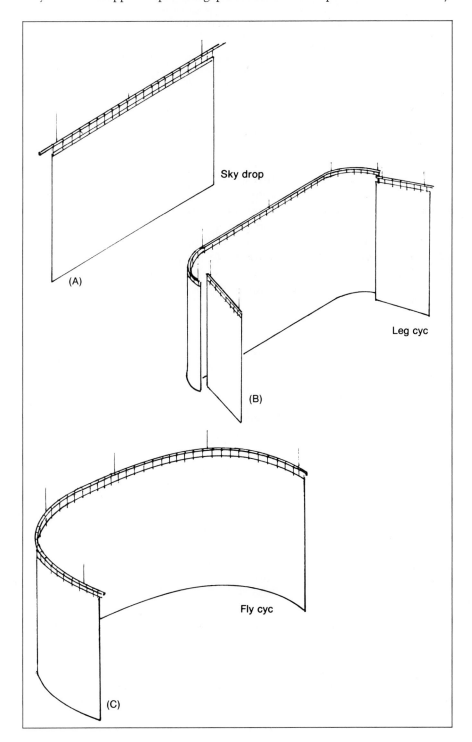

Figure 4.21 A sky drop and two types of cycloramas.

Sky drop

(A)

Leg cyc

(B)

Fly cyc

(C)

The **fly cyc** (Figure 4.21C) is made from one unbroken expanse of cloth. It is hung on a counterweighted pipe located outside the other counterweighted battens to reduce any possible interference between the two systems.

Sometimes sharkstooth **scrims** are used in conjunction with both sky drops and cycloramas. Sharkstooth scrim is a knit fabric that is actually composed of more open spaces than thread. Because of this structure the fabric possesses some very interesting properties. When light is projected onto the front of sharkstooth scrim, it is reflected back toward the viewer, and the fabric appears to be opaque. When the front light is turned off and any objects behind the scrim are lit, the sharkstooth scrim becomes transparent, and the objects in back of it are clearly visible. When those same objects are lit, and light also strikes the scrim, it becomes translucent, and the objects, while still visible, are hazy and less distinct.

A white scrim hung in front of the cyc helps smooth out any wrinkles, dirty spots, and imperfections on the cyc. If the scrim is hung on a batten a foot or two downstage of the cyc, additional lights can be focused onto the scrim to provide very interesting, and sometimes spectacular, multilayer cyclorama lighting.

A black sharkstooth scrim can also be used to enhance the sky drop or cyc lighting. Used in the same manner as the white scrim, it improves aerial perspective by reducing the intensity and saturation of objects that are lit behind it.

A great deal of stage lighting equipment could be considered a part of the permanent stage equipment. It will be discussed in Chapter 14, *Lighting Production*.

Fly cyc: A single drop, hung on a U-shaped pipe, that surrounds the stage on three sides.

Scrim: A drop made from translucent or transparent material.

THRUST STAGE

As we saw in the last chapter, the thrust stage (see Figure 4.22) isn't a new development. Medieval audiences gathered on three sides of the pageant wagons and platform stages to watch passion plays, and research indicates that the Globe theatre also had a thrust stage. The thrust stage was rediscovered by directors who wanted to move the action of the play out of what they felt were the artificial and limiting confines of the proscenium stage. Whatever the reasons, the mid-twentieth century saw the birth of a large number of thrust stage theatres in the United States.

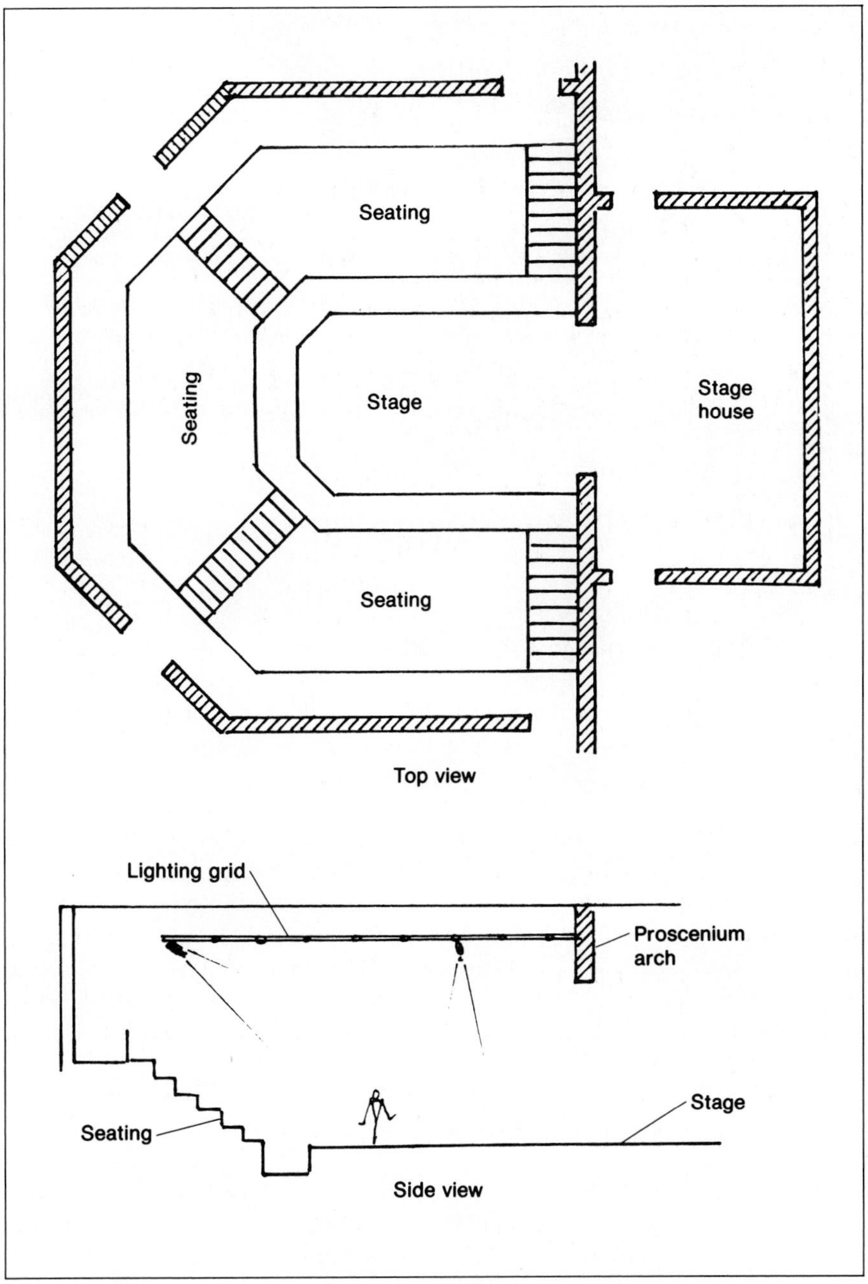

Figure 4.22 A typical thrust stage arrangement.

Seating

Seating

Stage

Stage house

Seating

Top view

Lighting grid

Proscenium arch

Seating

Stage

Side view

The stage of the thrust theatre projects into, and is surrounded on three sides by, the audience, so tall flats, drops, and vertical masking can't be used where they would interfere with the spectators' view of the stage (see Figure 4.23). But on the fourth, or upstage, side of the stage, drops and flats can be placed to help visually describe the play's location. Although entrances are frequently made through openings in the upstage wall, the house is also used for this purpose.

The **lighting grid** in a thrust theatre is usually suspended over the entire stage and auditorium space, so instruments can be hung wherever necessary to effectively light the playing area. Lighting grids vary in complexity from designs that hide the lighting instruments from the spectators' view to simple pipe grids from which the lights are hung in full view, as shown in Figure 4.24.

Lighting grid: A network of pipes from which lighting instruments are hung.

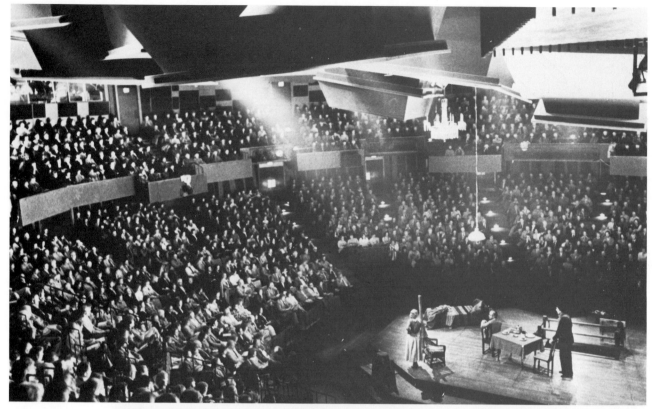

Figure 4.23 Thrust theatre. Tyrone Guthrie Theater, Minneapolis, Minnesota. Seating an audience of 1,441, no seat is further than 52 feet from the stage. Photo by Robert Ashley Wilson.

Figure 4.24 Lighting grids for thrust theatres are frequently exposed pipe grids. The Contemporary Theatre, Seattle, Washington. Photo by Chris Bennion.

CHAPTER 4: THE STAGE AND ITS EQUIPMENT

I t can be somewhat frustrating trying to tell an actor what direction to move or telling a technician that "I want the sofa a little farther to the left." "My left?" he asks. "No, that way. Over there." Through the years a system of stage directions has evolved to help clear up these problems.

On the American proscenium and thrust stages, stage directions are understood to mean that you are standing on the stage and looking into the auditorium. Stage left is to your left and stage right is to your right. Upstage is behind you, and downstage is in front of you. The terms *upstage* and *downstage* probably evolved in the sixteenth or seventeenth century during the era of raked stages, when you literally went up the slope of the stage in moving upstage.

Stage directions in Europe are noted in a slightly different manner. Upstage and downstage are the same, but right and left are reversed from the American system, being given in reference to the auditorium rather than the stage.

Stage directions for arena stages can't use this system, since the audience surrounds the stage. When this happens, it is much easier to describe the stage directions by referring to one direction as north, and then the remaining directions are understood to be south, east, and west.

Stage directions.

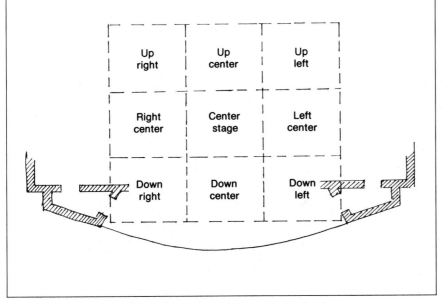

Access to the simpler pipe grids is usually from a rolling ladder placed on the stage. The more complex grids frequently have walkways above the pipes to allow electricians to adjust the lighting instruments from above. In addition to the grid there are usually some additional **hanging positions** above the house, either open pipes or some type of semiconcealed location.

Some thrust theatres retain a vestigal proscenium arch on the upstage wall as well as a small backstage area. Although battens are frequently **dead hung** above this backstage space, some theatres have installed **rachet winches,** rope sets, or counterweight sets so the battens can be raised and lowered.

The lighting and sound booths are generally located at the back of the

Hanging position: A location where lighting instruments are placed.

Dead hang: To suspend without means of raising or lowering.

Ratchet winch: A device, used for hoisting, with a crank attached to a drum; one end of a rope or cable is attached to the drum, the other end to the load; by turning the crank the load can be moved; a ratchet gear prevents the drum from spinning backward.

house directly facing the stage, although nothing stronger than tradition prevents them from being placed at any location in the auditorium that provides an unobstructed view of the stage. Again, as in the proscenium theatre, and for the same reasons, the sound operator frequently chooses to run the mixing board from a position in the house rather than from the sound booth.

ARENA STAGE

The arena stage (Figure 4.25) is another step in the development of an intimate actor-audience theatre. The audience surrounds the stage and is much closer to the action of the play than in either the proscenium or thrust theatres (see Figure 4.26).

Figure 4.25 A typical arena theatre configuration.

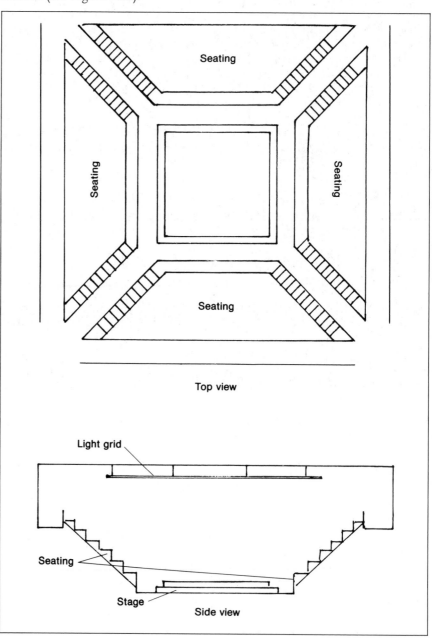

CHAPTER 4: THE STAGE AND ITS EQUIPMENT

The scenery used on an arena stage is extremely minimal. Because the audience surrounds the stage, designing for the arena theatre provides a challenge to all the designers. Anything used on an arena stage—sets, costumes, makeup, props—must be carefully selected to very clearly specify the period, mood, and feeling of the play. Additionally, everything must be well constructed, because the audience sits almost on top of the stage and can see every construction detail.

As in the thrust stage theatre, the space above the arena stage has a lighting grid rather than a fly loft. The lighting grid frequently covers not only the stage but the auditorium as well.

The stage manager and the lighting and sound operators need to have a clear view of the stage. Many arena theatres have an elevated deck running around the perimeter of the auditorium to provide these people with a variety of potential work locations. Some arena theatres have a traditional lighting booth and sound control booth rather than flexible work stations.

Figure 4.26 Arena theatre. The interior of the 827-seat Arena Stage in Washington, D.C.

Figure 4.27 Converted theatre space. The stage/auditorium of the Yale Repertory Theatre, housed in a former church.

BLACK BOX THEATRES

The flexible staging of black box theatres encourages, and demands, ingenuity from the production design team. These new design-it-yourself performance spaces are a direct result of a number of experimental theatre movements that sought to break down the visual and psychological barriers created by the proscenium stage.

In black box theatres (so named because they are usually painted black and have a simple rectangular shape) the seating is generally on movable bleacherlike modules that can be arranged in any number of ways around the playing space. Although the space can be set up in traditional proscenium, thrust, or arena configurations, it can also be aligned into excitingly different staging arrangements that support the production concept for particular productions. This type of theatre is fun to work in, and every production creates a very real challenge to the ingenuity of the production design team.

The black box theatre was developed partially as a reaction against the artistic confines of more formal types of stage space. Consequently, there isn't a great deal of specific stage equipment associated with it. However, there is a lighting grid, very similar to that of the arena theatre, located above the stage and auditorium space, and there is usually a variety of additional hanging locations.

"FOUND" THEATRE SPACES

Found theatre spaces lend a great deal of credence to the statement that all theatre really needs is "two boards and a passion." These theatres are housed in structures that were originally designed for some other purpose. Almost every conceivable type of space has been, or could be, converted for use as a theatre. In Tucson, Arizona, alone, a supermarket, movie house, lumber yard, feed store, office building, and restaurant have been converted to theatrical use, all within the past fifteen years. The Lafayette Square Theatre in New York City houses five theatres in what used to be a library. The only criteria for conversion seem to be sufficient square footage in the building to house a stage and its audience and sufficient nearby parking or public transportation (see Figure 4.27).

Found theatre spaces are frequently converted into black box theatres, but a number of converting companies have opted for the more traditional arena or thrust stage configurations. For some producing groups the appeal of the converted space lies in the intimacy of the audience-actor relationship that is inherent in these generally small theatres. For others, the lower production costs of the smaller, more intimate theatre forms are an asset.

5

A designer needs to communicate, to share his or her information and ideas both verbally and visually. In Chapter 2 you were introduced to the verbal language of # Composition and Design

the designer—that is, the questioning process and the dynamics of group discussion, which are vital to the interaction among members of the production design team. In this chapter you are introduced to the other, equally important language of the designer—the visual language.

ELEMENTS OF DESIGN

What is design? Design is concerned with the processes of planning and drawing, specifically, planning an overall concept and drawing sketches, patterns, and other visualizations of the design. The drawings produced by every designer (scenic, costume, lighting, and, to a certain extent, sound) need to be guided by the elements of design—line, form, mass, value, and color. These elements, which are taken up next, are manipulated and adjusted to create a visual composition.

Line

The properties that define the characteristics of a line are dimension, quality, and character.

DIMENSION Dimension refers to the length and width of a line, as shown in the examples in Figure 5.1.

Figure 5.1 Lines can have different dimensions, quality, and character.

Figure 5.2 The quality of a line is defined by its shape.

Figure 5.3 Varying the character of a line changes its connotative meaning.

Figure 5.4 Form is created by enclosing space within a line.

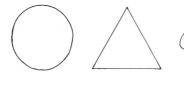

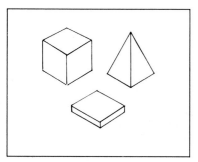

Figure 5.5 Mass is the three-dimensional manifestation of form.

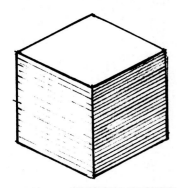

Figure 5.6 Value helps the designer create apparent depth in a drawing.

QUALITY The quality of a line refers to its intrinsic shape. Lines can be straight, curvilinear, or anything in between, as shown in Figure 5.2.

CHARACTER The character of a line refers to its emotionally evocative characteristics, whether soft, hard, harsh, or sensuous. The lines shown in Figure 5.3 all have different character, because they elicit different emotional reactions from the viewer.

Form

Any line that encloses a space creates a form. The drawings shown in Figure 5.4 create form by enclosing space within the boundaries of their lines. Form generally refers to a two-dimensional composition that has height and width but no apparent depth. The character of the form is further defined by the quality of the line used in creating it.

Mass

Mass is the three-dimensional manifestation of a form. The three-dimensional counterpart of a square would be a cube. Several examples of mass are shown in Figure 5.5.

Value

Value refers to the relative lightness or darkness of a line, form, or mass. The value of the sides of the cube illustrated in Figure 5.6 helps to create its apparent depth.

Color

There are various definitions of color. In one sense color is a perception created by the brain as a result of the stimulation of the retina by light waves of a certain length. In another sense it can be thought of as a term to describe all wavelengths of light that are contained in the visible spectrum. Because color is such a complex subject it will be discussed separately in Chapter 6, *Color.*

CHAPTER 5: COMPOSITION AND DESIGN

To be a really effective designer you must understand the basic principles of composition. They can guide you to an understanding of how the visual elements of a design, whether scenic, costume, or lighting, are coordinated. Good composition usually results when the line, form, mass, value, and color are arranged in a cohesive and unified manner.

The principles of composition are relatively simple. They are harmony, rhythm, and balance, achieved through the adjustment of relationship of line, form, mass, value, and color.

Harmony

Harmony is the sense of blending and unity that is obtained when all elements of a design fit together to create an orderly, congruous whole. Harmony is achieved when a combination of design elements seem to naturally blend or flow together, avoiding discordant or incompatible contrasts. Although harmony is primarily concerned with congruity, it doesn't require that all lines, forms, masses, values, and colors within a design be of one particular style, shape, or character. What it does mean is that those elements should be chosen to complement one another. For example, the **profile,** or **silhouette,** for the walls of the set of *A Member of the Wedding* (Figure 5.7) is actually composed of two basic lines. The more apparent is the slightly jagged silhouette of the short vertical cuts. The second is the long, gentle sweep of the silhouette itself. The jagged line was chosen for two reasons, one aesthetic, the other logical. The jagged line is evocative of the emotional stress that is felt by Frankie, the play's main character. The more mundane reason for selecting this line is that the short, vertical breaks can be thought of as the ends of the clapboards that cover the outside of the house. The long, sweeping line was chosen to reinforce the romantic, nostalgic nature of the play.

Profile (silhouette): The outline of a form, which determines the form's quality and character.

Rhythm

Rhythm refers to the orderly and logical interrelationship of successive parts of a composition. It can be the logical progression of a motif through all the

Figure 5.7 Harmony is created when the various elements in a composition seem to blend and flow together. *A Member of the Wedding* scenic design by the author.

elements of a composition, as in the vase and chain design illlustrated in Figure 5.8. It can also be demonstrated through the placement of physical features of the design in an arrangement that directs the eye toward the focal point, or center of attention of the design, as shown in the costume in Figure 5.9.

Balance

Balance can be established by the arrangement of the design elements to give a sense of restfulness, stability, or equilibrium to the design. Balance can be either symmetrical or asymmetrical.

Symmetrical balance means that if you were to draw a line down the center of the design shown in Figure 5.10, the objects on the left would be a mirror image of the objects on the right. Symmetrical balance has an ordered,

Figure 5.8 Rhythm is created when there is a logical interrelationship between the parts of a composition.

Figure 5.9 A focal point is created when the dominant compositional lines direct your eye toward a specific point, such as the gold collar of this costume design by Peggy Kellner for the University of Arizona production of *The Maid's Tragedy.*

TERMINAL ACCENTS

Carefully selected terminal accents—the lines that define the profile, or silhouette, of a form or mass—can be used to help portray emotional quality. In some productions the upper parts of the set walls are cut off. The quality and character of the line chosen to form this terminal accent on the upper edge of the wall (form) can help shape the audience's understanding of the emotional atmosphere of the play. If the play is a light comedy, a "fun" sort of curlicue line will reinforce the happy nature of the play. If the production is more romantic, a gentle, sensuous line may be more appropriate. If the play is serious and heavy, straight lines with sharp, angular corners are probably more appropriate.

The emotional quality of the terminal accent can also be used to good advantage in costume design. The hems of the sleeves and skirts of witches' costumes are frequently designed with sharp points (dags) to visually support the menacing nature of the characters wearing those costumes. The unadorned neckline of a collarless smock provides a visual clue to the stiff, unyielding nature of its wearer. But add a soft, frilly, lace collar to that same dress, and our perception of its wearer will similarly be softened.

Asymmetrical balance: A sense of equipoise achieved through dynamic tension created by the juxtaposition of dissimilar design elements (line, form, mass, value, color).

nondynamic quality. It is very common in costume design, so that the right side of the costume almost always matches the left. If the costume designer wants to make a visual statement about the dynamic quality of a character, however, a diagonal sash can be placed on the costume, or the line of the dress can be draped at a dramatic diagonal angle.

Because of its basically placid evocative properties, symmetrical balance is frequently avoided by scene designers; however, the staid, placid quality can sometimes be supportive of the production concept.

More frequently, scenic designers make use of the inherently dynamic properties of **asymmetrical balance** (see Figure 5.11A). The dissimilar forms on opposite sides of the frame create a dynamic balance. Your eye is alter-

Figure 5.10 Symmetrical balance results when the left side of a design is a mirror image of the right side, as in this scene design for *Lady Precious Stream* by A. S. Gillette.

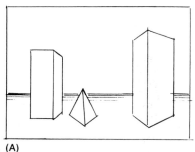

(A)

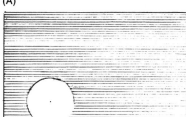

(B)

Figure 5.11
Asymmetrical balance occurs when dissimilar forms appear to be balanced within the framework of the composition. Costume design by Peggy Kellner.

(C)

nately drawn to both objects but ultimately comes to rest in the relative center of the picture. Figure 5.11B is another example of asymmetrical balance. The darker value of the background form creates a dynamic balance with the lighter form on the left of the frame. Figure 5.11C is an illustration of asymmetrical balance in costume design.

CREATING INTERESTING DESIGNS

Once you've mastered the basic principles of composition, three other design considerations—position, theme, and contrast—will help you turn a nicely composed design into a masterful, interesting, and unified one.

Position

Position refers to the relative placement of objects within a visual composition. To a great extent positioning will determine the focal point of the audience's attention.

Figure 5.12 Scenic design for *Death of a Salesman*. From the Billy Rose Theatre Collection, The New York Public Library at Lincoln Center; Astor, Lenox, and Tilden Foundations.

In scenic design the most important acting areas will be placed in the most prominent positions. The design for *Death of a Salesman* (Figure 5.12) has a number of different playing areas. All of them are distinctly visible, but the kitchen and the foreground area outside of the house, where a variety of other scenes are played, are the most prominently positioned. Whereas important playing areas are prominently positioned, the details that help create the character of the set are normally placed in a subordinate or background position. Notice how the peripheral detail such as the tall buildings crowding in on the house and the general state of disrepair of the yard help to set the mood of despair and defeat for the set of *Death of a Salesman*.

Theme

The importance of theme in design is significant. Theme refers to the repetitive use of a specific combination of line, form, mass, value, and color to create a central visual core for a particular design. Variations on the theme can enhance its interest, but the root theme is always the dominant feature of the design. In the set for *Nicholas Nickleby* (Figure 5.13) the primary visual theme is the strong vertical lines of the posts. These verticals are intersected by the horizontal lines of the platforms and the diagonals of the stairs, but the arrangement of these subordinate lines only reinforces the strength of the verticals.

Regardless of the design field in which you are working, if you select and express a specific visual theme, such as the vertical posts in *Nicholas Nickleby,* you will have created a dominant central element in the composition that ties together all of the other design elements to strengthen the overall effect.

Figure 5.13 *Nicholas Nickleby,* produced at the University of Arizona, directed by Harold Dixon and Dianne Winslow, scenic design by Tom Benson, lighting design by Michael Renken and Joel Young. Photo by Robert F. Walker, University of Arizona Photo Center.

Contrast

Contrast can be defined as the juxtaposition of dissimilar elements. In composition this juxtaposition refers to differing types of line, form, mass, value, and color. The following general guidelines apply equally to the use of contrast in all the design elements.

The greater the contrast between elements of a design, the greater the level of tension, or dynamic stress, created within that design. Conversely, the lower the contrast, the lower the tension. There is more visual interest, life, or tension in the illustration with lines of varying height (Figure 5.14A) than in

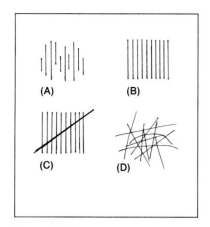

Figure 5.14 Generating visual interest through contrast of line.

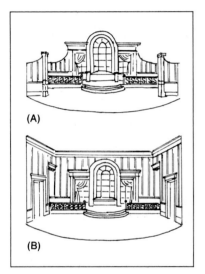

Figure 5.15 The use of an interesting silhouette can increase visual interest and connotative meaning in a scenic design.

Figure 5.16 Visual interest can be increased by using a contrasting line, such as the diagonal of a shawl.

the one with lines of uniform height (Figure 5.14B). The visual tension is substantially increased when the parallel lines of Figure 5.14B are cut by a diagonal line, as shown in Figure 5.14C. But contrast, like spice, must be used in moderation; too much can overwhelm and destroy the flavor of your creation. In Figure 5.14D the sequence and harmony of the composition have been destroyed by making every line contrast with every other line.

To be genuinely effective, contrast must be able to work in opposition to the major, or dominant, visual theme in the composition, such as the horizontal and diagonal lines of the platforms and stairs in the scenic design for *Nicholas Nickleby* illustrated in Figure 5.13.

The scenic design shown in Figure 5.15A creates more visual interest than the design in Figure 5.15B. Both designs use the same ground plan, but the heightened visual interest of Figure 5.15A is created by using a cutout line to eliminate portions of the walls. (The general guidelines on the use of cutout lines were covered in the discussion of harmony earlier in this chapter.)

Contrast is also used in costume design. A standard cliché can be seen in almost every "B" western ever made—the black hats of the villains versus the white hats of the heroes. This very obvious use of contrast allows the viewers to distinguish at a glance between good guys and bad guys. Many costume designers make very effective use of color contrast. In 1968 Danilo Donati received an Oscar for his costume design for Franco Zeffirelli's film production of *Romeo and Juliet*. In that design Donati dressed the Capulets in varying shades of reds and yellows and the Montagues in shades of blue and gray. Through this simple chromatic contrast he identified for the audience where the political and familial allegiances of the various characters lay.

Contrast of line can also be used to good advantage in costume design. Figure 5.16 shows a design for a simple dress (center) and then illustrates how the addition of a shawl, with its contrasting lines cutting across the bodice, provides a more visually stimulating design.

Contrast in line and color can greatly enhance the visibility of a given character. If you want to make your lead character stand out from the crowd, for example, dress him or her in something that will contrast strongly in color or line with what the crowd is wearing.

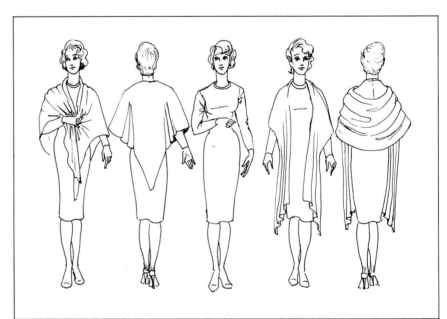

CHAPTER 5: COMPOSITION AND DESIGN

Contrast is equally important to the lighting designer. Within any given scene the average audience member will focus on the brightest area. This principle is amply demonstrated through the traditional use of followspots in the musical theatre. During a typical musical number the general stage lights dim or change color, and the lead singer is picked up by a followspot. The followspot beam is two or three times brighter than the surrounding stage areas. Because of the contrast in intensity, the spectators are effectively forced to look at the lead singer.

The lighting designer can achieve a similar, but more subtle, use of contrast for less stylized productions. By making one area of the set slightly brighter than the rest, the designer can focus the spectators' attention on the brightest of the areas. It is amazing how uniformly an audience will react to even a slight contrast in lighting. This instinctive reaction can be played on by the designer to help shift the attention of the spectators from one area of the set to another.

The sound designer also uses contrast. Any sound that contrasts sharply with its aural surrounding, or ambient sound, will be noticed. The cry of a gull will intrude on the otherwise lulling effect of gentle waves lapping on a beach because the pitch and quality of the gull's call is substantially different from the low murmur of the waves. Similarly, a shift in tempo can alter the level of audience awareness solely by its contrast with the tempo that preceded it. An example may help to explain this phenomenon. Many scary movies have sinister, I'm-going-to-get-you music playing as the hero unwittingly wanders toward the dark alley in which the villain is hiding. Just before the hero reaches the alley, the music almost reaches a climax—then abruptly stops. This drastic change (music to silence) creates a strong contrast with the previously existing condition (music) that triggers our instinctive defensive reaction to be on the alert. If the perceived change in tempo is small, the shift to heightened awareness will be minimal because the contrast is slight. If the contrast is large, however, the change in audience awareness will be correspondingly large.

Texture is another form of contrast. Designers can make a variety of statements about the nature and character of their designs through the use of texture. In costume design smooth-textured fabrics (silk, satin) have traditionally been the province of the upper class and good guys, and the harsher-finished fabrics (homespun, burlap) have been primarily relegated to villains and the lower classes. Fabrics with delicate textures such as frothy lace and chiffon are frequently used to denote delicate, vulnerable characteristics in the wearer, and heavier, rougher-textured fabrics such as fur, leather, and heavy velvets are usually worn by more rugged types.

As have costume designers, scenic designers have traditionally used texture to provide visual reference to the play's psychological environment. Although it is all but impossible to describe texture without reference to other design elements such as line and form, certain psychological reactions to texture are reasonably uniform. Generally speaking, smooth surfaces reflect a finished, orderly type of environment when compared with the harsher, less polished atmosphere created by rough textures.

In lighting design **gobos** are used to create texture by breaking up the otherwise smooth output of the lighting instrument into shadow patterns. (See Chapter 14, *Lighting Production,* for more information on gobos.) These patterns provide an effective tool to increase the dramatic tension in the lighting by providing the only effective means of creating textural contrast in lighting.

A *void,* or unfilled empty space, is another type of contrast that has sig-

Texture: The relative roughness or smoothness of the finish of an object.

Gobo: A thin metal template inserted into an ellipsoidal reflector spotlight to project a shadow pattern of light.

nificant application in theatrical design. The most obvious use of this design element is by the sound designer. The use of a sound void is sometimes more important than the music or sound that precedes or follows the silence. The quiet that follows the elimination of a background soundtrack can create a feeling of suspense or relief, depending on the nature of the sound or music that precedes it. In the example of the I'm-going-to-get-you music previously discussed, the music created a psychological atmosphere of anticipation and suspense. When the music stopped, the audience knew that something was going to happen because of the nature of the music preceding the silence. If, on the other hand, the sound had been a very loud jackhammer instead of suspenseful music, the audience's reaction would probably have simply been relief that the noise had stopped.

A scenic designer can help to stimulate the audience's interest in the play by placing a setting within a black void. The design for *The Birthday Party* shown in Figure 5.17 is an example. The conscious selection of this empty blackness helped create a sense of claustrophobic isolation and separateness. The spectators' focus would have been diffused and the stage area would have seemed much larger if the design had been surrounded by a white background.

STEP-BY-STEP ANALYSIS OF THE KITCHEN

A working knowledge of the elements of composition and of techniques that can be used to create interesting and vital designs are very important for all theatrical designers. A step-by-step analysis of the illustrated design for Arnold Wesker's *The Kitchen* (Figure 5.18, page 82) may help explain how all of these elements are used in creating a design.

Line

As you will recall, line is defined by three characteristics: dimension, quality, and character. The lines used in *The Kitchen* design to create the outline of the set are relatively long and narrow in dimension, whereas the lines used to define the interior space (the space confined within the outline of the set), the furniture, and the equipment are equally narrow and considerably shorter. The dominant lines in this design are the straight horizontals and verticals used to form the outline of the set and define its interior space and furnishings. This quality of sharp angularity is occasionally modified by bold curves. The character of the sharply etched horizontal and vertical lines connotes the relatively serious nature of the play. The curves soften some of this seriousness.

Form, Mass, and Value

A specific discussion of form, mass, and value would not be of particular value, since their visual meaning is contingent on their application according to the principles of composition. These principles (harmony, rhythm, and balance) are discussed a little later.

Color

The walls of the set, with the exception of the short hallway stage center, are painted a dingy off-white to look as though they had started out white years ago but had accumulated successive layers of smoke and grease. The short hallway is painted a medium dirty green above the off-white color of the ceramic tile wainscoting. The floor is painted a dull red to resemble the floor tiles that are frequently found in older commercial kitchens. The stoves are a dull metallic black, and the hot plates and other counters are finished to resemble well-used brushed stainless steel. The entire set is placed inside of a black cyclorama, which effectively creates a void.

Harmony

Harmony refers to the blending, flow, and unity of the design. The strong horizontal and vertical lines of the set walls create a dynamic tension that is softened by the curves that join the horizontal and verticals on the outside wall and the central arch. The lines of the set flow rhythmically outward from the tall combination chef's office-hallway-bakery structure located up center, and cascade downward to virtually disappear behind the banks of stoves and ovens on each side of the set.

Rhythm

Rhythm refers to the orderly and logical interrelationship of successive parts of the design. The ground plan, or layout, of the set is predicated on the working patterns of a functional restaurant kitchen. The office-hallway-bakery structure provides a logical, functional visual background for the downstage stove-hot plate primary playing area. The double swinging doors lead to the dining room, and the hallway upstage left leads to the steam room, washroom, and other parts of the kitchen.

A logical unity among the individual portions of the design is achieved in several ways. The off-white walls and the dull-red floor are used to visually unify the various segments of the design. The black void effectively focuses the spectators' attention on the set, because there is nothing to look at in the void. Finally, the use of lines of similar quality and character provide sequence for the form and mass of the design.

Balance

Balance contributes a sense of stability, or restfulness, to the design. The almost symmetrical balance of the design is primarily dictated by the physical demands of the play's blocking. During the majority of the play the kitchen is in action, with the cooks working at the stoves. Since several of the cooks are

Figure 5.18 *The Kitchen,* produced at the University of Arizona, directed by Robert C. Burroughs, scenic and lighting design by J. Michael Gillette.

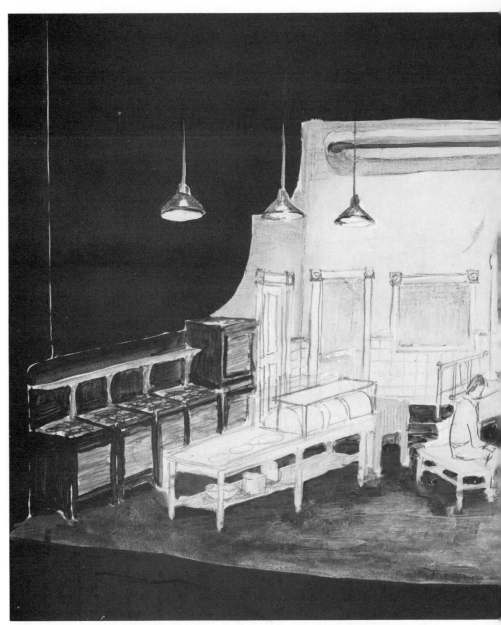

Figure 5.18 *The Kitchen,* produced at the University of Arizona, directed by Robert C. Burroughs, scenic and lighting design by J. Michael Gillette.

the central characters in the play, it is essential to position the stoves so the spectators can see their faces and watch them cook. Although symmetrical balance could easily have been achieved, the slightly asymmetrical design was selected to mirror the dynamic tension of the play. This tension was subtly enhanced by placing the set about nine inches off the center line of the stage. The asymmetrical placement was so slight that it was more felt than seen. When you looked at the set, it gave you the feeling that something wasn't quite right, but you couldn't readily identify it. This sense of malaise was an appropriate visual expression of the production concept.

Position

Since the overwhelming majority of the action of this play takes place as the cooks are preparing and cooking meals, a primary goal in creating this design was to position the stoves in a prominent downstage position so all twelve cooks could be observed by the audience. Although there was almost continu-

CHAPTER 5: COMPOSITION AND DESIGN

ous action in the chef's office, the hallway, and the bakery, it was of secondary importance to the main action of the play.

Theme

Theme refers to the repetitive use of a specific combination of line, form, mass, value, or color. The cascading effect of the horizontal-vertical-curved cutout lines is repeated on each side of the set to create the basic line of the set. This visual motif is repeated in the silhouette of the stoves. To a lesser extent the interrelationship of horizontal, vertical, and curved lines is also faintly echoed in the rectangular form and circular windows of the swinging doors that lead to the dining room. Ceramic tile wainscoting is used to visually unite all areas of the kitchen. Only the chef's office does not have the ceramic wainscoting, which helps set that area apart from the rest of the kitchen. The dull-red tile floor is used to visually tie all elements of the design together.

Contrast

Contrast, as we have seen, is the juxtaposition of dissimilar elements. Although the vertical, horizontal, and curved lines certainly contrast with one another in quality and character, color is a dominant element of contrast in this design. The dingy, off-white walls contrast strongly with the black void in which the set is placed. This stark contrast effectively focuses audience attention on the "pressure cooker world" of the kitchen. The hallway leading to the dining room is painted in a medium dirty green for two reasons, both related to contrast: The contrasting color helps to physically separate it from the off-white of the kitchen; the darker color helps reduce the prominance of this physically dominant location, which is used only for entrances and exits.

The foregoing example used scenic design to explain the uses of the various elements of design and principles of composition. An understanding of these tools of the designer will provide you with the basic artistic resources to be able to create effective designs in not only scenery but also costumes, lighting, and sound.

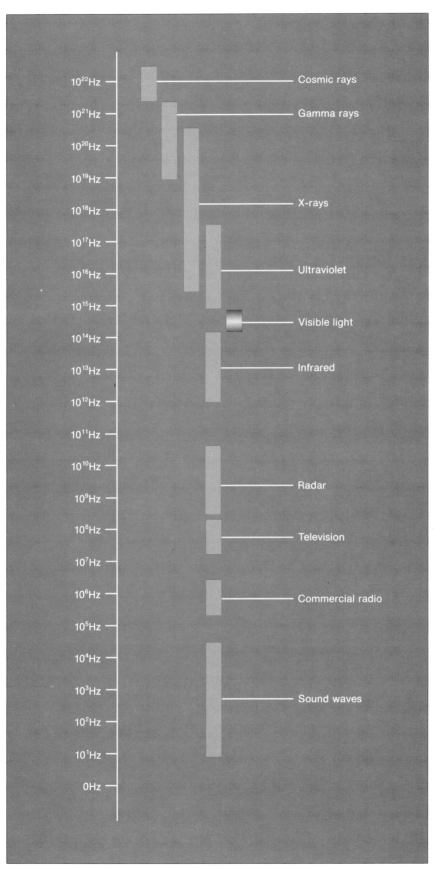

Cosmic rays

Gamma rays

X-rays

Ultraviolet

Visible light

Infrared

Radar

Television

Commercial radio

Sound waves

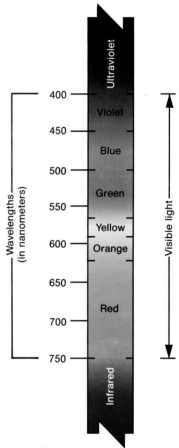

Color Plate 1 The frequency range of selected energy forms contained in the electromagnetic radiation spectrum.

Color Plate 2 The frequency range of visible light.

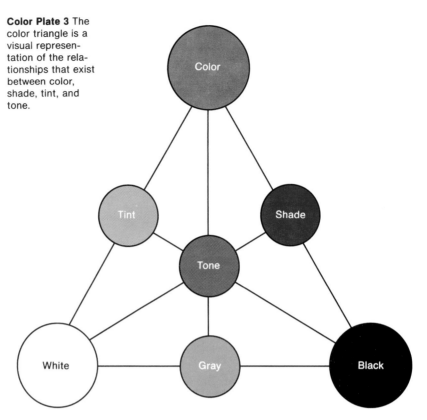

Color Plate 3 The color triangle is a visual representation of the relationships that exist between color, shade, tint, and tone.

Color

Tint

Shade

Tone

White

Gray

Black

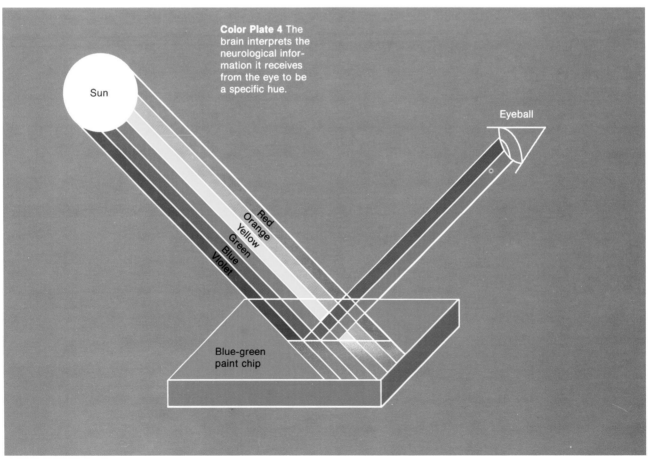

Color Plate 4 The brain interprets the neurological information it receives from the eye to be a specific hue.

Sun

Eyeball

Red
Orange
Yellow
Green
Blue
Violet

Blue-green
paint chip

Color Plate 5 Color wheels for (A) light and (B) pigment.

Red

Magenta

Yellow

White

Green

Blue

Cyan

(A)

Red

Orange

Purple

Black

Yellow

Blue

Green

(B)

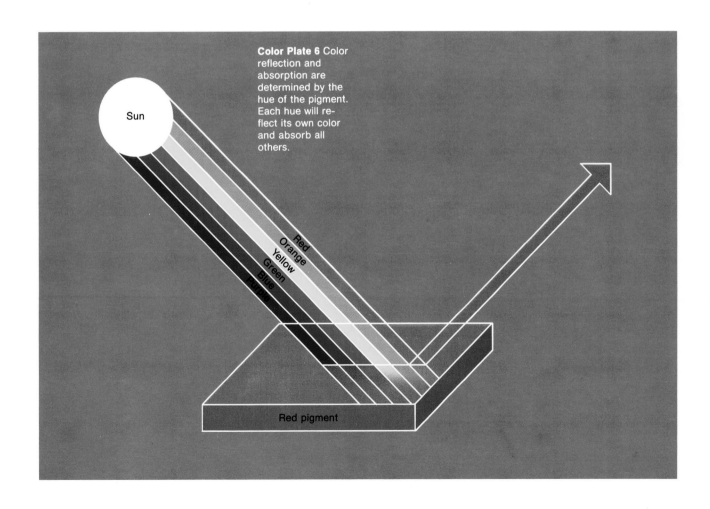

Sun

Red
Orange
Yellow
Green
Blue
Purple

Red pigment

Color Plate 6 Color reflection and absorption are determined by the hue of the pigment. Each hue will reflect its own color and absorb all others.

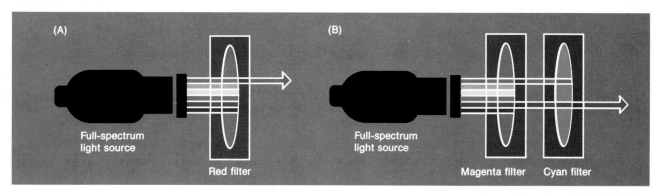

(A)

Full-spectrum light source

Red filter

(B)

Full-spectrum light source

Magenta filter   Cyan filter

Color Plate 7 Subtractive color mixing in light. A colored filter will allow its own color to pass but will absorb all others.

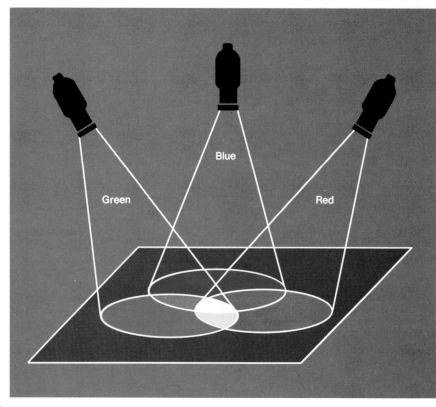

Green

Blue

Red

Color Plate 8 Additive color mixing in light. The eye sees each separate color; the brain interprets the ratio of the color mix to be a specific hue.

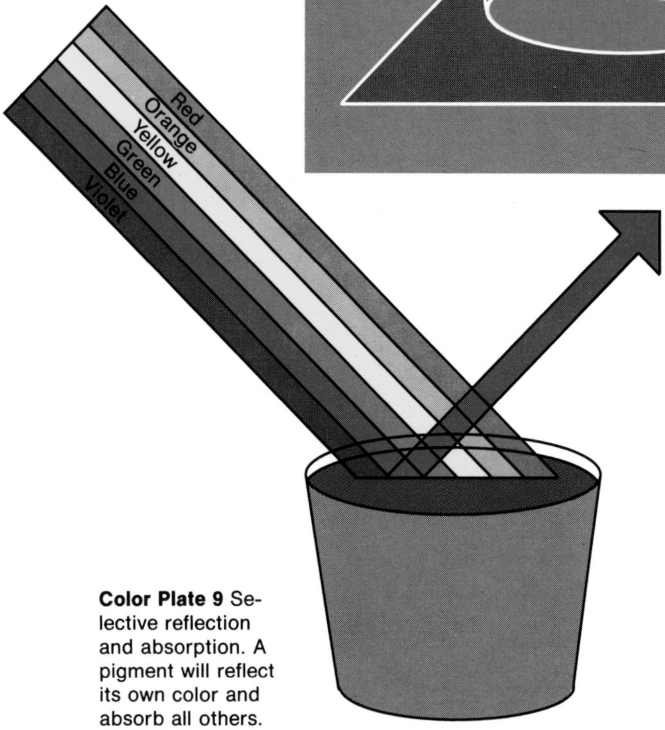

Red
Orange
Yellow
Green
Blue
Violet

Color Plate 9 Selective reflection and absorption. A pigment will reflect its own color and absorb all others.

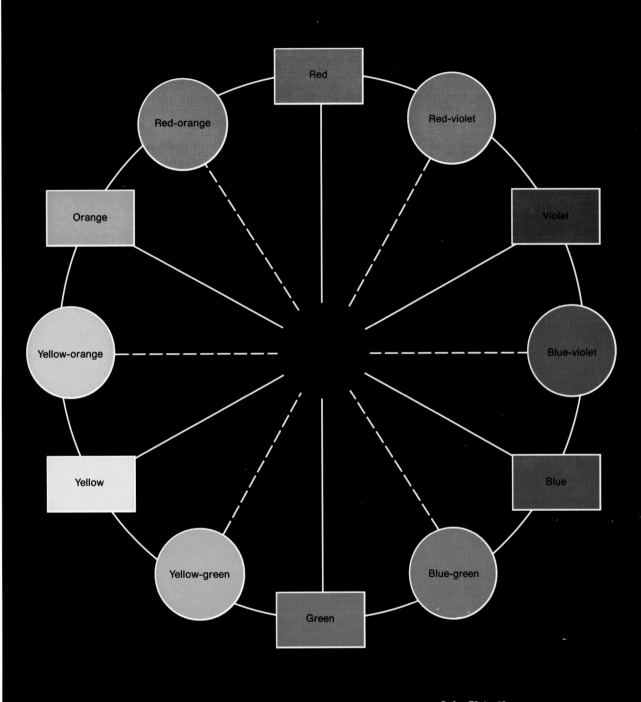

Red

Red-orange

Red-violet

Orange

Violet

Yellow-orange

Blue-violet

Yellow

Blue

Yellow-green

Blue-green

Green

- - - - - - - - - - = Light

――――――――― = Pigment

Color Plate 10
Integrated color
wheel. This device
is used to help
clarify the relation-
ships that exist be-
tween the primary
and secondary
hues in both pig-
ment and light.

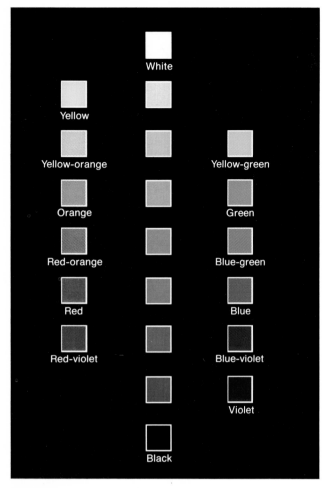

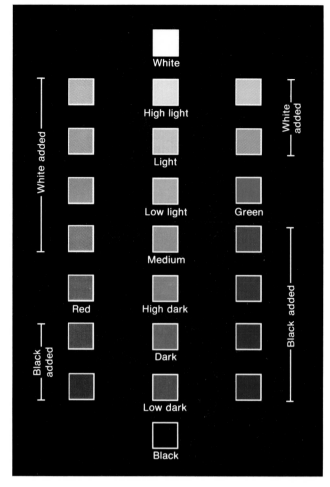

Color Plate 11 A hue-value relationship chart. Since fully saturated colors do not all have the same value, this chart helps explain the relative values of the indicated colors. The values of the colors on the outside columns correspond with the values of the adjacent gray blocks on the center gray-scale column.

Color Plate 12 Complementary hue-tone relationships. The value of a specific hue changes as white or black is added to it. The values of the resultant tints and shades on the outside columns correspond with the values of the adjacent gray blocks of the central gray scale.

Color Plate 13 The use of an additive mix of complementary tints results in a more lively, vibrant light.

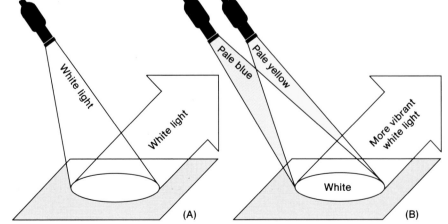

An audience can only see objects as a result of those objects reflecting or emitting light. Since the overwhelming majority of objects in a play (actors, costumes, sets, props) reflect rather than emit light, an analysis of the use of color in a design concept would logically stem from an analysis of the effects of the hues used in the lighting design on the various other elements of the total design for the production.

This section will analyze the use of color in two distinctly different types of color designs: a muted, predominantly low-saturation, closely coordinated palette in the University of Arizona production of Ted Tally's *Terra Nova*; and a vibrant, highly saturated, full-range color design for the University of Arizona production of the Masteroff/Kander/Ebb musical *Cabaret*.

THE ENVIRONMENT OF THE PLAY.
The primary location is the vast frozen whiteness of Antarctica, but numerous vignettes take place in a variety of other locations: an English country garden in spring, a banquet hall, and several nonspecific memory locations. It is essential for the continuity of the play that scenes flow smoothly from location to location without a break in the action.

THE SCENIC DESIGN.
The color design helped to create the cinematic flow required for the production. To bring to life the vast coldness of Antarctica, the set, which was a jumble of platforms arranged to create an abstraction of the ruptured surface of an ice floe, was painted an off-white (Color Plate 14). On the upstage side of the platforms a large expanse of unpainted, unbleached muslin was suspended from an abstracted ship's spar (Color Plate 15). This sail was used as a projection surface for color washes, visual effects, and photographic images of Scott's ill-fated expedition to the South Pole. The entire set was surrounded by a black cyclorama to help focus the audience's attention on the set and actors.

THE COSTUME DESIGN.
The costumes and properties were ultrarealistic. The natural earth tones (primarily shades of browns and grays) of the properties and the men's costumes stood out in strong contrast against the whiteness of the set. Scott's wife, the only woman in the play, was seen only in Scott's memory scenes of home. She was dressed in a warmly colored floral print (Color Plate 16) to present a stark contrast with the muted patterns and solids that were worn by the men.

Terra Nova

Director: Harold Dixon; scenic and lighting design: J. Michael Gillette; costume design: Jerry D. Allen; property design: Peter Wexler—the properties were designed and constructed for the original production of *Terra Nova* at the Mark Taper Forum in Los Angeles, produced by the Center Theatre Group.

Color Plate 14 The color of the set and sail (white) was selected for two reasons: (1) Antarctica is overwhelmingly white; (2) the highly reflective neutral color makes an excellent projection surface for the various colors and images that make up a large segment of the design concept.

Color Plate 15 The sail was backlit with color washes (left) to provide primary atmospheric and psychological keys about the nature of the individual scenes. It was also used as a projection surface for black-and-white slides of Scott's actual expedition (right).

Color Plate 16 The warmly colored, floral-print summer dress worn by Scott's wife provided a strong color contrast with the predominantly muted patterns of gray and brown worn by the men.

THE LIGHTING DESIGN.

The lighting used color as a primary device to create psychological keys in support of the emotional content of the various scenes. Color Plate 17 provides a color key of the lighting used in this production indicating the direction and color of the various light sources. (Note that the numbers indicate Roscolux color numbers.) Color Plates 18–21 show how the various design elements (scenic, costume, properties, lighting) blended to create the color impact of the production design.

The scenes in Antarctica were lit with almost painfully brilliant white light (Color Plate 18), which resulted in the colors of the costumes and properties being portrayed very closely to their true hues.

The memory scenes were lit with textured top lights and color washes selected for their psychological impact: deep blue for Scott's heavier memories (Color Plate 19); soft pastels for the romantic memories of his wife (Color Plate 20); amber candlelight for the banquet scene (Color Plate 21).

The use of low-saturation complementary colors to light the acting areas from the front and sides significantly reduced the color-shifting effects of the stage lights on costumes and skin tones. The clear, textured top lights, when used in conjunction with the heavily saturated top washes, created significant changes in the visual appearance of the set. These elements working together created a subtly effective color design that worked for the support of the production.

Explanations of how the color palettes of the various design elements (scenic, costume, property, and lighting) interacted are contained in the captions for each illustration.

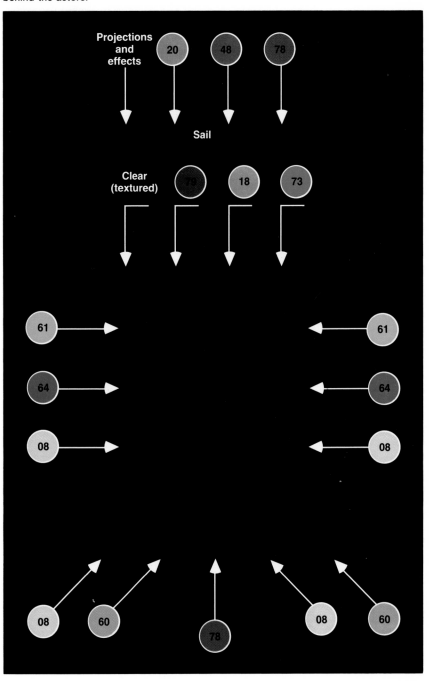

Color Plate 17 The color key for the lighting design. The arrows indicate the direction from which the light is traveling toward the stage. The horizontal flags on the arrows at the upper part of the illustration indicate that those lights are coming from above, rather than behind the actors.

Color Plate 18
Complementary colors (Roscolux 08 and 60 from the front and 08 and 61 from the sides) were used at high (but equal) intensity to provide a white, very bright, slightly cool color mix. The clear (white) top light helped to edge the actors' heads and shoulders with white as well as wash out any color shadows created by the individual hues in the front and side lights. The rendering of the skin tones as well as costumes and property colors was slightly cooler than if white light (as opposed to the complementary mix) had been used. The "cooler" look was a desired effect.

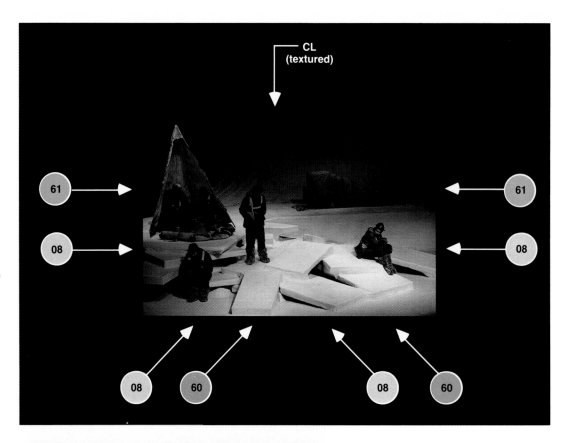

Color Plate 19 The textured light was created by bathing the stage with saturated blue (78 and 79) from the front and top. The texture was created by introducing the clear, textured toplight at relatively low intensity. Scott's face was framed with a low-intensity followspot whose beam diameter was only shoulder wide. Skin tones and upper-torso costume colors were rendered naturally by the warm followspot (at low intensity the light from the uncolored beam is naturally warm) combining with, and overriding the effects of, the deep blue.

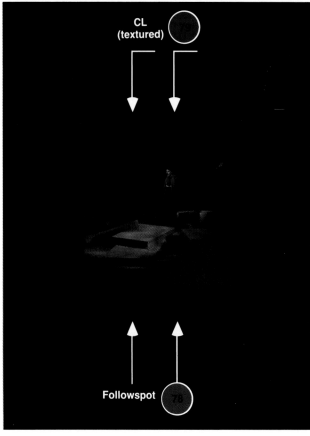

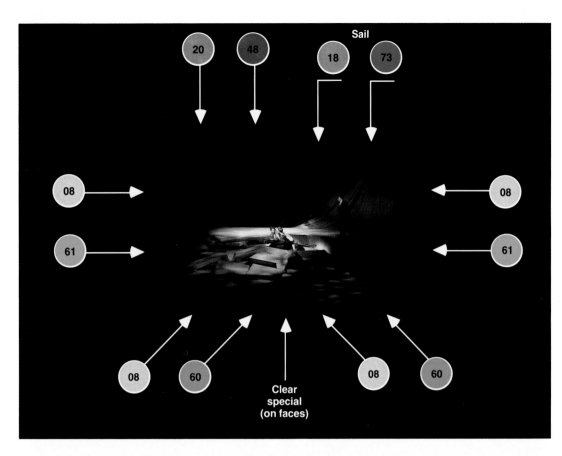

Color Plate 20
The atmosphere of England was created by using textured toplights colored in warm, soft hues (18 and 73) and the back-lights on the sail (20 and 48) to provide a striking contrast with the blue-white cold-ness of the lights for Antarctica. Scott and his wife (down stage) were lit with warm-white combinations of 08 and 60 from the front and 08 and 61 from the sides. The figure in the background was side lit with a warm, dim, front/side light. The warm-white light on Scott and his wife provided accurate color rendering of their costumes. The warm light striking the background figure created a fairly accurate color rendering of his tuxedo.

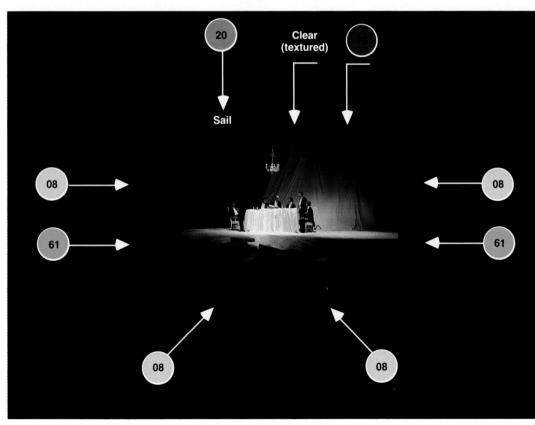

Color Plate 21
Primary color for this scene was provided by the warm amber (20) on the sail in the background. The banquet table was lit with a warm-white blend of 08 and 61 from the sides and 08 from the front and un-colored, textured toplight. A little blue toplight (79) was used to en-hance the edging effect of the top-light on the black tuxedos. This created a candle-lit feeling with warm skin tones, table cloth and floor, and black tuxedos.

THE ENVIRONMENT OF THE PLAY.
The primary location of this musical
is a seedy, second-rate night club, the
Kit Kat Klub, in Berlin, Germany in
the years 1929–30. Additional scenes
take place in several other locations: a
railroad car, various rooms in a
rooming house, and a fruit shop.

THE SCENIC DESIGN.
The scene design created a startling ca-
cophony of contrast through the juxtaposition of line, color, and finish
(Color Plate 22). The strong contrast
was appropriate because it helped to
heighten the dramatic tension inherent
in the script and the production concept. The dominant element of the design was the Kit Kat Klub, which was
painted in medium saturation earth

tones. However, the color was applied
in a erratically angular pattern on the
vertical face of the runway as well as
on the floor of the audience portion
of the nightclub. The zigzag motif
was continued with the busy herringbone pattern on the floor of the runway and the rest of the stage.

The floor and four upstage columns were finished with a high-gloss
glaze to heighten the contrast between
those elements and the remainder of
the set, which was painted with a traditional matte finish. The shimmering
aluminized mylar curtain (Color Plate
23) provided another dazzling type of
contrast during one of the production
numbers.

Small white lightbulbs were used
to spell CABARET and outline the
arches. These little pinpoints of light
played against the black void created
by the surrounding black cyclorama to
create another type of emphatic
contrast.

The fully saturated secondary colors (amber, cyan, and magenta) used
in the double rows of vertical striplights on either side of the stage and
the six-inch fresnel spotlights hung
from the upper-level railings of the
set created another jarring note of
color contrast.

The color and contrast treatment
of the other locations, which slid in
on a shuttle stage just upstage of the
nightclub runway, were more muted
than the Kit Kat Klub because, in gen-

eral, scenes that took place in those locations were emotionally "softer" and more intimate.

THE COSTUME DESIGN.

Contrast was also readily evident in the costume design. The designs for the Kit Kat Girls were based on vibrant, fully saturated colors (Color Plate 24) and high-sheen fabrics. A powerful statement was made by the contrast between the actresses' pale skin and the skimpy, heavily saturated, highly reflective surfaces of the costumes.

The costumes for Sally (the two on the left and the two on the right in Color Plate 25) used a change in saturation and hue as a device to mirror her emotional progression through the play. In the beginning she was dressed in the vibrant, shocking colors and styles of the Kit Kat Girls. As she fell in love with Cliff, she dressed in softer, more muted tones. When Sally chose to stay in Germany as Cliff left, her reimmersion in the world of the cabaret was mirrored in the high contrast of a floorlength black sequin evening dress that she wore in the final scene.

The men's costumes, while being faithful to the period, also mimicked the emotionally based use of high contrast employed for the women's costumes. The Master of Ceremonies and the cabaret ensemble men were costumed in black-and-white evening wear, while Cliff and Herr Schultz were dressed in suits of muted hues selected to mirror their emotional warmth.

THE LIGHTING DESIGN.

The colors selected for the lighting design were dictated by three primary considerations: (1) the full-spectrum colors of the costumes and set; (2) the heavy, smoke-filled, sensuous atmosphere needed for the cabaret; and (3) the need for a lighter, more realistic atmosphere for those scenes outside the cabaret (Color Plate 26).

Complementary colors of light-to-moderate saturation (Roscolux 62 and 02) were selected for the front lights for the acting areas because they would be appropriately neutral for both the cabaret scenes and those more

Cabaret

Director and choreographer: Richard Hanson; scenic design: Tom Benson; costume design: Peggy Kellner; lighting design: J. Michael Gillette.

Color Plate 22
Scenic design for *Cabaret*, by Tom Benson. A number of hues were used on this production, but they were all in a relatively close tonal range. Contrast was achieved primarily by pattern variation and gloss finish coats applied to selected elements of the set.

intimate scenes outside the cabaret. However, those colors had enough saturation to enhance the costume and set colors in both locations. By balancing the color mix between the 02 and 62, the stage could be made neutral, cool, or warm as appropriate. The full saturation necessary for the scenes inside the cabaret was supplied by the Roscolux 20, 57, and 93 used on the vertical striplights and fresnels on either side of the stage. These saturated color washes, used in conjunction with the acting-area lights, enhanced the full-spectrum, strongly colored palettes of the costumes and scenery used in the cabaret scenes, as well as creating the heavy atmosphere necessary within the cabaret. (Specific hues of strongly saturated light create an impression of more vibrant color than do similar hues of less saturation. If two or more of these relatively saturated hues are additively mixed to cre-

ate a white light, the resultant white light will create a similar vibrant color reaction from the full color spectrum.)

During production numbers, the set was generally lit with psychologically appropriate color washes, and the six followspots, using white or lightly tinted light, were used to highlight the various leads.

The downstage area of the cabaret audience was lit with a top wash of textured white light to support the concept that the area was lit by the individual table lamps. During the out-of-the-cabaret scenes, the textured top wash was combined with a deep blue wash to reduce the area's apparent visibility. (The deep blue looks like a shadow color but allows the "real" audience to see the shadow detail.)

Color Plate 24
Costume designs
by Peggy Kellner.
The full-saturation,
high-contrast
"glitzy" materials of
the Kit Kat Girls'
costumes were
enhanced by the
strongly saturated
hues used to light
the cabaret
scenes.

Color Plate 25
Costume designs
by Peggy Kellner.
The color progres-
sion of Sally's cos-
tumes mirrored her
emotional progres-
sion through the
production. See
text for details.

Color Plate 26
Color key for the lighting design. Low-saturation colors (02, 62, 08, 99) were used for general acting-area lights, while strong-saturation color washes (20, 57, 93, 78) were added for psychological emphasis. See text for details.

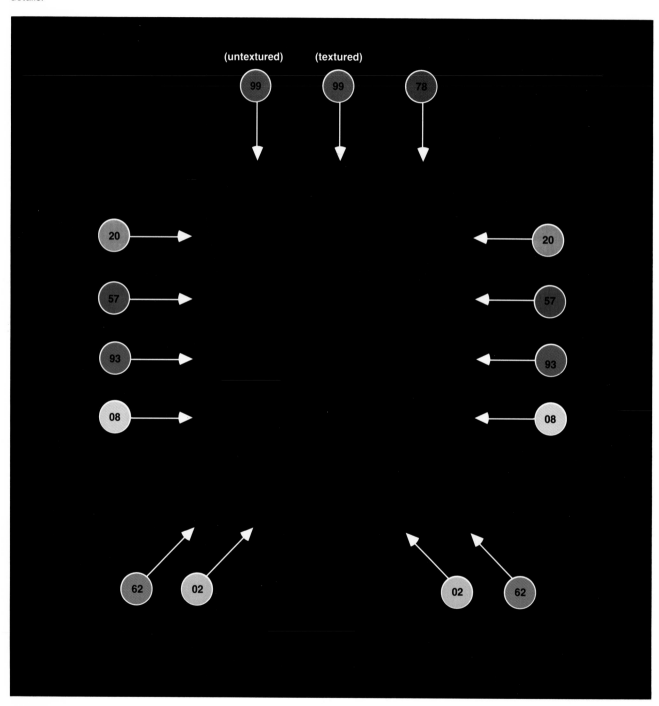

(untextured) (textured)

6

Color is easily the most noticeable of the design elements and is arguably the most dominant. It is also the least understood. We grow up with color all around us, and we see and use it every day. It is probably because of our constant contact with  color that we accept it without really thinking about it. This chapter attempts to help you understand the actually rather complex subject of color.

DEFINING COLOR

Color has a variety of definitions. As we saw in the last chapter, it can be defined as a perception created in the brain as a result of stimulation of the retina by light waves of a certain length. It can also be thought of as the intrinsic physical properties of specific objects that allow those objects to reflect and absorb light waves of a certain length. The common denominator for any definition of color is light, because all color is derived from light. The phenomenon that we call light is actually the very narrow portion of the spectrum of electromagnetic radiation that is visible to the human eye. Color Plate 1 shows the position of visible light on this spectrum, as well as that of some of the other types of radiation. The visible spectrum stretches in frequency from approximately 750 nanometers to 400. (A nanometer is one billionth of a meter.) Color Plate 2 shows the approximate wavelengths for the various colors of the visible spectrum.

Color Terminology

Without a specific set of terms to describe the various properties of color, almost any discussion of it would quickly degenerate into rather meaningless comparisons. An example will help explain this phenomenon. If you provided each member of a group of twenty people with one hundred **paint chips,** all yellow, but each slightly different, and asked them to identify

Paint chip: A small rectangle of paper or thin cardboard painted in a specific hue.

canary yellow, they would probably select twenty different chips. This is because the connection between the description of any specific color, such as canary yellow, and the brain's understanding of the physical appearance of that color differs, sometimes significantly, from person to person.

The terms that we will be using in our discussion of color are as follows:

HUE Hue is the quality that differentiates one color from another, such as blue from green or red from yellow.

SATURATION Saturation, also known as chroma, refers to the amount, or percentage, of a particular hue in a color mixture. Fire-engine red has a high, or strong, saturation, because there is a lot of fully saturated color in the mixture. Dusty rose, in contrast, has a low, or weak, saturation, because there isn't a lot of fully saturated color in the mixture; instead, the majority is white or gray.

VALUE The relative lightness or darkness of a color is referred to as value. Pale blue has a high value, and dark brown has a low value.

TINT A color with a high value is referred to as a tint. It is usually achieved by mixing a hue with either white pigment or white light.

SHADE A color with a low value is known as a shade. It is usually created by a mixture of one or more hues and black.

TONE A color of middle value is frequently referred to as a tone. It is a mixture of a hue with black *and* white.

The color triangle in Color Plate 3 shows the relationships among hue, white, black, gray (the product of mixing black and white), tint, shade, and tone.

SEEING COLOR

Before we learn how color works, we should understand how we see color. Human sight comprises a complex series of events. When you look at an object, elements within your eye are stimulated by the light being emitted by, or reflected from, the viewed object. An electrochemical reaction occurs in specialized nerve cells in the retina. Two distinct types of light-receptor nerves, **rods** and **cones,** emit minute charges of electricity that are relayed to your brain, where the received data are interpreted as a "picture" that you have seen. The cones are divided into three primary groups: those that respond to the wavelengths of light that correspond to red, blue, and green, respectively.

If a red light enters the eye, the red-responsive cones are stimulated but the others are not. If a light that contains both red and blue wavelengths enters the eye, both the red- and blue-responsive cones are stimulated. In this case the message that is sent to the brain corresponds to the ratio of red and blue light contained in the light mixture that the eye receives. If the light contains more red than blue light, that information is transmitted.

Notice that the eye can only send information to the brain corresponding to the input it has received. The brain is the organ that does the interpretative mixing of the colors. In the example of the red and blue light, the amount of

Rods: Nerve cells in the retina that are sensitive to faint light.

Cones: Nerve cells in the retina that are sensitive to bright light; they respond either to red, blue, or green light.

CHAPTER 6: COLOR

red and blue in the mixture will be interpreted by the brain to be a particular color such as violet, magenta, or purple.

All perceived color is transmitted to the eye by light. If the light is dim, the cones (color sensors) do not function. The best way to demonstrate this effect is by standing outside on a moonlit night and looking at your surroundings. Everything you see will be a monochromatic gray, with perhaps a slight tint of blue or green if the moonlight is sufficiently bright. You will see no vibrant reds, blues, or greens, because the cones require more light than is being transmitted to your eye. If you look at the same scene during the daytime, the bright sunlight will activate the cones in your eye. Unless your eye has some physical dysfunction or the color-interpretative segment of your brain is impaired, you will see colors.

To further illustrate how the eye sees and the brain interprets color, let's assume that you are standing outside in the sunlight looking at a turquoise (blue-green) color chip, as shown in the Color Plate 4. The sunlight, which contains all of the electromagnetic wavelengths of the visible spectrum, strikes the blue-green surface of the color chip. Some of that light is reflected, and some of it is absorbed by the pigment on the paint chip. The majority of those wavelengths of light that correspond to the color of the chip (blue and green) are reflected. The majority of all other wavelengths of light are absorbed by the paint chip. The reflected blue and green light is received by the eye. The blue and green cones are stimulated by the light, causing them to send electrical impulses to the brain. The relative strength of these signals from the blue and green cones is proportionate to the specific amount of blue and green in the color mix. When the color-sensitive area of the brain is stimulated by these impulses, it interprets that information as a specific color known to that particular brain as turquoise.

COLOR MIXING

Before examining color mixing we must understand some additional terms.

Primary Colors

Primary colors are those hues that cannot be derived or blended from any other hues. In light, the primary colors (Color Plate 5A) are closely related to the color sensitivity of the red, blue, and green cones in the eye.

Secondary Colors

Secondary hues are the result of mixing two primary colors. In the color wheel for light (Color Plate 5A) the mixing of adjacent primaries creates the secondary hues yellow, magenta, and cyan (blue-green). The primary colors in **pigment** (Color Plate 5B) are red, blue, and yellow. The secondary colors in pigment are purple, green, and orange.

Complementary Colors

Complementary colors can be described as any two hues that, when combined, yield white in light or black in pigment. They can also be described as colors opposite each other on a color wheel. The color wheel for light (Color Plate 5A) shows that the complementary hue for red is cyan. When the two are combined

Pigment: A material that imparts color to a paint or dye.

---

they form white light. In the color wheel for pigment (Color Plate 5B) the complementary of red is green. When the two are mixed, they form black.

Filtered Light

When white light passes through any type of filtering material, such as glass, plastic, or air, a certain portion of the spectrum is absorbed. To fully understand this type of absorption you need a little background about the nature of light and energy.

Light, as we have seen, is a form of radiant energy (part of the electromagnetic spectrum). According to the laws of physics, energy can be neither created nor destroyed, but its form can be changed or converted. This principle can be demonstrated by touching a window through which the sun is shining. The glass will be warmer than a similar window that isn't in the direct sunlight. This is because the energy being absorbed by the glass is being converted from light into heat.

SUBTRACTIVE COLOR MIXING IN LIGHT If the glass in the window mentioned above is colored, another type of filtering takes place. Colored filters allow only their own hue to pass through the filtering medium; they absorb all other wavelengths of light.

Color Plate 7A shows a red filter placed in front of a full-spectrum light source. The white light emitted by the lamp is composed of wavelengths from all portions of the visible spectrum. The red filter allows only the wavelengths of light that correspond to its own color to pass. All other light is stopped by the filter and converted into heat.

When two or more filters, such as the secondary hues magenta and cyan, are placed in front of a single source (Color Plate 7B), each filter removes all but its own segment of the spectrum. The resulting blue light is caused by successive filtration. The magenta filter allows only red and blue light to pass through it. The cyan filter absorbs the red portion of the magenta light but allows the blue portion to pass. In practical application, it is usually preferable to use a single filter, rather than multiple filters. By selectively removing portions of the visible spectrum, subtractive color mixing actually reduces the intensity of the output of the source. A yellow or amber color medium of

---

THEORETICAL VERSUS PRACTICAL COLOR MIXING

According to color theory, the combination of complementary pigments yields black. The reason is straightforward. Each pigment reflects the wavelengths of light that correspond to its own hue and absorbs all others, as shown in Color Plate 6. Complementary hues are composed of one primary color and a secondary color. The secondary color is created from a mixture of the other two primary hues. The resultant blend of all three primaries should, theoretically, absorb all light that strikes it. This absence of reflected color means no light, which is the same as blackness.

In the practical mixing of pigments you will be dealing with paints that are not pure colors. There are fillers, extenders, and impure colors in every commercially prepared paint. These impurities will result in a deep gray instead of the theoretically correct black when mixing complementary hues.

CHAPTER 6: COLOR

minimal saturation may reduce intensity by about 5 percent, for example, and a heavily saturated dark blue may reduce it by as much as 85 percent. If more than one filter is used, the output of the source can be significantly reduced.

ADDITIVE COLOR MIXING IN LIGHT When several individual hues are transmitted to the eye, added together, and interpreted by the brain, the process is called additive color mixing. Color Plate 8 illustrates color mixing in light. The beams of the three lights are being projected onto a neutral or white surface. When a primary hue, such as red, is mixed with an adjacent primary, such as green, a secondary hue, yellow, is created. (It is interesting to realize that this hue is *not* created on the projection surface but is the result of the red and green cones in our eye being stimulated by the red and green light and our brain interpreting this neurological information as the hue yellow.) This same phenomenon occurs when any two or more hues are additively mixed.

All color is perceived in the same way. The subtle tones, tints, and shades of the various hues that you see are all determined by the level of stimulation that the red, blue, and green cones receive from the light reflected to your eye and by your brain's interpretation of that information.

Color Mixing in Paint

Color mixing in light and paint rely on the same principles of color reflection and absorption. Color mixing in paint is primarily a subtractive process, because pigments and dyes of specific hues reflect the wavelengths of light that correspond to their own hue and absorb all others. The primary hue blue provides a good example of how this subtractive process of color absorption works. When the white light strikes the blue surface illustrated in Color Plate 9, the various wavelengths of light are either reflected or absorbed depending on the particular hue of blue paint. Since the dominant color of the surface is blue, the blue light is reflected to your eye, and the other wavelengths of light are either reflected or absorbed according to their proportions in the blue paint.

The selective absorption characteristics of the individual hues in a paint mix cause a reduction in the saturation, or chroma, of the resultant hue. If yellow and red paint are mixed, for example, the result is an orange. But since the yellow pigment absorbs some of the red light and the red pigment absorbs some of the yellow light, the resultant orange paint is not so fully saturated as either original color.

Integrated Color Wheel

Sir Isaac Newton demonstrated that six principal hues (violet, blue, green, yellow, orange, and red) can be generated when sunlight is passed through a prism. These hues can be placed on a color wheel, as shown in Color Plate 10. Additional hues, which are full chroma equivalents to a mixture of adjacent original hues, can be created and placed between the six principal colors to create a color wheel with twelve specific, fully saturated, hues.

This integrated color wheel can help clarify the interrelationships between pigment and light. For years a semantic problem has hindered easy understanding of these relationships. The use of the same words to describe some of the primary and secondary hues for pigment and light has tended to create some confusion. Although the words red, blue, green, and yellow are used to describe colors in both pigment and light, the specific hues are not identical. The integrated color wheel resolves this problem by renaming the primary colors in light to more accurately reflect the true color relationship that exists between the various hues in pigment and light.

Fully saturated colors don't all have the same value. The twelve principal hues of the integrated color wheel have been arranged in Color Plate 11 in their appropriate relationships to a value scale.

A wide variety of interesting and useful tones can be created by mixing complementary pigments with black and white. Color Plate 12 demonstrates this effect with the complementary hues red and green. The value and saturation (chroma) of the resultant hues change as they are mixed with either black or white. **Neutralization** occurs in mixing complementary hues of the same value.

A Practical Postscript to Color Theory

Any discussion of color theory necessarily revolves around hues of 100 percent purity and saturation. Colors of this strength and value are not used in theatrical work, for two primary reasons: they would be incredibly expensive, and the use of fully saturated colors isn't particularly appropriate in the theatre, simply because the colors would visually dominate anything else on the stage.

THE APPLICATION OF COLOR IN THE THEATRE

In any discussion of color there is bound to be a disparity between theoretical principles and practical results. Although the principles of color theory are certainly applicable in the practical use of color, the end results of mixing paints, dyes, or lights will be somewhat different from the results projected by the theory. This is because of the impurities and contaminants found in all stage paints, dyes, lamps, and color media.

Meaning of Color

People react to color. Sometimes that response is subtle and subconscious, and at other times it is overtly physical. Doctors and drug rehabilitation counselors have discovered that an extremely violent patient will often become calm and manageable in about fifteen or twenty minutes if placed in an all-pink environment. Many hospitals now have "pink rooms" in which everything— the floor, ceiling, walls, doors—is painted the same hue of pink.

The meanings of color are constantly changing. Color meanings are influenced by many factors: cultural background, personality, adjoining colors, and individual mood. The variability of these factors is the primary reason that the following list of affective meanings is necessarily ambiguous. Moreover, these definitions are simply common interpretations of the meaning of specific colors and should not be thought of as being the "correct" ones.

> yellow: stimulating, cheerful, exciting, joyful, serene, unpleasant, aggressive, hostile
>
> orange: warm, happy, merry, exciting, stimulating, hot, disturbed, distressed, unpleasant
>
> red: happy, affectionate, loving, exciting, striking, active, intense, defiant, powerful, masterful, strong, aggressive, hostile
>
> green: youthful, fresh, leisurely, secure, calm, peaceful, emotionally controlled, ill

blue: pleasant, cool, secure, comfortable, tender, soothing, social, dignified, sad, strong, full, great

violet: dignified, stately, vigorous, disagreeable, sad, despondent, melancholy, unhappy, depressing

black: sad, melancholy, vague, unhappy, dignified, stately, strong, powerful, hostile, distressed, fearful, old

white: pure, tender, soothing, solemn, empty

brown: secure, comfortable, full, sad, disagreeable

Practical Color Use

Designers in the theatre normally follow some general color guidelines. The following discussion provides a survey of examples and general practices. Any competent designer will advise you that there are many occasions when it is appropriate, logical, and right to ignore the normal and the conventional if doing so will support the visualization of the production concept.

PIGMENT Scenic designers generally use hues of medium saturation and value, because most sets serve as a background environment for the action of the play, and the set needs to recede from the audience's consciousness after it has made its original visual statement. For the same reason costume designers generally work in a less constricted palette. Colors of full saturation and brilliance will direct the audience's attention to the actors. The only proviso for their use is that the hue and value be an appropriate reflection of the actor's character.

Color proximity—the placement and relationship of specific hues—has a great impact on the spectators' perception of a scene. Strongly contrasting colors create a greater dynamic tension than do less conflicting hues. A set that had a highly saturated yellow sofa placed in front of a brilliant blue wall would be visually shocking. The startling color contrast would indicate that the owner of that particular apartment was dynamic, eccentric, possibly volatile, and probably wacko. Similarly, a man dressed in an electric blue suit with a brilliant yellow vest would also be thought of in the same basically antisocial way. But if the saturation of those contrasting colors was reduced and modified—a soft-yellow, floral-print sofa against a dusty powder-blue wall of the same or similar value—our perception of the owner of that apartment would be similarly softened.

Accent colors, which are basically small touches of contrasting colors, are continually used by both scenic and costume designers. The color dynamics of an otherwise relatively lifeless set can be enhanced by setting a vase of colorful flowers on a table, hanging a painting on the wall, or accenting a table through the use of a white or color-coordinated tablecloth. Costumers frequently provide accent colors in their designs with accessories such as jewelry, scarves, purses, and shoes. Accent colors generally are interpreted in the same way as other contrasting colors: greater contrast creates increased dynamic tension.

LIGHT There are some very pragmatic reasons for using colored light onstage. The light from theatre spotlights is relatively bright and harsh. In its uncolored state, and at close to full intensity, it will tend to bleach any color out of the scenery, costumes, and makeup. If colors that are compatible with the scenery and costumes are used to filter the stage lights, however, the scenic designer's and costume designer's color palettes and values will be maintained.

As we have seen, the mixing of complementary hues creates white light. In the discussion on color theory this principle was demonstrated with fully saturated hues. In practical application fully saturated hues are rarely used because of their adverse effect on the other designers' palettes and on actors' skin tones. Complementary hues of low chroma are frequently used, however, because pigments lit with additively mixed white light are enhanced rather than bleached. This color enhancement is caused by the brain's interpretation of retinal stimulation, as demonstrated in Color Plate 13. Color Plate 13A shows white light striking a white surface. Since the white light is composed of all wavelengths of light, the white surface simply reflects all the light rather than absorbing or filtering out any specific portion of the spectrum. Color Plate 13B shows two complementary hues of low saturation (light blue and light yellow) striking the same white surface. These low-saturation hues emphasize a relatively narrow portion of the spectrum (blue and yellow), although there is still a large proportion of the full spectrum (white light) in the mix. The white surface reflects the pale blue and pale yellow, as well as the white light, to your eye. Because blue and yellow are complementary, your brain interprets the mixture of those two lights as white. However, the cones are more strongly stimulated by the blue and yellow light than they would be with plain white light. Interestingly, the brain interprets this stronger color stimulation as a richer, more vibrant color. This phenomenon works for all complementary color mixes. Although the specific color reflectivity and absorption of any colored light from any particular costume or set color will depend on the characteristics of that particular hue, the principles of color vibrancy remain constant.

The palettes used by the scenic and costume designers generally dictate the specific complementary hues that are chosen by a lighting designer. The lighting designer usually selects specific hues that will enhance the primary palettes of the other designers, using the guideline that every hue heightens its own color and supresses its complementary. If the scenic or costume designer is using a full-spectrum palette, the lighting designer may combine three or more colors to create white light. When more specific hues are used to create the white light mix, the range of hues affected by the color-enrichment characteristics of a complementary mix are similarly broadened.

The lighting designer can also produce a white light mix that is not exactly complementary—either slightly warm or cool—to create a corresponding warming or cooling of the stage environment. This type of not-quite-complementary color mixing is very helpful in establishing an atmospheric feeling of heat or cold on the stage.

The difference between the theory and practice of color mixing is only a matter of degree, not principle. Although an understanding of the laws of physics that govern the mixing of color is very helpful in using color in the theatre, the only way that a designer can develop any real understanding of, and facility in, the use of color is through experimentation and experience. Additional information on the practical application of color can be found in Chapter 10, *Scene Painting*, Chapter 12, *Lighting Design,* and Chapter 20, *Rendering.*

7

Scenic Design

Scenery helps the audience understand and enjoy a play by providing a visual reinforcement of the production concept. However, the scenery hasn't always been designed with a production concept in mind.

Before about 1875 no one paid any great attention to specifying the elements (period, country, locale, socioeconomic status, and mood) that we in the late twentieth century believe make up a well-conceived stage setting. Greek and Roman productions were performed out of doors with little or no scenery. Medieval drama used standardized scenic elements (heaven, hell, the courtyard, and so on) that represented the various locations needed for almost all productions. The Renaissance was a period of evolutionary development in scenery. Some theatres had permanent sets built as part of the theatre architecture (Teatro Olympico). Other theatres (the Globe) had bare, open stages with no scenic elements. From the Restoration (1660) until the mid–nineteenth century plays were performed in front of stock sets. Only in the last one hundred years has scenery evolved into its present form.

STYLES IN SCENIC DESIGN

At the end of the nineteenth century scenic design entered a period of development and experimentation unparalleled in the history of the theatre, and the spirit of experimentation and stylistic growth fostered at that time is still very much alive today. The various design styles that evolved—naturalism, realism, expressionism, and the like—are not ends in themselves. They are just convenient reference points on the continuum of design style that moves from **representational** (Figure 7.1) on one end to **nonrepresentational** (Figure 7.2) on the other. Nonrepresentational design escapes the pictorial con-

Representational design: A style in which the portrayed elements represent some recognizable object, such as a room, a forest, or a street corner.

Nonrepresentational design: A style in which the portrayed elements do not represent a physically identifiable object.

93

(A)

(B)

Figure 7.1 Representational sets. (A) Gary Merrill and Maureen O'Sullivan in Elizabeth McCann, Nelle Nugent, and Ray Larson's production of *Mornings at Seven;* scenic design by William Ritman, costume design by Linda Fisher; photo © 1986 Martha Swope. (B) Jamie Horton (left) and Mike Regan in *Ringers,* Denver Theatre Center Company; set design by Richard L. Hay, costume design by Andrew V. Yelusich; photo by Larry Lazlo.

(A)

(B)

(C)

Figure 7.2 Nonrepresentational sets. (A) *Romance Languages,* Mark Taper Forum (Los Angeles); scenic design by Lauren Sherman, costume design by Sheila McLamb-Wilcox; photo by Jay Thompson. (B) Kermit Bloomgarden's production of *Equus,* the Plymouth Theatre (New York); costumes and scenery by John Natier, lighting by Andy Phillips; American supervisor of scenery and lighting, Howard Bay; photo by Van Williams. (C) Bradford Wallace (left) and Eric Travers in Asolo State Theatre's (Sarasota, Florida) production of *Waiting for Godot;* set design by Bennet Averyt, costume design by Catherine King; photo by Gary W. Sweetman Photography.

fines of realism by creating abstract environments in a variety of interesting forms. It encourages every member of the audience to create his or her own meaning for the abstraction.

For all practical purposes it is almost impossible to tell where one style stops and another begins. A designer frequently makes use of two or more styles in combination to create a visual representation of the production concept for a particular play. Regardless of the style that a designer chooses, the finished product—whether sets, costumes, lights, or sound—needs to be a faithful, logical, and natural outgrowth of the production concept.

A great number of terms are used to discuss and analyze design. Misunderstanding of the specific meanings of two key terms—*style* and *form*—can lead to confusion and consternation.

Style refers to the specific compositional characteristics that distinguish the appearance of one type of design from another. Using this definition, the various design styles—realism, expressionism, surrealism, and so forth—are delineated by the differences in their compositional principles (see Chapter 5).

Form, on the other hand, simply refers to elements that have similar physical characteristics. For example, arena, thrust, and proscenium theatres have different forms of stage configuration.

Using these definitions it becomes relatively clear that the form of a design doesn't necessarily dictate the style of the design; for example, the set for an arena production (form) could be designed naturalistically, realistically, or in any other style.

CONSIDERATIONS FOR THE SCENIC DESIGNER

Before we look at the various elements that must be considered to create a quality scenic design, a cautionary digression seems appropriate. Beware of any so-called rules of design. There aren't any. What works in one design situation may not work in another. If every design choice we make is a rational, considered decision, there is no need for rules such as "Never paint a set white," "Don't use green light," "Never wear taffeta on stage," and so forth. In terms of creativity these rules are debilitating, because they arbitrarily limit our ability to select from the full breadth of our knowledge and experience.

Although we should be wary of arbitrary rules, most good scenic designs do comply with a majority of the principles discussed in this section.

In addition to the scenery, the scenic designer is responsible for designing the stage properties. Props are an important element of the stage picture, and they subscribe to all of the qualities discussed in this section. In black box and arena theatres, furniture props take on added significance as the primary visual elements of the scenic design, since flats, drops, and other vertical elements of scenery generally aren't used. Additional information on stage properties is available in Chapter 11, *Stage Properties*.

Mood and Spirit of the Play

One guideline works for all plays: the design should be expressive of the **mood** and **spirit** of the play. Within this context mood usually refers to the dominant emotional quality of the production. Spirit is generally interpreted to refer to the production concept—the way in which the production design team (producer, director, and scenic, costume, lighting, and sound designers) decide that the play is going to be presented.

For the design to effectively express mood and spirit the designer needs to incorporate some elements that suggest the emotional characteristics of the play, as shown in Figure 7.3. If the play is a gentle romance, it might be

Mood: The feeling of a play—comic, tragic, happy, and so forth.

Spirit: The manner and style in which a play is presented to the audience.

CHAPTER 7: SCENIC DESIGN

(A)

(B)

Figure 7.3 Scenic designs can provide reinforcement of the mood and spirit of the play. (A) *Flea in Her Ear,* Florida State University; scene design by Park Warne, costume design by Abby Lillethun, lighting design by Michael Murphy; photo by Robert M. O'Lary. (B) John Bottom and Ben Halley, Jr., in *Endgame,* produced by the American Repertory Theatre (Cambridge, Massachusetts); scene design by Douglas Stein, costume design by Kurt Wilhelm, lighting by Jennifer Tipton; photo by Richard Feldman.

appropriate to use soft curves to define the outline of the set, and the scenery could be painted with delicate pastel to reinforce the romantic qualities of the play. If the play is an intense tragedy, hard lines, sharp angles, and a palette of dark colors would express the heavy mood that the production concept seeks to project.

Assume that an old melodrama is being considered for production. The play has many situations that are essentially serious (the heroine, her widowed mother, and her seriously ill little brother are being thrown out of their house for nonpayment of rent), and most of the characters are likable people who just happen to be down on their luck. Unhappiness, sadness, and despair seem to be the general emotional qualities of the play. Instead of emphasizing these rather depressing qualities, however, the director decides to change the emotional tone of the play. He or she chooses to concentrate on the comic aspects. The serious and dramatic situations are exaggerated to the point that they no longer seem believable, and the whole spirit of the production changes.

The design work should mirror this change in the mood and spirit of the production. For the original mood the settings would have been realistically depressing, and the color palette would probably have been muted and somber. For the reinterpretation the settings can be simplified and exaggerated in a cartoon style that supports the same spirit of overemphasis and artificiality that is evident in the acting and business of the play.

Historical Period of the Play

A scenic designer must provide historically accurate visual clues that will help the audience identify the period of the play. To provide these clues the designer needs to do historical research.

Historical research may mean that the set designer actually looks at furniture, rooms, knickknacks, and buildings from the period of the play. Or the

Figure 7.4 Historical detail helps provide visual keys to the period of the play. (A) John A. McQuiggan's production of *The Foreigner* at the Astor Place Theatre (New York); scenic design by Karen Schulz, costume design by Rita Ryack, lighting by Paul Gallo; photo by Van Williams. (B) Asolo Theatre (Sarasota, Florida) production of *Misalliance;* scenic design by Jack Doepp; photo by Gary W. Sweetman Photography.

(A)

(B)

CHAPTER 7: SCENIC DESIGN

designer may search the library for pictures of furniture, room design and decoration, architecture, landscape photos, paintings, and so forth in books and periodicals. Such background research is extremely important, because the style of the trim, furniture, and furnishings, as well as their arrangement within the room or building, varies tremendously from generation to generation and from one geographical area to another. It is this change of appearance that helps the audience identify the period, country, and locale of the play, as shown in Figure 7.4.

Although it is vital that you do historical research, don't assume that your design must adhere to every stylistic quirk of the period in which you are working. It isn't necessary to make exact copies of furniture pieces and trim styles. You will need to understand the general motifs and idiosyncracies of the period and use them in a way that creates a faithful visual representation. But you don't have to duplicate every variation and nuance. A scenic design is not a reproduction; it should be a creation that mirrors the essence of a period to provide a physical environment that will enhance the mood and spirit of the play.

Locale of the Play

Geography has a significant impact on the design of buildings and their furnishings. In the days before air conditioning and central heat, climate shaped the buildings. For example, steeply pitched gables helped the snow slide off the roofs of houses built in the North. Homes in the warmer climates had lower-pitched roofs and large overhanging eaves to keep the summer sun off the walls and out of the windows. By using these and similar visual keys, the scenic designer can help the audience identify the play's location.

Styles in the design of houses and business structures change relatively rapidly. These changes stem more often from socioeconomic circumstances than from architects' aesthetic yearnings. Thus, the oil crisis of the 1970s strongly influenced American architecture. As the cost of heating oil, natural gas and electricity rose, the size of the average residential dwelling decreased accordingly. The all-glass designs for commercial buildings of the 1960s and early 1970s were replaced by structures that could be heated and cooled more economically.

Even more noticeable than the differences in the exterior design of houses and buildings are the differences in interiors. Depending on the historical period and the socioeconomic status of the occupants, ceilings may be high or low. Walls may be plain, painted, or covered with wallpaper. They may contain window arrangements, recessed bookcases, or ornamental niches. The only guideline for their inclusion in the design is that they be appropriate for the period of the play and the social status of the characters.

The walls of the room in which the action of the play takes place may be made from rough logs, finished boards, or lath and plaster. They may also have a variety of decorative trim, for example, baseboards, wainscoting, chair rails, plate rails, picture rails, or cornices (see Figure 7.5). Depending on the type of room and the period of the play, there may be a fireplace. The fireplace may be built into the wall, or it may project into the room and be surrounded by a plain or decorative hearth.

In addition to the shape, arrangement, and details of the walls, the furnishings also provide the scenic designer with an excellent opportunity to help create an appropriate environment for the play. In selecting furniture the designer should study the types of arrangement appropriate for the period and adapt them to the **blocking** needs of the play. In selecting the appropriate

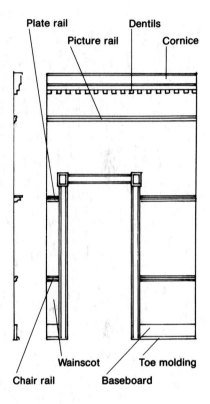

Figure 7.5 Various types of wall trim.

Blocking: The actors' movements on the stage.

number of chairs, sofas, or other seats to be used on a set, for example, always have enough places for everyone to sit if all the principal actors are on stage at the same time.

Decorative properties can also aid in creating a believable environment. Decorative props are generally considered to be those furnishings that aren't used by the actors and serve no specific purpose in the business of the play but that help project atmosphere and feeling. Small pieces of furniture such as occasional chairs and end tables, pictures, wall hangings, rugs, knickknacks, lamps, lighting fixtures, and similar decorative articles all fall into the category of decorative properties.

The floor needs to be considered when doing historical research. It provides a unifying visual element that ties the whole set together and can provide the foundation for the color scheme for the entire design. The stage floor can be covered with one-quarter-inch Masonite for a relatively small expense, and it can be painted in whatever treatment (boards, earth, stone) is appropriate for the design. Painted ground cloths, rugs, or some similarly individualized, moveable treatment can be used for the individual scenes of a multiset production.

Socioeconomic Level of the Characters

Most sets give some indication of what sort of characters will inhabit the environment of the play. The designer normally uses set and decorative props as tools to achieve this effect. A living room that is decorated with inexpensive but reasonably tasteful furnishings suggests one type of occupant, and the same room furnished with expensive but incredibly gaudy things indicates that a completely different sort of person lives in the room. If either of the preceding rooms were littered with a month's accumulation of dirty dishes, clothes, and other junk, it would seem likely that a completely different type of character was living there.

Selecting furniture can be a bit complex, simply because so many factors can influence what furniture should be used. The status of the "owners" of the furniture greatly affects not only the style but also the amount of furniture. If the principal character is a "pack rat" type, it is usually appropriate to have more furniture on the set than if the lead is a more fastidious type.

There are, of course, many situations that prevent a scenic designer from giving any indication of the socioeconomic level or personalities of the characters. But when the circumstances permit, this is another means by which the designer can enhance the audience's understanding and enjoyment of the play.

Season of the Year

Normally it is rather difficult for the scenic designer to provide anything other than a cursory indication of the season in which the play is happening. If the play takes place in summer, the designer can suggest heat by having the doors and windows open and using screen doors and windows. The selection of light colors and fabrics for any upholstery and curtains can help create a feeling of summer, but by and large the projection of seasonal atmosphere is usually left to the lighting and costume designers.

Elements of Composition

Full discussions of composition and color were presented in Chapters 5 and 6. However, this is an appropriate time to remind you that it is essential that scenic, property, and costume designers be able to draw freely and easily. This is a skill that can be learned, and instructions for basic perspective drawing and sketching are included in Chapter 19, *Perspective,* and Chapter 20, *Rendering.* Although these instructions will provide you with a beginning point, the best way to become really adept at drawing and painting is to take art classes.

Manipulation of the compositional elements (line, form, mass, value, and color), as we have seen in Chapter 5, is the root of any design. We will now explore the applicability of this principle to scenic design.

LINE Line defines form. The characteristics of any line are defined by its physical properties (dimension, quality, and character). These properties, especially character, give any particular line its emotional content.

Cartooning is almost always based on the principle of line simplification. Walt Disney's cartoon characters Mickey Mouse and Donald Duck are simplified outlines of a mouse and a duck. There is no mistaking the objects for anything else, yet their simplicity gives them distinctive personalities that are uniquely their own.

Simplifying or altering the line of a natural form within a scenic design creates the same type of unique character definition as does line simplification in cartooning. The personality of the object created by this process is directly related to the emotional quality of the line style chosen by the designer. Generally, an object drawn with strong (heavy, sharply angular, bold) lines creates an emotional response that the object is more powerful, dominant, and purposeful than if it were drawn with weak (soft, curvilinear, lightweight) lines.

FORM In compositional terms form refers to a space enclosed by a line. The evocative characteristics of the line defining any form will dictate the emotional qualities of that form. The character of the chosen line, (heavy, light, straight, squiggly, softly curving, sharply angled) will create a perceptual key that helps explain the psychological nature of the object being depicted (Figure 7.6).

Figure 7.6 *Peter Pan,* produced at Florida State University; scenic design by Robert Barnes, costume design by Erin Wertenberger of Costume Crafters, Inc., lighting design by Lauren Schoemaker.

MASS Within the context of composition, mass is defined as the three-dimensional manifestation of an enclosed form, and the perceived meanings of mass are very closely related to those of form. The exaggeration of either form or mass can be used to stylize a design. By exaggerating the height, width, or depth of the natural dimensions of an object, we can change the character of that object. The illustrations from almost any book or cartoon version of *Alice's Adventures in Wonderland* serve to illustrate this point. Once Alice encounters the March Hare and enters the strange land ruled by the Queen of Hearts, hardly anything is seen in its normal size or shape.

VALUE Value refers to the relative lightness or darkness of a line, form, or mass. The emotional reaction to the value or reflectance of an object has become ingrained in the core of Western thought, although no one is really sure why white has come to symbolize purity, truth, and honor. Its opposite in terms of reflectance or brilliance, black, has similarly come to symbolize evil, dishonesty, and dishonor. These evocative differences can be used by the scenic designer when selecting the color palette for use in a production. Although the values of white, gray, and black are obvious, the value differences within specific hues—pink, medium red, and deep red, for example—are more subtle but have the same emotional effect on the audience. The color pink generally evokes a response that is allied to the emotional response to white—purity, truth, honor. Its counterpart—dark red—evokes an emotional reaction that is more closely related to black—evil, dishonesty, dishonor.

COLOR Although scenic objects are normally painted to appear as they are in life, interesting results can be achieved by substituting an unexpected hue for the natural color. Any production of the musical *Brigadoon,* which centers on time travel of the hero to the mythical pseudo-Scottish country of Brigadoon, needs a set to show the countryside of Brigadoon for several of the scenes. The drop for this scene usually shows a typical Scottish glen complete with hills, heather, and sylvan glade. The audience will be alerted that all is not quite normal in Brigadoon if, rather than natural colors, the hillside is painted in a gaily colored plaid.

Practicality of the Setting

A sketch for a scenic design can be both absolutely beautiful and totally worthless, because a design doesn't exist just on paper. It must also be practical. Any scenic design must fulfill four utilitarian functions before it can be considered anything more than a pretty picture. The designer must take into consideration the needs of the director and actors, the demands of construction, and budgets of money and time.

NEEDS OF THE DIRECTOR The set design must meet the needs of the director. The form of the setting(s) must be designed to accommodate the blocking and other stage business that the director has in mind. If the director wants the heroine to make a grand entrance down a flight of stairs, it is the responsibility of the scenic designer to place the stairs in a prominent position. The director and scenic designer discuss these directorial needs during the early production conferences so that they can help to shape the set in the scenic designer's mind.

NEEDS OF THE ACTORS To fulfill the actors' needs the set must function properly, efficiently, and as planned. Actors have to be able to concentrate in

GOOD DESIGN: A CHECKLIST

Here is a concise list of those qualities that can be found in a good design. It is equally applicable to scenic, property, costume, and lighting design.
  Does the design express

- the mood and spirit of the play?
- the historical period of the play?
- the locale of the play?

- the socioeconomic status of the characters?
- the season of the year?

  Is the design based on the elements of good composition?
  Practically, does the design meet

- the needs of the director?
- the needs of the actors?
- the technical demands of the production?
- the fiscal and time budgets?

---

order to perform their roles properly. The last thing that they need is anything that would break that concentration, such as slippery floors, doors that won't open or stay closed, windows that jam shut, and supposedly solid floors that wiggle.

CONSTRUCTION DEMANDS OF THE DESIGN Every scenic design presents certain technical demands when it is constructed. Their complexity is directly related to the intricacy of the design. Elements within the design, such as a spinning staircase or a cantilevered platform, may create construction challenges that cannot be solved by ordinary scenic construction techniques. The designer must be aware of these and must determine how these pieces can be constructed and rigged. It can be disastrous for a production if the designer and director plan on a specific piece of equipment, such as an elevator or large wagon or revolve, and then discover during the technical or dress rehearsals that the unit won't function as planned.

Additional technical demands are imposed because scenery must be portable, and the scenic designer needs to specify how the sets should be broken down into manageable units. Even the scenery for plays that require a single set must be portable, since the scenery is usually built in one place and transported to the stage for setup. The unit breakdown of the scenery for a multiscene production must be carefully planned to ensure that there will be room to store everything in the wings and flies.

Before construction starts, the scenic designer reviews the plans with the lighting designer to be sure that the set can be lit as effectively as possible. Sometimes portions of the scene design are slightly rearranged or modified to give the lighting designer room to hang and focus the lighting instruments. Sets with full ceilings normally preclude the use of top and side light, but if the scenic designer can include a beam or similar architectural feature in the ceiling, an opening can be cut on the upstage side of the beam and the instruments focused through the slot.

TIME AND FISCAL BUDGETS The administration of the actual construction schedules and fiscal budgets varies from organization to organization, but the scenic designer is ultimately responsible for the timely construction of the

Many theatres maintain an inventory of standard-sized flats and platforms. This inventory is referred to as stock scenery. Found objects are simply that—objects retrieved from a salvage yard, a garbage can, or a dark corner of the prop room.

Designing for stock scenery or found objects can be cost-efficient and sometimes even inspirational. If your budget is small, using stock flats for the walls of the set will allow you to save a good deal of money. If the flats aren't the right height, small flats called headers can be attached to the top of the stock flats to increase their height. Jogs, which are narrow flats less than a foot wide, can be made to modify the width of the flats. Stock platforms, which are normally four feet wide by eight feet long, are another cost-efficient scenic element. Although the shape of a raised stage area may be irregular, the majority of the elevated platform can be constructed using the four-foot-by-eight-foot platform modules. The remaining spaces can be filled in with irregular platforms specifically constructed for the production.

Designing for found objects requires that you look at utilitarian objects in a slightly different way. Jim Gray sculpts dinosaurs of amazing anatomical accuracy from old auto parts. He looks at a junkyard and doesn't see piles of broken cars, but the bones of long-vanished animals just waiting to be resurrected.

Using this same kind of different vision Peter Wexler created a backdrop for the Theatre Center Group's production of *Godspell* from old doors, pipe, and chain-link fencing. Designing for found objects can be fun, effective, and efficient.

Other people's junk can be turned into art. Twentieth Century Dinosaurs sculpted by Jim Gray. Photo by Tova Navarra courtesy of the *San Francisco Chronicle.*

Scenic design for *Godspell,* produced by the Center Theatre Group at the Mark Taper Forum, Los Angeles. Scenery designed by Peter Wexler.

scenery and properties. It is the designer's responsibility to produce the best possible design that the budgets will allow.

In the New York professional theatre the scenic costs and construction schedules are determined in a fairly straightforward manner. The scenic designer submits the plans to the producer, who approves the plans and then solicits bids for the construction and painting of the scenery and properties from a number of independent scenic studios. The contract is generally awarded to the lowest bidder. If the actual costs of the scenery are above the estimated budget for scenic construction, the producer and scenic designer discuss cost-cutting procedures. These generally involve eliminating some part of the design or redesigning various elements to reduce their construction costs.

In regional professional companies that construct their own scenery, and in educational and community theatres, the responsibility for formulating cost and time estimates is a little less clear. Generally, the producer or managing director determines the estimated budget, and the scenic designer and technical director work within those estimates to determine the actual time and fiscal budgets for the construction, finishing, and mounting of the scenic and property elements. To accomplish this relatively complex task the scenic designer is in almost constant communication with the technical director during the design phase. The whole process of budgeting is immeasurably improved if the scenic designer can produce fairly accurate estimates of costs and construction time.

Figure 7.7
Thumbnail sketches.

VISUAL PRESENTATION OF SCENIC DESIGNS

To communicate effectively the scene designer must be able to present his or her visual concepts to the other members of the production design team in some clearly understandable manner. Two methods are used to fulfill this vital function, sketches and models.

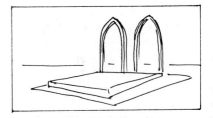

Sketches

Thumbnail sketches and renderings are the two basic types of sketch that the scene designer produces.

THUMBNAIL SKETCHES Thumbnail sketches (Figure 7.7) are rough drawings, usually made in pencil, that show the general composition of the set but very little detail. They are generally made while the designer is developing various concepts for the set while doing conceptual research.

Thumbnail sketches are almost always unfinished drawings. Their purpose is to provide a rough visualization of the various scenic concepts on which the designer is working. They are drawn rapidly for two primary reasons. The quick sketching seems to lessen the inhibitions that other members of the production design team feel when suggesting changes in the various elements of the design; and the lack of time spent on the drawing also seems to keep the designer from getting locked into one particular design concept too soon.

RENDERINGS Renderings are finished color sketches of the set. They are normally drawn to scale in **mechanical perspective** so they are an accurate representation of the actual size, shape, and color of the setting. The renderings are also complete in terms of the type, style, and location of any

Mechanical perspective: A drafting technique that provides an illusion of depth.

furniture, as well as all trim and decorative touches that will be used on the actual setting. Quality renderings also show the scenic designer's thoughts regarding the lighting for the set. These sketches generally include a figure or figures to help the viewer determine the scale of the design.

Renderings can be produced using any media, but watercolor and acrylic paints, pastels, colored pencils, and markers are used most frequently. Specific "how-to" information on scale drawing, perspective drawing, and rendering techniques is contained in Chapter 18, *Mechanical Drafting,* Chapter 19, *Perspective,* and Chapter 20, *Rendering.*

Models

Two specific types of scenic models are used to present the visual ideas of the scenic designer—functional models and production models. Scenic models are attractive, interesting, and fun to look at, but they are most useful when they are placed within an accurate scale model of the stage space (proscenium, thrust, or arena) for which they are designed. The scale model of the theatre needs to be used because it is difficult to understand the relationship between the set and stage unless both those spaces are very clearly defined.

Figure 7.8 The functional model is usually constructed from thin cardboard, and any detail is drawn with pen and ink. *As You Like It: The Forest,* produced at the MacLeod Theatre, Southern Illinois University; designed by Darwin Reid Payne. This illustration and Figure 7.9A are from *Theory and Craft of the Scenographic Model* by Darwin Reid Payne, copyright 1985 by the Board of Trustees, Southern Illinois University, Carbondale. Reprinted by permission of the publisher.

FUNCTIONAL MODELS The functional model is the three-dimensional equivalent of a thumbnail sketch. Its purpose is to help the scenic designer and other members of the production design team visualize the basic composition of the scenic design. It is usually quickly constructed from stiff paper (file folders) or cardboard and held together with tape. It is made to scale (usually one-quarter or one-half inch to one foot) so that it will be an accurate representation of the finished set.

Because the purpose of the functional model (Figure 7.8) is to show the general shape and form of the set and not the detail, any indication of trim and decoration is usually limited to pencil sketches indicating the location and general style of the major architectural trim elements. The functional model is rarely painted.

The functional model is an excellent aid to the scenic designer. Most designers begin the execution step of the design process with a series of thumbnail sketches. Then they frequently construct functional models of these sketches as a means of verifying and solidifying their design concepts.

The use of a functional model is particularly important when working on a design that is difficult to represent with a sketch, such as a setting that is more sculptural than decorative. The functional model is also a great aid when dealing with any set that makes use of forced perspective, because it is much easier to see the effect of the visual distortion on the model than it is in a drawing. Additionally, it is very easy to create the exact angle of desired distortion by cutting down, or adding to, the height and angle of the thin cardboard walls of the model.

The functional model also provides an excellent method of presenting visual concepts to other members of the production design team. It is usually much easier for everyone to understand the scenic designer's concept and intentions when a model is used to supplement the scenic sketches.

The director can use the functional model as a visual aid while explaining the set concept to the actors. Furthermore, he or she can use it when planning the blocking for the production.

The scenic designer and technical director use the functional model to help plan complicated scene shifts. Problems of limited storage space or complex movements of the various scenic units can be solved with its aid.

To check on the accuracy of plans after they have been drawn, simply

(A)

(B)

Figure 7.9 The production model is usually painted and furnished to provide an accurate miniature version of the finished set. (A) *Suddenly Last Summer,* scenic design by Darwin Reid Payne. (B) *A Member of the Wedding,* scenic design by the author.

glue the plans onto thin cardboard, and make a functional model from the plans. If no errors have been made in drawing the plans, the model should fit together perfectly.

PRODUCTION MODELS The production model (Figure 7.9) provides a complete visualization of the scene designer's concept. The production model is also built to scale (usually one-quarter or one-half inch to one foot), is fully painted, and completely decorated with all of the furniture, props, and set dressing that will be used during the production.

Because it is complete in every detail the production model provides an excellent method of explaining the full scenic concept to the other members of the production design team. For the same reason it is also used by the property master to help guide the design and selection of props and set dressing for the production.

The production model also provides a good means of keeping a record of the scenic design for the production. When security permits, it can also be used during the production as a decorative display in the lobby of the theatre.

These sketches and models are tools, not end products. The thumbnail sketches, renderings, and models that are made by the scenic designer help him or her discover workable solutions to specific design challenges. They are also the primary tools used to communicate those solutions to other interested members of the production team. They are, to a very real degree, working drawings.

Designer's Plans

The colored sketch or production model for a scenic design may be a thing of beauty, and it may give a clear picture of the designer's intentions, but it does not give the technical director or carpenters all of the information they need to build the set. This information is contained in a series of mechanical drawings, called designer's plans, that depict every detail of the set as well as providing exact measurements of its components. These plans are prepared by the set designer and consist of a ground plan, front elevations, detail drawings, full-scale drawings, sight-line drawings, and painter's elevations.

GROUND PLAN The ground plan (Figure 7.10) is the key drawing on which the remainder of the designer's plans are based. It is a scale mechanical drawing showing the top view of a setting in its proper position on the stage. It clearly shows the form of the set and its relationship to the physical structure of the theatre. The location and measurements are given for all architectural features of the set, onstage and off, such as doors, windows, fireplaces, columns, stairs, and ramps. Additionally, the position and measurements for all **backing, ground rows,** wings, borders, and cycloramas are indicated.

A majority of the work done in planning a production depends on the information provided by the ground plan. During the rehearsal period the director has the stage manager, using the ground plan as a guide, tape or chalk the outline of the design onto the rehearsal room floor. Then the actors can rehearse and perfect their blocking in a space that corresponds to the actual set.

The lighting designer, when drawing the light plot, uses the ground plan to provide information about the shape and placement of the set within the theatre. This type of information is needed when making decisions about the **hanging positions** for the various instruments that will light the production.

The technical director uses the ground plan for a wide variety of functions. Together with the **center line sectional** it tells the TD where the set will sit on the stage and where to place the masking. It also indicates a great deal of information about the amount of materials that will be needed to construct the set(s).

Information on how to draw a ground plan, as well as the other drawings that make up the designer's plans, is contained in Chapter 18, *Mechanical Drafting*.

FRONT ELEVATIONS Front elevations (Figure 7.11) show a front view of the set as if it were flattened into a single plane. The main purpose of these scale drawings (normally one-half inch to one foot) is to indicate all of the vertical measurements that cannot be shown on the ground plan. These dimensions include the height of walls, doors, and windows as well as the location of any features on the walls such as baseboards, wainscoting, chair rails, cornices, paintings, or other decorative features.

Even if the scenic designer has constructed a functional model of the set, he or she will actually be designing as much with the drafting of the elevations as when producing the thumbnail sketches, renderings, or models, be-

Backing: Flats, drops, or draperies on the offstage side of doors and similar openings to prevent the audience from seeing backstage.

Ground row: Low, horizontal flats used to mask the base of cycs or drops; frequently painted to resemble rows of buildings, hedges, or similar visual elements.

Hanging positions: The various locations around the stage and auditorium where lighting instruments will be placed.

Sectional: A drawing, usually in scale, of an object that shows what it would look like if cut straight through at a given plane.

Center line sectional: A sectional drawing whose cutting plane is the center line of the stage and auditorium, showing the height of the various elements of the theatre; usually drawn in the same scale as the ground plan.

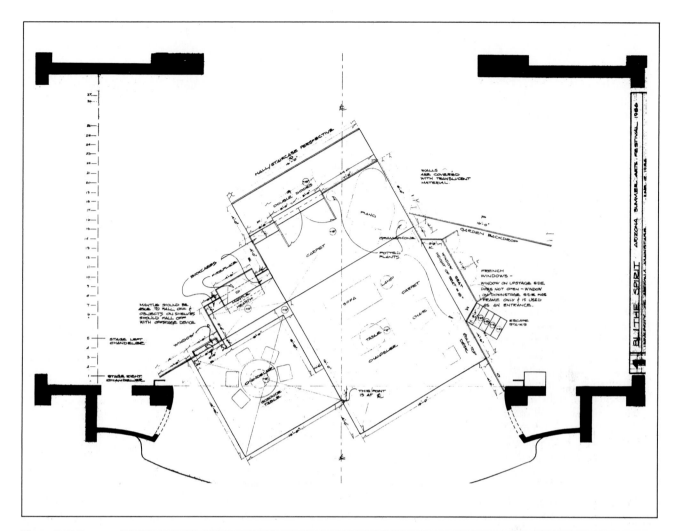

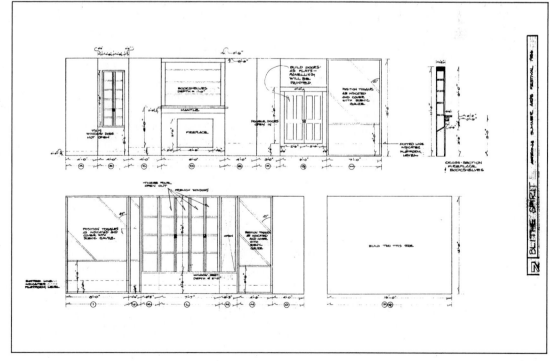

Figure 7.11 Front elevations for *Blithe Spirit,* produced at the University of Arizona; scenic design by K. Pistor.

COMMITMENT

As in any other design field, you have to make a commitment to yourself to do your best possible work on the assignment.

ANALYSIS

To help clarify the challenge of scenic design, you need to read the script, talk to other members of the production design team, and ask questions. Find out everything you can about the play (see the material on script analysis in Chapter 2), the director's production concept, and the production circumstances (type of stage, budget, and so forth).

A ground plan and center line sectional of the theatre in which the play will be produced provide information regarding the stage configuration, sight lines, general stage equipment, and other aspects of the physical structure of the theatre. Many times these drawings are accompanied by a specification sheet that provides other pertinent data regarding the auditorium, stage equipment, and policies. The producer or theatre manager should be able to supply you with these drawings and specification sheets.

While you are scurrying around asking questions, you will identify areas that require additional research. For example, if you are designing *Terra Nova,* which is set in Antarctica, you will have to know what that frozen continent looks like. Because the chances are pretty good that you've never been there, you will have to study the geography, climate, and appearance of that continent. This kind of information is usually available in books and periodicals at the library.

RESEARCH

Background research in scenic design involves several things. If the production concept requires a realistic setting, the scenic designer must delve into the architectural, sociological, and cultural background of the environment of the play. If the setting is to be non-realistic, it won't be necessary to probe as deeply into these details. You may need to examine the psychological roots of the play more closely, however, because a non-representational setting ideally should be a physical extension of the psychological environment of the play.

This research will necessitate a trip or two to the library or museum(s) to look at books, periodicals, paintings and other sources that provide visual information about homes, buildings, furniture, and other details of the period of the play.

Up to this point in the design process, your primary function has been the stockpiling of information, which has helped clarify the challenge and pointed out areas requiring further research. In the next phase of the design process—conceptual research—you start to synthesize and utilize the information you have been gathering.

The object of conceptual research is to create as many potential solutions to the design challenge as possible. Now is the time to start producing thumbnail sketches or functional models based on a synthesis of your information. It is also appropriate, and almost inevitable, that you experiment with differing combinations of elements from the various design concepts you have evolved. This sort of experimentation is the real key to a creatively vital design, because creativity in theatrical design is basically the combination of existing forms and elements into new arrangements or orders.

INCUBATION

After you have conjured up as many solutions to the design challenge as possible, you need to set the whole project aside for a while, and go do something else.

SELECTION

The next phase of the design process involves selecting the one solution that seems to best fit the parameters of the design challenge. In actual practice the solution that you finally settle on will undoubtedly be a combination of bits and pieces from several of the design concepts that you evolved during the conceptual research phase.

IMPLEMENTATION

During the implementation phase you produce the plans, drawings, and models that will allow the design idea you have selected to be constructed. At this time you produce the rendering of the set or sets, build the presentation model(s), and prepare the ground plan, front elevations, detail drawings, painter's elevations, and any other drawings or notes that will help the shop to build the set and properties as they were conceived.

EVALUATION

In the evaluation phase of the design process you take an objective look at how the scenic design worked in relationship to the production concept and objectively review the communication that took place between yourself and the other members of the production design team. You need to examine the methods that you used, as well as the materials that you selected to reach the goal of your scenic design. You also need to evaluate your communication with the other members of the production design team. Did you do everything you could have to foster good communication? Did you consult with the other designers when you made adjustments to your design after construction had begun?

cause what appears on the elevations is actually a proportional reduction of the appearance of the finished set. If the designer wants to change or adjust any element, it is relatively easy to erase and redraw the elevations. A corresponding change needs to be made on the ground plan whenever the changes made on the elevations, such as widening or moving a flat, affect its accuracy.

The primary purpose of the front elevations is simply to describe the appearance of the set; they don't tell how to build it. For this reason no attempt is made to indicate the width of the individual flats that will be used to construct the various wall units. This breakdown of the wall segments into manageable units is the responsibility of the technical director or, in the professional theatre, the scene shop foreman. The actual construction of the flats is made from rear elevations, which are drawings that show the reverse side of the flats depicted in the front elevations. These scale drawings show the framework of the flat, including the placement and dimensions of all of its various parts. The structure and nomenclature of flats will be discussed in Chapter 9, *Scenic Production Techniques,* and the drawing of rear elevations is taken up in Chapter 18, *Mechanical Drafting.*

DETAIL DRAWINGS The scale of one-half inch to one foot normally used in drawing the front elevations reduces the size of some of the smaller features to the point that it is difficult, if not impossible, to draw all of their details. Detailed pieces, such as an elaborate fireplace or an intricately designed stained-glass panel, need to be drawn in a larger scale (Figure 7.12).

Many features of a setting cannot be fully described by drawing them in top and front (or rear) views only. Three-dimensional objects often require a third view to supplement the other two. There are several methods of drafting (orthographic projection, isometric drawing, oblique drawing, and cabinet drawing) that show more than two sides of an object. The techniques of these methods of drafting are discussed in Chapter 18, *Mechanical Drafting.*

FULL-SCALE DRAWINGS A few of the smallest features of a set should be drawn in full scale, or actual size. If the design is unusually intricate or the object rather small, such as the pattern for a turned bannister or a wallpaper pattern, it is usually both easier and faster to draw it in full scale. It is also easier to construct something from a full-scale drawing than one that has been proportionally reduced.

SIGHT-LINE DRAWINGS An improperly or inadequately masked set is a sign of a second-rate production. Most people come to the theatre to be entertained, to escape into the world of the play. When they can see backstage and watch actors waiting for their cues, stagehands lounging around, or any of the backstage paraphernalia, their concentration on the substance of the play is broken. All of these unnecessary distractions can be avoided if the scenic designer just takes the time to draft some **sight-line** drawings.

The sight lines of any set can be checked through the use of two drawings, a ground plan and a vertical section of the stage and auditorium, with the set in its proper position on the stage (Figure 7.13). The horizontal section, or plan view, shows the view of the stage, or sight line, of the people sitting in the extreme side seats of the first and last rows of the auditorium. The vertical section shows a side view of the sight line for the same seats.

The little time required to draft sight-line drawings is time well spent. Too often the scenery is built, painted, and assembled on stage before the sight lines are checked. The sight lines may be perfectly satisfactory, but occasion-

Sight line: A sighting extending from any seat in the house to any position on stage; used to determine how much of the stage and backstage area will be visible from that auditorium seat.

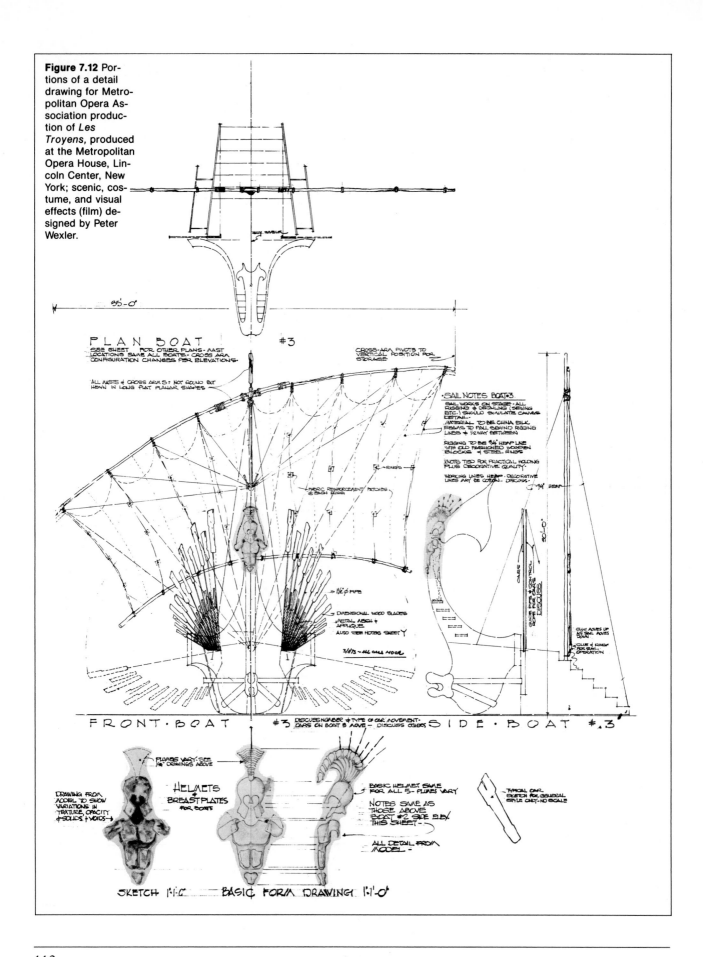

Figure 7.12 Portions of a detail drawing for Metropolitan Opera Association production of *Les Troyens,* produced at the Metropolitan Opera House, Lincoln Center, New York; scenic, costume, and visual effects (film) designed by Peter Wexler.

CHAPTER 7: SCENIC DESIGN

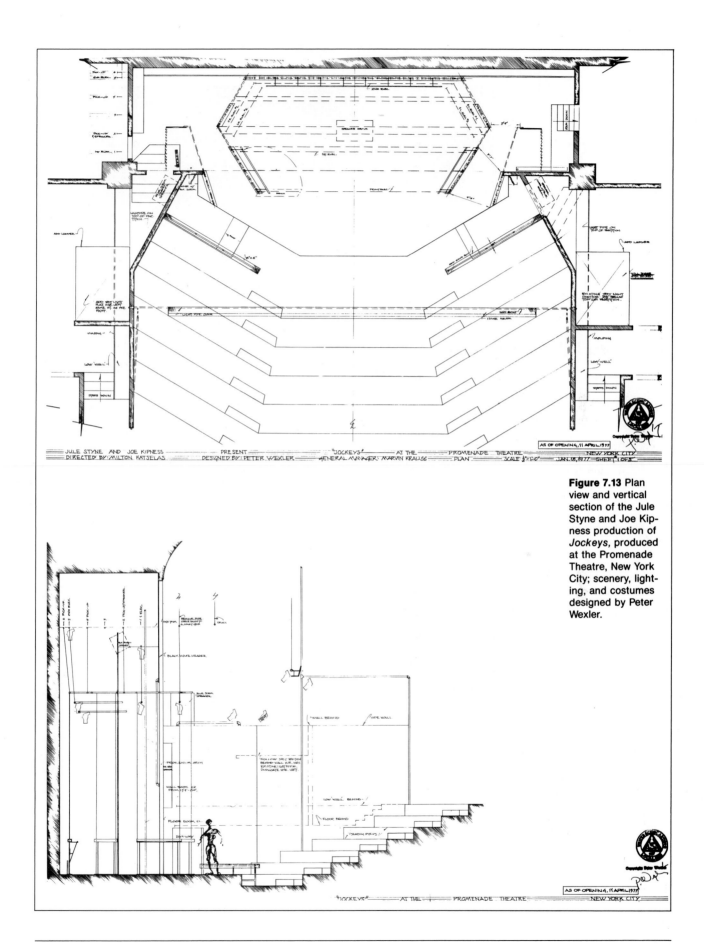

Figure 7.13 Plan view and vertical section of the Jule Styne and Joe Kipness production of *Jockeys,* produced at the Promenade Theatre, New York City; scenery, lighting, and costumes designed by Peter Wexler.

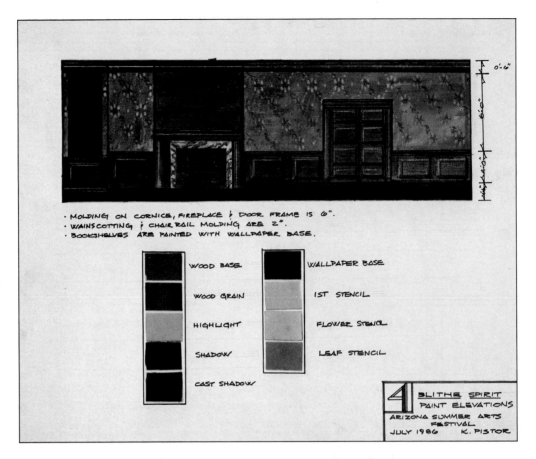

Figure 7.14 Painter's elevations for *Blithe Spirit,* produced at the University of Arizona; scenic design by K. Pistor.

ally some area of the set is out of sight of the audience, the backing flats are too small, or the masking drapes have been hung in the wrong position. Sightline drawings can reveal any potential problems with masking in sufficient time to correct them.

PAINTER'S ELEVATIONS Painter's elevations are front elevations of the set, but they are drawn on watercolor board and painted to show not only the colors but also the painting techniques that will be used in finishing the set. The painter's elevations (Figure 7.14) are the actual plans that the scenic artist and paint crew use when painting the set. The scenic artist mixes the colors to match the palette used on the painter's elevations, and the crew applies the paint using techniques that will duplicate the style illustrated in the painter's elevations. Information on the materials and techniques of scene painting is contained in Chapter 10, *Scene Painting.*

Scenic design is both a demanding and rewarding practical craft. In order to create a quality scenic design you have to use your imagination, sketch, paint, construct scale models, and produce accurate mechanical drawings. Although this process may seem to be an almost overwhelming task, seeing your design actually standing on the stage as tangible proof of a viable production concept is an extremely rewarding experience.

8

Almost any material can be used to make scenery. Wood, fabric, metal, and plastics are commonly used, but almost anything else can be, or has been, used in scenic construction. The majority of these nontraditional construction materials are generally applied to a basic

Tools and Materials

scenic form as decoration. Most basic scenery is made by constructing a supporting form from wood or metal and covering that structure with wood, fabric, or both. These structures will be covered in Chapter 9, *Scenic Production Techniques*. This chapter introduces the tools and materials used in scenic and property construction.

HAND TOOLS

Almost any type of scenery can be built with just a few hand tools; after all, people were building scenery long before the discovery of electricity and the development of power tools. The only advantages that power tools provide are speed and reduced effort.

Measuring Tools

Measuring tools are used to measure dimensions and angles.

TAPE MEASURE Metal tape measures (Figure 8.1A) are housed in either a plastic or a metal case. Most have a self-return spring to retract the tape into the case. They should have a lock to hold the extended tape in position. Available in a variety of tape lengths from six feet to twenty-five feet, they are appropriate for general scenic measuring. The steel tape (Figure 8.1B),

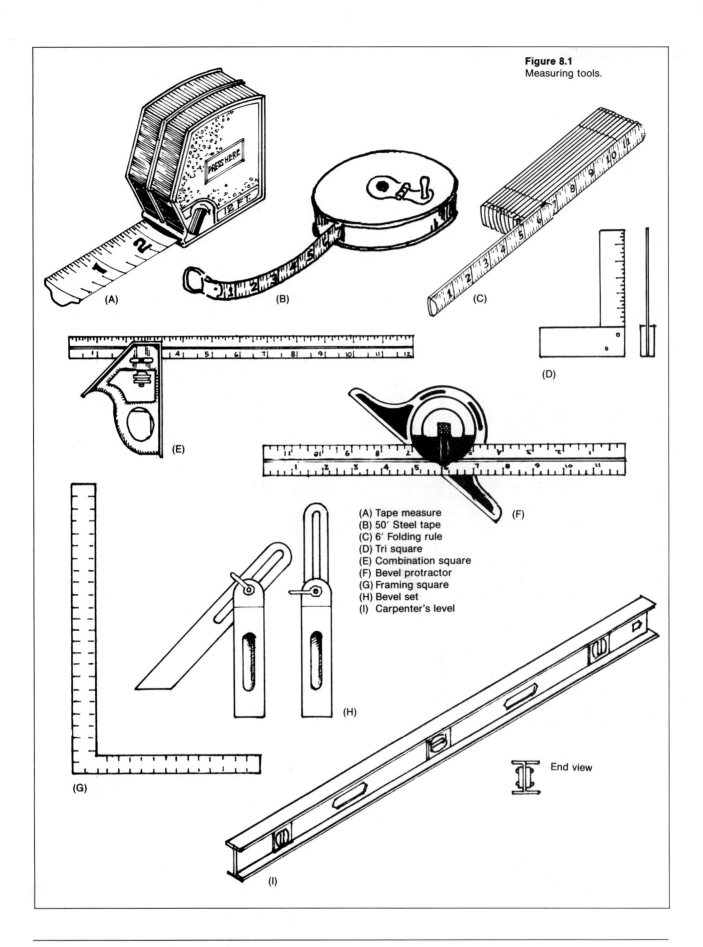

Figure 8.1
Measuring tools.

(A) Tape measure
(B) 50' Steel tape
(C) 6' Folding rule
(D) Tri square
(E) Combination square
(F) Bevel protractor
(G) Framing square
(H) Bevel set
(I) Carpenter's level

End view

which comes in lengths between fifty feet and two hundred feet, is manually retracted into the case with a built-in crank. It is used for measuring long distances, as when laying out the dimensions of the set on the stage floor.

FOLDING WOOD RULE Folding carpenter's rules (Figure 8.1C) are six feet long, are quite fragile, and must be treated with care to avoid breaking. They are suitable for general measuring.

TRI SQUARE A tri square is a small, rigid, hand square with a steel blade and either steel, composition, or wooden handle, as shown in Figure 8.1D. It is used as a guide for marking ninety-degree angles across narrow (under six inches wide) materials.

COMBINATION SQUARE The larger combination square is a twelve-inch steel rule with a movable handle angled at forty-five and ninety degrees, as shown in Figure 8.1E. It is used for marking those two angles, and the steel rule can also be used for measuring.

BEVEL PROTRACTOR The bevel protractor is similar to a combination square, except the angle is adjustable, allowing it to be set anywhere between zero and ninety degrees (Figure 8.1F).

FRAMING SQUARE The framing square is a large steel **L** (Figure 8.1G), typically sixteen inches long on the bottom leg and twenty-four inches on the vertical leg. It is normally used for checking the accuracy of ninety-degree corner joints in flat construction.

BEVEL SET The bevel set (Figure 8.1H) has a combination wood and metal case housing a movable metal blade that can be locked in position at any angle. It is also called a bevel gauge. The set is used for transferring angles from one piece of work to another.

CARPENTER'S LEVEL The carpenter's level is used to determine true horizontal and vertical angles. A two- to three-foot-long carpenter's level, as shown in Figure 8.1I, is appropriate for stage use.

Marking Tools

Marking tools are used in conjunction with measuring tools to mark dimensions and angles.

SCRIBE Also called a scratch awl, the scribe (Figure 8.2A) has a sharp metal point and is used for marking on wood, metal, and plastic. It can also be used for enlarging smaller holes or making **starter holes** for wood screws.

CHALK LINE A tool used to mark straight lines is the chalk line (Figure 8.2B). A metal or plastic housing holds a length of cotton twine on a reel. The housing is filled with dry scenic pigment, which coats the twine. The twine is stretched between two points and lightly snapped to leave the straight line.

Hammers

Hammers are used for nailing and starting screws, as well as shaping and forming metal.

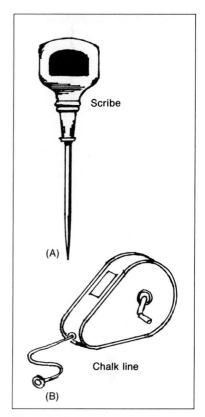

Figure 8.2 Marking tools.

Starter hole: A small hole bored into a piece of wood to hold the tip of a screw or drill bit; also called a pilot hole.

CLAW HAMMER Designed for inserting and removing nails, the claw hammer has two sharply curved claws projecting from the back of its head, as shown in Figure 8.3A. The curved claws facilitate nail removal. Claw hammers are available with a variety of head weights and shaft and grip compositions.

RIP HAMMER Sometimes referred to as a straight claw hammer, the rip hammer (Figure 8.3B) has straighter claws than the claw hammer. They can be used for prying or ripping apart previously nailed wood. This hammer is also available in a number of head weights and shaft and grip compositions.

BALL PEEN HAMMER Primarily used for bending and shaping metal and seating rivets, instead of pounding nails, the ball peen hammer (Figure 8.3C) is made of harder steel than the claw or rip hammer and has a rounded striking face instead of claws on the back of the head.

MECHANIC'S HAMMER Also known as a blacksmith's or heavy-duty hammer, the mechanic's hammer (Figure 8.3D) has a heavy head (one to three pounds). It is used for shaping metal.

TACK HAMMER Used for inserting tacks, the lightweight tack hammer (Figure 8.3E) has two faces. The smaller face is magnetized to hold the tacks for insertion, and the larger face is used to seat the tacks.

MALLET A mallet (Figure 8.3F) can have a wooden, plastic, or hard rubber head. The wooden and hard plastic mallets are generally used for driving chisels. All three can be used for shaping thin sheet metal when you don't want to leave hammer marks on the work.

Figure 8.3
Hammers.

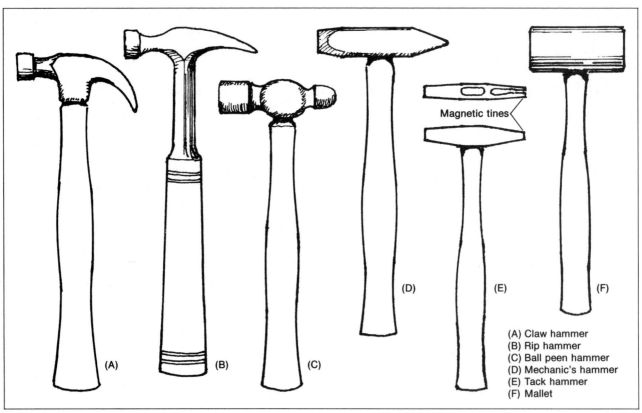

Magnetic tines

(A) Claw hammer
(B) Rip hammer
(C) Ball peen hammer
(D) Mechanic's hammer
(E) Tack hammer
(F) Mallet

CHAPTER 8: TOOLS AND MATERIALS

Cutting Tools

Kerf: The width of the cut made by a saw blade.

SAWS Saws are used to cut materials such as wood, metal, and plastic. The material that a saw is supposed to cut is generally dependent on the number of teeth per inch in the blade, with wood-cutting blades having the fewest number of teeth.

CROSSCUT SAW The crosscut saw (Figure 8.4A) is used to cut across the grain of wood. Alternate teeth on the blade are bent outward so the **kerf** is wider than the width of the blade. This is done to prevent the blade from binding. A saw with a twenty-six-inch blade and ten to twelve teeth per inch is suitable for most scenic purposes. (A blade with a higher number of teeth per inch will give a smoother cut.)

Figure 8.4 Saws.

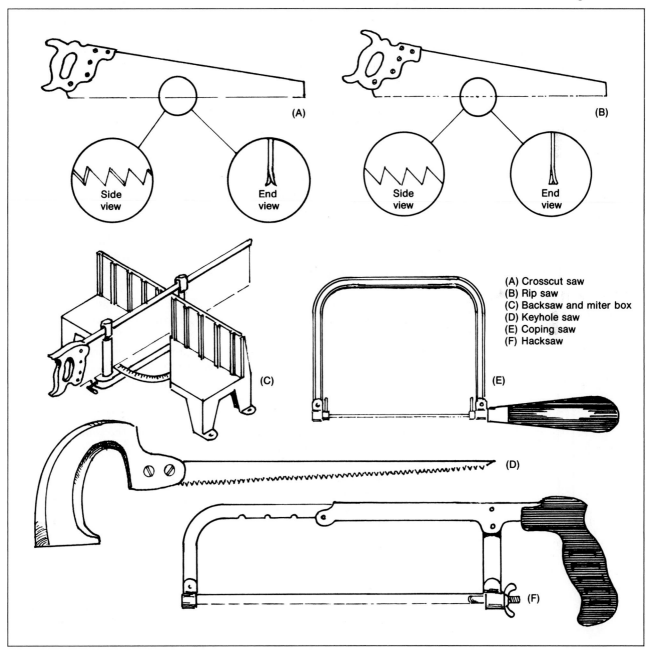

Side view
End view
(A)

Side view
End view
(B)

(C)

(E)

(A) Crosscut saw
(B) Rip saw
(C) Backsaw and miter box
(D) Keyhole saw
(E) Coping saw
(F) Hacksaw

(D)

(F)

Miter: An angle that is cut in a piece of work, usually in pairs to form a corner.

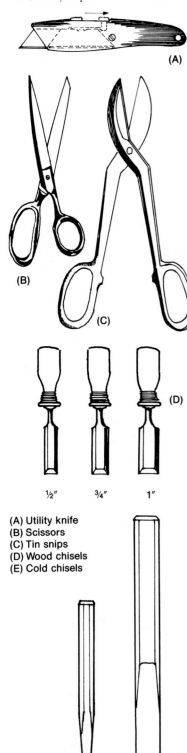

(A) Utility knife
(B) Scissors
(C) Tin snips
(D) Wood chisels
(E) Cold chisels

Figure 8.5
Miscellaneous cutting tools.

RIP SAW Similar in appearance to the crosscut saw, the rip saw (Figure 8.4B) is designed to cut parallel with the grain of the wood. It has fewer teeth per inch—usually around six—and the teeth are filed straight across the blade to give a chisel-like cut.

BACKSAW AND MITER BOX The backsaw (Figure 8.4C) is a fine-toothed (twelve to fourteen teeth per inch) crosscut saw with a strong spine on its back. The spine stiffens the blade for more accurate cuts and also fits into a guide on the **miter** box. The miter box is a guide for making accurate cuts at forty-five- and ninety-degree angles. Some miter boxes have adjustable guides to permit cutting other angles.

KEYHOLE SAW With its narrow, tapering blade of ten to twelve teeth per inch, the keyhole saw (Figure 8.4D) is used for making curvilinear cuts in stock lumber or plywood.

COPING SAW The lightweight coping saw (Figure 8.4E) is used for making fine, curvilinear cuts in thin plywood. The replaceable blades have sixteen to eighteen teeth per inch and are easily broken. For making interior cuts, the blade can be snapped out of the frame, inserted through a hole in the work, and reinserted in the frame.

HACKSAW The hacksaw is an adjustable frame saw for cutting metal (Figure 8.4F). The extremely fine-toothed (20–25 per inch), replaceable blades are available in a number of configurations for cutting mild steel and nonferrous metals such as copper and aluminum.

UTILITY KNIFE Also called a matte knife, the utility knife (Figure 8.5A) has a replaceable blade. It is generally used to trim excess muslin from the edges of flats but can also be used for cutting out stencils and for other light-duty cutting or carving projects.

SCISSORS Heavy-duty scissors (Figure 8.5B) are used for cutting a wide variety of papers and fabrics that are commonly used in scenic construction.

TIN SNIPS There is a variety of tin snips, some that cut on a straight line (Figure 8.5C) and others that cut either left- or right-hand curves. Compound-leverage snips multiply the force that is applied to them with your hand. All snips are designed for the same purpose—to cut thin (generally under eighteen-gauge) ferrous and nonferrous strap and sheet metals. Snips should not be used to cut nails, wire, or similar small objects, because the small surface area of the object may pit or nick the cutting edge of the blades.

WOOD CHISEL The wood chisel's steel blade, sharpened at a thirty-degree angle, is used for gouging, paring, or smoothing wood (Figure 8.5D). It has either a wooden or plastic handle. The chisel is struck lightly with a mallet or the heel of the hand. It is available in a variety of blade widths, with the one-half, three-quarters, and one-inch widths the most useful in scenic construction work.

COLD CHISEL The cold chisel, made of very hard steel, is used for cutting through, or shearing, mild steel and nonferrous metals (Figure 8.5E). It is struck with a ball peen or mechanic's hammer.

PLANES Planes are knife-bladed tools used to smooth or round the edges or corners of wood. The lumber being planed must be firmly anchored in a vise or clamped to a solid surface like a workbench.

Sole: The bottom plate of a plane, with a slot through which the tip of the blade projects.

BLOCK PLANE The small block plane (Figure 8.6A) is used to smooth the ends (across the grain) of boards. The blade is set at an angle of approximately fifteen degrees to the plane's **sole** (this angle varies with the manufacturer). The depth of the cut can be adjusted by raising or lowering the blade.

SMOOTHING PLANE Larger and heavier than the block plane, the smoothing plane (Figure 8.6B) is applied parallel to the grain of the wood. The blade is set at a steeper angle (approximately 25 to 30 degrees), and the depth of cut can be adjusted.

SPOKE SHAVE Whereas the block and smoothing planes are pushed across the wood to make their cuts, the spoke shave (Figure 8.6C) is pulled across the surface of the work. It has an adjustable blade to regulate the depth of cut, and the blade angle is approximately twenty to twenty-five degrees. The sole is slightly rounded rather than flat, since the spoke shave is used to soften or round sharp edges rather than to smooth flat surfaces.

SURFORM TOOLS The trademarked Surform tools (Figure 8.6D) fall between the cracks of traditional definitions: they aren't really planes, and they aren't really files. They are based on the Surform blade, a thin, disposable strip of spring steel honeycombed with sharpened protrusions projecting from the surface. The Surform tool is pushed across the work, cross-grain or parallel with the grain. The serrated blade face doesn't leave a smooth finish, so the work generally has to be smoothed after the tool has been used.

FILES Files are used to rasp or grind wood, metal, plastic, and other materials. The teeth of a file are formed in diagonal ridges or rows across its face, with the more coarsely grained files having distinctly individual teeth. The spacing and height of the teeth determine the type of material for which the file is designed. Coarse teeth are used with wood, medium teeth with wood and plastic, and fine teeth with metal and some plastics.

WOOD RASP An extremely coarse-toothed file, with individually discernible teeth, the wood rasp (Figure 8.7A) is usually flat on one face and curved on the other. It is used for rough shaping of wood.

WOOD FILE The wood file (Figure 8.7B) has smaller teeth than the wood rasp. It is available in three cross-sectional configurations—flat on both faces, flat on one surface and curved on the other, and round. It is used for smoothing wooden and plastic surfaces.

RAT-TAIL FILE The rat-tail file (Figure 8.7C) is also known as a round file. It is available in a variety of surface finishes and diameters appropriate for use with wood, plastic, and metal.

METAL FILE Metal files have very fine teeth for use on metal. As shown in Figure 8.7D, they are available in a variety of configurations.

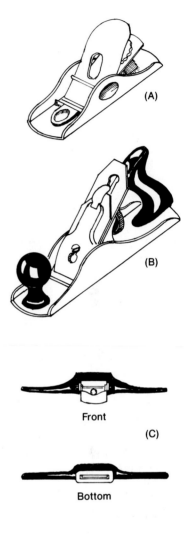

Front

(C)

Bottom

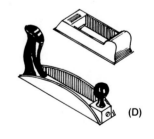

(A) Block plane
(B) Smoothing plane
(C) Spoke shave
(D) Surform tools

Figure 8.6 Planes.

Figure 8.7 Files.

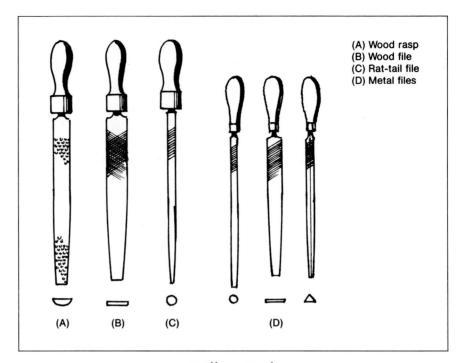

(A) Wood rasp
(B) Wood file
(C) Rat-tail file
(D) Metal files

(A) (B) (C) (D)

Drilling Tools

Center punch: A pointed tool made from a similar type of hard steel as the cold chisel and used for indenting shallow holes in wood and metal.

Chuck: The adjustable jawed clamp at the end of a drill that holds the drill bits.

Several tools provide the motive force to spin the bits for drilling holes in wood, plastic, and metal. When drilling you usually need to make a starter hole, so the hole will be drilled exactly where you want it. When working in wood you can make the starter or pilot hole with a nail and hammer or a push drill (described later in this section). With steel the starter hole is usually made with a **center punch.**

HAND DRILL The hand drill is a cranked device (Figure 8.8A) for making small-diameter holes in wood. The bit is inserted into the **chuck,** which is driven by a small-geared crank. The chuck will accept only bits that have a shaft diameter of one-quarter of an inch or smaller.

BRACE The brace, another hand-cranked drill for wood (Figure 8.8B), is used for holes larger than one-quarter of an inch in diameter. The wood bits are held by the chuck, which is driven by an offset handle. The handle works as a lever to increase the twisting power applied to the bit.

PUSH DRILL The push drill (Figure 8.8C) has a spring-loaded shaft that spins the chuck as you push downward on the drill handle. Designed for light usage, it can accept bits from ⅟₆₄ to ³⁄₁₆ of an inch in diameter. The push drill is very useful for making starter holes.

BITS

TWIST DRILL BITS Twist drill bits (Figure 8.9A) are designed for use with either wood or metal. Available in a variety of sizes from ⅟₆₄ to approximately ⅜ of an inch in diameter. When using these bits in metal (mild to medium steel and common nonferrous metals) the work should be lubricated with cutting oil. The cutting oil not only lubricates the bit and the work but also helps to dissipate friction-generated heat, which would otherwise quickly dull the bits.

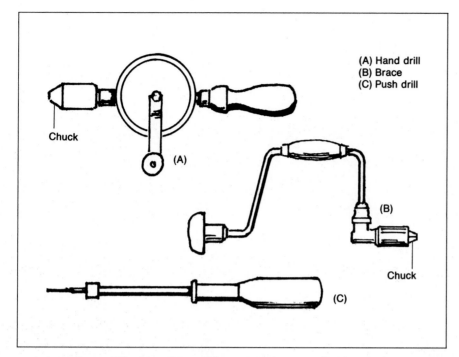

(A) Hand drill
(B) Brace
(C) Push drill

Chuck

(A)

(B)

Chuck

(C)

Figure 8.8 Types of hand drills.

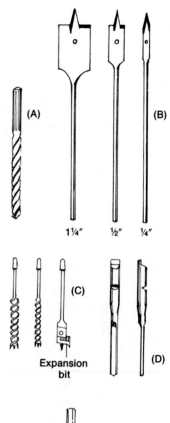

(A)

1¼"   ½"   ¼"

(B)

(C)

Expansion bit

(D)

(E)

(A) Twist drill bit
(B) Wood bits for power drill
(C) Auger bits
(D) Push drill bit
(E) Hole saw

Figure 8.9 Drill bits.

WOOD BITS Paddle-shaped wood bits, sometimes called spade bits (Figure 8.9B), are designed for use in wood, although they can be used in some soft plastics. They must be used with power hand drills or drill presses, because they require high-speed rotation to do their work. They are generally available in diameters from ¼ to 1¼ inches.

AUGER BITS Designed to be used with the brace for cutting holes in wood, auger bits (Figure 8.9C) are available in diameters from ¼ to 1 inch. A modification of the auger bit, the expansion bit, has an adjustable cutting head that can be set to drill holes with 1- to 2½-inch diameters.

PUSH DRILL BITS Push drill bits (Figure 8.9D) have very sharp points and straight, fluted indentions running up the side of the bit shaft to carry away the wood chips loosened during drilling. Because of the very narrow bit diameter (1/64 to 1/8 of an inch) and the strong downward pressure on the drill itself, push drill bits seem to punch rather than drill holes in the wood.

HOLE SAWS Although not really bits, hole saws (Figure 8.9E) are saw-toothed cylinders of hardened steel with a drill bit in the center that is used to center the hole saw in the work. Generally available in sets of six to eight diameters, hole saws are used to cut holes up to 2 inches in diameter in wood that is 1½ inches thick or less.

Clamping Tools

Clamping tools cover a wide variety of devices, ranging all the way from vises to pliers to C clamps. Regardless of the type of clamp, they are designed to firmly hold wood, metal, or plastic.

CARPENTER'S VISE The carpenter's vise (Figure 8.10A) is attached to the edge of a workbench and is designed for holding wood. One or both faces are covered with hardwood to prevent the vise from scratching, denting, or marring the surface of the work.

Figure 8.10
Clamping tools.

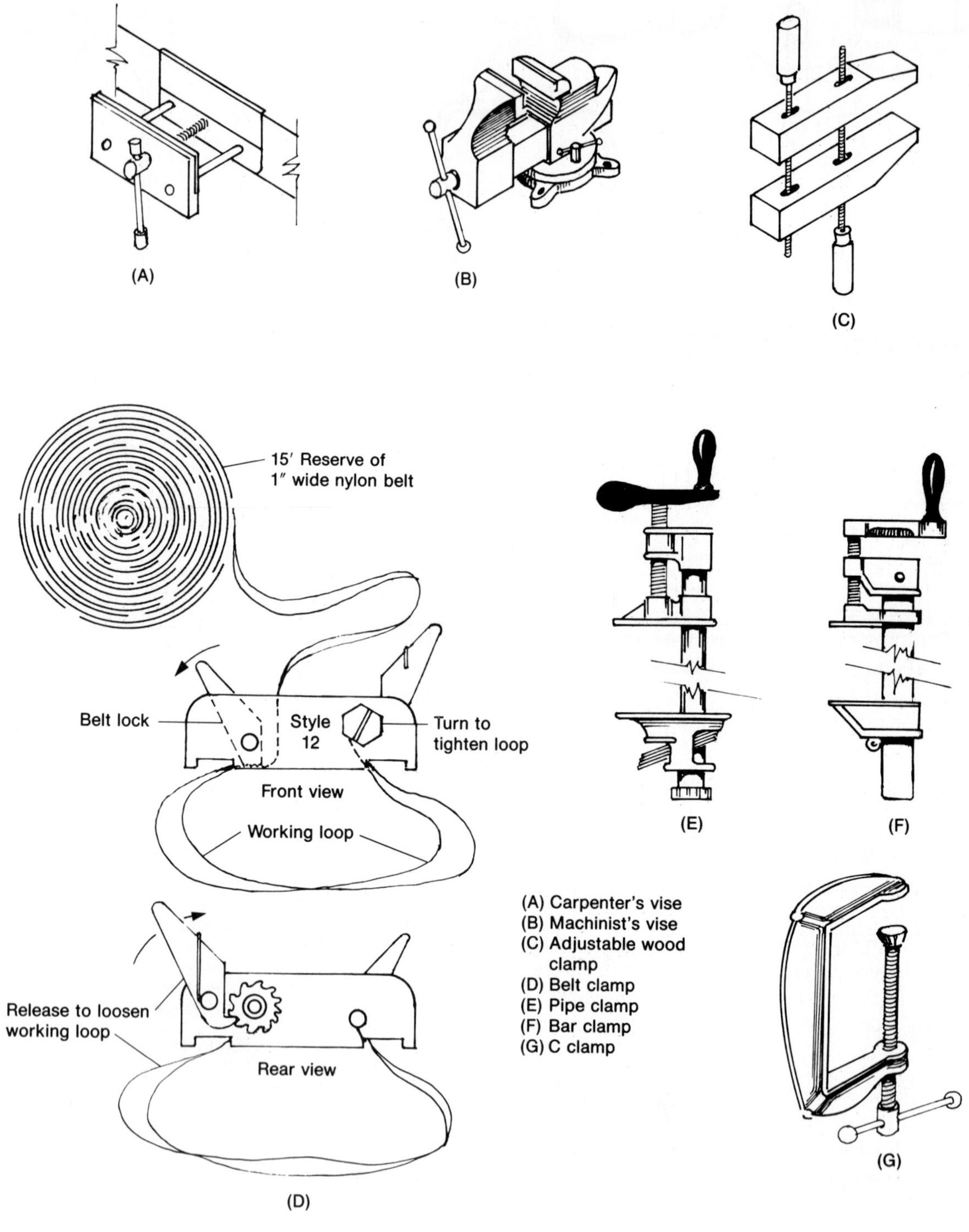

(A)

(B)

(C)

15′ Reserve of
1″ wide nylon belt

Belt lock

Style
12

Turn to
tighten loop

Front view

Working loop

Release to loosen
working loop

Rear view

(D)

(E)

(F)

(A) Carpenter's vise
(B) Machinist's vise
(C) Adjustable wood
    clamp
(D) Belt clamp
(E) Pipe clamp
(F) Bar clamp
(G) C clamp

(G)

MACHINIST'S VISE Used to clamp and hold metal, the machinist's vise (Figure 8.10B) has toothed steel faces to help grip the work. The machinist's vise can be used for clamping and holding wood, but it will score or mar the surface of the work unless protective blocks of wood are used to sandwich the object.

ADJUSTABLE WOOD CLAMP The adjustable wood clamp (Figure 8.10C) is a versatile tool used primarily in furniture construction. The two jaws can be adjusted to a variety of angles that are useful in holding various parts of furniture frames together while the glued joints are drying.

BELT CLAMP A belt clamp (Figure 8.10D) is a woven nylon belt that can be used to clamp irregularly shaped pieces together. It uses a ratchet device to tighten the belt after it has been placed around the object. It is very helpful in furniture construction. Some belt clamps substitute a nylon rope for the web belt.

PIPE CLAMP Pipe clamps (Figure 8.10E) are composed of a threaded pipe, a movable end plate, and an adjustable head plate. The bar clamp (Figure 8.10F) is the same as the pipe clamp except that a notched bar is substituted for the pipe. Both pipe and bar clamps are used to clamp furniture frames, table tops, and similar wide objects together while their glue joints dry.

C CLAMP C clamps are available in an almost bewildering array of configurations (Figure 8.10G). The most useful sizes for scenic and property construction have an opening from 4 to 8 inches and a minimum throat depth of 2½ inches. They are used for a wide variety of jobs, such as holding work together while the parts are being assembled or while glue joints are drying.

PLIERS Pliers are used for a variety of gripping, clamping, bending, and cutting jobs in scenic and property construction. There are almost as many styles and types of pliers as there are potential uses.

SLIP-JOINT PLIERS Slip-joint pliers (Figure 8.11A) are very common. They have an adjustable pivot point that provides two ranges of jaw openings. They can be used for clamping, gripping, bending, and cutting light wire.

LONG-NOSE PLIERS Extremely useful for holding small objects in hard-to-reach locations, long-nose, or needle-nose, pliers (Figure 8.11B) should not be used for bending anything other than the lightest wire, because the jaws can be forced out of alignment very easily.

ADJUSTABLE ARC-JOINT PLIERS Known by a variety of other names, such as slip-joint pliers and alligator pliers, arc-joint pliers are truly versatile (Figure 8.11C). They have a series of jaw ranges that allows them to be used for a wide variety of purposes. The jaw design and long handles enable the worker to grip both square and round objects with a great deal of leverage. These pliers are used for holding metal pipe and tubing and for similar gripping jobs.

LOCKING PLIERS Generally known by its tradename of Vise Grip, locking pliers (Figure 8.11D) are available in a number of configurations to fit a variety of shapes. Their primary function is to grasp, lock, and hold almost

Figure 8.11 Types of pliers.

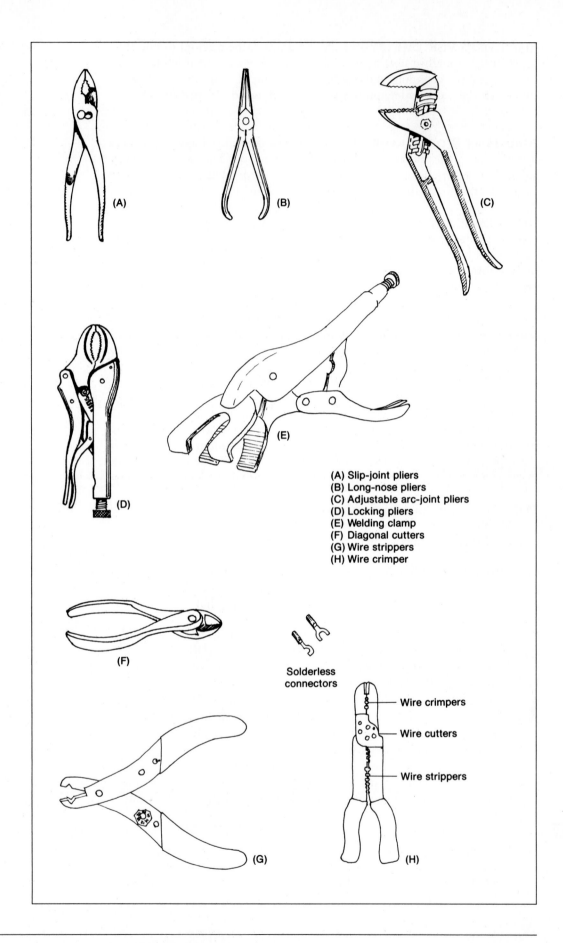

(A) Slip-joint pliers
(B) Long-nose pliers
(C) Adjustable arc-joint pliers
(D) Locking pliers
(E) Welding clamp
(F) Diagonal cutters
(G) Wire strippers
(H) Wire crimper

Solderless connectors

Wire crimpers

Wire cutters

Wire strippers

any object. The size of the jaw opening and the amount of pressure applied by the jaws are adjustable by the screw at the base of the handle.

The welding clamp (Figure 8.11E) is a variation of the locking plier that can be used to clamp almost any combination of metal shapes together.

DIAGONAL CUTTERS Available in a variety of sizes, diagonal cutters (Figure 8.11F) are primarily used by electricians for cutting soft wire.

WIRE STRIPPERS Wire strippers (Figure 8.11G) are used for stripping insulation from electrical wires without cutting the wire.

WIRE-CRIMPING TOOL The wire crimper (Figure 8.11H) is used to pressure-clamp solderless connectors to electrical wire.

WRENCHES Many wrenches are useful in the scene shop. They are used to tighten nuts and bolts.

OPEN-END WRENCH Nonadjustable open-end wrenches have smooth jaws (Figure 8.12A). These wrenches are designed to fit nuts of a specific standard or metric diameter.

BOX-END WRENCH Also made in standard and metric sizes, box-end wrenches have a closed, toothed head that must be fit over the nut. The head of the box-end wrench is frequently offset, as shown in Figure 8.12B.

ADJUSTABLE-END WRENCH Also known by the trade name Crescent Wrench, the adjustable-end wrench (Figure 8.12C) has smooth jaws that adapt to fit almost any small- to medium-sized nut. The six-, eight-, and ten-inch sizes are the most suitable for stage work.

Figure 8.12 Types of wrenches.

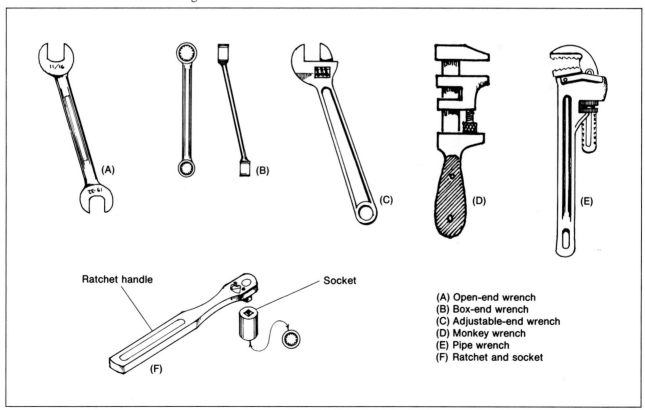

(A) Open-end wrench
(B) Box-end wrench
(C) Adjustable-end wrench
(D) Monkey wrench
(E) Pipe wrench
(F) Ratchet and socket

Ratchet handle

Socket

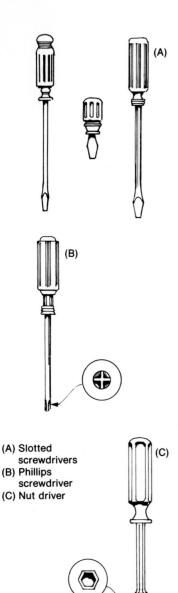

(A) Slotted
 screwdrivers
(B) Phillips
 screwdriver
(C) Nut driver

Figure 8.13 Types
of screwdrivers.

MONKEY WRENCH The monkey wrench is a heavyweight, smooth-jawed, adjustable wrench (Figure 8.12D) for use on large nuts and work that is too large for adjustable-end wrenches.

PIPE WRENCH Similar in shape to the monkey wrench (Figure 8.12E) has jaws that are serrated to bite into the soft metal of pipes. It is used to hold or twist pipes and their associated couplings.

SOCKET SET AND RATCHET HANDLE Sockets are cylindrical wrenches used with a ratchet handle (Figure 8.12F). The design of the reversible ratchet handle allows you to tighten or loosen nuts without removing the socket from the nut. The tool is very useful for working in confined spaces.

A deep-throated nine-sixteenths-inch socket is very useful in attaching or removing platform legs that have been bolted with three-eighths-inch carriage bolts.

Screwdrivers

Screwdrivers are used for inserting and removing screws. They are available in a variety of configurations and sizes.

STANDARD SCREWDRIVER The standard, or slotted, screwdriver (Figure 8.13A) is available in sizes from approximately three inches long with a blade width of one-eighth of an inch to large screwdrivers sixteen inches long with a blade width of one-half inch or larger. The handle is usually made of wood or plastic and sometimes has a thin jacket of rubber to provide electrical insulation. The smaller screwdrivers are useful for working on electronic devices and for similar lightweight applications. The largest screwdrivers are primarily for uses other than scenic construction. Screwdrivers six and eight inches long with one-quarter-inch tips are the most useful for scenic construction.

PHILLIPS SCREWDRIVER The Phillips-head screwdriver (Figure 8.13B) has a four-flanged tip that matches the crossed slots on Phillips-head screws. The design of the Phillips screw allows more rotational force to be exerted on it when seating it in wood or metal. The six- and eight-inch sizes are most useful in the scene shop.

NUT DRIVER Similar in appearance to a screwdriver, with a cylindrical socket instead of a slot or Phillips head, the nut driver (Figure 8.13C) is used for tightening small hex nuts (six-sided nuts) on bolts. It is available in a variety of socket sizes from approximately one-eighth to three-eighths of an inch in diameter.

Miscellaneous Hand Tools

There are several useful hand tools that don't fit conveniently into any particular category.

SANDPAPER Various weights of sandpaper are useful for smoothing wood, metal, and plastic before painting or varnishing. Garnet or silicon grit sandpaper with fine (220), medium (120), and coarse (80) ratings are the ones most often used in the scene shop. Garnet and silicon grit papers work equally well, but garnet grit paper lasts a little longer because its pores better resist clogging with wood dust.

WRECKING BARS Various tools are used to pry wood apart and remove nails (Figure 8.14A). The crowbar and pinch bar have flattened metal claws that can be used to pry wood apart. The claws have **V**'s cut in them so they can be used as nail pullers. The rip bar has slightly rounded tips that provide a little more leverage when it is inserted between pieces of nailed wood. All three wrecking bars are extremely useful for prying nailed boards apart and dismantling platforms.

NAIL PULLER The nail puller (Figure 8.14B) is a tool for extracting nails that have been driven flush with the surface of the wood. The sliding handle is used as a hammer to drive the jaws into the wood to grasp the nail. The handle is then used as a lever to pull the nail out.

GROMMET SET The grommet set (Figure 8.14C) consists of a hole punch, a small anvil, and a crimping tool. The set is used to seat grommets, which are brass reinforcing rings, on drops, stage draperies, and the like.

OIL STONE The oil stone (Figure 8.14D) is an indispensable part of a shop inventory. It is used to sharpen knives, chisels, and other cutting tools. It is usually made of silicon carbide, has coarse and smooth faces, and should be lubricated with oil when it is being used.

STAPLE GUN The staple gun (Figure 8.14E), also known as a hand stapler, uses a spring-driven piston to drive staples. The staple legs vary in length from three-sixteenths to five-eighths of an inch. The stapler is used for attaching muslin to flat frames and fabric to furniture, and for similar jobs.

Figure 8.14
Miscellaneous
hand tools.

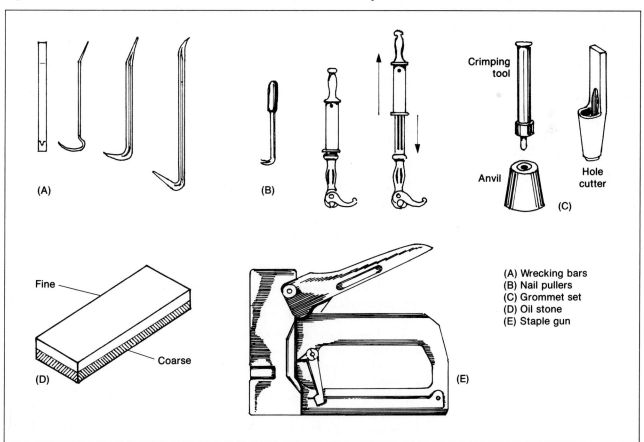

Crimping tool

Anvil

Hole cutter

(A)

(B)

(C)

Fine

Coarse

(D)

(E)

(A) Wrecking bars
(B) Nail pullers
(C) Grommet set
(D) Oil stone
(E) Staple gun

Metalworking Hand Tools

Although many of the basic woodworking tools are equally useful when working with metal, there are a few additional tools designed specifically for metalwork.

ANVIL A heavyweight anvil (Figure 8.15A) is an essential tool for bending metal. It is a solid metal device with varying shaped faces. Strap metal and rod can be shaped by bending it around these faces. Sheet metal, rod, and strap can also be formed by holding the material against the anvil and pounding it with a blacksmith's or mechanic's hammer. The metal will take on the shape of the particular facet on which it is being worked.

CONDUIT BENDER Thin-wall conduit (used in nonscenic construction as a housing for electrical wires) can be bent into curves with a conduit bender (Figure 8.15B). The notch at the end of the curved face of the conduit bender holds the conduit, and the bend is made by pulling on the pipe handle of the conduit bender.

CENTER PUNCH Made of hardened steel, the center punch (Figure 8.15C) is used to make small indentations in metal that can be used as "hole starters" for drill bits in both metal and wood.

BOLT CUTTER Bolt cutters (Figure 8.15D) are heavy-duty shears that use a great deal of leverage to cut through mild steel bolts and round stock up to one-half inch in diameter.

PIPE CUTTER A pipe cutter (Figure 8.15E) is used to make clean, right-angle cuts through steel pipe of half-inch and larger diameters. A smaller version, called a tubing cutter (Figure 8.15F), is designed for cutting half-inch and smaller tubing.

TAP AND DIES Tap and dies (Figure 8.15G) are used to cut threads on pipe and rod stock. The tap is used to cut threads on the inside of pipes (internal threads), and the die is used to cut threads on the outside of pipe and rod stock (external threads). Dies used to cut threads on pipes three-quarters of an inch in diameter and larger are also called pipe threaders.

POWER TOOLS

Power tools by and large perform the same function as hand tools. But they usually do it quicker and with less effort. However, the use of power tools does increase the safety hazards that are present in the shop. Before you work with any power tool, you must be certain that you have received thorough instructions in its safe operation. As a general safety rule you should remember that any power tool, if improperly used, has the potential to cause severe injury.

Although almost all power hand tools are commonly available with 120-volt electric motors, many are also made with pneumatic drives (pneumatic tools are discussed a little later in the chapter), and an increasing number of power hand tools run on rechargeable batteries.

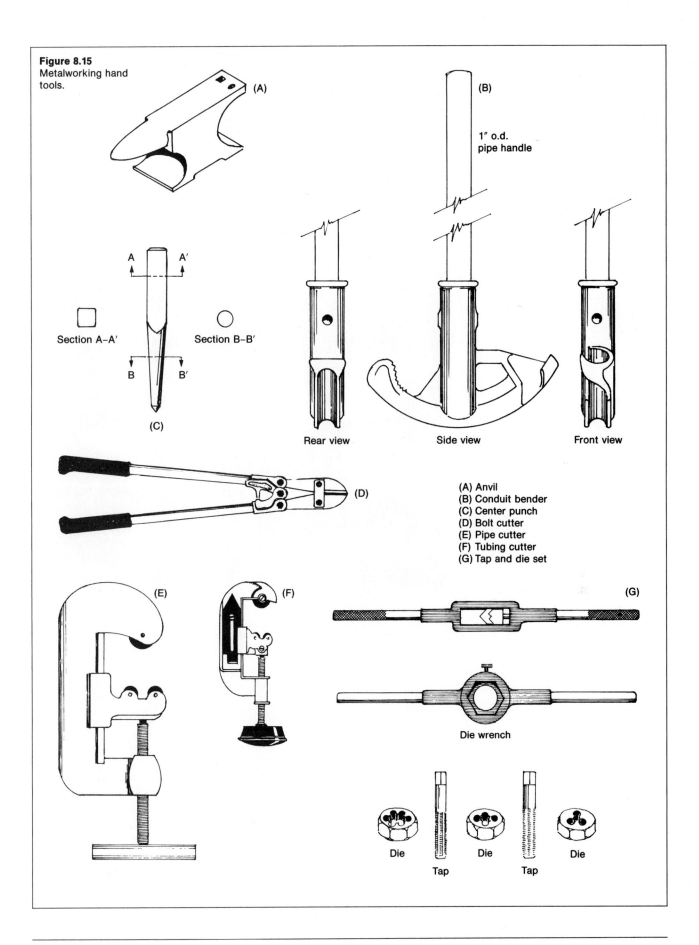

Figure 8.15
Metalworking hand tools.

(A)

(B)

1" o.d. pipe handle

A ◄──────► A'

Section A–A'

Section B–B'

B ◄──────► B'

(C)

Rear view

Side view

Front view

(D)

(A) Anvil
(B) Conduit bender
(C) Center punch
(D) Bolt cutter
(E) Pipe cutter
(F) Tubing cutter
(G) Tap and die set

(E)

(F)

(G)

Die wrench

Die   Tap   Die   Tap   Die

Dado head: A saw accessory consisting of a set of toothed blades that sandwich a chisel-like chipper; the blades smooth-cut the outside edges of the kerf while the chipper gouges out the wood between the blades; the distance between the blades is variable.

Molding cutter head: A heavy cylindrical arbor in which a variety of matched cutter blades or knives can be fit.

Stationary Power Saws

Stationary power saws are mounted on a stand and are normally located in a fixed position in the shop.

TABLE SAW   The circular blade of the table saw (Figure 8.16A) projects through a slot in the table of the saw. The height and angle of the saw blade can be adjusted. Primarily used for ripping lumber, the table saw also can be equipped with a **dado head** to cut wide slots (technically, a dado cut runs across the grain of the wood, whereas a groove runs parallel with the grain) or a **molding cutter head** for making a variety of decorative moldings. Blade diameters vary between seven and twelve inches. Commercial quality table saws with ten- or twelve-inch blades are appropriate for almost all scenic work.

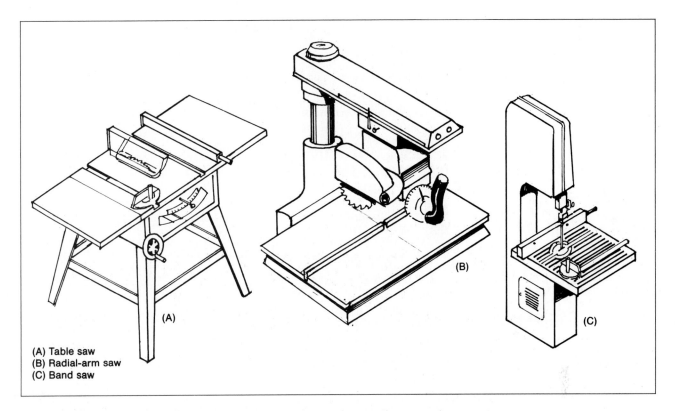

(A) Table saw
(B) Radial-arm saw
(C) Band saw

Figure 8.16
Stationary power
tools.

RADIAL-ARM SAW The radial-arm, or pullover, saw (Figure 8.16B) is probably the most versatile power tool in the scene shop. The housing containing the circular blade and motor is suspended from an arm above the surface of the work table. The height of the blade is adjusted by raising or lowering this supporting arm. The angle of the cut can be adjusted by swinging the arm or rotating the angle of the housing. Although primarily used for cross cutting and angle cutting, the radial-arm saw can also be used for ripping. Commercial quality saws with blade diameters of ten or twelve inches are appropriate for theatrical work. Accessories are available for converting this saw for use as a router, planer, or grinder.

BAND SAW Whereas the table saw and radial-arm saw are used to make straight cuts in lumber, the band saw (Figure 8.16C) is used to make curvilinear cuts. The narrow, continuous loop (or band) blade passes through a table that supports the work to be cut. If the band saw has either mechanical or electronic speed-reduction capability, an appropriate blade can be substituted for the wood-cutting blade, and the band saw can be used to cut mild steel, nonferrous metals, and plastics.

Power Hand Saws

Some power saws are hand held rather than being mounted on a bench or stand.

CIRCULAR SAW The portable circular saw (Figure 8.17A) normally has a blade diameter between seven and eight inches. The angle and depth of cut can be adjusted, and the saw has a guard that completely covers the blade when it is removed from the work. The portable circular saw is used for straight-line cross cutting and angle cutting as well as ripping of stock lumber, plywood, and composition board.

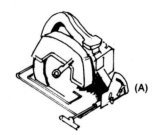

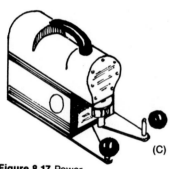

(A) Circular hand saw
(B) Saber saw
(C) Cut Awl

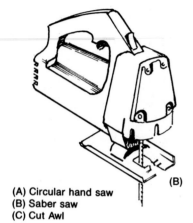

Figure 8.17 Power hand saws.

SABER SAW The saber saw (Figure 8.17B) uses a reciprocating action with stiff, narrow blades to make curvilinear cuts. With a speed control and appropriate blades the saber saw can cut metal and plastics as well as wood. It is excellent for cutting curved lines in plywood, composition board, and stock.

CUT AWL Also used for making curvilinear cuts, the Cut Awl (a registered trade name) combines reciprocating cutting action with a swiveling blade mount (Figure 8.17C). Available with both toothed and knife-edged blades, the Cut Awl can be used to make very intricate, smooth-edged cuts in wood, plywood, and composition board as well as plastic, paper, and cloth.

Power Drilling Tools

Power drills speed the process of drilling holes.

DRILL PRESS Mounted on a stand or bench, the drill press (Figure 8.18A) has variable speeds and is very accurate. The chuck usually accepts bit shanks up to one-half inch in diameter as well as a variety of accessories that enable the operator to polish and sand as well as cut mortise and tenon joints for furniture construction.

ELECTRIC HAND DRILL The electric hand drill (Figure 8.18B) is a lightweight, hand-held drill that accepts bits up to one-quarter or three-eighths of an inch in diameter. Many electric hand drills have variable speed and reverse controls. The electric drill is generally used for light-duty drilling on lumber 1½ inches thick or less and on light metals.

HEAVY-DUTY HAND DRILL Heavy-duty hand-held drills (Figure 8.18C) generally have more powerful motors and a lower gear ratio (which turns the chuck more slowly). They can accept drill bit shanks up to one-half of an inch in diameter. They are used for heavier work such as drilling through multiple layers of wood, three-sixteenth-inch and thicker mild steel, and concrete.

Pneumatic Tools

Pneumatic tools perform the same functions as electrically powered tools, but they are driven by air pressure. To effectively use pneumatic tools, a shop

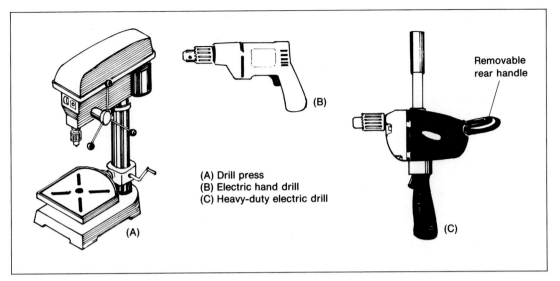

(A) Drill press
(B) Electric hand drill
(C) Heavy-duty electric drill

Removable
rear handle

needs to have a large-capacity compressor and air tank as well as an efficiently designed system for distributing the compressed air to convenient locations around the shop and stage.

Figure 8.18 Power drilling tools.

PNEUMATIC STAPLER The pneumatic stapler (Figure 8.19A) uses air pressure to drive the staples. The length of the staple legs that can be used with the pneumatic staplers varies from about ¾ to 1½ inches depending on the manufacturer. Staples are available in a variety of styles: straight-leg staples go straight into the work; coated-leg staples have a heat-activated adhesive; and the legs of divergent-leg staples spread in opposite directions when they enter the wood. The pneumatic stapler is used for the same types of job as a hammer and nails. It can be used for assembling flat framing, putting tops on platforms, and performing similar functions.

Figure 8.19
Pneumatic tools.

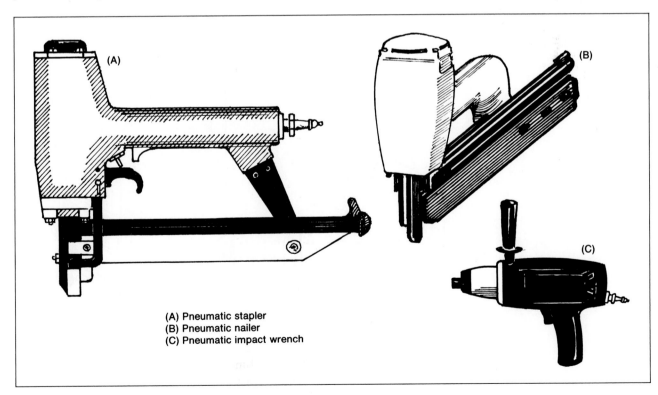

(A) Pneumatic stapler
(B) Pneumatic nailer
(C) Pneumatic impact wrench

Figure 8.20
Welding
equipment.

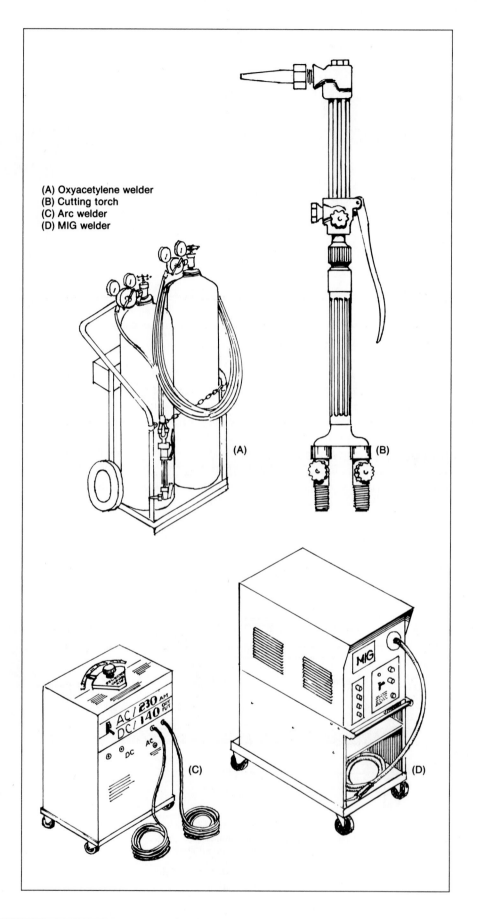

(A) Oxyacetylene welder
(B) Cutting torch
(C) Arc welder
(D) MIG welder

(A)

(B)

(C)

(D)

CHAPTER 8: TOOLS AND MATERIALS

PNEUMATIC NAILER The pneumatic nailer (Figure 8.19B) uses clips of coated nails in much the same manner that the pneumatic stapler uses staples. It can be used for rapid assembly of platforms and similar structures.

IMPACT WRENCH The pneumatic impact wrench (Figure 8.19C) uses air pressure to tighten or loosen nuts. If you have ever watched someone change a tire in a service station you have probably seen a pneumatic impact wrench in action. In the scene shop this device is very useful when you are "legging" (bolting legs onto) platforms. The impact wrench is also available in an electrically powered version.

Other pneumatically driven tools, such as sanders, grinders, and drills, work exactly as their electrically powered counterparts do.

Metalworking Tools

WELDERS Several types of welder are used for fusing metal in the scene shop.

OXYACETYLENE WELDER The oxyacetylene welder (Figure 8.20A) combines oxygen and acetylene to produce a very hot flame (approximately six thousand degrees Fahrenheit) capable of melting most metals. The oxygen and acetylene are stored under pressure in steel tanks. The amount of each gas in the mixture is controlled by pressure regulators attached to the top of each tank. The gas is fed to the torch, where the mixture is again adjusted with the small valves at the end of the torch.

A cutting torch (Figure 8.20B) has an extra lever that introduces more oxygen into the mix, enabling the flame to burn through the metal. (See Chapter 9, *Scenic Production Techniques*, for a discussion of using welding equipment.)

ARC WELDER The arc welder (Figure 8.20C) consists of a power housing unit, cables, and a welding handle. It works by creating an electrical arc that melts the metals being welded. There are several power settings, which can be adjusted for the heat range that is appropriate to the composition and thickness of the metal being welded.

MIG WELDER The MIG (metal insert gas) welder (Figure 8.20D) is an arc welder that focuses a flow of inert gas (usually carbon dioxide or argon) on the welding zone as the weld is being made. The electrode of the MIG welder is a thin piece of wire that is automatically fed through the welding handle from a spool stored in the housing of the power unit.

SOLDERING EQUIPMENT Soldering provides a relatively low-strength bond between most common metals such as steel, copper, and brass. It is frequently used to bond wires together in an electrical circuit. Aluminum can be soldered, but it requires high heat and a special **flux.**

Various soldering pencils, guns, and irons are used to heat solder to its melting point. Soldering pencils (twenty-five to forty watts) are used for lightweight projects such as working on the circuitry of electronic equipment (Figure 8.21A). Soldering guns (fifty to two hundred watts) are trigger-operated, rapid-heating, medium- to heavy-usage devices (Figure 8.21B). Soldering irons (Figure 8.21C) are larger versions of soldering pencils with proportionally higher wattages (eighty to five hundred). They are used for heavy-duty

Flux: A chemical that reduces surface oxidation, which would prevent the solder or filler rod (welding) and the metal being soldered or welded from flowing together.

soldering projects in which the iron is required to heat a relatively large mass of metal.

PROPANE TORCH The propane torch (Figure 8.21D) consists of a small bottle of propane gas and a nozzle with a number of fittings designed to produce different flame shapes. The heat produced by the torch is sufficient for soldering most heavy-duty scenic jobs. It is also useful for heating thin-gauge steel for bending or shaping.

POWER HACKSAW A motorized gear assembly provides the forward and backward movement necessary for the blade of the motorized hacksaw (Figure 8.22A) to cut through various types of metal stock.

CUTOFF SAW Also called a motorized miter box, the cutoff saw, equipped with a wood-cutting blade, (Figure 8.22B) can also be equipped with a metal-cutting blade to make either straight or angle cuts through various types of metal stock.

POWER PIPE CUTTER The power pipe cutter (Figure 8.22C) performs the same functions as the manual pipe cutting tools—cutting and threading metal pipes with diameters from approximately one-half to two inches.

Figure 8.21 Soldering equipment.

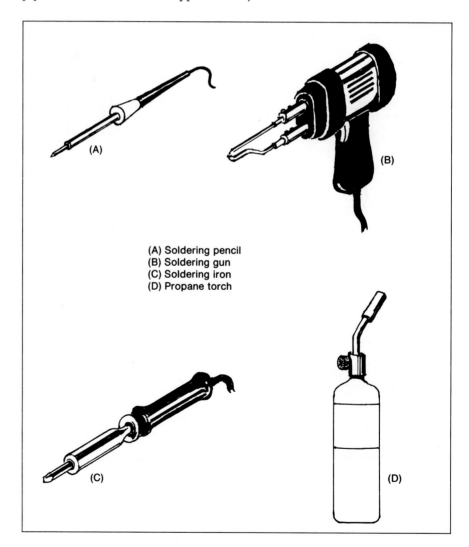

(A) Soldering pencil
(B) Soldering gun
(C) Soldering iron
(D) Propane torch

CHAPTER 8: TOOLS AND MATERIALS

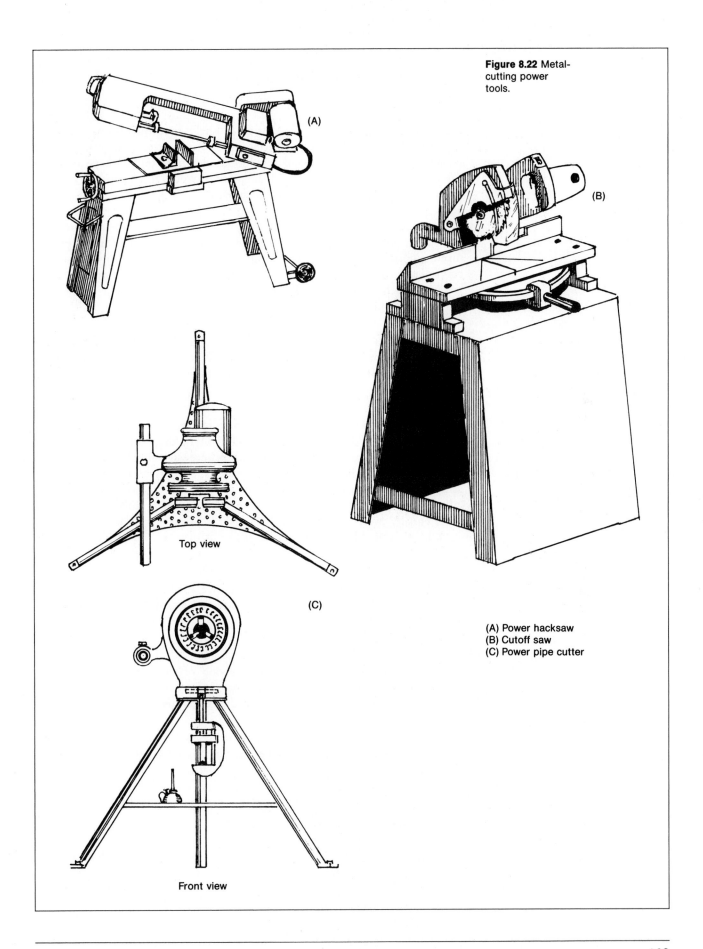

Figure 8.22 Metal-cutting power tools.

(A)

(B)

Top view

(C)

Front view

(A) Power hacksaw
(B) Cutoff saw
(C) Power pipe cutter

Miscellaneous Power Tools

Some additional power tools cannot be neatly placed into any particular category.

ROUTER A router (Figure 8.23A) is a hand-held, motor-driven tool used for shaping wood. The chisel-like rotating bit is driven at extremely high speed (generally twenty-five thousand revolutions per minute) to shape or carve designs from the surface or edge of the piece of wood. It is primarily used for shaping decorative moldings and trim pieces.

WOOD LATHE The wood lathe (Figure 8.23B) is a bench-mounted tool that holds and spins wood rapidly so it can be shaped by carving. Special wood-turning chisels are used to carve the wood. The speed is variable and is controlled either by mechanical or electronic means. In the scene shop the lathe is used for turning bannisters, table legs, and the like. The wood lathe can also be modified for use in turning Styrofoam.

BENCH SANDER A variety of sanders is available, but the bench sander (Figure 8.23C) is normally mounted and is usually a combination of belt sander and disk sander. It is used to bevel or smooth the surface or edges of wood and some plastics.

ELECTRIC SCREWDRIVER One very handy tool bears a strong visual resemblance to an electric hand drill, but instead of holding drill bits its special chuck holds the magnetized tip of a Phillips screwdriver. Electric screwdrivers (Figure 8.23D) have variable-speed motors, so the screws can be started slowly, and a clutch that stops the chuck from turning when the screw is fully seated. It is designed for use with case-hardened Phillips screws that work equally well in wood and metal with no starter hole. The electric screwdriver is used for assembling flats and platforms and in similar situations where assembly and the strength of a screw fastener are needed.

BENCH GRINDER The bench grinder (Figure 8.23E) is used for grinding and sharpening metal. It is normally equipped with a grinding wheel and a wire brush (for polishing), although a cloth buffing wheel can be used for polishing metal to a high luster.

HAND POWER GRINDER A portable version of the bench grinder is the hand power grinder (Figure 8.23F). It is particularly useful for pieces that are too heavy or awkward to be worked on the bench grinder.

HAND POWER SANDER Basically a slightly less powerful version of the hand power grinder, the hand power sander (Figure 8.23G) uses a rotating disk of sandpaper to sand wood, metal, and plastic.

BELT SANDER The powerful belt sander (Figure 8.23H) uses belts of sandpaper for rapid sanding of (primarily) wood.

HOT MELT GLUE GUN One of the most versatile tools in the shop, the hot melt glue gun (Figure 8.23I) uses sticks of heat-activated adhesive for making rapid-hold glue bonds on and between just about every type of material—wood, plastic, paper, cloth, metal, dirt, sand, and so on.

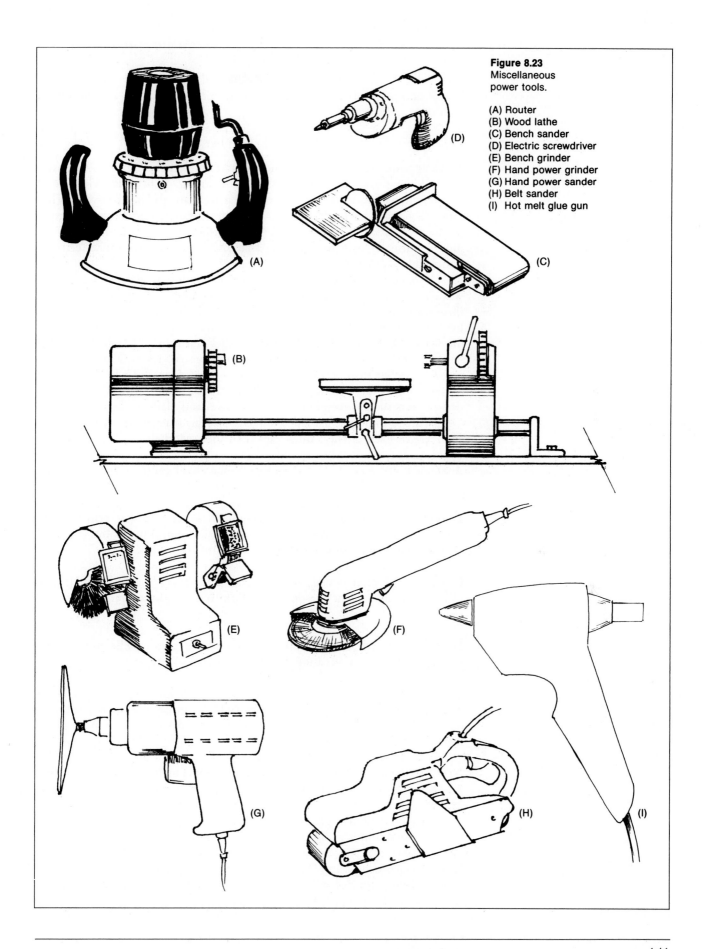

Figure 8.23
Miscellaneous
power tools.

(A) Router
(B) Wood lathe
(C) Bench sander
(D) Electric screwdriver
(E) Bench grinder
(F) Hand power grinder
(G) Hand power sander
(H) Belt sander
(I) Hot melt glue gun

WOOD

Three categories of wood are used in scenic construction—stock lumber, moldings, and sheet goods.

Stock Lumber

To be appropriate for use in scenic construction, stock lumber must possess the following characteristics. It should be strong, light, relatively free of knots, splinter resistant, easily worked, and relatively inexpensive. White pine, a generic name applicable to a number of separate species of pine grown in the western United States, generally satisfies these requirements. White pine is normally used to build the frames of flats and in similar relatively lightweight construction projects.

Unfortunately for the theatrical technician, white pine isn't always called white pine. The name varies considerably depending on the locale. Because of these regional name variations it isn't possible to simply call up your friendly lumber store and order "white pine." First visit the lumber yard and look for the wood that has the required characteristics. Then find out what it's called.

Another commonly used wood in scenic construction is Douglas fir. This wood is heavier than white pine, is stronger, and generally sells for one-half to one-third the cost of white pine. It is normally used for heavier construction projects such as weight-bearing structures and platform legs.

All stock lumber is graded. There are two primary grades of wood, *select* and *common*. Each of these categories is further subdivided.

A SELECT "A select" wood is free of all knots, blemishes, erratic graining, and warps.

B SELECT Also known as "B or Better," "B select" wood is primarily the same as A select except that the grain can be less uniform and the wood can contain more pitch, which increases its weight.

C SELECT "C select" wood can have a few tight knots (that will not fall out) of less than one-half inch in diameter, slightly less-uniform graining, and still more pitch.

D SELECT "D select" wood can have more tight knots, (still only one-half inch in diameter), an occasional pitch pocket, and some warping.

NO. 1 COMMON No. 1 common lumber can have knots up to $1\frac{1}{2}$ inches in diameter. The knots do not have to be tight; in other words, they may fall out, leaving a knothole in the plank. Warping and twisting are more prevalent in this grade of lumber.

NO. 2 COMMON The knots in No. 2 common lumber can be greater than $1\frac{1}{2}$ inches in diameter, and the edges can show an occasional strip of bark. The wood will probably be warped and twisted.

The cost of lumber goes down as you move down the scale from A select to No. 2 common. It is difficult to find A select in most lumber yards. When it is available, it is almost always very expensive. Most stage construction can be accomplished by using "C select" or "D select." The occasional knot, split end, or slight warp that will be found in these grades can usually be trimmed to prevent it from interfering with the construction project. The common grades of lumber are not particularly suitable for stage purposes, although they can be used for applications where their appearance and structural weakness would not adversely affect the looks or safety of the set.

DIMENSIONS OF STOCK LUMBER The Department of Agriculture determines the standards for the thickness, width, and length of all stock lumber sold in the United States. Since the sizing of lumber is done before the boards are milled to a smooth surface, the actual dimensions of the lumber that we buy are smaller than the indicated size, as shown in Figure 8.24. Slight variations in the actual dimensions of the lumber can be measured on almost any piece of stock because of milling variations and shrinkage. Because of these discrepancies it is a good practice to measure every piece of lumber before you use it. The typical scenic uses of the various sizes of lumber are described in Table 8.1.

DETERMINING THE COST OF LUMBER The cost of stock lumber is normally calculated in one of three ways—by the piece, by the linear foot, or by

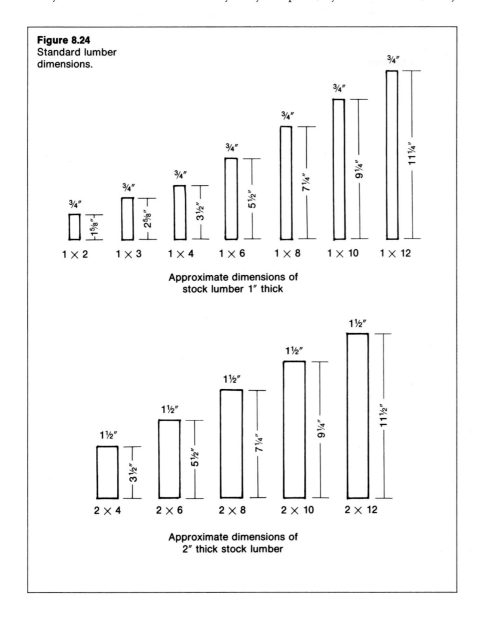

Figure 8.24
Standard lumber dimensions.

Approximate dimensions of stock lumber 1″ thick

Approximate dimensions of 2″ thick stock lumber

Table 8.1
Standard Uses of Lumber in Scenic Construction

Indicated Size (Cross Section)	Actual Size	Typical Stage Uses
1 × 2	¾ inch × 1⅝ inches	small flats; lightweight corner bracing of flats
1 × 3	¾ inch × 2⅝ inches	standard flat framing (6–14 feet); diagonal bracing of platform legs
1 × 4	¾ inch × 3½ inches	large flat framing (over 14 feet)
1 × 6	¾ inch × 5½ inches	door and window frames and similar architectural trim work; narrow sweeps
1 × 8	¾ inch × 7¼ inches	
1 × 10	¾ inch × 9¼ inches	stair treads, sweeps, profile cutouts, furniture
1 × 12	¾ inch × 11¼ inches	
2 × 4	1½ inches × 3½ inches	platform framing, platform legs, and similar weight-bearing structures
2 × 6	1½ inches × 5½ inches	
2 × 8	1½ inches × 7¼ inches	
2 × 10	1½ inches × 9¼ inches	temporary scaffolding; some stair carriages
2 × 12	1½ inches × 11½ inches	not normally used for stage scenery

Board foot: A unit of measurement equivalent to a piece of stock lumber that is twelve inches long, twelve inches wide, and one inch thick (12 × 12 × 1).

the **board foot.** When buying a large quantity of lumber the price is normally quoted as a specific dollar figure per one thousand board feet. Unfortunately, the technical director rarely figures the lumber requirements for a set in board feet. Normally when reviewing the designer's plans the TD determines the lumber requirements for the production in terms of linear feet of 1 × 3, 2 × 4, and so on. To determine the cost of the lumber it will be necessary to convert the linear feet into board feet.

Let's assume that we want to buy twelve pieces of 1 × 3 white pine that are fourteen feet long (1 × 3 × 14). To determine the number of board feet in the order, multiply the number of pieces times the width (in inches), times the thickness (in inches), times the length (in feet), and divide that answer by twelve:

$$\frac{12 \times 3 \times 1 \times 14}{12} = \frac{504}{12} = 42$$

The cost per one thousand board feet is $180. To determine the cost per board foot simply move the decimal point three places to the left. This gives us a board foot price of $0.18. To determine the cost of our lumber order, multiply the board-foot cost times the number of board feet in the order:

$$\$0.18 \times 42 = \$7.56$$

(The cost of plywood is normally based on a price per sheet, and specialty items such as the trim and molding are based on a cost per linear foot. Metal is normally priced per linear foot for tube and rod stock and per square foot for sheet stock.)

Molding and Trim

In addition to stock lumber there are a number of standard trims and moldings (Figure 8.25) that can be used in theatrical production. Decorative moldings are normally manufactured from white pine and are used extensively for architectural trim on and around door and window casings as well as to provide visual interest on baseboards, chair rails, cornices, wall panels, and similar locations.

CHAPTER 8: TOOLS AND MATERIALS

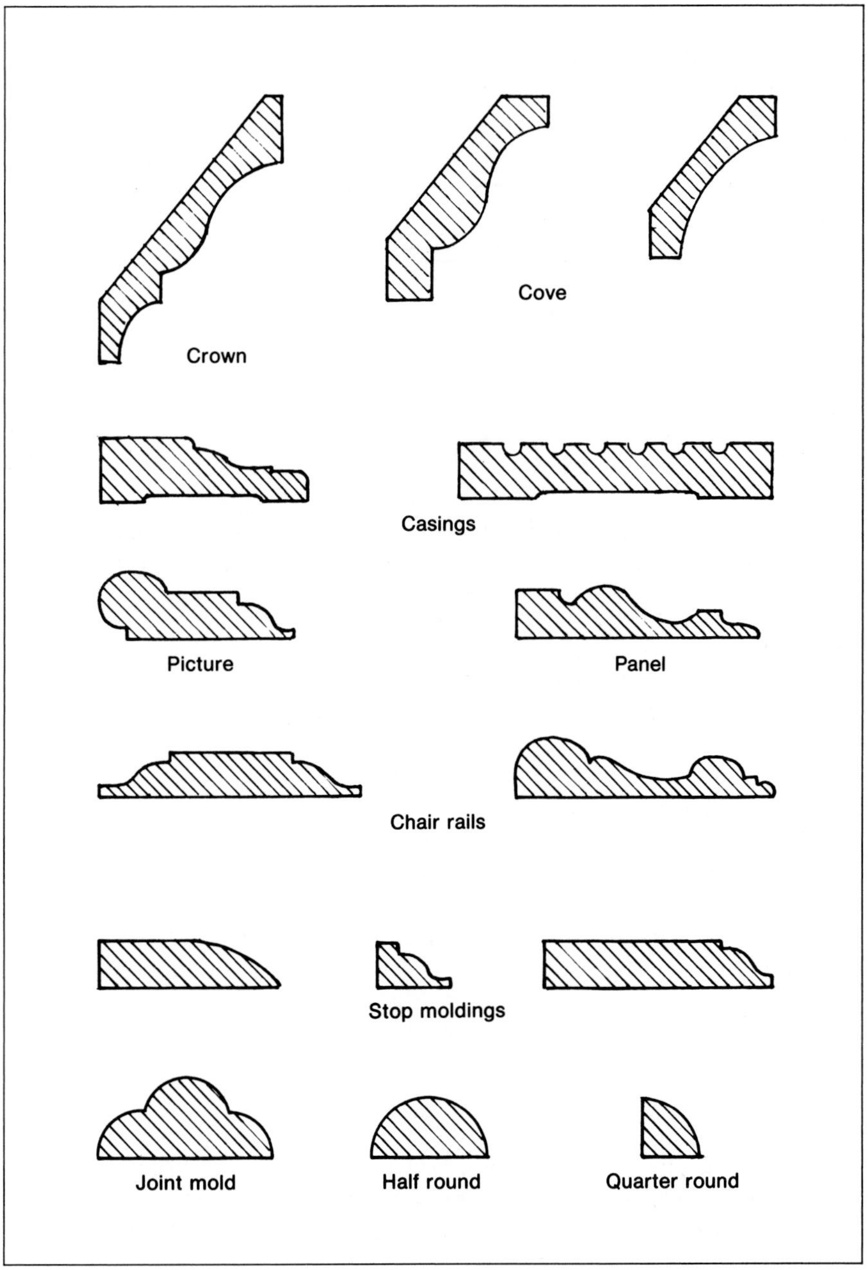

Figure 8.25
Specialty cut
lumber and
moldings.

Crown

Cove

Casings

Picture

Panel

Chair rails

Stop moldings

Joint mold

Half round

Quarter round

Sheet Stock

Various materials fall into the general classification of sheet stock, or lumber products that are manufactured in sheet form.

PLYWOOD Plywood is made by laminating several layers of wood. Most plywood used in the theatre is composed of either three or five layers of wood. The direction of the grain of each successive layer lies at a ninety-degree angle to the layers immediately above and below it, as shown in Figure 8.26. Because the strength of wood lies across its grain, plywood is much stronger than solid wood of a similar thickness.

Plywood is manufactured in interior and exterior grades. The only difference between them is that the exterior grade is laminated with a waterproof glue, whereas the interior grade uses a glue that is water soluble.

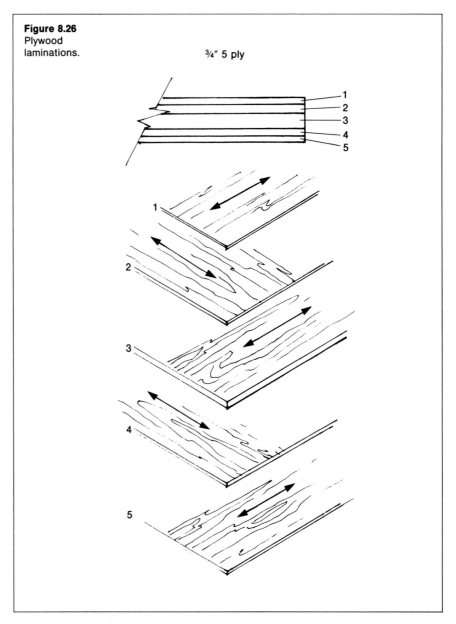

Figure 8.26
Plywood laminations.

¾″ 5 ply

Plywood is available in most lumber yards in thicknesses of ⅛, 3/16, ¼, ⅜, ½, ⅝, and ¾ of an inch. Almost all plywood, unless precut by the lumber yard, is sold in 4-by-8-foot sheets. The only general exception to this rule is ⅛-inch plywood, which is generally sold as "door skin" and is normally marketed in 3-foot-by-6-foot-9-inch or 7-foot sheets.

Plywood is graded according to its surface finish, as shown in Table 8.2. Although there are other grades of plywood, those listed in the table are the most common and are readily available.

AD plywood, despite the fact that it has **plugs,** small knotholes, and grain irregularities on one face, is the standard grade for almost all theatrical construction purposes. The AA grade is rarely used because of its high cost. **Keystones** and **cornerblocks** are made from one-quarter-inch AD plywood. Sweeps, profile pieces, and other curvilinear forms can be cut from any appropriate thickness of AD plywood. Three-quarter-inch AD plywood (A side up) is often used to make platform tops. CD plywood costs less than AD, and its inherent strength is not reduced by its surface imperfections. It can be

Plug: A wooden insert used to replace a knothole or other imperfection in the surface layer of a sheet of plywood.

Keystones and cornerblocks: Pieces of one-quarter-inch AD plywood used to reinforce joints in the construction of stage flats.

Table 8.2
Plywood Grading System

Grade	Surface Appearance
AA	smooth sanded on both sides; both faces free from knots, plugs, or grain irregularities
AD	smooth sanded on both sides; one face (A) is free from imperfections, and the other (D) is not
CD	rough sanded on both sides; each face may have many surface imperfections, some open knotholes, and grain irregularities; whole sheet may be slightly warped

used for platform tops if the rough surface is going to be covered with some other material or if it is not going to be seen by the audience.

Furniture-grade plywood is manufactured with higher quality filler layers. The outer surfaces are usually AA or AD and are made from hardwoods such as mahogany, birch, oak, or walnut. There is also a wide variety of plywoods, usually three-sixteenths or one-quarter-inch thickness, that have prefinished, painted, or hardwood veneer surfaces. These prefinished panels can be used to cover flats as well as in other applications.

PARTICLE BOARD Particle board (Figure 8.27A) is composed of wood chips and sawdust mixed with a glue binder and compressed into four-by-eight-foot sheets. Particle board is usually available in three-eighths, one-half, five-eighths, and three-quarter-inch thicknesses. It is much heavier than plywood of similar thickness and isn't nearly so strong, but it can be used for subflooring, cabinet shelves, and similar structures.

WAFER BOARD Similar to particle board but composed of much larger chips, wafer board (Figure 8.27B) is actually as strong as plywood and is lighter and cheaper. It is finished with one smooth face and one that has a slight texture. Because it is a fairly new addition to the wonderful world of wood, it has not been extensively used as a platform-covering material. However, it should prove to be a valuable new material for scenic construction.

MASONITE Masonite, a registered trade name, is manufactured from wood pulp that is compressed into four-by-eight sheets of one-eighth-, one-quarter-,

Figure 8.27
Closeup views of particle board and wafer board.

(A)   (B)

and three-eighths-inch thickness. It is available in two degrees of hardness, untempered and tempered. Untempered Masonite, which is light brown, has a soft, easily gouged surface. Tempered Masonite is dark brown and has an extemely hard surface.

Although Masonite is quite brittle and can be broken easily with a sharp blow, the one-eighth-inch board can be used as a facing surface for counters, stair risers, and other vertical surfaces that may receive moderate physical abuse during the production. It is flexible enough to be bent around slightly curved forms. Either one-quarter- or three-eighths-inch tempered Masonite can be used to cover the permanent wooden stage floor, because the hard surface resists the abuse caused by heavy stage equipment and can easily be painted with casein, latex, or acrylic paint.

UPSON BOARD Upson board is basically paper pulp and binder that have been mixed and compressed into four-by-eight sheets. It is available in thicknesses of one-eighth, three-sixteenths, and one-quarter inch. The material is relatively flexible and has very little inherent strength. Unless the edge of a piece of Upson board is supported by a wooden framework, it can be easily bent, broken, or frayed.

Upson board one-eighth of an inch thick, also known by the trade name of Easy Curve, is used to cover fairly sharply curved surfaces such as columns or curved walls. The three-sixteenths and one-quarter-inch Upson board can be used as a hard cover for flats or profile cutouts if they won't be subject to too much physical abuse.

Fabrics that are normally used for covering scenery are discussed in Chapter 9, *Scenic Production Techniques,* and typical drapery and upholstery materials are dealt with in Chapter 11, *Stage Properties.*

METAL

Metal is being used with increasing frequency in scenic construction. This popularity can be attributed to two specific factors: (1) the increasing cost of wood has eliminated what was once a significant cost difference between wood and metal, and (2) metal is inherently stronger than wood.

The greater strength of metal allows the construction of frameworks for platforms and large flats that are as strong as or stronger than, but weigh less than, similarly sized wooden units. Additionally, metal's strength encourages its use in the fabrication of delicate or irregular shapes that would be impossible to duplicate in wood.

Although there are literally hundreds of metals and alloys, only two types—mild steel and aluminum—are used extensively in scenic construction. Other metals, most notably, bronze, brass, and copper, are occasionally used in prop construction, but their relatively high cost and working characteristics argue against their being used for other than decorative purposes.

Mild Steel

Mild steel is the most common type of steel. It is quite malleable and is relatively easy to cut, bend, and drill. It is also very easy to weld, and its strength is sufficient for most general scenic uses such as flat and platform frameworks. It is readily available from local steel suppliers in the shapes illustrated in Figure 8.28 as well as in sheets of varying sizes and thicknesses.

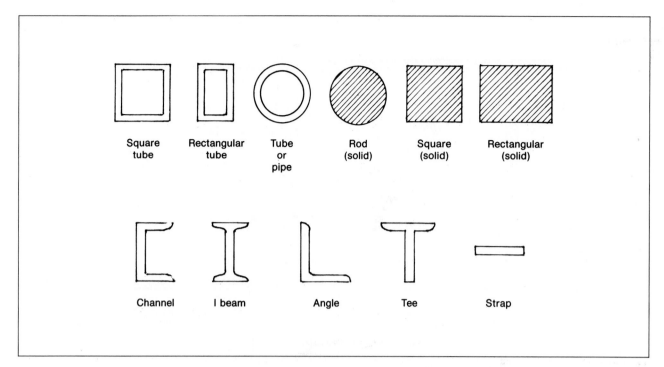

Square
tube

Rectangular
tube

Tube
or
pipe

Rod
(solid)

Square
(solid)

Rectangular
(solid)

Channel

I beam

Angle

Tee

Strap

Aluminum

Aluminum is manufactured in the same shapes as mild steel. Additionally, decorative panels made of aluminum can be purchased in many hardware or lumber stores.

Aluminum is not used as extensively as mild steel, primarily because it is more expensive and is more difficult to weld than steel. It is used mainly for decorative purposes in scenic construction.

Figure 8.28 Basic forms of metal.

PLASTICS

Various plastics are useful in technical production, but more substantial safety hazards are involved in forming and processing plastics than in dealing with any other common construction material.

Friction between a saw or knife blade and plastic creates heat. This heat liberates gases from the plastic. Some of these fumes simply smell bad; some are noxious, or unhealthy; others are toxic or poisonous; and still others can be lethal.

Because it is frequently difficult to determine the level of toxicity of these various fumes, it is vital that you work with plastics only in a well-ventilated area. If your workshop isn't equipped with a good fresh-air circulation system, create your own. Set up a cross-ventilation pattern, illustrated in Figure 8.29, between outside windows and doors. Use box fans or similar large-bladed fans set on high speed to move a large volume of air. When you first open the windows or doors, check the natural direction of the air flow and reinforce it with your fans. However, be sure that you ventilate the fumes to the outdoors rather than simply blowing them into another part of the building. If your shop doesn't have direct access to outside fresh air, don't work on plastics in the shop. Work on them outdoors, or if that isn't possible, appropriate a room that can be properly ventilated. The necessity for a high

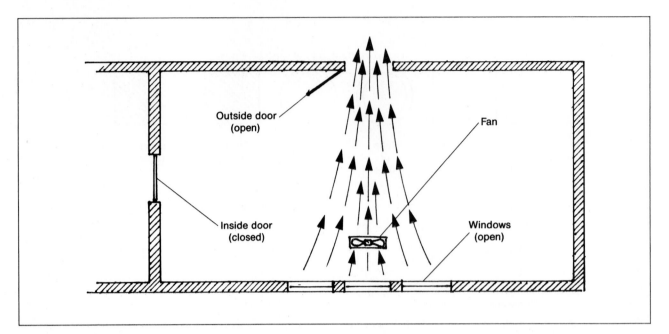

Figure 8.29 Cross-ventilation air-flow pattern for a shop.

volume of air movement cannot be stressed too much. Your physical health, and the health of everyone else in the shop, depends on it.

When working with plastics be sure to wear a respirator. This mask filters the air through activated charcoal and removes many of the harmful elements from the air. The use of a respirator and an effective fresh-air ventilation system, when combined with the commonsense rules of shop safety, can make working with plastics safe.

Acrylic

Frequently identified by one of its trade names, Plexiglas, acrylic is available in rigid sheets of varying sizes and thicknesses in clear, translucent, textured, and colored finishes. It is also available in rods, tubes, and bars and in a liquid form for use as a **casting resin.** It is commonly used as a glass substitute, and the casting resin can be used to make decorative baubles for costumes, props, and stained glass. The sheets, rods, and tubes can be formed by heating and bending the material to the desired shape.

Epoxy

Epoxies are available in a variety of formulations to suit a number of purposes, but in theatrical construction the most commonly used types are those for adhesives and casting resins. All epoxies are extremely durable and moisture resistant. Depending on the particular formulation, epoxies can be worked with either wood- or metal-cutting tools.

Epoxy adhesive is very useful for scenic and property construction projects that require strength or water resistance. Epoxy auto body putty is very useful for molding and sculpting decorative detail on sets and props. The casting resin can be used to make objects that are much stronger than those cast with either acrylic or polyester casting resins.

Fluorocarbons

Teflon is probably the best known trade name in this family of tough, durable, low-friction, nonstick plastics. Although it is commercially available in

Casting resin: Any of a number of liquid plastics used for casting forms in molds.

a variety of forms, the most useful for theatrical purposes are the sheets and tapes.

Teflon makes an excellent bearing surface because of its extremely slippery qualities. It can be used for turntables or for covering the tracks and runners of **skids.**

Skid: A low-profile substitute for a wagon; usually a piece of three-quarter-inch plywood on which some small scenic element is placed.

Polyesters

There are two types of polyester, saturated and unsaturated. All polyesters have a characteristically smooth surface and great tensile strength.

SATURATED POLYESTERS Saturated polyesters are used to form the fiber from which polyester fabrics such as Dacron are made. Saturated polyesters are also used to manufacture films such as Mylar.

Polyester fabrics have a variety of uses in both scenic and costume construction, and they can be worked with normal fabric-cutting tools. The film, which is available in a variety of textures, treatments, and colors, has many uses in the scene shop. Aluminized Mylar film is frequently used as a lightweight, unbreakable stage mirror, and Mylar film is used as the base material for several lines of lighting instrument color media as well as audio and video recording tape.

UNSATURATED POLYESTERS Unsaturated polyesters can be used in casting or to create the multipurpose material known as fiberglass.

The unsaturated polyester casting resin can be used for the same purposes as the acrylic and epoxy casting resins. Fiberglass, also called glass fiber plastic, is used in situations where its great strength and flexibility of form are an advantage.

Unsaturated polyesters can be worked with both woodworking and metalworking tools. A basic introduction to working with glass fiber plastics can be found in Chapter 11, *Stage Properties.*

Polyethylene

Polyethylene plastics are available in a variety of formulations, but the forms most commonly used in the theatre are film and foam. All polyethylenes have a characteristically slick, waxy surface.

Polyethylene film, generally available in black, white, and clear, can be used for such things as drop cloths and projection screens. Polyethylene foam, generally known by the trade name Ethafoam, is very flexible and is generally available in sheets and rods. It is frequently used for architectural trim and similar nonstructural functions. It rejects every type of paint except acrylic, and even acrylic will chip off if the surface of the foam is flexed. Ethafoam can be painted if, after it is applied to the scenery, it is covered with several layers of cheesecloth that have been coated with white glue. Sheets of polyethylene foam, sold under the trade name of Bubble Board, make excellent rear-screen projection surfaces.

Polystyrene

As with other plastics, the strength of polystyrene is directly dependent on the density of its molecular structure. High-impact polystyrene has a fairly dense molecular structure and a hard surface and is moderately flexible, fairly strong, and somewhat brittle. It becomes very limp when heated, and it is the primary plastic used in vacuum forming (to be discussed in Chapter 11).

Polystyrene foam, commonly known by the trade name Styrofoam, does not have a dense molecular structure, yet it retains the basic characteristics of all polystyrenes—a hard surface, moderate flexibility, strength, and brittleness. It is frequently used for making decorative trim such as cornices and statuary. Techniques for carving Styrofoam will be discussed in Chapter 11.

Polyvinyl Chloride

Although there are probably more formulations of vinyls than any other family of plastics, arguably the most useful formulations for stage purposes are those members of the polyvinyl chloride group. Characteristically, polyvinyl chlorides (PVCs) are strong, lightweight, and rigid.

PVC pipe has those characteristics. Normally used in lawn sprinkler systems, it can also be used for a variety of decorative scenic purposes. PVC is available in a variety of other forms (sheet, rod, and so forth) that are useful for the theatre artisan.

PVC pipe, and its other forms, can be formed using heat. Heat forming will be discussed in Chapter 11.

Pyroxylin

Felt treated with pyroxylin is sold under the trade name Celastic. The material becomes extremely limp and flexible when dipped in acetone and can be formed into a wide variety of shapes. When the acetone evaporates, the Celastic becomes rigid again.

Urethanes

Urethane plastics have a number of uses in technical production. Flexible urethane foam is commonly used for cushions and padding in furniture. The rigid foam, which has a tighter cell structure than polystyrene foam, is used as the modeling block in floral displays and has also been used as an insulation material in building construction. Urethane is also available as a casting resin.

Kits for hand-mixing rigid or flexible foams can be purchased from building insulation companies and scenic or plastics supply houses. Two types of kit are generally available. The hand-mix, or pour-in-place, forms are two-part compounds that are mixed together and poured into molds. Spray-pack foams, such as the Insta-Foam Froth Pak, are also two-part formulations, but they are automatically mixed as they are sprayed. Both molds and casting techniques are discussed in Chapter 11.

FASTENERS

Fasteners in a variety of forms are used in scenic and property construction.

Nails

Nails are the most commonly used mechanical fasteners. They are driven into two or more pieces of wood with a hammer to hold them together. The strength of the fastening depends on the gripping pressure that the wood exerts on the shaft of the nail.

The size of nails is designated by the term *penny,* which is symbolized by the letter *d.* There is a rough equivalency between the length of the shaft, or shank, of a nail and the penny designation: the higher the number, the longer the shaft.

With the exception of the clout nail, all of the nails, screws, and bolts listed below are commonly used in nontheatrical construction and are readily available at lumber yards.

COMMON NAIL The common nail (Figure 8.30A) has a large head and thick shank. It is used for heavier general construction—platforms, bracing, and the like.

BOX NAIL Similar in shape to the common nail, the box nail (Figure 8.30B) has a narrower shaft that reduces the chance of splitting the lumber.

COATED BOX NAIL Similar to the box nail but with a slightly narrower shaft, the coated box nail has an adhesive applied to the shaft. The friction generated when the nail is driven activates the adhesive to tightly bond the nail to the wood.

FINISH NAIL The finish nail (Figure 8.30C) has a slender shaft and very narrow, almost nonexistent head. It is designed so the head can be driven below the surface of the wood and the resultant hole filled with putty or filler. The finish nail is not normally used in general scenic construction but is employed in the building of props or furniture and at any time that it is desirable to hide the nail head.

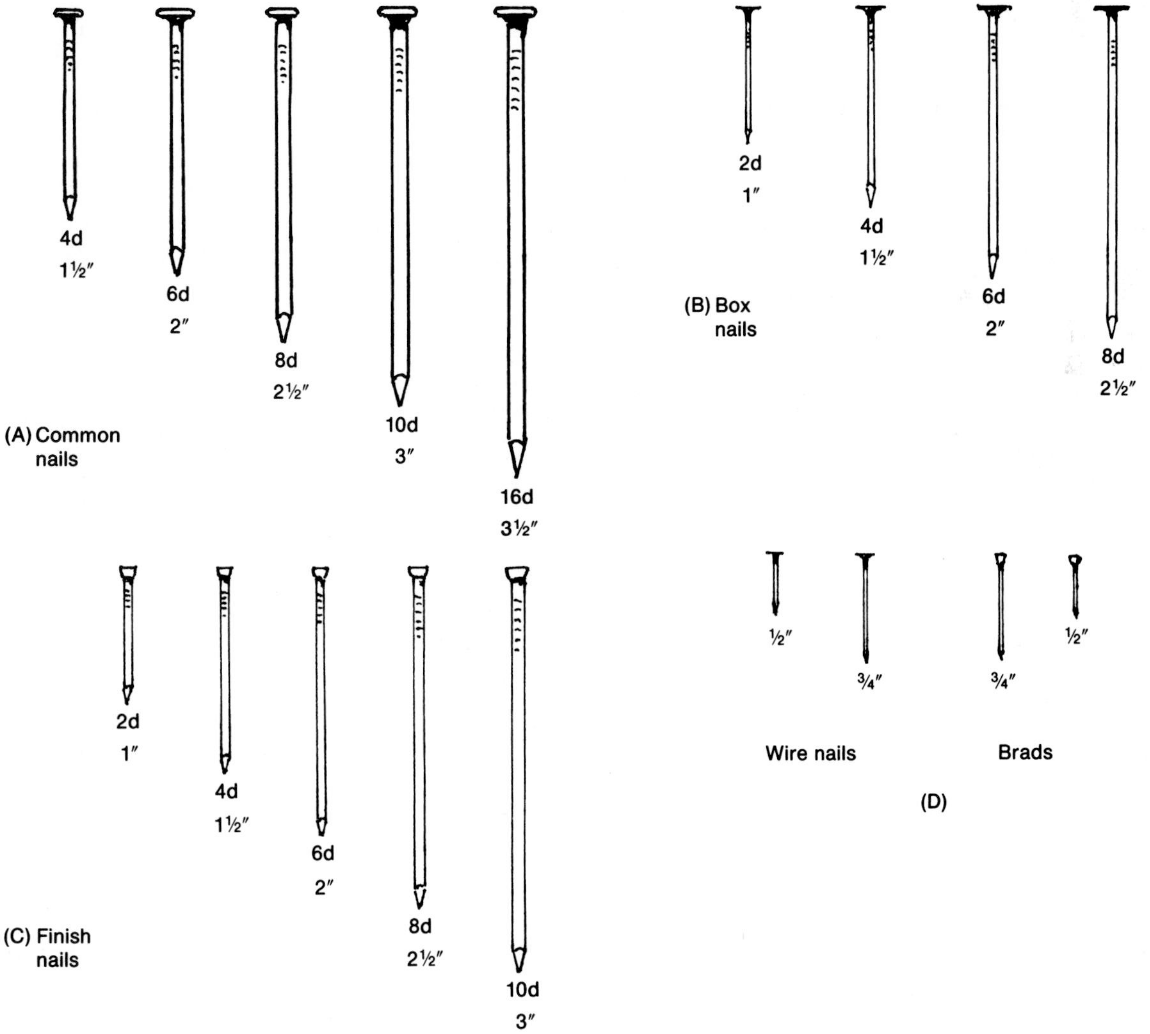

Figure 8.30
Standard nails.

(A) Common nails

4d 1½"
6d 2"
8d 2½"
10d 3"
16d 3½"

(B) Box nails

2d 1"
4d 1½"
6d 2"
8d 2½"

(C) Finish nails

2d 1"
4d 1½"
6d 2"
8d 2½"
10d 3"

(D)

Wire nails
½"
¾"

Brads
¾"
½"

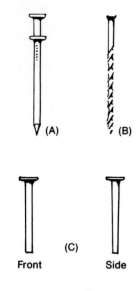

Front Side

**Flat side of clout nail
at right angle to wood grain
to prevent splitting**

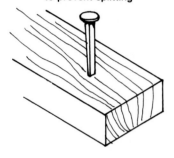

(A) Double-headed nail
(B) Screw nail
(C) Clout nail

Figure 8.31
Specialty nails.

WIRE NAIL AND BRAD Wire nails and brads (Figure 8.30D) are small (under one inch long) finish or box nails with very slender shafts. They are used in property construction or for attaching delicate decorative moldings or panels to larger scenic elements.

DOUBLE-HEADED NAIL Double-headed nails (Figure 8.31A) are also known as scaffolding nails. They are driven into the wood until the lower head is flush with the surface, leaving the upper head exposed so that it can be pulled out easily. As the secondary name implies, these nails are used for scaffolding or any temporary structure that you may want to dismantle quickly.

SCREW NAIL The screw nail (Figure 8.31B) has a threaded shank that rotates as it is driven into the wood. It has more holding power than a common nail and is used for attaching platform tops and for similar jobs where the greater holding power would be useful.

CLOUT NAIL A specialty nail known as a clout nail is used in flat construction (Figure 8.31C). It is made from soft iron, is wedge shaped, and is 1¼ inches long. It is used to attach cornerblocks and keystones to the framing of a flat. The clout nail is driven through the wood onto a steel backing plate, which curls the end of the nail back into the lumber. This process, called clinching, is what gives the nail its strong grip. Clout nails can be purchased from scenic supply houses.

The use of clout nails is declining because of problems in obtaining and using them and because coated box nails and power-driven staples can achieve relatively the same gripping power with less fuss, muss, and bother.

TACK Various tacks are used in scenic construction. Carpet tacks (Figure 8.32A) have very wide heads and tapered shafts varying from approximately three-eighths to three-quarters of an inch in length. Carpet, gimp, and thumb tacks (Figure 8.32B) are generally used for attaching fabric to some type of wooden backing, for example, tacking carpeting to the floor, upholstery fabric to furniture frames, and so forth. Decorative tacks have rounded heads and straight shanks, as shown in Figure 8.32C. Although they do hold upholstery fabric to its wooden frame, their primary purpose is simply decoration. They are also very useful to the property master in the decoration, or "glitzing," of various stage props.

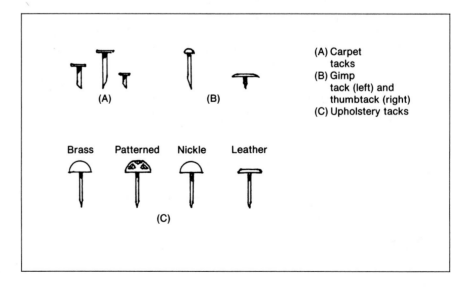

(A) Carpet
    tacks
(B) Gimp
    tack (left) and
    thumbtack (right)
(C) Upholstery tacks

Brass   Patterned   Nickle   Leather

Figure 8.32 Tacks.

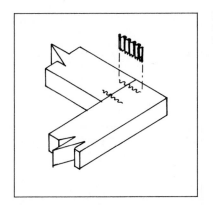

Figure 8.33
Corrugated fastener.

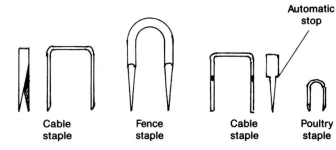

Screen staple
Cable staple
Fence staple
Cable staple
Automatic stop
Poultry staple

Figure 8.34
Staples.

CORRUGATED FASTENER Corrugated strips of metal about ⅝ of an inch tall and 1⅛ inches wide, shown in Figure 8.33, are primarily used to hold light-weight frames together.

STAPLE Staples are U-shaped fasteners sharpened at both ends. Fence, screen, and poultry staples (Figure 8.34) are driven with a hammer and can be used to attach wire, rope, cording, chicken wire, screening, and similar materials to supporting wooden frameworks.

Spring-powered and electrically powered staple guns use short-legged staples (¼ to ½ inch) to attach fabric to wooden frames. Relatively long-legged staples (¾ to ½ inches), when driven by a pneumatic stapler, are used to fasten various types of wooden structures together.

Screws

Screws provide a stronger method of joining than nails, because their auger-like thread digs into the material on the sides of the screw hole to mechanically bind them to the material. Various screws are used in scenic construction. The type of screw appropriate for an individual job is dependent on the type and thickness of the material being worked and the strength needed in the particular joint. Most screws are designed with either a slotted or Phillips head (Figures 8.35A and 8.35B), although some are manufactured for use with an **Allen wrench** (Figure 8.35C) or have a combination slotted hex head (Figure 8.35D).

FLAT-HEAD WOOD SCREW The flat-head wood screw (FHWS) is probably the most common type of screw used in the scene shop (Figure 8.36A). It has a flat head that is beveled on the underside to easily dig into the wood. This countersinking action allows the upper face of the head to be flush with the

Allen wrench: An L-shaped piece of steel rod with a hexagonal cross-sectional shape; used for working with Allen head screws and bolts.

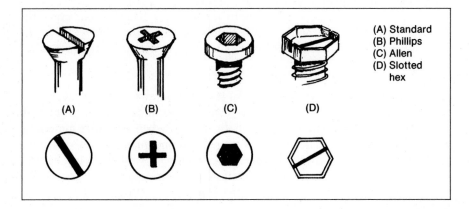

(A)   (B)   (C)   (D)

(A) Standard
(B) Phillips
(C) Allen
(D) Slotted hex

Figure 8.35 Types of screw heads.

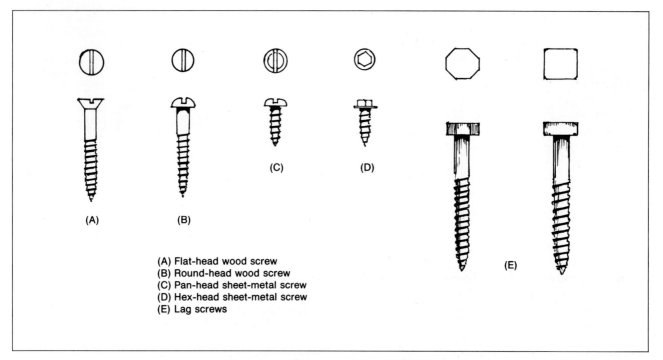

Figure 8.36
Screws.

(A) Flat-head wood screw
(B) Round-head wood screw
(C) Pan-head sheet-metal screw
(D) Hex-head sheet-metal screw
(E) Lag screws

surface of the work. Common uses for the FHWS are attaching hardware (hinges, doorknobs) and joining various wooden elements together. FHWS's range in length from about ½ to 3 inches, although the most common sizes used in the shop vary from ¾ to about 1¼ or 1½ inches, with a screw shank diameter of No. 8 or No. 9. (The numerical rating of screw shank sizes is roughly dependent on their diameter: the higher the number, the larger the diameter.)

ROUND-HEAD WOOD SCREW Identical in most respects with the FHWS, the round-head wood screw (RHWS) has a head with a flat underside and a rounded upper surface (Figure 8.36B). The RHWS is used in those situations in which you do not want to have the top of the screw flush with the surface of the work, such as when you are attaching thin metal or fabric to a wooden frame.

SHEET-METAL SCREW As the name implies, sheet-metal screws are used for joining sheets of metal. They are commonly available with either a pan head (Figure 8.36C) or a hex head (Figure 8.36D). Most jobs using sheet-metal screws in the scenic or property shop require shank lengths between one-quarter and three-quarters of an inch.

When pieces are to be joined with the use of a hand-driven screw, the metal must be predrilled with a hole slightly narrower than the width of the screw shank. If a power screwdriver is used, it is not necessary to predrill the work.

LAG SCREW Lag screws are very large wood screws with hexagonal or square heads (Figure 8.36E). They are used where the lack of access to both sides of the work prevents the use of bolts, such as when attaching something to a wall or the floor. Shaft diameters range from one-quarter to one-half inch with shaft lengths varying from one to six inches. A washer should be used under the head of the lag screw to increase the bearing area and prevent the head from biting into the surface of the work.

Unless you are using a power screwdriver, a screw is much easier to use if you drill a starter, or pilot, hole. Ideally this hole should be the same diameter as the solid shaft of the threaded portion of the screw (not counting the flange of the screw thread).

Specialty drill bits called screw starters, designed for use with electric drills, can drill starter and countersink holes in the same action. They are available for most common sizes of screws.

The starter hole for a bolt should be the same diameter as the full diameter of the bolt (including the screw flange).

Bolts

Bolts are used when you want the strongest type of mechanical fastening. In using a bolt, a hole is drilled in both members of the work, the appropriate type and size of bolt is inserted into the hole, a washer is slipped onto the bolt shaft, and a nut is threaded onto the bolt shaft and tightened (Figure 8.37).

CARRIAGE BOLT The upper face of a carriage bolt head has a rounded surface, and the underside has a slightly tapered square collar a little wider than the diameter of the bolt shaft, as shown in Figure 8.38A. The carriage bolt is used to join either wood to wood or wood to metal. After the bolt has been inserted into the hole, the head is struck with a hammer to make the square collar seat, or bite into, the surface of the wood to prevent it from turning. This type of bolt is commonly used to fasten legs to platform frames and in similar types of work. Carriage bolts range in diameter from one-quarter to three-quarters of an inch and in length from one to twenty-four inches.

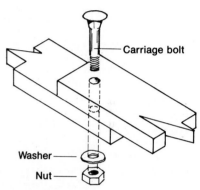

Figure 8.37 Bolts are the strongest form of mechanical fastener.

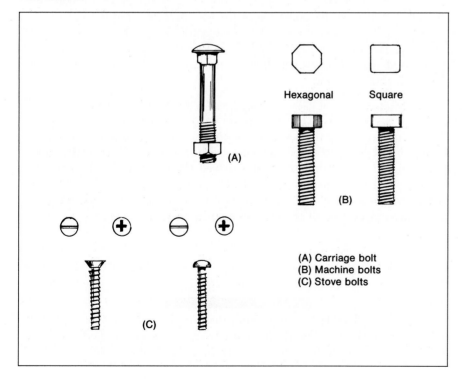

Hexagonal   Square

(A)

(B)

(A) Carriage bolt
(B) Machine bolts
(C) Stove bolts

(C)

Figure 8.38 Bolts.

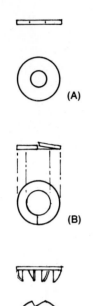

(A) Washer
(B) Lock washer
(C) Torque washer

Figure 8.39
Washers.

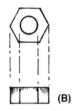

(A) Square nut
(B) Hex nut
(C) Wing nut

Figure 8.40 Nuts.

MACHINE BOLT Machine bolts are designed to join metal to metal, although they can be used to join wood to wood if a washer is used under the head of the bolt as well as under the nut. Machine bolts are manufactured with both square and hexagonal heads, as shown in Figure 8.38B. The bolt shaft diameters range from one-quarter to one inch and the lengths from one to six inches.

STOVE BOLT Stove bolts (Figure 8.38C) are smaller than carriage or machine bolts and have threads on the entire length of the shaft. They have head shapes identical to flat- and round-head wood screws to serve similar purposes. Sizes appropriate for general scenic purposes range from diameters of one-eighth to five-sixteenths of an inch, with shaft lengths ranging between one and six inches. Much smaller stove bolts (shaft diameters less than one-eighth of an inch and lengths under one inch) are available from hobby or electronic stores.

Stove bolts are generally used for attaching stage hardware, hinges, and similar items in situations that might require the extra fastening strength available with the use of bolts instead of screws.

Washers

Washers are flat steel disks with a center hole cut for the bolt shaft. When placed between either the nut or the head of the bolt and the material being joined, a washer (Figure 8.39A) increases the bearing surface of the nut or bolt head and prevents the head from cutting into the surface of the work. Lock washers (Figure 8.39B) are made from spring steel and are cut and slightly spread apart to form a compression tension when the nut is tightened. The purpose of the lock washer is to hold the nut in place after it has been tightened.

Torque washers (Figure 8.39C) are designed to prevent carriage bolts from twisting once they have been seated. The torque washer is slipped onto the shaft of the carriage bolt before it is inserted into the predrilled bolt hole. The square collar on the underside of the bolt head fits into the square hole on the face of the torque washer. When the bolt is seated, the four prongs bite into the surface of the wood. By firmly seating the head of the carriage bolt in the wood, the torque washer allows more torque, or pressure, to be applied when tightening the nut.

Nuts

Nuts are applied to the threaded ends of bolts to close and tighten this type of fastener. Nuts designed to be tightened with wrenches are generally either square (Figure 8.40A) or hexagonally shaped (Figure 8.40B). The wing nut (Figure 8.40C) is designed to be tightened with your fingers. Nuts are available in sizes and metallic compositions identical to the shaft diameters and composition or coating of their corresponding bolts.

GLUES AND ADHESIVES

Myriad glues and adhesives are manufactured today, and many of them have applications in theatrical work, particularly in the area of property construction. Although the following list is certainly far from exhaustive, it does

introduce you to the glues and adhesives commonly used in scenic and property construction.

There are general guidelines for using all glues and adhesives. Be sure that the faces being glued are clean, dry, and free from oil and dust. Most glues, except contact cement, require some type of clamping. The amount of pressure and the time that it must be maintained are dependent on heat and humidity as well as the type of glue being used. The working characteristics of each glue and adhesive are discussed in the following sections.

Glues

Glue is made of, or primarily derived from, natural substances.

ANIMAL GLUE Animal glue is just what the name implies. A by-product of the meat packing industry, it is purchased in a dry form (granular or flaked) and must be prepared in the theatre shop before it can be used. The dry glue is poured in an electric glue pot or double boiler, covered with water, and soaked (no heat added) until it becomes a gelatinous mass (about six to ten hours). It is then heated until it reaches the consistency of syrup, at which time it is ready for use. It is one of the prime ingredients of scenic glue, which is one of the formulas used to glue muslin or canvas to flats and other scenic elements. It is also used as a binder in the mixing of scene paint. These formulas are discussed in the section of Chapter 9, *Scenic Production Techniques,* on covering flats.

Animal glue can be used to join most natural substances—wood, paper, cloth. When dry it has a glossy, smooth surface that is stiff and brittle. It is not effective for any project that requires a flexible joint. It can be purchased from scenic paint and supply houses as well as some paint and hardware stores. Animal glue sets when it cools. If it is diluted with water, the drying time varies between one and four hours depending on the heat and humidity.

FLEXIBLE GLUE Flexible glue is animal glue with glycerine added. It must be prepared in the same manner as animal glue and can be used for projects requiring flexibility. It is available from scenic supply and paint houses. The drying characteristics of flexible glue are the same as those of animal glue.

WHITE GLUE White glue (widely known by the trade name of Elmer's Glue-All) is a casein or milk-based glue that is used extensively in scenic construction. It is reasonably fast drying, is slightly flexible, and adheres to wood, paper, cloth, Styrofoam, and some other plastics as well. When dry it leaves a slightly glossy surface. It can be purchased from almost any lumber, paint, or hardware store. White glue dries in about one or two hours depending on heat, humidity, and air circulation around the glue joint, but for the joint to develop strength the glue must be allowed to cure for about twenty-four hours.

WHEAT PASTE Wheat paste is made from a mixture of unrefined wheat flour and water. Although it looks like flour, wheat paste shouldn't be used for cooking, because it is usually laced with rat poison to prevent it from being eaten when it is in storage. It is used for hanging wallpaper, as the glue in papier-mâché, and as one of the ingredients in the glue used for attaching **dutchmen** to wall units. After wheat paste has dried, it is reasonably flexible and has a dull, or matte, surface finish. It can be purchased at paint and wallpaper stores, hardware stores, and lumber yards.

Dutchman: A five- to six-inch-wide strip of cloth of the same material as the flat covering; applied over joints between flats to give the appearance of a smooth, unbroken wall unit.

Adhesives

Adhesives perform the same functions as glues but are primarily composed of synthetic materials. They have a distinct advantage over natural glues in that they will not spoil, rot, or turn sour, and they generally come in ready-to-use formulations.

Drying and curing times for adhesives vary considerably depending on type and manufacturer. Read the label of the specific product to determine its particular characteristics.

LATEX CEMENT A milky-white, flexible cement commercially used in laying carpet, latex cement can be used whenever a very flexible glue joint is required. It adheres to cloth, paper, wood, and many other materials and can be purchased from many carpet shops, some furniture stores, and scenic supply houses.

CONTACT CEMENT Contact cement is an adhesive for bonding nonporous surfaces together. As the name implies, the surfaces being joined are bonded as soon as they come in contact with each other. Each surface to be joined is spread with a light coating of the contact cement and allowed to dry for a few minutes; then the pieces are brought together and are immediately bonded. There are two basic types of contact cement: one has a highly volatile, extremely flammable base, and the other has a water-soluble latex base. Although the adhesion of the volatile-base cement appears to be slightly better, in the interest of safety it is recommended that the latex-base contact cement be used whenever possible.

POLYVINYL GLUE A white liquid adhesive that resembles white glue in appearance, polyvinyl glue is a synthetic with excellent adhesion to porous surfaces and good flexibility. It can be used for a number of jobs, ranging from furniture repair and construction to use as the binder for scene paint.

CYANOACRYLATE CEMENT Cyanoacrylate cements are a relatively new family of very powerful adhesives that will bond almost any porous or nonporous surface to almost anything else. Therein lie their strengths and dangers. Sold under trade names such as Super Glue, Krazy Glue, and so on, these powerful adhesives are too expensive for use in general scenic construction but are excellent for use in property construction. Like contact cement, cyanoacrylate cements bond very rapidly. However, they also bond skin to skin or skin to anything else just as rapidly. When using cyanoacrylate cements be sure to follow the instructions very carefully.

EPOXY RESIN ADHESIVE Two-part epoxy resin adhesive is available in a number of formulations that enable the user to do gluing, filling, and painting. The bond created by an epoxy adhesive is extremely strong and waterproof. It is used in the shop in situations where its strength can be an advantage, such as furniture construction and property work.

Almost all of the adhesives discussed in this section can be purchased at any well-stocked hardware store. If you are involved in scenic construction, particularly property construction, it would be to your advantage to spend some time wandering around a hardware store familiarizing yourself with the really vast range of adhesives.

A great deal of hardware is used in the construction of stage scenery. Most of this hardware is also used in building construction and can be purchased at a lumber yard or hardware store. The specialized hardware designed for specific stage applications is usually not available locally and must be purchased from a scenic supply house.

Construction Hardware

EYE BOLT Eye bolts (Figure 8.41A) can be used for almost any situation that requires attaching lines or ropes to an object, such as the pull rope for a stage wagon or a guide for the piano wire or cable on a piece of flying scenery. The diameter of the steel rod used to manufacture the eye bolt varies from approximately one-eighth to three-eighths of an inch. The shaft length varies from about one to six inches.

Figure 8.41
Common construction hardware.

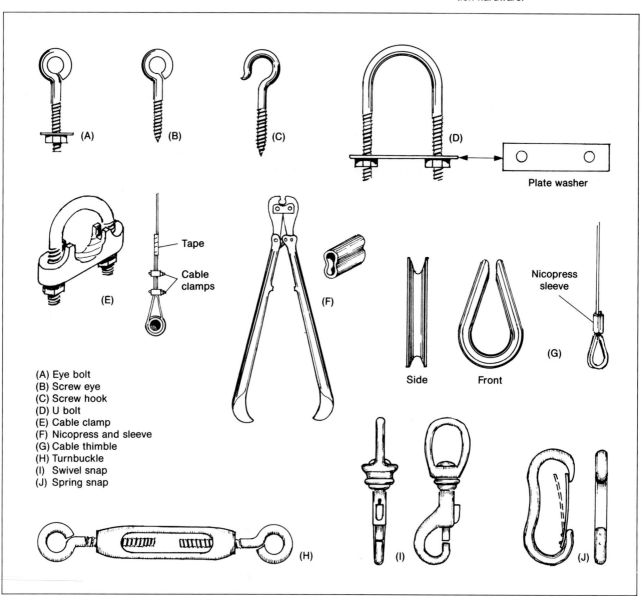

(A) Eye bolt
(B) Screw eye
(C) Screw hook
(D) U bolt
(E) Cable clamp
(F) Nicopress and sleeve
(G) Cable thimble
(H) Turnbuckle
(I) Swivel snap
(J) Spring snap

Plate washer

Tape

Cable clamps

Nicopress sleeve

Side   Front

Screw Eye Screw eyes (Figure 8.41B) are similar to eye bolts but are used when the additional strength of the bolt fastener isn't necessary or when the back of the surface to which the screw eye is being attached cannot be reached. Screw eyes are available in a wide range of sizes: shaft diameters vary from about one-sixteenth to three-eighths of an inch and lengths from one-half to four inches.

Screw Hook Screw hooks (Figure 8.41C) are similar to screw eyes but have a hook instead of an eye so that items hung from the hook can be removed quickly. Size variations are similar to those of screw eyes.

U Bolt U bolts (Figure 8.41D) are made from metal rod that has been bent in a **U** shape and threaded on both ends. They are typically used to secure or fasten pipe, tube, or rod to a flat surface.

Cable Clamp Another type of U bolt, the cable clamp (Figure 8.41E), also known as a cable clip, has a grooved metal clamp that fits over the bolt shafts. The size of the grooves corresponds to the diameter of the wire rope or cable that is used to hang scenery and battens. For safety reasons cable clamps should always be used in pairs.

Nicopress Tool Another cable fastener, the Nicopress tool (Figure 8.41F), provides a permanent, nonremovable friction clamp for wire rope or cable. Nicopress sleeves, which are thin, soft metal tubes approximately one-half to three-quarters of an inch long, are designed for specific diameters of cable and must be crimped or tightened with a Nicopress tool. Like the sleeves, the Nicopress tools are designed to work with only one diameter of cable.

Thimble The thimble (Figure 8.41G) is a narrow, grooved, teardrop-shaped piece of sheet metal used to protect wire rope or cable from sharp bends or kinks when the cable is attached to a ring or similar device.

Turnbuckle A turnbuckle (Figure 8.41H) has a long, oval body with a threaded eye bolt protruding from either end. When attached as a link in a cable it can be used to lengthen or shorten that line system. This property makes it an excellent device to place between a flying line and a flown piece of scenery to adjust the trim of the flown unit.

Snaps There are various types of snaps—some with swivel bases (Figure 8.41I), some designed for use with rope, and others intended for use with cable, chain, and curtains (Figure 8.41J). But they all have the same purpose—they provide a quick means of attaching a line to its associated load.

Hinges A hinge is composed of two joined metal plates that swing around a pivot point. A number of types of hinge have applications in scenic construction.

Strap Hinge Strap hinges (Figure 8.42A) are composed of two tapering leaves that are joined by either a loose or a fixed pin. Strap hinge **leaves** vary in length from 2½ inches to 8 inches. Each leaf is drilled and countersunk to accept flat-head wood screws or stove bolts. They are commonly used to hinge stage doors by bending one leaf, attaching it to the depth piece of the casing, and attaching the straight leaf to the back of the door.

Leaf: The movable flap of a hinge.

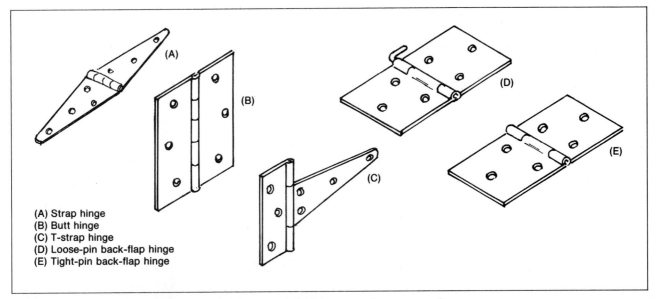

(A) Strap hinge
(B) Butt hinge
(C) T-strap hinge
(D) Loose-pin back-flap hinge
(E) Tight-pin back-flap hinge

Figure 8.42 Hinges.

BUTT HINGE Butt hinges (Figure 8.42B) are available in a wide variety of sizes and finishes, but they are all used for the same general purpose—hanging doors. They are composed of rectangular leaves joined by either a fixed or a loose pin. The holes are countersunk to accept flat-head wood screws or stove bolts.

T-STRAP HINGE A combination of one leaf from a strap hinge and an elongated leaf from a butt hinge, the T-strap hinge (Figure 8.42C) is used for hanging doors, gates, and box lids.

LOOSE-PIN BACK-FLAP HINGE Loose-pin back-flap hinges (Figure 8.42D) have square leaves in sizes ranging from approximately 1¼ to 2½ inches in width. The 1½- and 2-inch sizes are the most commonly used in scenic construction. These hinges can be used as "regular" hinges, but in scenic construction they are primarily used for joining scenery. The individual hinge leaves are attached to the separate pieces of scenery, and the pin is inserted to hold the unit together. The pin can be removed whenever it is necessary to break the unit into its component elements for shifting or storage.

TIGHT-PIN BACK-FLAP HINGE The tight-pin back-flap hinge (Figure 8.42E) is primarily used for the same purposes as its loose-pin companion whenever a permanent joining is desired. It is frequently used when two or more flats are joined to form an unbroken expanse of wall. Details of this type of wall construction are covered in Chapter 9, *Scenic Production Techniques.*

Stage Hardware

LASHING HARDWARE Lashing, the technique of joining flats together by a process that is closely akin to lacing your shoes, requires some very specific stage hardware. Lashing is done with a lash line, which is a piece of one-quarter-inch cotton clothesline approximately eighteen inches longer than the height of the flats being lashed together. The location of lashing hardware is illustrated in Figure 8.43. For safety purposes all lashing hardware should be attached to the flats with one-inch (No. 8 or 9) flat-head wood screws or stove bolts.

Figure 8.43
Locations for
lashing hardware.

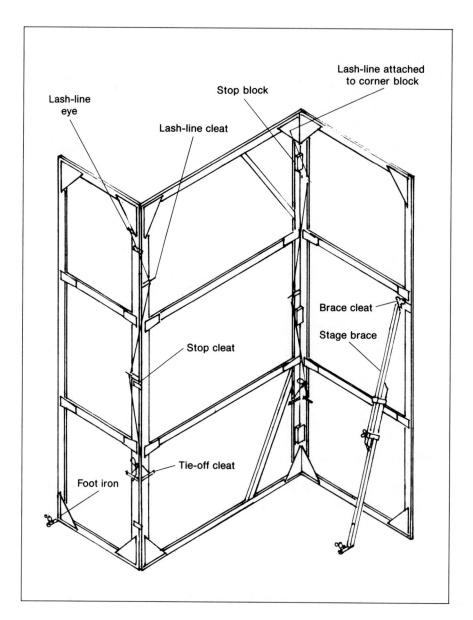

Lash-line
eye

Lash-line cleat

Stop block

Lash-line attached
to corner block

Brace cleat

Stage brace

Stop cleat

Tie-off cleat

Foot iron

LASH-LINE EYE The lash-line eye (Figure 8.44A) is used to attach the lash line to the flat. It is placed on the inside edge of the stile (the vertical framing member of a flat) just beneath the cornerblock.

LASH-LINE CLEAT The lash-line cleat (Figure 8.44B) is attached to the flat so its pointed end projects over the inside edge of the stile. The lash-line cleat is used to hold the rope in place so the flats can be lashed together.

LASH-LINE HOOK The lash-line hook (Figure 8.44C) serves the same purpose as the cleat. However, it is used when the construction of the flat prevents the use of a cleat, as when the stile is extra wide or is next to an opening in the flat (window, doorway) or some type of projection. It can also be used in place of a tie-off cleat.

TIE-OFF CLEAT Tie-off cleats (Figure 8.44D) are used in pairs approximately thirty inches above the stage level to tie off the line after the flats have been lashed together. Regular cleats or hooks can also be used for this purpose.

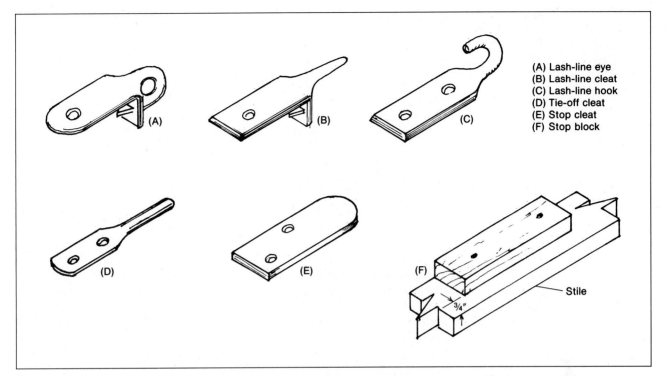

(A) Lash-line eye
(B) Lash-line cleat
(C) Lash-line hook
(D) Tie-off cleat
(E) Stop cleat
(F) Stop block

Stile

¾"

Figure 8.44
Lashing hardware.

STOP CLEAT Stop cleats (Figure 8.44E) are attached to the back of the flats with their ends projecting three-quarters of an inch past the outside edge of the stiles to prevent the flats from slipping past each other when they are being lashed together in an outside corner configuration.

STOP BLOCK Although it is not an actual piece of lashing hardware, a stop block (Figure 8.44F) is a small piece of scrap wood that is attached to the **stile** of a flat to prevent flats from slipping past each other when they are being lashed together in an inside corner configuration.

FLYING HARDWARE Several pieces of stage hardware aid in flying scenery and stabilizing flown scenery. For reasons of safety all flying hardware should be attached with bolts (or screws if the scenery is reasonably light).

HANGER IRON The hanger iron (Figure 8.45A) is a metal strap with a D ring at the top. It is attached to the stile at the top of the flat in a position that keeps the D ring hidden behind the top of the flat. The hanger iron, also called a top hanger iron, is used in conjunction with a bottom hanger iron for flying heavy scenery, but it can be used by itself for flying lightweight pieces.

BOTTOM HANGER IRON The bottom hanger iron (Figure 8.45B) is a metal strap with a hooked foot at the bottom and a D ring at the top. The bottom hanger iron, also called the hook hanger iron, is attached so the bottom of the flat rests on the hooked foot. The flying line is attached to the D ring so the flat will, in effect, be picked up from the bottom or lifted under compression.

When rigging a heavy or tall flat for flying, use the bottom hanger iron in conjunction with a hanger iron. The hanger iron is attached to the top of the flat in a line directly above the bottom hanger iron. The flying line is fed through the D ring of the hanger iron and attached to the D ring of the bottom hanger iron. If the flat is very small, a screw eye can be substituted for the top hanger iron.

Stile: A vertical side member of a flat.

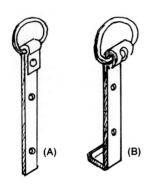

(A) Hanger iron
(B) Bottom hanger iron
(C) Ceiling plate

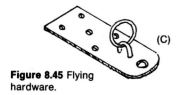

Figure 8.45 Flying hardware.

Dowel: A short cylinder of hardwood (usually birch).

CEILING PLATE The ceiling plate (Figure 8.45C) is bolted to primary structural members of the ceiling to provide a means of attaching the flying lines to the ceiling.

BRACING HARDWARE Most flats need some type of external support to be able to stand up. If the flats don't need support to stand, they will probably need some type of bracing to prevent them from wiggling. The normal positions for placing these pieces of hardware are shown in Figure 8.43.

STAGE BRACE The stage brace is the mainstay of scenic bracing. It is an adjustable wooden (Figure 8.46A) or aluminum (Figure 8.46B) pole that can be quickly attached to a brace cleat on the back of a flat. The other end of the stage brace is secured to the stage floor by one of the several methods to be described.

BRACE CLEAT Attached to the stile of a flat with the end projecting past the inside edge of the stile, a brace cleat (Figure 8.46C) provides a point of attachment between the scenery and the stage brace.

RIGID FOOT IRON The rigid foot iron (Figure 8.46D) is an L-shaped piece of metal. The long leg is attached to the bottom of the scenery with screws or bolts. The horizontal foot sticks out and is secured to the stage floor with a stage screw inserted through the ring at the end of the foot.

HINGED FOOT IRON The hinged foot iron is similar to the rigid foot iron. Its horizontal foot (Figure 8.46E) is hinged to fold out of the way when the scenic unit is being shifted or flown.

STAGE SCREW The stage screw is a very coarse-threaded, large, hand-driven screw used to anchor a foot iron or the foot of a stage brace to the wooden stage floor. Although stage screws (Figure 8.46F) provide an effective means of anchoring stage braces, they leave ragged holes and splinters wherever they are used.

IMPROVED STAGE SCREW The improved stage screw (Figure 8.46G) doesn't tear up the stage floor nearly so much as its unrefined cousin. A steel plug, threaded on the outside and inside, is inserted into an appropriately sized hole that has been drilled into the stage floor. The improved stage screw screws into the plug. When the production is over, the plug can be removed from the floor, and the hole patched by gluing a small piece of hardwood **dowel** into the hole.

FLOOR PLATE It is rather difficult to use either a stage screw or improved stage screw if your stage floor is concrete or if the building owner or administrator has said, "Thou shalt not put any holes in the stage floor." Fortunately, all is not lost, because a floor plate (Figure 8.46H) can come to the rescue.

The lower end of the stage brace is secured to the floor plate, which is a block of wood with a nonskid material (foam, rubber) attached to the bottom. Sandbags or counterweights are piled on the plate to anchor it to the floor.

S HOOK Also known as a latch keeper, the S hook (Figure 8.46I) is used to hold stiffening battens on the back of wall units that are made up of two or more flats. Normally used on flats that must have the stiffening battens removed for shifting, S hooks can be purchased or made in the shop from ⅛- or ³⁄₃₂-by-1-inch mild steel strap.

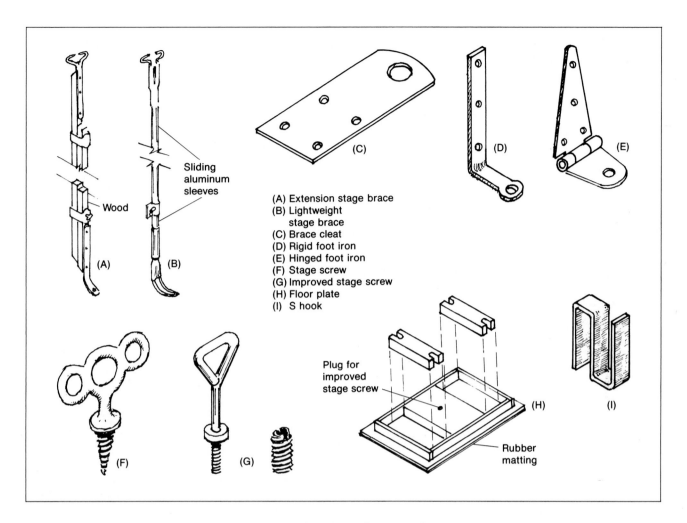

Figure 8.46 Bracing hardware.

(A) Extension stage brace
(B) Lightweight stage brace
(C) Brace cleat
(D) Rigid foot iron
(E) Hinged foot iron
(F) Stage screw
(G) Improved stage screw
(H) Floor plate
(I) S hook

Sliding aluminum sleeves

Wood

Plug for improved stage screw

Rubber matting

MISCELLANEOUS HARDWARE There are several additional pieces of stage hardware that cannot be neatly categorized because their use is not necessarily limited to a single purpose.

CORNER PLATE The corner plate (Figure 8.47A) is an **L**-shaped piece of one-sixteenth-inch galvanized steel, available in a variety of sizes. Each leg is pre-drilled, or tapped, for use with No. 8 or No. 9 flat-head wood screws. Corner plates are used to reinforce the corners of doors, windows, door or window casings, and picture frames and in similar applications.

TEE PLATE Made of the same galvanized steel as the corner plate, the tee plate (Figure 8.47B) can be used as a substitute for keystones or in similar applications.

PICTURE HOOK AND EYE Picture hooks and eyes (Figure 8.47C) are shop-made pieces ($3/32$-by-$3/4$-inch or 1-inch mild steel strap) that facilitate the rapid hanging and removal of decorative draperies on a set. They are used in sets of two or more. The sockets are attached to the face of the flat with screws or bolts, and the hooks are similarly attached to the drapery rod.

CASKET LOCK The casket lock (Figure 8.47D) is a heavy-duty hidden lock that is used to hold platforms together or in similar applications. Its use as a platform lock is detailed in Chapter 9, *Scenic Production Techniques*.

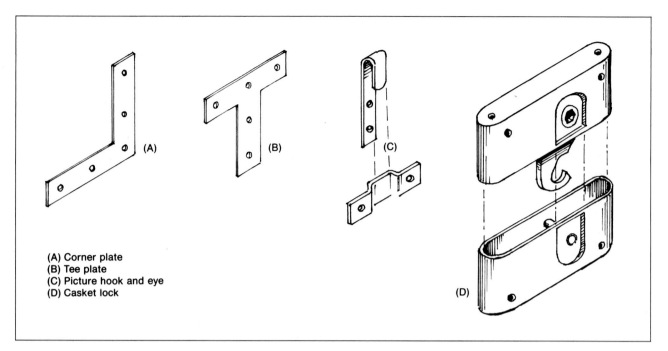

(A) Corner plate
(B) Tee plate
(C) Picture hook and eye
(D) Casket lock

Figure 8.47
Miscellaneous
stage hardware.

CASTERS Casters come in a bewildering array of sizes, styles, and load ratings. To be useful for stage purposes casters should meet a few specific requirements. They should have hard rubber tires, should have a load rating of at least three hundred pounds, and should be sturdily constructed. Although stage casters can be purchased from theatrical equipment supply houses, it is sometimes advantageous to buy your casters at a local building equipment supply firm.

Swivel casters (Figure 8.48A) are mounted on a bearing plate that allows the wheel to pivot around a vertical axis. To turn easily under a load the pivot should be supported by ball bearings. For use with stage wagons the overall height of the caster should be four to five inches. The tires on a swivel caster should be made of rubber to reduce the rumble that inevitably accompanies the movement of a stage platform. The wheel of the caster should be metal, and it should have some type of bearing (ball, tube) to decrease the friction between the axle and the wheel. The axle should be removable, so a metal strap can be attached to the axle and the platform to lock the swivel caster in a stationary position. Some swivel casters are equipped with built-in pins that can be used to hold the caster stationary.

Rigid casters (Figure 8.48B) are permanently locked in position so they cannot pivot. The specifications for the swivel caster regarding the structure of the tire, wheel, axle, height, and load rating are applicable to the stationary caster.

Furniture casters do not have the same rigorous specifications as stage casters. They should be sturdily constructed, but because they are often seen by the audience, they need to look as if they belong to the period being depicted in the production. Furniture casters can be purchased at furniture and hardware stores.

A revolutionary type of compressed-air lifter literally floats heavy objects on a thin cushion of air. The *air caster* or *air bearing* (Figure 8.48C) is an inflatable, saucer-shaped disk of rubberized fabric. The air caster works as follows: compressed air inflates the doughnut-shaped bearing to raise the load; the compressed air continues to flow, creating an air cushion under the bearing. Three or four air casters are needed to raise an object. Although they are

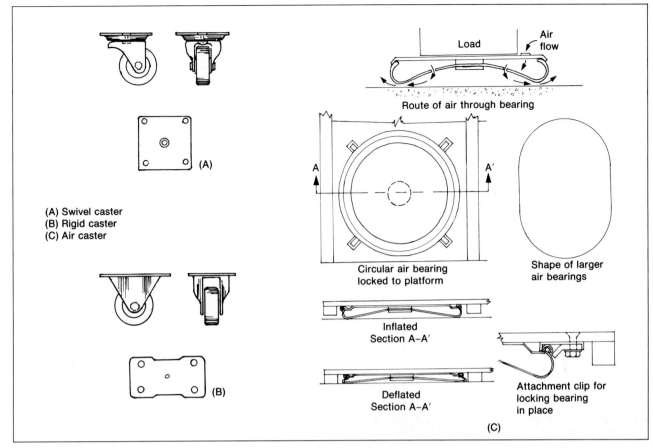

(A) Swivel caster
(B) Rigid caster
(C) Air caster

Load

Air flow

Route of air through bearing

A   A'

Circular air bearing locked to platform

Shape of larger air bearings

Inflated Section A–A'

Deflated Section A–A'

Attachment clip for locking bearing in place

(C)

Figure 8.48 Types of casters.

available in a variety of diameters ranging from one to four feet, the one-foot size, which is load rated at approximately two thousand pounds, is adequate for almost any theatrical use. A drawback to the air caster is the noise of the compressor needed to supply the low-compression, high-volume air. The noise problem can be solved, however, if the compressor (a shop vacuum cleaner works well) is located in an adjacent space (not on stage) and air hoses are run to the casters.

ROPE, CABLE, AND WIRE

Several types of rope are used for a variety of purposes in the theatre.

Manila Rope

Manila is the primary type of rope used for raising and suspending loads (scenery, equipment) in the theatre. It is used as the operating line for counterweight systems and for rope set (sandbag counterweight) systems. Manila rope is strong and flexible, but it is affected by humidity, which causes it to stretch when the weather is damp and shrink when it becomes drier. Table 8.3 provides some information about the relative strengths of differing diameters of manila.

You will probably notice that there is a discrepancy between the information in this table and general guideline of using the ten-to-one safety margin recommended in the accompanying box. The information in this table is calculated for unused manila rope, whereas the safety factor is a "guesstimate" that takes into account the wide range of rope types, uses, and conditions.

Traveler: Any drapery that moves horizontally; generally, travelers are composed of two sections of stage drapes that split in the middle, with each section retracting in an opposite offstage direction.

Table 8.3
Manila Rope Data

Diameter	Feet per Pound	New Rope Breaking Point (Pounds)	Working Load (Pounds)
¼ inch	50	540	54
⅜ inch	24	1215	122
½ inch	13	2385	264
⅝ inch	7.5	3960	496
¾ inch	6	4860	695

Sisal Rope

Sisal looks like manila, but the fibers are much stiffer, and the rope deteriorates rapidly when subject to the sharp-angle bending caused by running it over pulleys and tying it in knots. For these reasons it should not be used as a substitute for manila.

Clothesline

Clothesline is a braided cotton rope that should never be used to raise a load over the stage. It simply isn't strong enough for that type of use. It can and should, however, be used as the operating line on **travelers** and as the line for lashing flats together.

Nylon Rope

While very strong, nylon and other synthetic ropes generally stretch too much or are too expensive to be used for most applications in the theatre.

Monofilament Line

Commonly sold in sporting goods stores as fishing line, monofilament line is basically a single-strand plastic string. It is transparent, comes in a variety of breaking strengths ranging from two to over one hundred pounds, and is used whenever an "invisible" or "trick" line is needed.

Aircraft Cable

Aircraft cable is frequently used in the theatre, because it is very flexible and very strong. One-eighth-inch aircraft cable is often used for flying heavy stage scenery because its breaking strength is approximately one ton.

SAFETY TIP

Rope

Regardless of the type of rope being used, there are several general safety rules. Any rope that is suspending a load over the stage should have a breaking strength at least ten times the weight of the load that it is required to bear. Any rope should be carefully inspected before use—at least annually and more frequently if the rope is part of a permanent system (counterweight, rope set and the like) or is in constant use—for signs of abrasion, cuts, gouges, seriously worn or broken fibers, discoloration, kinks, or twists. If any of these conditions is evident, the rope should be replaced. Any rope used as the operating line for a counterweight system should be replaced at least every three years, even if it appears to be in good condition. The strain that has been placed on the rope during those years will have broken down the fibers enough to significantly decrease its effective working strength.

Wire

Wire is used for a variety of purposes in both scenic and property construction.

STOVEPIPE WIRE Soft iron stovepipe wire is approximately one-sixteenth of an inch in diameter and is generally colored black. It is quite flexible but has very little tensile strength. It is normally used for tying or wiring things together. It shouldn't be used for flying scenery, because it isn't strong enough to support a load. Stovepipe wire of slightly greater diameter is known as baling wire. Soft iron, or stovepipe, wire is also manufactured with a galvanized finish to prevent rust.

PIANO WIRE Piano wire is made from spring steel and is frequently used to fly scenery because of its remarkable tensile strength in comparison with its diameter. Care should be taken to avoid making sharp bends in piano wire, because kinking greatly reduces its strength.

BLOCK AND TACKLE

The term *block and tackle* refers generically to arrangements of pulleys and ropes that provide a mechanical advantage. A pulley has one specific job; it changes the direction of travel of the rope passing through it. An ideal pulley accomplishes this task with no friction and little noise. Unfortunately, this ideal pulley doesn't exist. All pulleys create friction and make noise. But, as in all things, some pulleys are better than others. The small galvanized pulleys found in a hardware store can be used for lightweight applications such as the curtain pull for some decorative set drapes, but they are rather noisy. A better solution can be found in the marine hardware section of a boat supply shop. These stores usually stock high-quality pulleys that are very quiet and have relatively little friction loss.

For heavy-duty use the best pulleys are available from scenic supply houses or, sometimes, from well-stocked hardware stores. These pulleys have wooden bodies, have well-matched sheaves (wheels) and axles, and are relatively quiet in operation. Three common tackle rigs were illustrated and explained in Chapter 4.

SAFETY EQUIPMENT

There is a variety of protective equipment for working in the shop. The specific device depends on the materials with which you are working.

Clear-lensed goggles, safety glasses, and face shields will protect your eyes from flying wood and metal chips as well as chemical splashes. Specially tinted eye shields such as welding goggles or (preferably) welding masks need to be worn when welding.

A **dust mask** should be worn when working with any material that produces dust. A **respirator,** equipped with an appropriate type of filter, should be worn any time that you are working with materials that produce fumes or vapors.

Proper hand protection is necessary to prevent possible injury: chemically resistant rubberized gloves for working with chemicals; heavy leather gloves

Dust mask: A device covering the nose and mouth that filters particulate matter from the air.

Respirator: A mask covering the nose and mouth that filters out gases as well as particulate matter.

for welding; heat-resistant gloves (not asbestos) for handling heated objects; and regular light leather or cotton work gloves for handling manila rope such as that found on the operating lines of the counterweight system.

When working with noise-producing objects, wear hearing protectors such as noise-abatement earmuffs or earplugs. When working with heavy objects such as metal pipe, tubing, or sheet or when moving or building large stage platforms, you should wear steel-toed shoes or steel shoe caps. When there is any danger of something being dropped from above the stage floor, all personnel should wear protective headgear, such as a plastic helmet that meets or exceeds the minimum federal standards.

This chapter has outlined the tools and materials used in the construction of scenery and properties. Chapter 9, *Scenic Production Techniques,* will discuss basic techniques of scenic construction, and Chapter 11, *Stage Properties,* will take up some of the more specialized techniques and materials used to make stage properties.

9

Scenic Production Techniques

Playwrights have set their plays in almost every imaginable environment. Thousands of plays have been set in ordinary rooms in homes or buildings, and thousands more have been set in representational settings like caves, mountaintops, river beds, lakesides, wheat fields, war zones, and even the gondolas of hot air balloons. Nonrepresentational scenery can be, and frequently is, beautifully imaginative, evocative, and representative of the emotional content of the play. Whether wheat field or moonscape, representational or nonrepresentational, the setting must work as conceived by the scenic designer and director—and it's the technical director's job to see that it does.

Technical production refers to the very broad field concerned with the processes and techniques used in making this setting work. Specifically, the field encompasses the construction and painting of the scenery and properties, the assembly of the set or sets onstage, the shifting of those sets and props during the production, and the tools that are used to accomplish those tasks. The specific organization and assigned responsibilities vary considerably depending on the type of producing unit.

In the Broadway theatre the personnel are hired for a single production. After the producer has approved the construction bids, the designs are constructed and finished by independent professional scenic and property studios. During construction and painting the scenic designer is in frequent contact with the scene shop foreman to answer artistic and practical questions about the scenery. When the scenery is completed, it is moved from the studio to the theatre and set up on the stage. This **load-in** is carried out by union stagehands under the supervision of the production's stage manager. The scenic designer and the stage manager work together to choreograph any scene

Technical production: All organizational and procedural aspects of the construction, painting, and operation of scenery and properties.

Load-in: The moving of scenery and associated equipment into the theatre and the positioning of them on the stage.

The production calendar (see Figure 1.8) helps the technical director keep track of progress on the various productions. It specifies pertinent information (tryouts, design due dates, construction and painting schedules, rehearsals, and performances) for every play being produced by the theatre during the season. It also provides a visual reference that shows at a glance the status of each production. The production calendar is usually developed by the technical director in conjunction with the producer or managing and artistic directors with input from the resident directors and designers.

shifts, and the stage manager is responsible for supervising the actual work of the union crews that will be shifting the scenery.

The Broadway theatre's single-production concept is the exception rather than the rule in the American theatre. Most theatre in the United States is produced on a limited-run, multiple-production basis by colleges, universities, community theatres, and regional professional theatre groups. Almost all of these theatres produce three or more productions a year. They are almost always working on more than one production at any given time. This situation creates a definite need for some very specific organization to keep all of the production activity flowing smoothly. The primary organizer of the technical aspects of production is the technical director. Probably the most important skills that the TD must possess are the ability to effectively organize time and resources and the ability to manage people. The technical director is an expediter. He or she needs to know the current status of the work being produced by every member of the production team. This task is compounded because most technical directors are keeping track of two, three, or more productions simultaneously.

The technical director's work on scenic and property construction cannot really begin until the designer provides plans (ground plan, front elevations,

SCENIC CONSTRUCTION PRIORITIES

It takes a tremendous number of hours to construct the scenery for even a simple production. The following list provides a construction sequence that makes very efficient use of available construction time.

1. Build practical elements of the set that will be needed by the actors in the early rehearsals.

2. Build and hang flying units, including any masking, that either will be flown over the set or will use counterweighted battens hanging above the set.

3. Build anything that will have a complicated or time-consuming paint job.

4. Base the construction schedule for any remaining scenic elements on the complexity of the item. The least complex scenic elements, such as flats, should be built last.

5. Allow some time at the end of the construction sequence for adjustments, repairs, and the inevitable changes that will be made in the set.

Rear elevations are scale mechanical drawings that show the back of the flats depicted on the front elevations. These drawings:

1. show the construction details of the framework of the flats.
2. indicate which flats are to be joined to form wall units.
3. show the unusual construction challenges.

In professional scene shops the foreman is responsible for drawing the rear elevations. In practice very few are drawn, because the carpenters working in these scenic studios are very knowledgeable about construction methods and techniques.

In educational theatres, however, the construction crews are usually students who are just learning how to build scenery. Rear elevations should be drawn to provide the student carpenters with all of the information needed to build the scenery.

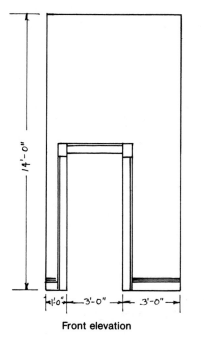

Front elevation

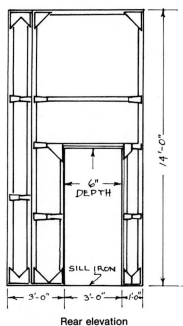

Rear elevation

Rear elevations show the framework of a flat.

detail sheets, functional models, painter's elevations) for the production. After studying the plans the technical director draws any necessary rear elevations or construction drawings that will facilitate the building of the scenery and props.

After drawing the rear elevations the TD needs to order construction materials. At this same time he or she also creates a construction calendar. This calendar specifies the amount of time scheduled for the construction, painting, and assembling of the individual elements of the sets.

SCENIC CONSTRUCTION TECHNIQUES

Although the overall construction plan, as well as the specific methods used to build each piece of scenery, should be guided by the basic tenets of the design

The complexity of the construction calendar depends on the complexity of the play. A single-set production will not be so difficult or time consuming as a multiset musical. The following construction calendar shows a reasonable work schedule for a production of a single-set show.

February	27	Receive designer's plans. Begin analysis of the plans. Order any special building materials. (This calendar assumes that the theatre shop maintains an inventory of standard building materials in the scene shop at all times. If all building materials are ordered on a per-show basis, additional time will be needed at the beginning of the calendar to allow for their delivery.)
	28	Begin drafting working drawings.
	29	Finish drafting working drawings.
March	1	Begin construction: platforms, properties.
	2	Construction: platforms, stairs, properties.
	3–4	Weekend (no work)
	5	Construction: platforms, stairs, properties. Hang flying units and masking above area occupied by the set.
	6	Construction: same as preceding day. Hang and circuit lights above set.
	7	Construction: same as preceding day.
	8	Construction: same as preceding day. Erect platforms; begin platform facings.
	9	Construction: platforms, stairs complete. Build facings, railings.
	10–11	Weekend
	12	Construction: same as preceding day. Begin painting offstage. Hang lights.
	13	Construction: same as preceding day.
	14	Construction: same as preceding day.
	15	Construction: major construction complete. Paint floor. Build and paint props.
	16	Construction: same as preceding day.
	17–18	Weekend
	19	Construction: all scenic construction complete. Focus lights. Paint props.
	20	Construction: same as preceding day.
	21	Construction: all set and prop construction and painting complete. Lighting rehearsal.
	22	Touch-up and detail work. Decorate set. Adjust lights. Load in sound.
	23	Detail work. Final property adjustments.
	24	Technical rehearsal: make necessary adjustments.
	25	Sunday (no work)
	26	Dress rehearsal: make necessary adjustments.
	27	Dress rehearsal: make necessary adjustments.
	28	Dress rehearsal: make necessary adjustments.
	29	Opening of play.

process (see Chapter 2), some fairly standardized construction techniques are used to fabricate stage scenery.

Woodworking

Wood is used extensively for building two- and three-dimensional scenery. It is relatively inexpensive and can be worked easily with a variety of tools, which were described in Chapter 8.

Various wood joints are used. The following are most common in scenic and property construction.

BUTT JOINT The butt joint is made when two pieces of wood are cut square at the end and fitted together, as shown in Figure 9.1A–D. Because the area of contact between the two pieces of wood is relatively small, a butt joint isn't very strong unless some type of reinforcement is applied.

BATTENED BUTT JOINT A battened butt joint (Figure 9.1E) is created when two pieces of stock lumber are butted end to end, and an eighteen- to twenty-four-inch piece of lumber of similar width is attached directly over the joint with glue and screws.

Specialized battened butt joints (Figures 9.1F and 9.1G) are used in flat

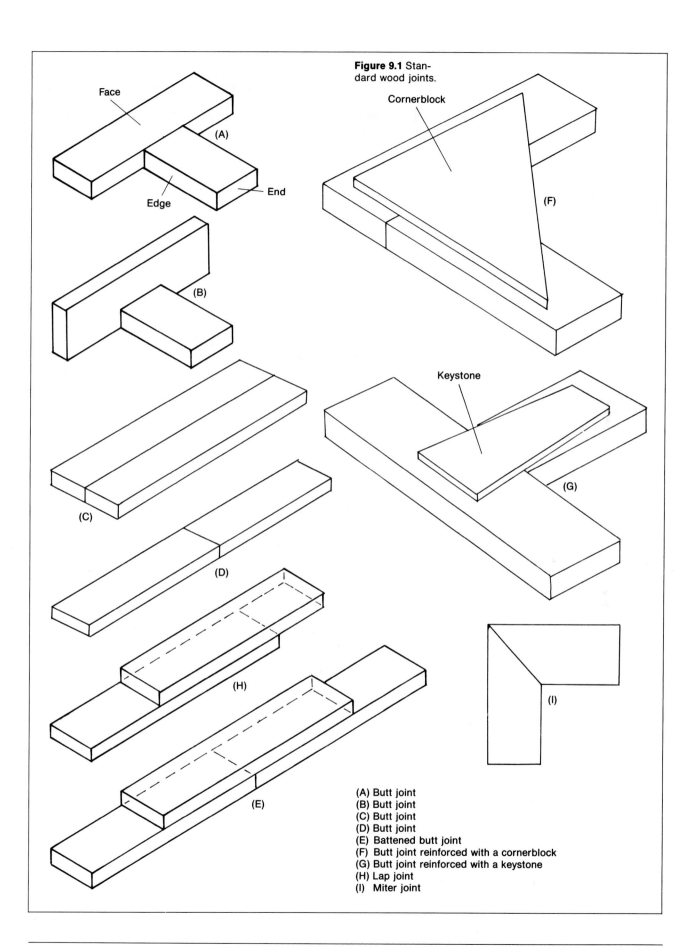

Face

(A)

Edge

End

Figure 9.1 Standard wood joints.

Cornerblock

(F)

(B)

(C)

(D)

Keystone

(G)

(H)

(E)

(I)

(A) Butt joint
(B) Butt joint
(C) Butt joint
(D) Butt joint
(E) Battened butt joint
(F) Butt joint reinforced with a cornerblock
(G) Butt joint reinforced with a keystone
(H) Lap joint
(I) Miter joint

The Scene Shop

Any workplace that uses electricity, flammable and toxic materials, and tools capable of cutting, gouging, and sawing is an inherently dangerous environment. With a healthy dose of common sense and a few safety rules, however, working in the scene shop can be safe, efficient, and enjoyable.

1. Wear clothing suited to the work: long pants, short- or long-sleeve shirt, and hard-toe, hard-sole shoes (not sandals or sneakers). Clothing should be reasonably close fitting. Don't wear flowing robes—they might get caught in power equipment.

2. Tie back, put under a cap, or otherwise contain long hair so it won't get caught in a power tool.

3. Always get instructions before operating any power or hand tool. Be sure you know what you're doing before you do it.

4. Pay attention to what you are doing. Don't operate any tool unless you are giving it your undivided attention. Watch your work area for potential hazards such as wood with protruding nails and potential fire or electrical hazards. Either correct the hazard (if you know how) or report it to your supervisor.

5. Keep your work space clean. If the shop is kept neat, clean, and organized, accidents are reduced and you can find the tools and supplies you need.

6. Know where the first aid materials are kept. Disinfect all cuts and splinters and bandage even minor cuts. Report all accidents to your supervisor.

7. When working with materials that emit dust or fumes make sure that the work area is well ventilated and that you wear an appropriate mask.

construction. Cornerblocks of one-quarter-inch plywood are used to reinforce the butt joints at the corners of the flats. Keystones, also made from one-quarter-inch plywood, are used to reinforce the butt joints made for any internal bracing on the flats.

LAP JOINT A lap joint (Figure 9.1H) is probably the simplest of all joints. Two pieces of lumber are joined face to face and fastened together. This type of self-reinforcing joint is used when attaching legs to platforms.

MITER JOINT A miter joint (Figure 9.1I) is a type of butt joint. The only difference is that the wood being joined is cut on an angle instead of square. A miter joint is used when making **irregular flats** and picture frames.

DADO JOINT A dado joint (Figure 9.2A) is made by cutting a slot across the face of one piece of lumber to receive the edge of another. The slot is cut only halfway through the depth of the lumber. Fastened with glue and nails, the dado joint is frequently used for shelving and similar applications.

The dado slot can be cut with several passes of a regular blade in a radial-arm saw or with a dado blade. The width of the kerf on the dado blade can be adjusted so the dado slot can be made in a single pass.

HALVED JOINT A halved joint (Figures 9.2B and C), also called a halved lap joint, is made by removing half of the thickness of each piece of lumber from the area to be joined, so the thickness of the finished joint will be no greater than the stock from which it is made. This is a very strong joint when secured with glue and nails, screws, or staples, and it can be cut relatively easily with a dado blade. It is used in making the **muntins** and **mullions** of windows and in similar applications.

NOTCHED JOINT A notched joint (Figure 9.2D) is created when the edge or face of one board is inserted into a notch cut in another. The size of the notch

Irregular flat: A flat having nonsquare corners.

Muntin: A horizontal crossbar in a window.

Mullion: A vertical crossbar in a window.

CHAPTER 9: SCENIC PRODUCTION TECHNIQUES

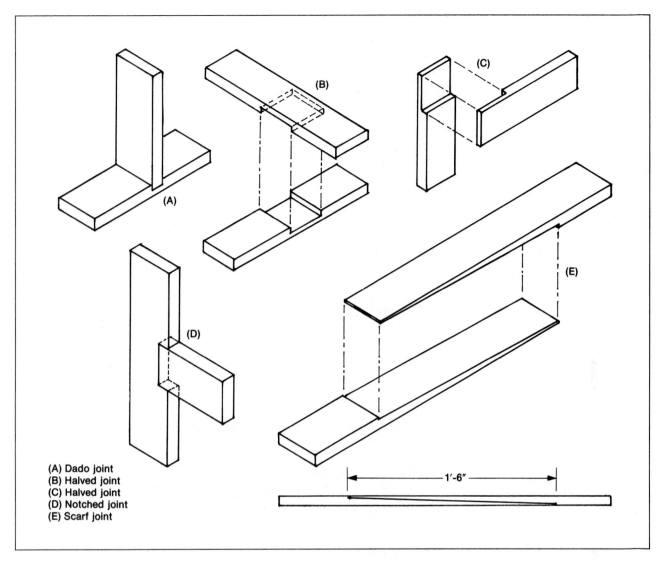

(A) Dado joint
(B) Halved joint
(C) Halved joint
(D) Notched joint
(E) Scarf joint

1'-6"

is determined by the width and thickness of the piece that the notch will receive. The notched joint is used for shelving and similar applications.

Figure 9.2 Specialty wood joints.

SCARF JOINT The scarf joint (Figure 9.2E) is used to make one long board from two short ones with no increase in the thickness of the lumber. The angled surface of the joint should be at least eighteen inches long. It can be cut using a band saw (with a wide, newly sharpened blade to rough-cut the diagonal cut). A plane or power sander should be used to smooth the surface of the cut so the faces of the joint will be **flush** when joined. Each face is coated with glue, and the unit is clamped together and fastened with screws or bolts and allowed to dry.

MORTISE AND TENON JOINT A square hole, the mortise, can be chiseled into one of the pieces to be joined. This is much easier than it sounds if a **mortise drill bit,** which drills square holes, is used. The other piece of wood has the edges cut back to create the tenon. The tenon must snuggly fit into the mortise. The mortise and tenon joint (Figure 9.3A and B) is normally secured only with glue.

An open mortise and tenon joint has the tenon exposed; a closed mortise and tenon joint looks from the outside just like a butt joint. Because of their

Flush: Smooth, level, even.

Mortise drill bit: A drill bit housed inside of a square hollow chisel; used with a drill press to make square holes; available in a variety of diameters.

Figure 9.3 Internally supported wood joints.

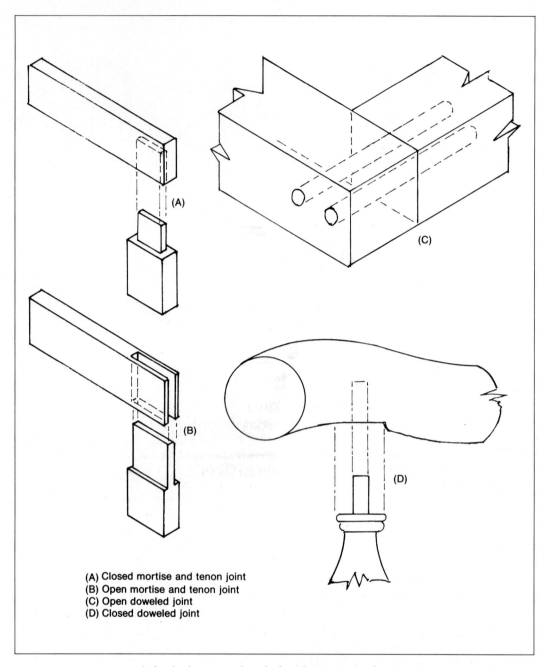

(A) Closed mortise and tenon joint
(B) Open mortise and tenon joint
(C) Open doweled joint
(D) Closed doweled joint

strength both the opened and closed mortise and tenon joints are used extensively in furniture construction.

DOWELED JOINT A doweled joint is a butt joint that is reinforced with small pieces of hardwood dowel. An open doweled joint (Figure 9.3C) has the end of the dowel exposed; a closed doweled joint (Figure 9.3D) shows no outside evidence of its existence.

Welding

Welding is the process of fusing metal by heating the pieces being joined to their melting temperature and inducing the metal to flow together before it cools. During this high-temperature process a certain amount of the metal is vaporized or otherwise lost. The **filler rod** is used to replace the lost metal.

Filler rod: Metal piece, of the same composition as material being welded, used to replace the metal lost during the welding process or to fill a hole or groove in the work.

Welding

There are some basic safety rules for welding:

1. Use appropriate eye protection. Welding produces a very intense light and a shower of sparks. Both can severely damage your eyes. Wear welding goggles (for oxyacetylene welding only) or a welding mask (for either arc or oxyacetylene welding). The goggles or mask should be equipped with lenses of appropriate darkness for the type of welding you are doing. Arc welding requires the darkest lenses; oxyacetylene requires only slightly less dark lenses; brazing requires the least lens darkness.

2. To protect your body from the heat and sparks, wear leather welding gloves with gauntlets, a long-sleeve work shirt made of denim or similar heavy material, long pants, and leather boots or shoes.

3. A leather welding jacket and apron will provide even better protection from the sparks. This additional safeguard is essential when working with a cutting torch, because the stronger flame can create heavy splatters of molten metal.

SURFACE PREPARATION Before welding, the surface of the metal must be cleaned of all oil, grease, paint, rust, and any other contaminants. This can be done by polishing the welding zone with a wire brush, by sanding, by grinding, or by cleaning with commercial chemical removers.

WELDING TECHNIQUES Several welding techniques have been developed to use with the various types of welder (see Chapter 8 for a description of welding equipment).

OXYACETYLENE WELDING Oxyacetylene welding uses the **two-handed welding** technique. With this method the welder holds the torch or welding handle in one hand and the filler rod in the other. As the flame melts the pieces being joined, the operator feeds the filler rod into the welding zone. The rod melts, flows into the joint, and replaces the lost metal. The filler rod is frequently dipped into flux to facilitate the flowing together of the molten metal from the rod and the materials being welded.

In oxyacetylene welding (Figure 9.4) the strength of the weld is dependent on a chemically neutral flame. This neutral flame is achieved through a proper mix of the oxygen and acetylene gas. After the torch flame has been lit (using acetylene gas only), oxygen is introduced to the mix. When the oxygen is first introduced a small white cone appears at the base of, and inside, the flame. At first this cone is rather long. Sometimes it is a double cone. As more oxygen is added, the cone gets smaller. A neutral flame is produced when this white cone is short and slightly rounded. An oxidizing flame, which will burn the molten metal, is produced when more oxygen is added to a neutral flame.

A cutting torch (see Chapter 8) is equipped with a lever-actuated valve that introduces additional oxygen to the flame, creating an oxidizing flame. This flame burns the metal, resulting in a cut.

ARC WELDING The arc welder utilizes electricity to generate an **arc** that has a temperature of approximately thirteen thousand degrees Fahrenheit. This extremely high heat almost instantaneously melts most common types of metal.

To use an arc welder the ground cable from the welding machine is attached to the work, effectively turning the work into an electrode. When a flux-coated **welding rod,** which is connected to the power side of the weld-

Two-handed welding: A technique in which the torch or welding handle is held in one hand and the filler rod in the other.

Arc: An electric current that leaps the gap between two closely placed electrodes.

Welding rod: A rod, usually covered with flux, that serves as the positive electrode in arc welding.

Figure 9.4 Oxy-acetylene welding technique. For portability the oxygen (tall) and acetylene tanks are normally secured to a rolling cart (A). To light the welding torch, close the valves on the handle of the torch, then turn on the oxygen (B) to approximately 30–35 pounds and the acetylene (C) to 5–7 pounds. (The pressure settings will vary with the composition and thickness of metals.) Open the acetylene valve on the torch handle and light the torch (D). Adjust the acetylene flame until the base of the flame just touches the tip of the torch (E), then slowly open the oxygen valve on the torch and adjust the flame until the small inner cone at the base of the flame is approximately ¼" long (F). Be sure to wear protective clothing and use dark goggles or a welding mask (G) when you weld.

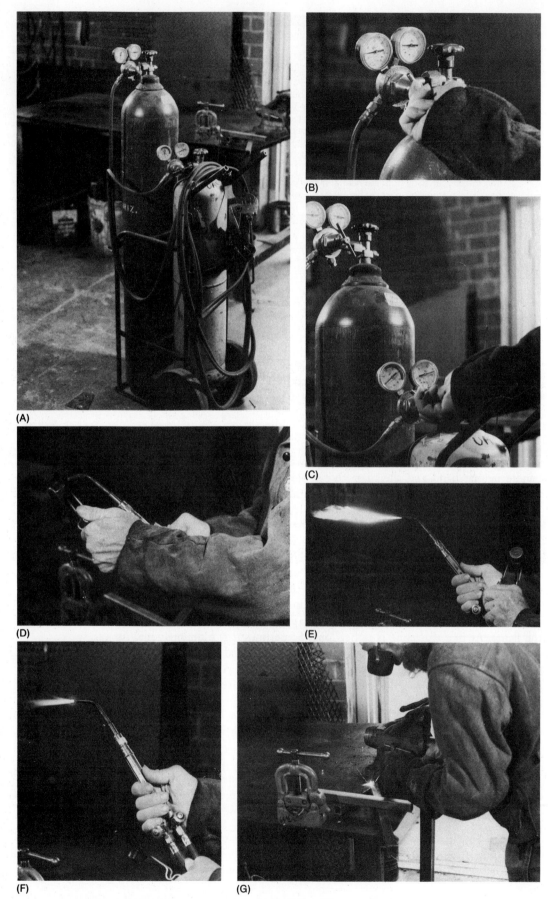

(A)

(B)

(C)

(D)

(E)

(F)

(G)

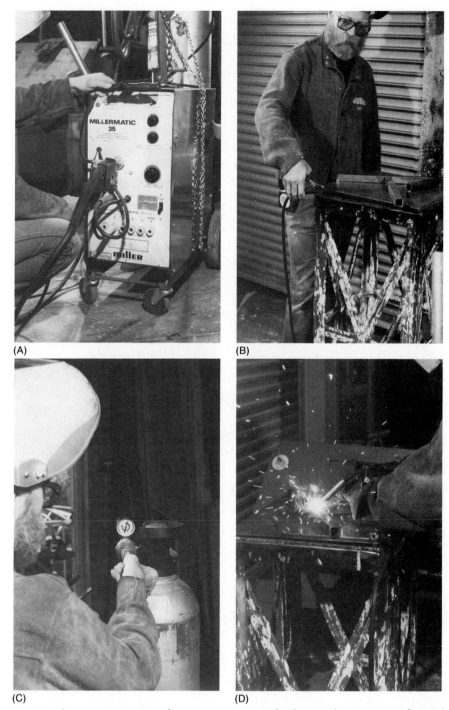

(A)

(B)

(C)

(D)

Figure 9.5 MIG (metal inert gas) welding technique. (A) Adjust the power setting of the welder to suit the composition and thickness of the metal being welded (consult the welding machine's instruction book). (B) Attach the ground cable to the welding table or the work. (C) Turn on the gas (carbon dioxide or argon) to 5–9 pounds (consult the welder's instruction book for appropriate setting for your specific equipment). (D) Bring the welding wire close to the welding zone, press the trigger, and weld. Be sure to wear appropriate protective clothing.

ing machine, comes into close proximity with the work, an arc is formed across the gap. The resultant heat melts the metal, and the weld is made. The electrode, which also acts as a filler rod, is consumed in the welding process. Since the welding handle is held with only one hand, the process is called **single-hand welding.**

The MIG (metal inert gas) welder (discussed in Chapter 8) is another single-hand arc welder. It differs from the arc welder in that the welding handle focuses a flow of inert gas on the welding zone (as shown in Figure 9.5) as the weld is being made, and it has a wire electrode. The inert gas reduces **oxidation,** which can substantially weaken the weld. The thin wire electrode of the MIG welder is automatically fed to the handle from a spool

Single-hand welding: A technique in which one hand holds the welding handle and the other hand is not used.

Oxidation: A chemical reaction between the metal and air that forms a very thin, discolored "skin" over the metal; this skin effectively prevents heat transfer and reduces the strength and conductivity of the joint.

in the housing of the power unit. A flux coating for the wire electrode isn't used because of the oxidation-reducing properties of the shielding gas.

When equipped with a steel wire electrode and carbon dioxide or argon gas, the MIG welder does an excellent job of welding steel. It can be used for welding aluminum if aluminum wire and argon gas are used.

Although the single-hand welding technique used with the arc and MIG welder is the same, the MIG welder is easier to use. It is probably the easiest welder on which to learn how to weld, because the electrode is automatically fed to the welding zone, and the shielding gas yields a substantially better weld than either an arc or an oxyacetylene welder.

The TIG (tungsten inert gas) welder uses a nonconsumable tungsten rod as the electrode and requires a two-handed welding technique. A filler rod of the same composition as the materials being welded is held in the other hand and fed into the welding zone as the weld is being made.

Figure 9.6 Types of welded joints.

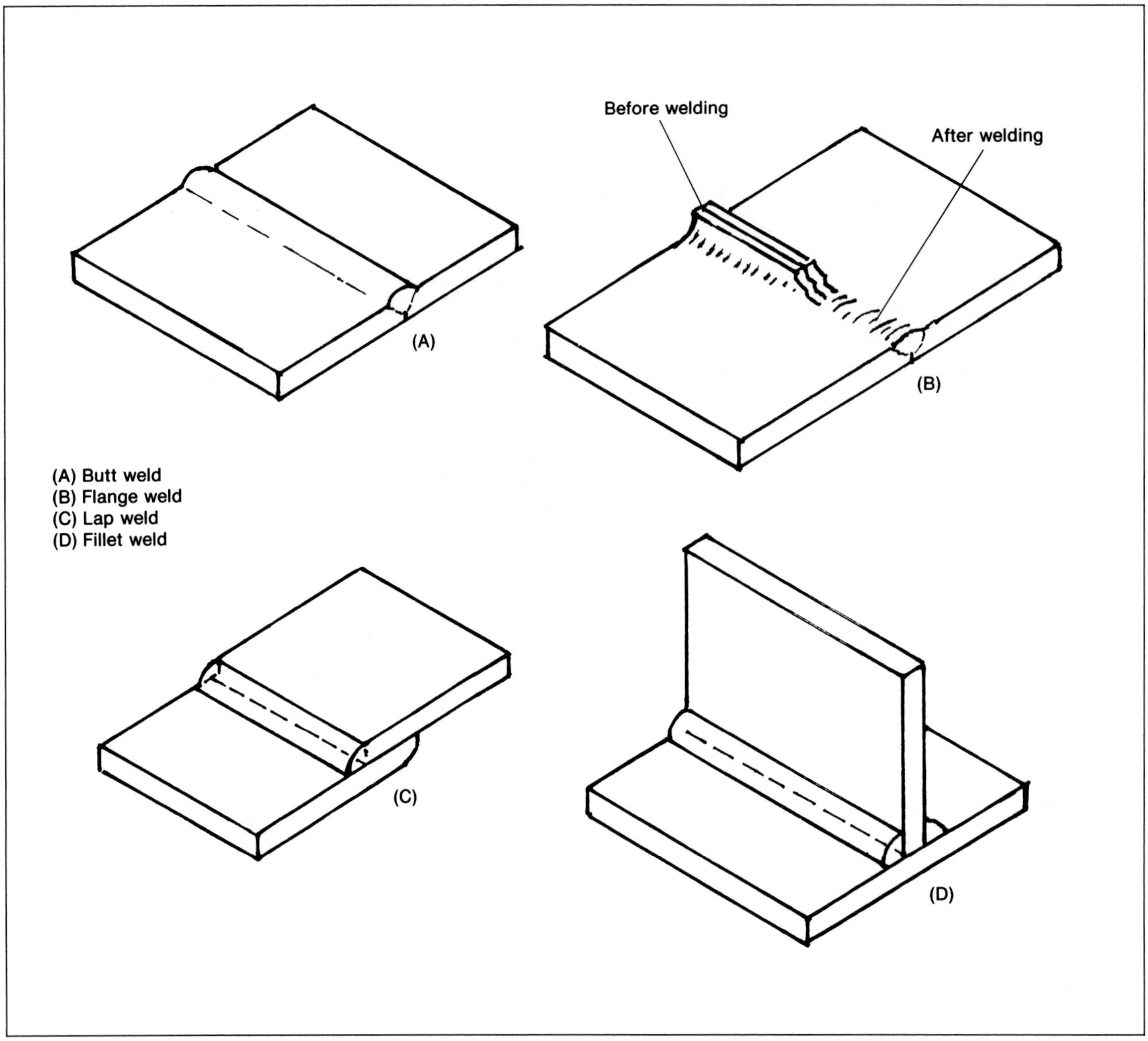

TYPES OF WELD Common welding joints are described below and illustrated in Figure 9.6.

(A) Butt weld
(B) Flange weld
(C) Lap weld
(D) Fillet weld

BUTT WELD The butt weld is probably the most common, and strongest, type. The edges of the materials to be joined are clamped edge to edge with a narrow space (one-sixteenth to one-eighth of an inch) between them. If the material is between three-sixteenths and one-half inch thick, the edges should be ground to form a **V**, as shown in Figure 9.6A. If the metal is less than three-sixteenths of an inch thick, the **V** will not be needed.

FLANGE WELD A flange weld is similar to a butt weld, except the edges of the material being joined are bent up, as shown in Figure 9.6B, before the sheets are clamped in place. The weld is made by melting the upturned flanges. Although it is necessary to apply flux to the welding zone, the flange weld can frequently be made without the use of a filler rod.

LAP WELD A lap weld is made when two pieces are overlapped, as shown in Figure 9.6C. Both of the overlapped edges must be welded.

FILLET WELD A fillet weld (Figure 9.6D) is made when the edge of one piece is joined to the face of another. Both sides of the angled piece should be welded to create the strongest possible weld.

Soldering

Soldering is the process of heating metal (usually lightweight steel, copper, or brass) until it is hot enough to melt **solder.** The solder flows over the surface of the metal and bonds the pieces together. For an effective soldering bond to be made there must be a good mechanical connection between the parts being soldered. The parts must be clean and free of grease, oxidation, and other contaminants.

Soldering flux is applied to further clean the metal and prevent oxidation when the joint is heated. Flux is manufactured in solid, powder, paste, and liquid forms. The type of flux used depends on the project. Rosin flux is non-corrosive and should be used on all electrical work. Soldering wire with a rosin flux core can be purchased at almost any hardware store. Acid fluxes are very effective, but the acid is corrosive so the work must be washed with warm water to prevent corrosion. Be sure to wait for the solder joint to cool before you wash it.

If you aren't using a soldering wire with a flux core, it will be necessary to apply flux to the joint before it is heated. After the joint has been fluxed, heat is applied to the work. The solder should be melted by touching it to the work, not the iron. The melted solder should freely flow over and through

---

MAKING A GOOD SOLDER JOINT

A good solder joint can be made only if you heat the work to the melting point of the solder. If the work is not heated sufficiently and the solder is melted by touching it to the soldering iron, the solder will just sit on top of the work rather than bonding with its surface. This produces what is known as a "cold" solder joint. A cold solder joint isn't very strong, and it doesn't conduct electricity very well. A cold solder joint can be identified by its appearance. The solder looks dull, whereas a good solder joint will appear bright and shiny. A cold solder joint can generally be fixed by adding a little flux to the joint and reheating the work until it is sufficiently hot to make the solder flow freely.

---

the joint where the hot solder bonds with the surface of the metal and fuses the joint together.

TWO-DIMENSIONAL SCENERY

Two dimensional scenery can be divided into two basic subgroups, hard scenery and soft scenery. Hard scenery generally refers to flats, and soft scenery to unframed units such as drops and draperies.

Flats

Flats are lightweight frames made of wood or steel tubing. They are normally covered with muslin or, when the circumstances require, with Upson board, paper, Masonite, plywood, velour, or other fabrics and materials.

The various pieces that make up the framework of a flat have specific names, as shown in Figure 9.7. The top and bottom horizontal members are called **rails,** the outside vertical elements are called **stiles,** and the interior horizontal members are referred to as **toggle bars. Corner braces** are located in the upper and lower corners of the same side of flats over three feet wide.

Rail: A top or bottom framing member of a flat.

Stile: A vertical side member of a flat.

Toggle bar: An interior horizontal framing member of a flat.

Corner brace: A diagonal internal framing member that helps keep a flat square.

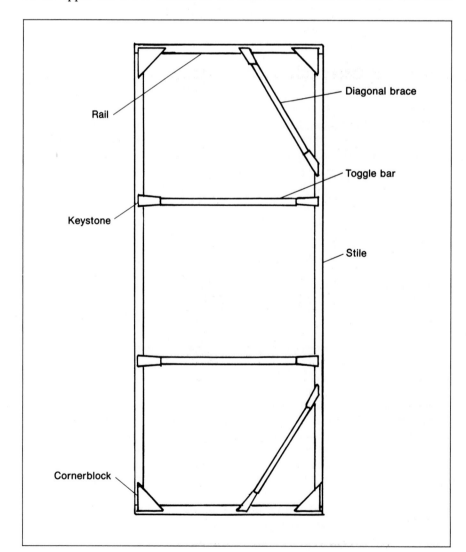

Figure 9.7 The parts of a flat.

CHAPTER 9: SCENIC PRODUCTION TECHNIQUES

Flats can be designed to be almost any size and shape, but the vast majority resemble tall rectangles from one to six feet wide and eight to sixteen feet high. The wooden framework for a flat up to fourteen feet tall is usually made of 1 X 3 white pine ("B or better" or "C select"). This wood needs to be light in weight, straight grained, relatively free of knots, and, most importantly, straight.

Flats over 14 feet tall will probably need the additional strength offered by ⁵⁄₄ X 4 **stock.** ("Five-quarter" stock is lumber that is 1¼ inches thick; thus, ⁵⁄₄ X 4 stock actually measures 1¼ inches thick by 3½ inches wide.) Outsized flats can also be built from 18-gauge, one-inch-square steel tubing. The face of the steel frame is covered with ¼- or ⅛-inch plywood that is attached with power-driven screws.

Toggle bars are used to keep the stiles parallel. If toggle bars were not used, fabric shrinkage (caused when the flat is painted) would cause the stiles to twist and bow in toward each other. Toggles should be spaced approximately four to five feet from the nearest toggle bar or rail.

Any flat wider than six feet is rather awkward to handle and takes up a lot of storage space. Flats less than two feet wide are generally referred to as **jogs,** and jogs less than one foot wide are normally made from solid stock rather than fabric-covered framework. The solid jog is covered with the same fabric as other flats so it will look the same when painted.

BUILDING FLATS To build a standard wooden flat fourteen feet tall and four feet wide, you can follow a standard procedure outlined in fifteen steps:

1. Select good, straight white pine 1 X 3 ("B or better," "C select") for the rails, stiles, and toggle bars.
2. Trim and square the end of one of the boards, and cut two pieces four feet long for the rails. (Note that the rails are cut the full width of the flat.)
3. Trim and square the boards, and cut the two stiles fourteen feet (the height of the flat) minus the combined width of the two rails.
4. Square the boards, and cut two toggle bars four feet (the width of the flat) minus the combined width of the two stiles.

KEYSTONES AND CORNERBLOCKS

Keystones and cornerblocks are used as reinforcement for the butt joints commonly used in flat construction.

The *cornerblock* is a triangle of one-quarter-inch AD plywood with eight- or ten-inch legs. To provide effective reinforcement position the cornerblock so its grain runs perpendicular to the joint between the rail and the stile.

Also made of one-quarter-inch AD plywood, the *keystone* is six inches long and shaped like a keystone of an arch. The small end is slightly narrower (one-half inch)

than the width of the toggle bar that it is covering; the wide end is approximately one-half inch wider than the toggle bar.

Some technicians prefer rectangular strips of plywood, called straps, to keystones. These straps should be cut approximately one-half inch narrower than the width of the toggle bar. Both keystones and rectangular straps provide about the same amount of bracing for the joint, but many technicians think that keystones are prettier, so they continue to use them in preference to the plywood straps.

Stock: Regularly sized lumber that can be purchased from a lumber yard.

Jog: A flat less than two feet wide.

Figure 9.8 Positioning of butt joints on a flat.

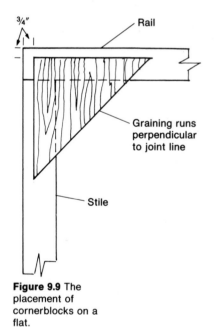

Figure 9.9 The placement of cornerblocks on a flat.

Figure 9.10 The placement of keystones on a flat.

5. Before you begin to assemble the flat, cut the keystones and corner-blocks.

6. Although a flat can be assembled using mortise and tenon or halved joints for extra strength, most shops use butt joints when putting flats together. Butt the stiles against the edge of the top and bottom rails, as shown in Figure 9.8. By assembling the flat in this manner the rail will be the only framing element making contact with the floor when the finished flat is set upright. If the flat were assembled with the end of the stile touching the floor, it would be splintered and broken whenever the flat was moved or skidded along the floor.

7. Use a framing square to make sure that the corner joint between the rail and stile is square. Lay a corner block on top of the joint with its grain running perpendicular to the line of the joint (parallel to the grain of the stile), and inset three-quarters of an inch from the outside edge of both the rail and stile, as shown in Figure 9.9. Secure the corner blocks (as well as the keystones or straps) with clout nails and a clinch plate, coated staples, or screws. This routine is repeated for each corner of the flat.

8. Center the toggle bars at four feet eight inches and nine feet four inches, so they will be equidistant from the top and bottom of the flat and from each other, as shown in Figure 9.8. Use the framing square to make sure that the toggle bars are square to the stile, and secure them with keystones that are also inset three-quarters of an inch from the edges of the stiles, as shown in Figure 9.10.

9. Because the flat is wider than three feet, place diagonal corner braces made of 1 X 2 in the upper and lower corners of the same side of the flat. Secure these corner braces with plywood straps ripped in half and angle cut so they can be inset three-quarters of an inch from the outside edge of the flat, as illustrated in Figure 9.11.

10. To cover the flat you will need to turn it over so it is lying on the cornerblocks and keystones (Figure 9.12A). Stretch a piece of heavyweight muslin (128- or 140-thread count) over the frame (see the box on page 190). The muslin should be slightly larger than the height and width of the flat, as shown in Figure 9.12B. Using a hand stapler or tack hammer and tacks, attach the muslin along the inside edge of the face of one of the stiles. Place the staples about one foot apart.

11. Move to the center of the other stile, and pull the muslin until it barely sags across the face of the flat. Staple it on the inside edge of the face of that stile. Be sure that you don't stretch the muslin until it is tight; you need to allow room for fabric shrinkage when you paint the muslin. (On a four-

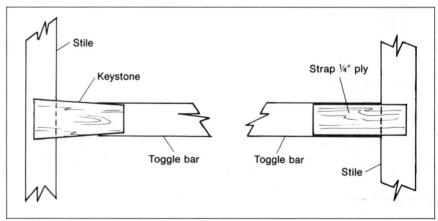

CHAPTER 9: SCENIC PRODUCTION TECHNIQUES

by-fourteen-foot flat the completely tacked muslin should just brush the work surface underneath it.) Work your way toward the end of the flat, alternately pulling and stapling or tacking the material. Do this in both directions from the tack or staple that you placed in the center of the stile.

12. In a similar fashion pull and tack the fabric to the inside edge of the face of both rails, as shown in Figure 9.12C. If there are any wrinkles or puckers in the fabric, the staples or tacks can be pulled and the fabric re-stretched until the wrinkles are removed.

13. To finish covering the flat, the muslin needs to be glued to the frame.

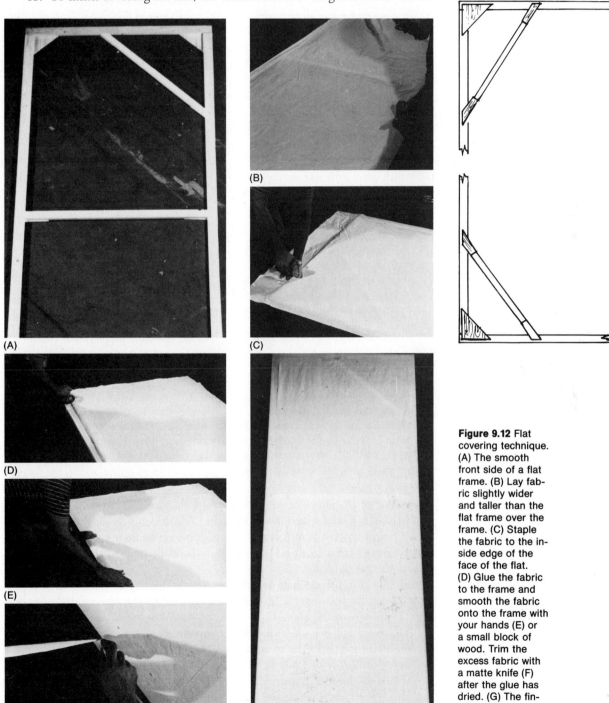

(A)
(B)
(C)
(D)
(E)
(F)
(G)

Figure 9.11 The placement of reinforcement for diagonal braces on a flat. Be sure that all corner blocks are placed with their outside edges ¾″ from the outside edge of the flat.

Figure 9.12 Flat covering technique. (A) The smooth front side of a flat frame. (B) Lay fabric slightly wider and taller than the flat frame over the frame. (C) Staple the fabric to the inside edge of the face of the flat. (D) Glue the fabric to the frame and smooth the fabric onto the frame with your hands (E) or a small block of wood. Trim the excess fabric with a matte knife (F) after the glue has dried. (G) The finished flat.

FLAT-COVERING FABRICS

A variety of fabrics can be used to cover flats.

UNBLEACHED MUSLIN

Heavyweight unbleached muslin is an excellent, relatively low-cost flat-covering material. It is available in a variety of widths—72, 81, 90, and 108 inches and 33 feet. The narrower widths are used for flat covering, and the 33-foot material is usually used for making seamless drops and cycloramas.

This type of muslin, which is available from scenic supply houses, has a high thread count—128 or 140 threads to the inch—which gives sufficient strength for flat covering and most other scenic uses. Muslin accepts all scenic paints well and has a uniform shrinkage rate.

Although bleached muslin is available in fabric stores, it isn't particularly useful for scenic purposes, because the bleaching process weakens its fibers, it isn't available in sizes wider than forty-eight inches, and it is more expensive.

LINEN CANVAS

Linen canvas is an excellent flat-covering material, because it is extremely durable and has a coarse weave similar to artist's canvas. The fabric is sixty-nine to seventy-two inches wide and weighs twelve to sixteen ounces per square yard. It accepts paint well and doesn't shrink very much. Unfortunately, it is also the most expensive of the flat-covering materials, is not always available, and can be purchased only from scenic or fabric supply houses.

COTTON CANVAS

Cotton canvas is an excellent substitute for linen canvas, because it has many of the same properties, is approximately the same weight—nine to sixteen ounces—is readily available, and is much less expensive. It is the preferred type of canvas for making platform covers and ground cloths.

It is available in widths up to seventy-two inches, is sometimes available from tent and awning suppliers, and can also be purchased from scenic or fabric supply houses.

COTTON DUCK

Cotton duck is a lighter weight—five- to eight-ounce—cotton canvas. It has the same properties as cotton canvas and is generally available locally, although it may be difficult to find in sizes wide enough for stage purposes (generally sixty-nine inches or wider). It is available from local fabric stores, tent and awning suppliers, and scenic or fabric supply houses.

Regardless of the shape of the flat, you should glue the covering only to the face of the rails and stiles. If the covering fabric is not glued to any internal pieces (toggle bars, corner braces), it will be able to shrink evenly when the flat is painted. This uniform shrinkage will result in fewer wrinkles on the face of the finished flat.

14. To glue the cloth to the flat turn back the flap of muslin around the edge of the flat and apply a light coating of glue to the face of the stiles and rails, as shown in Figure 9.12D. Be sure that you use a thorough but *light* coating, because if it soaks through the muslin, it may discolor or darken the ensuing paint job. Fold the muslin back onto the wood, and carefully smooth out any wrinkles with your hand (Figure 9.12E) or a small block of wood.

15. After the glue has dried, you will need to trim the excess fabric from the flat. The easiest way to do this is to pull the fabric tight and run a matte knife down the edge of the flat, as shown in Figure 9.12F.

SCENIC CANVAS AND MUSLIN GLUE FORMULAS

There are several effective methods of gluing covering fabric to flats.

PAINT

Probably the easiest method of gluing muslin to a flat frame is with casein, acrylic, or latex paint. Either use white paint (which is close to the color of muslin) or mix a color that closely approximates the prime coat that you will be using to paint the set. Simply paint the stiles and rails with the paint, apply a light coat of paint to the underside of the fabric flap, flop the fabric back onto the wood, and smooth it out. The binders in the paint will glue the fabric to the wood. This method works well if the flat is going to be used for a single production. The binders in the paint are not really strong enough to tightly bond the fabric to the flat. If the flat is going to be reused, one of the following glues would be more appropriate.

ANIMAL GLUE AND WHITING

Animal glue is combined with whiting (a thickening agent made of low grade chalk) in the ratio of one part prepared animal glue (see Chapter 8 for instructions) to one part whiting paste. To make whiting paste put the dry whiting in a container, and stir in enough water to make a paste the consistency of sour cream. Add the glue to the whiting paste, and use while it is hot. The mixture dries when it cools, but it can be reheated in a double boiler or glue pot to make it workable again.

WHITE GLUE AND WATER

A mixture of two parts of white glue thinned with one part of water makes a good muslin glue. Take care to use a light coat of glue, because if the white glue bleeds through to the surface of the fabric, it can leave a glaze coat that may discolor any subsequent coats of paint.

DOOR AND WINDOW FLATS All wooden flats can be constructed and covered using the general principles just listed. The stiles of all flats (regular, irregular, door, window) are always placed inside their respective rails to prevent splintering of the stiles. The size of any interior openings in the flats (doors, windows, and so forth) are determined by the position of the toggle bars and door or window stiles, as shown in Figures 9.13 and 9.14.

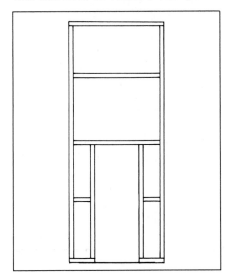

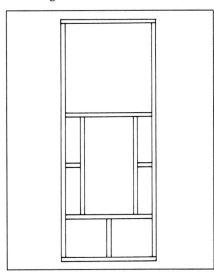

Figure 9.13 Standard door flats.

Figure 9.14 Standard window flats.

Figure 9.15 A sill iron is used to replace the bottom rail that is cut out when constructing a door flat.

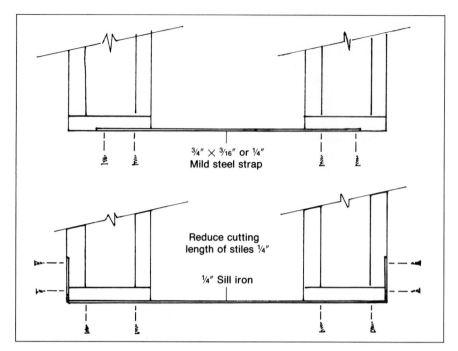

Figure 9.15 A sill iron is used to replace the bottom rail that is cut out when constructing a door flat.

Sill iron: A strap of mild steel attached to the bottom of a door flat to brace it where the rail has been cut out.

Sweep: A wooden curvilinear form, generally used to outline an arch or irregular form in door and window flat openings.

Door flats have one construction variation. The bottom rail across the door opening is removed and replaced with a **sill iron,** which is a mild steel strap three-sixteenths or one-quarter of an inch thick and three-quarters of an inch wide, as shown in Figure 9.15. The sill iron should extend at least one foot on either side of the doorway, and for maximum strength it can run to the outer edges of the door flat, bent at right angles, and run up the outside edge of the stile. With either method a thin strip of wood the thickness of the sill iron needs to be removed from the bottom of the rail or the outside edge of the stile so the sill iron can be recessed. The sill iron is attached with 1- or 1¼-inch No. 8 or 9 flat-head wood screws.

Arches and irregular openings in flats are made by insetting **sweeps** in regular door and window openings, as shown in Figure 9.16. Sweeps can be made from three-quarter-inch stock or plywood. Stock is preferable, because it will better hold the nails driven into its edge to support the depth pieces. Sweeps that are used to create arches in either doors or windows should be notched into the door or window stiles. If they aren't, the end of the sweep will have to be cut to a feather edge, and the chances of breaking that slivered end will be very good. Insetting the sweep approximately one-half to three-quarters of an inch into the stile can prevent potential breakage.

Trim enhances the realistic appearance of a door or window flat. Depth pieces create the illusion that the flat has actual thickness. Straight-line depth pieces can be made from 1 × 6 stock, one-quarter-inch Masonite, or similarly rigid material, as shown in Figure 9.17; curved depth pieces can be made from one-eighth-inch Easy Curve, three-sixteenth-inch Upson board, or one-eighth-inch Masonite. The actual depth of the door or window depends entirely on the style and architectural period chosen by the scenic designer. The appearance of the window or door is similarly dependent on its architectural model.

There are two types of stage window and door, dependent and independent. The basic difference between the two is that the dependent unit is fixed to the flat, whereas the independent unit is largely self-contained and can easily be attached to or removed from the flat. Figure 9.18 shows exploded views of dependent doors and windows, and Figure 9.19 shows similar illustrations of independent doors and windows.

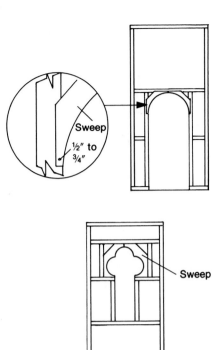

Figure 9.16 Sweeps are used to create irregularly shaped openings in door and window flats.

Sweep

½" to ¾"

Sweep

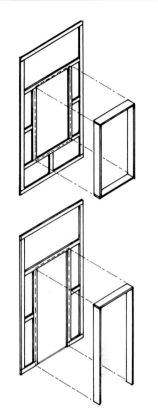

Figure 9.17 Depth pieces help create the illusion of wall thickness.

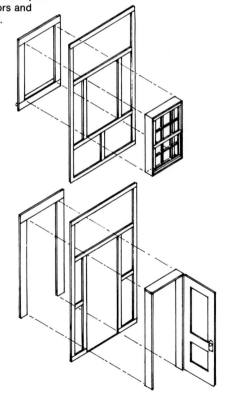

Figure 9.18 Dependent doors and windows.

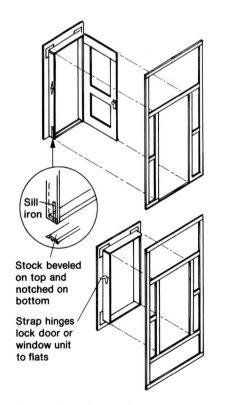

Figure 9.19 Independent doors and windows.

Sill iron

Stock beveled on top and notched on bottom

Strap hinges lock door or window unit to flats

There isn't really a single, "correct" way to build either stage doors or windows. The appearance and function of doors and windows are determined by the scenic designer, and their appearance largely determines how they need to be built.

It is fairly standard practice to design doors to pivot on their upstage side and swing offstage (Figure 9.20), because, with this arrangement, they are self-masking. Self-masking doors block the spectators' view of the backstage area, they don't mask the actors' entrances, and they don't cut off the spectators' view of any part of the set. Because doors usually swing offstage, the spectators normally see only one side of them. For this reason it is fairly common to build them on a base piece of one-quarter-inch plywood. Decorative trim can be applied to the face of the plywood (Figure 9.21). If both sides of the door are going to be seen, the same type of trim is applied to the back.

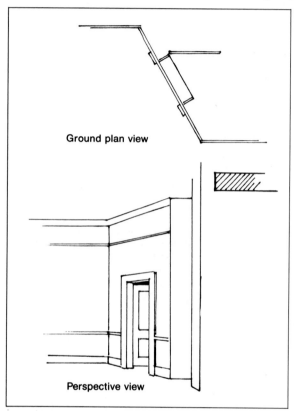

Figure 9.20 Stage doors are usually hinged to swing offstage.

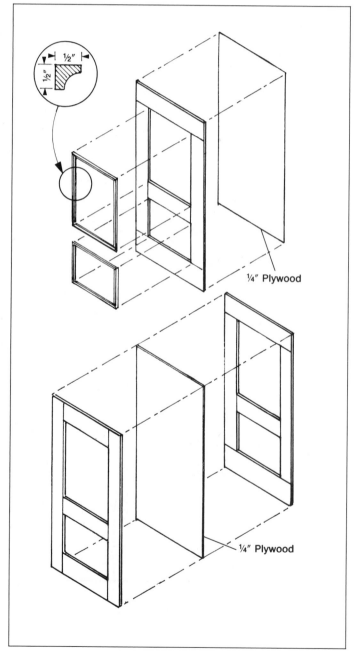

Figure 9.21 Trim is attached to a plywood door to provide appropriate decoration.

CHAPTER 9: SCENIC PRODUCTION TECHNIQUES

Although the appearance of any door is the province of the scenic designer, certain dimensions and characteristics of doors are fairly standard.

1. Doors that people will pass through need to be at least two feet six inches wide. Set doors normally vary in width from two and a half to three and a half feet, depending on the height and style of the door. Closet doors are often narrower. Double doors are usually five to seven feet wide.

2. Door heights vary between six feet nine inches and seven feet six inches.

3. Doorknobs are generally placed around three feet above the floor, although certain European styles place the doorknob closer to four feet.

4. Doors normally swing offstage. They are usually hinged on the upstage side of the doorway unless other needs (stage business, architectural faithfulness) dictate that the door be hung in some other manner.

JOINING FLATS Up to this point the discussion has been confined to constructing individual flats no more than six feet wide. But most designs call for walls that are considerably wider. To construct such a larger wall individual flats are joined. As shown in Figure 9.22, varying styles of door, window, and plain flats can be joined to form a wall unit.

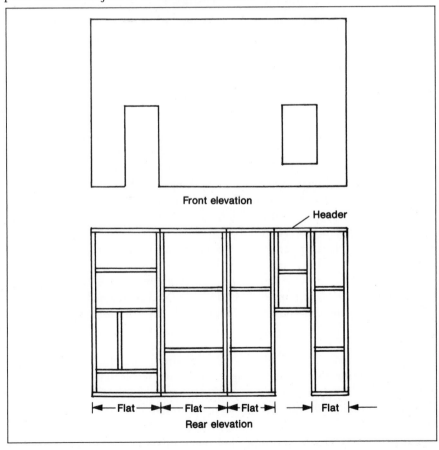

Figure 9.22 Flats can be joined together to create a wall unit.

Front elevation

Header

Flat → ←— Flat —→ ←Flat→ ←— → ← Flat ←—

Rear elevation

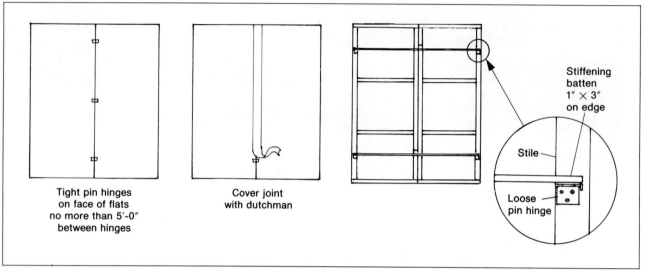

Tight pin hinges
on face of flats
no more than 5'-0"
between hinges

Cover joint
with dutchman

Stiffening
batten
1" × 3"
on edge

Stile

Loose
pin hinge

Figure 9.23 Rigid
flat-joining
techniques.

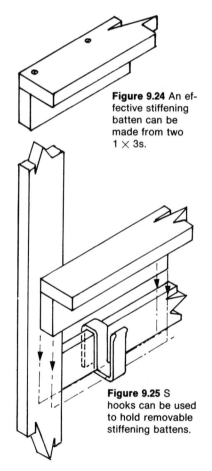

Figure 9.24 An effective stiffening
batten can be
made from two
1 × 3s.

Figure 9.25 S
hooks can be used
to hold removable
stiffening battens.

Prime coat: The first coat of paint applied
to the flats, to develop a relatively uniform
color and surface to the wall units.

Stiffening batten: A length of 1 × 3
attached to a multiflat wall unit to keep it
from wiggling.

There are two primary methods of joining flats to form wall units, rigid and flexible. The rigid joining method is used when the wall unit doesn't have to be folded for shifting or storage. The flexible method is used when it is necessary to fold the wall.

RIGID JOINING If the multiflat wall does not need to fold, the flats can be joined to form a rigid unit (Figure 9.23) in the following manner:

1. Lay the flats face up in their proper order. Where adjacent flats butt together, attach tight-pin hinges to the stiles, as shown in Figure 9.23.
2. Cover the joint and hinges with a dutchman. Fray one-quarter of an inch of the edges of a five- to six-inch-wide strip of cloth (the same material as the flat covering), and attach it to the flat by coating one side of it and the stiles with latex, acrylic, or vinyl paint the same color as the **prime coat.** Apply the dutchman to the joint, smooth out any wrinkles, and allow to dry. (You don't have to put the dutchman on at this time. You can wait until you are doing the other painting.)
3. Turn the hinged wall unit onto its back, and attach **stiffening battens.** Stiffening battens are 1 × 3s, on edge, that are attached to the back of a multiflat wall as stabilizers. The stiffening battens are held in place with tight-pin hinges. One flap of the hinge is attached to the batten and the other to a stile or toggle bar of the flat. To keep the stiffening batten in the proper position the hinges are attached alternately to opposite sides of the batten.

Some technicians prefer to lay the stiffening battens on their sides and attach them to the flats with screws. Although this method holds the flats together, it does not provide nearly the stiffening effect that is supplied by the 1 × 3 standing on edge. However, if another 1 × 3 is attached to the edge of the stiffening batten, as shown in Figure 9.24, the stiffening effect will be regained.

FLEXIBLE JOINING Flexible joining uses the same principles as rigid joining, with the exception that the stiffening batten is removable. The flats are joined with tight-pin hinges on the faces of the flats, and the joint is covered with a dutchman. To make the stiffening batten removable it is attached with loose-pin hinges. To remove the batten take the pins out of the hinges. S hooks provide another method of attaching a removable batten, as shown in Figure 9.25.

CHAPTER 9: SCENIC PRODUCTION TECHNIQUES

If more than two flats are going to be **booked,** you will have to use a **tumbler.** A tumbler is basically a miniflat. It is a piece of three-quarter-inch stock the full height of the flats but only one inch wide. It acts as a spacer between two flats and allows the flats to be fully closed, as shown in Figure 9.26. It is attached to the other flats with tight-pin hinges and covered with a dutchman.

When joining flats, **headers** can be used to create doors or archways simply by placing them between two regular-sized flats, as shown in Figure 9.27.

CEILINGS Ceilings for sets are primarily used on proscenium stages. They are really large, horizontal flats, but they do provide some special challenges simply because of their size. The **book ceiling** (Figure 9.28) is a permanent piece of stage equipment in many proscenium theatres. It is composed of two large flats approximately the same width as the proscenium arch. The depth of the opened book ceiling is normally about sixteen to twenty feet. It can be stored on a single counterweight line.

Book: To fold hinged flats together (so that they resemble a book).

Tumbler: ¾-inch-thick-by-1-inch-wide piece of stock used as a spacer when three or more flats are going to be booked.

Header: A small flat that can be placed between two standard-sized flats to create a doorway or window.

Book ceiling: Two large flats about the same width as the proscenium arch, stored in a booked position in the flies; when needed to create a ceiling, they are opened and lowered onto the walls of the set.

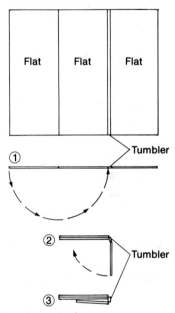

Figure 9.26 A tumbler permits the flats being booked to fold completely.

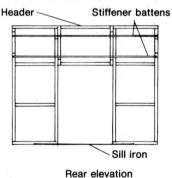

Figure 9.27 A header can be used to create a doorway.

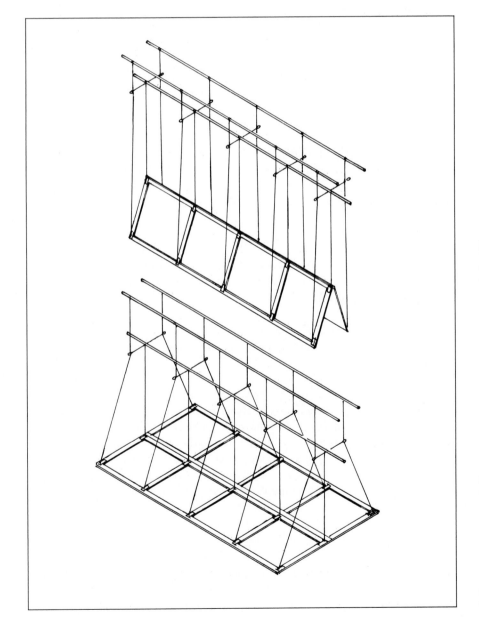

Figure 9.28 A book ceiling.

Figure 9.29 An
irregular ceiling.

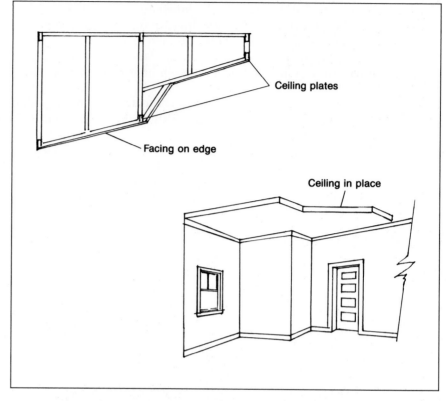

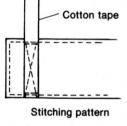

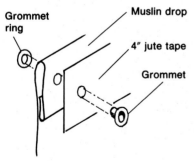

Muslin drop

½" cotton
tape tie—
36" long

4" jute tape

Cotton tape

Stitching pattern

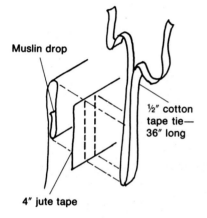

Grommet
ring

Muslin drop

4" jute tape

Grommet

Figure 9.30 Methods of attaching
drops to battens.

Irregular ceiling pieces (Figure 9.29) that do not completely cover the set can be built just as any other flat is. They are normally built of 1 × 4 stock for additional strength. Spot lines of piano wire can be dropped from the grid or a batten to support the downstage edge of the ceiling.

Soft Scenery

Soft scenery refers to unframed fabric units such as drops and draperies, which are usually suspended from the grid, a batten, or some type of structure capable of supporting their weight.

DROPS Drops are large, flat curtains that have no fullness. There are two primary methods of attaching drops to their respective supporting battens, ties and batten clamps.

TIE-SUPPORTED DROPS Probably the easiest way of hanging a drop is to tie it to the batten. Ties (which can be made from strips of scrap muslin, one-half-inch heavy cotton tape, thirty-six-inch shoelaces, or similar materials) are attached to the top of the drop and then tied to the batten. Cotton tape ties can be sewn to the four-inch jute backing tape at the top hem of the drop, as shown in Figure 9.30. The other kinds of ties are used in conjunction with grommets in the jute tape backing of the drop. The grommet-reinforced holes are usually spaced on one-foot centers across the width of the drop. The ties (ideally thirty-six to forty inches long) are looped through the grommet holes and tied to the batten.

BATTEN-CLAMP DROPS Drops are sometimes attached to a counterweight batten with batten clamps. The batten clamp facilitates rapid hanging or removal of a drop from the batten. The top of the drop is sandwiched be-

CHAPTER 9: SCENIC PRODUCTION TECHNIQUES

tween two 1 × 3s, as shown in Figure 9.31. The batten clamp is designed to hold the wooden batten "sandwich" without touching the drop.

A variety of effects can be achieved with drops. Drops are generally hung on an upstage batten and provide a background such as a forest, street scene, or the upstage wall of a ballroom. To an extent the effects the drops create are dependent on the type of material from which the drop is made and the manner in which it is painted and lit.

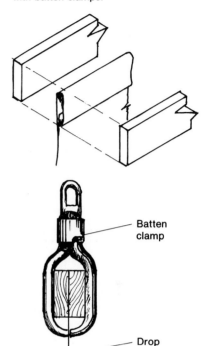

Figure 9.31 A drop that has to be quickly removed from the batten can be supported with batten clamps.

Batten clamp

Drop

SCENIC SPECIALTY FABRICS

A variety of fabrics can be used for special scenic construction purposes. These fabrics are not normally available in local fabric stores and must be purchased from scenic supply houses.

SHARKSTOOTH SCRIM

The thirty-foot-wide, seamless cotton material called sharkstooth scrim has a unique property. When lit from the front the material is opaque. When light is taken off the fabric and objects behind it are lit, the scrim becomes transparent, because the material has a very open weave that creates rectangles of open space about 3/32 of an inch wide by 3/16 of an inch high.

A close-up view of sharkstooth scrim.

It is available from scenic fabric supply houses in natural (a creamy white), white, and black. It can be painted with dye or paint, although if paint is used, care must be taken to avoid filling the open spaces.

Sharkstooth scrim is used for transparent drops, in illusion effects, and in similar applications. It can also be used as a diffusion drop (a drop that softens light) for cyc lighting. If sharkstooth scrim is hung in front of a muslin cyc, it diffuses and softens the effects of the cyc lighting and creates a greater illusion of depth.

BOBBINET

Another thirty-foot-wide, open-weave cotton material is bobbinet. It is lighter in weight than sharkstooth scrim, is more transparent, and has a hexagonal weave. It is also available from scenic supply houses in natural, white, or black. It can be used as a substitute for glass in windows, as a diffusion drop for cyc lighting, as net backing for cutout drops, and in similar applications.

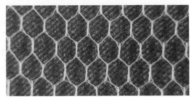

A close-up view of bobbinet.

THEATRICAL GAUZE

Theatrical gauze is a cotton fabric with a fine-mesh weave similar to cheesecloth, but its threads are thicker, and the weave is slightly tighter. It is seventy-two inches wide and can be purchased from scenic fabric supply houses in natural, black, and a limited range of colors. Its applications are similar to those of sharkstooth scrim with the exception of those situations where the seams every six feet would prove objectionable.

A close-up view of theatrical gauze.

OPAQUE DROPS Commonly made of heavyweight muslin, opaque drops are painted with opaque paints (scene paint, casein, latex, acrylic, and so on) and are lit from the front. The audience cannot see through them.

TRANSLUCENT DROPS Made of heavyweight muslin, translucent drops are painted with dyes or a combination of dye and opaque paint and are lit from both front and back. This makes the areas that have been dyed translucent, increasing the apparent depth of the scene. Since any seams would show when such drops were back-lit, they are frequently made from seamless muslin thirty-three feet wide. If the translucent area is relatively small, the drop can sometimes be made so that any seams fall in the opaque painted areas.

SCRIM DROPS Made from sharkstooth scrim or theatrical gauze, scrim drops have the unique ability to become transparent when the scene behind the drop is lit. The material can be painted with dyes or thinned paint. Be sure that the paint does not fill the large holes in the fabric.

CUTOUT DROPS Cutout drops have sections or pieces of the drop actually cut out of the material. The sense of depth in a design can be greatly enhanced by the use of a series of cutout drops placed in back of one another. The drops are painted before they are cut to keep the cut edges from curling. Bobbinet or similar loose-weave netting can be glued to the back of the drop to support the cut-out areas if necessary.

DRAPERIES The two types of drapery used in the theatre are discussed elsewhere in this book. Stage draperies were covered in Chapter 4, and the drapes and curtains used to decorate sets will be discussed in Chapter 11, *Stage Properties.*

THREE-DIMENSIONAL SCENERY

Although flats and architectural trim actually have three dimensions, the term *three-dimensional scenery* generally refers to the construction of platforms, stairs, and similar objects.

Stage Platforming

Directors love multilevel stage floors, because they make it easy to create interesting blocking pictures. Platforms are used to create these levels. There are several types of platform and a number of techniques for joining them.

RIGID WOODEN PLATFORM Probably the easiest stage platform to build, the rigid wooden platform, is also the least expensive. An added bonus is that the legs are detachable, so its height can be varied easily.

The framing for a rigid platform is generally made of 2 × 4 although 1 × 6 or 2 × 6 can also be used. The frame is a ladderlike construction with the rungs, or **joists,** spaced no more than two feet apart, as shown in Figure 9.32. Rigid platforms can be easily constructed in almost any irregular shape, but standard rigid platforms that are kept in a theatre's inventory of stock scenery are normally four feet wide by eight feet long.

Joists: Parallel beams that support flooring.

CHAPTER 9: SCENIC PRODUCTION TECHNIQUES

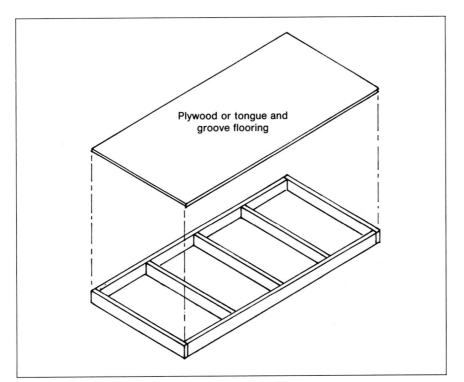

RIGID STEEL-TUBING PLATFORM Steel tubing can also be used to fabricate rigid platforms, as shown in Figure 9.33.[1] The framework is made from sixteen-gauge 1 × 2 steel tubing, and the top from three-quarter-inch plywood. **Gussets** inset into each corner of the frame or steel plates one-quarter inch thick designed to accept casters or legs are welded to the frame. These are predrilled in a pattern that matches the hole pattern on a caster flange or shop-built leg base. Casket locks are attached to the underside of the platform in a uniform pattern so the platform can be locked to an adjacent unit.

Gusset: A triangular piece of material used to reinforce a corner joint.

Figure 9.33 Steel tube platforms are similar in appearance to rigid wooden platforms.

1. This design is based on Stancil Campbell, "Steel Framed Stock Platforming," *Theatre Design and Technology* (Summer 1984): 16–20.

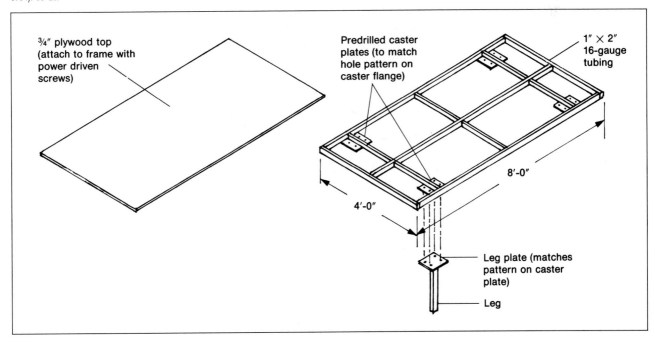

¾" plywood top (attach to frame with power driven screws)

Predrilled caster plates (to match hole pattern on caster flange)

1" × 2" 16-gauge tubing

8'-0"

4'-0"

Leg plate (matches pattern on caster plate)

Leg

RIGID PLATFORM LEGS Legs for rigid platforms can be fabricated from a variety of materials, as shown in Figure 9.34. All platform legs over eighteen inches tall should be braced, regardless of whether they are wooden or metal, because the sideways forces exerted on the platform by the movement of the actors can very easily break either the joint between the leg and the platform or, possibly, the leg itself.

Braces should be placed so that they form a triangle between the leg and the rail to take advantage of the structural strength of the triangular form, as shown in Figure 9.35A. Braces will be effective if placed at any angle between thirty and sixty degrees, as shown in Figure 9.35B, although forty-five degrees provides the maximum strength. There should be no more than four feet between bracing support points, as shown in Figure 9.35C.

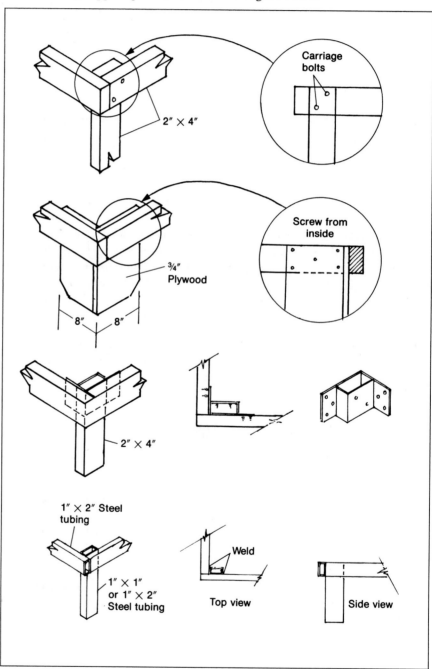

Figure 9.34 Types of platform legs and methods of attachment.

CHAPTER 9: SCENIC PRODUCTION TECHNIQUES

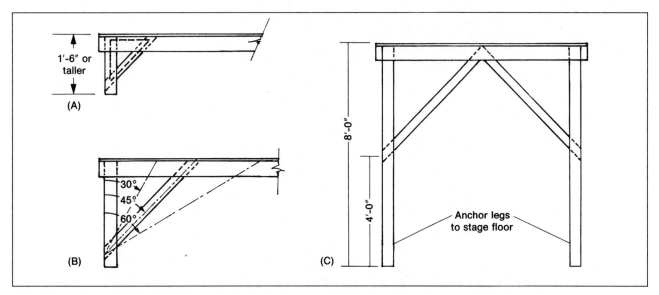

Figure 9.35
Platform-leg
bracing
techniques.

The strength of the rigid wooden platform is primarily based on the depth of the wood used to construct the frame. There are pragmatic limits to the size of a rigid wooden platform that are loosely based on the weight of the assembled platform and the platform storage space available in the theatre. Rigid platforms are generally made no larger than four by eight feet.

STRESSED-SKIN PLATFORM Stressed-skin construction involves securely gluing and screwing plywood **skins** to an internal framework that is nailed and glued, as shown in Figure 9.36. In this type of construction, in which the frame and covering are interlocked, the load is distributed over the entire unit instead of just on the joists. Since the skins can be **laminated** from two sheets of easily warped one-quarter-inch plywood, stressed-skin construction can be used for making curved-surface platforms. With this technique platforms longer than eight feet can be made that require support only at the platform ends.

The strength of stressed-skin construction depends on the secure interlocking of all the components, so it is essential that all the edges of the plywood skins be supported by the internal framework.

Skin: A top or bottom plywood covering for a platform.

Laminate: To build up an object from several layers.

SIZE OF JOISTS

A rule of thumb for estimating wooden joist spans such as the longitudinal, or lengthwise, joists of a rigid platform is:

span = 24 × joist depth

For example, if you build a rigid platform frame from 2 × 4, the practical limit for the length of the platform would be eight feet:

24 × 4 = 96 inches, or 8 feet

Other factors—such as the spacing between joists, the number of support points (legs), and the load and type of activity that will be imposed on the platform—must be factored in to help determine the actual design of the platform. But the above formula provides a rough guide for determining the size of wood that should be used for the construction of a rigid platform.

Figure 9.36
Stressed-skin construction techniques.

Figure 9.37
Honeycomb-laminate platform construction techniques.

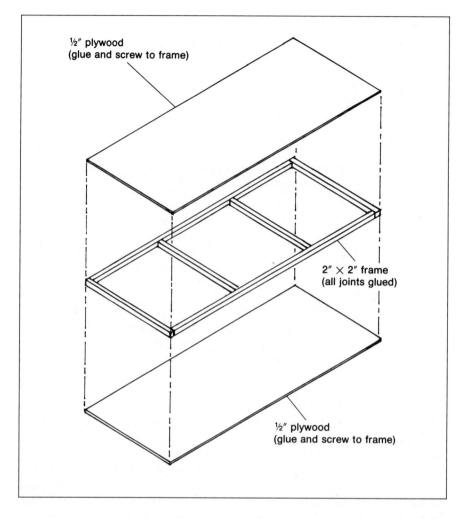

½" plywood
(glue and screw to frame)

⅜" plywood glued to paper core

2" honeycomb paper core

2" × 2" frame
(all joints glued)

⅜" plywood glued to paper core

½" plywood
(glue and screw to frame)

Enlarged view
of honeycomb paper

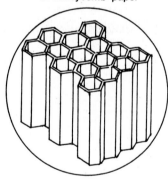

Honeycomb paper: A manufactured paper product with a hexagonal structure similar to a honeycomb.

Cure: To harden and reach full strength (in reference to glue).

HONEYCOMB PAPER LAMINATION Another lamination method is based on the principles used to fabricate the extremely strong, lightweight wings of supersonic aircraft. The strength of the platform is dependent on a continuous glue bond between the **honeycomb paper** and its covering skins.

These platforms are made by sandwiching honeycomb paper between two sheets of plywood, as shown in Figure 9.37. A liberal coat of a strong adhesive such as polyvinyl glue, foaming polyurethane glue, or white glue must be applied to the inside faces of both the top and bottom skins as the platform is being assembled.

To further ensure uniform bonding, pressure has to be maintained on the platform until the adhesive dries. Large pieces of one-quarter-inch steel plate that completely cover the platform's surface can be placed on top of it. Counterweights can be used if the steel plate isn't available. Vacuum pressure can be used instead of weights. The assembled platform is covered with heavyweight plastic sheeting, the plastic is taped to the shop floor with gaffer's (duct) tape, and a vacuum pump is used to remove the air under the cover.

Clamping pressure, whether from weights or vacuum, must be maintained on the platform for at least two hours or until the glue has set. The glue has usually partially **cured** enough after twenty-four hours so the units can be moved, but no weight or stress should be placed on the platforms for at least thirty-six to forty-eight hours. The curing time depends on a number of variables, such as the type of glue, relative humidity, heat, and amount of air circulation within the unit.

CHAPTER 9: SCENIC PRODUCTION TECHNIQUES

After the glue has dried at least overnight, a facing should be put around the open sides of the platform to protect the exposed paper core from possible damage that would reduce the platform's strength. The facing can be made of stock lumber, plywood, or **hardboard** and attached to the edge of the skins.

To make platforms larger than four by eight feet, the top and bottom skins can be laminated from two thicknesses of plywood. When making these laminated skins be sure that the butt joints between sheets in adjacent layers are separated by at least eighteen inches, as shown in Figure 9.38.

The flexibility of the honeycomb paper encourages its use for the development of free-form, curvilinear platforms.[2] Basic forms can be developed by laminating several layers of **butcher paper** and gluing the honeycomb paper to it. This form can be draped, honeycomb paper up, over forms until the desired shape is achieved. Additional layers of butcher paper are laminated to the top of the honeycomb paper to make a rigid structure. If necessary, after the unit has dried, it can be covered with fiberglass (see Chapter 11, *Stage Properties,* for a discussion of application techniques) to make it strong enough to walk on.

Honeycomb laminate platforms present an additional advantage: they are quiet. The vibrations of footsteps and caster rumbling are absorbed by the honeycomb paper, which significantly reduces the "drumming" phenomenon associated with other types of platforming.

PARALLELS Another type of platforming, the parallel, comes in two varieties, standard and continental. In both the top is removable, the framework (made of 1 × 3) folds for compact storage, and the height of the framework is not variable. The folding patterns of the two types are different, and the center support of the continental parallel is removable. Although parallels can be built in almost any size, they are normally four feet by eight feet.

STANDARD PARALLEL The standard parallel is hinged to fold like a giant parallelogram (see Figure 9.39). This is done by placing the hinges in the

2. Tom Corbett, "Laminating Stage Platforms Using Honeycomb Paper," *Theatre Design and Technology* (Winter 1980): 24–25; 57–58.

Hardboard: Generic term for composition sheet goods such as Masonite, particle board, and the like.

Butcher paper: A medium-weight brown paper, available in thirty-six-inch-wide rolls; also known by its trade name, Kraft paper.

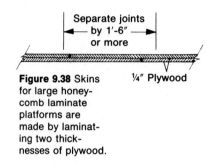

Figure 9.38 Skins for large honeycomb laminate platforms are made by laminating two thicknesses of plywood.

Figure 9.39 The standard parallel hinging pattern.

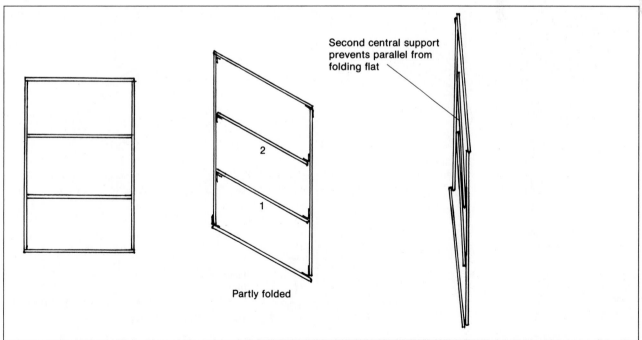

Second central support prevents parallel from folding flat

Partly folded

Cleat: A piece of wood used to brace, block, or reinforce.

specific pattern shown in the Figure 9.40. The framework for the standard parallel is locked open with the 1 × 3 **cleats** on the underside of the top. These cleats fit snuggly into the corners of the framework and prevent it from moving. The standard parallel can be set up or moved fairly quickly, because after the top is removed, the framework collapses into a single unit.

CONTINENTAL PARALLEL The continental parallel is hinged differently than the standard parallel, as shown in Figure 9.41. Although it folds into a more compact unit than the standard parallel, its center support frames must be removed before it can be collapsed. The framework is locked open in the same manner (with cleats on the underside of the top preventing the hinges from moving).

PLATFORM AND PARALLEL TOPS Platform and parallel tops are usually made from three-quarter-inch AD plywood or five-eighths-inch waferboard. The top can also be made of 1 × 6 white pine tongue and groove, but most TDs prefer to use plywood or waferboard, because these sheet stocks are stronger, are less likely to squeak, and take less time to construct.

To help muffle noise it may be appropriate to cover the platform top with some type of padded surface. Old rugging (either jute- or foam-backed) or jute rug padding (not foam) can be tacked to the upper face of the top, as shown in Figure 9.42. The rugging is covered with scenic canvas. Muslin—even heavyweight muslin—should not be used, because it will not stand up to the physical abuse the platform tops are likely to receive. When covering the

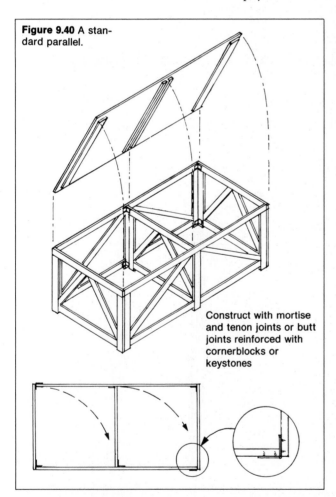

Figure 9.40 A standard parallel.

Construct with mortise and tenon joints or butt joints reinforced with cornerblocks or keystones

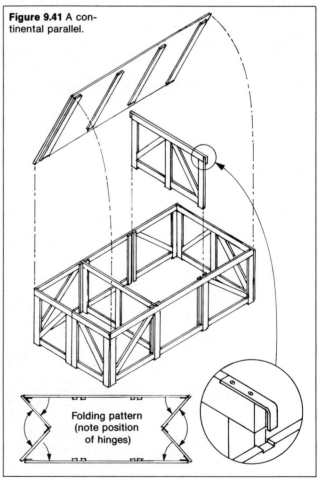

Figure 9.41 A continental parallel.

Folding pattern (note position of hinges)

CHAPTER 9: SCENIC PRODUCTION TECHNIQUES

platform top the scenic canvas should be stretched over the outside edge of the top, pulled around to the underside, and tacked with heavy carpet tacks.

Care should be taken that all platform tops are covered with rugging or padding that is the same thickness, to avoid the possibility of creating an uneven floor when several platforms are tied together to be used as a unit. If a hard, shiny surface is needed, the platform tops should be covered with Masonite, as discussed in Chapter 4.

CONNECTING PLATFORMS When more than one platform is used to create a new floor level, the platforms must be connected to improve the lateral stability of the unit. Tying them together can be accomplished in a number of ways.

BOLTING Wooden platforms or parallels can be bolted together by drilling through the framing members of adjacent units and using three-eighths-by-four-inch bolts, as shown in Figure 9.43. Two or three bolts per long side and one at each end are usually sufficient.

CLAMPING If the platforms or parallels need to be shifted during the production, C clamps can be substituted for the bolts described in the process above, as illustrated in Figure 9.44.

CASKET LOCKS Casket locks can be inset into the framing members of rigid wooden platforms or parallels, as shown in Figure 9.45, to tie the platforms together. Casket locks can also be welded to the bottom of the frame on steel-framed platforms.

If casket locks are attached to every stock platform in a standard pattern (Figure 9.46), it will be easy and quick to lock any platform to an adjacent unit of the same height. Because platforms equipped with casket locks can be locked or unlocked quickly, they can be used for either permanent or temporary staging.

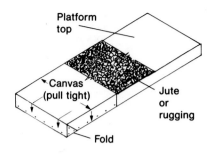

Glue and tack canvas to sides of platform

Figure 9.42 A platform-top padding technique.

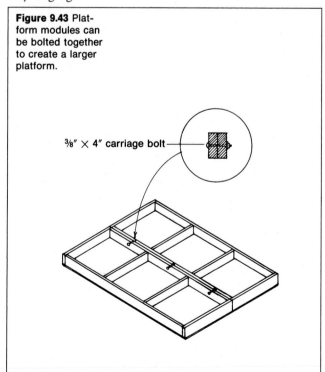

Figure 9.43 Platform modules can be bolted together to create a larger platform.

⅜″ × 4″ carriage bolt

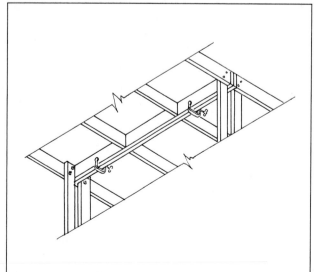

Figure 9.44 Platforms can be temporarily joined together with C clamps.

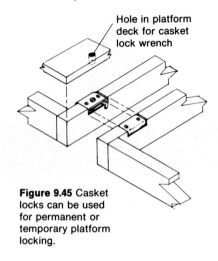

Hole in platform deck for casket lock wrench

Figure 9.45 Casket locks can be used for permanent or temporary platform locking.

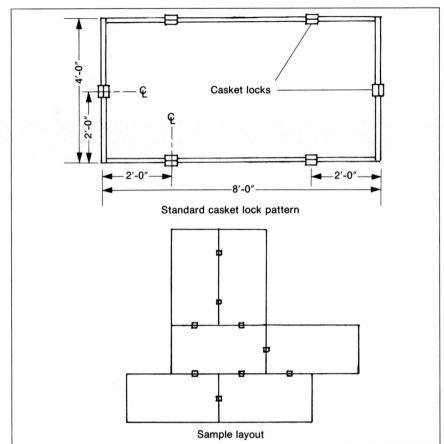

Casket locks

Standard casket lock pattern

Sample layout

Figure 9.46 A standard casket lock pattern.

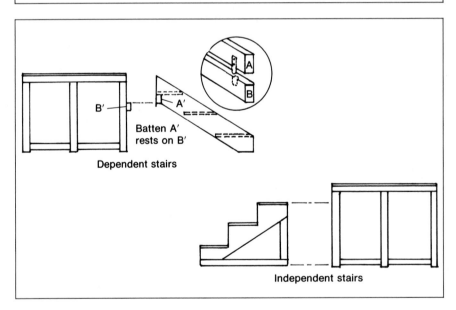

B'

A'

Batten A' rests on B'

Dependent stairs

Independent stairs

Figure 9.47 Dependent and independent stair units.

Stairs

Two basic types of stairs are used in scenic construction, dependent and independent. The dependent units require support from some other element, usually a platform, for support; the independent units are self-supporting, as shown in Figure 9.47. Although the primary difference between independent and dependent staircases is in their method of support, the actual units are built in much the same manner.

The **carriage** can be built in a variety of ways, as shown in Figure 9.48. Carriages can be cut from 1 × 12 for stair runs of less than six feet. For runs over six feet or in those instances where the stairs must support an unusual amount of weight, 2 × 12 should be used.

The **treads** can be made from three-quarter-inch stock or plywood. They should be cut with the grain running parallel with the long side of the tread (Figure 9.49A) to take advantage of the strength of the wood. For safety reasons the unsupported span of a tread should never exceed two feet six inches. **Risers** are usually made from one-quarter-inch tempered Masonite or plywood. If the riser has to curve, one-eighth-inch Masonite or plywood can be used, and the back of the quarter-inch sheet stock can be **scored** so the wood can be bent more easily. Scoring can be done by adjusting the blade height of the radial-arm saw so it cuts about halfway through the wood. Depending on the arc of the anticipated bend, cuts are spaced between three-eighths and one inch apart.

Carriage: The part of a stair unit that supports the tread and risers.

Tread: The horizontal surface of a stair.

Riser: The vertical face of a stair.

Score: To cut partially through.

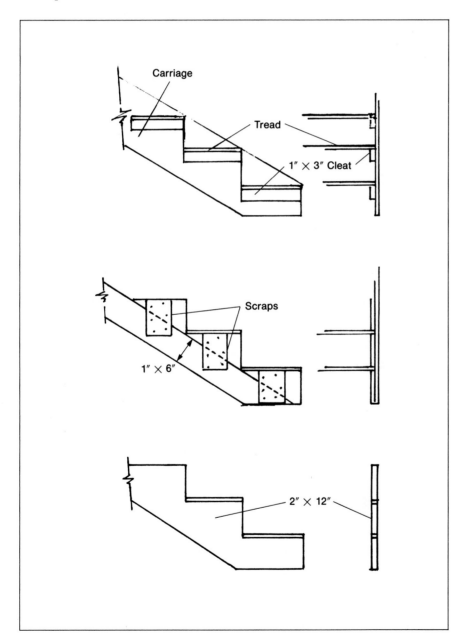

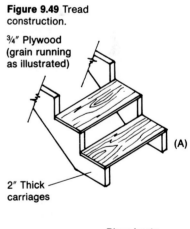

Figure 9.48 Carriages can be built in a variety of ways.

Figure 9.49 Tread construction.

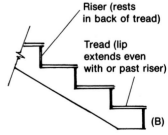

Although the size of treads and risers varies considerably, ten to twelve inches could be considered a fairly normal tread depth, and a riser of six to seven inches would be typical and appropriate. The important point is that the actors need to be comfortable and secure when moving on the stairs. Figure 9.49B shows the usual construction method of butting the treads into the bottom of the risers.

Staircase Railings

Although the design of any staircase railing is the province of the scenic designer, some seemingly universal challenges are encountered in the construction of these units. Unless **handrails, banister,** and **newel posts** are firmly anchored to the stair unit, they will wiggle and detract from the action of the play. For this reason it is generally preferable to firmly attach at least every other banister post to the stair riser with screws or bolts, as shown in Figure 9.50A. If the design indicates that the banisters and lower newel post cannot be butted against the risers, the base of the banister posts should be extended through the tread and screwed or bolted to the carriage, as shown in Figure 9.50B.

The lower newel post should be firmly anchored to the bottom tread, and the top newel post and handrail should be solidly attached to the flat at the top of the stairs, as shown in Figure 9.51.

Wagons

Wagons are usually rigid platforms (although parallels can be used) that rest on casters instead of legs (Figure 9.52). They can vary in size from very small (one foot square or less) to very large. (The slip stage is a huge wagon slightly larger than the normal playing area of the stage. It can hold an entire set.)

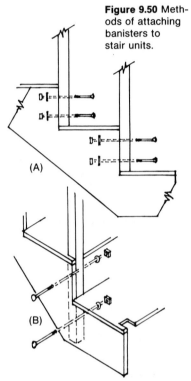

Figure 9.50 Methods of attaching banisters to stair units.

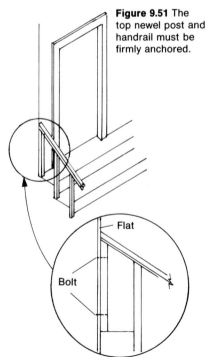

Figure 9.51 The top newel post and handrail must be firmly anchored.

Flat

Bolt

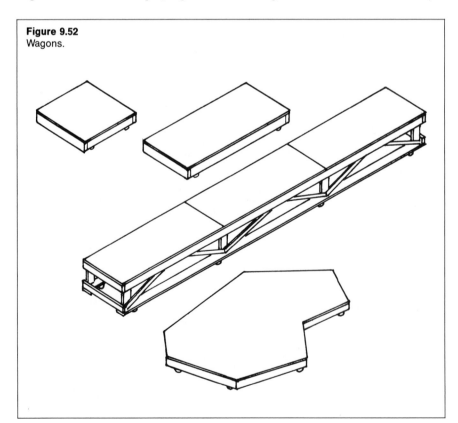

Figure 9.52 Wagons.

Casters, either rigid or swivel, are usually bolted onto caster plates attached to the underside of the platform (Figure 9.53). The caster plates should be sufficiently tall to create ½ to ¾ of an inch of clearance between the bottom edge of the platform and the stage floor. Unless the platform framing is very stiff (2 × 6 or 2 × 4 reinforced with 1½- to 2-inch by ³⁄₁₆″ or ¼″ mild steel strap—see Figure 9.54) the casters should be spaced no more than 48 inches apart to prevent the platform from bouncing when it is walked on.

Wagons can also be made from stressed-skin and honeycomb laminate platforms. With both types of platform the mounting bolts for the casters will have to penetrate both skins to ensure a strong attachment, as shown in Figure 9.55A. Figure 9.55B shows a caster mounting jig and bearing plate that can be used to increase the strength of the caster mount.

Trusses

Many times it is necessary to bridge a relatively large span between supporting points. A wooden or welded-steel truss (Figure 9.56) offers another solution to this challenge.

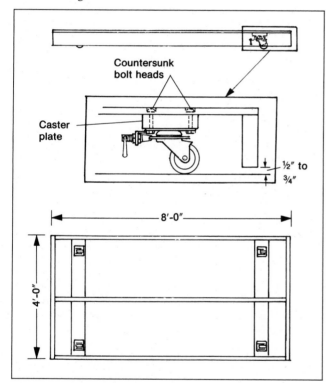

Figure 9.53 Caster mounting techniques for rigid platforms.

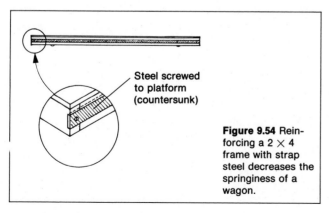

Figure 9.54 Reinforcing a 2 × 4 frame with strap steel decreases the springiness of a wagon.

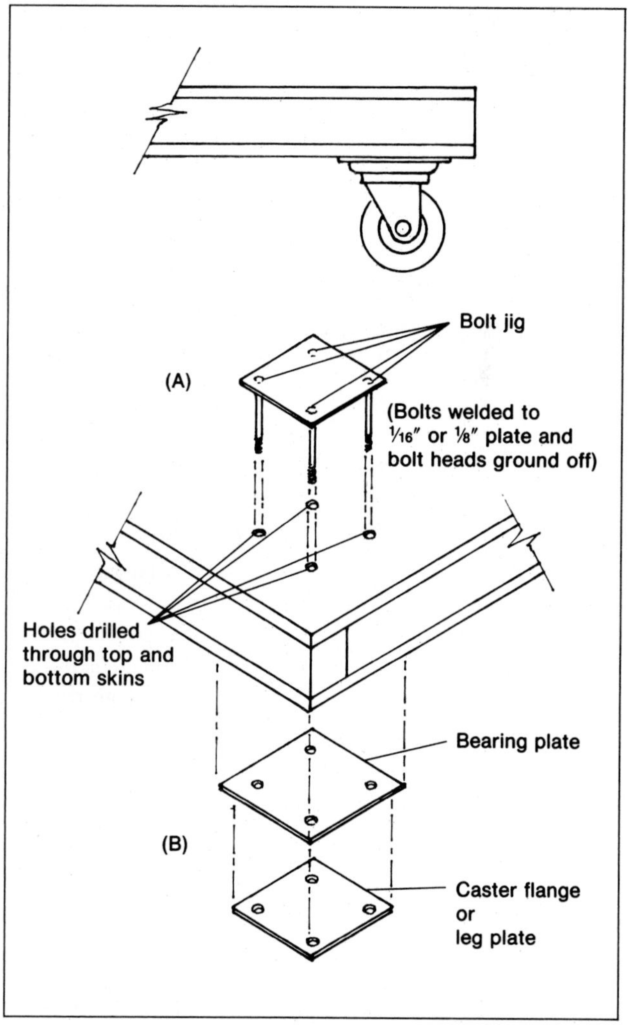

Figure 9.55 Caster mounting techniques for stressed-skin and honeycomb-laminate platforms.

Figure 9.56 Principles of truss bracing and types of
trusses.

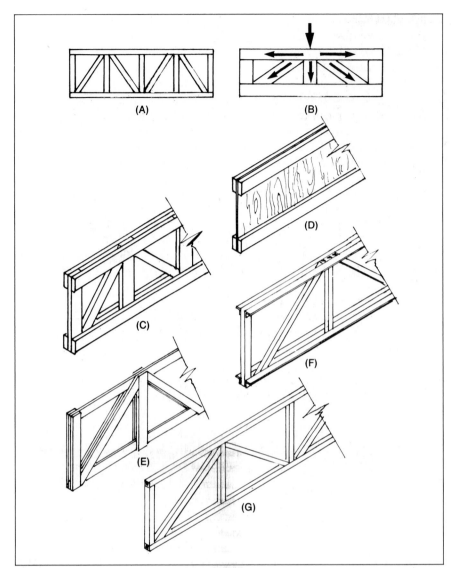

The truss derives its strength from a redistribution of forces, as shown in
Figure 9.56B. The downward force on the truss is channeled and redirected
into a horizontal force by the legs of the triangle. Since the truss is composed
of a series of interlocking triangles, a downward force anywhere on its top
will be distributed over its full width.

Trusses, as noted, can be made from either wood or metal. Wooden
trusses can be made by sandwiching the vertical and diagonal support pieces
between the two longitudinal joists, as shown in Figure 9.56C. A more easily
constructed, but heavier and more expensive, wooden truss can be made by
substituting three-eighths-inch plywood for the diagonal bracing. Be sure that
the grain of the plywood runs vertically, as shown in Figure 9.56D. The top
and bottom rails of the truss can also be made by sandwiching 2 × 4 rails
with the diagonal and vertical elements, as shown in Figure 9.56E. All joints
in any type of wooden truss should be fastened with a high-quality synthetic
adhesive (polyvinyl or epoxy glue) and nails, screws, bolts, or staples.

Metal trusses can be made by using bar stock for the diagonal supports and
angle stock for longitudinal rails, as shown in Figure 9.56F. Again, to keep the
truss from twisting, the rails should sandwich the diagonal bar stock. Metal
trusses can also be made from square tubing, as illustrated in Figure 9.56G.

In the interests of strong and safe welds use an arc welder (preferably MIG), rather than oxyacetylene for this type of weight-bearing, welded structure.

Trusses should be spaced no farther than two feet apart if the **decking** attached to the top of the truss is three-quarter-inch plywood. If the truss is to be decked with rigid, stressed-skin, or honeycomb laminate platforms, the spacing between the trusses can be varied accordingly.

Decking: The covering surface of a structure on which people will walk.

Revolves

Revolves, also called turntables, are large, circular platforms that pivot on their central axis. The primary challenges in constructing a smooth-turning revolve are (1) attaching the casters so the wheels are absolutely perpendicular to the radii of the turntable and (2) placing the center pivot in the exact center of the revolve.

Revolves can be built using any of the standard platform construction techniques, although the rigid platform method, shown in Figure 9.57, seems to work best, particularly if the scenery that will be placed on the revolve requires that you cut through its surface for support points.

If the revolve is going to be rotated with a winch drive (discussed later in the chapter), the outer edge of the revolve will have to be smoothly finished to provide a uniform bearing surface for the cable. Figure 9.58 shows a method that can be used to finish the edge of the revolve. The curved 2 × 8 sweeps create a smooth bearing surface for the drive cable, and the curved one-quarter-inch-plywood sweeps that form the three-quarter- to one-inch lip around the lower edge of the revolve prevent the drive cable from falling off.

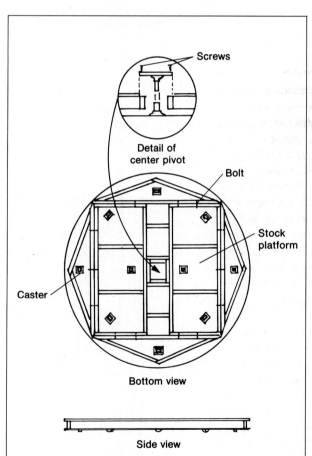

Figure 9.57 Revolve construction principles.

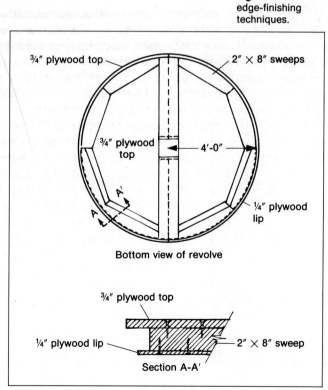

Figure 9.58 Revolve edge-finishing techniques.

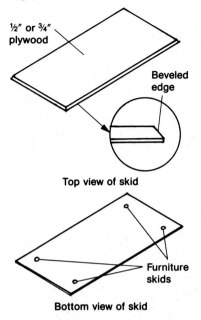

Figure 9.59 Skids.

½" or ¾" plywood

Beveled edge

Top view of skid

Furniture skids

Bottom view of skid

Figure 9.60 Hand-cranked winch.

Skids

Skids are low-profile, casterless substitutes for wagons. They are generally pieces of one-half- or three-quarter-inch plywood that are "skidded" across the stage. Although skids (Figure 9.59) can be pushed across the stage with a pole or pulled with a monofilament fishing line, they are frequently propelled by a winch and cable system. Skids are normally used to shift relatively light-weight scenic pieces such as chairs and tables or small set elements.

Winch-Drive Systems

Figure 9.60 shows designs for hand-cranked or motorized winches that can be used in scene shifting. Figure 9.60A is a hand-cranked version, and Figure 9.60B illustrates a version that uses a variable-speed motor.

When working with a cable drive system it is important to provide some means of adjusting the tension on the cable, because a loose cable might tangle, wrap around a pulley, or otherwise foul up the works. Figure 9.60C shows a technique that makes adjusting the cable fairly easy.

To turn a small revolve, a plastic-covered steel cable is served around the circumference of the revolve and attached to the winch drum, as illustrated in Figure 9.61. The plastic covering on the steel cable increases the friction on the finished edge of the revolve, reducing slippage. By constructing a false floor with stock platforms, as shown in Figure 9.62, you can feed cable through the slot and attach it to steel tongues extending from the underside of the wagon or skid.

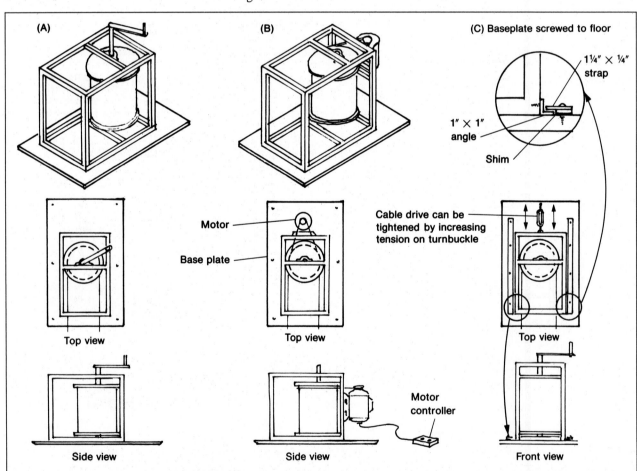

(A)

(B)

(C) Baseplate screwed to floor

1¼" × ¼" strap

1" × 1" angle

Shim

Motor

Base plate

Top view

Top view

Cable drive can be tightened by increasing tension on turnbuckle

Top view

Side view

Side view

Motor controller

Front view

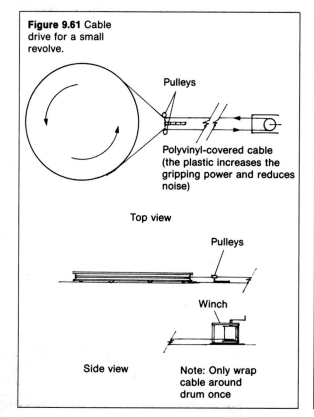

Figure 9.61 Cable drive for a small revolve.

Pulleys

Polyvinyl-covered cable (the plastic increases the gripping power and reduces noise)

Top view

Pulleys

Winch

Side view

Note: Only wrap cable around drum once

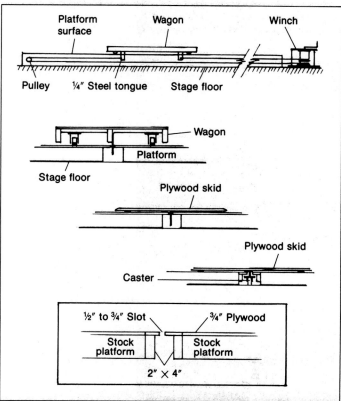

Platform surface   Wagon   Winch

Pulley   ¼" Steel tongue   Stage floor

Wagon

Platform

Stage floor

Plywood skid

Plywood skid

Caster

½" to ¾" Slot   ¾" Plywood

Stock platform   Stock platform

2" × 4"

Figure 9.62 Winch-driven wagons and skids.

Platform-Anchoring Techniques

Large, three-dimensional scenic elements are frequently mounted on wagons to facilitate shifting. Once the wagon is in place, however, the casters will still wiggle or roll unless the wagon is anchored. Figure 9.63 illustrates a number of methods that can be used to anchor platforms.

LIFT JACK The lift jack (Figure 9.64) is another platform-anchoring technique. The casters are placed in contact with the stage floor when the platform needs to be moved, but the platform rests directly on the stage floor when it is stationary. Lift jacks are normally equipped with swivel casters.

TIP JACK The tip jack (Figure 9.65) can be used when a large wall unit cannot be conveniently shifted in another manner. The tip jack is simply two large interconnected jacks that are fitted with swivel casters. When the flat is tied into the rest of the set, the casters don't touch the stage floor. But when the lashing is released, the wall unit leans back, and the weight of the flat rests on the casters for easy shifting.

Rocks, Irregular Platforms, and 3-D Trees

Rocks, irregular platforms, and three-dimensional trees are all built in approximately the same manner. The basic principles of platform construction (three-quarter-inch plywood top, 1 × 4 or 2 × 4 framing, 2 × 4 legs) are followed when building stage rocks and other irregular platforms, as shown in Figure 9.66. Although the actual shape of these units will be determined by the scenic designer, the only significant construction difference is that surfaces of the rocks and irregular platforms are not straight, square, and level. The irregular quality is achieved by tilting the platform tops and covering the

Figure 9.63 Wedges and blocks.

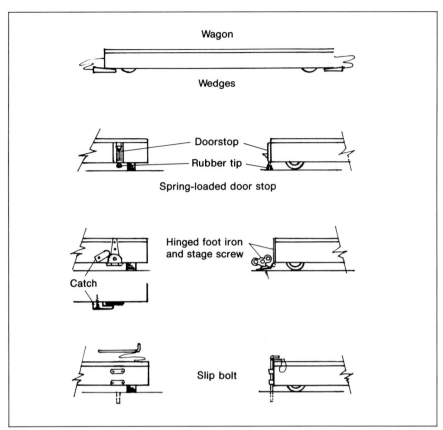

Figure 9.64 Lift jacks.

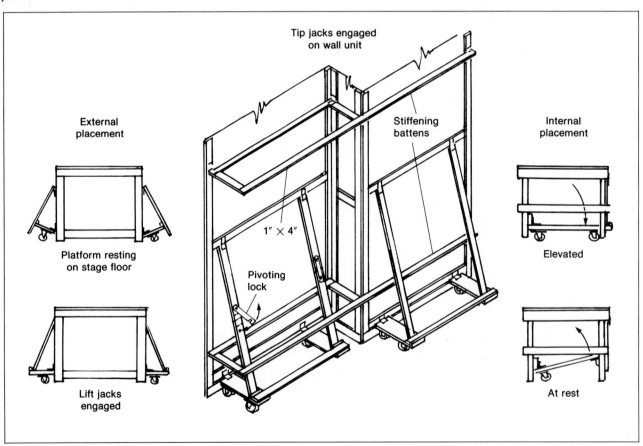

CHAPTER 9: SCENIC PRODUCTION TECHNIQUES

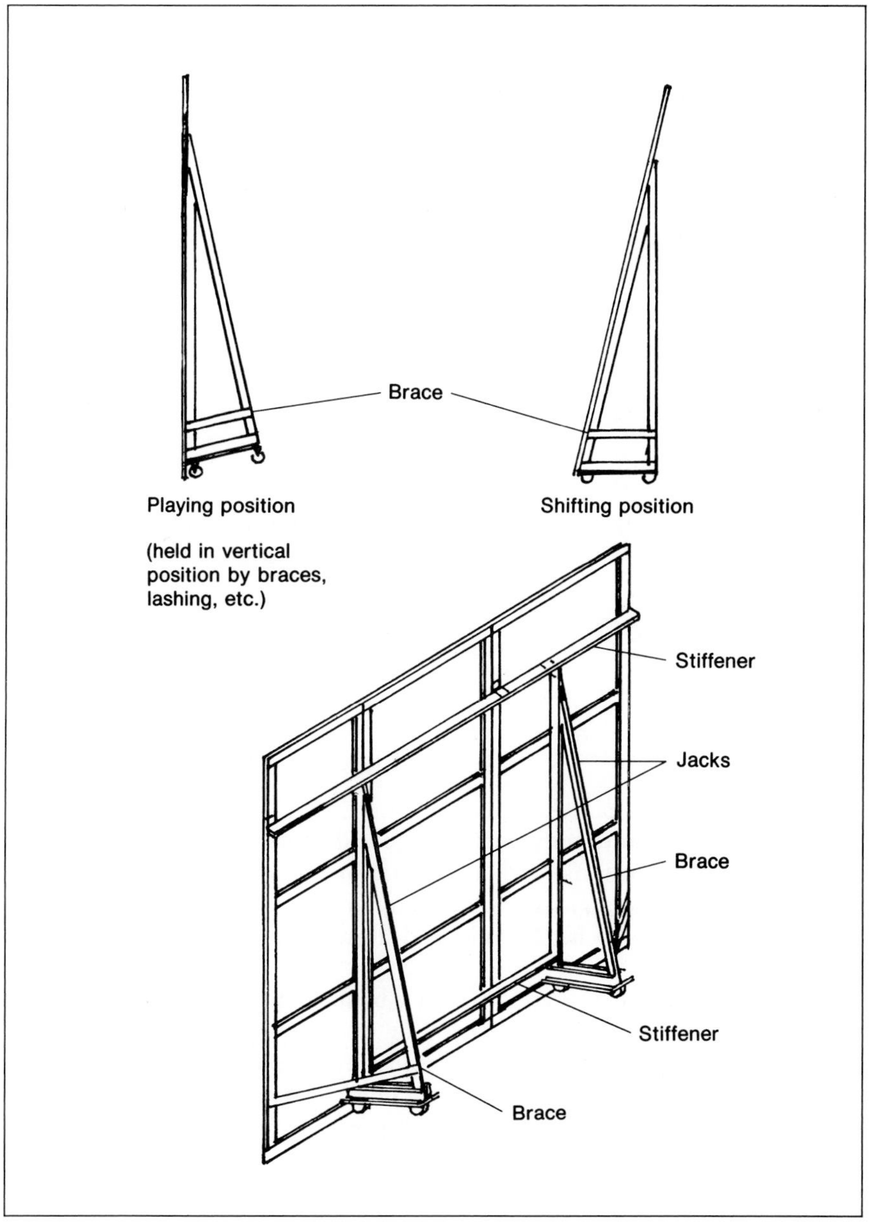

Figure 9.65 Tip jack.

Brace

Playing position

Shifting position

(held in vertical position by braces, lashing, etc.)

Stiffener

Jacks

Brace

Stiffener

Brace

Figure 9.66 Rigid platforms can be modified to look like rocks.

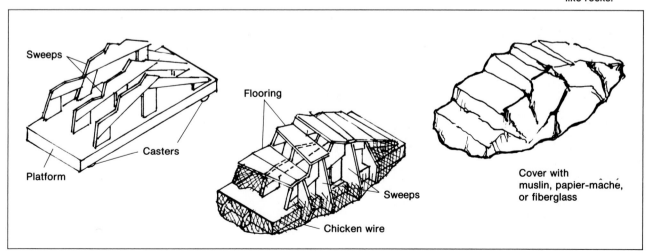

Sweeps

Flooring

Casters

Platform

Sweeps

Chicken wire

Cover with muslin, papier-mâché, or fiberglass

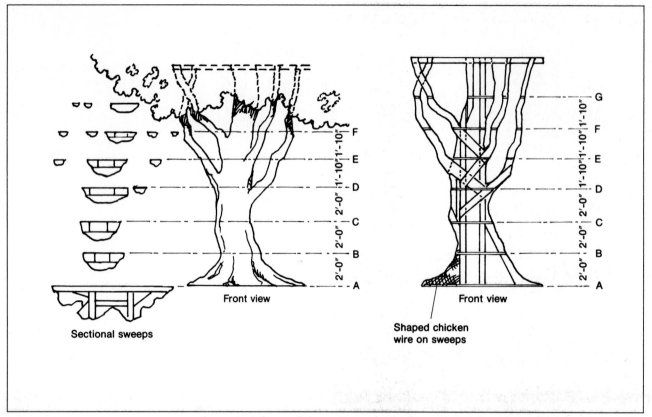

Sectional sweeps

Front view

Shaped chicken
wire on sweeps

Front view

Figure 9.67 A
three-dimensional
tree.

vertical faces of the units with chicken wire and papier-mâché or some more-substantial covering material such as Celastic or fiberglass. The chicken wire is supported by a basic armature of plywood or stock sweeps. Techniques for working with papier-mâché, Celastic, and fiberglass are discussed in Chapter 11, *Stage Properties.*

Three-dimensional trees are built on a basic framework that utilizes the principles of flat construction. Plywood or stock sweeps are attached to the framework (Figure 9.67), which is subsequently covered with chicken wire, papier-mâché, and burlap or some similar rough-weave fabric to give the appearance of bark. The character of the bark can be created by forming the burlap into ridges that resemble the actual type of bark that you are simulating.

10

Scene painting is the crowning touch on the realization of any scenic design. Through the techniques and materials described in this chapter the scenic artist can make the various elements of the set—walls, floors, furniture, beaches, rocks, trees—look as if they belong to the play. Scene painting is the primary method used to create character in the set. Like any other craft field, scene painting can be divided into two primary areas, materials and techniques.

Scene Painting

MATERIALS

The basic materials that are used in scene painting can, in turn, be divided into two main areas, paints and applicators.

Scenic Paints

Experience has proven certain types of paint to be more effective for theatre work than others. All paints are composed of four elements: **Pigment, filler, vehicle,** and **binder.** The pigment is that portion of the mixture that provides the paint with color. The type and amount of filler and, to a certain extent, the hue of the pigment determine the opacity of the paint. The vehicle is the liquid in which the pigment, filler, and binder are suspended. The binder is the adhesive that bonds the pigment and fillers to the painted surface.

When the paint is mixed, the pigment, filler, and binder are suspended in the vehicle. When you paint something, the vehicle evaporates, and the binder bonds the pigment and fillers to the painted surface.

Almost all paints used for general scenic purposes are water-vehicle (water-base) paints, because they are generally nonflammable, less expensive, easier to mix, quicker to dry, lighter in weight, and easier to clean up than

Pigment: A material that imparts color to a paint or dye.

Filler: A material that creates opacity (covering power) in paint.

Vehicle: The liquid medium—water, oil, lacquer, and the like—in which pigments, fillers, and binders are suspended to create a paint mixture; after the paint is applied, the vehicle evaporates.

Binder: An adhesive in paint that "glues" the pigment and fillers to the painted material after the vehicle has evaporated.

their oil-base counterparts. However, some oil- and lacquer-base paints are used in scene painting for specific applications, such as creating metallic trim and highlights.

DRY PIGMENT AND BINDER Probably the oldest type of scene paint is dry pigment and binder, otherwise known as scene paint. The pigment and filler are premixed at the factory. To create scene paint this powder is mixed with **size water** in the shop. With some pigments—generally the fully saturated mineral colors—a little more glue will have to be added to the mix. The exact water-glue ratio varies from pigment to pigment, because the amount of binder needed in the mix is related to the weight of the pigment and the amount of pigment used in the paint mix. The best way of determining the correct amount of glue in the paint is with the "finger test." After the paint has been mixed, dip you finger and thumb in the mix and then touch them together. If they feel slightly tacky or sticky you have enough binder; if they don't, add some more.

Dry pigments are available in a wide range of hues, as shown in Table 10.1. They are inexpensive in comparison with the other types of scenic paint and will store indefinitely. These scene paints have moderate covering properties and a matte finish. More glue added to the size water will make the finish become slightly glossy.

Dry pigment and binder, although still quite serviceable for many applications, is becoming somewhat obsolete. This is primarily because other types of paint are easier and less messy to mix, cover better, and have a wider range of available hues.

CASEIN PAINT Casein is a water-base paint with a milk-base binder. Anyone who has tried to clean dried milk out of the bottom of a glass has had firsthand contact with the bonding properties of casein. It is generally available in one- and two-gallon cans of concentrate that are diluted approximately two to one with water.

Casein is easily mixed, has excellent covering properties, and yields a matte finish. When fully dry it is water repellent, so it can be used on outdoor scenery.

LATEX PAINT Although water-base, latex-binder paint is not often thought of as a scenic paint, it serves that purpose very well. Latex is a synthetic liquid plastic with the flexible qualities of natural latex, or rubber. It not only bonds well but is reasonably flexible. White latex paint is available at a reasonably low cost in five-gallon buckets and provides a very workable base for mixing tints with the more saturated, and more costly, casein paints. Dry pigment, **aniline dyes,** and highly saturated **vinyl acrylic concentrates** can also be used to tint latex paint. The dry pigment or dye is mixed into a little water and a couple of tablespoons of wood alcohol to form a paste about the consistency of sour cream. The paste is stirred into the latex paint. The acrylic concentrates can be stirred directly into the paint. Fully saturated colors and custom-mixed hues are available from most paint stores. Latex paint formulated for use as an interior wall paint adheres to wood and fabric very well and has a matte finish when dry.

VINYL ACRYLIC PAINT Another water-base paint that has a vinyl acrylic binder. It has excellent adhesion, is extremely flexible, and is suitable for painting wood, fabric, and most metals and plastics. After the paint has dried for approximately twenty-four hours, it becomes quite water resistant.

Size water: A mixture of one cup of hot animal glue and one tablespoon of Lysol per gallon of warm water; white glue can be substituted for the animal glue in approximately equal measure.

Aniline dye: A transparent pigment made from aniline, a poisonous derivative of benzene; characterized by brilliant hues and full saturation.

Vinyl acrylic concentrate: A highly saturated pigment with a vinyl acrylic binder; mixed with an opaque base (for tints) or a transparent base (for fully saturated hues) to create a working paint.

CHAPTER 10: SCENE PAINTING

The paint is mixed by combining the concentrated, fully saturated pigments with either a clear or white base. If a fully saturated hue is desired, the pigment is mixed with the clear base; if a tint is needed, the white base is used. Two parts of concentrated pigment are normally mixed with one part of water before being mixed with the base. To create a transparent wash, or **glaze,** the mixed paint (pigment and base) can be diluted with eight to ten parts of water. The clear base can be used to provide a matte finish glaze coat over painted scenery.

Aniline Dye

Aniline powders form transparent, brilliant, saturated dyes when mixed with water. A very strong dye solution can be made by mixing approximately one teaspoon of dye with a quart of boiling water.

Aniline dyes can be used by themselves to paint scrims and muslin drops or cycs. They can also be used to tint water-base scene paints. To keep the dye from **bleeding** by capillary action, add a little binder such as gum arabic, animal glue size, or clear vinyl acrylic base to the dye solution.

VARNISH Varnish is a transparent coating made of synthetic or natural resinous materials suspended in an oil (oil varnish), alcohol (spirit varnish), or synthetic (polyurethane, vinyl acrylic) vehicle. It is used to provide a sealing coat over other types of finish. In the world ouside the theatre varnish is frequently used as a finish coat on stained wooden furniture and other woodwork. In the theatre it is used in this way and also as a satin- or gloss-finish glaze coat over matte-finish scene paint.

Varnish is formulated in matte, satin, and glossy finishes. The amount of gloss on the finished surface can be controlled in two ways: by mixing portions of the various finish types together or by increasing the amount of thinner in the mix (more thinner lessens the gloss).

Varnish is thinned with—and the equipment used to apply it must be cleaned with—an appropriate type of solvent; mineral spirits or paint thinner for oil- or polyurethane-base, alcohol for alcohol-base, and water for vinyl acrylic. The polymer-base varnishes, such as polyurethane varnish, are generally better for stage use, because they are easier to apply and dry faster than their oil-base counterparts.

SHELLAC Shellac is a transparent finish coating made of resinous material (lac—the secretions of certain scale insects) suspended in alcohol. Similar in appearance to high-gloss varnish, shellac must be thinned with wood alcohol, usually about two parts to one. Because of the extreme volatility of wood alcohol great care must be exercised when working with the shellac.

Shellac can be used as a high-gloss finish for painted floors and furniture.

Glaze: A transparent, usually lightly tinted, slightly glossy coating.

Bleeding: The characteristic of dyes and thinned paints to spread through cloth in the same way that water spreads through blotter paper.

SAFETY TIP

Flammable-Base Paints

Any of the oil-, alcohol-, and lacquer-base paints and some synthetic-base paints are flammable. Polyester resin and its catalysts are also flammable. The volatile liquids used for thinning and cleaning these materials—turpentine, mineral spirits, alcohol, acetone—are extremely flammable. Fire codes require that any flammable liquids (including aerosol spray paints) be stored in a special fire-resistant metal cabinet.

Be sure to work carefully with these materials. Never use them in the vicinity of an open flame. Absolutely never smoke while working with them; make sure the area in which you are working is well ventilated, and, if at all possible, work with them outdoors.

Table 10-1
A Representative Listing of Scene Paints

	Dry Pigments	Protein Paints		Latex, Acrylic, and Vinyl Paints		
	Gothic Scenic Colors*	Iddings Deep Colors	Gothic Casein Fresco Paints	Flo-Paint Scenic-Decorator Colors (vinyl)	Cal-Western Show & Display Colors (acrylic)	Rosco Paint Super Saturated (vinyl acrylic)
Whites	Pemanent white 171 Danish whiting	Priming white 5550 White 5551	White	White gloss 5055 White flat 5033	White 520 Blockout white 565 Texture white 568 Hi gloss white 5119	White base 6002
Black	Ivory black 169 Hercules black 170	Black 5552	Black	Black gloss 5079 Black flat 5034	Black 519 Hi gloss black 5120	Velour black 6003
Yellows	Lt. chrome yellow 103 Med. chrome yellow 104	Lemon yellow 5566 Golden yellow 5567	Lemon yellow Golden yellow	Lemon yellow flat 5050 Lt. yellow gloss 5075 Golden yellow flat 5051 Med. yellow gloss 5069	Acacia 506	Chrome yellow 5981
Oranges	French orange mineral 110	Orange 5563	Orange	Orange flat 5052 Orange gloss 5068	Orange 507	Moly orange 5984
Reds	Turkey red lake 121 American vermilion red 113 Solferino red 126 Lt. maroon 127 Dk. maroon 124	Bright red 5562 Red 5560 Dark red 5561 Magenta 5569	Bright red Red Dark Red Magenta	Bright red Flat 5044 Gloss 5076 Deep red Flat 5054 Gloss 5077 Magenta Flat 5048 Gloss 5065	Phthalo red 533 Fire red 503 Magenta 502	Red 5965 Spectrum red 5977 Magenta 5975
Violets	Purple lake 130 Royal purple 132	Purple 5568	Purple		Violet 505	
Blues	American ultramarine blue 141 French cobalt blue 142 Italian blue 143 Prussian blue 144 Celestial blue 146	Turquoise blue 5570 Cerulean blue 5572 Ultramarine blue 5559 Navy blue 5573	Turquoise blue Cerulean blue Ultramarine blue Navy blue	Cerulean blue flat 5049 Medium blue gloss 5067 Ultramarine blue flat 5045 Navy blue flat 5047 Dark blue gloss 5066	Ultramarine blue 538 Phthalo blue 508	Green shade blue 5968 Ultramarine blue 5969

*This is an incomplete listing of Gothic Dry Pigments but indicates the range of colors available.

Source: Richard L. Arnold, Scene Technology, © 1985, pp. 150–151. Reprinted by permission of Prentice-Hall, Englewood Cliffs, N.J.

Table 10–1
Continued

	Dry Pigments	Protein Paints		Latex, Acrylic, and Vinyl Paints		
	Gothic Scenic Colors*	Iddings Deep Colors	Gothic Casein Fresco Paints	Flo-Paint Scenic-Decorator Colors (vinyl)	Cal-Western Show & Display Colors (acrylic)	Rosco Paint Super Saturated (vinyl acrylic)
Greens	Lt. chrome green 150 Med. chrome green 152 Dk. chrome green 153 Emerald green 151 Hanover green 154	Emerald green 5564 Chrome oxide green 5565 Dark green 5571	Emerald green Chrome oxide green Dark green	Emerald green flat 5088 Light green gloss 5060 Chrome oxide green flat 5037 Medium green gloss 5061 Dark green flat 5039 Deep green gloss 5063	Phthalo green 504 Green oxide 501	Chrome green 5971 Phthalo green 5973

Earth Colors	French yellow ochre 160
	Golden ochre 161
	Italian raw sienna 165
	Italian burnt sienna 164
	Raw turkey umber 163
	Burnt turkey umber 162
	Van Dyke brown 166
	Eng. venetian red 123
		Yellow ochre 5553
		
		Raw sienna 5555
		Burnt sienna 5556
		Raw umber 5557
		Burnt umber 5554
		Van Dyke brown 5558
			Yellow ochre
			
			Raw sienna
			Burnt sienna
			Raw umber
			Burnt umber
				Raw sienna
				  Flat 5040
				  Gloss 5056
				Burnt sienna
				  Flat 5041
				  Gloss 5057
				Raw umber
				  Flat 5042
				  Gloss 5058
				Burnt umber
				  Flat 5043
				  Gloss 5059
					Raw sienna 517
					Burnt sienna 516
					Raw umber 514
					Burnt umber 515
					Venetian red 513
						Yellow ochre 5982
						
						Burnt sienna 5987
						Raw umber 5986
						Burnt umber 5985
						Iron Red 5980

Other		Acrylic/latex gloss 5580
		Acrylic/latex flat 5581
				Clear gloss 5080
				Clear flat 5053
				Krom-o-key blue 5046
				Peel paste 5083
				Strip coat 5084
				Heat resistant blue-white 5027
				Battleship gray
				  Flat 5035
				  Gloss 5064
					Clear acrylic glaze 574
					Acrylic artist paste 588
					Acrylic gel (hi gloss) 539
					Five fluorescent colors
					Four metallic finishes
						Gloss medium

It is also used as a sealing coat to prevent previous coatings of aniline dyes, and certain pigments that have dyes in their chemical structure (such as cerulean blue), from bleeding through successive coats of scene paint, varnish, or enamel. Knots in pine boards can also be sealed with shellac to prevent the resin in the knots from bleeding through the finish coat. Shellac can also be used as the vehicle and binder for the application of bronzing powders (metallic powders—aluminum, bronze, gold, and the like) to impart a metallic appearance to smooth-finish surfaces.

LACQUER Lacquer is actually a form of shellac or varnish (depending on the type of resinous material used as the binder and filler) that has been diluted with alcohol or other quick-drying solvents. It is used for the same purposes as shellac.

POLYESTER RESIN Although not an actual paint, polyester resin is the plastic coating that is used with glass fiber reinforcement to form those materials generically known as fiberglass. When cured, the resin has a very smooth, high-gloss, metallic finish. Dry pigment, bronzing powders, and commercial colorants can be added to the resin to give it color. Almost any natural material (dirt, sand, sawdust) can be added to impart texture. Polyester resin is probably the quickest finishing method available that will cover the grain of wood to give it a realistic metallic appearance.

Polyester resin must be mixed with the catalyst-hardener methylethylketone (MEK) to harden. Since the amount of MEK added to the polyester resin determines the time it takes the resin to "set," or harden, pay particularly close attention to the instructions on the resin container. Always mix the resin and hardener in wax-coated paper or metal containers. Don't use Styrofoam, because the resin will melt it. Be sure to use disposable containers, because the resin is all but impossible to remove after it has begun to cure.

ENAMEL Enamel is an opaque paint with an oil, lacquer, or synthetic base. It has a hard surface and excellent covering power. Enamel is usually formulated so it dries with a smooth satin or gloss finish. It is used to paint any surface on which this type of hard finish is needed or desired (furniture, door and window casings, and so on).

Any object that is to be enameled should first be painted with enamel undercoat so the surface will be properly sealed. If the surface isn't sealed, the finish of the enamel will not have the desired smooth, softly glowing appearance.

Applicators

A number of different types of applicators are used in scene painting.

BRUSH Good-quality scene-painting brushes are expensive. But it is also axiomatic that good scene painting demands good brushes.

Brushes that are to be used with the various types of water-based scene paint should have 100 percent natural bristles of the highest available quality. These bristles are fairly long and have good springiness when wet. Scene-painting brushes generally have to be ordered from scenic supply houses.

There are three general types of scene-painting brush: priming, lay-in, and detail, as shown in Figure 10.1. The priming brush is used for applying the prime coat, or first covering coat, of paint. It is quite large (six to seven inches wide), so it can carry a great deal of paint. The lay-in brush is used to apply

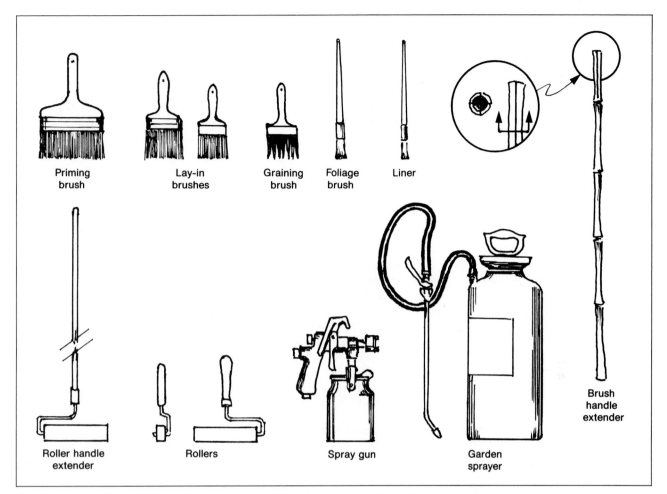

Priming brush

Lay-in brushes

Graining brush

Foliage brush

Liner

Brush handle extender

Roller handle extender

Rollers

Spray gun

Garden sprayer

Figure 10.1 Paint applicators.

the base coat, which follows the prime coat. This brush is smaller (four to five inches wide), because the application techniques frequently used with base coats require quick manipulation of the brush, and it is much easier to change the position of a smaller and lighter brush. The detail brushes (one-quarter to two inches wide) are used for fine work such as painting lines and leaves.

A push broom can be effectively used for painting floors. Paint is simply poured directly onto the floor and pushed around and smoothed out with the broom.

Several specialty brushes are extremely useful to the scenic artist. The wood-graining brush is actually several small brushes in one. Each of the approximately six China-bristle artist's brushes are flexibly mounted in a four-inch-wide ferrule. As the brush is used, the individual tips move independently of one another to give a random wood-grain appearance. The badger brush is made with the very limber bristles of the badger. Rather than being used to apply paint, it is used to feather and blend paint applied with other techniques. Lettering brushes, which can be purchased at most art stores, are very useful for lettering and similar sign-work applications.

SPONGES Both natural and synthetic sponges have many uses in scene painting. Natural sponges, which hold a great deal of paint, can be gently pressed against the scenery to create an irregularly textured pattern. Synthetic sponges are also used for texturing, and they can be cut into a pattern (using a band-saw, scissors, or knife), mounted on a backing board such as a small piece of

BRUSHES: DOS AND DON'TS

You'll need to follow several suggestions to help your brushes last a long time and provide you with the best possible results.

DOS

1. Always thoroughly clean the brush in the appropriate type of solvent. Water-base paints are cleaned with warm water and liquid dish soap. The appropriate solvent for non-water-base paints will be printed on the container label. To remove the paint from the ferrule (the metal cap that binds the bristles to the handle) load the brush with solvent and repeatedly press the bristles sideways in alternate directions.

2. After cleaning, hang your brushes to dry in a clean, well-ventilated place (preferably a brush cabinet) with the bristles pointing down. Lay-in and priming brushes usually have a hole in the handle for this purpose. Detail brushes don't. Either drill a hole in the end of the brush or hang it vertically with a spring-loaded clip.

3. Use the right kind of bristle for the job. Natural bristles (white China bristles) are best for detail work (lining, foliage) with water-base paints. High-quality polyester bristles are good for lay-in and priming brushes (four to seven inches wide). General-purpose brushes (one to three inches wide) can have either natural or polyester bristles.

4. Use natural-bristle brushes only when working with polyester resin. The resin will melt most synthetic bristles into a totally useless blob.

DON'TS

1. Don't use a natural-bristle watercolor brush (liner, foliage brush) in anything but water-base paints. The solvents in oil- or lacquer-base paints will deteriorate the bristle spine and make the brush floppy and basically useless.

2. Don't use synthetic-bristle brushes in polyester resin.

3. After cleaning your brushes don't put them anywhere where the bristles will be bent.

plywood with latex contact cement, and used as a stencil to form a repetitive pattern.

ROLLERS Paint rollers, with extending handles, can be very helpful for a variety of scene-painting jobs, ranging from floor painting to detail work on drops. Generally, the wider rollers are used for applications on large areas, such as floors and similar hard surfaces, and the narrower rollers are used for detail work. Regardless of the application technique, the rollers should be covered with quality material designed for use with water-base paints.

AEROSOL SPRAY CAN Spray cans of paint are amazingly useful items for the scenic artist. Available in a wide range of metallic and nonmetallic colors, these paints are very useful for painting props, plastics, and metals, and they can be used to apply highlights and shadows to decorative elements on the sets. Aerosol fabric sprays are frequently used in the costume shop to **distress,** or age, costumes and costume accessories.

Distress: To create a worn or aged appearance, as with fabric, wood, or metal.

SPRAY GUN Compressed-air spray guns can be used in a variety of ways for scene painting. They are used for painting furniture and applying a dusting of shadow or highlight color to both drops and scenery.

Garden sprayers can also be used for applying glaze coats, fire-retardant solutions, and **spattering.** You will need to use a high-quality sprayer for spattering, simply because these more expensive models produce a relatively smooth pattern from one edge of the spray cone to the other.

Auxiliary Scene-Painting Tools

A number of other tools are also part of the craft of scene painting.

CHARCOAL AND CHALK Although hardly unique to scene painting, charcoal and white or lightly colored chalk are invaluable tools for drawing parts of the design on the scenery during various phases of the painting process. The choice between charcoal and chalk is usually dictated by whether the background color on the item to be painted is light or dark.

HANDLE EXTENDER Handle extenders can be made for almost every scene-painting brush to allow you to paint scenery that is lying on the stage floor while you are standing up. The extenders, generally three feet long, are frequently made from bamboo. The end of the bamboo is split so it will slide over the end of the handle. The extender is then secured to the brush handle with either heavyweight rubber bands or tape. If bamboo isn't locally available, broom handles or similar three-quarter- to one-inch-diameter dowels taped to the handle of the brush make acceptable extenders. Broom handles with threaded tips can be used as extenders for roller handles, or you can purchase extendable handles in paint stores.

BUCKET Small, lightweight, one-gallon plastic buckets are very useful for carrying small amounts of scene paint. (Number 10 tin cans are very useful, usually free, substitutes for these buckets.)

Larger buckets (over one gallon) should be made from either heavyweight plastic with a wire-reinforced lip or galvanized metal, simply because the weight of the paint will break a lightweight plastic bucket. Casein paint is often sold in heavyweight one- or two-gallon plastic pails that make ideal paint buckets. The sturdy five-gallon metal or plastic buckets in which interior latex wall paint is sold are perfect for mixing large batches of paint.

STRAIGHT EDGE A straight edge is used as a guide while painting straight lines. Although it can be made in any length, it is normally 3 to 6 feet long and about 2½ inches wide. A handle is attached to the center of the straight edge (Figure 10.2) so you can balance it while working. The underside of the straight edge should be beveled to prevent the paint from creeping under it.

CHALK LINE The chalk line, also called a snap line, is a tool borrowed from the carpenters (see Chapter 8 for details). The bow snap line, which looks like an archery bow, is a shorter version of the chalk line that can be used easily by one person. Dry pigment is rubbed on the snap line, the bow is held in place with one hand, and the line is snapped with the other hand.

PAINT CART When painting detail work it is usually necessary to mix a little bit of a number of different color paints to achieve the right hue. The paint cart (Figure 10.2) provides a convenient method of carrying those different colors, as well as the other paraphernalia used by the scene painter.

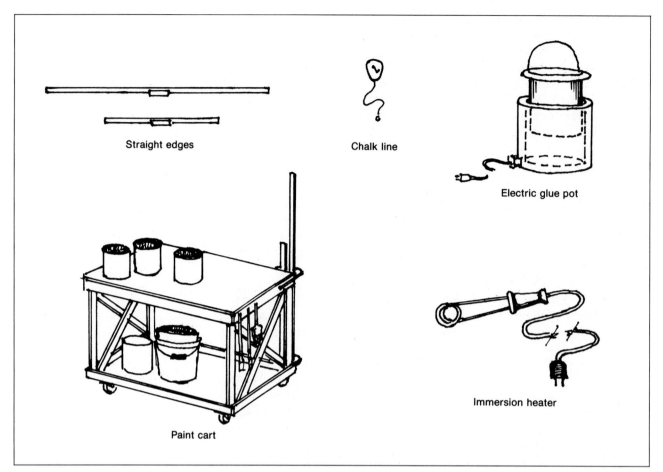

Straight edges

Chalk line

Electric glue pot

Immersion heater

Paint cart

Figure 10.2
Painting
accessories.

ELECTRIC GLUE POT The electric glue pot (Figure 10.2) is an indispensable tool for melting animal glue. A good-quality glue pot is thermostatically controlled to heat the glue to its melting point without burning or scorching. Although animal glue can be melted in a double boiler or by placing the container of glue in a water-filled pan on top of a hot plate, the electric glue pot all but eliminates the potential fire and horrendous odor hazards associated with these improvised solutions.

IMMERSION HEATER An electric immersion heater is a handy device for heating water for any of the paint-mixing chores that require hot water (starch mixtures, aniline dye, flameproofing, and so on). It is simply inserted into the bucketful of water and turned on. It can heat the water to boiling in a relatively quick time.

When using an immersion heater you must take care that it is always in excellent working condition—that the electrical cord, plug, and watertight seal between the unit and the cord are not damaged in any way. After using be sure that the heater is placed on a heat-resistant surface in a location where no one will accidentally touch it.

PREPARING SCENERY FOR PAINTING

A certain amount of preparation needs to be done before scenery can be painted.

Repairing Holes

Any holes in the fabric covering of the flats should be repaired. First, fray the fabric for about one-quarter of an inch back from the edge of the hole. Then cut out a piece of the same type of material (muslin, scenic canvas) approximately twice as large as the hole. Cover the patch with animal glue, casein, or vinyl acrylic paint and place it over the hole *on the back* of the flat. On the face of the flat, smooth the frayed edges of the hole, and blend them into the surface of the patch.

Applying Dutchmen

As we have seen, dutchmen are four- to six-inch-wide strips of muslin used to cover the joints between flats in a single wall section. Fray about one-quarter of an inch along the edges of the dutchman. Paint the joint (the full width of the dutchman) with a compound made of three parts water and one part hot glue. (This compound won't bleed through the dutchman to stain the finished paint job.) Quickly apply the dutchman over the joint, and smooth the frayed edges to blend into the surface of the flats. Be sure to select dutchman material that is of the same composition and condition as the flats that it is covering.

Flameproofing

All scenery needs to be flameproofed. Although more and more items that are used for building scenery and props are being flameproofed at the factory, it is a good precaution to apply a flame-retardant solution to all scenery constructed in the shop. There are a variety of commercially manufactured flameproofing solutions, but a formula that has been used for years, and is generally effective, is as follows: one pound of borax, one pound of sal ammoniac, one-half pint of vinegar, and one gallon of hot water. This solution is liberally sprayed, brushed, or rolled onto both the fabric and wood of the scenery before any coats of paint are applied. The materials for this flameproofing solution are generally available locally. When this shop-built flameproofing solution is used, its effectiveness should be tested and the results verified by the local fire inspector. Washing or dry cleaning removes the salts that give any flameproofing solution its effectiveness, so scenery that is cleaned will have to be treated again.

Horizontal and Vertical Painting

Traditionally, two-dimensional scenery has been painted while lying flat. There are several advantages to this method of painting: a number of painters can work simultaneously; all portions of the set are accessible; some texturing techniques are more suited to this horizontal application; and a wooden floor provides excellent uniform support for drops and other unframed scenery. But horizontal painting has some disadvantages: it requires a lot of floor space; you have to walk on the fabric to get to the center of a large piece; the toggle bars in flats may leave horizontal drying lines if the paint is applied heavily; if the humidity is high, drying time for a drop is lengthened (although warm air forced under the drop will solve this challenge); and unless the shop is equipped with a loft or some elevated vantage point, it is very difficult to move away from the paint job to see what it looks like.

Vertical painting is usually done on a paint frame (Figure 10.3A). The frame is either permanently fixed to one wall, or it is counterweighted and lowered into a paint well. In either case the framed or unframed scenery is

Figure 10.3 Vertical scene painting tools.

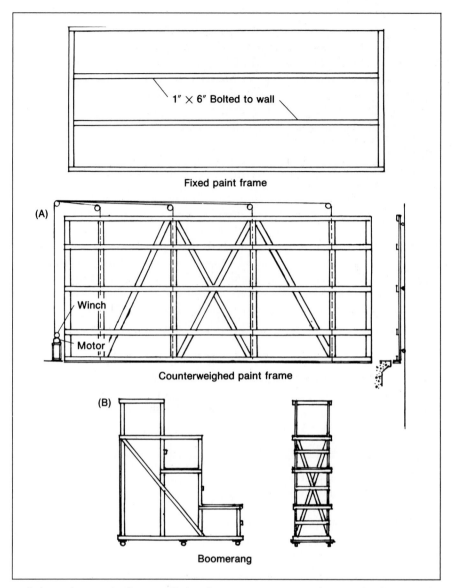

nailed to the paint frame. If the frame is permanently mounted, painting above floor level is done from ladders or a multilevel rolling platform called a boomerang (Figure 10.3B). The counterweighted paint frame is lowered into the paint well to bring the upper parts of the scenery to the painter's eye level. Almost all painting techniques can be used when the scenery is in a vertical position; it just takes a little more care and skill to avoid drips and runs.

PRELIMINARY COATING

Two basic coatings are normally applied to scenery before the application of the specialized texture and detail coats.

Size Coat

If the muslin or other fabric covering has never been painted, you will need to size it before proceeding with the rest of the paint job. Sizing does two things: (1) it shrinks the fabric, which tightens it on the flat frame, and (2) it

I f you are painting over scenery that has been previously painted with dry pigment and binder, you can prevent bleedthrough (caused when the moisture from the new paint loosens the binder in the old paint, allowing the two coats to blend) by mixing about one-quarter of a cup of alum per gallon of paint. A mixture of approximately fifteen parts of water to one part of white glue can also help prevent bleeding.

If small areas of the undercoat continue to bleed through, or if a persistant stain won't stay covered with the alum or white glue coat, you can brush the offending area with white shellac. White shellac will also stop the staining caused by pine knots.

fills the surface of the cloth, which prepares the fabric for the ensuing coats of paint. The sizing can be brushed or sprayed onto the fabric.

Sizing can be made from water and hot glue (sixteen to one), with whiting and a little pigment added to let you see where you've painted. It can also be made by thinning inexpensive latex interior paint with water (approximately two to one).

If you want to create a translucent effect when painting with dye, size the fabric with cornstarch (about one pound of starch in one gallon of hot water). A semitranslucent effect can be created with dyes if you do not size the fabric before painting. However, you will need to brush the material with water first to tighten it on the flat.

Prime Coat

The prime coat, also called the ground coat, is the first layer of paint that is applied to all of the scenery to provide a uniform base for the rest of the paint job. If the scenery is going to be painted with casein or vinyl acrylic paints, the prime coat can be eliminated as long as the colors on the previously painted parts of the set are not too wildly divergent in hue or brilliance.

The prime coat provides a golden opportunity to use any **garbage paint** that may be in the shop. Garbage paint is composed of those remnants of paint that are inevitably left after a paint job has been completed. As long as the paint hasn't spoiled and the various hues are not too saturated, these remnants can be mixed together, neutralized to a medium gray or brown by adding a complementary pigment, and used as the prime coat.

Several techniques are used in mixing the various types of paint.

Dry Pigment and Binder

The only real way of determining the amount of pigment needed per gallon of paint is based on the particular situation (new versus old material, type of previously applied paint, and so on). Generally speaking, however, the paint is "right" when it is the consistency of coffee cream.

Some general guidelines may help you mix this type of paint. Mix a little alcohol and water with the pigment to form a paste the consistency of sour

Garbage paint: Any paint left over from previous paint jobs; the various hues are mixed to create a (usually) rather ugly light brown color.

cream. (The alcohol helps the pigments go into solution.) Add enough size water to the paste to get it to painting consistency.

Casein

Although the exact ratio varies with hue, manufacturer, and specific application, one part of paste is generally mixed with two to four parts of water.

Latex

Most frequently used in its undiluted state, latex paint can be extended with up to approximately one pint of water to one gallon of paint before its covering power is adversely affected.

Vinyl Acrylic

The many techniques for mixing vinyl acrylic paint were covered under the discussion of this extremely versatile paint earlier in this chapter.

No paints look the same wet as they do dry. Dry pigment and binder looks much lighter when it's dry than when wet. For this reason mix the pigments to match the painter's elevations before you add the size water. The variations between the wet and dry appearance of the other paints aren't quite so dramatic, but it is still necessary to make dry test samples (chips) and check them against the painter's elevations whenever you are mixing colors. (A hand-held hair dryer speeds the drying process immeasurably.)

SCENE PAINTER'S PALETTE

The scene painter's color palette (Figure 10.4) provides a practical guide to the use of readily available scenic paints. (A full-color version of the same palette can be found in Chapter 6.) As we have seen, complementary colors produce the greatest contrast in a comparison between any two hues on a color wheel. Additionally, if complementary colors are mixed in equal proportion, the resultant hue will be a neutral gray. (Theoretically, the mix should produce black, but impurities in the paints prevent a theoretically perfect mix.) Many scene painters prefer to mix gray this way, because a gray mixed with complementary hues has more visual vibrancy and life than a gray produced from a black and white mix. When **related colors** are mixed, they produce a hue that is an approximate average of the two original hues. However, this resultant hue has a lower value than either of the original colors. Mixtures of hues other than complementary or related will create colors that fall somewhere between these two extremes.

The mixing of colors to match the various hues on the painter's elevation is a very specialized craft that has to be practiced to be learned. The principles of color theory discussed in Chapter 6 provide the base from which all practical pigment mixing stems. However, there are a few practical hints that may help as you try to translate theory into practice.

1. Be sure that all individual component paints are thoroughly stirred and all lumps of color completely dissolved before you start mixing the final paint.

2. To reduce the value or saturation of any hue, add a complementary hue, add a less saturated pigment of the same color, or, as a last resort, add

Related colors: Colors that are adjacent to each other on the color wheel.

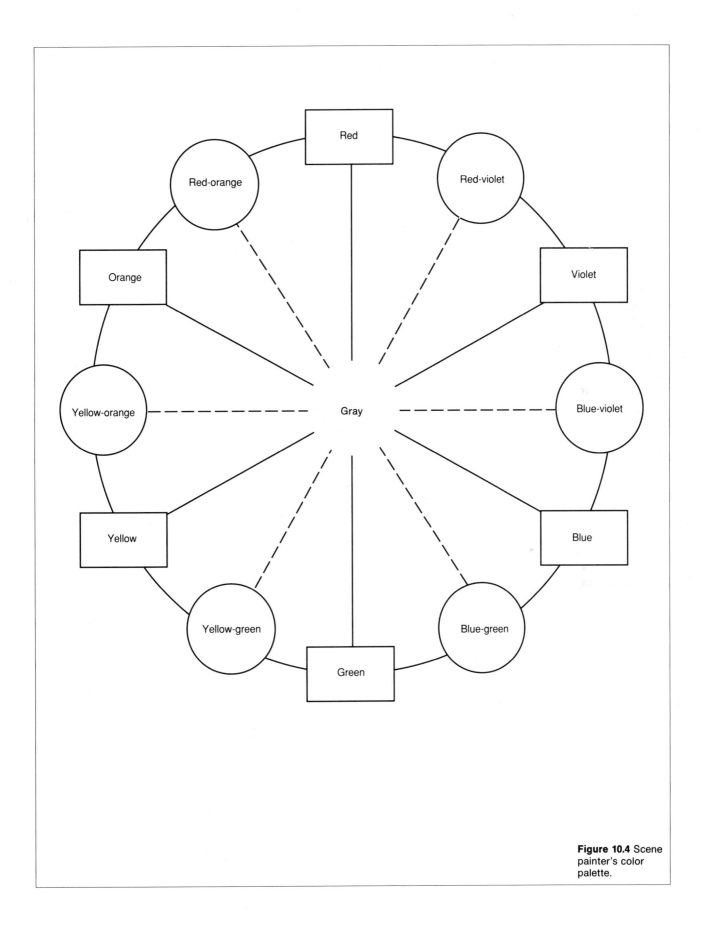

Figure 10.4 Scene painter's color palette.

Box: To pour paint back and forth between buckets to ensure a complete and uniform mix.

black. The addition of black should be done very carefully, and only to hues of relatively low value (shades: dark blue, dark green, purple, and the like), because the black has a tendency to kill the vibrancy and life in any color. It will turn tints (light yellow, pink, and the like) into really ugly mud colors.

3. To increase the value of a color, add a pigment of the same hue but higher value, or add white. The addition of white should also be done judiciously. If added to hues of relatively low value, it will tend to bleach out the color and make them look chalky. When it is added to tints, the "bleaching" effects are less dramatic, but still prevalent. To counteract the reduction in saturation caused by the addition of white, add a small amount of a more fully saturated version of the original color to restore the level of saturation.

4. If the hue that you are mixing is of high value, start mixing with the lightest pigment, and slowly add the other components.

5. When mixing dark colors start with the darkest hue, and slowly add the lighter colors.

6. If mixing a batch of paint that fills more than one bucket, be sure to **box** the paint.

7. Almost all paints appear lighter when they are dry than when they are wet. Make test patches of the various hues on the same type of material that is to be painted. Use a hair dryer or a heat gun to speed up the drying process.

Regardless of how many helpful hints you can get from a textbook, the only way that you will learn the craft of color mixing is to go into the paint shop and actually mix paint. A little practice and experimentation will show you that it probably isn't so difficult as you originally thought.

PAINTING TECHNIQUES

A variety of painting techniques is traditionally used in scene painting. Almost all of them are relatively simple, but as with most seemingly easy craft skills they generally take a good deal of practice to master.

Base Coats

The base coat is the foundation for the remainder of the paint job, so it is imperative that it match, as closely as possible, the hue and value of the desired finished color of the set. The specific hue of the base coat, and any other color used in the scenic design, should be mixed using the scenic designer's painter's elevations as the color guide. The method used to apply a base coat can be varied to create different visual effects.

SMOOTH BASE COAT A smooth base coat results from a uniform coat of paint of a specific hue and value being applied to the scenery, as shown in Figure 10.5. There are several guidelines that should help you to apply a smooth base coat.

1. It is generally more efficient to begin painting vertical scenery such as flats at the top. This way you pick up any drips and splashes as you work your way down the scenery. Begin painting horizontal scenery (platforms, floors) at a narrow edge and work your way across the surface.

2. Keep the brush fully loaded with paint. Don't dip more than three-quarters of the length of the bristles into the paint, and lightly press the brush against the inside wall of the bucket to remove any excess paint. Think of

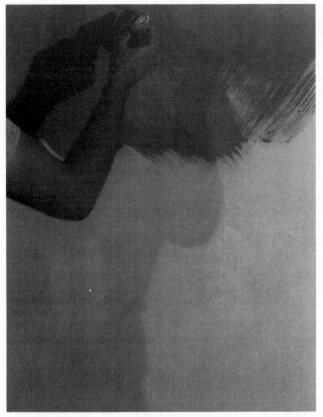
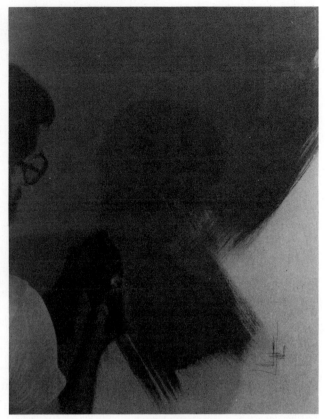

Figure 10.5 Applying a smooth base coat is normally done with a cross-hatch technique.

the paint as flowing from the tips of the bristles onto the surface that you're painting. When the bristles begin to drag across the surface, reload your brush.

3. Keep a wet edge. If the edge of the paint is allowed to dry, it will generally show up as a line or a slight darkening in the finished color. If it becomes necessary to stop painting in the middle of a surface, feather the edge, as shown in Figure 10.5. When you start again, begin painting in an unpainted area of the surface, and feather back into the previously painted surface.

4. Don't scrub the surface with your brush. Scrubbing can loosen old paint and cause a variation on the finished surface of the base coat.

5. When using dry pigment and binder apply the paint in a cross-hatch pattern, as shown in Figure 10.5, to significantly reduce the chances of having any brush marks appear on the finished surface of the base coat. Cross-hatching isn't quite so important when using casein, latex, or vinyl acrylic paints, simply because they are generally more opaque than dry pigment and binder paints and don't show brush marks so easily.

GRADED BASE COAT A graded base coat is one that gradually changes hue or value over the height or width of the painted surface, as shown in Figure 10.6. Graded base coats are frequently used to help make a set look used and worn with age.

The secret to a good graded base coat is speed. The blending must be done while the paint is still wet. Use a separate brush for each color, work rapidly, blend a small area at a time, and progressively work your way around the set.

SCUMBLING Scumbling is similar to a graded base coat in that it involves the blending of several hues. Scumbling provides the illusion of texture by

Figure 10.6 A graded base coat. The pigments to be blended are painted in proximity to each other (A). Using a separate brush for each pigment and working quickly so the paint will stay moist, the painter brings the edges of the dark and light pigments together and merges them (B), to yield a smoothly blended coat of paint (C).

Figure 10.7 Scumbling techniques. (A) A sharply textured, high-contrast curvilinear scumble created by using separate brushes for each pigment and not blending the pigments. (B) A softly textured, low-contrast curvilinear scumble created by using separate brushes for each pigment and over-brushing the surface to blend and merge the separate pigments. (C) A high-contrast linear scumble created by applying separate pigments with a linear brush stroke. (D) A low-contrast linear scumble created by overbrushing the separate pigments.

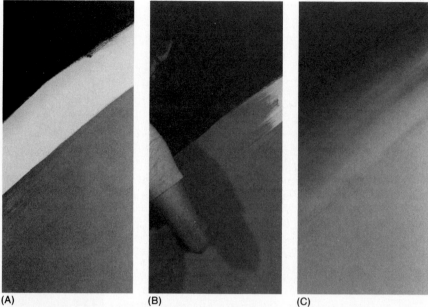

(A)　　　　(B)　　　　(C)

creating an irregular, multihued (or multivalued) base. Instead of creating a smooth blending from one area to the next, scumbling yields a roughly blended base coat of relatively indistinct pattern, as shown in the examples illustrated in Figure 10.7. The type of pattern created is primarily dependent on the style and number of brush strokes used when scumbling. Any type or combination of large or small, circular, swirling, cross-hatch, straight, or curved strokes can be used. Actually, any manipulation of the brushes that slightly blends the varying hues or values of paint is a valid scumbling technique. For scumbling to be effective you will need to follow these two general guidelines.

1. Use a separate brush for each color, in order to maintain the integrity of the individual hues.
2. Work rapidly, because the paints must be wet for the blending to take place.

Depending on the hue and value of paints and the type of brush strokes used when blending them, scumbling can be used to create the appearance of rough plaster, wood, stone, dirt, and a myriad of other surfaces.

(A)　　　　(B)　　　　(C)　　　　(D)

Spraying Techniques

Spraying is the fastest method of applying paint. It is ideal for applying a base coat to ornate forms such as wicker chairs, picket fences, and wrought iron forms. If can also be very effectively used to apply a graded base coat.

The texture of the **spray cone** of most **spray guns** can be adjusted from a fine mist to light droplets. The width of the cone pattern can also be adjusted from narrow to wide.

A spraying system is composed of three separate parts: the spray gun, the paint container, and the compressor. The regular spray gun has a one-quart paint reservoir and is designed for continuous-duty applications—painting flats, floors, houses, and so forth. Touch-up guns have much smaller containers (two to six ounces) and are designed for light-duty jobs such as painting chairs and picture frames and for situations in which the color will have to be changed frequently. Air brushes are equipped with small paint containers (one-half to two ounces) and are used for fine detail and lining work. Most air brushes can be varied to spray a hard- or soft-edged line as well as a typical misty cone.

Compressors provide the motive power for most spray guns. The smallest serviceable compressor for general theatrical spraying would have an electric motor of approximately one horsepower and a ten-gallon air tank. The larger, permanent compressor systems found in many shops provide an excellent air source for spray painting. Much smaller one-eighth- or one-sixteenth-horsepower compressors, as well as disposable compressed-air cans, are frequently used to power air brushes. Small electrically powered airless spray guns such as the Wagner Power Painter can be used in most theatrical applications as an effective substitute for the more expensive compressed air systems.

Spray cone: The pattern of paint emitted from the nozzle of a spray gun.

Spray gun: A pistol-like device that shoots out a cone of paint.

Compressor: A pump, typically electric- or gasoline-powered, that drives air into a tank; output pressure from the tank is controlled by a valve called a regulator.

SPRAY PAINTING TIPS

If these general guidelines are followed, you should find that your spray-painting experiences will be productive and relatively trouble free.

1. Always rinse the spray gun before using it to make sure that there is no dust or grit that could clog the nozzle in the gun or paint container.

2. Be sure to strain the paint with a commercial strainer or small-mesh nylon, such as the material in stockings or pantyhose. Straining the paint will remove any little globs of paint that might clog the nozzle.

3. Run a momentary blast of compressed air through the hoses before attaching them to the gun to remove any dust or grit from the hoses.

4. Don't "fan" the gun at the work; keep the gun a uniform distance from the work, and move it parallel with the surface to deposit a uniform coat of paint.

5. Be sure to wear a dust mask or respirator to filter out the atomized paint from the air you breath; wear goggles to keep the airborne paint out of your eyes.

6. Be sure to keep the compressor pressure within the recommended levels for the gun and type of paint you're using.

Cartooning

Some scenic designs have a great deal of detail that must be transferred to the scenery after the prime and base coats have been applied. Cartooning refers to the process of making these transfers. Large, simple designs can usually be applied simply by taking scale measurements of the object on the painter's elevation and transferring them to the scenery. Any further details can usually be duplicated by freehand sketching with frequent references back to the painter's elevation. If the object is quite detailed, one of the following methods can be used to duplicate it accurately on the scenery.

GRID TRANSFER In the appropriate scale, draw a one-foot-square grid on the painter's elevation. (To preserve the elevation cover it with a sheet of acetate, and use a fine-point acetate marker or well-sharpened grease pencil to draw the grid.) Also draw a full-scale one-foot-square grid on the scenery, as shown in Figure 10.8. If the scenery is small, this grid can be drawn using a straight edge and charcoal or chalk. If the scenery is large, the grid can be created by tacking four-penny box nails, one foot apart, around the edge of the scenery. String is laced back and forth between the nails to create the grid. Be sure to use the same beginning point for both grids, such as the lower left corner or some other readily identifiable point, on both the painter's elevation and the scenery.

If the horizontal grid lines on both the painter's elevation and the drop grid are designated with letters and the vertical lines with numbers, as shown in Figure 10.8, it becomes a relatively rapid process to accurately transfer the points of intersection between the drawing on the elevation and the eleva-

Figure 10.8 Grid transfer technique.

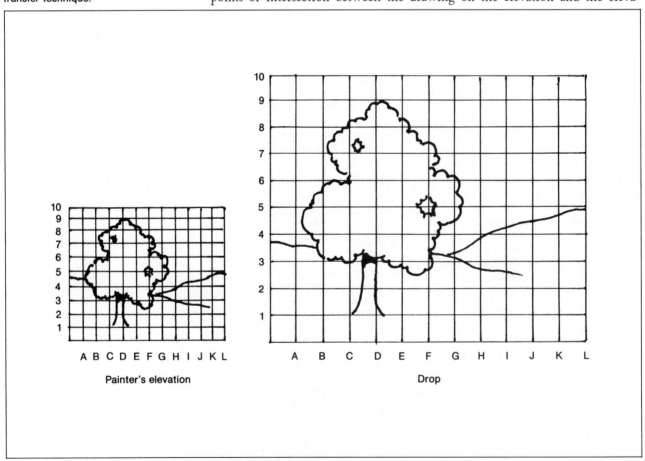

Painter's elevation

Drop

CHAPTER 10: SCENE PAINTING

tion's grid to the full-scale grid on the scenery. When those points have been located, connect the dots using a piece of charcoal or chalk to complete the transfer of the design to the scenery.

PROJECTION TRANSFER An opaque projector can also be used to project the painter's elevation onto the scenery. The projector is placed far enough from the scenery to project a full-scale image of the object onto the scenery, and the design is traced in charcoal or chalk.

There are two drawbacks to this method: the shop needs to be relatively dark while the projection transfer is being made; and, unless the projector is placed perpendicular to center point of the drop, or flat, **keystoning** will occur. (A full discussion of keystoning and how to avoid it is contained in Chapter 15, *Projections*.) If you can avoid these two pitfalls, projection cartooning is generally much faster and more accurate than a grid transfer.

Standard Texture Coats

The following techniques are normally applied on top of the base coat to provide visual interest, variety, depth, and patina to the scenery.

SPATTERING Spattering is the process of applying small drops of paint to a surface. Spattering is done over the base coat to help age the paint job, slightly alter the hue, or smooth out any apparent irregularities in an unevenly applied base coat. Spattering can be done either by hand or with a garden sprayer and with the scenery in either a vertical or a horizontal position. It is a very effective painting technique that can be mastered with a little practice.

Hand spattering is done by slapping a lightly loaded paintbrush against the heel of your hand. Dip only the tips of the brush in the paint, and scrape most of the paint off on the lip of the bucket. Stand three to five feet from the surface, and slap the **ferrule** of the brush against the heel of your hand. As the bristles snap forward, they throw tiny paint droplets at the scenery. The amount of paint in the brush and the distance that you stand from the object being spattered will determine the size and density of the individual droplets. By constantly changing the relative position of the brush you will make a cross-hatch design that creates an appropriately neutral spatter pattern, as shown in Figure 10.9.

Keystoning: The distortion that occurs in a projected image when the projector is placed at some angle other than perpendicular to the center of the projection surface.

Ferrule: The metal part of a brush that binds the bristles to the handle.

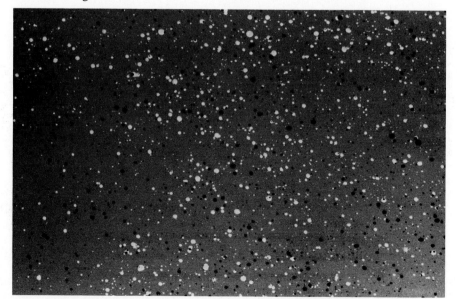

Figure 10.9 Spattering is created when drops of paint are applied to a surface. This is an example of a two-tone spatter.

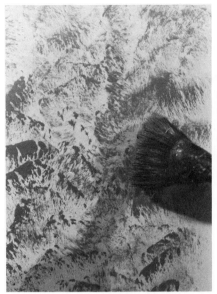
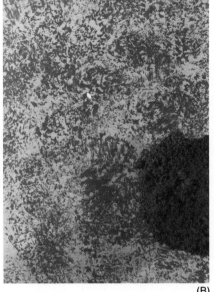

(A) (B) (C)

Figure 10.10 Stippling with a brush (A), with a sponge (B), and with a feather duster (C). Stippling is frequently used to create the appearance of surface texture.

Figure 10.11 Dry brushing is often used to create the appearance of wood grain. The tip of the brush is dipped in paint, scraped across the lip of the bucket (to remove excess paint), and lightly dragged across the surface of the work.

A garden sprayer can also be used to spatter. The nozzle of the sprayer can be adjusted to spray a pattern that varies in density from a fine mist to medium-sized droplets. The sprayer handle should be moved in a circular pattern as you spatter to avoid any tendency to create a linear pattern. To avoid clogging the nozzle you should strain the paint before putting it into the sprayer. Be sure to thoroughly clean the sprayer after each use.

STIPPLING Although similar to spattering, stippling applies a heavier texture to the scenery. As shown in Figure 10.10, stipling can be done with the tip of a brush, a sponge, or a feather duster. It can also be done with the frayed end of a rope or the edge of a piece of burlap.

Stippling is accomplished by loading one of these applicators with paint and touching it to the scenery. To avoid making an obvious pattern you need to constantly change the position of the applicator and the pressure with which you apply it to the scenery.

DRY BRUSHING Dry brushing is painting with a brush that holds very little paint. Just the tip of the brush is dipped in the paint. Any paint that has been picked up by the bristles is scraped off on the lip of the bucket. The brush is then lightly drawn across the surface to deposit a linear, irregular pattern of paint (see Figure 10.11).

Dry brushing is very effective in creating the appearance of wood. If the dry brushing paint(s) is fairly close in hue and value to the color of the base coat, the result will look like smooth wood. If the contrast between the hue and value of the base and dry brush paints is greater, the result will look more rough hewn.

LINING Lining involves painting narrow, straight lines of varying width. The lines are painted with lining brushes, which were illustrated in Figure 10.1, with larger brushes creating wider lines. A straight edge is used in conjunction with the lining brush, as shown in Figure 10.12A.

Lining can be used to create the appearance of depth, as shown in the Figures 10.12B and C. The illusion is primarily achieved through the use of highlight and shadow lines. The effect of the **source light** on an object will determine where the highlight and shadow lines need to be painted. On the bricks, notice the highlight at the top edge and the shadows below. On the paneling, see how the placement of the highlight and shadow lines creates the illusion of depth. Both of these examples are effective because the highlight and shadows look as if they were created by some specific source light. The location of the source light should appear to be some specific source within the design—either a practical onstage lamp or a specific position and angle (agreed on by the scenic and lighting designers) for an offstage, unseen source such as the sun.

Source light: The apparent source of light that is illuminating a scene or object.

Applications of Painting Techniques

Figure 10.13 shows a potpourri of fairly standard applications of the various painting techniques that have been discussed in this section. Careful study of the individual pictures can be helpful in understanding how the images were created.

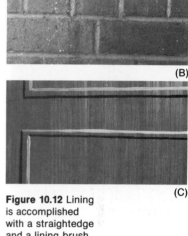

(A)

(B)

(C)

Figure 10.12 Lining is accomplished with a straightedge and a lining brush (A). It is frequently used to create the illusion of highlight and shadow, as shown in B and C.

(A)

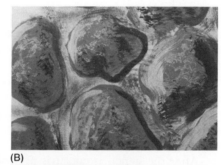

(B)

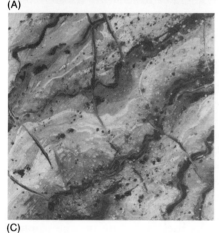

(C)

(D)

Figure 10.13 Scene-painting techniques can be combined to create a variety of realistic forms. Wood grain (A) is primarily accomplished with successive layers of dry brushing in (generally) two or three tones of paint and an overcoat of glaze(s) in one or more tints. Stone (B) is usually created by scumbling two or three tones of a similar hue with a light uneven overlay of stippled or spattered highlight and shadow to provide a slightly rougher texture. Marble (C) is created by wet blending (scumbling with a lot of paint) several tones or related hues in a loose, vaguely linear pattern and overspattering with large drops of the same paint. Foliage (D) uses a combination of all techniques; the tree trunk and branches are created by scumbling and drybrushing, the foliage and grass with scumbling, stippling, and spattering, and the distant bushes with stippling and a light spatter.

Whiting: A white powder extender, basically low-grade chalk, used to increase the covering power of dry pigment and binder paint.

Stencil paper: Stiff, water-resistant paper used for making stencils.

Vacuforming: The process of shaping heated plastic, usually high-impact polystyrene, around a mold through the use of vacuum pressure.

Stencil brush: A relatively short, squat brush with a circular pattern of short, stiff bristles; the bristles are pressed onto, rather than stroked across, the work, to prevent the paint from bleeding under the edges of the stencil.

Figure 10.14 Stencils are often used to apply repetitive patterns, such as for wallpaper.

The following techniques are not used so frequently as the previously discussed methods of painting, but when the design opportunity presents itself, they can provide dazzling and effective results.

TEXTURING Texturing refers to the use of additives in paint to give actual depth and texture to the surface being painted. Anything can be used for texturing, but organic materials such as sawdust, wood shavings, **whiting,** and sand are commonly used. An alternative form of texturing is to build up a surface using papier-mâché (see Chapter 11, *Stage Properties,* for how-to information on papier-mâché) or some other method and then paint that surface with textured or untextured paint.

A variety of surface textures and forms (bricks, stone, stucco, adobe, tree bark) can be created using the texturing techniques described above. The secret to creating a realistic texture is to carefully study an example of the real thing and then duplicate its general shape, surface quality, and color.

STENCILING Stencils are large, cut patterns that facilitate the creation of repetitive, intricate designs such as wallpaper patterns. The stencil can be cut from **stencil paper,** a commercial product made of heavy, stiff paper impregnated or coated with oils that make the paper water resistant. Stencil paper can be made in the shop by painting thin illustration board with a water-resisting coating such as shellac, lacquer, or spray varnish. Be sure to coat the paper *after* you have cut the design. The high-impact polystyrene plastic used for **vacuforming** is completely waterproof and is excellent for use as stencil material.

After the stencil is cut, it is normally framed with 1 × 2 stock to hold it flat and make it easier to handle. The paint can be applied with a brush, **stencil brush,** roller, paint sprayer, or sponge, as shown in Figure 10.14. Generally, spraying works best, simply because it is gentler on the stencil. Regardless of the application tool used, the stencil will have to be cleaned frequently to remove any excess paint that could be accidentally transferred to the scenery.

FRONT-BACK PAINTING An incredible depth can be created when you paint, and light, both the front and back of muslin-covered scenery. Although this technique is normally used with drops, equally effective results can be achieved on flats and other framed scenery.

Imagine you are painting a landscape on a small drop that will be hung upstage of a window of an interior set. The normal tendency is to paint the entire scene with paint and light it from the front. However, if you paint the solid objects (ground and trees) with paint and the translucent or transparent things (sky and clouds) with dye, you can light the drop from both the front and the back. The apparent depth that is created with this technique is really amazing.

The technique is particularly effective if the scene involves a sunset effect. If the front lights are dimmed and the back lights are up, the painted areas will appear in silhouette. The hue of the backlights, and projections, can be used to create spectacular sunset or night-sky effects.

Front-back painting can also be used to create stained-glass windows and similar effects. Be sure to work with the paint before the dye, because the paint will act as a "dam" to prevent the dye from creeping into other areas of the fabric.

GLAZING Glazing is simply applying a clear top coat to an existing finish. The finish of the glaze coat is usually satin or gloss, but it can also be matte.

Stain and gloss glazes are generally used on furniture and natural woods, and matte glazes are frequently used to protect painted designs. However, there aren't any laws that dictate the particular uses of glaze coats. Use the type of finish that is appropriate to the specific design need.

Glazing can be done with a variety of materials. Extra-strength size water (one part animal glue to eight parts water), thinned white glue, clear vinyl acrylic, lacquer, shellac, and polyurethane varnish are all frequently used for glazing. The choice of which material to use is predicated on the use that the particular piece will receive. Finishes that are more water- and scratch-resistant (shellac, clear vinyl acrylic, polyurethane varnish) should be used for those objects that may be subjected to water or abrasive physical treatment.

Glaze coats can also be tinted to tone down the brilliance or slightly change the hue of the undercoat over which they are being applied.

METALLIC FINISHES The types of material that can be used to create metallic finishes have been discussed in various other sections of this chapter. Briefly, bronzing powders, which are powdered metal (available from scenic supply houses or well-stocked art stores), are mixed with a vehicle and applied to the work. High-gloss materials such as shellac, clear vinyl acrylic, varnish, and polyester resin all work very well as vehicles for the bronzing powders.

The secret to a good metallic finish is the undercoat. The wood, plastic, or fabric to which you are applying your alchemy must be filled until there is absolutely no evidence of any wood grain or other texture. The best undercoat is polyester resin. Generally, one coat of resin will fill any but the roughest surface.

After the undercoat has dried or cured, the bronzing powders or colorants are mixed with vehicle and applied to the work. For small areas, metallic spray paints create a nice metallic appearance if they are used on top of a smooth undercoat.

Wallpapering

As an alternative to painting, particularly in theatres where the audience is sitting very close to the stage, real wallpaper can be used. Although wallpaper can be applied to muslin-covered flats, the finished job will look much better if the flat is covered with a hard covering such as Upson board, Masonite, or plywood. The wallpaper is applied with vinyl acrylic wallpaper paste or wheat paste.

Drop Painting Techniques

Drops need to be stretched and framed in some manner before they can be painted. The stretching not only produces a smooth surface on which to paint but also minimizes shrinkage. The drop can be stretched on a vertical paint frame by:

1. nailing a framework of boards the same width and height as the drop to the paint frame.
2. attaching the drop to the framework. Staples with one-half-inch legs, spaced one foot apart, normally secure any muslin drop to the framework. If the drop is going to be saturated with dyes or paint (which causes it to shrink a great deal), it will be better to secure it with roofing nails.

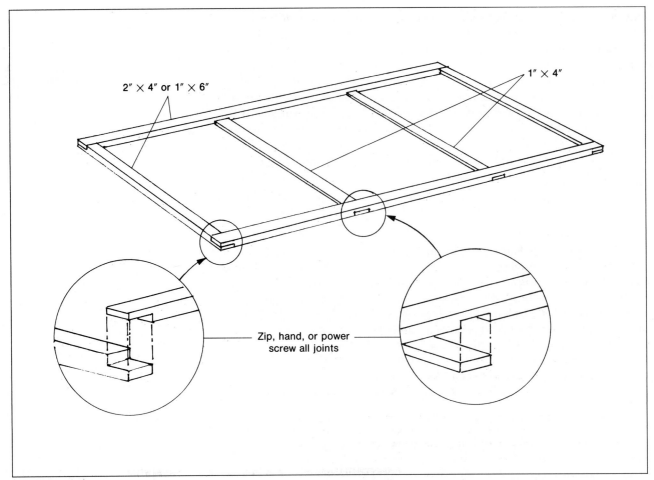

2" × 4" or 1" × 6"

1" × 4"

Zip, hand, or power screw all joints

Figure 10.15 Temporary drop stretcher.

Some painting techniques are more easily executed with the drop in a horizontal position. In these cases the drop will need to be stretched on a wooden floor and secured to the floor with staples or roofing nails spaced on one-foot centers. Be sure to put a layer or two of Kraft or other butcher paper underneath the drop to protect the floor and the drop. (The paints or dyes may stain the floor, or the back of the drop may pick up some staining from old paint or dye already on the floor.)

If you do not have a wooden floor large enough to accommodate the size of the drop, you will need to build a temporary frame large enough to stretch the drop. The frame can be made of notched 2 × 4 or 1 × 6 so it will hold its shape against the rather strong force created when the fabric shrinks. As shown in Figure 10.15, the toggle bars of this oversized frame are made of 1 × 4s. Before you stretch the drop and nail it to the framework, don't forget to cover the area under the drop with butcher paper.

In the final analysis any scenic paint job is dependent on the talent and ingenuity of the scenic artist. The materials and techniques suggested in this chapter provide only a beginning point for the scene-painting artist. Although each of the materials has specific properties, there aren't any artistic "rules" to which the painter must adhere. Experimentation, trial and error, and learning from your happy accidents are the only guidelines that need to be followed as you work to develop your skill in the challenging field of scene painting.

In the proscenium theatre the stage properties are the icing on the scenic designer's cake. Although the set usually creates the dominant visual motif, the properties are really coequal design elements. They are generally the primary design tool used to provide clues about the personality and socioeconomic status of the inhabitants of the set. Figure 11.1 demon-

Stage Properties

strates these principles. Figure 11.1 is a relatively nondescript living room that is furnished in three different ways. In Figure 11.1A, it is furnished with utilitarian props that don't provide many indications of the nature and character of the inhabitants or to the period of the play. Figure 11.1B illustrates how changing the style of the properties to late Victorian changes our perception of the social class and characteristics of the room's inhabitants. Additionally, it suggests a relatively clear idea of the period of the play. These visual clues are again demonstrated in Figure 11.1C, where the absence of any furnishings other than the stacked boxes, broom, and a crumpled newspaper suggest that the room's inhabitants are either moving in or moving out.

The visual importance of stage properties increases significantly when the play is produced in either a thrust or arena theatre or any of the other configurations that preclude or restrict the use of vertical scenic elements such as flats and drops. In these intimate theatre spaces where the audience is usually sitting close to the stage, the furniture and decorative props are frequently the major visual elements of the scenic design.

Although the duties and responsibilities of the members of the prop department were covered in Chapter 1, it bears repeating that the property master needs to have a detailed working knowledge of every craft area in theatre; woodworking, metalworking, electrical wiring and electronics, mold making, ceramics, sewing, upholstery, furniture construction, and scene painting are but a few of the craft areas in which a true property master will be competent.

(A)

(B)

(C)

When you understand the actual impact of properties on the appearance of a design and the scope of knowledge that a prop master must possess, it becomes obvious that a full discussion of how to construct stage properties cannot be contained in this chapter. Probably more than in any other single craft area in theatre production, someone who is interested in property design and construction needs to know it all—the history of fashion, architecture, furniture, and decoration; design theory and practice; and craft construction techniques.

WHAT IS A PROP?

Stage properties have traditionally been divided into three categories: (1) set props, (2) hand props, and (3) decorative props.

Set Props

Set props are generally defined as larger movable items, not built into the set, that are used in some way by the actors. This group would include such things as furniture, floor lamps, rugs, stoves, tree stumps, swings, and so forth.

Hand Props

Hand props refer to small items that are handled or carried by the actors. This group includes plates, cups, letters, books, fans, lanterns, and similar items.

Decorative Props

Into the category of decorative props fall all the things that are used to enhance the setting visually but are not specifically touched by the actors. Such items as window curtains, pictures, doilies, table lamps, bric-a-brac, and the books in a bookcase are typical of decorative, or dress, props.

PROPERTY DESIGN

In the New York professional theatre properties are normally designed by the scenic designer and either purchased from stores or constructed by studios that specialize in property construction (Figure 11.2). In educational and regional professional theatres props are also bought, but they are frequently borrowed or rented, and if they are built, they are usually constructed in the organization's own shops. In these theatres the prop master, working closely with the scenic designer, usually designs and either makes or supervises the construction of the props. After consultation with the scenic designer on the general appearance and categories of the props, the prop master does background research by studying books, paintings, and other sources that contain pictures of the objects needed for the production. If there is a museum in the area that has examples of the actual objects from the period, the prop master investigates that source as well. After researching the appearance of the objects the prop master normally makes design sketches and checks them with the scenic designer. When the scenic designer has approved the sketches, the prop master builds, buys, rents, or borrows the props for the production.

Real or Fake?

If an actor is going to touch or pick up a prop, it should feel real. For example, assuming that you are trying to project a realistic or naturalistic appearance, a book should look and feel like a real book and, if it is going to be opened, it should have pages. The scene designer and the property master may want to alter the appearance of the book by painting or staining the cover, covering it with cloth or leather, or hot-gluing jewels or appliqués to it.

Props can be faked if they aren't going to be used by the actors. If the prop book discussed above isn't going to be touched by an actor, it may simply be a cigar box or piece of wood that is painted and decorated to look like a book. Frequently, the books in a bookshelf are the spines of books that have been attached to a frame. Other types of prop can be treated in the same way.

Property Acquisition

To create an aura of authenticity property masters frequently try to find actual objects appropriate to the period of the play to use as props. For a

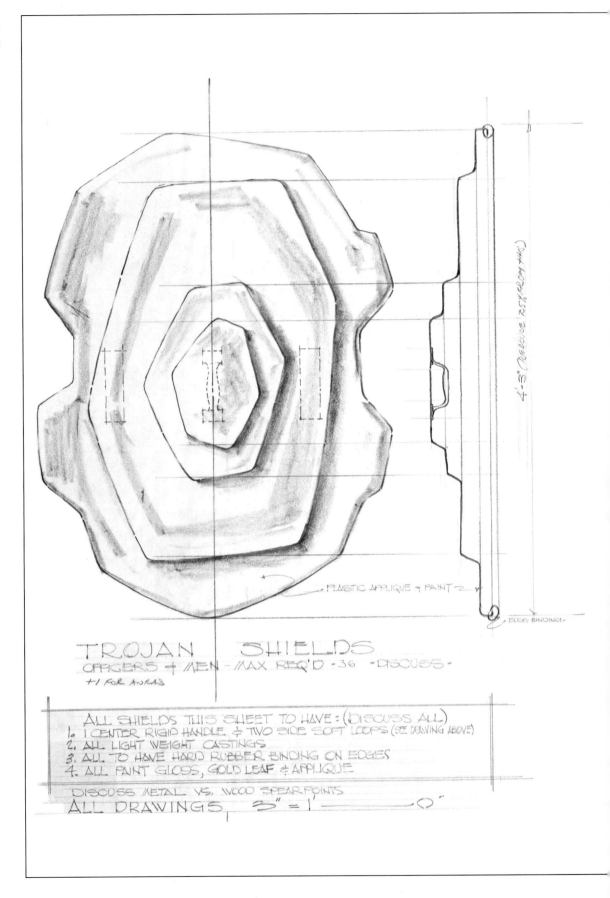

TROJAN SHIELDS
OFFICERS + MEN - MAX REQ'D - 36 - DISCUSS -
+1 FOR ANKAS

ALL SHIELDS THIS SHEET TO HAVE: (DISCUSS ALL)
1. 1 CENTER RIGID HANDLE + TWO SIDE SOFT LOOPS (SEE DRAWING ABOVE)
2. ALL LIGHT WEIGHT CASTINGS
3. ALL TO HAVE HARD RUBBER BINDING ON EDGES
4. ALL PAINT GLOSS, GOLD LEAF + APPLIQUE

DISCUSS METAL VS. WOOD SPEAR-POINTS
ALL DRAWINGS 3" = 1' ————— 0"

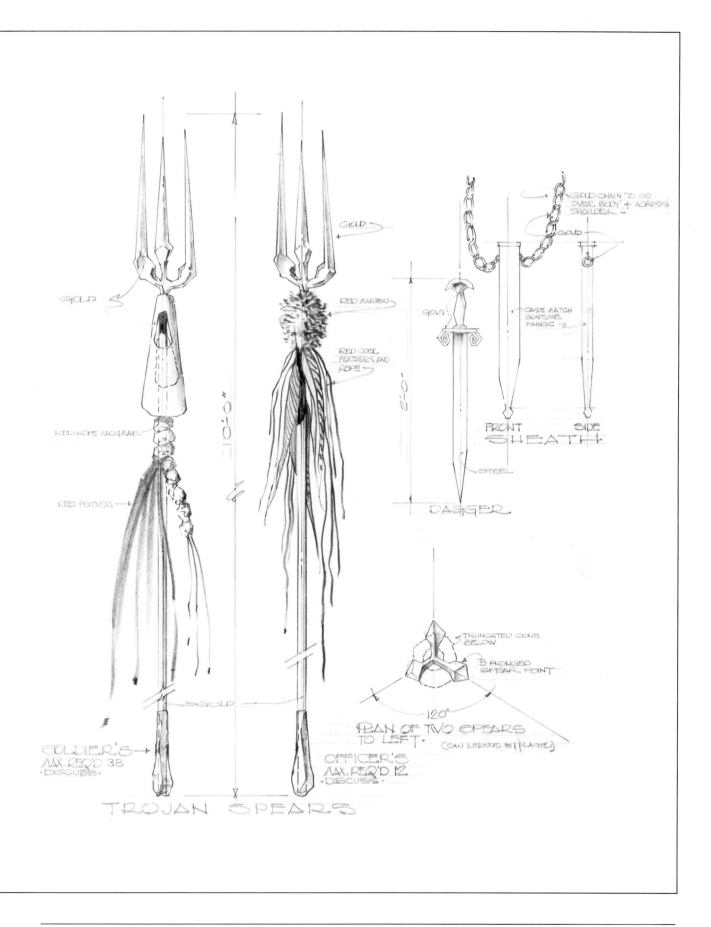

GOLD

GOLD

GOLD

RED MARABU

RED COCK
FEATHERS AND
ROPE

RED ROPE MACRAME

RED FEATHERS

10'-0"

GOLD

SOLDIER'S →
MAX. REQ'D 38
·DISCUSS·

OFFICER'S
MAX. REQ'D 12
·DISCUSS·

TROJAN SPEARS

GOLD CHAIN TO GO
OVER BODY & ACROSS
SHOULDER·

GOLD

CASE MATCH
COSTUME
FABRIC·2

GOLD

2'-0"

FRONT   SIDE
SHEATH

STEEL

DAGGER

TRUNCATED CONE
BELOW

3 PRONGED
SPEAR POINT

120°

PLAN OF TWO SPEARS
TO LEFT·
(CAN REDUCE TO 1 PLASTIC)

contemporary production props can usually be purchased or borrowed from local stores. For a play set twenty or thirty years ago it is relatively easy to find most props in junk shops or used furniture stores. However, when producing a period play such as *Amadeus,* which moves in time between 1780 and 1820 and is set in Vienna, it is very difficult to find actual furniture or decorative props of that period. Even if you could find them, you wouldn't want to put them on the stage for fear that they might be damaged. In these situations the property master frequently builds the props or acquires reproductions.

BORROWING OR RENTING PROPS Some special challenges need to be considered when borrowing props. Any type of prop used in the theatre is subject to unusual stresses and wear. Furniture, which is designed to sit in one location in a room in someone's house and occasionally be moved for cleaning, will be moved around the stage as the scenery is shifted. Even if it isn't moved, the director may block someone to stand on it, flop on it, run across it, or spill a drink on it. It should be obvious that if any of the above are going to take place, the furniture involved shouldn't be borrowed or rented.

If you are borrowing furniture, you should be able to assure the lending party that it will be returned intact. Lenders are frequently more at ease if a lending agreement (Figure 11.3) is executed. This agreement stipulates that the object will be returned in good condition and that the borrower will be responsible for any necessary repairs resulting from accidental damage.

BUILDING PROPS Some props, such as antiques, are best not used on stage. It is usually more appropriate either to use a reproduction or to build the piece in the shop. Other props such as fantasy pieces and antiques, for which there are no reproductions, will have to be built.

Figure 11.3 A lending agreement form.

LENDING AGREEMENT FORM

1. Old Time Productions agrees to return the below listed borrowed items in the same condition in which they were borrowed.

2. If any item is damaged while in the possession of the theatre, Old Time Productions will be responsible for its repair.

3. The items will be borrowed on_____ and returned no later than_____.

ITEMS
_____

For Old Time Productions: _____   Date: _____

Lender: _____   Date: _____

CRAFT TECHNIQUES

Many props can be built using the construction methods that were explained in Chapter 9. A number of additional construction techniques that are primarily used in building stage properties are discussed in the rest of this chapter.

Furniture

Furniture construction, alteration, and upholstery aren't really as difficult as they seem. Carpenter-style furniture (Figure 11.4) can be built using ordinary woodworking tools and techniques. The illustrated table will be very strong if it is assembled with open doweled joints. Because of its strength and ease of fabrication, the open doweled joint can be used for reinforcing almost any joint in furniture construction.

Upholstery

Many times the apparent age or period of a fabric-covered piece can be altered simply by changing the upholstery fabric. For example, the relatively square silhouette of the tuxedo-style sofa (Figure 11.5) has been in continuous fashion since the 1920s. Although the dust ruffle has been in and out of vogue and floral prints have come and gone, the basic style and shape of the sofa have remained basically unchanged. The fabric covering for **stock furniture** is normally altered in two ways: by slipcovers or reupholstery.

Figure 11.4
Exploded view of a carpenter-style table and the finished product.

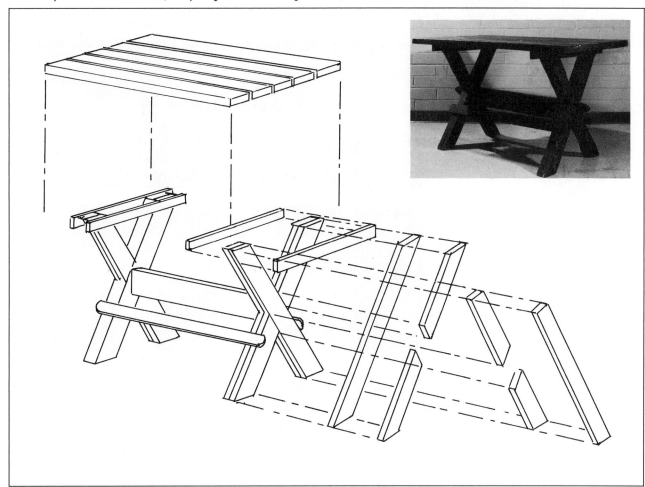

OPENED DOWELED JOINTS

The extremely strong doweled joint, which was introduced in Chapter 9, is used extensively in the furniture industry. The closed, rather than open, doweled joint is preferred for assembling fine furniture, because the dowel is hidden inside the wood. The open doweled joint is just as strong and is actually very easily made, as shown in the accompanying illustrations.

The open doweled technique can be used for making any joint in furniture construction. Even if the joint is on exposed wood, the dowels will rarely be noticed, even in arena productions, because the spectators won't be close enough to see the exposed dowel, particularly if the joint has been sanded, filled with wood putty, stained, grained, and varnished.

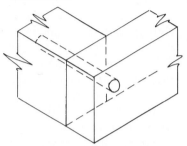

Open doweled joint

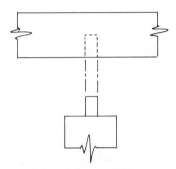

Closed doweled joint

(A)

(B)

(C)

(D)

Open doweled construction technique. Clamp together the parts to be joined (A), and drill a hole through the top piece and approximately 1 to 1½ inches into the second piece (B). Squirt glue into the hole and insert a dowel the same diameter as the hole (C). The finished open dowel joint (D) creates a very strong joint.

SLIPCOVERS A slipcover is upholstery fabric that is tailored to fit a particular piece or type of furniture and is applied over existing upholstery. Slipcovers are normally used on fully upholstered furniture rather than on pieces that have exposed wood. They should be used only if the underlying fabric, padding, and frame are in good condition. Slipcovers can be used on borrowed furniture, since the existing upholstery material is left in place.

REUPHOLSTERY Reupholstery involves removing the existing fabric covering and replacing it with new fabric. The existing fabric should be carefully removed, as shown in Figure 11.6, so it can be used as a pattern to cut the new

Figure 11.5 Changing the upholstery can change the apparent period of a furniture piece.

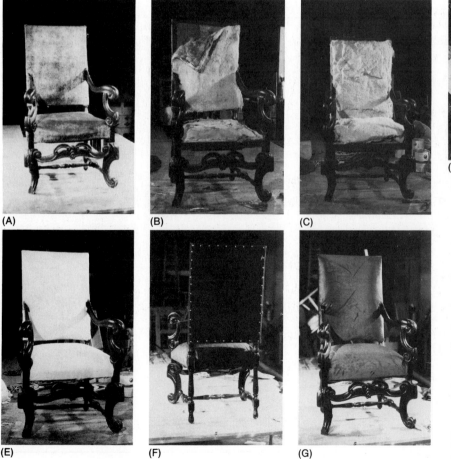

Figure 11.6 Basic reupholstery technique. (A) A chair in need of reupholstery. (B) Carefully remove and save the old fabric and torn elements of padding. (C) Apply new padding. (D) Use the old fabric as a pattern. (E) Cover the padding with muslin to hold the padding in place and to provide a smooth surface over which the covering fabric can slip. (F) Attach the new fabric with staples or decorative tacks. (G) The finished chair.

Dress: To place decorative props such as curtains, doilies, knickknacks, or magazines on the set to help make the environment look lived-in and provide clues to the personality of the set's inhabitants.

Valance: A horizontal element at the top of a drapery arrangement that covers the curtain rod.

Drape: A vertical element of heavy fabric that frames the sides of a window or archway; can usually be pulled across the opening.

Sheer: A thin gauze curtain that hangs across the opening of a window to soften the "sunlight" and obscure the view into a room.

material. Once the old fabric is removed, the padding, springs, and webbing should be examined and repaired as necessary. Depending on the age of the piece, the padding may be either urethane foam, cotton batting, or horsehair. Any damaged or compressed padding should be replaced with the same type of material if possible.

Before applying the new upholstery fabric the padding should be covered with muslin. The muslin holds the padding in place, allows the upholstery fabric to move freely without snagging the padding, and serves as a base for any future reupholstery jobs.

Decorative Curtains and Draperies

Decorative curtains are used by the scenic designer to help **dress** the set. The type and style of drapery or curtain selected should be dictated by the period that is being represented in the design. Background research is done by looking at paintings, drawings, or photographs that show drapery styles of the period being represented. Figure 11.7 illustrates several typical styles of curtain.

A variety of materials is used in making draperies. The specific type of material is dictated by where it is used in the drape. The **valance, drapes** (also called overdrapes), and **sheers** are the primary elements of any window curtain arrangement. The valance is generally made from heavy drapery material, although it can be made of wood painted or covered with fabric. A wooden valance is called a valance box. Heavy, soft drapery materials like those used for stage drapes (velour, velveteen, corduroy, commando) are generally used for the drapes, and lightweight, translucent materials such as chiffon and netting (see Chapter 16) are used for making sheers.

Figure 11.7 Several styles of curtains.

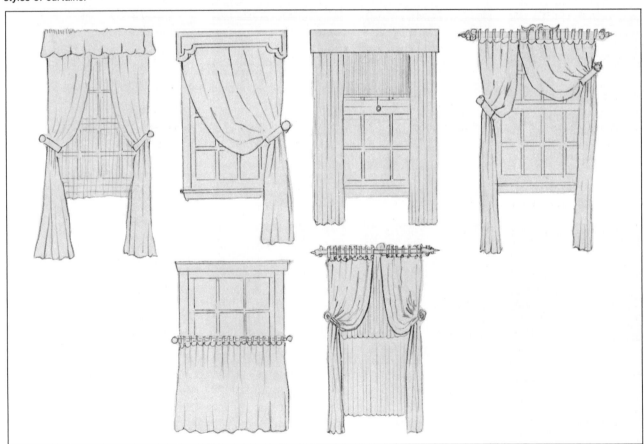

All materials used for stage draperies have roughly the same characteristics. They generally have a soft, non-reflective surface and are available in a variety of colors. Upholstery and decorative drapery materials are not nearly so limited. They are available in a variety of finishes and a panoply of colors.

Factory flame-retardant treatment for the stage drapery materials is essential; it is also desirable for any other materials that are used on the stage. If the materials aren't flameproofed when you buy them, they will have to be treated by hand, and most flameproofing solutions, if applied by hand, will darken the fabric in an uneven pattern.

VELOUR

Velour is a cotton-backed material with a deep surface pile generally made from cotton, rayon, or nylon. It is available in a variety of weights ranging from twelve to twenty-five ounces per square yard and widths from forty-five to fifty-four inches. The material is available in a wide variety of colors, has a rich, lustrous appearance, and absorbs light well. It is generally the preferred material for stage drapes as well as rich, heavy decorative curtains and some upholstery applications. Crushed velour, in which the nap is compressed to create an irregular textural pattern, is a common upholstery material.

VELVETEEN

Velveteen possesses the same general characteristics as velour, but it is much lighter—six to eight ounces. It has a lustrous pile finish and is generally available in forty-five- to forty-eight-inch widths from local fabric stores. It is normally used for decorative curtains and upholstery. The material, which wrinkles easily, is not durable enough to be used for stage drapes.

PLUSH

The pile of plush is softer and longer than that of velveteen but has the same characteristically silk-like sheen. Available in a variety of colors and widths from forty-five to fifty-four inches, plush can be purchased from local fabric and upholstery shops. It is used as an upholstery or drapery material.

COMMANDO

Commando cloth, also known as duvetyn, is a lightweight cotton fabric with a very short, feltlike, almost matted pile. It is available in two widths and weights—thirty-six-inch (lightweight) and forty-eight-inch (heavyweight). The heavyweight material is good for stage drapes but is a little stiff to be used for decorative drapes. The lightweight is suitable for decorative drapes but is a little too delicate for the rugged treatment that most stage drapes receive. Neither type is particularly appropriate for upholstery applications. Commando cloth is available in a variety of colors and can be purchased from scenic fabric supply houses.

COTTON REP

Cotton rep is a tough cotton fabric with a ribbed finish that is similar to a very-narrow-wale corduroy. It reflects light more than other drapery materials. Rep is available in a wide range of colors from scenic fabric supply houses. It can be used for stage or decorative drapes.

DAMASK

Damask achieves its rich appearance from the raised patterns of high-luster yarn that are normally woven into the matte finish of the background cloth. The heavy material is available from local fabric houses in a wide range of colors and in widths ranging between forty-five and fifty-four inches. It is primarily used for decorative drapes and upholstery.

BROCADE

Brocade is similar to damask but lighter in weight. The pattern, which can be either raised or flat, is generally created through the use of high-luster yarn that contrasts with the matte finish of the background. Forty-five to fifty-four inches wide, brocade is available in a wide range of colors and patterns in fabric and drapery shops. It is primarily used for decorative drapes and upholstery.

SATIN

Satin is a heavy, stiff fabric with a smooth, shiny finish on the front and a dull finish on the back. If it is patterned, the design is generally printed on, rather than woven into, the fabric. Available in a wide range of colors and pattern designs, it is normally between forty-five and fifty-four inches wide and can be purchased at local fabric and drapery shops. It is usually used for decorative drapes and upholstery.

CORDUROY

Corduroy is a cotton material whose pile ridges, called wales, alternate with a low-luster backing. The width of the wale varies from only one-thirty-second to approximately three-sixteenths of an inch. The weight of the material also varies considerably, with the lighter-weight versions suitable for costumes and the heavier weights more appropriate for upholstery. Corduroy is available in a wide selection of colors and in fabric widths from forty-five to fifty-four inches. It can be purchased from local fabric and upholstery shops. Waleless corduroy (similar to a very-short-nap velour) or very-narrow-wale corduroy can be used as a substitute for velvet in draperies, costumes, and upholstery; the wider-wale fabrics are primarily used for upholstery purposes.

Papier-Mâché

Papier-mâché is one of the oldest craft techniques used in the theatre. It is also one of the cheapest. It is used to make, or cover, a wide variety of shapes and objects that range from logs to statues, clubs, and various types of fake food.

Papier-mâché is made by building up a form with successive layers of paper that are bound together with a wheat-paste binder. The normal method of working with it is to tear newspaper into strips about one inch wide, dip them in the wheat-paste mixture, and form them over the mold. Between three and six layers of paper are usually applied to the form. After the object has dried (usually twenty-four to forty-eight hours), it can be painted with any of the paints used in the shop.

Craft stores frequently sell a prepared mixture of very finely shredded paper and wheat paste. You only need to add water to this papier-mâché mix to create a pastelike substance that can be used for sculpture or as a smooth finish coat over rough objects. It can also be formed in molds.

Vacuum Forming

Vacuum forming, or vacuforming, is the process of shaping plastics through the application of heat and vacuum pressure. Shapes can be formed with a vacuforming table of the type shown in Figure 11.8.

The vacuum forming machine consists of a heating oven, a forming table, and a pump to evacuate air from a tank to create a vacuum reservoir. A sheet of plastic is heated by the oven until it becomes quite limber. While it is still hot, it is placed over a mold on the forming table, and the valve to the vacuum reservoir is released. The pressure of the outside air trying to reach the vacuum reservoir forms the plastic around the mold. When the thermoplastic cools (in a few seconds), it retains the shape of the mold.

This very flexible system can be used to form a variety of shapes such as banisters, decorative cornices, wall panels, and masks, as shown in Figure 11.9.

Figure 11.8 A vacuforming table.

High-impact polystyrene .020 of an inch thick is the most commonly used material in vacuum forming, because it is thick enough to be reasonably strong after it has been stretched over the mold during forming. The material can be painted with acrylic vinyl, casein, and most oil- or lacquer-base paints. Other types of plastic that can be vacuum formed include thin sheets (.010 to .025 of an inch thick) of acrylic, vinyl, and cellulose acetate butyrate (CAB). (See Chapter 8 for a discussion of the various types of plastic.) Nicholas Bryson's book *Thermoplastic Scenery for Theatre* provides a wealth of information about the various thermoplastic materials, as well as detailed plans for the construction of a vacuum forming machine.

Molds

In scenic and property construction, molds are generally used to create multiple copies of a wide variety of items such as fake loaves of bread, decorative panels for cornice molding, and costume jewels.

Molds can be divided into two categories—open and closed. The only significant difference between the two is that the open mold has an open top or port, whereas the closed mold is enclosed on all sides and has one or more ports into which the casting material is poured.

Molds can further be subdivided into rigid and flexible. Rigid molds (Figure 11.10 top) are generally made from materials such as wood, plaster of paris, fiberglass, or rigid urethane foam. Flexible molds (Figure 11.10 bottom) can be made from a variety of synthetic materials such as room-temperature-vulcanizing (RTV) silicone rubber. RTV silicone rubber and other mold-making materials can usually be found at local craft or art supply shops. Instructions for their use are found on the material containers.

In order to remove the cast object from the mold, the inside of the mold must have been treated with a release agent before being filled with the casting material. The release agent needs to be compatible with the type of

Figure 11.10 Rigid (top) and flexible (bottom) molds.

Model: An object that is being used as the subject of a mold casting.

Undercut: An indentation in a form that leaves an overhang or concave profile—for example, the nostrils in a mask of a face.

material being cast. A silicone release agent, commercially available in spray cans, will work well for polyester, acrylic, and epoxy resins, but the heat generated by the urethane casting resins requires that a urethane mold release be used with both pour-in-place and spray foams. Both types of release agent are generally available at craft or hobby shops.

MAKING A MOLD Rigid molds of objects that don't have a great deal of detail can be made relatively quickly by coating the **model** with a urethane release agent and then covering it with either pour-in-place or spray urethane foam (rigid formulation), as shown in Figure 11.11. This type of mold works well for objects that are free from **undercuts,** such as bricks and planks. Rigid molds can also be made in the same manner from plaster of paris or fiberglass.

Figure 11.11 Rigid mold making technique. (A) The object being cast: a brick. (B) Attach a collar to create a box for the mold, and coat the brick and box with a silicone release agent. (C) Coat the brick and box with spray urethane foam (rigid formula). (D) The finished mold.

(A)

(B)

(C)

(D)

If there are undercuts on the object being cast, a flexible mold is needed. This type of mold can be made with RTV silicone rubber, as shown in Figure 11.12.

A flexible mold that reveals a great deal of detail of the object being cast can be made by coating the model with silicone release, followed by several layers of liquid latex. Three to five coats are generally required. After the latex has dried, the inside of the box is coated with urethane release agent or lined with polyethylene film (urethane won't adhere to polyethylene), and flexible urethane foam is poured into the mold box. The flexible urethane foam will bond with, and provide a strong backing for, the latex mold.

CASTING MOLDED OBJECTS It is fairly easy to cast objects from molds. The inside of the mold is coated with an appropriate release agent, and the molding material is poured into the mold and allowed to dry or set. After the material has cured (the time required varies depending on the material, heat, and humidity) the cast object is taken out of the mold. Depending on the complexity of the mold and the material being cast, some finishing details such as sanding or trimming may be required.

In order to paint the cast object, you will generally need to remove all traces of the release agent. Read the label on the release agent's container to determine the type of cleaner that will be needed.

(A)

(B)

Figure 11.12 Flexible mold making technique. (A) The object being cast: a brooch. (B) Place the brooch in a cardboard box and spray both with a silicone release agent. (C) Pour RTV rubber into the box until it covers the top of the brooch to a depth of about ⅛ inch. (D) The finished mold and the brooch.

(C)

(D)

"Tubed" building adhesive: An adhesive product, such as Liquid Nails, packaged in a caulking tube and designed to be dispensed with a caulking gun.

Hot-wire cutter: A tool for cutting foam that consists of a wire heated to incandescence.

Gesso: Plaster of paris in a semiliquid state approximately the consistency of sour cream; dries to a hard plaster finish.

Foam Carving

Expanded polystyrene foam, generally referred to by its trade name, Styrofoam, is frequently used in the fabrication of statues, columns, cornices, and other types of appliqué. Styrofoam is available from almost any lumber or insulation dealer in thicknesses ranging from one-half to two inches. The light blue Styrofoam is fire resistant, but the white variety is not. Thicker blocks can be made by laminating sheets with polyvinyl glue, latex contact cement, or several different types of **"tubed" building adhesive.**

Styrofoam is easily cut with any power saw. Knives with serrated edges seem to work better than those with smooth cutting edges. Soaping the blades will help to reduce friction and possible scorching or melting of the foam. The foam can also be shaped with **hot-wire cutters** of the types shown in Figure 11.13. The molding jig can be used to cut cornices or other architectural trim by shaping the cutter into the appropriate cross-sectional outline of the desired finished form. The block of foam is then slowly pushed through the jig, and the foam is cut into the finished shape.

Foam can also be cut into irregular forms by the direct application of heat with a propane torch or hot-air gun; by a soldering iron; or by a solvent such as mineral spirits, acetone, or lacquer thinner.

When the Styrofoam has been carved to the desired shape, it can be finished in a variety of ways. The soft surface will normally need to be protected in some manner. A coating of white glue will slightly toughen it, and cheesecloth glued to it will make it quite durable. To create a smooth, reasonably durable surface the foam can be coated with two or three coats of acrylic **gesso** or plaster of paris. If the foam-carved object is going to be subject to a good deal of physical abuse, it should be covered with auto body putty. Styrofoam and all of the above-mentioned finishing materials can be painted with latex or vinyl acrylic water-base paints and most oil- or lacquer-base paints.

Heat Forming

Heat forming generally refers to warming plastic until it becomes flexible enough to bend. Sheet and rod acrylic or PVC can be heated and formed without any preparatory work. Tubes should be filled with sand before they are heated, to prevent them from crimping or collapsing as they are being bent.

If the pieces of acrylic or PVC are small enough, it will be possible to heat the plastic in the oven of a kitchen stove. Remove any paper or protective covering from the plastic, and put the plastic on a cookie sheet. Preheat the oven to 300 degrees, and heat the plastic for a couple of minutes, or until

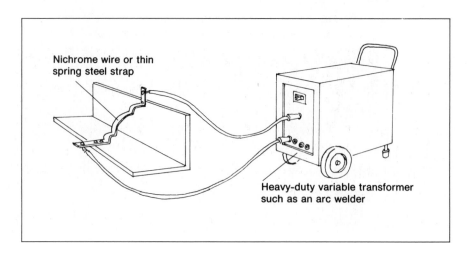

Nichrome wire or thin spring steel strap

Heavy-duty variable transformer such as an arc welder

Figure 11.13 Hot-wire cutters.

CHAPTER 11: STAGE PROPERTIES

Polyester resin does not dry the way paint or varnish does. It will remain in its liquid state until a catalyzing agent, methylethylketone (MEK), is added and thoroughly stirred into the resin. The catalyst initiates a change in the molecular structure of the resin from liquid to solid.

When the resin "kicks off" (begins to change its physical state), heat is released. If you carefully follow the suggested recipe that is printed on the resin container, you should have between ten and twenty minutes to work with the catalyzed resin. When the resin kicks off, it turns to a jellylike consistency very quickly. From this point it will take twelve to twenty-four hours for it to fully cure.

Disposable paper cups make excellent mixing containers for resin, since you can throw them away after the resin has kicked off. Apply the resin with natural-bristle brushes, because it will dissolve synthetic bristles. Thoroughly clean any application equipment with acetone before the catalyzed resin gels; you won't be able to clean it after the resin has begun to cure.

it is limber enough to bend. The plastic can be formed over a mold or clamped in position until it has cooled. Be sure to wear heavy gloves when heat-forming plastics.

Armature: A basic skeletal form that holds the covering materials in the desired shape or alignment.

Fiberglass

Fiberglass is formed by coating glass fiber reinforcement with polyester or epoxy resin, as illustrated in Figure 11.14. Polyester resin is normally used, because it is less expensive. The most common types of glass reinforcement are (1) a woven glass fiber cloth in either sheet or tape form and (2) a glass mat that closely resembles felt cloth. The great strength of fiberglass results from the tensile strength of the glass reinforcement being locked into place by the resin.

For most applications in property construction the cloth or mat is draped over an **armature** and held in place with clothespins, wire, or tape. It is also possible to form the fiberglass by using molds.

When the glass fiber cloth is formed, it is saturated with a coating of catalyzed resin. A second layer of cloth or mat can be added for additional strength after the resin has cured for twelve to twenty-four hours. Be sure to lightly sand the surface between coats. Generally, two to three coats will be strong enough for most scenic or property applications.

Most water-base paints won't adhere directly to cured fiberglass. If you

Figure 11.14 Fiberglass construction techniques. (A) "Flesh out" a wooden skeleton with newspaper to create the basic form. (B) Cover the armature with aluminum foil and (C) drape fiberglass cloth over it to create the line of the sculpture and coat it with catalyzed resin. (D) The finished form. It can be reinforced with additional coats of glass cloth or mat as necessary and painted or finished as desired.

(A)

(B)

(C)

(D)

first paint it with an automotive type primer, however, you will be able to finish it with any scene paint except dry pigment and binder.

Wood Turning

Wood turning is done on a lathe. Various prop and scenic items such as banisters, newels, and chair and sofa legs are frequently turned on a lathe.

Because hardwoods such as walnut, oak, mahogany, and cherry have a relatively dense structure, they are usually considered the best candidates for turning, although carefully selected, knot-free, tight-grained pine or fir can be used. To turn wood securely mount it in the lathe, and as the lathe spins the stock, carve it using special chisels called turning tools.

SAFETY TIP

The Wood Lathe

A wood lathe is inherently dangerous. However, the following precautions should make working with a lathe safe.

1. Never wear loose clothing. It might get caught in the spinning wood.
2. Wear goggles or a face shield.
3. Be sure the wood doesn't have any defects (knots, weak spots) that might cause it to break while spinning.
4. Be sure that all glue joints on stock that is going to be turned are very carefully and thoroughly made and that the glue is completely dry before turning.
5. Center the work, and be sure that it is securely mounted between the spindles.
6. Keep the tool rest as close to the stock as possible. Before starting the motor revolve the stock by hand to make sure it doesn't hit the tool rest. Adjust the position of the tool rest to keep it close to the stock as the turning progresses.
7. Turn stock over six inches in diameter at a slow speed, that from three to six inches at medium speed, and that under three inches a little faster.
8. Don't make any adjustments to the tool rest or other mechanical elements of the lathe while the motor is running.
9. Run all stock at the slowest possible speed until it is rounded.
10. Hold tools firmly with both hands.
11. Remove the tool rest before sanding or polishing the work. If you don't, your fingers may become caught between the stock and the tool rest.

Foam can be turned on a wood lathe by using a relatively slow speed and using sandpaper rather than cutting tools. It can also be shaped with a hot-wire cutter. Urethane foam shouldn't be turned because of the toxic gas it emits when heated. Styrofoam sheets will probably have to be laminated to provide stock of sufficient thickness. Since Styrofoam is not very dense, pieces of one-quarter-inch plywood of the same size as the ends of the work will need to be securely glued to the ends so the lathe's **spindle chucks** will have something to bite into to hold the work in the lathe. If the foam turnings are to be very narrow, a wooden armature (a ⅜-inch or ½-inch dowel or ¾-by-¾-inch white pine stock) may need to be sandwiched into the foam laminate to provide sufficient strength for the unit to be turned. Be sure that the wooden armature is absolutely straight.

The design and construction of stage properties is a genuinely fascinating field. If your interest in this field has been piqued, you should undertake further study of the almost innumerable design and craft areas such as painting, furniture construction, upholstery, electricity, metalworking, ceramics, and sewing that are part of this theatrical specialty.

12

Lighting Design

Any dramatic production, unless it is performed outdoors in the daytime, needs some kind of artificial light. On the other hand, if illumination were the only function of stage lighting, you could hang a bank of fluorescent lights over the stage and forget about all the dimmers, control boards, cables, instruments, and other complicated paraphernalia of stage lighting.

Obviously, there is something more to stage lighting than simply bathing the stage with light. Effective stage lighting not only lets the spectators see the action of the play but also ties together all the visual elements of the production and helps create an appropriate mood and atmosphere that heighten the audience's understanding and enjoyment of the play.

CONTROLLABLE QUALITIES OF LIGHT

Tharon Musser, a prominent professional lighting designer, has said, "If you ask most people who walk in and tell you they want to be lighting designers, what kind of weather are we having—what's it like outside?—half of them won't know how to describe it, if they remember it at all. They simply don't know how to see."[1] Learning how to see—to understand how light shapes and modifies people and objects—is absolutely essential in learning to understand lighting design.

A lighting designer can "see" how the lighting should look for a production only if he or she has an understanding of the controllable qualities of the

1. "Tharon Musser," *Lighting Dimensions* 1(1977):16.

Followspot: A lighting instrument with a high-intensity, narrow beam; mounted in a stand that allows it to tilt and swivel so the beam can "follow" an actor.

medium. The qualities of light that the lighting designer can control are divided into four categories: distribution, intensity, movement, and color.

Distribution

Distribution is a catchall term that refers to several elements: (1) the direction from which the light approaches an area, actor, or object; (2) the shape and size of the area that the light is covering; and (3) the quality of the light—its diffusion or clarity.

Intensity

Intensity is the actual amount, or level of brightness, of light that strikes the stage or actor. Intensity can range from total darkness to painfully brilliant white light.

Movement

Movement can be divided into three general categories: (1) the timed duration of the light cues; (2) the movement of onstage lights, such as a lantern or candle that an actress carries across the stage; and (3) the movement of an off-stage light source, such as a **followspot.**

Color

Color, which was discussed at length in Chapter 6, is an extremely powerful tool of the designer. The judicious use of appropriately tinted light can greatly assist the audience's understanding of, and reaction to, the play.

FUNCTIONS OF STAGE LIGHT

To increase the audience's understanding and appreciation of a play, stage lighting needs to perform several basic functions.

Visibility

A reasonably accurate adage in the theatre holds that "if you can't see 'em, you can't hear 'em." Stage lighting needs to make everything on stage—the actors, costumes, and setting—clearly visible to the spectators. At the same time, however, the concept of "designed," or controlled, visibility dictates that those actors and objects be seen only in the manner that the designer and director intend. One of the real challenges of lighting design is to create a selective visibility that subtly directs the spectators' attention. The number of lighting instruments and other sources used to light a scene, the color of those lights, and their direction and intensity all affect visibility.

Selective Focus

Selective focus means directing the spectators' attention to a specific place. The lighting designer can selectively focus attention in a number of ways, but the primary method is by manipulating our instinctive response to light. Everybody has a strong instinct to look at an area of brightness or movement in an otherwise neutral scene. By simply making one part of the stage brighter than the rest of the set, the lighting designer forces the spectators to look there (Figure 12.1). This technique of emphatic focus is amply demonstrated, for example, whenever a followspot is used in a musical number.

Modeling

Modeling is the revealing of the form of an object through the pattern of highlight and shadow that is reflected from that object to the eye. The distribution and intensity of the light will, to a great extent, determine our visual understanding of that object. Anyone who has ever yelped, "But that doesn't look like me!" when confronted by a flash snapshot of himself has just had a demonstration of this effect. The light from a camera-mounted flashbulb or strobe approaches us from a very unnatural angle—straight from the front and parallel with the floor. Light coming from this direction fills in the areas where we normally expect to see shadows—under the eyebrows, cheekbones, nose, and jaw line. It also puts highlights in rather unexpected places. Because of this redirection of the expected pattern of highlight and shadow, the picture doesn't look like the face that we remember.

Direction is the primary element used in modeling, although intensity, movement, and color all affect modeling to a lesser degree. A change in any or all of these variables will inevitably result in an apparent change of form and feeling of the object being lit.

Mood

Creating a mood with light is one of the easiest and, at the same time, most difficult aspects of stage lighting. It is relatively easy to create a spectacular sunset effect or a sinister feeling of lurking terror; the difficulty comes in integrating these impressive effects with the other elements of the production. Effective stage lighting is subtle and rarely noticed. Although it is fun to create a sunset or similar breathtaking visual display, the opportunity to do so legitimately does not present itself in many plays. Within the parameters of the production concept, stage lighting is usually designed to enhance the mood of the play as unobtrusively as possible.

DESIGNING WITH LIGHT

Before you can create with light you have to *see* the light. Let's explore (with visual aids) the effects that can be achieved by manipulating the first two controllable qualities of light—distribution and intensity—to affect the four functions of light—visibility, selective focus, modeling, and mood.

Figure 12.1
Selective focus with light. Notice how your attention moves from person to person in the photo on the left, whereas your attention is directed to the highlighted actress in the photo on the right.

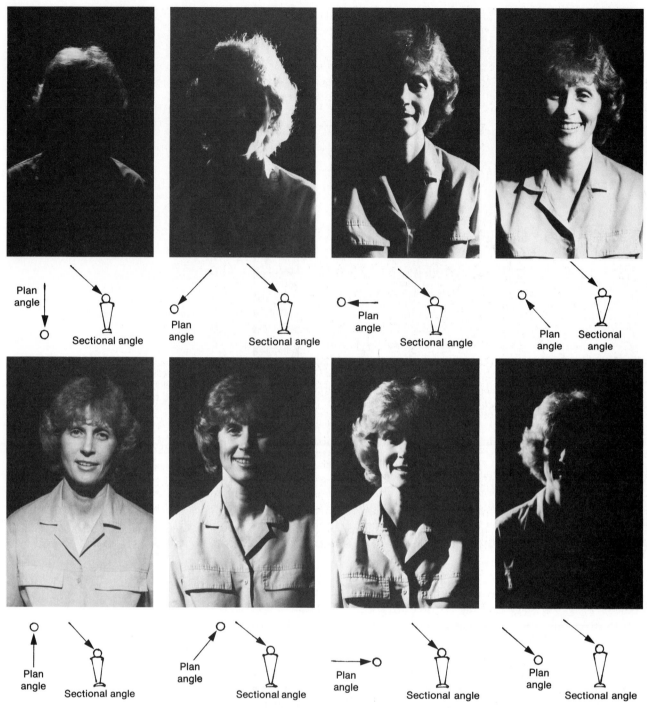

Figure 12.2 Effects of varying the direction of light.

The series of photographs in Figure 12.2 illustrates how varying the direction of light affects the face of an actress. Each photograph is accompanied by a drawing that shows the relative **plan angle** of the light. The **sectional angle** of the light is forty-five degrees and shows the angle of the light relative to the actor's face.

Surrounding an actor with a number of light sources provides the potential for modeling with light. In Figure 12.3 the direction of the light varies, but the intensity remains the same. A front light (Figure 12.3A) by itself is unflattering; it tends to flatten and compress facial and bodily features. Both side lights (Figure 12.3B) and top lights (Figure 12.3C) create highlights

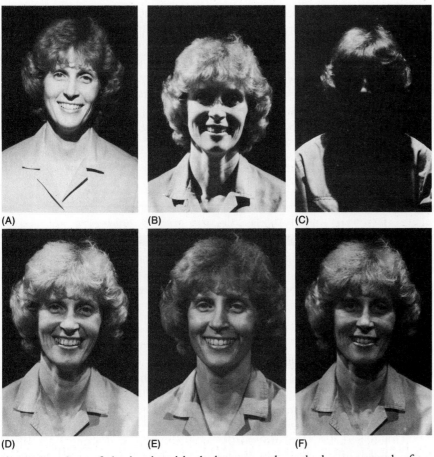

(A)   (B)   (C)

(D)   (E)   (F)

Figure 12.3 Surrounding an actor with light creates the most potential for modeling.

along the edges of the head and body but cause deep shadows across the face and front of the body. A combination of side and top lights (Figure 12.3D), together with a front light that fills in the shadows created by the side and top lights, reveals the form of the model by surrounding her with light.

When lit from the side-front at about forty-five degrees in both plan and section (Figure 12.3E), the model is smoothly illuminated, but her facial and bodily features are slightly compressed. If a top light or back light is added to the side-front light (Figure 12.3F), the resultant rim or edge light creates a highlight that adds depth to the face and body. As you can see the greatest potential for modeling is achieved when the model is surrounded with light.

Plan angle: The ground-plan view of an object.

Sectional angle: The angle of intersection between the axis of the cone of light emitted by an instrument and the working height—usually the height of an average actor's face (about five feet six inches)—of the lighting area.

Key and Fill

The terms *key light* and *fill light* are frequently used to describe the relationship between the direction and relative intensity of light striking an object. The key light is the brightest light on the scene, and the fill light is used to fill the shadows created by the key light.

Psychological Effects of Light

In lighting design, just as in literature, the concepts of good and evil are often associated with light and darkness. When a scene is lit with dark and murky shadows, most people instinctively react with a sense of foreboding. The suspicion that something could be lurking unseen in the shadows is almost universal. When a scene is brightly lit, we instinctively relax, because we realize that nothing can sneak up on us unseen.

(A)

(B)

Figure 12.4
Psychological
effects of varying
the angle of light.

Hanging: The process of placing lighting instruments in their specified locations.

Instrument schedule: A form used to record all of the technical data about each instrument used in the production; also known as a hookup sheet.

Pipe: A counterweighted batten or fixed metal pipe that holds lighting instruments.

First electric: The onstage pipe for lighting instruments that is closest to the proscenium arch.

The direction from which light strikes an object has a direct effect on our perception of that object. Light striking a face from a low angle (Figure 12.4A) effectively creates a "monster" light, because such light does not occur in nature. Any light that places the face in heavy shadow, such as the back light shown in Figure 12.4B, will create an uneasy reaction in viewers, because they cannot see the facial expression of the person in the shadows and so cannot read his or her intentions.

Those who are interested in being lighting designers should become more fully aware of these instinctive, and learned, responses. More information on the psychology of color can be found in Chapter 6.

THE LIGHT PLOT AND RELATED PAPERWORK

Because the product of lighting design—light—is probably the most intangible and abstract of all the theatrical design elements, some specialized paperwork is needed to help in carrying out the design.

The Light Plot

The light plot is a scale mechanical drawing—a "road map"—that indicates where the lighting instruments should be placed (Figure 12.5, page 270). More specifically, it is a "horizontal offset section with the cutting plane passing at whatever levels are required to produce the most descriptive view of the instrumentation in relation to the set(s)," according to the USITT's graphic standards for stage lighting.

Although there is no universally accepted style of drafting light plots, some general information must always be included. Depicting the location of all lighting instruments being used in the production is the primary purpose of the light plot. The lighting designer specifies, to scale (usually one-half or one-quarter inch to one foot), where the instruments should be placed. The master electrician uses this scale drawing as a guide in **hanging** the plot.

The Legend

A legend, or instrument key (Figure 12.6, page 272), provides complete identification information about each instrument used on the plot. In addition to identifying the particular type or style of instrument that is denoted by each symbol, the legend should also contain an explanation of the peripheral information (Figure 12.7, page 272) that is associated with each instrument symbol. The USITT recommended standards for this type of instrument notation are shown in the box on page 269. The types of peripheral information that can be used with each lighting instrument symbol are explained below.

INSTRUMENT NUMBER Each instrument needs to be assigned an identification number so it can be cross-referenced with the **instrument schedule,** or hookup sheet. Figure 12.8 (page 272) shows how lighting instruments are numbered on the light plot. The specific number recorded for each lighting instrument on the instrument schedule is determined by two factors: (1) its hanging location and (2) its position relative to the other instruments on that **pipe.** The first segment of the number is an abbreviation of its hanging location. The number "1E," illustrated in Figure 12.9 (page 272), indicates that the instrument is hanging on the **first electric.** The second part of the number indicates the instrument's sequential position on the pipe. In a proscenium

LIGHTING SYMBOLS

Because so much data must be included on a light plot or lighting section, the United States Institute for Theatre Technology has developed a system of symbols for use on these drawings. The following information on lighting symbols is based on those recommendations.

INSTRUMENT NOTATION

The normal procedure in drawing a light plot is to use symbols to represent the various types of lighting instrument being used. The USITT-recommended symbols are illustrated in the figure below. A great deal of information is usually associated with each lighting symbol.

LIGHTING TEMPLATES

Lighting templates are used to help in drawing the various symbols for the stage lighting instruments and practical lamps used in most productions. The photo below shows examples of both plan and sectional lighting templates.

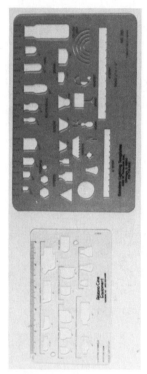

Lighting templates.

3" Fresnel		Par 38
6" Fresnel		Par 56
8" Fresnel		Par 64
12" Fresnel		10" Scoop
2-panel barndoor		14" Scoop
4-panel barndoor		14" Scoop
Floor-mounted strip light		Followspot
Pipe-mounted strip light		35mm slide projector
10" Beam projector		Practical
16" Beam projector		
Effects projector		

USITT recommended lighting symbols.

		3½" × 6" ERS
		3½" × 8" ERS
		3½" × 10" ERS
		6" × 9" ERS
		6" × 12" ERS
		6" × 16" ERS
		6" × 22" ERS
		4½" × 6½" ERS
		8" × 9" ERS
		8" × 10" ERS
		8" × 11" ERS
		ERS designated by degree
		Variable focal length
		Gobo
		Iris
		Top hat

Templates are readily available in scales of one-quarter of an inch to one foot and one-half inch to one foot (which are the most commonly used scales for drafting light plots).

LETTERING

The lettering used on the drawings associated with lighting design need to follow the same criteria of clarity and uniformity outlined in Chapter 18, *Mechanical Drafting*.

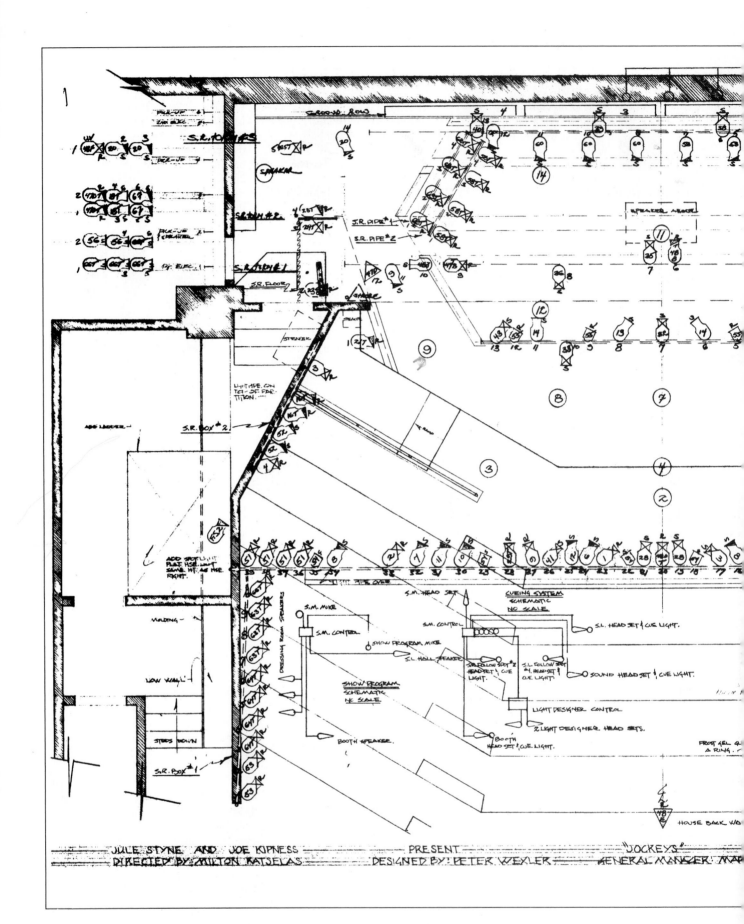

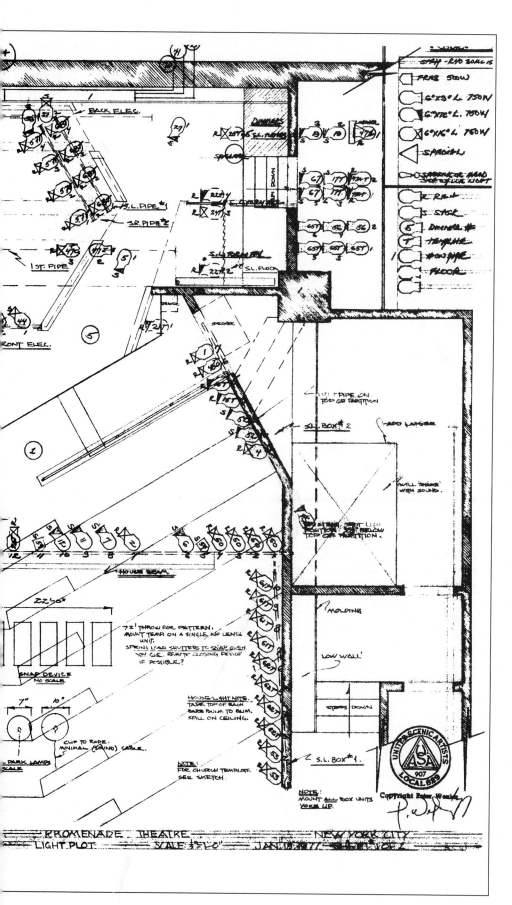

Figure 12.5 The
light plot from
Jockeys for the
Jule Styne and Joe
Kipness production
at the Promenade
Theatre, New York.
Designed by Peter
Wexler.

Figure 12.6 A sample legend.

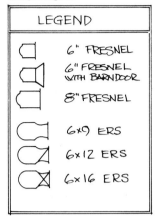

Figure 12.7 Peripheral information notation standard.

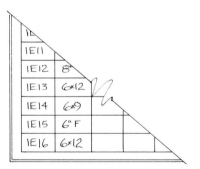

Figure 12.9 Details of instrument notation technique.

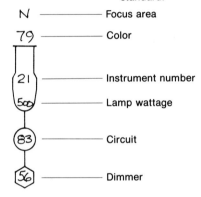

Figure 12.8 Instruments are numbered according to two factors: the pipe on which they are hanging and their position relative to other instruments on the pipe.

theatre, the numbering of any **electric** starts at the left end of the pipe when viewed as if you were standing with your back against the upstage wall of the stage house.

FOCUS AREA The focus area for each instrument is identified by a letter placed in front of the lens housing of the symbol for that instrument. This letter corresponds to the same letter that identifies a specific lighting area on the light plot.

CIRCUIT NUMBER The circuit number identifies the stage circuit into which the lighting instrument should be plugged. Although the lighting designer may assign the circuit number for each instrument, this particular decision is usually left up to the master electrician.

DIMMER NUMBER The **dimmer** number identifies the specific dimmer that will control the instrument. The assignment of the dimmer is frequently determined by the lighting designer, although this decision may also be left to the discretion of the master electrician.

INSTRUMENT COLOR The instrument color number refers to the specific color media that will be used with that particular instrument.

The Lighting Section

The lighting section is a scale drawing, usually drawn in the same scale as the light plot, that isn't really a sectional drawing at all. It is actually a composite side view of the set, masking, and lighting instruments (Figure 12.10). It is used for several purposes: (1) to check sight lines of the lighting instruments, (2) to assist in determining the appropriate trim height for the horizontal masking, and (3) to ensure that the lighting instruments will not interfere with any scenic elements and vice versa.

The Instrument Schedule

The instrument schedule, also known as the hookup sheet, is a specification sheet that contains everything that you might want or need to know about every instrument that is used on the production (Figure 12.11, page 274). It identifies each instrument by its instrument number and specifies its type, hanging location, focus area, circuit, dimmer, lamp wattage, and color. A section for special remarks is used to note anything else that might be appropriate, such as focusing notes, auxiliary equipment that needs to be attached to the instrument, and so forth.

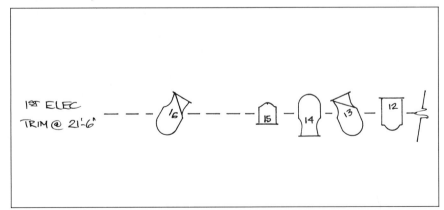

CHAPTER 12: LIGHTING DESIGN

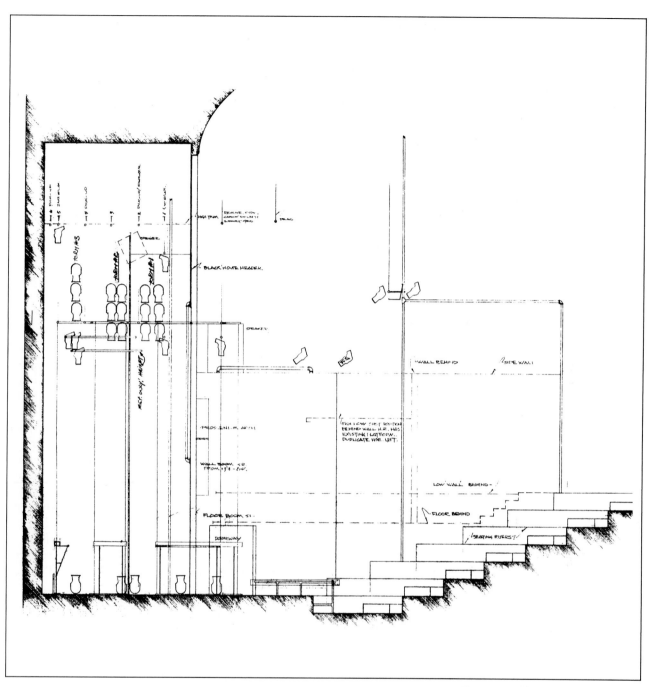

Figure 12.10 The lighting section for *Jockeys*; designed by Peter Wexler.

THE IMAGE OF LIGHT

The image of light is a picture or concept of what the light should look like for a production. The following discussion makes reference to the image of light as a pictorial vision. For the majority of lighting designers these images are pictorial, but they can also be auditory or emotional. It is essential that you develop some type of core image. The mental manifestation of that concept isn't nearly so important.

The analysis of the image of light for its distribution and intensity is probably the prime creative factor in determining the hanging positions for

Electric: Any pipe that is used to hold lighting instruments.

Dimmer: An electrical device that controls the intensity of a light source connected to it.

Figure 12.11 The instrument schedule contains all the technical data about each instrument used in the production.

Show: THE TUNNEL				INSTRUMENT SCHEDULE				Page 4 of 4
Inst #	Type	Location	Area	Circuit	Dimmer	Color	Lamp	Remarks
1 E13	30°	1ST ELEC	L	64	12	61	500w	
1 E14	30°	"	M	67	64	21	500w	SHUTTER ON ARCH EDGES
1 E15	6x16	"	SIGN SPEC	68	65	02	750w	SHUTTER ON SIGN
1 E16	8"F	"	C	69	27	79	1000w	BARNDOOR
2 E1	30°	2ND ELEC	R	128	21	61	500w	
2 E2	30°	"	R	129	22	18	500w	
2 E3	8"F	"	I	130	28	79	1000w	BARNDOOR
2 E4	30°	"	S	131	23	61	500w	
2 E5	30°	"	S	132	24	18	500w	
Boom 1R1	6x9	DR BOOM	A-C	165				
1R2	6x9	"	A-C	166				
1R3	6x9	"	A-C	167				
Boom 2R1	6x9	RC BOOM	F-H	185	44	18	500w	OVERLAP THROUGHOUT F-H
2R2	6x9	"	F-H	186	45	51	500w	
2R3	6x9	"	F-H	187	46	62	500w	

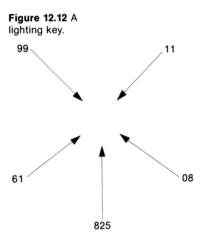

Figure 12.12 A lighting key.

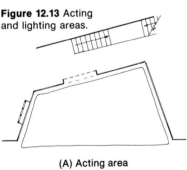

Figure 12.13 Acting and lighting areas.

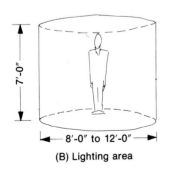

(A) Acting area

(B) Lighting area

the lighting instruments. To analyze the image of light for its distribution and intensity you have to see the image of light and then analyze its appearance to determine the angles and relative intensities of the various sources that are illuminating that image. However, all is not lost if you cannot actually see some type of image in your mind's eye. You can create a nonvisual image (a phrase, a melody, some set of stimuli) that provides you with a central thought or concept that can then be analyzed for its quality (mood, texture, color, intensity) of light.

Analysis of the image of light for its component colors is easier than the analysis for distribution, if for no other reason than that people usually have an emotional reaction to a play that can be translated into specific colors.

As movement is probably the least tangible, and most easily adjusted, of the qualities of light, the timing of the cues is customarily developed during the lighting rehearsal and adjusted during the technical and dress rehearsals. It isn't of great concern to the designer during the selection phase of the design process.

The Lighting Key

The analysis of the image of light to determine its controllable qualities is not just an idle intellectual exercise. The lighting designer codifies that information to create a very pragmatic tool called the lighting key. The lighting key (Figure 12.12) is a drawing that indicates the plan angle and color of the various sources that illuminate the image of light. The lighting key is used by the designer as the primary guide for locating the hanging positions of the lighting instruments.

ACTING AND LIGHTING AREAS To fully understand the purpose and function of a lighting key it will be necessary to digress momentarily and discuss acting areas and lighting areas. Acting areas are those spaces on the stage where specific scenes, or parts of scenes, are played. The shape and size of an acting area (Figure 12.13A), although roughly determined by the shape of the setting, are specifically determined by the blocking patterns used by the actors.

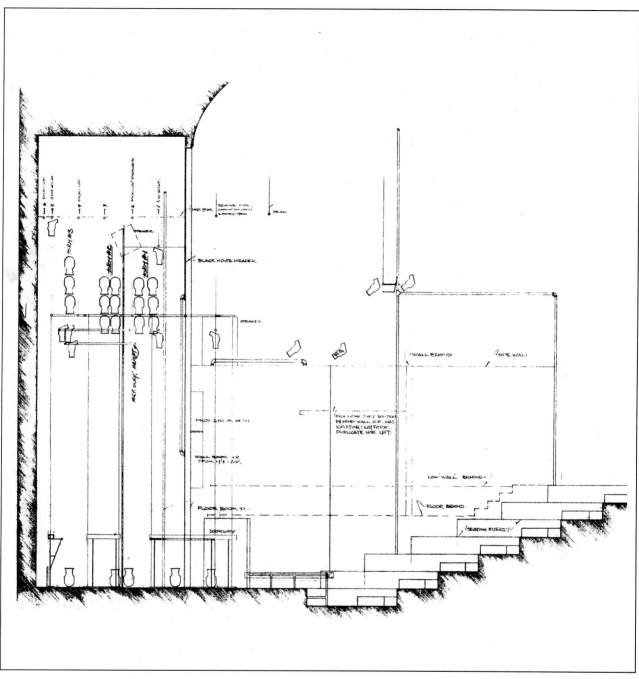

Figure 12.10 The lighting section for *Jockeys*; designed by Peter Wexler.

THE IMAGE OF LIGHT

The image of light is a picture or concept of what the light should look like for a production. The following discussion makes reference to the image of light as a pictorial vision. For the majority of lighting designers these images are pictorial, but they can also be auditory or emotional. It is essential that you develop some type of core image. The mental manifestation of that concept isn't nearly so important.

The analysis of the image of light for its distribution and intensity is probably the prime creative factor in determining the hanging positions for

Electric: Any pipe that is used to hold lighting instruments.

Dimmer: An electrical device that controls the intensity of a light source connected to it.

Figure 12.11 The instrument schedule contains all the technical data about each instrument used in the production.

Show: THE TUNNEL		INSTRUMENT SCHEDULE						
Inst #	Type	Location	Area	Circuit	Dimmer	Color	Lamp	Remarks
1E13	30°	1ST ELEC	L	64	12	61	500w	
1E14	30°	"	M	67	64	21	500w	SHUTTER ON ARCH EDGES
1E15	6x16	"	SIGN SPEC	68	65	02	750w	SHUTTER ON SIGN
1E16	8"F	"	C	69	27	79	1000w	BARNDOOR
2E1	30°	2ND ELEC	R	128	21	61	500w	
2E2	30°	"	R	129	22	18	500w	
2E3	8"F	"	I	130	28	79	1000w	BARNDOOR
2E4	30°	"	S	131	23	61	500w	
2E5	30°	"	S	132	24	18	500w	
Boom 1R1	6x9	DR Boom	A-C	165				
1R2	6x9	"	A-C	166				
1R3	6x9	"	A-C	167				
Boom 2R1	6x9	RC Boom	F-H	185	44	18	500w	OVERLAP THROUGHOUT F-H
2R2	6x9	"	F-H	186	45	51	500w	
2R3	6x9	"	F-H	187	46	62	500w	

Figure 12.12 A lighting key.

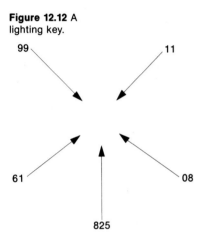

Figure 12.13 Acting and lighting areas.

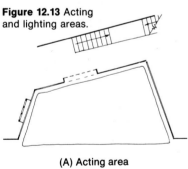

(A) Acting area

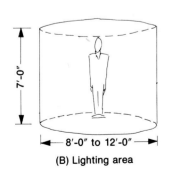

(B) Lighting area

the lighting instruments. To analyze the image of light for its distribution and intensity you have to see the image of light and then analyze its appearance to determine the angles and relative intensities of the various sources that are illuminating that image. However, all is not lost if you cannot actually see some type of image in your mind's eye. You can create a nonvisual image (a phrase, a melody, some set of stimuli) that provides you with a central thought or concept that can then be analyzed for its quality (mood, texture, color, intensity) of light.

Analysis of the image of light for its component colors is easier than the analysis for distribution, if for no other reason than that people usually have an emotional reaction to a play that can be translated into specific colors.

As movement is probably the least tangible, and most easily adjusted, of the qualities of light, the timing of the cues is customarily developed during the lighting rehearsal and adjusted during the technical and dress rehearsals. It isn't of great concern to the designer during the selection phase of the design process.

The Lighting Key

The analysis of the image of light to determine its controllable qualities is not just an idle intellectual exercise. The lighting designer codifies that information to create a very pragmatic tool called the lighting key. The lighting key (Figure 12.12) is a drawing that indicates the plan angle and color of the various sources that illuminate the image of light. The lighting key is used by the designer as the primary guide for locating the hanging positions of the lighting instruments.

ACTING AND LIGHTING AREAS To fully understand the purpose and function of a lighting key it will be necessary to digress momentarily and discuss acting areas and lighting areas. Acting areas are those spaces on the stage where specific scenes, or parts of scenes, are played. The shape and size of an acting area (Figure 12.13A), although roughly determined by the shape of the setting, are specifically determined by the blocking patterns used by the actors.

CHAPTER 12: LIGHTING DESIGN

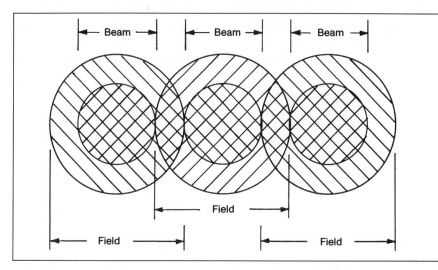

Figure 12.14
Lighting areas are overlapped in an acting area to facilitate the creation of a smooth wash of light.

A lighting area (Figure 12.13B) is a cylindrical space approximately eight to twelve feet in diameter and seven feet tall.

To achieve a smooth wash of light throughout an acting area, individual lighting areas are overlapped by approximately one-third, as shown in Figure 12.14. This overlapping of adjacent areas takes advantage of the optical properties of the **beam angle** and **field angle** of the stage lighting instruments to create a smooth wash of light throughout the acting area.

Beam angle: That point where the light emitted by an instrument is diminished by 50 percent when compared with the output of the center of the beam.

Field angle: That point where the light output diminishes to 10 percent of the output of the center of the beam.

CREATING THE LIGHTING KEY The process of converting the image of light into a lighting key is best explained through example. To illustrate this process we will create a lighting key for *The Playboy of the Western World* by John Millington Synge.

Let's assume that the image of light for this production could be stated as "a bright, twinkling Irish morning." Our analysis of this statement leads us to the conclusion that to achieve the concept of a bright, twinkling Irish morning on the stage it will be necessary to create the following: (1) a light and cheery atmosphere, (2) no shadows, and (3) thin tints of springlike colors.

If an actor in our play were surrounded with light, as shown in Figure 12.15, we would have achieved one of our stated objectives—no shadows. If we adjusted the dimmers that control those lights to a fairly bright setting, we would achieve another of our objectives—a bright atmosphere. By selecting happy, springtime, pastel colors we would also meet the third objective—a "cheery" springlike atmosphere.

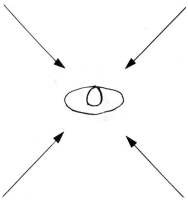

Figure 12.15 Four-source lighting key for *Playboy of the Western World*.

BEAM AND FIELD ANGLES

The field angle for an ellipsoidal reflector spotlight (the most commonly used stage lighting instrument) is approximately twice the beam angle for any given design or make of instrument. In practical terms this relationship between the beam and field angles means that when the lighting areas are overlapped by one-third, the beam angle of each instrument lights the central, or "un-overlapped," portion of each lighting area, and the field angles of adjacent lighting areas overlap. The result is an additive effect that brings up the intensity level of the overlapped areas to approximately that of the area covered by the beam angle.

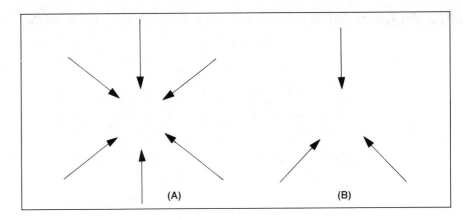

Figure 12.16 Six- and three-source lighting keys for *Playboy of the Western World*.

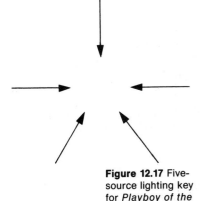

Figure 12.17 Five-source lighting key for *Playboy of the Western World*.

With this brief analysis of the image of light we have already determined a great deal of the information that is needed for completing the basic lighting key for our production. Specifically, we have determined the distribution for the basic lighting of each lighting area (four diagonal cross lights) and the basic range of the color palette (pastel tints). Let me hasten to add that this particular solution is not the "correct" analysis of the image of light. There are myriad other possibilities, all of them equally "correct." You could have light from more or fewer directions (Figure 12.16A and B). You could also interpret the concept of "springtime pastel colors" to mean thin tints of cool colors as opposed to warm—it just depends on your personal understanding of the idea of a springtime atmosphere.

With the foregoing proviso firmly in mind, we make the conscious decision that our lighting key is going to be based on a five-sided distribution pattern (Figure 12.17). We made this decision because this pattern will provide a smooth, shadowless light that will support our interpretation of the image of light. Additionally, the top or back light (the arrow at the top of the pentagon) will provide a nice rim or halo light around the head and shoulders of the actors to prevent them from blending into the set.

Before selecting specific colors for the lighting instruments, the color palettes of the scenic and costume designers must be studied. This "color study" normally occurs during the various production conferences as each designer (scenic, costume, lighting) presents his or her design and color concepts. The reason that the lighting designer must know what colors the other designers are using is relatively simple. Colored light can drastically alter the apparent color of the sets and costumes, and it isn't in the interests of a unified production concept (or the lighting designer's physical well-being) to change the other designers' work without their knowledge and consent.

During the initial conferences of our hypothetical *Playboy* production, the design team decided that the play would be produced in a realistic style. Based on this concept the lighting designer will want the set to appear as though it were being lit by the source lights that are located on the set. To determine the nature of these sources, and their locations, it will be necessary to look at a scenic rendering or model of the set. The scenic sketch (Figure 12.18) shows that there are oil lamps on the counter and each table, there is a peat fire glowing in the fireplace, and the window and door are open. Each of these sources would provide light of differing hues. The sunlight, according to our analysis of the image of light, is cool-white, bright, and cheerful. The fireplace is warmer and redder than the sunlight, and the oil lamps give off a soft, amber glow.

Using this analysis and information as a guide, Roscolux 61, Mist Blue, is selected to represent the bright, clean sunlight. Roscolux 02, Bastard Amber,

Figure 12.18 The set design for *Playboy of the Western World*.

is chosen for the firelight, and Roscolux 09, Pale Amber Gold, is selected to represent the color emitted by the oil lamps. (Roscolux colors, a common brand of theatrical lighting instrument media, are being used to identify the specific hues selected for this exercise. These colors are identified by the manufacturer with a name and number.)

Now that the colors have been selected to represent the various sources, they need to be applied to the lighting key. The application of color to the basic distribution pattern of the lighting key should support the thesis that the source lights are providing the light for the environment of the play. To achieve this goal the light from stage left should be colored to represent the fireplace color, Bastard Amber, because the fireplace is on the stage-left side of the set. The oil lamp color (Pale Amber Gold) is used from a direction (stage right) that supports the visual impression that the oil lamps are primarily on the downstage-right part of the set. The light approaching the stage from an upstage direction should represent the sunlight (Mist Blue), because the window and doorway are on the upstage wall of the set.

Figure 12.19 shows the colors assigned to the specific distribution pattern that we had previously determined from our analysis of the image of light. The stage-left side light is assigned Bastard Amber, to support the concept that the fireplace is lighting the room from this direction. The top-back light is colored with Roscolux 61, Mist Blue, because this supports the idea that any light approaching the stage from this direction would be sunlight coming through the window or door. The stage-right side light and the stage-right front light are colored with Pale Amber Gold, to support the notion that the primary source light for this side of the stage comes from the oil lamps.

This leaves the stage-left front light as the only uncolored instrument. Since there is no specific source light coming from this direction, it will be necessary to refer back to the image of light to determine the appropriate color for this instrument. The image of light specifies that the atmosphere should resemble a "twinkling spring morning." Roscolux 51, Surprise Pink, is selected for use from this direction, because this bright, cheerful color will

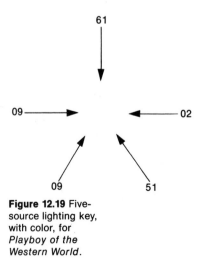

Figure 12.19 Five-source lighting key, with color, for *Playboy of the Western World*.

blend with the Pale Amber Gold (used in the other front light) to produce a warm white light that supports the concept of a cheery morning that is dictated by the image of light.

Using the Lighting Key to Draw the Light Plot

The lighting key is the primary tool in drawing the light plot. The shape of the acting areas determines the number and arrangement of the lighting areas. In our hypothetical production of *The Playboy of the Western World* the whole set is a single acting area. In order to draw the light plot it will be necessary to subdivide that acting area into lighting areas, as shown in Figure 12.20.

Figure 12.20 Acting (top) and lighting areas for *Playboy of the Western World*.

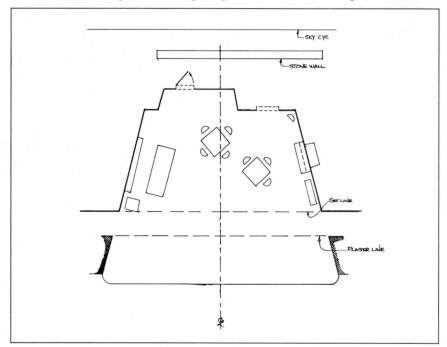

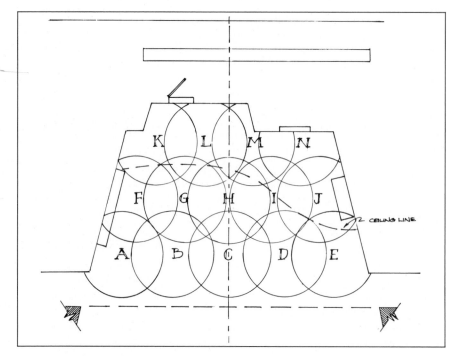

CHAPTER 12: LIGHTING DESIGN

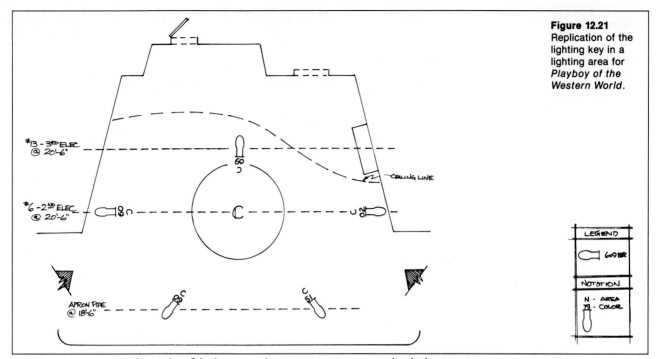

Figure 12.21
Replication of the
lighting key in a
lighting area for
*Playboy of the
Western World.*

To create a smooth wash of light over the entire acting area the lighting designer needs to replicate the lighting key in each of the lighting areas. This process of duplication is demonstrated for a single lighting area in Figure 12.21.

Unfortunately, it isn't always possible to achieve an exact duplication of the lighting key in every lighting area, because the walls of the set prevent the use of side light in the lighting areas that are adjacent to the walls, and the ceiling interferes with a great deal of the top and back light. More challenges are imposed by the physical limitations of the auditorium, which generally inhibit some of the front-of-house hanging positions.

When a situation occurs that makes it difficult to place an instrument exactly where it is needed, the lighting designer must make a design decision. If the light can't be placed in a position where it will replicate the angle specified in the lighting key, the compromise solution should be guided by the principles outlined in the lighting key and the designer's interpretation of the image of light. For example, it isn't possible to use direct stage-left side light for Area J (see Figure 12.22), because the wall gets in the way. Two possible compromise solutions to this challenge might be: (1) Put an instrument on the stage-left end of the first electric, as shown in Figure 12.22. (2) Eliminate the instrument. The choice of which solution to use should be guided by your interpretation of the image of light and the lighting key.

To complete the basic, or first, layer of the lighting design it will be necessary to duplicate, as closely as possible, the lighting key in every lighting area. This process of replication results in a basic light plot that creates the atmosphere and look dictated by the image of light.

Layering

A lighting design exists in time as well as space. It ebbs and flows as the mood of the play changes. To create a temporal development in the lighting design, mechanisms must be designed into the light plot.

Layering is primarily an organizational tool of the lighting designer. It refers specifically to the process of designing layers of light.

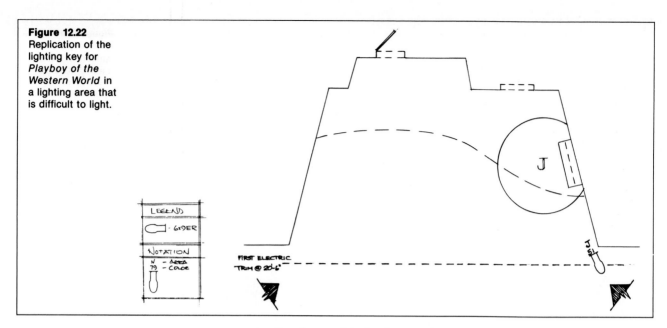

Figure 12.22
Replication of the lighting key for *Playboy of the Western World* in a lighting area that is difficult to light.

The first layer of light for our hypothetical production of *Playboy* was created when we implemented our interpretation of the image of light—"a bright, twinkling Irish morning." This image works well for Acts II and III, which take place in the morning and afternoon, respectively. However, Act I takes place in the early evening. The "twinkling morning" look simply doesn't translate as night. In order to create an appropriate look of early evening for Act I it will be necessary to do one of two things: (1) create a completely separate lighting key and design for Act I or (2) create some supplemental "early evening" lighting that can be used in conjunction with the basic "twinkling Irish morning" lights.

From an aesthetic standpoint a completely separate plot for Act I would be the preferred solution, but a separate design would necessitate a very large instrument inventory.

The supplemental lighting solution would achieve relatively similar results with a considerably smaller number of instruments. The instruments used to create this second layer of light need to be positioned and colored to create the look of "indoor evening" in the pub, where the principal sources of light are oil lamps and the peat fire. Any light coming in the window and door should have the appearance of "night light" rather than daylight.

Since this second layer of light needs to be integrated with the "twinkling Irish morning" lights to achieve the look of "early evening," it will be necessary to select angles and colors that work to support the premise that the pub is actually lit by the oil lamps and the peat fire.

A wash of "night" colors (Roscolux 79, Bright Blue) could be used to flood the stage from the front-of-house positions, as shown in Figure 12.23A. By balancing the intensities of these night colors with those of the basic lighting key we can ensure that the blue lights won't override the basic hues that were selected for the lighting key. They will, however, provide a blue wash over the whole acting area that will fill any shadow or underlit areas with a blue light to help create the illusion of nighttime.

Additional instruments could be hung to augment the color selected to reinforce the source lights—the oil lamps and peat fire—in the first layer of the plot. These instruments, as shown in Figure 12.23B, should be colored in more fully saturated hues than their "first layer" counterparts, and they should be hung in positions that will support the effects of the source lights.

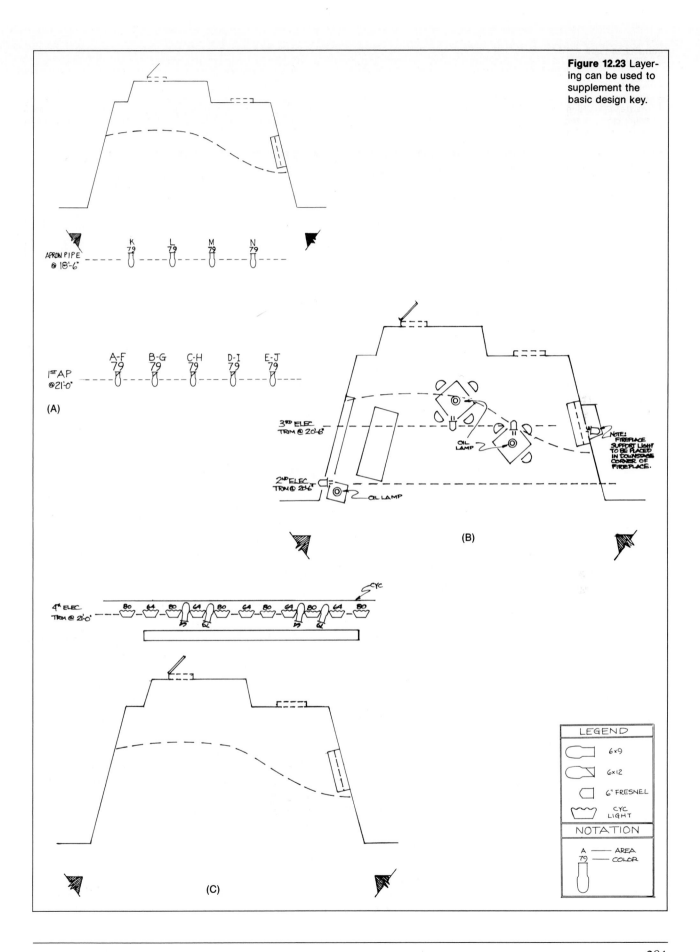

Figure 12.23 Layering can be used to supplement the basic design key.

Figure 12.24 Light plot for a proscenium production of *Playboy of the Western World*.

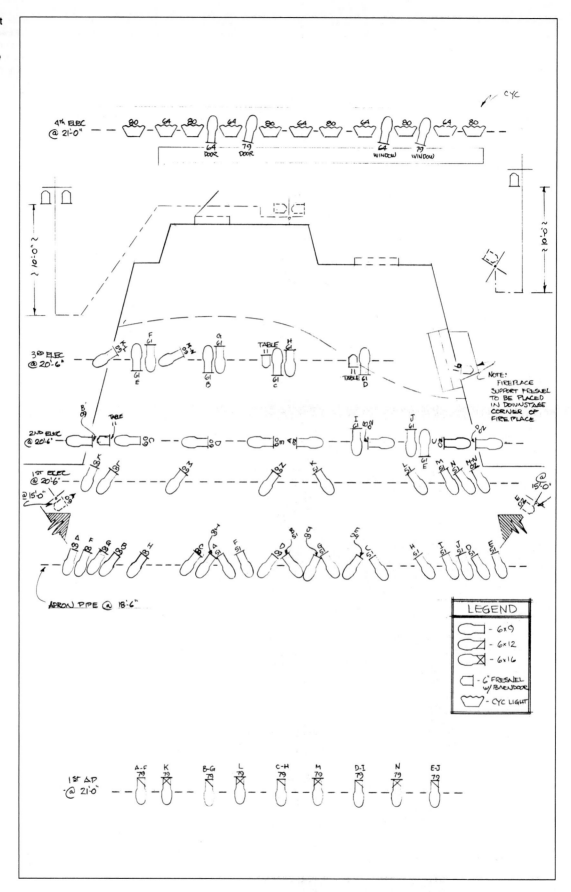

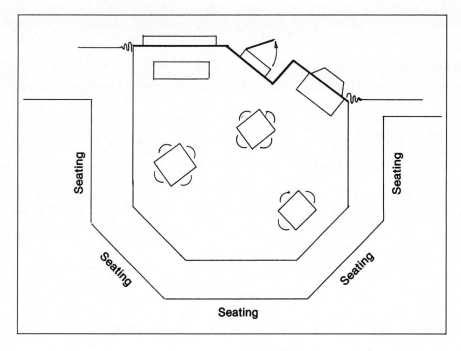

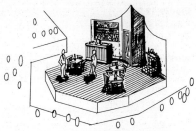

Figure 12.25
Scenic design for a thrust production of *Playboy of the Western World*.

Additional layers of light can be used for a variety of purposes. Figure 12.23C shows the location of those instruments that are used to create the "daylight" and "night light" that come through the window and door.

As indicated at the beginning of this discussion, layering is primarily an organizational tool of the lighting designer. It isn't really necessary to divide your thinking about the design into segments, but many designers find that this compartmentalization of the design into specific segments, or layers, makes it easier to concentrate on solving the challenges imposed by the individual elements of the design. Figure 12.24 on page 282 shows the finished light plot for *Playboy of the Western World*.

Designing Lights for Thrust and Arena Stages

Designing lights for an arena or thrust stage is not significantly different from designing for a proscenium theatre. The only substantive difference is the location of the audience. In the thrust configuration, as you will recall, the audience sits on three sides of the stage, and in an arena theatre it surrounds the stage. It is the lighting designer's responsibility to light the stage so that all spectators, regardless of where they are sitting, are able to see the production equally well.

We can use our hypothetical production of *The Playboy of the Western World* to demonstrate the relative lack of difference between designing lighting for the three modes of stages. Figure 12.25 shows a sketch of the modified scenic design that would work for a thrust production of our play. Note that the side walls have been removed so the spectators sitting on the sides of the thrust stage can see all of the action. Also notice that because the walls are gone, the ceiling has been eliminated.

The image of light remains the same as before, simply because the concept of how we are going to produce the play hasn't changed. The distribution of the design key has been slightly modified because of the position of the audience relative to the stage. We are still surrounding the actors with

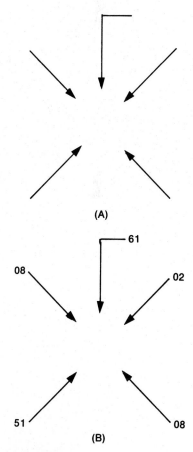

Figure 12.26
Lighting key for thrust production of *Playboy of the Western World*.

Figure 12.27
Additional layers
for lighting key for
thrust production
of *Playboy of the
Western World*.

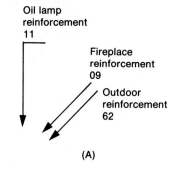

Oil lamp
reinforcement
11

Fireplace
reinforcement
09

Outdoor
reinforcement
62

(A)

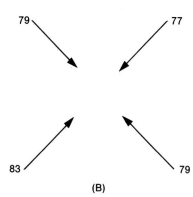

79   77

83   79

(B)

light to recreate our "bright, twinkling Irish morning" as shown in Figure 12.26A. The color of the design key also remains relatively unchanged, although we will lower the saturation of the "warm" color because of the proximity of the audience, as shown in Figure 12.26B.

The second layer for our thrust production could concentrate on enhancing the source lights—oil lamps, fireplace, window, and door (Figure 12.27A). The third layer (Figure 12.27B) would concentrate on creating the "night" wash.

The lighting design for an arena production of our play would be very similar to the thrust design. The set for the arena production is shown in Figure 12.28. Notice how all of the walls that might in any way interfere with the spectators' sight lines have been removed. The scenic design has been essentially reduced to a furniture arrangement, with just enough set left to provide a hint of what the cottage or pub actually looks like. The set has been shifted to a diagonal angle so the entrances are lined up with the auditorium entryways.

The distribution of the lighting key for the arena production is slightly different from the other two configurations (Figure 12.29A). The color portion of the design key is also different, but only because we want everyone looking at the play to get the same feeling. For the proscenium and thrust productions we were able to have the light coming from the direction of the door and window gelled with colors that would support the "outdoors" look of the light coming through the window and door. Because we now have the audience surrounding the stage however, we need to create the same feeling of "interior" lighting from all angles. These changes are shown in the color selection for the design key illustrated in Figure 12.29B.

Similarly, the "night" layers must place lights in positions that will enhance the idea of "night" for all of the viewing audience, as shown in Figure

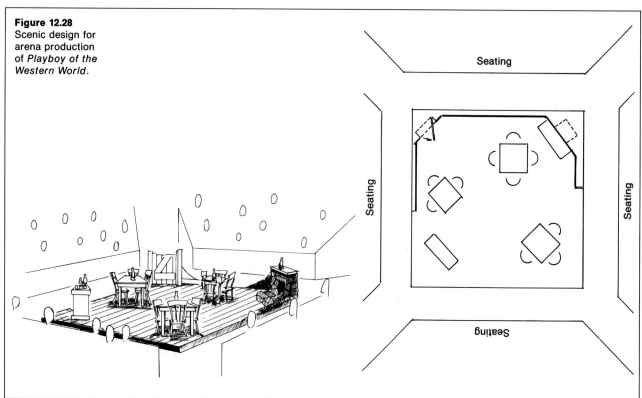

Figure 12.28
Scenic design for arena production of *Playboy of the Western World*.

Seating

Seating

Seating

Seating

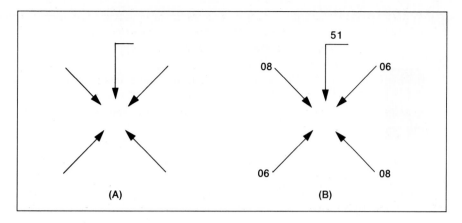

Figure 12.29
Lighting key for
arena production
of *Playboy of the
Western World*.

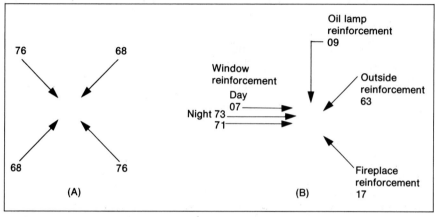

Figure 12.30
Additional layers
for lighting key for
arena production
of *Playboy of the
Western World*.

12.30A. In this particular design the third layer of light is used to support both the internal and external source lights. These lights need to be reasonably directional, as shown in Figure 12.30B, because the apparent source lights that they are reinforcing (sunlight, moonlight, peat fire) are also directional. The instruments that are reinforcing the oil lamps are placed over the general area of the lamps, simply because the light from the oil lamps illuminates everything around it.

The only other type of design modification that needs to be made when working in an arena theatre is that the instruments are probably hung considerably closer to the actors than in either a thrust or proscenium configuration. Because of this you will want to use less-saturated color media, because the closer the instrument is to the actor, the stronger the effect of any color that is used with that instrument.

Other than these relatively minor adjustments required by the positioning and proximity of the audience, there really aren't any significant changes in philosophy, practice, or techniques when designing for thrust or arena theatres.

DRAWING THE LIGHT PLOT AND LIGHTING SECTION

The lighting designer needs to acquire several specific drawings from other members of the production design team before he or she can start to draw the light plot:

1. the ground plan(s) of the scenic design
2. the sectional(s) of the scenic design

As we have seen, the lighting designer uses two principal mechanical drawings to record the information that is needed to hang, circuit, and focus the lighting design, the light plot and the lighting section. The purpose of these drawings is to guide the master electrician and crew. The amount and kind of information shown on the paperwork associated with a lighting design varies greatly from production to production and designer to designer. But a set of basic criteria pertains to the drawings associated with any lighting design.

1. The light plot and lighting section should be drawn to scale.

2. The light plot should show the location of the lighting instruments in relationship to the set and the physical structure of the theatre.

3. All drawings should adhere to the tenets of good mechanical drafting techniques (see Chapter 18, *Mechanical Drafting*).

4. Lighting instrument symbols and associated lettering should be represented by a thick line; all other elements should be drawn using a thin line, unless a thick or extrathick line is needed for emphasis.

5. A legend should be used to explain all symbols used on the plot.

6. Each lighting instrument or fixture should be numbered to allow for its easy identification on the hookup sheet, or instrument schedule.

7. All pertinent data regarding each instrument should be included on the instrument schedule.

8. The title block should adhere to the criteria noted for scenic and technical production in Chapter 18.

3. a scale ground plan of the stage and auditorium

4. a sectional of the stage and auditorium

5. a layout of, and specifications for, the stage lighting system(s) of the theatre

The ground plans of the theatre and set are traced, using a thin line, onto the light plot. The layout of the stage lighting system provides information about the location of the various stage circuits (connecting strips, floor and wall sockets, and so on). The sectionals of the set and the stage and auditorium are traced to create the basic visual information necessary for the lighting section.

Information regarding the lighting key, beam and field angles, and lighting areas was presented earlier in this chapter. However, some additional technical information may prove helpful when you start to draw the light plot.

Determining the Sectional Angle

The lighting key codifies the plan angle and color for each instrument, but it doesn't provide any information about the sectional angle for each instrument. Although the sectional angle should be determined from an analysis of the desired appearance of the light, in fact the sectional angles of most light-

Throw distance: How far light from an instrument travels from its hanging position to the center of its focus area.

Working sectional: A drawing showing the sectional angle for a lighting instrument; used to determine its trim height; not to be confused with the lighting section.

ing instruments used in the theatre will usually be somewhere between thirty and sixty degrees. The reason for this apparently arbitrarily selected angle is that people living in temperate climates are used to seeing objects illuminated by the sun within this angle range, so we perceive of this angle range as being natural, normal, and appropriate.

Dance and other applications in which the revelation of form is more important than the visibility of the face are notable exceptions to this generalization about the sectional angle. Dance lighting normally makes very effective use of side lighting with an angle of approach parallel with the stage floor.

Figure 12.31A shows the plan view of a single lighting instrument. Figure 12.31B shows a sectional view taken at right angles to the axis of that same instrument. Since the lighting instruments are usually hidden from the spectators' view, the lighting designer will set a specific trim height (height above the stage floor) for the instrument. Since any point along the axial line will produce the "correct" sectional angle, the sectional line can be extended until it reaches the predetermined trim height (x). At that point a vertical line can be dropped to the stage floor, and the distance from that point to the center of the lighting area can be measured (y). This information is recorded on the light plot by placing the symbol for the instrument at the measured floor distance from the center of the lighting area, as shown in Figure 12.31C. The trim height for the pipe is noted, at the end of the pipe, on the plot.

Selecting Instrument Size

At the same time that the sectional angle is being determined, the lighting designer can also determine the appropriate size of instrument to use. From the beam and field angle information (see page 275) or from the manufacturer's specification sheets for specific lighting instruments, templates of the beam and field angles can be constructed for each instrument. These are simple triangular, scale, acetate, or cardboard templates that contain the **throw distance** and the beam and field angles of the light emitted by each instrument.

Figure 12.32 shows how to use the beam and field angle template. After the **working sectional** for the instrument has been drawn, the apex of the template is placed at the specified trim height for the instrument. The appropriately sized instrument will have a field angle that slightly overlaps the

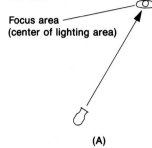

Figure 12.31 A sectional view of the hanging position of a lighting instrument provides an accurate picture of the angle from which the light will strike the actor.

Focus area (center of lighting area)

(A)

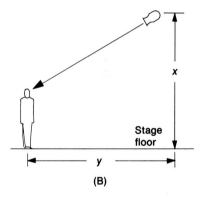

x

Stage floor

y

(B)

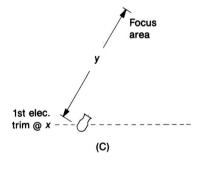

Focus area

y

1st elec. trim @ x

(C)

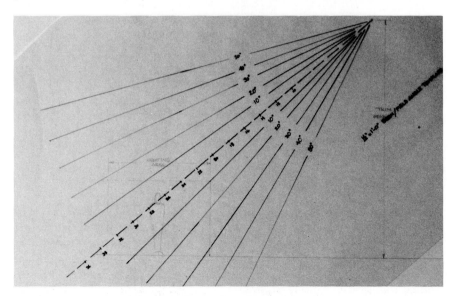

Figure 12.32 How to use a beam and field angle template.

LIGHTING INSTRUMENT SPECIFICATION SHEETS

It is extremely useful for a lighting designer to assemble a collection of data sheets that specify the photometric data (beam, field angle, light output at specific throw distances, and the like) for the instruments of the various manufacturers (see example). The maximum throw distance is the farthest distance at which the instrument can effectively be used. At this distance the light emitted by the instrument measures fifty footcandles, which is used as the industry standard and is considered to be the lowest effective illumination level for stage use.

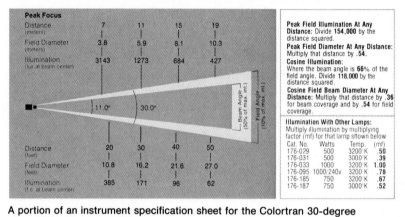

A portion of an instrument specification sheet for the Colortran 30-degree ellipsoidal reflector spotlight.

lighting area and a maximum throw distance that is longer than the required throw distance.

This method of instrument selection is suggested only as a general guide. In the final analysis the designer needs to make instrument selections based on what is aesthetically appropriate for the particular situation.

REHEARSAL AND PERFORMANCE PROCEDURES

It has been said that any lighting design is only as good as its paperwork. The light plot, lighting section, and instrument schedule are only about half of that paperwork. The rest of it is associated with the recording of the dimmer intensity levels and other data that are used when running the lights for a production.

This section will present a series of rehearsal and performance procedures, forms, and practices that can be used to assist in the running of the lighting for any production. Every action involving the adjustment of one or more lighting instruments needs to be recorded to ensure that the intensity settings for those dimmers and the timing of each **lighting cue** remain the same from rehearsal to rehearsal and performance to performance.

The forms and practices suggested in this section are not sacrosanct; they are just one of many methods that can be used to record the information that is needed to run the lighting for a production. Any well-organized system that works for the lighting designer and electrician can be used. The important point is the necessity of having a clearly written, systematic method of recording the necessary information.

Lighting cue: A command to take some type of action involving lighting, usually, to raise or lower the intensity of one or more instruments.

Electrician's Cue Sheet

The electrician's cue sheet is the **board operator's** bible. It contains the primary operating instructions (cue number, what specific action the board operator takes, the timing of the cue, and so forth) for every lighting cue, as shown in Figure 12.33. It is also important to note what information the electrician's cue sheet does not contain. It doesn't give the specific dimmer intensity level settings (commonly referred to as dimmer settings) for major shifts in the lighting. That information is written on the preset sheet, which will be discussed a little later in this section. But the electrician's cue sheet is often used to record the dimmer levels for minor shifts of intensity that involve only one or two dimmers.

If you carefully study the information written on the electrician's cue sheet shown in Figure 12.33, you will be able to follow the progress of the lighting from the lowering of the house lights through the end of the first scene of the play.

Recording Dimmer Intensity Levels

There are actually two methods of recording lighting cues: electronically and in writing.

ELECTRONIC CUE STORAGE Electronic cue storage is probably the primary advantage of the computer-assisted light board. Although the capabilities of computer-assisted lighting consoles (more commonly known as "computer boards") vary from manufacturer to manufacturer, they all provide a basic level of computer memory that allows them to electronically store the intensity levels of each dimmer that is used in each cue. Many of them can also store the time associated with each cue. If a production company doesn't have a computer board to electronically record and store the data associated with each cue, that information will have to be recorded manually.

PRESET SHEET The preset sheet (Figure 12.34) is also used to record the intensity levels for each dimmer during major shifts in lighting. The layout and content of the preset sheet is dependent on the type of control system used for the production. But regardless of the exact form of the sheet, it will have an open space adjacent to each dimmer number for recording the intensity level of that particular dimmer for that particular cue.

ELECTRICIAN'S CUE SHEET

Show _____ Script Page _1-25_

Cue	Preset	Count	Notations
1	1	—	HOUSE PRESET @ 7:30
2	—	8	HOUSE TO HALF
3	—	4	HOUSE OUT
4	2	6	APARTMENT ↑ (MORNING)
5	3	1	KITCHEN ↑ WHEN HAL HITS SWITCH
6	4	5	FADE TO BLACK (END OF SCENE)

Figure 12.33 An electrician's cue sheet.

Figure 12.34 A
preset sheet.

PRESET SHEET

Production:_____

Preset Bank:_____ Cue:_____

1		16	
2		17	
3		18	
4		19	
5		20	
6		21	
7		22	
8		23	
9		24	
10		25	
11		26	
12		27	
13		28	
14		29	
15		30	

Each time a major shift in the lighting involves more than two or three dimmers, a preset sheet is completed for that cue. The sheet provides the board operators with the information necessary to accurately adjust the dimmers.

Preset sheets are used in conjunction with electrician's cue sheets. The electrician's cue sheets tell the board operator what action is necessary for any particular cue, and the preset sheets are inserted between the cue sheets where they are needed. To keep everything tidy, the cue sheets and preset sheets are usually kept in a three-ring binder.

Designer's Cue Sheet

After the designer has a general idea of the intensity levels for each cue, the levels are recorded on a designer's cue sheet similar to the one illustrated in Figure 12.35. The designer's cue sheet allows the designer to record the rough intensity levels and timing of each cue in a systematic manner. Using one page per cue, the designer records the intensity level for each dimmer that is used within the cue so that he or she will have a clear indication of what changes are being made to each dimmer for every cue. Notations can be made on the sheets to indicate the purpose, function, or effect of that particular cue. Designer's cue sheets can also be kept in a loose-leaf binder so that cues can be easily added or deleted by inserting or removing sheets from the binder.

It is essential that the lighting designer and master electrician devise some

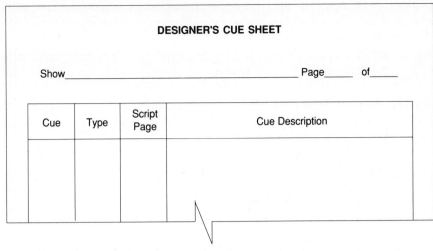

Figure 12.35 A designer's cue sheet.

DESIGNER'S CUE SHEET

Show_____ Page_____ of_____

Cue	Type	Script Page	Cue Description

type of organized system that will ensure that the lighting designer's concepts are accurately recorded and reproduced during each rehearsal and performance of the production. It is of the utmost importance that the various cue and preset sheets be clear and current; any changes in the timing, intensity, or location of any cue must be recorded so they can be duplicated during the next rehearsal or performance.

Lighting Rehearsal

The lighting rehearsal is a period devoted to setting the intensity levels and timing for each lighting cue. The lighting designer, electrician (board operator), stage manager, a small crew to shift the scenery (if necessary), and the director are the only members of the production team that need be present for this rehearsal.

Before the lighting rehearsal the lighting designer will have noted the position of any motivated or unmotivated lighting cues that he or she may want to use in the production. (Motivated cues are those prompted by an internal action of the play—for example, a sunset, a character's turning on a light, and the like. Unmotivated cues are prompted by an action external to the play—for example, changing the intensity of an instrument to shift the focus of action.) The designer will have discussed these cues with the director during one of the production conferences. The extent of this discussion varies greatly. Some directors want to know the exact location, purpose, and function of every cue, whereas other directors will leave the matter entirely up to the lighting designer. The lighting designer and board operator will have "roughed in" the intensity settings for each cue before the lighting rehearsal.

There are two primary reasons for holding a lighting rehearsal: (1) It provides the director and lighting designer with a specific time to discuss the effect, purpose, and content of each cue when they are relatively unencumbered by other elements of the production. Additionally, it gives them an opportunity to discuss any additions, deletions, or other changes that they feel should be made in the location or duration of the cues or anything else affecting the lighting design. (2) It provides the designer, director, stage manager, and board operator with an opportunity to make sure that the paperwork affecting the lighting design is correct. Since the stage manager will be calling all of the cues, he or she can use the lighting rehearsal to make sure that the lighting cues have been noted in their appropriate positions in the prompt script. It also gives the board operator a chance to check the accuracy of the electrician's cue sheets and preset sheets.

Figure 12.36 A
dimmer instrument
check sheet.

DIMMER/INSTRUMENT CHECK SHEET			
Dimmer	Number of Instruments	Instrument Location(s)/Color(s)	Area of Focus

Technical and Dress Rehearsals

Changes and adjustments to the timing, content, and positioning of lighting cues are normal during the technical and dress rehearsals. Although this can be a very frustrating time, it is essential that the lighting crew understand that the majority of the lighting cues will probably have to be adjusted; intensities and timing will be changed, entire cues will probably need to be added or deleted, instrument focus may need to be shifted, and the color in various instruments may also have to be changed. These adjustments should be considered as normal, rather than extraordinary, because it is part of the lighting designer's responsibility to develop the lighting design to work with the production concept that has evolved during the rehearsal period.

Instrument and Dimmer Check

Several routine equipment checks should be conducted before each technical or dress rehearsal and each performance. All dimmers and instruments need to be checked to determine that they are functioning properly. With the aid of a check sheet (Figure 12.36) two crew members can test all the instruments and dimmers in a short time. As the board operator turns on each dimmer, the other electrician checks to see that all of the instruments assigned to that dimmer are functioning properly. At the same time the person checking the instruments can see if any of the color media are bleached out, torn, or otherwise in need of replacement. Each instrument should also be tested to determine if it is focused into its respective area.

The dimmer and instrument check is normally made about an hour and a half before curtain time to allow any necessary repairs, replacements, or adjustments to be made.

13

As theatre (and everything else) bounds rapidly toward the twenty-first century, it has become a pragmatic reality that students of technical theatre simply have to comprehend the function of electricity and electronics. The discussion that follows differentiates between the terms; electricity generally pertains to the use of the electromotive force to perform work—make lamps glow, motors run, and so on; electronics generally refers to the low-voltage circuits and devices used to control the flow of electricity.

Electrical Theory and Practice

ELECTRICITY—WHAT IS IT?

The study of electricity has to begin with a brief excursion into the not so mysterious realm of basic atomic theory. This is because some very fundamental laws of electricity are based on the laws of atomic structure. For this reason we need to know a little bit about the **atom.**

The atom is the smallest complete building block in nature. But an atom is composed of even smaller particles: **protons, neutrons,** and **electrons.** The subatomic particles possess specific electrical properties. The proton has a positive charge, the neutron a neutral charge, and the electron a negative charge. The physical structure of any atom is very similar to the configuration of our solar system. In the same manner that the earth rotates around the sun (Figure 13.1A) electrons follow a slightly elliptical orbit as they whirl around the nucleus of an atom (Figure 13.1B).

Atom: The smallest particle of a chemical element that retains the structural properties of that element.

Proton: A fundamental particle in the structure of the nucleus of an atom; possesses a positive charge.

Neutron: A fundamental particle in the structure of the nucleus of an atom; possesses a neutral charge.

Electron: A negatively charged fundamental particle that orbits around the nucleus of an atom.

293

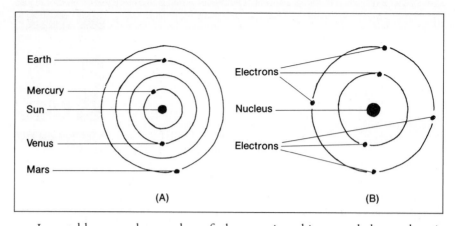

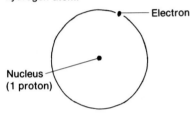

Figure 13.2 A hydrogen atom.

Electron

Nucleus (1 proton)

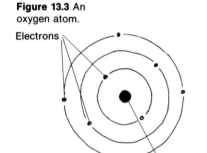

Figure 13.3 An oxygen atom.

Electrons

Nucleus

Valence shell: The outermost plane of orbiting electrons in the structure of an atom.

In a stable atom the number of electrons in orbit around the nucleus is equaled by the number of protons in the nucleus. Hydrogen, the lightest and least complex atom, is a perfect example of this principle. Figure 13.2 shows the single electron of the hydrogen atom in orbit around the nucleus, which is composed of a single proton. Since the orbiting electron has a negative charge and the proton in the nucleus has a positive charge, an electrical attraction exists between them. The electron is prevented from being pulled into the nucleus by the centrifugal force of its orbital movement. At the same time the electron is restrained from breaking out of orbit and flying away by the attraction. This attraction is an important underlying principle of electricity and is the basis for the first important law of electricity, the Law of Charges: *like charges repel, and unlike charges attract.*

If it were physically possible to isolate two protons, they would defy all attempts to bring them together. The same results would occur if attempts were made to push two electrons together. But if an electron and a proton were placed in proximity, they would zip toward each other until they met. The Law of Charges is the "electrical glue" that actually holds the atom together.

In atoms that are more complex than hydrogen, such as oxygen (Figure 13.3), additional electrons orbit in several planes around the nucleus. These electrons are counterbalanced by an equal number of protons in the nucleus, so the atom remains in an electrically balanced, or stable, condition. These additional orbiting electrons occupy orderly spherical shells at specific distances from the nucleus. Each of these shells can hold only a certain number of electrons. When each shell is filled with its quota of electrons, a tight bonding takes place, and no additional electrons can be added. Although it is possible to dislodge an electron from one of these filled shells, it takes a relatively large amount of energy to do so.

As the structure and weight of the atom grow, the number of protons in the nucleus increases, as does the corresponding number of electrons orbiting around it. Since the electrons cannot force their way into the already filled shells, they must orbit at a greater distance. The increased distance between the orbiting electron and its counterbalancing proton in the nucleus decreases the attractive force that holds the electron in orbit.

An atom of copper has twenty-nine electrons in orbit around its nucleus. Because of copper's particular atomic structure, only a very weak force holds its outer electrons in orbit, and only a very weak force is needed to dislodge them from the outer shell, or **valence shell,** of the copper atom.

A strand of copper wire is composed of billions upon billions of copper atoms, all having the same characteristically weak valence electron. The atoms in the wire are in such close proximity to one another (most of them are intertwined with their neighbors) that the nuclei of adjacent atoms can actually exert the same or more attractive force on their neighbors' valence electrons than they do on their own. Consequently, many of the valence electrons break away from their "home" atoms, momentarily attach themselves to other atoms, or simply float freely within the confines of the wire.

If this cloud of **free electrons** meandering in the wire could be organized to move in the same direction, an **electrical current** would be generated, simply because an electrical current is defined as the flow of electrons from one point to another. The unit of measurement for this electron flow is the **ampere.**

How can free electrons be motivated to move from one point to another? The answer lies in a practical application of the Law of Charges (like charges repel, and unlike charges attract). Since the electrons have a negative charge, they are attracted to a body that has a positive charge. However, it isn't possible to create a positive charge by itself. A negative charge must be created simultaneously with the creation of a positive charge, because electrical charges are produced by the transfer of electrons from one point to another. (In the process, electrons are neither created nor destroyed but simply transferred.) Figure 13.4 simplistically illustrates the principle that the positive charge is created by the removal of electrons, and the negative charge is the result of an accumulation of electrons.

If two bodies of opposite charge are created, an electrical current could be generated if a conductor, such as a copper wire, were connected between them. Free electrons would flow from the negatively charged body to the positively charged body, as shown in Figure 13.5. The flow, or current, would continue as long as there was a difference in charge between the two bodies. This difference in the electrical charge between the bodies is called **potential** and is measured in **volts.**

Free electron: An electron that has broken away from its "home" atom to float free.

Electrical current: The flow or movement of electrons through a conductor.

Ampere: The unit of measurement of electrical current.

Potential: The difference in electrical charge between two bodies; measured in volts.

Volts: The unit of measurement of electrical potential.

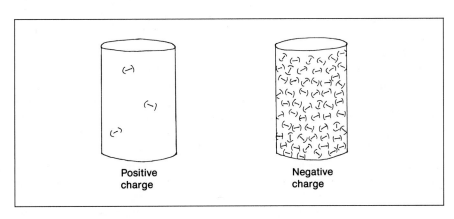

Figure 13.4 An electrical charge is created when electrons are transferred from one place to another.

Positive charge

Negative charge

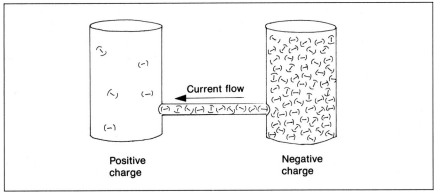

Figure 13.5 Electrical current flows from a negatively to a positively charged body.

Current flow

Positive charge

Negative charge

Source: The origin of electrical potential, such as a battery or 120-volt wall outlet.

Load: A device that converts electrical energy into another form of energy: a lamp converts electrical energy to light and heat; an electrical motor converts electricity to mechanical energy.

Circuit: A conductive path through which electricity flows.

Resistance: The opposition to electron flow within a conductor, measured in ohms; the amount of the resistance is dependent on the chemical makeup of the material through which the electricity is flowing.

The amount of voltage, or potential strength of the electrical system, is directly related to the difference in potential between the charged bodies. The greater the difference in potential between the charges, the greater that system's capacity to do work. A system with a rating of 220 volts has a greater potential capacity to do work than a 117-volt system.

ELECTRICITY AT WORK

Every electrical system must have three parts: a **source,** a **load,** and a **circuit.** The source is a mechanism that provides a difference in potential, or voltage. The load is a device that uses the electricity to perform some function. The circuit is a pathway that the current follows as it flows from the negative to the positive terminal of the source. (A negative terminal is created by an excess of electrons; a positive terminal, by a dearth of electrons. In batteries this electron transfer happens through a chemical reaction.)

A practical demonstration of the interrelationship between the three elements of any electrical system is provided by the example of a very simple battery and lamp, as shown in Figure 13.6. The source of this system is an ordinary flashlight battery. The load is a small incandescent lamp. The circuit is composed of copper wire. When the wires are attached to the lamp and the terminals of the battery, electrons flow from the negative to the positive terminal of the battery. As the electrons pass through the filament of the lamp, resistance to their flow causes the filament to heat up and incandesce, or give off light. The current will continue as long as the circuit is intact and there is enough voltage left in the battery to overcome the resistance within the circuit and lamp filament. When the voltage is reduced to the point that it cannot overcome the circuit resistance, the current will stop, and the lamp will no longer glow.

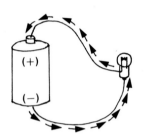

Current flow

Figure 13.6 A lamp will incandesce when current flows through it.

Ohm's Law

Although it's interesting to know that electrons flow within a circuit, unless there is some way of determining how the various parts of the circuit affect one another, there is no real way to understand and predict what will happen in any electrical circuit. Fortunately, a German physicist, Georg Simon Ohm, discovered in the nineteenth century that some very basic rules apply to the functioning of electricity in a circuit. These relationships have been formalized as Ohm's Law, and they are the primary mathematical expressions used in determining electron action within a circuit. Ohm's Law states: *as voltage increases, current increases; as resistance increases, current decreases.*

The diagrams in Figures 13.7 and 13.8 will help illustrate these relationships. They show very simple schematic diagrams or drawings that substitute symbols for the various parts of the circuit. The ⊣⊢ symbol represents a battery, and the -ᴠᴠ- symbol represents a **resistance,** or load, within the circuit. Figure 13.7 illustrates the first portion of Ohm's Law. The voltage of the battery in Figure 13.7A is ten volts. With this voltage the one-ohm resistance allows a current flow of one ampere. If the voltage is doubled to twenty volts, as shown in Figure 13.7B, and the resistance is not changed, the current will also double, to two amperes.

Figure 13.8 illustrates the second element of Ohm's Law. Figure 13.8A is a ten-volt system with a resistance, or load, of one ohm. This configuration allows a current flow of ten amperes. In Figure 13.8B the voltage remains

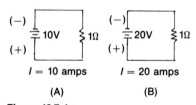

Figure 13.7 As voltage increases, current increases.

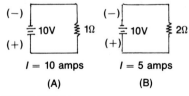

Figure 13.8 As resistance increases, current decreases.

CONDUCTORS, INSULATORS, GROUNDING, AND SHORTS

An electrical conductor is any material with an abundance of free electrons. Copper, aluminum, gold, and silver are excellent conductors. Water is also a very good conductor. Conversely, an insulator is a material with few free electrons. The lack of free electrons effectively prevents the flow of electricity through an insulator. Air, glass, paper, rubber, and most plastics are good insulators. In electrical wire the conductor (usually copper) is surrounded with an insulator (normally rubber or plastic) to keep the electrical flow confined to the conductor and to prevent the conductor from making contact with anything else.

Safety dictates that all electrical equipment be grounded. This involves making a direct mechanical connection between the conductive housing of an electrical device and the earth. This connection is made through the ground pin on the electrical cord of the equipment. (The ground pin protrudes farther than the circuit connectors on all late-model plugs.) The ground pin makes contact with the ground wire, which, if you followed it back to the point where it enters the house or building, would be clamped to a metal rod driven five or more feet into the ground or to a metal water pipe. The purpose of the ground wire is to provide a low-resistance path for the electricity to follow in case of a short circuit between the power circuit and the device's metallic housing.

The difference between an overloaded circuit and a short circuit is really just a matter of degree. An overload occurs when the current flowing through a circuit is greater than the maximum current for which the system was designed. A short circuit is created when a very large surge of current in an overloaded circuit causes a portion of the wire, insulation, and anything else at the point of the short to explode.

An overload is created when a too heavy load is placed on a circuit—as when a three-thousand-watt load is placed on a circuit that was only designed to safely carry a load of twenty-four hundred watts. A short circuit, or short, happens when a very-low-resistance alternative to the primary circuit is created. These alternate paths form when a wire breaks or comes loose from its terminal or when the insulation is worn away from the conductor, allowing it to touch another conductor or come into contact with the unit's metal housing.

If a short occurs in a grounded circuit, the very-low-resistance path between the circuit and the earth invites the surge of current to follow the ground circuit path. The high current flow activates a fuse or circuit breaker to shut off the electricity to the shorted equipment. If the circuit isn't grounded or the ground circuit doesn't function (perhaps because someone clipped off the ground pin from the plug), and you picked up the shorted device, you would be severely shocked, and possibly killed, because your body would act as the ground circuit to provide the path of least resistance between the shorted circuit and the earth.

You may find that some electrical hand tools do not have a grounding pin on the plug. The information plate attached to the tool's casing will probably carry the words *double insulated*. These tools don't need grounding, because the casing that you hold is actually a second, or outer, casing. These two layers of plastic insulators (casings) effectively isolate you from harm from any potential short.

constant at ten volts, but the resistance has been doubled to two ohms, which results in a reduction of the current to five amperes.

In both cases it is important to remember that the speed of the electron flow is constant. The increase or decrease in current flow is the result of an increase or decrease in the number of electrons flowing in the circuit.

Another way of looking at the relationships stated in Ohm's Law may help in understanding them. The voltage can be compared to the electrical pressure that causes the electrons to flow within the circuit. If more pressure (voltage) is applied, it would be logical for more electrons to flow. Since resistance is defined as opposition to the flow of electrons, any increase in the resistance would naturally cause the electron flow to decrease.

The relationships of Ohm's Law can be mathematically expressed as:

$$I = \frac{E}{R}$$

where I = current in amperes, E = voltage in volts, and R = resistance in ohms. This basic formula can be rearranged into two other forms. Each of these can be used to find the value of the other components of the relationship.

$$E = IR.$$

$$R = \frac{E}{I}.$$

These mathematical expressions of Ohm's Law are extremely valuable when working with low-voltage electronic systems such as those found in microphone and low-power speaker hookups as well as the control portion of electronic dimmers.

The Power Formula

Another formula, which is a derivation of Ohm's Law, is much more useful when dealing with higher voltage electricity. It is called the power formula. This formula is used when it is necessary to determine how much power will be consumed by an electrical circuit.

Household light bulbs, toasters, stage lamps, and electrical motors all convert electrical energy into mechanical energy, light, or heat in accomplishing their tasks. The amount of electrical energy converted, or consumed, is measured in watts. Usually the wattage figure is written on a label located somewhere on the device. Almost all household lamps have both the voltage and wattage printed on the top of the bulb. Toasters, electrical motors, and similar devices usually have a tag or label fixed on the bottom or back of the unit. The label states both the voltage and wattage of the unit. Stage lighting lamps have this information printed on either the metal lamp base or the top of the lamp.

The power formula is usually referred to colloquially as either the "pie" or the "West Virginia" formula:

$$P = IE$$

where

P = power in watts

I = current in amperes

E = voltage in volts.

$$W = VA$$

where

W = power in watts

V = voltage in volts

A = current in amperes.

The power formula can be rearranged as Ohm's Law can:

$$P = IE. \qquad\qquad W = VA.$$

$$E = \frac{P}{I}. \qquad\qquad A = \frac{W}{V}.$$

$$I = \frac{P}{E}. \qquad\qquad V = \frac{W}{A}.$$

With these three expressions of the power formula it is possible to find the unknown quantity in an electrical circuit if the other two factors are known.

An everyday example will help illustrate the point. You want to put a desk lamp on a table, but the power cord won't reach from the table to the wall outlet. You go to the hardware store to buy an extension cord, and the only information attached to the power cord indicates that it will safely carry 6 amperes of current. You know that the voltage in your apartment is 117 volts (standard household voltage in the United States). The lamp you plan to use is rated at 150 watts. To determine if the extension cord is safe to use, you will need to find out how many amperes of current the 150-watt lamp will create. To find the answer just plug the known information ($V = 117$, $W = 150$) into the appropriate variation of the power formula—the variation that has the unknown variable (in this case, A) located on the left side of the equal sign.

$$A = \frac{W}{V}$$

$$A = \frac{150}{117}$$

$$A = 1.28 \text{ amps.}$$

The lamp creates a current of 1.28 amperes, so the extension cord, which can carry 6 amperes, will be safe to use.

OUTPUT AND INPUT VOLTAGE

Input voltage is the voltage that is fed into a device (amplifier, dimmer). The output voltage is the voltage that comes out of the same device. In stage lighting systems input voltage refers to the voltage that is fed to the dimmer pack (used with portable dimming systems) or rack (used with permanently installed systems). The input voltage (usually 208–240 volts) is broken down (reduced) inside the dimmer pack so it can be used by the individual dimmers, which are designed to work at an output voltage of 117–120 VAC.

Electronic dimmers have two output voltages—a low-voltage control circuit and a high-voltage load circuit. The low-voltage control circuit (which varies between 8 and 28 VAC depending on the manufacturer) is used to regulate the output of the high-voltage (117–120 VAC) load circuit. This means that the intensity of the lighting instruments, which are connected to the load circuit, is controlled by the low-voltage control circuit.

PRACTICAL INFORMATION The output load voltage of dimming systems in the United States is 117–120 volts alternating current (VAC). The input voltage for most portable dimming systems is 220 VAC. The input voltage for most permanently mounted dimming systems is either 220 or 440 VAC. (The figure 220 VAC is a generic term used to describe voltage in the 208–240 range. The specific voltage is important for calculating purposes and varies from community to community. The figure 440 VAC is a similarly generic term.) The voltage figure that you will use in calculating the safe loading capacity for dimmers is the output voltage—117–120 VAC.

Electrical wires and cables are designed to carry specific current loads, as shown in Table 13.1.

Table 13.1
American Wire Gauge Current Capacity Chart

Gauge of Wire	10	12	14	16	18
Capacity in Amps	25	20	15	6	3

Any electrical system is designed to work within certain limits. If those safe limits are exceeded, the system will do one of two things: (1) If adequate protective devices (**fuses, circuit breakers**) have been placed in the circuit, those units will break the continuity of the circuit and stop the flow of electricity. (2) If there are no fuses or circuit breakers in the circuit, the various elements within the system will heat up. If the overload is sufficiently large, the elements within the system (dimmers, cables, plugs, and so on) will heat up to the point where they will either melt or burn up. If combustible material is in the immediate proximity of the overheated elements, it is very possible that a fire will be started.

The following problems illustrate how the power formula can be used to calculate the safe electrical load limits of typical stage lighting situations.

PROBLEM No. 1 The output voltage of a dimmer is 120 VAC. The dimmer can handle 20 amperes of current. What is the maximum safe load that can be placed on this dimmer?

$$\text{watts} = \text{volts times amperes } (W = VA)$$

$$W = 120 \times 20$$

$$W = 2{,}400 \text{ watts}$$

The dimmer can safely carry any load up to, but not exceeding, 2,400 watts.

PROBLEM No. 2 The system voltage is 120 VAC. The dimmer can carry 2,400 watts (2.4 kilowatts, or KW). The 14-gauge cable connecting the dimmer to the lighting instruments can carry 15 amperes (see Table 13.1). How many 500-watt lighting instruments can be safely loaded onto the dimmer (Figure 13.9)?

We already know that the dimmer can handle 2.4 KW, but we need to determine the load that can be safely carried by the cable.

$$W = VA$$

$$W = 120 \times 15$$

$$W = 1{,}800 \text{ watts}$$

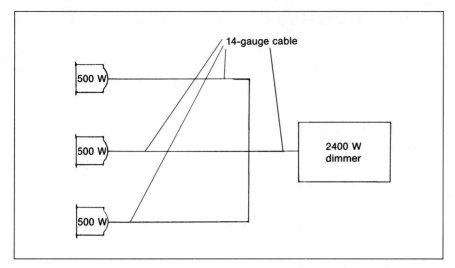

Figure 13.9
Problem number two.

The cable can carry a maximum load of 1,800 watts. To determine the number of 500-watt lighting instruments that can be carried by the cable, divide 500 into 1,800.

$$500 \overline{)1,800} \quad 3.6$$

Theoretically, the cable can safely carry 3.6 instruments. Pragmatically, it can safely carry 3 instruments. Even though the dimmer can safely carry 4 instruments, the single cable connecting the dimmer to the instruments can handle only the current flow generated by 3 500-watt stage lighting instruments.

Electrical Circuits

Two primary types of circuits, series and parallel, are used to distribute electricity. A third type, known as a combination circuit, combines the principles of the two.

SERIES CIRCUIT In a series circuit all of the electricity flows through every element of the circuit, as shown in Figure 13.10. In a series circuit if any of the lamps burn out, the circuit will be broken, the electricity won't flow, and the remaining lamps will go out.

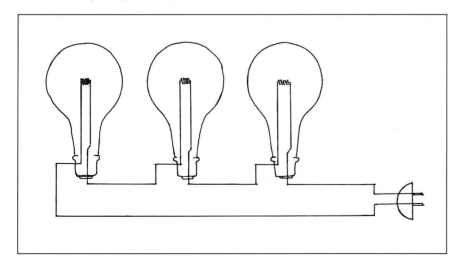

Figure 13.10 A series circuit.

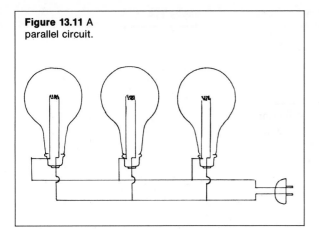

Figure 13.11 A parallel circuit.

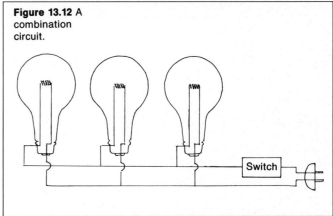

Figure 13.12 A combination circuit.

Switch

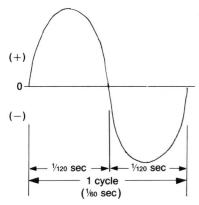

(+)

0

(−)

1/120 sec   1/120 sec

1 cycle
(1/60 sec)

Figure 13.13 An alternating current (AC) cycle.

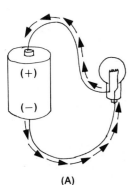

(+)

(−)

(A)

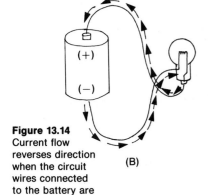

(+)

(−)

(B)

Figure 13.14 Current flow reverses direction when the circuit wires connected to the battery are reversed.

PARALLEL CIRCUIT In a parallel circuit only a portion of the electricity flows through each of the branches of the circuit. If one of the lamps shown in Figure 13.11 burns out, electricity will continue to flow in the rest of the circuit, and the other lamps will continue to glow.

COMBINATION CIRCUIT Any electrical circuit that uses a switch to control a light is a working example of a combination circuit. In a typical application of a combination circuit in stage lighting, a control device (switch, dimmer, fuse, circuit breaker) is used in series with the lamp load, and the lamps are wired in parallel, as shown in Figure 13.12. The series arrangement allows the switch or dimmer to exert control over the whole circuit, and the parallel wiring of the lamp outlets allows individual lamps to be inserted or removed from the circuit without affecting its operation.

Electrical Current

There are two types of electrical current, direct and alternating.

DIRECT CURRENT In direct current (DC) the electron flow is in one direction only. The battery demonstration discussed in a previous section is an example of direct current. The flow of the current is always from the negative terminal of a battery to its positive terminal. All batteries are examples of direct current sources.

ALTERNATING CURRENT The overwhelming majority of electrical power generated by power stations throughout the world is alternating current (AC). The electron flow in AC is the same as in DC with one exception—the current flow periodically changes polarity, which causes the electron flow to change direction. In the United States alternating current changes polarity at the rate of sixty cycles per second (60 Hz). This means that the electricity changes polarity (direction) every 1/120th of a second, as shown in Figure 13.13.

An example may help to explain this phenomenon. If the wires connected to the terminals of a battery, as shown in Figure 13.14A, were reversed (Figure 13.14B), the lamp would still emit light, but the current flow would have changed directions. Alternating current works like this example, except that the direction of current flow changes direction every 1/120th of a second.

When first confronted with the information that the current flow changes directions every 1/120th of a second, most people visualize the electrons as just sitting and vibrating. But they don't. Electricity travels at ap-

Before beginning this discussion of electric power service, remember: these high-voltage distribution systems can kill; if you don't fully understand how the systems work, call a supervisor or licensed electrician.

A number of wiring configurations are used to distribute AC power. Figure A illustrates a typical 120-VAC service system. According to National Electrical Code (NEC) practice, in the United States the insulation of one wire is normally colored black. It is called the "hot" wire. The insulation on the other wire is white, and it is called the "neutral."

The ground wire is not included in any of these illustrations, because it should not be used as part of the electrical distribution system. However, it needs to be included in the wiring of the system, and, according to code, its color should be green.

Figure B illustrates a three-wire, single-phase 120/240-VAC system. The voltage between either of the two hot wires (normally black) and the neutral (white) will be 120 VAC. The voltage between the two hot wires will be 220–240 VAC. Electrical service is delivered to most houses with this three-wire system. At the main service box (fuse box or circuit breaker panel)

the 120 VAC is distributed to the various lamp and wall outlets, and the 240 VAC service is usually routed only to the electric range and clothes dryer.

Figure C shows a three-phase, or four-wire, 120/208-VAC service system. The voltage between the neutral (white) and any of the three hot lines (black) will be 120 VAC. Although the input voltage measured between any of the hot lines and ground will be 240 VAC, the voltage measured between any two of the hot lines (phases) will be 208 VAC.

High-voltage distribution systems.

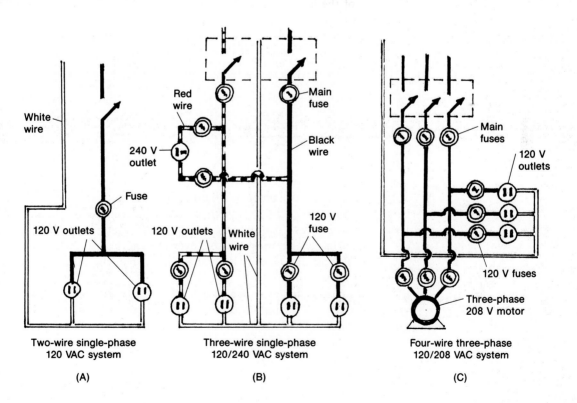

Two-wire single-phase 120 VAC system

(A)

Three-wire single-phase 120/240 VAC system

(B)

Four-wire three-phase 120/208 VAC system

(C)

Electrical Hazards

Electricity is extremely dangerous. It can burn, maim, and kill. Any piece of equipment that is connected to an electrical outlet should always be handled with caution and common sense. If you follow the safety procedures and work habits outlined below, your work with electricity can be safe and productive.

1. If you don't know what you're doing, don't do it. Ask your supervisor, or consult a trained electrician.

2. Use tools that are covered with plastic or rubber insulation when working with electricity.

3. Use wooden or fiberglass ladders when working on elevated electrical jobs. Electricity will always take the path of least resistance, and a metal ladder (and your body) provides a very-low-resistance path. If metal ladders must be used, insulate them with high-quality rubber foot pads. Movable metal scaffolds or adjustable ladders should have lockable rubber casters.

4. Disconnect any device (lighting instrument, motor, amplifier) from the circuit before you work on it. Unplug any lighting instrument before changing the lamp.

5. Use common sense: Don't touch any bare wires. Don't work in damp locations or put a drink where it could spill on an electrical or electronic component. Don't intentionally overload a circuit. Don't try to bypass fuses or circuit breakers.

6. Maintain the integrity of all ground circuits. Don't clip the ground plug off of any extension cord or power cord. When necessary, use ground plug adapters.

7. Check cables and connectors periodically, and replace any items that show signs of cracking, chipping, or other deterioration. Cracks in the insulation of cables and connectors increase the chances of receiving a shock from the device.

8. Keep the cables and connectors clean. Remove any corrosion, paint, grease, dust, or other accumulations as soon as they become evident. These substances can act as insulation between the contacts of the connector, and if flammable they can pose a fire hazard.

9. When stage or microphone cables are not in use, coil them and hang them up. A cable will stay neatly coiled if the connectors are plugged together or if it is tied with light rope or fastened with a Velcro loop.

10. Always disconnect a plug by pulling on the body of the connector, not the cable. Pulling on the cable puts an unnecessary strain on the cable clamp and will eventually defeat the clamp. When the cable clamp no longer functions, pulling on the cable places the strain directly on the electrical connections.

11. Be sure that all elements of a cable are of the same electrical rating: twelve-gauge cable (capable of carrying twenty amperes of current) should only have twenty-ampere-rated connectors.

proximately the speed of light—186,000 miles per second. At this speed an electron would travel about 1,550 miles in 1/120th of a second. Theoretically, in one complete cycle, or 1/60th of a second, an electron could travel the distance from New York to Los Angeles.

The principal advantages of AC over DC are that AC is easier and cheaper to generate and that there is less voltage loss when the electricity is transmitted over a great distance.

This chapter has provided a brief glance at the nature and uses of electricity. Anyone who is thinking about a career in any area of theatrical design or production would be wise to take a course or two in practical electronics as well as making an intensive study of standard electrical wiring practice.

14

Lighting Production

You might dream up the most imaginative lighting design ever conceived, but unless you knew how to execute that design, you wouldn't get very far as a lighting designer. In this chapter we explore the tools and technology that lighting designers use.

It is very easy to become enamored of the various tools (some would call them toys) of lighting design. The lighting instruments and dimmers as well as the control and distribution systems are not ends in themselves, however; they are simply the metaphorical mallet and chisels that lighting designers use to create their sculptures in light.

Ten years ago it wasn't really necessary for a practitioner of scenic or lighting design or technical production to have a thorough knowledge of electricity and electronics. Today that simply isn't true. Each of these technical areas uses an ever-increasing number of electronically controlled devices, and anyone who works in these areas needs to have a *thorough* working knowledge of both electricity and electronics. To help you prepare, the previous chapter presented a comprehensive discussion of the fundamentals.

LENSES

The angle of the beam of light emitted by the most frequently used stage lighting instruments is controlled by the optical properties of the lenses used with those instruments. Lenses refract light, which means that they redirect, or deflect, light from its normally straight path. The amount of deflection depends on the angle of intersection between the light ray and the surface of the lens, as well as the density of the medium through which the light is passing.

Figure 14.1 Light rays are deflected when they pass through a lens.

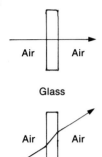

Air | Air

Glass

Air | Air

Figure 14.2 The greater the curvature of the convex face of a lens, the greater the angle of deflection, and vice versa.

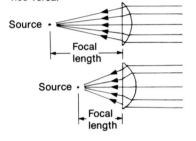

Source •

Focal length

Source •

Focal length

Figure 14.3 The focal length of a plano-convex lens is determined by the curvature of its convex face.

Long focal length

Short focal length

Figure 14.4 Double plano-convex lens train.

Focal length: The distance from the lens at which the light rays converge into a point; for lenses used in stage lighting instruments the focal length is most frequently measured in even inches.

Plano-convex lens: A lens with one flat and one outward curving face.

When a light ray passes from one medium into another medium of greater density (for example, from air into glass), it bends away from its original direction of travel. The direction of the deflection depends on the angle of intersection of the light ray and the boundary between the two mediums. When it passes through the glass and reenters the air (from more to less dense), it bends back toward its original direction of travel. Figure 14.1 provides an illustration of these principles.

The more pronounced the curvature of the convex face of the lens, the more quickly the parallel light rays will converge, as shown in Figure 14.2. The distance that it takes the light to converge into a single point is referred to as the **focal length** of the lens.

The focal length of a lens affects the angle of the beam of light emitted by that lens. When considered in relationship to the diameter of the lens, the shorter the focal length, the wider the beam of light emitted by that lens. A standard stage lighting instrument—the ellipsoidal reflector spotlight (ERS)—can be used to demonstrate this principle. If it is equipped with a lens six inches in diameter that has a focal length of nine inches (known as a 6 × 9), it will produce a wider beam of light than an instrument equipped with a 6 × 12 lens. Similarly a 6 × 12 ERS produces a wider beam of light than a 6 × 16 ERS.

The focal length of a **plano-convex lens** is determined by the curvature of the convex face of the lens, as illustrated in Figure 14.3. The greater the curvature, the shorter the focal length.

Three primary types of lens systems are used with theatrical lighting instruments: the double plano-convex lens train, the step lens, and the Fresnel lens.

Double Plano-Convex Lens Train

The double plano-convex lens train consists of two plano-convex lenses placed with their convex surfaces toward each other, as shown in Figure 14.4. This double configuration provides the same optical properties as a single lens of greater thickness and curvature, and the total thickness of the two lenses is less than the thickness of the optically comparable single lens. The single lens with short focal length is not used in lighting instruments, because its thickness makes it very susceptible to heat fracture. The thicker single lens also transmits less light than its thinner optical equivalent in the double plano-convex lens system.

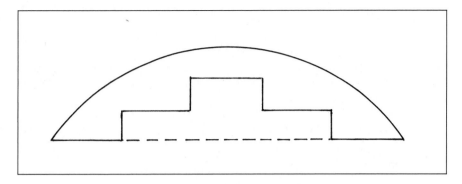

Figure 14.5 A step lens.

Step Lens

A step lens retains the optical characteristics and shape of a plano-convex lens, but the glass on the flat side is cut away in steps, as shown in Figure 14.5. The stepping process gives the lens the optical properties of a thick, short-focal-length, plano-convex lens while eliminating its negative characteristics.

An inherent property of step lenses is the prismatic effect caused by the steps themselves. Light passing through the steps at a shallow angle tends to create a spectral flare in the same manner that a prism breaks white light into a rainbow. Finishing the edges of the steps with a flat-black ceramic coating eliminates the spectral breakdown in most step lenses and does not interfere with the light passing through the rest of the lens (Figure 14.6).

Fresnel Lens

The Fresnel lens is a type of step lens with the glass cut away from the convex face of the lens instead of its plano side, as shown in Figure 14.7. The advantages of the Fresnel lens are the same as for the step lens; reduction of the thickness of the lens allows more light transmission and lessens the chances of heat fracture.

Fresnel lenses are used with both ERS and Fresnel spotlights. However, there are optically significant differences between the finishing of the two types of lens. Fresnel lenses for use with ERS's have black ceramic coating applied to the vertical faces of the steps to eliminate spectral flare. Fresnel lenses for use in Fresnel spotlights do not have such a coating, and the plano side of the lens is finished with a surface treatment to **diffuse** light. The diffusing treatment generally makes the plano side of the lens appear as though it has been sandblasted, or it may be finished with a series of small rectangular indentations. Regardless of the appearance of the treatment, its purpose is to soften the light to create the characteristically soft, luminescent light of the Fresnel spotlight.

Figure 14.6 A black ceramic coating prevents spectral breakdown.

Black ceramic coating

Diffuse: To soften the appearance of light by using a translucent filtering element to scatter the rays.

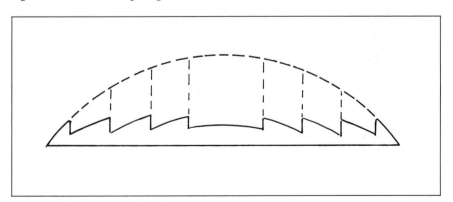

Figure 14.7 A Fresnel lens.

Figure 14.8 A standard incandescent lamp.

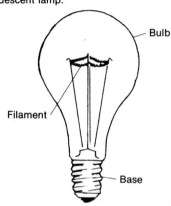

Bulb

Filament

Base

Figure 14.9 A tungsten-halogen incandescent lamp.

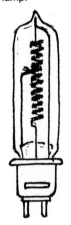

LAMPS

Each stage lighting instrument requires some type of lamp to produce light. The two primary sources used for stage lighting are the standard incandescent lamp and the tungsten-halogen lamp.

Incandescent Lamp

The standard incandescent lamp contains a tungsten **filament** that is placed in an inert gas environment inside the lamp **bulb,** as shown in Figure 14.8. The inert gas within the bulb is not pure and contains some oxygen. As an electrical current passes through the filament, heating it to incandescence, electrons are freed. The freed electrons unite with the oxygen to form carbon, which is deposited on the inside of the bulb or envelope. Eventually, the continued loss of electrons weakens the filament sufficiently to cause it to break. The average life expectancy of a regular incandescent lamp designed for use in stage lighting instruments ranges anywhere from fifty to approximately two hundred hours. The life rating for a lamp does not mean that the light will burn out in the rated time. It means that the original output of the lamp will be reduced by 40 percent by the carbon build-up on the inside of the bulb. Most lamps continue to burn long after their rated life, but at a significantly reduced output.

Tungsten-Halogen Lamp

Although it looks rather different than its cousin, the tungsten-halogen (T-H) lamp (Figure 14.9) is primarily the same as the standard incandescent lamp in all respects but one. That principal difference is that the atmosphere inside the bulb of the T-H lamp is a halogen, or chemically active, gas instead of an inert gas. As the electrons are released from the tungsten filament, they unite with the halogen gas to form a compound that is attracted back to the filament. The electrons reunite with the filament, and the halogen gas is released to repeat this chemical action. Because of the halogen cycle, carbon is not deposited on the inside of the bulb, and the filament of the T-H lamp is constantly being replenished. This results in a significantly longer life expectancy for the T-H lamp. Many T-H lamps designed for stage lighting instruments are rated from 150 to 2,000 hours, as shown in Figure 14.10.

The halogen cycle becomes active only in a high-temperature environment. To achieve this goal the T-H filament is encased within a small, highly heat-resistant synthetic quartz envelope. The heat generated by the filament is confined within the small space, and the resultant temperatures are much higher than if a larger bulb were used.

Arc Sources

An electric arc that produces a brilliantly blue white light is created when an electric current jumps the air gap between two electrodes. An arc is used as the source on some followspots.

When an arc is struck in an oxygen-rich environment such as air, the electrodes are consumed in the same way that a welding rod deteriorates during arc welding. If the arc is encapsulated in a noncorrosive atmosphere, however, the electrodes deteriorate extremely slowly. Encapsulated arcs such as the xenon and HMI (metal halide) lamps are frequently used in followspots. Neither arc nor encapsulated arc sources can be dimmed, so they are not used in "regular" stage lighting instruments.

Figure 14.10 The rated life of tungsten-halogen lamps varies according to their color temperature and output. Generally, the higher the output, the higher the color temperature and the shorter the life (and conversely). (Courtesy of Sylvania Lighting Products.)

ANSI Code	Watts	Volts	Bulb	Filament	Base	Lumens	Color Temp. (°K)	Avg. Rated Life (Hrs.)	LCL In.	LCL mm	MOL In.	MOL mm
EGC/EGD	500	120	T-4	CC8	Med. Pf.	13,000	3200	150	3½	88.9	5½	139.7
EGE	500	120	T-4	CC8	Med. Pf.	10,000	3000	2000	3½	88.9	5½	139.7
EGF	750	120	T-4	CC8	Med. Pf.	20,000	3200	250	3½	88.9	5½	139.7
EGG	750	120	T-5	CC8	Med. Pf.	15,000	3000	2000	3½	88.9	5½	139.7
DNT/FMD	750	120	—	—	Med. Pf.	17,000	3050	500	3½	88.9	6⅛	155.6
EGJ	1000	120	T-6	CC8	Med. Pf.	25,500	3200	400	3½	88.9	5¾	146.0
EGK	1000	120	T-6†	CC8	Med. Pf.	24,500	3200	400	—	—	5¾	146.0
DNV/FME	1000	120	—	—	Med. Pf.	27,500	3200	200	3½	88.9	6⅛	155.6

*Family of lamps which are replacements for existing incandescent T12 types primarily utilized in ellipsoidal reflector spotlights.
†Frosted

Color Temperature

All the standard light sources appear to be white. They are actually a variety of colors, however, and these colors can be identified by using the color temperature scale.

The color temperature scale was originally determined by heating a device known as a blackbody radiator. As the blackbody was heated, its color was read at specific temperatures by a **spectrometer.** The color temperature scale, measured in degrees, Kelvin (K), was the result of this experiment. Table 14.1 shows the color temperature of a number of standard sources.

Spectrometer: A device for measuring specific wavelengths of light.

Table 14.1
Color Temperature of Some Common Sources

Color Temperature	Light Source
6500	
6000	Xenon
5500	HMI (halide metal incandescent) — Sunshine
5000	
4500	Fluorescent (cool white)
4000	
3500	
3000	Theatrical Incandescent (standard and tungsten-halogen)
2500	
2000	

Gel: To put a color filter into a color frame and place it in the color frame holder of a lighting instrument.

There is a loose, but fairly constant, correlation among color temperature, light output, and lamp life. Generally speaking, the higher the light output of a lamp (which is measured in lumens), the higher its color temperature and the shorter its rated life. A comparison of the specifications for similar lamps such as the EGC/EGD and the EGE (the American National Standards Institute codes for two commonly used theatrical lamps) illustrates this relationship (Figure 14.10).

Although it isn't essential that the color temperature of all lamps used to light a production be the same, the instruments that are going to be **gelled** with color media of a specific hue are generally equipped with lamps of the same color temperature so the color of the resultant light will be uniform.

Lamp Structure

All lamps, regardless of shape or type, are composed of three basic parts: bulb, base, and filament, as shown in Figure 14.11.

BULB The bulb is the Pyrex or synthetic quartz envelope that encases the filament and acts as a container for the gas-filled atmosphere of the lamp. The shape and size of the bulb is determined by the position and shape of the filament, the burning position of the lamp within the lighting instrument, and the heat dissipation requirements of the lamp. Figure 14.12 illustrates common incandescent bulb shapes. Bulb sizes vary depending on individual lamp requirements.

BASE The lamp base secures the lamp in the socket and provides the electrical contact points between the socket and the filament. There are several styles of lamp base, as illustrated in Figure 14.13. Generally, large, high-wattage

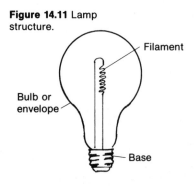

Figure 14.11 Lamp structure.

Figure 14.12 Common incandescent lamp shapes.

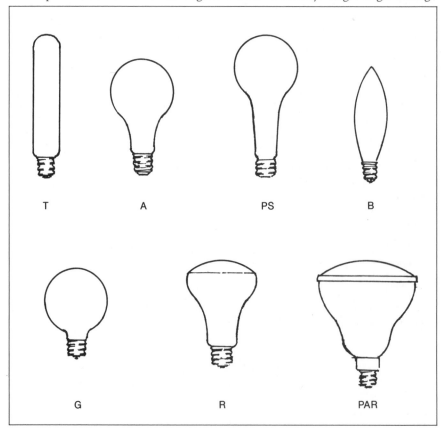

CHAPTER 14: LIGHTING PRODUCTION

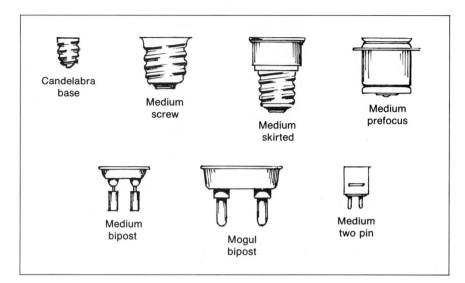

Figure 14.13
Typical lamp bases.

incandescent lamps have the larger bases. Figure 14.13 shows not only the different bases but also the relative size relationship that each base has to the others. The candelabra base is approximately ½ inch in diameter, the medium-size bases are approximately 1 inch in diameter, and the mogul bases are about 1½ inches across.

The prefocus, bipost and two-pin bases are used for instruments that need the filament in a specific location in relationship to the reflector—such as the ERS or Fresnel spotlight.

FILAMENT Various lamp filaments are available, each designed to perform a particular function. All filaments for stage lighting instrument lamps are made of tungsten wire, usually tightly coiled, and strung in one of the general configurations shown in Figure 14.14.

Figure 14.14
Filament styles.

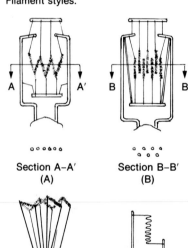

Light Output of Lamps

The output of an incandescent lamp, while related to the lamp wattage, is primarily a function of the size and composition of the filament. This output is measured in lumens. Generally speaking, if two lamps have the same wattage but one has a smaller filament, the smaller-filament lamp will have a higher lumen output but a shorter life expectancy, as shown in Table 14.2.

Table 14.2
Comparison of Same Wattage/Different Output Lamps

Watts	Sylvania Ordering Abbreviation	Other Designation	NAED Code	Standard Case Quantity	Volts	Color Temperature (°K)	Nominal Lumens	Average Rated Life (hrs.)	Filament Class	Fused Silica Bulb Finish	Lighted Length (in.)
1000	DXN	—	53993	12	120	3400	33500	30	CC-8	Clear	11/16
1000	DXW	—	53997	12	120	3200	28000	150	CC-8	Clear	13/16
1000	FBY	Frosted DXW	53996	12	120	3200	26000	150	CC-8	Frosted	—
1000	FBZ	Frosted DXN	53999	12	120	3400	31500	30	CC-8	Frosted	—
1000	BRH	—	54563	12	120	3350	30000	75	CC-8	Clear	—

Source: Sylvania Lighting Handbook, 7th ed.

LIGHTING INSTRUMENTS

A variety of lighting instruments is used in the theatre, but the ellipsoidal reflector spotlight and the Fresnel spotlight are the real workhorses for the lighting designer.

Ellipsoidal Reflector Spotlight

The light produced by an ellipsoidal reflector spotlight (ERS) has a relatively narrow beam width and is capable of traveling long distances. The quality of the light produced by this instrument, also known by the trade names Leko and Klieglight, can be characterized as generally hard edged with little diffusion. The shape of the beam is controlled by internally mounted shutters. The spill light from an ERS, that is, any light that escapes past the edge of the beam, is minimal. Because of all these characteristics, ERS's are the primary lighting tool of the designer. Several manufacturers' versions of the ERS are shown in Figure 14.15.

Figure 14.15
Ellipsoidal reflector spotlights. (Courtesy of Kliegl Bros., Colortran, and Strand Century.)

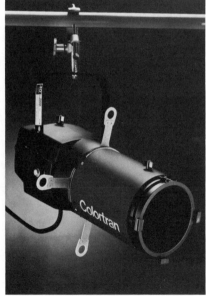

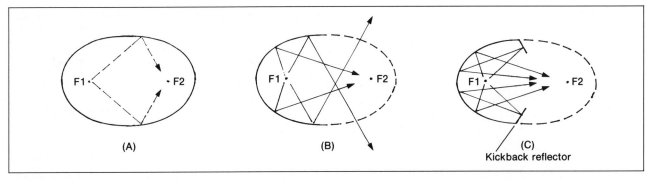

(A)   (B)   (C)
                                              Kickback reflector

Figure 14.16
Optical properties
of a conical ellipse
reflector.

GENERAL OPERATING PRINCIPLES The reflector of an ERS is a truncated conical ellipse, which has properties that are uniquely suited to focusing light. The conical elliptical reflector shown in Figure 14.16A has two focal points, F1 and F2. Light emitted by a light source at F1 will reflect off the walls of the conical ellipse and pass through F2. If half of the elliptical reflector were removed (Figure 14.16B), light emitted from the source at F1 would again pass through F2, although some of the light would pass out of the open end of the reflector and be lost.

The ERS operates on this basic principle of gathering light from one focal point (F1) and focusing it on the second focal point (F2). Some ERS's have a kickback reflector placed at the open end of the conical ellipse to redirect any spill light back into the reflector, as shown in Figure 14.16C. The shutters, made of stainless steel or some other highly heat-resistant metal, are located in a plane close to the second focal point to shape the light.

Figure 14.17 shows a cross section of an axial-mount ERS, so called because the lamp is placed on the optical, or centerline, axis of the instrument. This configuration was made possible by the development of the tungsten-halogen lamp. Compare the position of the lamp in the axial-mount instrument (Figure 14.17) with the instrument shown in Figure 14.18, an ERS

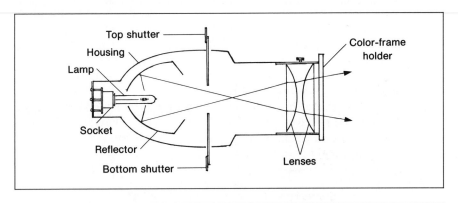

Top shutter
Housing
Lamp
Socket
Reflector
Bottom shutter
Color-frame holder
Lenses

Figure 14.17
Cutaway view of
an axial-mount
ellipsoidal reflector
spotlight.

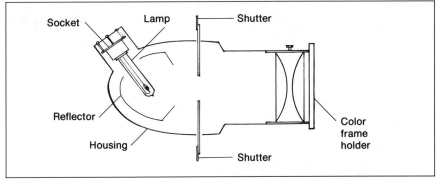

Socket   Lamp   Shutter
Reflector
Housing   Shutter
Color frame holder

Figure 14.18
Cutaway view of an
ellipsoidal reflector
spotlight designed
for a standard
incandescent lamp.

Figure 14.19 A continuously variable-focal-length ellipsoidal reflector spotlight. (Courtesy of Strand Century.)

Figure 14.20 A variable-focal-length ellipsoidal reflector spotlight. (Courtesy of Colortran.)

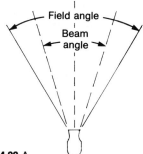

Figure 14.21 Beam and field angles.

Figure 14.22 A color frame.

Zoom ellipse: An ellipsoidal reflector spotlight with movable lenses that allow the focal length to be changed.

Color frame: A lightweight metal holder for color media that fits in a holder at the front of a lighting instrument.

designed for the incandescent T-shaped lamp, which predates the T-H lamp. Note how the lamp filament is still located at the focal point of the ellipsoidal reflector even though the lamp is mounted in a different position.

The lens is placed at a point in front of the shutters to focus the light into the desired field angle, as shown in Figures 14.17 and 14.18. ERS's are equipped with one of three lens systems: a double plano-convex lens train, a step lens, or a Fresnel lens. Although there may be slight differences in light output and quality, the three types work equally well.

The **zoom ellipse,** more officially known as the variable-focal-length ERS (Figure 14.19), is an extremely versatile instrument. This variation of the standard ERS has lenses that can slide forward or backward to change the focal length of the instrument. Changing the focal length affects the beam and field angles of the instrument, with those angles widening as the focal length becomes shorter. The field angle of most zoom ellipses can be varied between approximately twenty and forty-five degrees.

Figure 14.20 illustrates another type of variable-focal-length ERS. Its lenses can be moved between slots in the housing to change the field angle in ten-degree increments between twenty and fifty degrees.

Table 14.3 lists the beam and field angles in degrees of arc for several varieties of six-inch ERS's. As mentioned in Chapter 12, the beam angle (Figure 14.21) is that point where the intensity of the cone of light emitted by the instrument diminishes to 50 percent of its intensity as compared with the center of the beam. The field angle is that point where the light diminishes to 10 percent of the output of the center of the beam.

ACCESSORIES The most basic accessory designed for use with an ERS is the **color frame** (Figure 14.22), a lightweight metal holder for plastic colored media. The color frame is inserted into the holder on the front of the ERS to color the light.

The **gobo** (Figure 14.23), also known as a pattern, template, or cookie, is a lightweight metal cutout that turns the ERS into a pattern projector. Most ERS's are equipped with a built-in pattern slot located adjacent to the shutter plane. A wide variety of commercially designed gobos, usually made of stainless steel, are available from scenic and lighting supply houses. Gobos can be constructed from metal offset printing sheets or from heavyweight disposable aluminum cookware (roasting pans, pie plates), as shown in Figure 14.24. Offset printing sheets are thin, flexible aluminum sheets, which can usually be obtained from local newspaper publishers at low cost. They can withstand the heat generated by an ERS, are stiff enough to prevent flexing or buckling,

Table 14.3
Beam/Field Angles for Typical ERS's*

Instrument Type	Beam Angle	Field Angle	Maximum Effective Range†
6 × 9	16°	37°	35 feet
6 × 12	11°	26°	50 feet
6 × 16	9°	18°	60 feet
20°	10°	20°	70 feet
30°	12°	30°	60 feet
40°	15°	40°	55 feet

*All data is approximate but typical. Specific data varies with manufacturer.
†Determined by point at which output diminishes to 50 footcandles.

CHAPTER 14: LIGHTING PRODUCTION

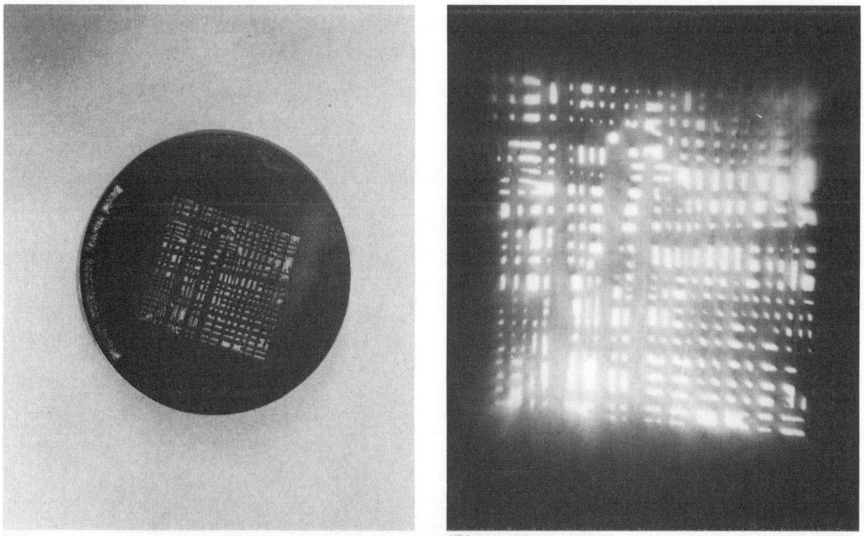

Figure 14.23 (A) A gobo, and (B) the pattern that the gobo projects.

(A)　　　　　　　(B)

Figure 14.24 Gobos can be built in the shop by cutting the pattern out of disposable aluminum cookware.

and can be worked quite easily with scissors, chisels, or a **Dremel tool.** The disposable aluminum pie plates are very satisfactory for making cloud gobos and similar patterns that have little intricate detail. The aluminum used in these products is about one-third as thick as the offset printing sheets and will vaporize under the high heat generated by the instrument lamp if the pattern is too detailed. It is much better to make intricately designed gobos from the offset printing sheets or from stainless steel.

Gobo: A thin metal template inserted into an ellipsoidal reflector spotlight to project a shadow pattern of light.

Dremel tool: A hand-held router similar to a dentist's drill, which can be equipped with a number of bits for grinding, cutting, or carving of wood, plastic, and metal.

Iris: A device with movable overlapping metal plates, used with an ellipsoidal reflector spotlight to change the size of the circular pattern of light.

Another useful accessory for an ERS is the **iris** (Figure 14.25). The iris varies the size of the circular pattern produced by an ERS. It is mounted in the shutter plane, and the size of the aperture is controlled by an external handle.

Fresnel Spotlight

The Fresnel spotlight produces a soft, diffused, luminescent light. Some Fresnel spotlights are shown in Figure 14.26. When the instrument is focused on narrow beam, or spot, as shown in Figure 14.27A, it produces a beam with a central hot spot that rapidly loses intensity toward the edge. When the instrument is focused on wide beam, or flood (Figure 14.27B), it produces a smooth wash of light.

Figure 14.25 An ellipsoidal reflector spotlight equipped with an iris.

Figure 14.26 Fresnel spotlights. (Courtesy of Kliegl Bros. and Colortran.)

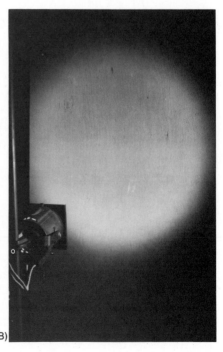

Figure 14.27 The Fresnel spotlight can be focused on spot (A), or flood (B).

(A)　　　　　(B)

The standard Fresnel spotlight is equipped with a Fresnel lens producing a circular beam of light. The oval-beam Fresnel lens (Figure 14.28) has the same luminescent and optical qualities as its round-beam counterpart but produces an oval, instead of round, beam of light.

GENERAL OPERATING PRINCIPLES The Fresnel spotlight is simple. The instrument housing holds the lens and provides a mounting platform for the socket, lamp, and small reflector assembly, which are mounted on a small sled that moves closer to or farther from the lens during focusing, as shown in Figure 14.29. Figure 14.30A shows the instrument on spot focus with the socket and reflector assembly moved toward the back of the instrument housing. In this position most of the light is concentrated into a hot spot in the center of the beam. Figure 14.30B shows the instrument on flood focus, with the socket and reflector assembly moved all the way forward. This creates a relatively smooth wash of light from edge to edge, with only a small, almost undetectable, hot spot in the center of the beam.

Figure 14.28 An oval-beam lens for a Fresnel spotlight.

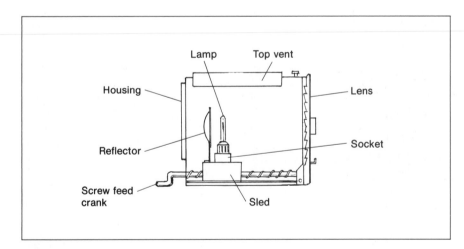

Figure 14.29 A cutaway view of a Fresnel spotlight.

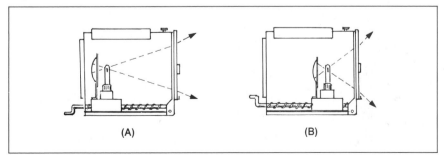

Figure 14.30 The sled holding the lamp/reflector assembly is (A) moved backward to produce a hot spot in the middle of the beam, or (B) moved forward to produce a relatively smooth wash of light.

Barn door: An accessory for a Fresnel spotlight whose movable flippers are swung into the beam to control it.

Funnel: An accessory for a Fresnel spotlight that masks the beam to create a circular pattern; also called a snoot or a top hat.

Gel: To insert color media in a color frame and place on a lighting instrument.

ACCESSORIES The primary, and almost indispensable, accessory for the Fresnel spotlight is the **barn door** (Figure 14.31). Its flippers are movable and can be swung into the beam of light until they cut off as much light as desired.

Another accessory is the **funnel** (Figure 14.32). The funnel, like the barn door, fits into the color frame slot on the front of the instrument. The circular pattern of light that it creates is dependent on the diameter of the funnel's cone.

Striplight

The *striplight* is used to create a smooth wash of light. It resembles a long trough with a series of lamps inside, as shown in Figure 14.33. Striplights are available in a variety of lengths and configurations, but they are most often between four and ten feet in length.

The individual lights within the instrument are wired in parallel to form three or four circuits, as shown in the block diagram of Figure 14.34. This type of configuration provides designers with the opportunity to mix and blend color if they **gel** all the lamps of each circuit with a separate color. By placing each circuit of the striplight on a separate dimmer, designers can manipulate the intensities of the individual colors to mix the desired resultant hue. To create the maximum potential for color mixing the individual circuits of a three-circuit striplight are frequently colored with the primary colors in light (red, blue, and green). If a four-circuit striplight is used, the fourth circuit is frequently gelled with amber. It is not mandatory that striplights be colored with red, blue, and green; if the designer knows that he or she will be working in a relatively narrow color spectrum, it is usually preferable to color the individual circuits in the appropriate hues.

Figure 14.31 A four-flipper barn door.

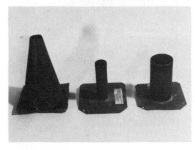

Figure 14.32 Funnels are used to create small circular patterns of light with a Fresnel spotlight.

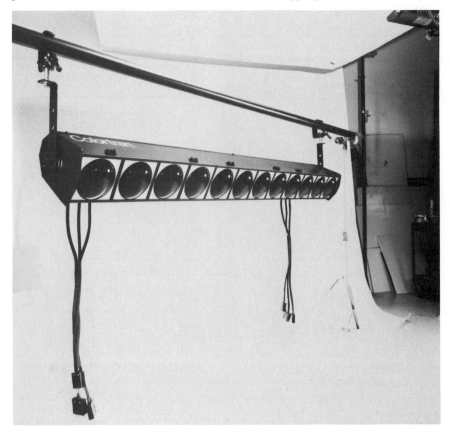

Figure 14.33 Striplights. (Courtesy of Colortran.)

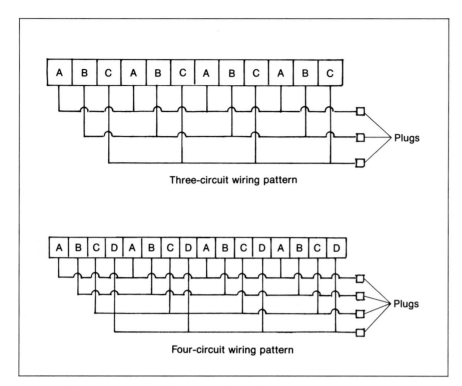

Three-circuit wiring pattern

Four-circuit wiring pattern

Figure 14.34
Circuiting pattern
for striplights.

Figure 14.35
Roundels are glass
filters used with
striplights.

Figure 14.36 A cyc
light. (Far Cyc
courtesy of
Colortran.)

Figure 14.37 An
ellipsoidal reflector
floodlight. (Cour-
tesy of Kliegl Bros.)

Striplights are primarily used to light background drops and cycloramas, although they can be used in any position wherever a diffused, general wash of light is desired. Striplights are equipped to hold plastic color media as well as **roundels** (Figure 14.35), which are glass color media that have diffusing properties to help blend the light. Roundels are available in the primary colors as well as amber, frosted, and clear.

Cyc Light

The cyc light (Figure 14.36) is superior to the striplight for creating a smooth wash of light over the expanse of a cyc or drop. This relatively new type of fixture uses an eccentric reflector to create such a wash from only seven or eight feet away. The cyc light emits a much smoother light than does the striplight, and it is equipped with a color frame holder so the light can be colored as desired.

Ellipsoidal Reflector Floodlight

The ellipsoidal reflector floodlight (Figure 14.37), also known as the scoop, is primarily used to light drops and cycloramas. It is a lensless instrument that has the light-focusing characteristics of a conical ellipsoidal reflector, which provides a wide, smooth wash of light. It is equipped with a large color frame holder that, in many cases, has wire restraining lines criss-crossed over the circular opening to prevent the color medium from falling out. The scoop is available in a variety of sizes, but in the theatre the fourteen-, sixteen-, and eighteen-inch diameters are most commonly used.

Beam Projector

The beam projector (Figure 14.38) is a lensless instrument with a parabolic primary reflector and a spherical secondary reflector. It produces a very intense shaft of light that has little diffusion and cannot be easily controlled or modified.

Roundel: A glass color medium for use with striplights; frequently has diffusing properties.

Figure 14.38 A
beam projector.
(Courtesy of Kliegl
Bros.)

The parabolic reflector focuses the light into parallel rays, and the spherical reflector redirects the light emitted from the front of the lamp back through the filament to the parabolic reflector. The beam projector's characteristically hard-edged, intense beam of light makes it desirable for creating shafts of sunlight and in similar situations.

PAR Can

The parabolic aluminized reflector, or PAR, is a sealed-beam lamp similar to the headlight of an automobile. The lamp housing, known as a PAR can (Figure 14.39), performs no function other than safely holding the lamp and its color media.

The most widely used size of PAR can is designed to hold the PAR 64, a one-thousand-watt lamp about eight inches in diameter. The PAR 64 lamp is available in a variety of beam shapes, as shown in Table 14.4. The PAR 64 produces a powerfully intense punch of light, yet it has a soft edge. It is used extensively in rock concert lighting and is finding increased usage in dance lighting because of its relatively low cost, portability, durability, and light weight.

Figure 14.39 A
PAR can. (Courtesy
of Strand Century.)

Table 14.4
Beam and Field Angles for Various PAR 64 Configurations

PAR 64 Lamp	Beam Angle (In Degrees) (Height × Width)	Field Angle (In Degrees) (Height × Width)
Very narrow	6 × 12	10 × 24
Narrow	7 × 14	14 × 26
Medium	12 × 28	21 × 44
Wide	24 × 48	45 × 71

Followspot

The followspot is used when a high-intensity, hard-edged beam of light is required to follow a moving performer. Followspots are manufactured in a variety of sizes and styles (see Figure 14.40). The smallest followspot is an incandescent model capable of a useful light throw of about thirty-five feet. The larger models use high-intensity xenon, HMI, or unencapsulated arc lamp sources and have a useful light throw of up to three hundred to four hundred feet.

All followspots function on the same general principles, illustrated in Figure 14.41. They have an illumination source—either incandescent, tungsten-halogen, HMI, xenon, or arc. Many have a forced-air cooling system that helps to dissipate the heat generated by the light source.

The iris and **shutter** are internal control devices used to shape the beam of light. By manipulating them simultaneously, the operator can create a variety of beam edge patterns.

All followspots have some type of lens or reflecting system to gather and shape the light. Portions of the system can be adjusted to focus the light and adjust the crispness of the edge of the beam.

Some followspots are equipped with a dimming device called a **douser.** Since the intensity of some of the light sources used in followspots (unencapsulated arc, xenon, HMI) cannot be adjusted, the douser provides the only way of smoothly dimming those sources. The douser can also be used to achieve a

Shutter: A lever-actuated device used to control the height of the top and bottom edges of a followspot beam; also called a chopper.

Douser: A mechanical dimming device used in followspots.

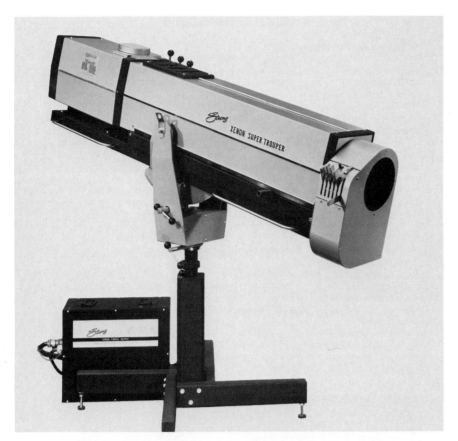

Figure 14.40 A followspot. (Courtesy of Strong International.)

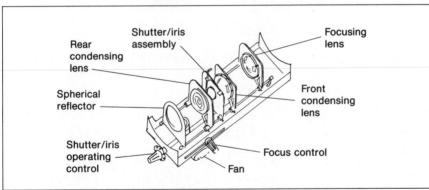

Rear condensing lens

Shutter/iris assembly

Focusing lens

Spherical reflector

Front condensing lens

Shutter/iris operating control

Focus control

Fan

Figure 14.41 Cutaway drawing of a followspot.

slow fade-in or fade-out of the light. Followspots are also equipped with a color boomerang, which holds five or six color filters that can be easily inserted into the beam of light to control its color.

Specialty Instruments

There are several lighting instruments that do not fall conveniently into other categories.

LOW-VOLTAGE SOURCES A number of specialty lamps use a voltage lower than the 120 output volts of most stage dimmers. The output of these low-voltage lamps is frequently as high as that of their 120-volt cousins. Aircraft landing lights (ACL's) have a very high output and high color temperature, and the parabolic reflector provides a very narrow beam spread. Automobile headlights provide another narrow-beam, low-voltage source.

Instrument Maintenance

To function effectively, the various instruments discussed in this chapter must be maintained in good working order, and, as with any delicate piece of equipment, they must be handled with care.

The position of the lamp filament and the reflector must be kept in alignment, particularly in an ellipsoidal reflector spotlight. If this relationship is disturbed, the light output from the instrument will be greatly reduced, and the hot spot will be moved from the center of the beam. One of the significant advantages of the PAR 64 is that the filament and reflector are permanently aligned during the manufacturing process, so when the lamp in a PAR can is changed, there is no need to check the relationship.

The lenses and reflectors need to be kept clean and free from dust and finger-prints, and all nuts and bolts on the housing, yoke, and pipe clamp should be maintained so that the instrument can be locked securely into place.

When not in use, instruments should be hung on pipes or on rolling racks, as shown in the photo, so they won't be knocked over. If the theatre does not have an instrument storage cage, the instruments can be stored on a counterweight batten above the stage.

Ellipsoidal reflector spotlights should be stored with the shutters pushed all the way in to prevent them from being accidentally bent. When the instruments are in storage, care should be taken that the electrical pigtails are not pinched between the yoke and the instrument housing. The electrical plug and pigtail must be kept in good working order.

Followspots are mounted on a yoke and swivel-stand base that must move smoothly to follow the action of a performer. The base and yoke need to be properly lubricated, usually with graphite rather than oil or grease, and all nuts and bolts must be properly tightened.

Instrument storage

A primary advantage of lower-voltage lamps is that their filaments can be much smaller than their higher-voltage counterparts. The smaller filament can be used effectively in some types of scenic projectors discussed in Chapter 15, *Projections.*

These low-voltage lamps require a **transformer** to decrease the 120-volt source voltage before it reaches the lamp, as shown in Figure 14.42. A step-down transformer of appropriate voltage and capacity to match almost any lamp can be purchased at any electrical supply store. For 12-volt lamps a heavy-duty automotive battery charger can be used as long as the current created by the wattage of the lamp does not exceed the rated capacity of the battery charger or its leads.

A number of lighting instruments and projectors have been designed to take advantage of the properties (small filament size, low heat output) of low-voltage lamps. These instruments normally have the required step-down transformer mounted inside of the instrument housing.

AUTOMATED LIGHTING INSTRUMENTS Devices have been introduced to automate certain functions on a lighting instrument. The Varimot (Figure 14.43A) is a motor-driven system that allows the operator to **pan, tilt,** manipulate the shutters, and focus the lens of the ellipsoidal reflector spotlight with a remote control device. The Vari-Lite (Figure 14.43B) is a computerized lighting system that lets the operator control the pan, tilt, beam size, color, and intensity of the instrument. A computer can be used to control a number of units simultaneously. A remote control color changer is another type of automated lighting instrument. It usually can be loaded with up to twelve colors, and the system operator can change the color as needed.

With the increased use of computer control the introduction of more remote focusing and color changing systems can be anticipated. Within ten years we can expect to find some theatres fully equipped with computer systems for remotely focusing and coloring their instruments. In these systems the only real job of the hanging crew will be to relamp the instruments and change the color media when they are burned out.

Transformer: A device that changes the voltage in an electrical system; the output voltage of a step-down transformer is less than its source; a step-up transformer increases it.

Pan: To rotate an object, such as an ERS, about its vertical axis.

Tilt: To rotate an object about its horizontal axis; to pan vertically.

Figure 14.42 A low-voltage lamp and transformer.

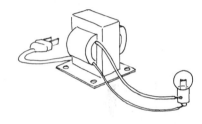

Figure 14.43 Automated lighting systems. (A) Varimot type HZM zoom followspot; (B) Varilite. [(A) Courtesy of Varilite; (B) courtesy of Emil Niethammer GMBH.]

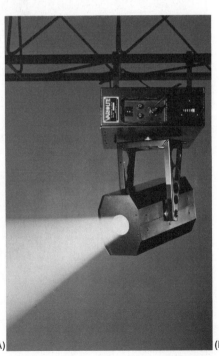

(A)

(B)

DIMMERS

In the relatively brief history of electrical stage lighting many different kinds of dimmer have been used to control the intensity of instruments. Some of the older dimmers, such as the salt water, saturable core, thyratron tube, and resistance dimmer, have dropped by the wayside. Other older dimmers, such as the autotransformer, have continued in use.

Dimmer Control Techniques

Dimmers can be divided into two groups based on the type of control used to regulate the current flow through them, mechanical or electronic.

MECHANICAL CONTROL Older types such as the resistance and autotransformer dimmers require direct mechanical manipulation of an axle running through the central core of the dimmer to adjust the intensity of a lamp, as shown in Figure 14.44. This method of dimmer control is awkward. When a number of dimmers are linked, as shown in the illustration of an archaic resistance board (Figure 14.45), the resultant dimmer board is noisy, is difficult to operate, and requires at least several rather muscular electricians to run

Figure 14.44 Some dimmers require a mechanical control technique.

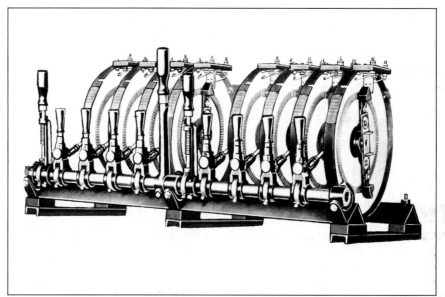

Figure 14.45 A resistance board.

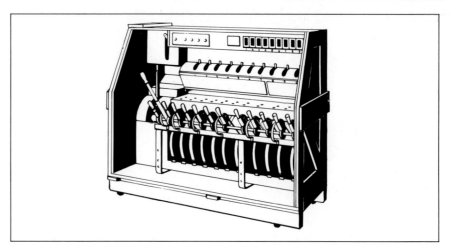

CHAPTER 14: LIGHTING PRODUCTION

even a moderately complex production. You can imagine that a certain delicacy of touch and smoothness of operation are lost when you have to control one dimmer with each hand and try to operate another one with your foot.

ELECTRONIC CONTROL The methods and operating principles vary according to the specific type of dimmer, but all electronically controlled dimmers use a low-voltage control current to regulate the high-voltage load current. The process of controlling the output of the dimmer by electronic rather than mechanical means lets the control console be located some distance away from the dimmers. Additionally, the low-voltage, low-amperage current of the control circuit allows all parts of this electronic circuit to be miniaturized.

Autotransformer Dimmer

Autotransformer dimmers increase or decrease lamp intensity by varying the voltage within the circuit. Although this type of dimmer is only rarely used to control stage lights, houselights in some theatres are controlled by a motorized autotransformer dimmer, as shown in Figure 14.46. A control switch, usually located in the light booth, is used to activate a motor, which runs a mechanical linkage that controls the dimmer and enables it to raise or lower the intensity of the houselights. The only drawback to the motorized auto-

Figure 14.46 A motorized autotransformer dimmer.

Figure 14.47 An SCR dimmer. (Courtesy of Kliegl Bros.)

transformer dimmer occurs when the motor runs at a single speed, so the fade time for the houselights cannot be varied.

Silicon Controlled Rectifier Dimmer

The silicon controlled rectifier (SCR) dimmer (Figure 14.47) is the most reliable and efficient unit that has been developed for stage lighting. The SCR dimmer operates on a gating principle, which is simply a rapid switching on and off of the power.

The SCR is a solid-state power transistor, which means that it has no moving parts and no filaments to burn out. The electronic circuitry necessary to switch the SCR to a conducting state is also relatively simple. These

---

SAFETY TIP

Dimmer Maintenance

The greatest enemy of an electronic dimmer such as the SCR is heat. To dissipate the heat some dimmers are equipped with large heat sinks. Heat sinks are metal—usually aluminum—structures that absorb the heat generated by an SCR and radiate it to the atmosphere. Other dimmer packs are equipped with fans.

It is vital for the longevity of dimmers that they have plenty of air circulating around them. Don't pile anything on top of a dimmer. If you are working with portable dimmers, be sure that the dimmer pack is raised off the ground so air can circulate under, as well as over, the case.

If your dimmer system is equipped with fans, be sure that they are running smoothly. The dimmers will frequently function for several hours even if the fan isn't working, but the heat buildup will cause a relatively rapid deterioration of the electronic equipment that will usually lead to premature dimmer failure.

Almost all SCR dimmers need to be adjusted periodically so they will smoothly increase or decrease their lamp loads. The specific methods vary from manufacturer to manufacturer, but they all involve an adjustment of the low, midpoint, and high-output voltage of the dimmer. These adjustments should be made by a qualified electrician at least annually.

CHAPTER 14: LIGHTING PRODUCTION

If, in a given period of time, you turn a lamp on, then off, then on, off, on, and off, you effectively control the amount of light it puts out for that specific amount of time. If the lamp is turned on, and left on, for one second, it burns at full intensity for that one-second period. If you turn the lamp on for half a second and turn it off for half a second, it burns at half intensity for the one-second span. If you turn the lamp on for three-quarters of a second and off for one-quarter of a second, it burns at three-quarters intensity for the one-second span. In each of these cases you will obviously see the lamp being switched on and off. But if the time span for the on-off cycle is reduced to 1/120th of a second, you perceive the on-off sequence as being a continuous level of illumination—an average of the on-off cycle ratio.

The SCR dimmer operates on this principle. The SCR is actually an electronic switch. The switch, or gate, opens and allows current to pass through the tube when it receives the proper electronic command. The gate stays open until the power to the tube is turned off. Sixty-cycle alternating current (AC), the standard current in the United States, alternates its polarity 120 times a second, or twice in each cycle, as illustrated in Figure A. Each time that it alternates its polarity, or crosses the zero point on the graph, there is actually no voltage. The effective result of this "no voltage" situation is that the electricity is turned off. If a command is fed to the SCR to start conduction at the beginning of the cycle, point A in Figure B,

the SCR will conduct for the full half cycle, or until the electricity is turned off when it changes polarity at point B. Similarly, if the command specifies that the SCR is to begin conducting halfway through the cycle (Figure C), the transistor conducts for only half the cycle, or half as long.

By varying the time that the SCR is able to conduct electricity, you vary the intensity of any lamp load connected to it. This means that if the SCR conducts for a full

half cycle, the lamp will glow at full intensity for the duration of that half cycle. If it conducts for only half of the half cycle, the lamp will be perceived to be glowing at half intensity. Similarly, a quarter-cycle electrical conduction means the lamp will appear to be glowing only one-fourth as brightly. Since each SCR conducts for only half a cycle, two SCR's, one for each half cycle, are necessary to make an effective dimmer.

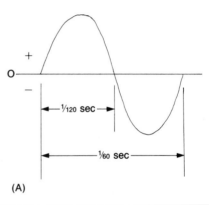

(A)

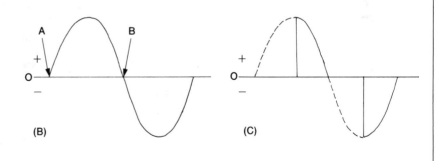

(B)   (C)

The gating principle.

properties result in a dimmer that is rugged, long lived, compact, relatively lightweight, moderate in cost, and reasonably quiet in operation.

With the rapid advancements being made in the electronics industry, discoveries will undoubtedly lead to even more efficient dimmers. At present, however, the SCR dimmer is recognized as the best solution.

Control Consoles

The design and style of any control console is dictated by the type of dimmer that will be used with the system. Because the mechanically controlled dimmers are for the most part outdated, their control consoles will not be discussed here. However, the types and designs of the electronic control consoles are predicated on the principles that were developed and refined with mechanically controlled dimmers. Electronic control consoles are divided into four main categories: (1) group master, (2) preset, (3) combination, and (4) computer-assisted memory.

GROUP MASTER The group master console design is a direct carryover from the control board configurations used with mechanically controlled dimmers. Individual dimmers are controlled by a submaster, which is subsequently controlled by a grand master, as shown in Figure 14.48.

Two general operating techniques are used with group master consoles. The first is to set individual dimmer intensity levels on a group of dimmers that are assigned to one particular submaster, as shown in Figure 14.49A. When the submaster is activated, the dimmers will fade up to the previously

Figure 14.48 Dimmers 1 through 6 are controlled by submaster A; dimmers 7 through 12 by submaster B; dimmers 13 through 18 by submaster C. The grand master acts as a master control for all submasters.

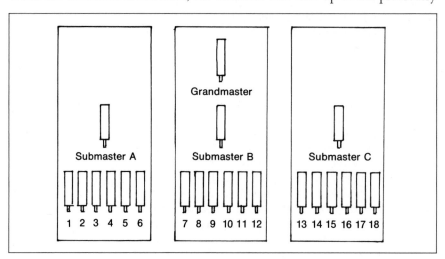

Figure 14.49 Group master operating principles.

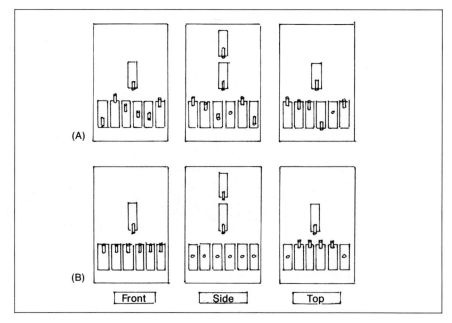

set levels. This technique is particularly useful when a designer wants to change the color blend of the lighting. For example, group A could be assigned all of the lights that are colored red; group B, blue; and group C, green. The color of the on-stage light can be changed by varying the intensity of the submaster control for each color group.

The second operating technique involves using the dimmers of one group to control the lighting instruments from a particular direction or location, as shown in Figure 14.49B. For example, group A might control all **front-of-house** instruments; group B, side lights; and group C, the top lights.

PRESET The primary advantage of a preset control console is that it allows you to keep ahead of the onstage action by presetting the intensity levels for each dimmer before it will be needed. Figure 14.50 is an example of a three-scene lighting control console. Although there may not actually be a control console that works like this one, all preset lighting boards work on the same basic principles being discussed for this hypothetical board.

The controls for dimmers 1 through 6 are repeated three times in the blocks of dimmer controls labeled Preset Scenes I, II, and III. In this simplistic example we will assume that the intensity levels of the lighting for the first cue will be preset on Preset Scene I, the second cue will be assigned to Preset Scene II, and the third cue will be set on Preset Scene III. After the board operator sets the appropriate intensity levels for each dimmer on the three preset scenes, he or she assigns control of Preset Scene I to **fader** A by pushing the button marked I next to fader A. When the cue is called by the stage manager, the operator brings up fader A, which automatically raises the intensity of the lights to the levels that had been preset on the dimmer controls of Preset Scene I. The second cue, preset on Scene II, is assigned to fader B. When the cue is called, the operator simultaneously moves fader B up and fader A down, which results in a cross-fade between the lights preset on Preset Scenes I and II. Similarly, before the third cue being called, the operator assigns control of Preset Scene III to fader A. When the cue is called, the operator cross-fades between faders B and A, which results in activation of the dimmer intensity levels associated with Preset Scene III.

Front-of-house: Describing lights that are hung on the audience side of the proscenium arch.

Fader: A device, usually electronic, that effects a gradual changeover from one circuit to another; in lighting it gradually changes the intensity of one or more dimmer circuits; in sound it changes audio circuits or channels.

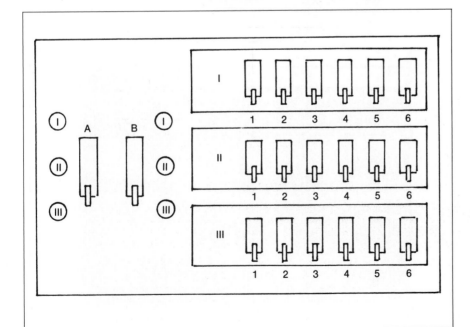

Figure 14.50 Preset board operating principles.

To preset the intensity levels for the fourth cue, the operator presets the appropriate intensity levels on Preset Scene I as soon as he or she has cross-faded into the second cue. To run the remaining cues in the show the process of presetting intensity levels on open, or nonactive, preset scenes is repeated as often as necessary. Many preset control consoles have mechanically or electronically interlocked faders, so when either fader A or B fades up, the other fader automatically dims down.

COMBINATION A fusion of the principles of preset and group master control provides an extremely flexible lighting control system. In the combination console (Figure 14.51) each dimmer channel has an associated switch capable of assigning the dimmer to preset, group master, or independent control. The combination control console provides an operator with more creative choices in controlling dimmer intensities, because it enables him or her to choose the control best suited to each individual production situation.

COMPUTER-ASSISTED MEMORY Computer-assisted memory control for stage lighting has become the standard for the industry. These systems offer much greater control flexibility than any other method of lighting control,

Figure 14.51
Combination boards. (Courtesy of Kliegl Bros. and Teatronics, Inc.)

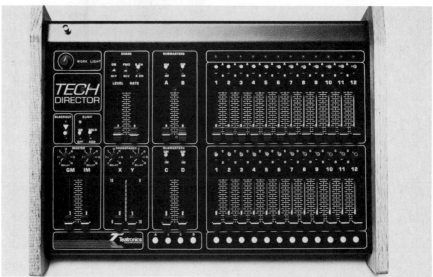

CHAPTER 14: LIGHTING PRODUCTION

Figure 14.52
Computer boards.
(Courtesy of Kliegl
Bros. and Strand
Century.)

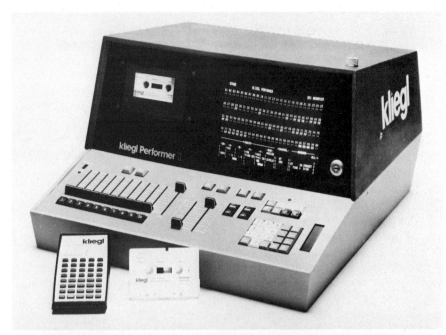

and they are less expensive to manufacture than a preset control console for a comparably sized system.

All "computer boards" (Figure 14.52) function in fundamentally the same way: a computer electronically stores the intensity levels of all dimmers for each cue. The computer memory replaces the cumbersome preset board and eliminates the chance of human error in the setting of intensity levels during a show. Even the most basic computer boards have a minimum of about one hundred memories for cue storage. More expensive boards have sufficient storage capacity for up to one thousand cues.

Since any computer will lose its memory when the power is turned off, most systems have some type of battery backup that provides enough power

Volatility: Nonpermanence; in computers, a volatile memory will be lost if the computer loses its power supply.

Floppy disk: A thin piece of plastic coated with metal oxide, used to record the information stored in a computer's memory.

Cassette tape: Audio recorder tape, used in computer storage.

Microcassette tape: A tape cassette approximately 1¼ by 2 inches, used in computer storage; identical to microcassette audio tape.

COMPUTER BOARDS: A COMPARISON OF FEATURES

SMALLER SYSTEMS
1. memory for up to several hundred cues
2. capability of controlling 100–150 dimmers
3. maximum of one video screen for displaying various system functions
4. a timed fader
5. some type of group or submaster control
6. control of dimmer intensity by individual sliders
7. keypad for addressing memory and functions
8. limited backup system in case of main computer malfunction

These smaller, less expensive systems work well in theatres that have modest production demands.

LARGER SYSTEMS
1. memory for approximately one thousand cues
2. control of one thousand or more dimmers
3. expanded functions
   A. two or more video screens to display more functions simultaneously
   B. advanced backup systems
   C. sophisticated group or submastering
   D. more control functions to permit simultaneous cues at different fade rates
4. dimmer and other functions addressed through a keypad
5. remote keypad
6. hard-copy printer for printing data about the lighting design
7. self-diagnostic program to identify malfunctioning component in case of breakdown

These larger and more expensive systems work well in facilities that have extensive production programs.

---

so the system can retain its memory for a reasonable length of time. This period varies from several hours to several days, depending on the manufacturer.

Because of the **volatility** and relatively limited storage capacity of the memories used in most systems, almost all but the lowest priced computer boards have some method of storing the cuing and programming information. This additional storage capability is generally referred to as library storage. The most common methods used for library storage are the **floppy disk,** the **cassette tape,** and the **microcassette tape.**

Computer boards have functions in addition to cue or preset memory capability. Almost all systems memorize the timed duration for each cue or preset. Most systems have two or more faders, so a cue can be assigned to each fader to allow two or more lighting actions to occur at the same time.

Whenever a system has an automatic, or timed, fader, it usually has a manual override feature that enables the electrician to interrupt the timed fade to increase, decrease, stop, or reverse the rate of fade. Almost all computer boards except very low priced ones have one or more video screens to display information about the various memory functions.

CABLES AND CONNECTORS

A flexible system of distributing electricity to lighting instruments is necessary, because the hanging position of the lights will be changed for each production. This section discusses the types of cables and connectors that make up this flexible distribution system, as well as several methods of circuiting, or connecting, the lighting instruments to the dimmers.

Electrical Cable for Stage Use

The National Electrical Code (NEC) stipulates that the only electrical cables approved for temporary stage wiring are types S, SO, ST, and STO. These cables have stranded copper conductors and are insulated with rubber (S and SO, shown in Figure 14.53) or thermoplastic (ST and STO). S and SO cables are more commonly used than ST and STO, because their thick rubber jacket can withstand more physical abuse than the thin, heat-resistant thermoplastic insulation of the ST and STO cable. Type S cable is generally used for stage lighting, because SO costs more and its only advantage is that it is impervious to oil and gasoline.

Wire Gauge

The American Wire Gauge (AWG) system rates wire according to the amount of current that a conductor of a particular size and composition can safely carry. The rated current capacity for any given gauge should never be exceeded. Most cables have the gauge and wire type imprinted every foot or so on the insulating jacket.

The amount of current that can be safely carried varies greatly, as we saw in Table 13.1. There is no standard size of cable for theatre use, because load requirements differ from one theatre to another. However, the NEC stipulates that receptacles used to supply incandescent lamps on stage must be rated at not less than twenty amperes and must be supplied by wires of not less than twelve gauge. Practical or decorative lamps are the only exception to this rule. These lamps may be wired with cable of smaller capacity as long as the lamp load doesn't exceed the rated capacity of the cable. This means that you can use eighteen-gauge wire (also known as lamp or zip cord) as long as the lamp load doesn't exceed 360 watts (assuming the system voltage is 120 volts: $W = VA$; $360 = 120 \times 3$).

Connecting Devices

Several different styles of connector are used in stage lighting, as shown in Figure 14.54. Twist-lock connectors (Figure 14.54A) are considered by many people to be the best type of stage connector. The male portion, or plug, fits into the female portion, or receptacle, and is twisted to lock the two halves together. This locking action prevents most accidental disconnections of the circuit.

Figure 14.53 An electrical wire.

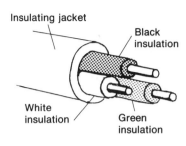

Figure 14.54 (A) A twist-lock; (B) grounded pin connector; (C) locking grounded pin connector; (D) grounded parallel blade (Edison) connector. [(B) and (C) Courtesy of Union Connector Co.]

(A) (B) (C) (D)

Figure 14.55
(A) Internal and
(B) external cable
clamps.

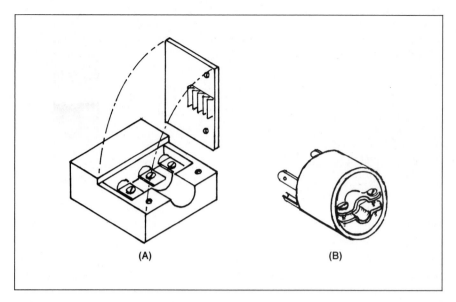

(A)   (B)

Pin connectors are probably more widely used than twist-lock connectors, primarily because they have been in existence longer. Older models of pin connectors (Figure 14.54B) have three distinct disadvantages: (1) they can be easily disconnected by accident; (2) the pins of the plug do not always make a good electrical connection with the receptacle; and (3) if the cable is connected to a live power source, it is very easy to be shocked, because the metal conductors in the receptacle are not deeply recessed.

Newer models of the grounded pin connector (Figure 14.54C) overcome the above-mentioned disadvantages. The new designs, which also meet the NEC guidelines, have an excellent locking device that prevents accidental disconnections, and the metal contacts within the receptacle are recessed quite deeply into the insulating body of the connector.

The Edison, or parallel blade, plug (Figure 14.54D), should be used only on decorative lamps or devices that carry a similarly small load.

All connectors, regardless of style, are designed to carry a specific amount of current. The maximum load is usually printed somewhere on the plug, and that limit should be strictly obeyed.

The NEC stipulates that each plug should be equipped with an effective cable-clamping device (see Figure 14.55). The purpose of the cable clamp is to secure the connector to the jacket of the cable. This clamping action transfers any physical strain from the plug casing directly to the cable jacket, which effectively eliminates any strain on the electrical connections inside of the plug.

Extension Cables

Extension cables can be purchased, or made in the theatre's electrical shop, in any reasonable length. As previously noted they are generally made of type S cable, although types SO, ST, or STO can also be used. Different theatres present differing requirements, but in general, if a theatre has a permanent lighting system, an inventory of cables five, ten, and twenty feet long should meet the needs of most operations.

Two-fer: An electrical **Y** that has female receptacles at the top of the **Y** and a male plug at the bottom leg of the **Y**; used to connect two instruments to the same circuit.

A **two-fer** is used to connect two instruments to the same circuit. When using two-fers (Figure 14.56) or any other device that can increase the electrical load on a circuit, take particular care not to exceed the maximum current rating of any element (cable, plug, dimmer, and so on) in that circuit.

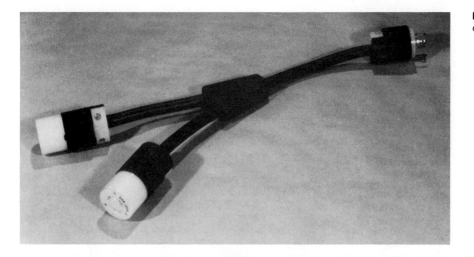

Figure 14.56 A "Y" or two-fer.

CIRCUITING

The distribution of electricity from dimmers to lighting instruments creates a complex system. Any complex system is built on compromise, simply because the maximum amount of efficiency that can be built into any system is finite. The compromises on which stage lighting systems are predicated are speed and ease of hanging and circuiting versus flexibility of hanging position. The following methods of stage circuiting demonstrate the effects of tinkering with the variables of this complex equation.

Permanent Wiring

The simplest method of circuiting is to permanently wire the instruments to the dimmers. In this system a few ellipsoidal reflector spotlights are usually hung somewhere on the ceiling of the auditorium, and some striplights or **work lights** over the stage. These instruments are permanently wired to specific dimmers. To operate the system you just turn on the dimmers. The only possible changes or adjustments within the system are changing the color or area of focus for each instrument.

Although this method is certainly the easiest to operate, it provides very little flexibility and just about eliminates any chance for creatively designing with light. Permanently wired lighting systems appear with great frequency in high school auditoriums, music halls, and other facilities where the lighting installation has been guided by criteria other than the needs and requirements of the creative use of designed light.

Spidering

Spidering, also known as direct cabling, involves running a cable from each lighting instrument directly to the dimmer to which it is assigned. It gets its name from the tangled web of cables created by circuiting a production in this manner.

Spidering is used extensively in Broadway theatres and on touring shows. It provides the greatest flexibility, because it allows the designer to put an instrument wherever it is needed. On the negative side, spidering requires an extensive inventory of electrical cable, and this method takes a relatively long time to hang unless the hanging crew is very experienced and the designer or master electrician has carefully planned the cabling requirements for the production.

Work light: A lighting fixture, frequently a scoop, PAR, or other wide-field-angle instrument, hung over the stage to facilitate work; generally not used to light a production.

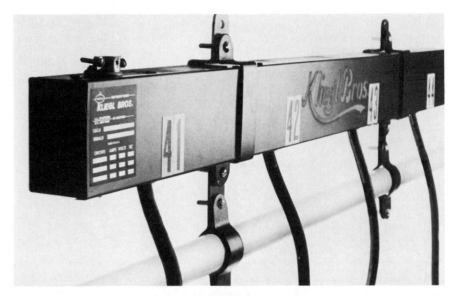

Figure 14.57 A connecting strip. (Courtesy of Kliegl Bros.)

Drop box: A small connecting strip, containing four to eight circuits, that can be clamped to a pipe or boom.

Floor pocket: A connecting box, usually containing three to six circuits, the top of which is mounted flush with the stage floor.

Wall pocket: A connecting box similar to a floor pocket but mounted on the wall.

Connecting Strips and Patch Panels

An electrical distribution system that utilizes connecting strips and a patch panel provides two advantages in a theatre that has an extensive production program: (1) the light plot can be hung and circuited quite rapidly and (2) the system provides a great deal of flexibility by enabling you to patch any circuit into any dimmer.

Two principal parts make up this system: the stage circuits and a patch panel. Most of the stage circuits are contained in connecting strips, which are sections of wireway, or electrical gutter, that contain a number of circuits (Figure 14.57).

The connecting strips are hung in a variety of positions about the stage and auditorium—counterweighted battens over the stage; various front-of-house positions (ante-proscenium cuts or slots, beamports, coves, boxes); and various locations on the walls of the stage house. Each circuit terminates in a receptacle that is usually mounted at the end of a two- to three-foot pigtail, although the receptacles are sometimes mounted flush on the gutter itself.

Additional stage circuit outlets are often contained in **drop boxes, floor pockets,** and **wall pockets** (Figure 14.58). Drop boxes are small connecting strips fed by cables that are attached to the grid above the stage. They usually contain four to eight circuits and are equipped with one or two pipe clamps so they can be easily attached to pipes or booms. Floor and wall pockets are recessed into the floor or wall and usually contain three to six circuits.

Figure 14.58
(A) Drop box;
(B) floor pocket;
(C) wall pocket.

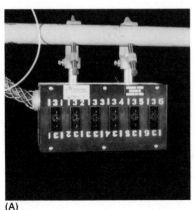

(A)

(B)

(C)

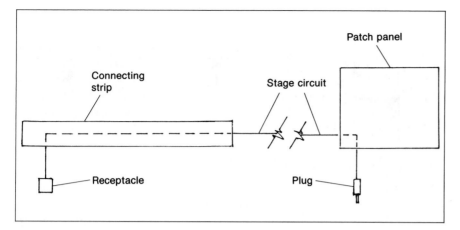

Figure 14.59 In a patch panel system the stage circuit runs from the female receptacle on the stage outlet to a male plug at the patch panel.

All of the circuits contained in connecting strips, drop boxes, and floor or wall pockets have certain properties in common. Each circuit is a rather long extension cable that, at the stage end, terminates in a female receptacle. Some connecting strips are designed to provide two receptacles for each circuit. In the patch panel system, the other end of the circuit terminates at the patch panel in a male plug, as shown in Figure 14.59.

The second part of the distribution system is the patch panel, or patch bay. It is an interconnecting device that provides the system with the capability of connecting, or patching, any stage circuit into any dimmer. Patch panels (Figure 14.60) are manufactured in a variety of styles and configurations.

Figure 14.61 illustrates the basic operational design of a patch panel. The lighting instrument is connected into a stage circuit, which terminates at the patch panel in a male plug. The dimmer, which is usually located in another part of the theatre, is permanently wired to a receptacle on the face of the patch panel. To enable the electricity to flow from the dimmer to the lighting instrument it will be necessary to complete the circuit. This is done by patching the circuit into the appropriate receptacle for the dimmer.

The patch panel is actually very simple to operate. What makes it seem so complex is that it contains many more than the one circuit and one dimmer cited in this example. In fact, a patch panel usually contains between sixty and several hundred stage circuits, and from forty to several hundred dimmers. In addition, each dimmer is usually provided with several receptacles on the face of the patch panel, so that more than one circuit can be patched into each dimmer.

Figure 14.60 Patch panels. (Courtesy of Colortran.)

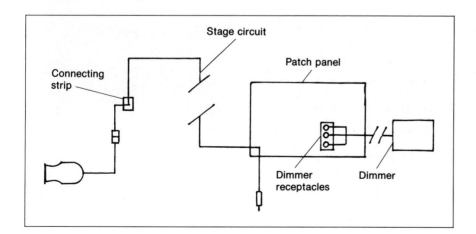

Figure 14.61 The patch panel allows you to plug more than one circuit into a single dimmer.

Figure 14.62
Circuit breakers
provide overload
protection for both
the stage circuits
and the dimmer
circuits.

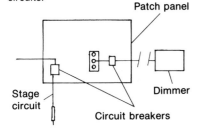

Patch panel

Dimmer

Stage
circuit

Circuit breakers

Patch panels usually have some type of electrical overload protection for both the stage circuit and the dimmer circuit. The circuit breaker automatically breaks the continuity of the circuit when an unsafe amount of current is passed through the line. Each stage circuit has a circuit breaker, as shown in Figure 14.62, that provides overload protection. Another circuit breaker is usually located either in the line connecting the patch panel to the dimmer or in the dimmer itself. This circuit breaker protects the dimmer circuit and dimmer from an overload.

Dimmer Per Circuit

The dimmer per circuit configuration is probably the most efficient electrical distribution system for stage lighting. It combines the efficiency in hanging and circuiting of the connecting strip with the ease of operation of the permanently wired system.

As in the connecting strip and patch panel system, the onstage end of each circuit terminates in an outlet on a connecting strip, floor pocket, or similar location. The other end of the circuit is directly wired to a dimmer instead of terminating in a male plug at the patch panel.

Before the introduction of the computer-assisted lighting control board it required a very large and unwieldy control system and three to six—or more—electricians to run all the dimmers required by this type of system. But the computer board makes control of the large number of dimmers associated with this type of system a relatively simple task for one person. The dimmer per circuit configuration, when combined with a computer-assisted light board, provides what is probably the most efficient electrical system for stage lighting available at this time.

SAFETY TIP

Cable and Connector Maintenance

The following steps are suggested to keep cables and connectors in good operating condition and in compliance with NEC and federal regulations.

1. When a cable is not in use, coil it and hang it on the wall of the lighting storage room. The cable will stay neatly coiled if the connectors are plugged together or if it is tied with heavy twine or narrow rope.

2. Check cables and connectors periodically, and replace any items that show signs of cracking, chipping, or other deterioration. Cracks in the insulation of cables and connectors increase the chances of someone's receiving a shock from the device. Also, dust can accumulate in the crack and may cause an electrical fire.

3. Always disconnect a plug by pulling on the body of the connector, not the cable. Pulling on the cable puts an unnecessary strain on the cable clamp and will eventually defeat the clamp. When the cable clamp no longer functions, pulling on the cable places the strain directly on the electrical connections.

4. Keep the connectors clean. Remove any corrosion, paint, grease, or other accumulations as soon as they become evident. These substances can act as insulation between the contacts of the connector and, if flammable, pose a fire hazard.

5. All elements of a cable should be of the same electrical rating; for example, twelve-gauge (AWG) cable (capable of carrying twenty amperes of current) should have only twenty-ampere-rated connectors, and so forth.

Cable storage.

15

Projections en-
hance the visual
texture of a design
immeasurably.
They can provide

Projections

the stage with seemingly unlimited depth or create an aura of surrealism as
one image dissolves into another. They can be used to replace or complement
other visual elements of the setting, or as an accent.

However, projections aren't a universal panacea. They are simply another
tool for the designer to use in the never-ending quest for an evocative visual
expression of the production concept.

Two basic systems of projection are used in the theatre, lens and lensless.

LENSLESS PROJECTORS

If you've ever made shadow pictures by holding your hands in the beam of a
slide or movie projector, you understand the principle of lensless projection.
As shown in Figure 15.1, a shadow image can be projected when an opaque
object is placed in the path of a light source. If the object casting the shadow is
colored and transparent rather than opaque, a colored image is projected instead of a shadow.

Several factors determine the sharpness of the projected image, but the
primary one is the size of the projection source. Although an arc can provide
a very small point source, it isn't particularly practical because its intensity
can't be varied through the use of a dimmer. There are two practical lamp
sources for lensless projectors:

1. For large-scale projections a 500-, 750-, or 1,000-watt, 120-volt, tungsten-halogen lamp normally used in an ellipsoidal reflector spotlight works
well. When selecting a specific lamp remember that the smaller the filament,
the sharper the image.

Figure 15.1
Principles of
lensless projection.

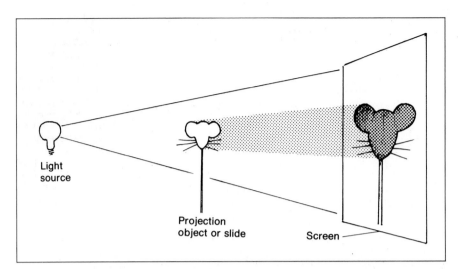

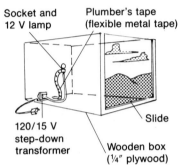

Figure 15.2 A low-voltage lamp can provide a high-intensity, small-sized source for a lensless projector.

2. For small-scale projections—under six feet wide—a single-filament, twelve-volt lamp (used for automotive brake and turning lights) can provide a high-intensity, small-filament source. For the lamp to provide enough output it must be run at about fifteen volts. This voltage is supplied to the lamp through a fifteen-volt step-down transformer, as shown in Figure 15.2. The transformer may not work properly, however, and the intensity of the twelve-volt lamp will probably flutter if you try to dim the unit with an SCR dimmer. The flicker occurs because the filaments of these twelve-volt lamps usually don't have sufficient mass to retain the heat necessary to give off light during the SCR's "off" cycles, particularly at low-intensity readings. (The operational principles of an SCR dimmer were discussed in the last chapter.) A smooth fade can be achieved only if the transformer is dimmed with an autotransformer or resistance dimmer.

Another important factor in determining image sharpness with a lensless projector is the distance between the slide and the projection surface. The closer the slide is to the screen, the sharper the image. Having the slide closer to the screen does not necessarily mean that the projector is closer to the screen. A relatively long, somewhat skinny projector, as shown in Figure 15.3A, can be built in the shop. If the ratio of the distance between the pro-

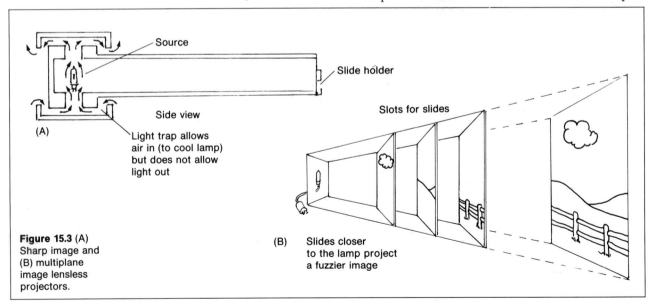

Figure 15.3 (A) Sharp image and (B) multiplane image lensless projectors.

jection surface and the slide and the distance between the slide and the lamp of this somewhat bizarre projector can be kept at approximately 1:1, an acceptably sharp image can be produced. The multiplane lensless projector (Figure 15.3B) is a natural adaptation of this development. As slides are placed closer to the lamp, the image they project becomes less focused. This phenomenon can be used to good advantage to create **aerial perspective.** In the projection of a landscape the clouds and distant objects could be painted on one slide and placed relatively close to the lamp to create a soft-edged image. Middle-distance objects, such as hills and a forest, might be painted on a second slide and placed farther from the lamp, so the image they project is more clearly defined. A third slide, with perhaps a fence row and the branch from an overhanging tree, could be painted on a third slide and placed farther away from the lamp, so its image is the sharpest of the three.

Although the multiplane projector might seem to be an ideal solution, there is one very basic problem: slide size. You will remember that for a slide to project a relatively sharp image it needs to be approximately the same distance from the screen as it is from the lamp. If you wanted to project an image twenty feet wide, the sharp-image slide would have to be ten feet wide! However, if you are only trying to project on a relatively small area (five feet wide or less), the multiplane projector can provide you with a very realistic aerial perspective effect.

A multiplane projector can be built in the shop using the techniques described a little later in the chapter for making Linnebach projectors. A 750- or 1,000-watt tungsten-halogen lamp from an ellipsoidal reflector spotlight will usually provide a more than adequate light for projections less than five feet wide, and the slides can be painted on one-eighth-inch Plexiglas with transparent acetate inks.

Linnebach Projector

The primary lensless projector used in the theatre was developed by Adolph Linnebach. All lensless projectors are based on its principles of operation, which are illustrated in Figure 15.4. The metal housing holds the lamp at a fixed distance from the open front of the projector, which is designed to securely hold a removable glass slide. The design is painted on the slide with transparent inks.

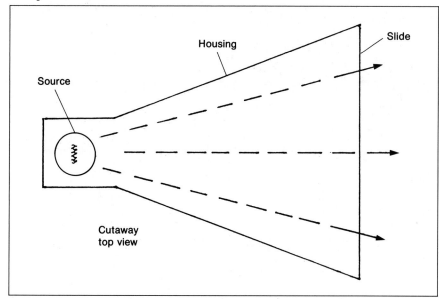

Aerial perspective: An optical phenomenon in which objects that are farther away appear less sharply in focus and less fully saturated in color.

Figure 15.4 Principles of operation of a Linnebach projector.

Figure 15.5 Shop-built Linnebach projector.

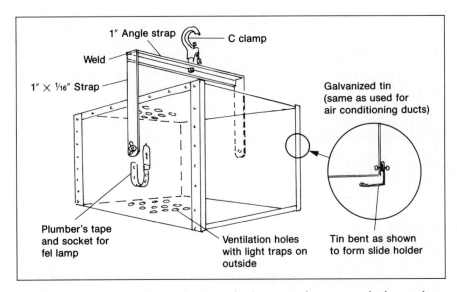

Projectors that work on the Linnebach principles can easily be made in the theatre shop using galvanized tin and a **pop riveter.** They can also be fabricated using plywood (Figure 15.5), but the inside of the back and top sides of the plywood box must be lined with tin or some other heat-reflecting or -absorbing material.

Linnebach projectors for use with curved cycs can also be shop-built, as shown in Figure 15.6. These projectors, while using only a one-thousand-watt FEL lamp, can project a patterned wash of pastel color over a full semicircular cyc. Slides for the curved-front Linnebach are made from twenty-mil acetate. These slides are fitted to the curved edge of the projector, and the image is painted on the slide using transparent acetate inks. Dr. Martin's Watercolors, when supplemented with a commercial additive that allows the paint to adhere to plastic, work extemely well for this purpose.

Other Lensless Projectors

Small lensless projectors can be made by removing the lens from Fresnel or plano-convex spotlights and inserting a slide (painted or photographic trans-

Figure 15.6 Curved-image Linnebach projector.

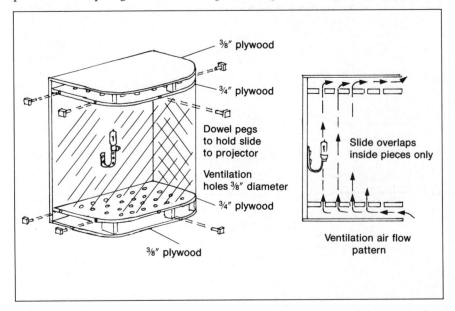

Scenic projector: A high-wattage instrument used for projecting large-format slides or moving images.

Slide projector: A reasonably high-output instrument capable of projecting standard 35-mm slides.

SLIDE TECHNIQUES FOR LENSLESS PROJECTORS

A number of systems based on mathematical principles can be used to lay out the slides for lensless, or Linnebach, projectors. However, the fastest and most accurate method is also the easiest. Put a slide into the projector, and place it and the projection screen (usually a cyc or sky tab) in the onstage positions that they will occupy during the production. Turn the projector on, and draw or paint the projection on the slide while watching the projection grow across the screen.

parency) in the instrument's color frame holder. Although these makeshift projectors won't cover a large surface, they are handy for making relatively soft projections on small surfaces.

LENS PROJECTORS

The second basic type of projector uses a lens to control the focus and size of the image on the projection surface. Two primary types of lens projector are used in the theatre, the **scenic projector** and the **slide projector.**

Scenic Projector

The scenic projector is composed of three basic parts: the lamp housing, the optical train, and the slide, as shown in Figure 15.7A.

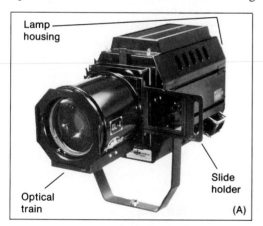

Lamp housing

Optical train

Slide holder

(A)

(B)

(C)

Figure 15.7(A) A scenic projector is composed of a lamp housing, the optical train, and the slide. (Courtesy The Great American Market.) (B) Scenic projector. (Courtesy Kliegl Bros.) (C) Slide projector. (Courtesy George R. Snell Associates.)

Figure 15.8 A typical scenic projector optical train.

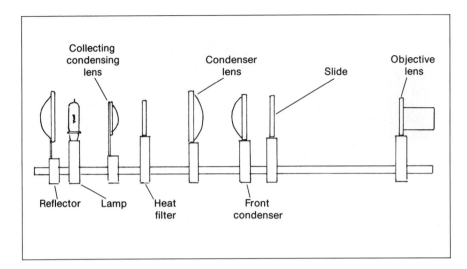

Collecting condensing lens

Condenser lens

Slide

Objective lens

Reflector   Lamp   Heat filter   Front condenser

LAMP HOUSING A lamp of high intensity is a prime requisite of a good scenic projector. Incandescent lamps of one thousand to two thousand watts are fairly typical, and some extremely expensive scenic projectors are designed for xenon or HMI lamps. The housings are frequently equipped with blowers that help dissipate the rather substantial heat that these powerful sources generate. Unfortunately, these fans are almost always noisy, so the scenic projector usually needs to be placed in some location that will mask the fan noise.

OPTICAL TRAIN The optical train, shown in Figure 15.8, is composed of several parts that perform specific functions. The reflector (usually ellipsoidal or spherical) and collector lens gather and concentrate the light. Some scenic projectors utilize a **heat filter,** which is a special type of glass that filters out a substantial portion of the infrared (heat) segment of the electromagnetic spectrum emitted by the lamp. The **condensing lenses** focus the light onto the **slide plane aperture,** which is the point where the slide or moving projection effect is placed. The **objective lens** is used to focus the material in the aperture onto the projection surface.

The reflector, lamp, collector lens, and aperture are normally mounted in fixed positions within the lamp housing unit. In contrast, the relative positions of the condensing lens and objective lens are variable on some models of scenic projector to allow the size of the projected image to be changed. Other

Heat filter: A glass medium that removes much of the infrared spectrum from light.

Condensing lens: A device that condenses the direct and reflected light from a source and concentrates it on the slide plane aperture of a projector.

Slide plane aperture: The point in a projection system where a slide or other effect is placed.

Objective lens: A device to focus a projected image on a screen or other surface.

CAROUSEL PROJECTOR TIPS

1. Use the slide tray that holds 80 slides rather than its larger-capacity (140-slide) cousin, because the greater space allocated to each slide in the 80 count tray significantly reduces the chances of the slides becoming stuck in the tray.

2. Mount the slides in plastic, rather than pasteboard, slide holders. The plastic holders are slicker and slightly heavier,

which makes it easier for them to be fed into the projector.

3. For the best image use the highest-wattage lamp designed for the specific model with which you are working.

4. Select a lens that will permit you to place the projector as close to the projection surface as possible.

scenic projectors are available with several **heads,** which hold the condensing and objective lenses in fixed positions to control the image size.

SLIDE Glass slides are frequently used with scenic projectors to project still images. The image can be painted on a single glass slide, or a photographic transparency can be sandwiched between two glass slides. The longevity of a painted or photographic image on the slide can be increased if a heat filter is placed between the collector lens and the slide.

A variety of moving effects can be created through the use of **effects heads.** These motorized devices are attached to the lamp housing in place of the slide holder. Effects heads move images in front of the aperture gate to create abstract or realistic moving images such as the lighted windows of a passing train on the projection surface. The speed of the control motor is usually variable, so the speed of the projected effect can be adjusted to suit the design need. Depending on the specific model, effects heads use either rotating disks or bands to create the specific effect desired. Most scenic effects projectors are equipped to use either Plexiglas or metal disks or plastic bands.

Head: A housing that holds scenic projector lenses in fixed positions to project images of a specific size.

Effects head: A motor-driven unit capable of producing relatively crude moving images with a scenic projector.

KEYSTONING

Unless the projector is placed on a perpendicular axis to the projection screen, some linear distortion will be introduced to the projected image. This phenomenon is known as keystoning, because the distortion generally resembles the shape of a keystone.

Keystoning results when the light from one side of the projected image (slide) has to travel farther than the light from the other side of the slide, as illustrated in the figure. Keystoning can be corrected in one of two ways: (1) the screen can be tilted so the projection axis is perpendicular to the screen, or (2) a distortion can be introduced to the slide that counteracts the effects of the projection distortion. To do this, determine the angle of intersection between the projection axis and the screen. To introduce the counterdistortion to the slide, place the camera at the same angle, but on the opposite side, when you are taking the picture of the slide material.

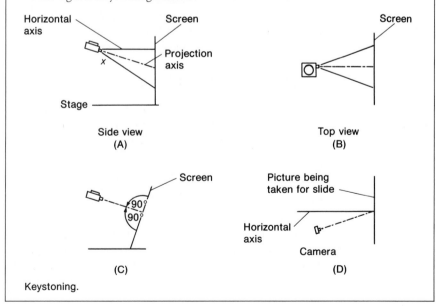

Keystoning.

Slide Projector

Projectors using 35-mm (two-by-two-inch) slides provide another excellent system for producing scenic projections. The challenge of using these projectors, which are designed for audiovisual, not theatrical, purposes, is that the lamp output is frequently not as bright as that of a scenic projector. If you work within the limitations that the lower lamp output imposes, however, the slide projector can be an extremely useful tool.

The Kodak Carousel equipped with a three-hundred-watt lamp provides sufficient light to create a readable image if the slide is of normal contrast and the maximum dimension of the projected image is kept at about six to eight feet.

Adaptations of the basic audiovisual (Ektagraphic) line of Kodak Carousel projectors provide higher-wattage lamps and a number of other interesting features. Although the three-hundred-watt lamp available on the basic models will work adequately, by all means acquire the higher-output models if your budget can afford them. The image can be significantly brighter.

Other types of 35-mm slide projector can be used, but the carousel types generally offer specific qualities that make them preferable for theatrical projection work: dependable and versatile slide-feeding capabilities, adequate light output, and interchangeable lenses.

Until recently the Buhl Optical Company manufactured a modification of a basic Kodak Ektagraphic Carousel projector that provided a high-output (twelve-hundred-watt) lamp. Unfortunately, citing reasons of modification to the basic Kodak projector model, Buhl has suspended production of the Hi-Lite.

Gobo

An ellipsoidal reflector spotlight can be converted into a pattern projector through the use of a gobo. A full discussion of gobos and how to make them can be found in Chapter 14.

PROJECTION SCREENS

Actors' bodies, painted scenery, dust motes, smoke, and fog have all been used as projection surfaces. However, they don't work nearly so well as scenic elements that have been specifically designed as projection screens. There are two basic types of screen material: front and rear.

Front-Screen Material

Front-screen projection materials are those surfaces that are designed to reflect light. The best front-projection materials are slide or movie screens. They are white and highly reflective, and the surface is often designed to focus the reflected light in a specific angular pattern. Unless you want a large, glaringly white screen sitting in the middle of the stage, however, it is essential that the screen be lit with either a projection or color wash at all times.

A smooth, white, painted surface (muslin, Masonite, and the like) provides a low-cost alternative to the commercial projection screen. Although the reflected image won't be so crisp as that from the projection screen, it will be more than adequate for most theatrical purposes. When the projections or color washes are turned off, however, the challenge of what to do with the "great white blob" continues.

Unless you are planning on using continuous projections or removing the screen from the set, it is frequently desirable to have the projection screen blend into the surrounding scenic elements until it is time to use it. In these cases the vertical or horizontal surfaces of the set itself can be used instead of a projection screen. When you are projecting on scenery, the sharpness and brightness of the reflected image will be directly related to the hue, value, and texture of the paint job used on the scenery. Surfaces with low saturation, high value, and little texture provide the best reflective surfaces for projected images.

Hot spot: An intense circle of light created when a projector lens is seen through a rear screen.

Rear-Screen Material

A major challenge of front-screen projection—actor shadows on the projection surface—is eliminated through the use of rear-screen projection. In this technique, illustrated in Figure 15.9, the projector is placed behind the screen, and the image is transmitted through the screen to the audience.

A significant challenge of rear-screen projection is created by the **hot spot.** If the projector is located within the audience's sight line, as illustrated in Figure 15.10, a small, intensely bright circle of light will appear on the screen. This bright circle is caused by seeing the actual lens of the projector through the screen material. The hot spot can be eliminated in one of two ways. You can position the projector so the hot spot is out of the audience's sight line, or you can use a screen material that eliminates the hot spot.

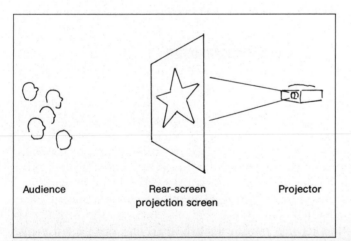

Audience   Rear-screen   Projector
                  projection screen

Figure 15.9 A typical rear-screen projection setup.

Figure 15.10 A hot spot, caused by seeing the lens of the projector through the screen, will result unless special rear-screen projection material is used.

Heat welding: The use of a heat gun (a high-temperature air gun, visually similar to a hand-held hair dryer) to fuse two pieces of plastic.

Commercial rear-screen materials transmit clear, crisp images while diffusing or eliminating the hot spot. Rosco Labs produces several types of reasonably priced flexible plastic rear-screen material in rolls fifty-five inches wide. Wider screens, with invisible seams, can be made by butting strips of the material edge to edge and taping the joints with No. 200 Scotch transparent plastic tape. Unless the atmosphere in your locale is of relatively low humidity, however, the tape seams are only a temporary solution. **Heat welding** of the seams will provide a permanent bond.

If the projector can be placed in a position that will eliminate the hot spot, a variety of translucent materials can be used to receive the projected image. Scenic muslin and other fabrics of similar weight and weave transmit light quite well. The muslin (which will present a crisper image if it is primed with a starch solution—one cup of starch per gallon of hot water) can be painted with dye if it is necessary or desirable for the screen to blend into the set. When using this technique be sure to use dye, not paint. Dye is transparent and won't interrupt the transmission of the image.

Plain white shower curtains provide another effective, low-cost rear-screen material. The plastic transmits light well, the larger-sized shower curtains are big enough for many scenic uses, and some of the plastics actually diffuse the hot spot.

White (not clear) polyethylene plastic sheeting, sold as plastic drop cloths in paint stores, is also an effective rear-screen material.

SLIDE PREPARATION

Slides for the various types of commercial and shop-built Linnebachs are generally made from one-eighth-inch clear Plexiglas. Slides for the curved-image Linnebach can be made from .020-inch acetate. Although still quite flexible, the .020 thickness provides enough stiffness so these slides don't bend or flop when secured to the projector.

The slide image can be painted on the acetate with a variety of materials. Transparent acetate inks, which are available in a wide range of colors, are a standard type of slide paint. If an additive, which makes the water-based dyes adhere to the plastic, is used, Dr. Martin's Watercolors are an excellent choice. As a last resort, the bottles of Magic Marker refill inks can also be used. Although the Magic Marker inks remain slightly tacky, they don't smear easily, but they do attract a great deal of dust.

Scenic projectors can use both photographic and painted slides. To be used in a scenic projector, photographic transparencies should be sandwiched between sheets of projection-grade glass. This type of glass is usually available from photography stores. This "sandwich" accomplishes two things: it keeps the heat of the lamp from crinkling or melting the slide, and it keeps the slide in a vertical plane. Painted scenic projector slides are also usually sandwiched for heat protection. The image is painted on a glass slide, and either that slide is sandwiched between two other clear slides or the painted surface is simply covered with a second slide. The transparent inks mentioned above will also work on glass. Additionally, silhouettes can be created by using opaque acetate inks. However, you must take care when using opaque inks, simply because they absorb more heat than do transparent ones. The additional heat may crack the glass or cause a deterioration of the other inks.

Thirty-five-millimeter slides shouldn't be used in the cardboard mounts in which they are placed by the film processors. These mounts don't really have enough weight to drop the slide into the projector if the projector is mounted at anything other than a perfectly horizontal angle. At a minimum the slides should be remounted in plastic slide mounts, and ideally you will sandwich them between two layers of slide glass. (The plastic mounts and 35-mm glass mounts are available at photography stores.)

OTHER PROJECTORS

A wide variety of other projectors can be used for special situations in the theatre. However, two of them, the overhead projector (Figure 15.11) and the opaque projector are arguably the most useful.

A relatively large transparent slide (most overhead projectors will accept slides up to eleven by fourteen inches) is placed on the light table of the overhead projector. A high-output lamp shines through the slide, and the image is redirected and focused on the screen by a mirror mounted in an optical head located a short distance above the light table. The luminance level of this projector is fairly low, but it can work well in short-throw, low-light situations.

The opaque projector works in generally the same fashion, except that the slide is opaque and the lamp is located above the slide so the light can be reflected, rather than directly transmitted, to the mirror and optical head. The output of the opaque projector is generally less than that of the overhead projector, because some of the lamp output is lost to absorption and scattering during the reflection process. Although this projector is effective on stage only for specific low-light applications, it is very helpful in the scene shop, where it can be used to project detail from painters' elevations and other drawings or photos onto scenic elements during the scene-painting process.

Figure 15.11 An overhead projector. (Courtesy of George R. Snell Associates.)

GENERAL PROJECTION TECHNIQUES AND HINTS

It is prudent to test the characteristics of any projection system, technique, or material (commercial or noncommercial) under actual stage conditions before you launch into a design concept that depends on projections. You will frequently discover that your vision of how the projections should look are at odds with the physical reality of how they actually appear on stage. Some general hints and guidelines may help you in working with projections.

1. To prevent the projected images from being washed out, keep ambient light off of the screen. Be sure that the stage lights for the acting areas in the vicinity of the screen(s) are placed at angles that minimize their effect (direct and reflected) on the screen.

2. To reduce the effects of ambient light and to keep the actors from blocking the spectators' view of the projected image, try to place the screen so its bottom edge will be no lower than five to seven feet above the stage floor.

3. To maximize the brightness of the image when working with an audiovisual slide projector:

    A. Keep the size of the projection as small as possible.

    B. Use a lens with a low f-stop (3.5 or less).

    C. Use a short-focal-length lens, and place the projector as close to the screen as possible.

4. Rear-screen projection is affected by ambient light less than front-screen projection is, so whenever possible try to work with rear-screen techniques.

5. Become thoroughly familiar with the equipment that you will be using well before technical rehearsals begin. Shoot your slides early, so you will have time to shoot and process additional slides if it becomes necessary.

16 Costume Design and Production

There may be some truth to the adage that "clothes make the man." A recent study, summarized in the book *The Four-Minute Sell,* by Janet Elsea, indicates that during the first four minutes of contact with a stranger your understanding of that person's nature and personality will be based on three primary, but unequal, factors: appearance, 55 percent; tone of voice, 38 percent; and what the person is saying, 7 percent.

Costume designers know these facts, either intuitively or from training. They know that when an actor walks onto the stage for the first time, the audience's feelings about the character will, to a great extent, be based on the information that guides all first impressions. The character's appearance is the predominant influence on the audience's basic understanding of his or her socioeconomic status, age, and personality.

This first, and extremely important, impression is the domain of the costume designer. He or she is responsible for the appearance of the clothes, makeup, hair styling, and **accessories** worn by every actor or actress in the production.

Conceptually, costume designers go through the same mental processes, procedures, and conferences as their colleagues in scenic and lighting design. They need to know how to draw with pencil and charcoal and work in watercolor and pastel to translate costume ideas into visual renderings or sketches. These sketches will be seen by the other members of the production design team during the production conferences, and they will also be used as general guides by the costume crew during construction of the costumes.

Accessory: In costuming, anything other than clothing that is worn or carried; includes wigs, hats, footwear, jewelry, and similar items.

STYLE IN COSTUME DESIGN

Costume design is almost always located at the representational end of the style spectrum, simply because of the primary function of clothes: to cover the human body. Although costumes should provide a visual extension of the character's personality, they must also be practical and allow the actor to move within the context of the character. Figure 16.1 illustrates the range of costume design style, from street clothes on one end to strangely abstracted constructions on the other end. Stylized animals and humanoid forms lie somewhere between representational and nonrepresentational style.

THE COSTUME DESIGNER'S CRAFT

In almost all general respects the design considerations for costumes are the same as those for scenic design. This section will first take up quality considerations and then examine practical aspects of costumes.

Requirements for a Quality Costume Design

All good costume designs adhere generally to the following guidelines, which were first detailed in Chapter 7.

Figure 16.1 A progression of style in costume design. Drawing by Peggy Kellner.

MOOD AND SPIRIT OF THE PLAY To support the mood and spirit of a play the costume design needs elements that evoke the play's emotional quality. For example, soft, pastel colors and light, flowing fabrics would be appropri-

ate for the women's dresses in a romantic musical comedy, whereas heavy, rough fabrics and dark, somber colors would be more suited to a tragedy (Figure 16.2).

Silhouette: The general outline of a garment.

Similarly, the **silhouette** of a garment can provide visual clues about the emotional qualities of a character. The curvilinear lines of the costumes in Figure 16.3A indicate that these characters are generally more light hearted and less serious than the people in Figure 16.3B.

Figure 16.2 Costume designs generally mirror the emotional quality of the play or characters. Costume designs for Elise Darling from Jerome Kern's *Very Good Eddie* and Queen Elinor from Shakespeare's *King John* by Paul D. Reinhardt, University of Texas, Austin.

(A)   (B)

Figure 16.3 The silhouette of a costume can provide visual clues about character. (A) Asolo State Theatre's (Sarasota, Florida) production of *Charley's Aunt*. Costume design by Catherine King, scene design by Gordon Miconis; photo by Gary W. Sweetman. (B) Jeri Leer, Candy Buckley, Linda Gehringer (left to right) and Michael O'Hara (background) in Dallas Theatre Center's production of *Three Sisters*. Designed by Leo Akira Yoshimura; photo by Linda Blase.

HISTORICAL PERIOD Since the vast bulk of a costume designer's work is rooted in representational style, the costumes must frequently be faithful to the historical period of the play. In costume design, as in all theatrical design areas, the degree of adherence to historical precedent is flexible. The costumes should be based on the silhouette of the period and should evoke the period and its style, but they don't have to be exact reproductions. The costume designer's historical research methods parallel those of the scenic designer, which were outlined in Chapter 7.

CLIMATE AND SEASON The climate and season have a significant impact on the design of clothing. Heavy, warm fabrics are used to keep out the cold, and light, relatively porous fabrics are used when the weather is hot. The costume designer generally uses the appropriate type of cloth to provide the audience with visual clues to the season of the play. Interesting inferences can be made about the personality of a character who is dressed "out of season," like the missionary preacher who wears long underwear and a woolen frock coat in James Michener's *Hawaii*.

LOCALE AND CULTURE More than any other design field, clothing exhibits variations that depend specifically on locale and culture, as shown in Figure 16.4. The costume designer can provide the audience with strong visual clues to the location and culture of the characters simply by employing these cultural and regional design characteristics.

SOCIOECONOMIC STATUS Throughout history it has been relatively easy to differentiate between master and servant simply by the style and quality of clothing that each is wearing. During some periods and in some circumstances the style of clothes worn by the master and mistress differed significantly from those of the servants. An example is the **livery** of butlers, maids, and chauffeurs. In other periods and situations the stylistic difference between servant and master was minimal. In those cases the *quality* of the clothing created the visual differentiation. Inevitably, the master wore clothes that had a better cut and more trim and were made of richer, more colorful fabrics. Appropriate historical research provides the costume designer with the necessary reference data. Again, the methods of conducting historical research for the costume designer are the same as for the scenic designer. Those techniques were discussed in Chapters 2 and 7.

Apart from the stylistic differences, costumers frequently **distress** the garments to give them character. If an actor appears in an elegant jacket but the cuffs are frayed and a pocket is ripped, the audience will frequently assume that the character is either a "good fellow" down on his luck, an eccentric, or a bum who has found himself a nice jacket. The play's dialogue and action usually reveal the correct characterization, but it is the distressed costume that creates the first impression.

Practicality of the Costume

To be practical a costume must meet the needs of the director and the actors and must be able to be made within the alloted construction schedule and fiscal budget.

Livery: Identifiable clothing associated with a specific occupation or trade.

Distress: To make something appear to be used, abused, and worn.

NEEDS OF THE DIRECTOR The director, in addition to having the same basic needs as the costume designer—that the costumes be a visual reflection of the characters' personalities and be functional as well as serviceable for the

Figure 16.4 (A) A sample of regional variations in costume design. (B) A sample of cultural variations in costuming within a particular country or region (American). Drawings by Peggy Kellner.

(A)

Tyrolean lederhosen

Modern Indian sari

Late nineteenth-century Java

Native Arab attire

Modern South African native

Japanese kimono

(B)

Skateboarding

Surfing

Aerobics

Biking

Jogging

actors—has some specific needs. Directors frequently ask the costume designer to help the audience identify who is on whose side, or who belongs to whom, in a production. As mentioned in Chapter 5, Danielo Donati made very effective use of color contrast (reds and yellows for the Capulets, blues and grays for the Montagues) to help delineate the political allegiances of the various cast members in Franco Zeffirelli's film production of *Romeo and Juliet.* In light comedies and musicals such as *The Boyfriend,* in which there are a number of romantically linked happy couples, the costume designer frequently dresses the couples in similar colors—for example, a pastel blue gown for the woman and the same hue as a trim color (hat band, tie, vest) for the man.

Directors may also want the actors to do certain bits of business that dictate special costume needs such as baggy pants, oversized pockets, hidden pockets, and breakaway sleeves and legs.

NEEDS OF THE ACTOR The actor's needs are relatively simple. The costume should fit, it should be reasonably comfortable, and it shouldn't inhibit any necessary and appropriate motion. Although a costume usually needs to be historically accurate, the search for authenticity cannot be allowed to restrain the actor's range of motion. In the long history of fashion there have been some rather strange clothing styles that in one way or another prevented movement. The circumference of the hem of a hobble skirt (Figure 16.5) was so small that women wearing them could take only very tiny steps, and it was all but impossible to move up or down stairs. For stage use hobble skirts, and

---

COSTUME COMFORT

Every costume should not only create the proper visual impression but also be practical for the actor or actress to wear. This does not mean that it must be delightfully comfortable. Period costumes, in particular, can be quite uncomfortable.

The tiny, wasplike waists of Victorian gowns were created by tightly bound corsets. These devices of medieval torture were in all probability the primary reason for the "swooning" that was so prevalent among "women of quality" during the latter half of the nineteenth century. The corset cinched in the lower portion of the lungs and tightly bound the diaphragm. The unhappy result of this cosmetic necessity was that women couldn't breathe deeply. If they became the least bit agitated, their natural reaction was to try to breathe deeply to calm themselves. Since the corset didn't allow that, they'd breathe more rapidly, which

caused them to hyperventilate. Then they'd giggle to mask their rising panic, and finally they would faint from lack of oxygen. It's a rather sad commentary that an undergarment—the corset— might have been a prime contributor to the shaping of the Victorian image of women as flighty, delicate, and faint hearted.

This example shows the lengths to which styles in various periods have influenced the lives of the fashion conscious. In theatrical costuming a reasonable blend should be achieved between historical accuracy and actor comfort. Obviously, the silhouette of the costumes from some periods requires that the clothes be less than comfortable, but at the same time the costume designer must remember that the actor needs to be able to perform his or her role in a fashion that will be relatively unimpeded by the fit and style of the costume.

This discussion is a capsulization of the specific applications of the design process to costume design. A review of Chapter 2 may be appropriate if you are a little hazy on the fundamentals of this problem-solving technique.

COMMITMENT
In order to accomplish your best work, you have to promise yourself that you will perform the task to the best of your ability.

ANALYSIS
The type of information that is needed to clarify and refine the challenge can be gathered by reading the script and asking questions of the other members of the production design team. Typical questions that relate specifically to costume design include:

1. What is the costume budget?
2. What is the production concept?
3. Are we going to be producing the play in the period in which it is written? What is that period?
4. When is the first dress rehearsal?
5. Does the director want a costume parade?
6. What does the set design look like? What is its color palette?
7. What is the lighting designer's color palette?

Some questions will be answered when you study the script. Others will be discussed and answered during the production conferences, in which the director and all designers freely exchange ideas and information.

The second phase of analysis involves discovering areas and subjects that will require further research. Note these areas so that you can investigate them during the next phase of the design process.

RESEARCH
Research is divided into two separate areas: background research and conceptual research. The primary function of background research is to answer the questions generated during the analysis phase. The vast majority of costume designs are based on a relatively realistic interpretation of the style of clothing worn during some particular period of history. Research sources used by the costume designer include texts on the history of costuming, photographs of actual garments of the period and country, paintings appropriate to the time and locale of the intended production, and museum displays of actual clothing and accessories.

The further back one goes in history, the greater will be the variations in the style of clothing from region to region and country to country. Before 1800 land transportation was either by foot, horse, carriage, or cart. Travel between continents was by sailing ship. With the development of steamships, railroads, and the telegraph, the time that it took for information to travel from one place to another shrank from months and years to merely minutes and days. Consequently, the readily identifiable regional variations in the style of clothing began to diminish as the interchange of ideas, goods, and services became easier.

Even in our own age of information, regional differences in dress are still alive and well. But the current variations in clothing between regions and countries are generally more subtle today than they were even one hundred years ago.

During conceptual research you need to visualize as many potential solutions to the design challenge as possible. Sketch a lot of ideas. Gather fabric samples that might be appropriate for material from which to construct the various costumes, and attach them to the sketches.

INCUBATION
Rest. Relax. Get away from the project. Work on something else. Go for a walk. Go to the library. Go see a play or movie. Do anything but work on or think about the project.

SELECTION
After you have selected the appropriate overall costume concept for the production, you will also need to select the appropriate design idea that will be used for each individual costume in the production.

IMPLEMENTATION
The implementation phase in costume design involves the drawing and painting of costume renderings, the selection of the appropriate fabrics for each design, and sometimes the supervision of the construction of each garment. (To be technically correct the costume designer is responsible for the appearance, not the construction, of the finished costume. It is the costumer, not the costume designer, who is responsible for the supervision of the actual making of the costumes. In some production companies these lines of responsibility become quite fuzzy.)

EVALUATION
Finally, take an objective look at the communicative process that has taken place between you and the other members of the production design team and your own use of the design process. The purpose of this evaluation is to discern ways in which you could improve your own communication with other members of the production design team as well as your use of the process.

similar movement-inhibiting clothes, are usually designed with authentic line and style but with slight modifications to allow for a little more freedom.

Actors come in all sizes and shapes. Since there is usually a variety of clothing styles for any particular fashion period, the costume designer normally selects a silhouette from the particular period that is appropriate to the body type of the individual actor. However, it occasionally becomes necessary to create a costume that will alter the actor's appearance. This is sometimes done to camouflage a flaw in the actor's body, but more frequently it is done to create a necessary feature for a specific characterization—a pregnant woman, a hunchback, an amputee, a potbellied lout, and so on.

CONSTRUCTION DEMANDS OF THE DESIGN Construction demands in costume design are generally predicated on the number of costumes in the production and the complexity of the individual designs. Obviously, if the production has only three costumes, it will be easier to build than a musical with a twenty-five-person chorus each of whom has three or four complete outfits. Similarly, costumes of certain periods are easier to construct than others. Some periods require fancy millinery and accessories, and others do not.

Although the first choice of most costume designers would be to construct all of the costumes, this sometimes isn't feasible because of time, fiscal, or other constraints. Alternative solutions include renting, buying, or modifying stock costumes.

RENTING COSTUMES Carefully tailored items made of expensive fabrics such as military uniforms and period men's suits are frequently rented. An advantage of renting uniforms is that the costume houses often have the appropriate accessories, such as swords, decorations, headgear, and footwear.

BUYING COSTUMES When producing a contemporary production, costume designers frequently buy clothes "off the rack" and tailor them to fit the specific actor. For productions that are set in the past twenty to thirty years costume designers can browse through used clothing stores and pick up appropriate period garments.

MODIFYING STOCK COSTUMES Educational and regional professional companies frequently have a stock of costumes that have been used in previous productions. Costumes can be pulled from stock and modified by the addition or deletion of trim and accessories. Significant variations in the appearance, and apparent period, of a costume can be made by something as simple as creating a lace **overlay** for the **bodice** of a gown. Similar changes can be effected by changing from lace to fur trim or vice versa.

COSTUME PRODUCTION

Overlay: A garment, usually made of lace or a similar lightweight, semitransparent fabric, designed to lie on top of another garment.

Bodice: The upper part of a woman's dress.

Tutu: The short, stiff skirt frequently worn by ballerinas.

Appliqué: A decorative item attached to a basic form such as a sweater or dress.

An incredible variety of fabrics and nonfabric materials can be used in constructing costumes. Some of these fabrics have already been described in Chapters 8 and 11.

Costumes, like scenery, can be made from just about any type of fabric or material. The only criterion to determine the appropriateness or suitability of any substance for use as a costume construction material can be summed up in two questions: "Will it look right?" and "Can the actor move as required by the part?"

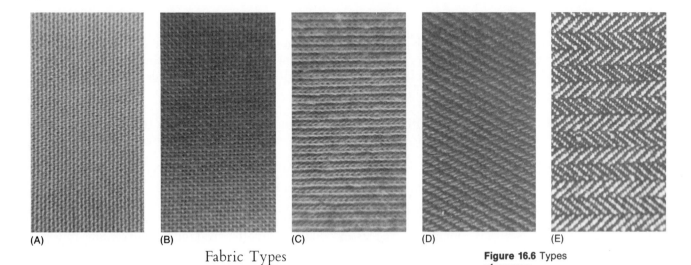

(A) (B) (C) (D) (E)

Figure 16.6 Types of weaves:
(A) plain,
(B) basket,
(C) rib,
(D) twill, and
(E) herringbone.

Fabric Types

Each type and weight of fabric has its own intrinsic characteristics. Some fabrics are crisp and stiff, and when draped they fall in stiff, angular lines. Other fabrics are soft and limp, and when draped they flow into smooth, sensuous curves. The costume designer must select the specific fabric or material that will most appropriately recreate the visual impression created in the costume rendering or sketch. If the design requires a hard, stiff line such as the skirt of a **tutu,** the costume designer would not use a soft, limp, flowing material unless he or she was trying to achieve a comic effect.

WOVEN FABRIC Weaving is achieved by interlacing yarns, threads, or filaments, as shown in Figure 16.6. Woven patterns include plain, basket, rib, twill, and herringbone, as shown in Figure 16.6A–E. Each type of weave imparts its own particular characteristic look and feel to the fabric.

KNITS Knit material is made with interlocking loops, as shown in Figure 16.7. Several common knits include purl, rib, tricot, and jersey. Again, each style has a tendency to produce a distinctive pattern, feel, and texture in the fabric.

FELTS Felting is the matting together of short fibers by the use of heat and water. Felt (Figure 16.8), which is the material formed through this process, has no discernable fabric structure and is relatively weak and floppy. Felt is primarily used in the costume shop to make **appliqués** and similar decorative items that will not be subject to any physical abuse. It is frequently used in the construction of both men's and women's hats.

FUSED FABRIC Fusing is the process of bonding of material together, generally through the application of heat and some type of adhesive agent. The process is used to manufacture laminated fabrics from synthetic materials such as drapery lining and the foam-backed duvetyn.

The lighter-weight fused fabrics are primarily used for lining dresses, suits, and drapes. The heavier-weight cloth can be used for robes, drapes, and the like that require a stiff fabric.

NETTING Netting is created by knotting or fusing yarn in a repetitive pattern, as shown in Figure 16.9. It is often used in millinery work, for tutus and other ballet skirts, and as a method of supplying weightless bulk in crinoline petticoats.

Figure 16.7 Knit material.

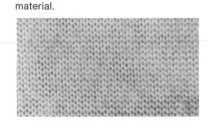

Figure 16.8 Felt.

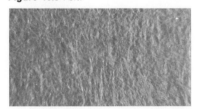

Figure 16.9 Netting.

Fabric Characteristics

A number of specific fabrics are typically used in the construction of stage costumes (and street clothes, for that matter). The samples described below and shown in Figures 16.10 and 16.11 illustrate the wide range of fabrics that are used in stage costuming.

CHIFFON Chiffon is a sheer, usually translucent, cloth frequently made from rayon or silk. It is used for scarves as well as diaphanous blouses and gowns.

CREPE A thin, crinkle-finished, soft cloth, crepe is frequently used in making women's blouses. It is often made from rayon, silk, or fine cotton.

MUSLIN Muslin is a plain, flat-surfaced cotton fabric. It is available in a number of weights and widths and is often used for making costume patterns.

HOMESPUN A coarse, loosely woven material, homespun is usually made from cotton, linen, or wool. It is often used for period men's shirts.

OXFORD CLOTH A flat-surface material with a basketlike weave, oxford cloth is used for making shirts and dresses.

TWILL Twill is a weaving pattern that results in parallel diagonal lines, or ribs. Cotton twill is a very durable, flat-surfaced fabric that can be used for making casual dresses, men's suits, and work clothes.

DENIM A fairly coarsely woven twill usually made of cotton or cotton-synthetic blends, denim was made famous by blue jeans.

FLANNEL Flannel is a lightweight, loosely woven material usually made with a soft-finish thread of wool, wool blend, or cotton. It is used for men and women's suits, trousers, and shirts.

CORDUROY A heavy material, frequently made from cotton or cotton-synthetic blends, corduroy has vertical wales varying from one-sixteenth to one-quarter of an inch wide. It is also available in a waleless weave that closely resembles a soft velvet. Waleless and pin-wale (very narrow) corduroy are used as lower-cost substitutes for velvet and velour. Wide-wale corduroy is most frequently used as an upholstery material.

Figure 16.10
Draping characteristics of several lightweight cloths: (A) chiffon, (B) crepe, (C) muslin, (D) homespun, (E) oxford cloth, (F) twill, (G) denim, and (H) flannel.

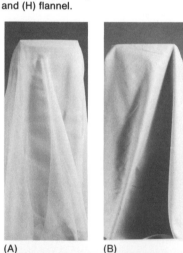

(A)   (B)

(C)   (D)   (E)   (F)   (G)   (H)

(A) (B) (C) (D) (E) (F)

(G)

Figure 16.11
Draping characteristics of several heavier cloths:
(A) corduroy,
(B) velvet,
(C) velour,
(D) damask,
(E) brocade,
(F) tweed, and
(G) worsted.

VELVET Velvet is a rich, lustrous material with a soft, thick pile. The pile is frequently made of rayon, with the backing cloth being cotton or cotton-rayon blend. It was originally, and sometimes still is, made from silk. Velvet is available in a variety of finishes—pile velvet (the pile loops are uncut), cut velvet (the loops are cut), and crushed velvet (the pile has been crushed between heated rollers). It is used in gowns, capes, upholstery—anywhere its rich, lustrous appearance would be appropriate. Velvet has a definite grain, so care must be taken that the grain is matched when cutting the fabric.

VELOUR Velour is similar to velvet but with a shorter nap. Available in a range of weights, the heavier fabrics are not very flexible, although lighter weight velours are very flexible. It is generally made of cotton or cotton-nylon blends. Although sometimes used in costuming as a substitute for velvet, velour is primarily used for stage draperies and upholstery. It has a grain similar to velvet's.

DAMASK A reversible, medium- to heavy-weight fabric, damask has a slightly raised pattern and is made from high-lustre yarn that is woven into the matte finish of the background cloth. It was originally made from silk and linen but is now most frequently made from synthetic yarns. Damask is used in constructing period costumes for aristocrats, as well as upholstery and draperies.

BROCADE Brocade can be used interchangeably with damask but is usually lighter in weight. The figured pattern in brocade is not necessarily raised but is woven into the material. Applications are similar to those for damask.

TWEED Tweed is a rough-surfaced woolen fabric in plain, twill, or herringbone weave in two or more shades of the same color. It is used for men and women's suits for cool to cold climates.

WORSTED A tightly woven, smooth-surfaced fabric of wool or wool blend, worsted is used for men and women's suits and trousers.

Fiber Characteristics

Two general categories of textile fiber are used to manufacture cloth—synthetic and natural. Each type of fiber has its own distinctive characteristics.

SYNTHETIC FIBERS Synthetic fibers are chemical compounds that are changed into hardened filaments by a variety of patented processes. Unless treated further these fibers have a tendency to be slick, smooth, and dense.

These properties are responsible for the characteristics of the fabrics that are woven or knit from synthetic yarns. Because of the slick, smooth yarn some woven synthetic fabrics tend to unravel easily. In general, fabrics made from synthetic fibers do not breathe (allow air to pass relatively freely through the fibers of the yarn) nearly so well as fabrics made from natural fibers. Thus, they trap body heat inside the costume. On the positive side, most synthetic fabrics have an inherent resistance to wrinkling.

Two or more synthetic and natural fibers are often blended to form a fabric that will take advantage of the best attributes of each while de-emphasizing their negative aspects. These blended fabrics are usually wrinkle-resistant and durable, and they breathe well.

The care of any fabric, as well as its fiber content, must, by law, be indicated on the **hang tag** of the bolt of fabric. Synthetic fabrics that have approximately 40 to 50 percent natural fiber content (cotton, linen, wool, and so forth) generally breathe well. Fabrics that are 100 percent synthetic generally do not breathe well. The costumer should be acquainted with the care of any fabric used in a stage costume, since those garments may need to be cleaned and pressed frequently during the run of the production.

NYLON Sold under the trade names of Antron, Celanese, Quiana, and others, nylon is characteristically woven or knit into fabrics that are strong, nonbreathing, stretchable, and strongly wrinkle-resistant. Nylon knits, such as Lycra, are stretchable and are frequently used for swimsuits, lingerie, and dance wear. Woven nylon blends are often made into shirts and socks. Nylon is also used to create some interesting specialty fabrics such as fake fur.

POLYESTER Fortrel and Kodel are two of the more popular trade names for polyester weaves and knits. This fiber is characteristically strong and reasonably wrinkle-resistant, and like most synthetics it does not breathe well. Another characteristic of polyester fabrics is that they can be heat set, which is the process that results in permanent press garments. Blends of polyester and natural fibers are frequently used in sports and dress clothing, where the polyester combines its heat-setting and wrinkle-resistant characteristics with the superior breathability of the natural fibers. One hundred percent polyester weaves are frequently found in lining, upholstery, and curtain materials. Polyester double-knit fabric has been used in the clothing industry for years.

RAYON Zantrel, Avril, and Fibro are some of the more common trade names for rayon, one of the first synthetic materials. Made of cellulose acetate, its fibers are relatively weak when compared with nylon and polyester. Unlike its stronger cousins, rayon breathes fairly well and will absorb moisture. Unfortunately, many types of rayon must be dry-cleaned. Rayon can be manufactured to have the appearance of either linen or silk and is most frequently used in the making of dresses and suits.

NATURAL FIBERS Before the twentieth century all fabrics were made from natural fibers. In terms of costume construction the primary advantage of natural fibers is their ability to breathe. But unfortunately, unless they are chemically treated or blended with some type of synthetic fibers, most natural fibers (except silk) have a pronounced tendency to wrinkle. Additionally, most natural fibers shrink rather dramatically when they are washed.

COTTON Cotton thread is spun from the white fluff contained in the pod of the cotton plant. Cotton material is characteristically strong, breathes very

CHAPTER 16: COSTUME DESIGN AND PRODUCTION

well, wrinkles easily, and accepts dyes quite readily. It can be used for both underclothing and outer garments and is suitable for year-round use. Commonly used stage fabrics made of cotton are corduroy, denim, muslin, and homespun.

LINEN Linen is made from the flax plant. Like cotton it is strong, breathes well, and wrinkles quite easily. Unlike cotton it does not dye well. Linen thread is usually slightly irregular in both size and color, which gives the material its characteristically nubbly appearance. Unbleached linen is used in the making of spring and summer suits for both men and women.

SILK Silk thread is made by laboriously unraveling the cocoons spun by silkworms. The resultant material is expensive, strong, and dyes well. Unlike the other natural fiber fabrics, silk is also wrinkle resistant. Because of its expense silk is usually confined to productions with rather large costume budgets. Silk is woven into a rich variety of beautiful fabrics ranging from sheer crepes and chiffons to luxuriously heavy brocades and damask fabrics.

WOOL Wool is made from the fleece of sheep. Woolen fabric is relatively weak, holds heat well, accepts dyes quite readily, and is a favorite food of moths. Wool and wool-blend materials are used for both men and women's suits and outer wear. Flannel, tweed, and worsted are typical materials made from wool.

Nonfabric Materials

A variety of materials other than cloth are used in costume construction. Some of these materials are substituted for fabric, and others are used to bind various costume materials together. This list is neither exhaustive nor exclusive. Almost any material can be, and has been, used to make costumes. In addition to the cloth and fabric materials that form the basis of most costumes, any number of decorative materials can be appliquéd to the fabric to enhance its appearance. The only limitations on appropriateness are commonsense rules of safety for the actors and those around them, and the suitability of the material to the design concept for that particular costume.

LEATHER Leather is often used for hats, shoes, and certain period pieces such as vests, armor, and belts. In the United States most leather is treated cowhide, although leather can be made from the hide of almost any animal. Leather has a smooth and rough side. The side that is used by the costumer is solely dependent on the particular look that is wanted. Most leather can be dyed with special leather dyes and sprays. It can be machine-stitched using a heavy-duty sewing machine equipped with a leather needle. It can also be hand-stitched. The surface of the leather can be tooled, and a variety of tools (awls, leather punches) can be used to punch holes in the material.

Leather can be formed into curves for items such as helmets and breastplates by steaming it and forming it to an appropriately shaped mold. Leather can be rather heavy, is extremely durable, and holds heat well. Complete costumes constructed of leather can become very warm and uncomfortable.

CELASTIC Celastic is a stiff, plastic-impregnated felt cloth. The plastic can be softened by dipping the Celastic into acetone. While it is limp, it can be formed into almost any shape. When the acetone evaporates, the Celastic again becomes quite stiff. It is frequently used for the construction of helmets, armor, masks, and jewelry, as shown in Figure 16.12.

Figure 16.12
Celastic is frequently used for making helmets and armor.

Care must be exercised when working with Celastic. The acetone solvent is extremely flammable and poisonous. The acetone fumes are toxic, and adequate ventilation must be provided. If possible, work outdoors. You should also use rubber gloves when working with Celastic, because the acetone and the plastic will remove the natural oils from your skin. Surgical gloves work very well, because they are thick enough to protect your hands from the drying effects of the acetone and yet they are thin enough to allow the "hands-on" feel that is necessary to good craft work.

Celastic can be sanded and painted with both water- and oil- or lacquer-based paints.

PLASTER BANDAGE Plaster-impregnated gauze can often be used as a substitute for Celastic. Available from surgical supply houses and some drugstores, it is the material that doctors use to make casts. It is water soluble, creates no toxic or noxious fumes, and can be formed as easily as Celastic. After the material has dried, it can be sanded and painted with both water- and oil- or lacquer-based paints.

FIBERGLASS As we have seen, fiberglass is an extremely strong material formed of two parts: glass fibers in the form of mat or woven cloth and a resin coat that cures into a hard plastic. It is used for constructing armor and helmets, while the resin can be used by itself in the production of jewelry. More information about fiberglass can be found in Chapter 11.

METAL Aluminum, copper, and brass appliqués and jewelry are often used in the construction of various accessories for gowns, armor, buckles, and similar applications. Metal appliqués (Figure 16.13) can usually be found in fabric

Figure 16.13 Metal is frequently used in the fabrication of decorative items such as appliqués and buckles.

stores, while thin sheet metal can be found in craft shops. The sheet metal can be formed using standard woodworking tools, and the copper and brass sheets can be soldered. All three metals can be riveted or glued with appropriate cyanoacrylate cements such as Super Glue or Krazy Glue. (See Chapter 8 for more information on adhesives.)

Costume Construction Tools

Just as in the other areas of theatrical production, a number of machines and tools are used to fabricate costumes and accessories.

POWER SEWING MACHINES The most basic piece of power equipment in the costume shop is the sewing machine. Costume shops are normally equipped with heavy-duty commercial-grade machines rather than the light-duty homemaker models, simply because the machines will receive a great deal of use. Figure 16.14 shows two of these machines. They are generally capable of making straight-line as well as zig-zag stitches, button holes, and one or more specialty stitches.

Some costumers like to have one or two power machines that can do high-speed, straight-line sewing. These machines have the power to stitch any fabric from chiffon to leather with equal ease.

The merrow machine (Figure 16.15) is another useful specialty tool of the costumer. This machine sews a seam, cuts both pieces of fabric about one-quarter of an inch from the seam, and makes an overcast stitch on the edge of both pieces of fabric to prevent it from raveling. The interesting thing about the machine is that it accomplishes all of these tasks in a single operation!

DRESS FORMS Dress forms, also known as mannequins or dress dummies,

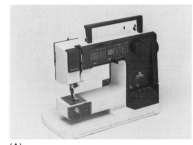
(A)

(B)

Figure 16.14
Sewing machines: (A) heavy duty machine (courtesy of Husqvarna Sewing Machine Co.), (B) power machine (courtesy of Chandler Sewing Machine Co.).

Figure 16.15
A merrow machine.

FABRIC FINISHES

Irrespective of the type or fiber content of a fabric, most textiles are treated with either a functional or a decorative finish or both.

FUNCTIONAL FINISHES
Functional finishes are normally applied to the fabrics before they leave the mill:

1. Permanent press processes enable permanent creases to be put into trousers and other garments while all but eliminating wrinkles from the finished fabric and clothes.

2. Mercerization is a chemical process that adds strength and shine to cotton thread.

3. Flameproofing is a chemical treatment of cloth that prevents it from supporting flames. It does not, however, prevent the cloth from charring and smoldering.

4. Preshrunken cloth, particularly cotton, has been bathed in water.

5. Cloth can be impregnated with antibacterial agents to reduce the severity of stains from perspiration and other natural substances.

DECORATIVE FINISHES
Decorative finishes alter the appearance of the fabric. These treatments include bleaching, dyeing, printing, and texturing. Although the vast majority of these treatments are applied to fabrics before they leave the mill, some decorative treatments, such as dyeing and fabric painting, are frequently performed in the costume shop.

Figure 16.16
An adjustable
dress form.

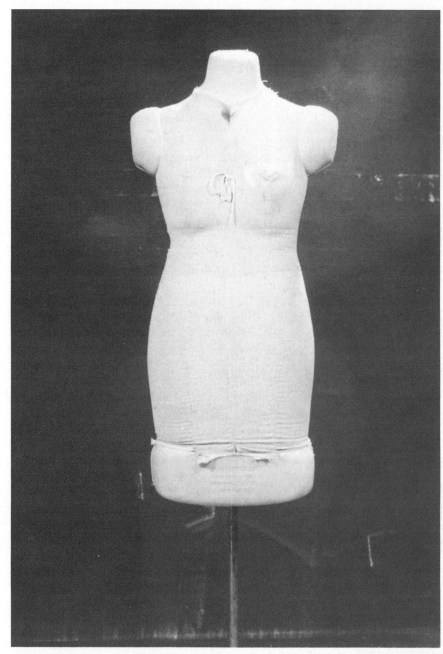

Figure 16.17
A heavy-duty
steam iron.
(Courtesy of
Sussman.)

Figure 16.18
A movable
clothes rack.

are available in a wide variety of sizes. Most costume shops will have a number of dress forms (Figure 16.16) that are adjustable to accommodate the wide size diversity of actors and actresses. These dress mannequins should have a padded cloth surface to which fabric can be pinned.

IRONS Every well-equipped shop will have a number of heavy-duty steam and dry irons (Figure 16.17) for pressing garments during construction and while the play is in production. Again, it is advisable to use commercial-quality rather than the light-duty models, simply because the irons will be subjected to almost continuous use when crews are working in the costume shop.

CLOTHES RACKS Several movable clothes racks will make the life of the costumer much easier. These racks, illustrated in Figure 16.18, can be moved

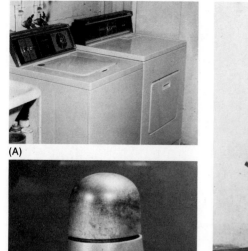

(A)

(B)

(C)

(D)

Figure 16.19
Miscellaneous
costume
equipment.
(A) washer and
dryer, (B) hat mold,
(C) dye vat,
(D) steamer
(courtesy of
Sussman).

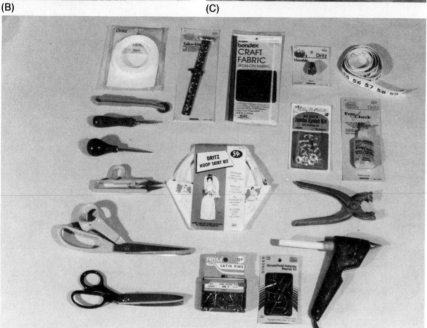

Figure 16.20 Hand
tools commonly
used in costuming.

to convenient locations and used to hang clothes under construction, in storage, or in production.

OTHER COSTUME EQUIPMENT Figure 16.19 shows some of the other equipment that greatly assists the costumer in constructing the wide range of garments made in a typical costume shop. Various hand tools (Figure 16.20) are used to mark, measure, and sew costumes. Adhesives are frequently used in costume, millinery, or accessory construction. The hot glue gun is an extremely versatile and useful tool, and the cyanoacrylate cements, white glue, and barge glue are also extremely useful. These adhesives were described more fully in Chapter 8.

JOINING HARDWARE Fabric and other materials used in costume construction can be joined in a variety of ways. The most common is by sewing. A

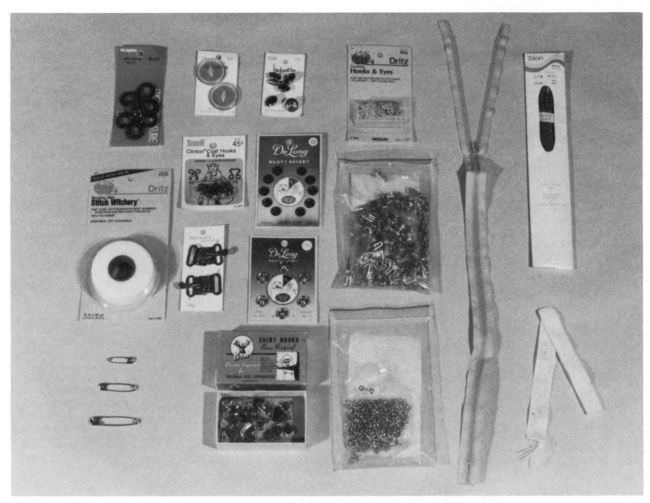

Figure 16.21
Fasteners used in costuming.

variety of materials and techniques can temporarily join fabric together. These devices are illustrated in Figure 16.21.

Costume Construction Procedures

After the costume designer has created the design for a particular garment and the costumer has purchased the material and made it ready for use by prewashing (if the fabric is to be cleaned by washing) and ironing, it is time to begin construction of the costume.

MEASUREMENTS At some time soon after the actors have been cast in the production, a member of the costume crew will take a thorough set of each actor's measurements, as shown on the forms illustrated in Figure 16.22, and will have one of the shop's dress forms altered to conform to those measurements.

PATTERNS If the costumes are not going to be borrowed or rented, the first order of business in making the costumes will be to procure the pattern. If the play is set in a contemporary period, it may be possible to purchase an appropriate ready-made pattern, in the actor's size, at a fabric store. These patterns can be altered slightly (by increasing or decreasing the widths of lapels or pants legs, the height of cuffs and hems, the fullness of skirts, and so on) to make the resulting costumes quite appropriate to almost any modern European or American period since the 1920s.

MEN

Name _____   Play _____

Address _____   Role _____

Phone _____ Taken by _____ Date _____

Head _____ Armhole _____ Outseam _____

Neck _____ Upper arm _____ Inseam _____ Rise/crotch _____

Chest _____ Forearm _____ Shoulder/waist _____ Shoulder seam _____

Chest exp _____ Wrist _____ Shoulders across front _____ Back _____

Waist _____ Sleeve inseam _____ F: Neck/waist _____ Fl _____

Hip _____ Sleeve outseam _____ B: Neck/waist _____ Fl _____

Thigh _____ Center back to elbow _____ Shoe size _____ Suit size _____

Knee _____ Center back to wrist _____ Pant size: W _____ Ins _____

Calf _____ Underarm/waist _____ Shirt size: N _____ Sleeve _____

Ankle _____ Sidewaist/knee _____ Ht _____ Wt _____ Eyes _____ Hair _____

WOMEN

Name _____   Play _____

Address _____   Role _____

Phone _____   Date _____

Head _____ Armhole _____ Inseam _____ Rise/crotch _____

Neck _____ Upper arm _____ Shoulder/waist _____ Shoulder span _____

Chest _____ Forearm _____ Shoulders across F _____ B _____

Under bust _____ Wrist _____ Shoulder tip to tip F _____ B _____

Waist _____ Bust point to bust point _____ Front: Neck/waist _____ Fl _____

Hip _____ Shoulder to bust point _____ Back: Neck/waist _____ Fl _____

Thigh _____ Sh/elbow _____ Wrist _____ Shoes _____ Tights _____ Bra _____

Knee _____ Underarm/waist _____ Ht _____ Wt _____ Eyes _____ Hair _____

Calf _____ Sidewaist/knee _____

Ankle _____ Outseam _____ Name of person who measured _____

Figure 16.22
Costume measurement cards.

Figure 16.23
Pattern-making
instructions. From
Douglas A. Russell,
*Stage Costume
Design: Theory,
Technique, and
Style,* 2nd ed., ©
1985, pp. 110–112.
Reprinted by
permission of
Prentice-Hall,
Englewood Cliffs,
New Jersey.

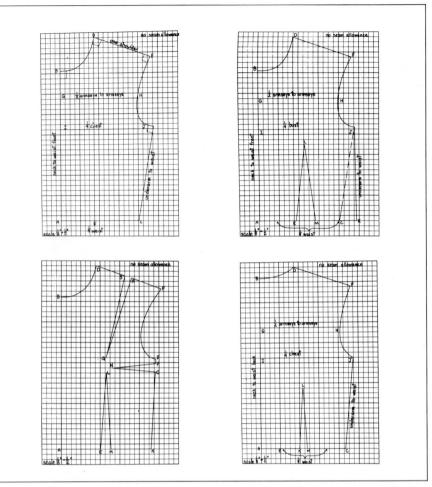

Figure 16.24
Draping technique.

Patterns for period costumes are not quite so easy to acquire and alter. A number of books contain basic period patterns (see the Bibliography). They provide detailed instructions for altering their patterns to fit actors of varying size.

Patterns are frequently made by the costumer. Contemporary patterns can be adapted to form a period garment, or patterns can be made by transferring the actor's measurements to paper or muslin, as outlined in Figure 16.23.

In a professional costume shop the costume designer provides the cutter or shop supervisor with a completed costume sketch (including fabric samples). The cutter then makes the pattern (or drapes the material) and cuts the fabric.

DRAPING Draping (Figure 16.24) in which fabric is actually draped on either the actor or a dress form adjusted to the actor's measurements eliminates the need for a pattern. After the desired look for the costume is achieved, the costumer can cut the material while it is still pinned to the actor or his or her dress mannequin. Draping works best with flowing gowns, robes, and cloaks. It isn't particularly well suited for suits and similarly tailored garments.

A muslin mock-up, called a **sloper** (Figure 16.25), can be cut from a pattern, **basted** and pinned together, put on the actor's dress form, and adjusted to fit exactly. The sloper is then taken apart and used as a pattern to cut the fabric from which the costume will be made. Occasionally, the sloper is eliminated, and the costume fabric itself is cut, basted and pinned to the dress form, and adjusted as necessary.

Sloper: A muslin mock-up of a costume; before cutting the expensive costume material, the pattern is cut from muslin, put on a dress form set to the actor's measurements, and adjusted to fit.

Baste: To loosely and temporarily stitch pieces of cloth together.

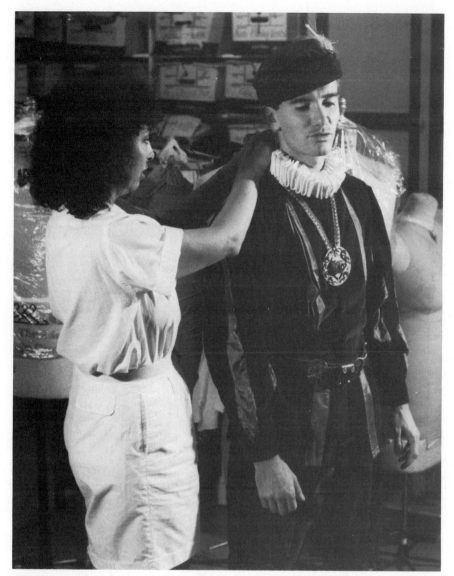

Figure 16.25
A sloper.

Figure 16.26 A
costume fitting.

FITTINGS After the basic **shell** of the costume has been basted, the actor will need to come to the costume shop for a fitting, as shown in Figure 16.26. The shell of the costume is placed on the actor, and all the seams, **darts,** and measurements are checked for accuracy, appropriate fit, and comfort. After any necessary adjustments are made, the costume is again basted, and the actor returns to the shop for the second fitting. The actor tries out the costume for fit and makes sure that none of his or her stage business is impeded by the garment. At this time the correct length of the hems is marked, and the fit of the garment is again checked and adjusted if necessary.

There is frequently a final fitting once the garment has been completed. The purpose is to check not only the fit and comfort of the garment but also the appearance and appropriateness of the accessories that will be carried or worn with the costume. At this time the costumer can also instruct the actor as to when during the play the costume is to be worn and other pertinent information.

To help the actors remember when to wear each costume and what accessories go with it, the costumer or costume designer frequently makes a costume chart. This chart is placed in a prominent position in the dressing room so the actors and dressers can easily refer to it.

Shell: The basic form of a costume, basted or pinned together, which covers the torso, arms, and legs.

Dart: A short, tapered seam resembling a very narrow **V**; used to make clothes fit more closely.

Dressed: To work with hair or a wig to create a specific style or look.

Accessories

In costuming the term accessory refers to anything other than clothing that is worn or carried by the actor or actress. Accessories include wigs, hats, jewelry, walking sticks, footwear, masks, purses, and many other items.

WIGS A wig can provide the crowning glory to almost any costume. It is often necessary to use a wig to achieve the correct hair style for a historical period, and a well-**dressed** wig can immeasurably enhance the appearance of contemporary costumes as well.

Modern wigs, of both synthetic and human hair, can be styled to achieve a period look, as shown in Figure 16.27. The hairdresser or stylist, working under the supervision of the costume designer, will need to consult appropriate source materials (paintings, photos, and so on) to determine a look that is appropriate for the particular period.

Figure 16.27 A progression of hair styles. Drawings by Peggy Kellner.

Sumerian 2900–2685 B.C.

Egyptian wig 1555–7330 B.C.

Second-century Greek

French c. 1150

Italian c. 1488

Spanish c. 1613

French c. 1660

French c. 1778

English c. 1831

American Gibson style c. 1895

American c. 1926

American bubble c. 1963

Assyrian

Roman

French c. 1150

Burgundy c. 1448

Elizabethan Van Dyke beard

English c. 1670

American c. 1776

English c. 1831

American mutton chops and handlebar moustache c. 1884

American Valentino look c. 1930

American crew cut c. 1942

American flower child c. 1960s

Human-hair wigs can be coiffed with conventional curlers, electric rollers, or curling irons. Synthetic wigs can be dressed by rolling the hair on a *cold* curling iron or cold rollers and gently heating it with the warm air from either a hand-held or capstyle hair dryer. Obviously, wig dressing is an exacting craft and should be attempted only under the supervision of someone with experience.

HATS In the same manner as wigs, hats are frequently a requirement for completing the costume in many periods of history (Figure 16.28). A number of books give the history of hats, and these provide the costume designer with excellent source material. Other books provide patterns for various period hats; some of these are listed in the Bibliography. Almost any period hat can be constructed from materials available in a well-supplied fabric store. It is also possible to adapt and modify a modern hat to resemble one from another period.

Figure 16.28 A progression of styles in hats, headdresses, and crowns. Drawings by Peggy Kellner.

Egyptian c. 500 B.C.   Byzantine c. 565 A.D.   French c. 950 A.D.   German c. 1275 A.D.   English c. 1476   German gable headdress c. 1563

French/English fontage c. 1695   French mobcap c. 1780   American bonnet c. 1830   American Lillian Russell hat c. 1910   American felt clóche hat c. 1927   English Princess Diana c. 1983

Egyptian—crown of Upper and Lower Egypt   Greek helmet c. fifth century   Viking helmet c. 1000 A.D.   English hood and liripipe c. 1325   German c. 1525

French tricorne c. 1650   French bicorne c. 1795   English top hat c. 1822   American Panama hat c. 1902

Early twentieth century   Later twentieth century   Twentieth-century American

Homberg   Derby   Fedora   Straw boater   Golf cap   Sport cap   Sweat band   Plastic visor   1980s cowboy hat   Baseball cap

Demi-mask: A mask normally mounted on a stick, that covers only half the face.

FOOTWEAR Just as many costumes would not be complete without a wig or hat, no costume is complete without the appropriate footwear. Examples of shoes from various periods are shown in Figure 16.29.

Although the ideal solution to this challenge is to contract with a cobbler or shoe company to custom-build footwear of an appropriate style and design, this prohibitively expensive solution is beyond the fiscal means of the vast majority of production companies. Instead, many companies adapt modern shoes by adding elements more appropriate to the desired period.

Figure 16.29 A progression of period shoe styles. Drawings by Peggy Kellner.

MASKS A wild variety of masks is used in the theatre (Figure 16.30). They vary in complexity from simple **demi-masks,** which are sometimes carried by women at fancy dress balls, to full head masks designed to look like an animal.

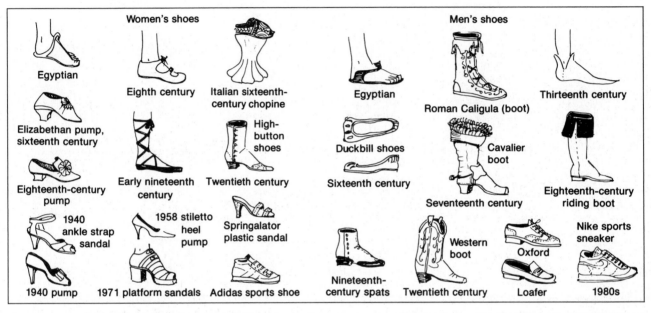

Figure 16.30 Styles of masks.

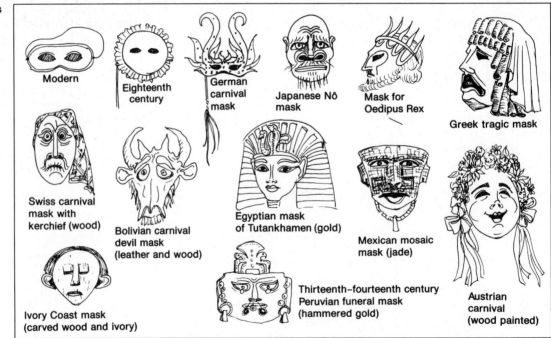

(A)

(B)

(C)

(D)

Figure 16.31 Papier-mâché mask construction technique. Cover the armature, a life mask (A), with aluminum foil. Apply several layers of glue-soaked strips of newspaper (B). Allow the finished mask to dry (24–48 hours) on the armature, and finish it as desired (D).

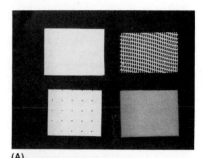

(A)

(B)

Figure 16.32 Low-temperature thermoplastics (A) used in mask and costume construction. (B) A mask made from plastic furnace filter foam hot glued onto a latex/gauze/celastic base.

Masks are made from a wide range of materials and fabrics, but the base layer of most masks is constructed on a clay or plaster mold, as shown in Figure 16.31. The mask is built up on the mold using papier-mâché, plaster bandages, Celastic, or some of the newer thermoplastic materials illustrated in Figure 16.32. These thermoplastics, available from medical supply houses under trade names such as Vara-form, Polyfoam, and Hexcelite, become limp and formable when heated in 160-degree water for approximately 30 seconds. They can also be heated with hand-held hair dryers. The nontoxic (unless burned) material can be worked, formed, and fused for approximately 2 to 4 minutes before it must be reheated. Although expensive, these materials are quite cost effective, as any waste scraps can be heated and fused together to form workable-sized pieces. These basic mask forms can be decorated with a variety of paints and appliqué materials.

Dyeing

Many times the costumer cannot buy a fabric in the color specified by the costume designer. This problem is solved by dyeing the fabric. Hot-water dyes in a variety of colors are available at most fabric stores. These dyes are excellent for working with most natural fabrics, but they are not strong enough to create really vibrant color. If a brilliant hue is needed, the fabric should be treated with aniline dyes, which were discussed in Chapter 10. Regardless of the type of dye used, it will be necessary to treat the fabric with a fixative to lock the dye into the fabric. Be sure to read the instructions for each dye you are using, as the specific type of fixing process varies according to the type of dye and manufacturer. After the dye has been fixed, be sure to wash the cloth several times to rid the fabric of any excess dye.

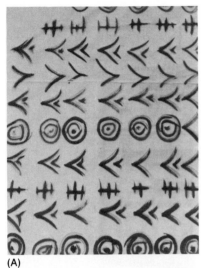

(A)

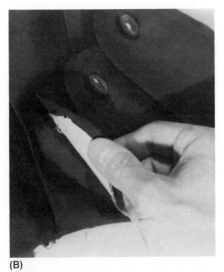

(B)

(C)

Figure 16.33 Fabric painting. Designs are frequently painted on fabric (A) prior to construction of the costume. Fabric painting is also used to give age and dimension to already constructed costumes (B and C).

Whereas most fabrics made of natural materials will accept dye readily, almost all synthetic fabrics have a nonporous surface finish that makes them difficult or impossible to dye.

Although fabric can be dyed using the hot-water cycle in the costume shop's washing machine, the dyes work better if the water is heated in a dye vat. The use of a vat also precludes the accidental dyeing of clothes in a washing machine that has been improperly cleaned after a dyeing session.

Painting

Fabric can be painted with designs or aged by painting the fabric with either cloth paint or dye, as shown in Figure 16.33. Spectacular effects can be achieved by painting designs on the fabric with flexible glue and sprinkling the wet glue with powdered metal or metal flakes.

MAKEUP

Makeup is a vital element in creating the total appearance of the actor. To a great extent the makeup design gives the audience its primary clue to the age, health, and vitality of the character. Although the overall appearance of the actor is the costume designer's domain, a makeup designer, under the artistic supervision of the costume designer, is often responsible for the design and execution of the makeup.

Stage makeup enhances the illusion that the actor has become the character. In almost every production some of the actors, for one reason or another, do not facially resemble the characters they are playing. Makeup can help solve this challenge by providing actors with the means to change their appearance. Through the skillful application of the various techniques of makeup, young faces can be made to look older, older faces younger, pretty faces less attractive, blemished skin clear, and rather plain faces ravishingly attractive.

A great deal of the communication process that transfers information from the actor to the audience takes place visually. To fully understand what the actors are saying (actually, what they are meaning) the audience must be able to read their facial expressions. In medium-sized and large theatres, many members of the audience are seated quite a distance from the stage. Therefore, a primary function of makeup is to enhance or exaggerate the actors' features.

(A)

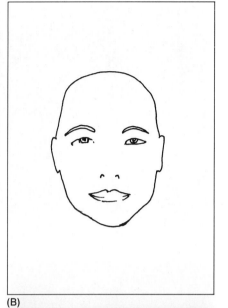

(B)

Figure 16.34 A makeup sketch is used to create the makeup design.

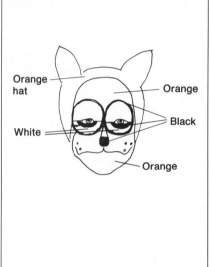

Orange hat

Orange

Black

White

Orange

(C)

(D)

Makeup designs usually begin with a sketch (Figure 16.34A–D). Using a photograph of an actor (A), a sketch (B) can be made following the general shape and features of the person's face. Although this personalized makeup sketch provides you with a clearer vision of how the finished makeup design (C) will appear, makeup designs can also be sketched on generic, or nonspecific, face drawings. Finished makeup is shown in Figure 16.34D.

Makeup Styles

There are four general stylistic categories of stage makeup—straight, remedial, character, and fantasy. As with style in other areas of theatrical design, the demarcation in practice between the various categories is unimportant; the labels are just convenient road signs for relative locations on the continuum of style.

STRAIGHT MAKEUP Straight makeup makes no attempt to significantly alter the appearance of the face. This style simply heightens the existing features

Figure 16.35
Straight or street
makeup.

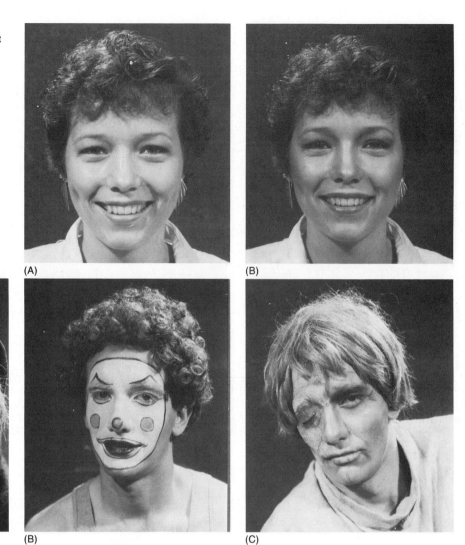

(A) (B)

(A)

Figure 16.36
Character makeup.

(B) (C)

and enhances skin tone. Street makeup (Figure 16.35A) is basically an application of makeup for street wear. It is frequently worn when the audience will be sitting close to the stage, as in most arena and black box theatres. The slightly exaggerated street makeup shown in Figure 16.35B heightens the facial features by highlighting the naturally protruding structures, such as the bridge of the nose and cheekbones, and aiding the areas where shadows naturally occur with an application of an appropriate shadow color. Enhanced street, or straight, makeup is normally worn when the distance between the actors and audience is great enough that the actors' natural features must be exaggerated to make their facial expressions clearly visible.

REMEDIAL MAKEUP Remedial makeup is simply straight makeup that is used to slightly change an actor's appearance. A broken nose will appear to be straight if the highlight on the bridge is applied in a straight line rather than following the nose's natural line. Uneven eyebrows can be balanced by applying the same pattern to both brows. Cheekbones and jawbones can be made more prominent simply by highlighting them. These and similar minor changes in the actor's appearance are classified as remedial makeup.

CHARACTER MAKEUP Character makeup significantly alters the appearance of an actor's face. These alterations can be made to create the appearance of

age (Figure 16.36A), a caricature or parody (Figure 16.36B), or disfigurement and disease (Figure 16.36C). The common link is that the actor's face is still the visible base for the designs.

FANTASY MAKEUP Fantasy makeup radically alters the appearance of an actor. The range of this style varies from fanciful animal designs to the full head masks and body parts created for movies like *Star Wars* (Figure 16.37).

Figure 16.37
Fantasy makeup.
Cantina creatures
from *Star Wars*,
courtesy of
Lucasfilm Ltd., ©
Lucasfilm Ltd.
(LFL) 1977. All
rights reserved.

Makeup Materials

Various materials are used for makeup base, liners, and prosthetic devices.

MAKEUP BASE As its name implies, the base is applied as the first layer of makeup. It has two primary purposes: (1) to cover any variations in skin tone and (2) to provide an appropriate tone for the application of further makeup. Three bases are commonly used in stage makeup: greasepaint, pancake, and liquid.

GREASEPAINT Greasepaint is the traditional makeup used in the theatre. Opaque and cream-based, it covers any variation in the actor's natural skin tone, hides blemishes, and provides a uniform base for subsequent layers of makeup. Greasepaint is manufactured in three forms, as shown in Figure 16.38: a creamy consistency that is packaged in tubes, a hard stick, and a formulation that is about halfway between the two and comes in small tins. The cream and stick formulations are available in a fairly wide range of Caucasian, Oriental, Indian, and black fleshtones and are used as a base. The greasepaint in tins is manufactured in a full range of heavily saturated colors and is used for highlighting and shadowing.

Figure 16.38 Types
of greasepaint
makeup.

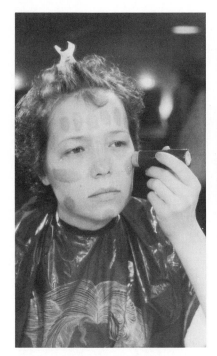

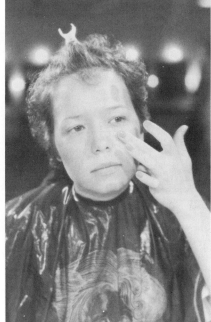

Figure 16.39
Application of
greasepaint base.

The base colors are very easily applied, either by putting little blobs of the tube cream or drawing lines with the hard stick on strategic points of the face (forehead, nose, cheeks, chin, jaw, and neck). Then these blobs or lines are smoothed and blended until the face and neck are uniformly covered with a thin coating, as shown in Figure 16.39.

If greasepaint is applied in sufficient quantity to conceal all skin irregularities and blemishes, it resembles an opaque mask instead of the translucent quality of a realistic or natural skin tone. If it is applied thinly, however, it reduces the evidence of blemishes and irregular skin tones while creating a smooth base of more natural quality.

In addition to being easy to apply, greasepaint is also the least expensive of the various types of stage makeup. Yet, it does have several drawbacks:

Figure 16.40
Pancake makeup.

1. Greasepaint smears easily and has a slightly greasy shine. These problems can be solved by an application of a facial powder. The powder "sets" the makeup (reduces its tendency to smear) and eliminates the greasy glow.

2. The cream base clogs the facial pores, promoting facial perspiration. If the perspiration is sufficiently heavy, it can cause streaks in the powder. Frequent reapplications of powder when the actor is offstage can usually solve this problem.

3. Greasepaint is not water soluble and must be removed with cold cream. It can cause skin irritation.

PANCAKE The second most common type of stage makeup is pancake. It is water soluble and is manufactured in cake and liquid forms (Figure 16.40). Pancake is applied with a moist sponge. If applied lightly, it can create a more natural appearing, translucent quality than greasepaint. If it is applied heavily, it produces the same opaque covering qualities as heavily applied greasepaint.

Pancake makeup does not block the pores, which reduces the incidence of facial perspiration, and it eliminates or significantly reduces the skin irritation associated with blocked pores. Additionally, it doesn't rub off so easily as

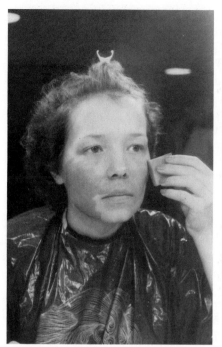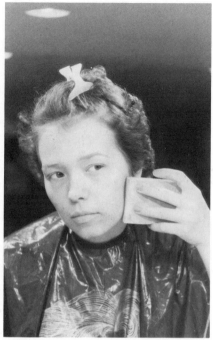

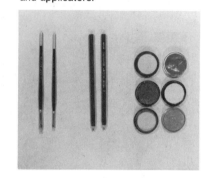

greasepaint. It does not need to be powdered, and it can be removed with soap and water. The negative aspects of pancake makeup are that it is a little more difficult to apply and blend than greasepaint, and it is also slightly more expensive. Figure 16.41 shows the basic techniques used in the application of pancake base.

LIQUID Liquid makeup manufactured for theatrical purposes is fairly well limited to body makeup. However, a variety of liquid bases formulated for street wear work perfectly well for the stage. The only problem in the use of liquid bases is that they dry quickly, which makes them difficult to blend if more than one color of base is being used.

LINERS The term *liner* refers to any of the saturated colors that serve as rouges and eye shadows or are used to create other areas of highlight or shadow. Liners are made in both greasepaint and pancake (Figure 16.42). Although it is generally preferable to work with greasepaint liners on top of a greasepaint base, and pancake on pancake, the two types can be used interchangeably.

Lining pencils are available in a fairly limited range of colors, and most makeup artists feel that they can get better control during application if, instead of using lining pencils, they work with a lining brush and the cream or pancake liners.

PROSTHETIC DEVICES Fake noses, beards, jowls, and cheeks, as well as other devices that alter the shape or appearance of the face, are referred to as prosthetic devices.

NOSE PUTTY Probably the most expedient way of altering the apparent structure of the face is through the use of nose putty. This material is approximately the same consistency as clay and can be used to create a variety of interesting effects, as shown in Figure 16.43.

Nose putty must be applied to clean skin, so any makeup must be removed and the area thoroughly cleaned with an astringent or other facial

Figure 16.43 Nose putty can be used to create a variety of prosthetic effects.

cleaner. After the putty has been applied and shaped into the desired form, it can be covered with an appropriate base color, and liners can be used to help blend it into the actor's natural facial structure.

Derma wax can be used instead of, or in conjunction with, nose putty. It is softer than nose putty, and it can be formed and blended into the skin more easily. It needs to be attached to the skin with spirit gum, and it is softer than nose putty and therefore more susceptible to damage from an inadvertent touch.

Both nose putty and derma wax normally have a smooth surface. To help match the natural texture of skin, the surface of the putty or wax should be roughened slightly by blotting it gently with a piece of nylon netting or similar lightly textured material.

LATEX The most versatile tool available to the makeup artist is probably liquid latex. It can be used as an adhesive to attach false mustaches, wigs, and masks; it can be used as a flexible base on which beards, hairpieces, and other devices can be made; and in its foamed state it can be used for the construction of prosthetic pieces.

FALSE HAIR False beards and mustaches are usually made from crepe hair, animal hair, or human hair. Crepe hair is the most commonly used material, because it is less expensive and provides generally satisfactory results.

For a prosthetic device made of false hair to look natural it should match the texture and thickness of the real thing. This usually entails the time-consuming task of making a beard or mustache one or a few hairs at a time (Figure 16.44).

The false beard or mustache can be applied directly to the actor's skin (be sure that the skin is free of makeup) using liquid latex or spirit gum. If the device is going to be reused, it will usually be more efficient to construct it on a latex base that can then be attached to the actor's face with either spirit gum or liquid latex.

Application Techniques

Although the principles of applying makeup are primarily the same for straight and character designs, some subtle differences should be noted.

STRAIGHT MAKEUP As we have seen, straight makeup designs usually begin with a base layer of either greasepaint or pancake. It is not essential that the base be of one color. If appropriate to the visualization of the character as sketched in the design, the base coat can be mixed from two or more colors.

After the base has been applied, the face's natural structure is either emphasized or deemphasized through the application of highlights and shadows. The highlights are normally applied where highlights would naturally occur, such as the bridge of the nose, the cheekbones, and the top of the eyebrows. The shadow colors are painted into those areas where shadows would naturally occur, such as wrinkle lines, eye sockets, and cheeks.

CHARACTER MAKEUP Although the process of makeup application is much the same for straight and character makeup, there is one significant difference. Any makeup base creates a greasy or powdery layer on the skin that prevents spirit gum or liquid latex from adhering. So any prosthetic devices need to be attached before the makeup.

A primary concern in creating a design that uses prosthetics is to make sure that the devices are blended into the actor's skin so they appear to be

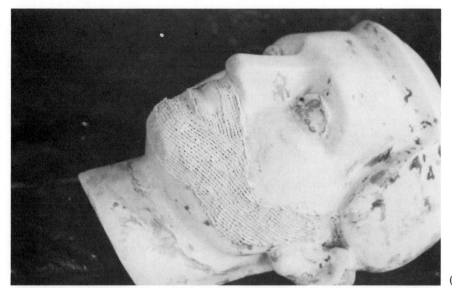

(A)

Figure 16.44 Basic beard construction technique. Join a base layer of gauze together with liquid latex (A). Individually attach small sections of hair to the gauze base with liquid latex (B) to create a finished beard (C). Be sure to separate the mustache from the beard so the actor can move his mouth in a natural manner.

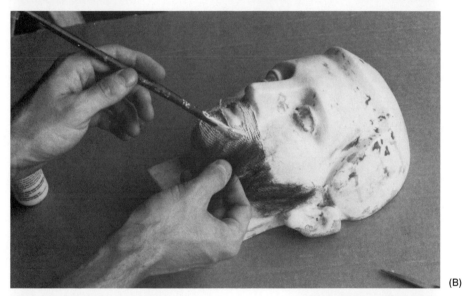

(B)

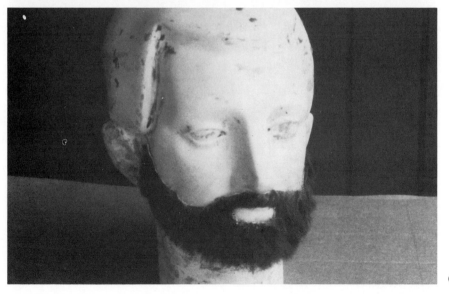

(C)

natural. This blending can be done by brushing a light coat of liquid latex from the device outward onto the skin. After the prosthetic pieces have been attached, the base, highlight, shadow, and lining are applied according to the instructions drawn and noted on the makeup design.

Makeup and Lighting

Advancements in the craft of lighting design have, in many instances, reduced the actor's need for an opaque makeup base. This has been done primarily by reducing the level of saturation of the colors used in the lighting instruments and increasing the use of side, top, and back light to supplement the existing front and side-front light.

Surrounding the acting area with light has also helped to create the appearance of a more naturally lit environment. This, in turn, has required that the actors make more extensive use of prosthetic devices and the subtle blending techniques of street makeup to create character designs, because the more natural lighting clearly reveals the false depth of a painted makeup design.

17

Sound Design and Technology

A few years ago sound in the theatre was fairly simple. If the director wanted some preshow music, you got some records that approximated the mood and spirit of the play and played them over the auditorium public-address system for about ten minutes before the curtain went up. You might get daring and play them again during the intermission.

If the script called for specific sound effects such as a doorbell or a telephone ringing, you either made the sounds live or consulted your sound-effects library, composed of low-fidelity 78-RPM records. If you used library effects, you either recorded them on your wire or tape recorder, or you cued the records up and played them just the way a disc jockey would.

Sound in the theatre has changed substantially since the bad old days. Instead of being an afterthought, sound is now frequently an integral part of the production concept. Increasing numbers of productions are giving credit to sound design as well as the traditional scenic, costume, and lighting design.

Arguably the most important reason for the increased use of sound is the improvement in sound equipment. A second reason stems from the tastes and expectations of the audience and of theatre craftspeople. Almost every member of the contemporary theatregoing public, as well as those of us who work in the theatre, have seen a lot more television and motion pictures than theatre. Our aesthetic expectations have been strongly influenced by what we have seen and heard in these media. For years both television and motion pictures have made very effective use of music and sound effects to focus the audience's attention and reinforce the dominant emotional theme of the material being presented. Higher-quality home and auto stereo systems have raised our sound expectations, too. It seems only natural, then, that designed sound and music should come to be expected in the theatre.

FUNCTIONS OF SOUND IN THE THEATRE

Theatre sound can be subdivided into three categories: music, effects, and reinforcement.

Music

The use of music in a nonmusical production has historically been limited to preshow, intermission, and postshow instrumentals that create an aural atmosphere selected to put the audience in the proper mood for the play. Comedies have been, and continue to be, accompanied by light and sprightly music, and full orchestrations of somber or ominous music have traditionally been associated with Shakespearean tragedies and plays of equally heavy subject matter. Plays that fall between these dramatic extremes are accompanied by music appropriate to their particular mood and subject matter.

Although this musical accompaniment has certainly been functional and effective, the contemporary use of music in the theatre has expanded in a variety of directions. Nonspecific musical effects, such as musical themes for specific characters or scenes, are now used to create or reinforce a particular psychological mood or feeling. Preshow selections have expanded to include almost any type of music or **constructed sound.** Lyrics, which used to be taboo, are now used whenever the production design team decides that their use would be appropriate. Furthermore, sections of many productions are now scored with music, the way motion pictures are, to reinforce the psychological content of particular moments in the script.

Effects

The creation of specific sound effects such as barking dogs, telephones, doorbells, and train whistles is still an important element of the sound designer's work, but it is no longer the sole element. Many production concepts now call for the creation of an effects track to provide an aural backdrop of appropriate sound for the environment of the play. For example, in the University of Arizona's production of Ted Tally's *Terra Nova*, which is set in Antarctica, the director wanted to create an effect that would emphasize the bitter cold and lonely emptiness of that hostile environment. Sound designers Mark Ruch and David Coffman, using a **synthesizer** (Figure 17.1), created a

Figure 17.1
A synthesizer.
(Courtesy of
Yamaha.)

CHAPTER 17: SOUND DESIGN AND TECHNOLOGY

very effective sound effect of wind sweeping across the empty frozen wastes. This sound effect, together with original music composed by Mark Ruch, was played, at varying levels of loudness, throughout all of the Antarctic scenes. When the sound was combined with the impact of an all-white set, the "cold" colors of the lights, and the cold-weather gear worn by the actors, the audience felt so chilly that it was necessary to turn the air conditioning to an above-average setting during the run of the production.

This type of fully scored effects design, which was extremely rare fifteen years ago, is not that unusual anymore. Arena, thrust, and black box productions frequently use specific sound effects, such as waves lapping a beach or "jungle noises," to provide aural images of specific locations.

Reinforcement

Reinforcement is used whenever there is a need to boost the loudness level of the actors' voices, as when the **acoustics** of the auditorium are not good or during musicals when the singers can't be heard over the orchestra. In the not-too-distant past actors projected loudly enough to be heard by every member of the audience in all but the largest theatres without the need for electronic reinforcement. Today most actors can still project loudly enough to be heard, but the growth in the use of background and effects sound has introduced a new challenge to theatrical production.

The audience wants and deserves to hear balanced sound. It shouldn't have to strain to hear the actors, nor should it be overwhelmed by the music or noise of a sound effect. The answer to these specific challenges has been to mike the actors' voices, then mix and **balance** the sound with the effects and background music before all three sources are amplified and sent into the auditorium.

Reinforced sound needs to be *balanced*. The various elements of the sound design, with obvious exceptions, should not call attention to themselves. The loudness level of any music or sound effect should not overwhelm the voices of the actors, nor should the content of the sound, either music or effects, be so vibrant or strident as to draw attention from the central focus of the scene.

THE NATURE OF SOUND

To develop a working knowledge of how sound systems operate, you'll need to understand the nature of sound. Sound is a pressure wave that moves, in air and at sea level, at about 1,130 feet per second. The pressure wave is instigated by a source such as the drum in Figure 17.2. The drum compresses the air immediately adjacent to the drumhead when the head is struck with the drumstick. This compression wave travels through the air until it strikes a receptor, in this case the ear. The ear converts the mechanical force of the pressure wave into a neurological impulse that is sent to the brain, where the stimulus is interpreted as a drum beat of a particular tone and quality.

Frequency

Frequency is the rate, measured in cycles per second (hertz, or Hz), at which an object vibrates. At one time or another most of us have strung a rubber band between our fingers and strummed it. The rubber band vibrated and made a sound. As we stretched the rubber band tighter, the vibrations of the rubber band seemed to get smaller, and the **pitch** of the sound increased. This

Acoustics: The sound transmission characteristics of a room, space, or material; also, the science that studies these qualities.

Balance: to adjust the loudness and equalization levels of individual signals while mixing, to achieve an appropriate blend.

Pitch: The characteristic tone produced by a vibrating body; the higher the frequency of vibration, the higher the pitch.

Figure 17.2
The transmission of sound in the air.

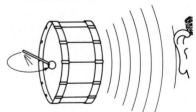

Decibel: A unit for expressing the intensity of sounds; an increase or decrease of one decibel is just about the smallest change in loudness that the human ear can detect.

was a demonstration of the direct relationship between frequency and pitch; as frequency increases, pitch increases.

To better understand the concept of frequency and its effect on pitch, let's assume that when the drumhead discussed above was struck with the drumstick, it took one second to complete twenty full vibrations, or cycles, as shown in Figure 17.3. We would hear this twenty-cycle vibration as a very low sound. If we were able to tighten the drumhead so that it vibrated at a frequency of two hundred cycles per second (200 Hz), we would hear this sound as a much higher pitched sound. Figure 17.4 illustrates the relationship between the frequency of a sound and its pitch.

The average human being can hear sounds that have a frequency range from 20 to 17,000 Hz, although people with very acute hearing can discern sounds from approximately 15 to 22,000 Hz. Figure 17.5 may help to clarify the relationship that exists between frequency and some readily identifiable sound sources.

Intensity

The intensity of a sound is synonymous with its loudness. Figure 17.6 is a demonstration of the fact that the intensity of a sound can change without having an effect on the pitch.

The intensity, or loudness, of sound is measured in **decibels** (dB). Figure 17.7 illustrates the relative loudness levels of a variety of sounds.

Figure 17.3
The higher the frequency, the higher the pitch. (A) A 20-cycle (Hz) sound; (B) a 200-cycle (Hz) sound.

Figure 17.4 As frequency increases, pitch increases.

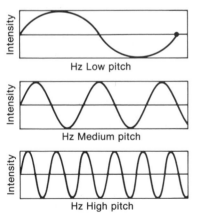

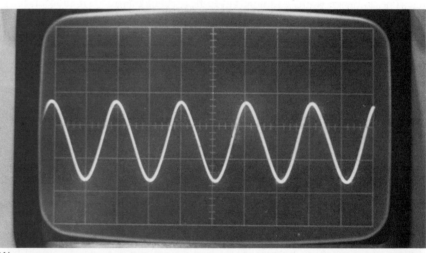

(A)

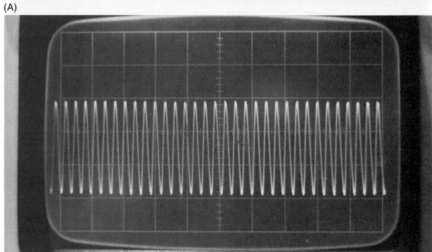

(B)

CHAPTER 17: SOUND DESIGN AND TECHNOLOGY

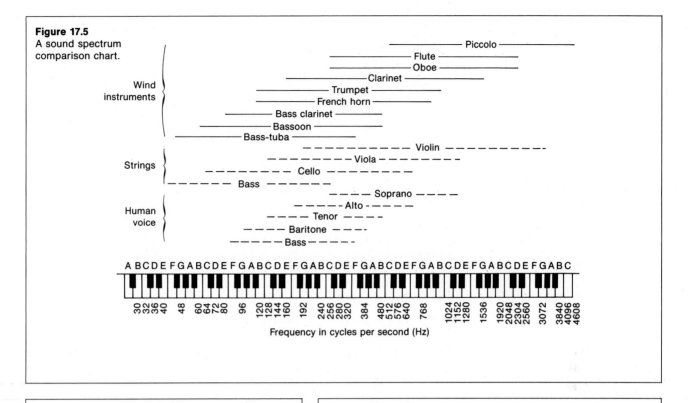

Figure 17.5
A sound spectrum comparison chart.

Wind instruments
- Piccolo
- Flute
- Oboe
- Clarinet
- Trumpet
- French horn
- Bass clarinet
- Bassoon
- Bass-tuba

Strings
- Violin
- Viola
- Cello
- Bass

Human voice
- Soprano
- Alto
- Tenor
- Baritone
- Bass

A B C D E F G A B C D E F G A B C D E F G A B C D E F G A B C D E F G A B C D E F G A B C D E F G A B C

30 32 36 40 48 60 64 72 80 96 120 128 144 160 192 240 256 280 320 384 480 512 576 640 768 1024 1152 1280 1536 1920 2048 2304 2560 3072 3840 4096 4608

Frequency in cycles per second (Hz)

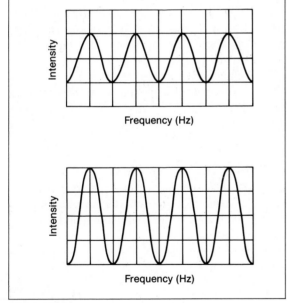

Figure 17.6
Intensity can change without affecting pitch.

Decibels	
130	Jet plane at 100 feet / Threshold of pain
120	
110	Loud rock band at 5 feet
100	Thunder
90	
80	Loud street traffic at 5 feet
70	Normal conversation at 5 feet
60	
50	
40	Quiet street noise
30	Quiet residence
20	Quiet whisper
10	
0	Threshold of hearing

Figure 17.7
Relative loudness of some common sounds.

Harmonics: Frequencies that are exact multiples of a fundamental pitch or frequency.

Reverberate: To reflect in a series of echos.

Timbre

Timbre refers to the distinctive quality of a sound that makes one voice sound different from another or a trumpet sound different from a violin. This qualitative difference is based on the **harmonics** of the sound-producing body.

Pure sounds, as shown in Figure 17.8A, rarely occur in nature. Most natural sound sources (voices, violins, pianos, surf noises) produce a variety of overtones, or harmonics, as shown in Figure 17.8B. These harmonic frequencies are based on the pitch of the fundamental, or base, frequency (Figure 17.9).

The amplitude, or loudness, of each harmonic will be less than the loudness of the fundamental frequency, and the amount of each harmonic in the final tone will be determined by the physical structure of the source. The reason that no two voices or instruments sound exactly alike is that each voice or instrument structure has minor, but significant, physical variations that affect the amplitude of the various harmonics it produces.

BASIC ACOUSTICS

Acoustics is the science that studies the absorption and reflection of sound. In the theatre, acoustics is concerned with the study of those qualities of the stage and auditorium space that affect the audience's hearing and understanding of the sound (language and music) of the play.

A theatre with good acoustics will allow every member of the audience to hear, and understand, the words being spoken by an actor standing anywhere on the stage. An almost limitless number of factors determine the acoustics of an auditorium. The room's shape vitally affects the reflection of sound. If the walls are parallel, the sound will **reverberate,** or bounce back and forth between them, reducing the intelligibility of the spoken word. Severe reverberation in an auditorium can so garble the sound that the audience cannot understand anything that the actor is saying. To reduce the reflection of sound waves, many architects slightly curve the auditorium walls so no wall will be parallel with any other.

The materials used to finish the walls, ceiling, and floor of the auditorium also have a great impact on the reflection of the sound. In general, hard-surface materials (wood, metal, plaster, and the like) reflect sound, and soft- or open-surface materials (cloth, foamed or loosely spun insulation, and the like) absorb sound, as shown in Figure 17.10.

Figure 17.8 (A) A pure tone and (B) its harmonics.

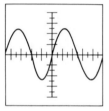

(A)

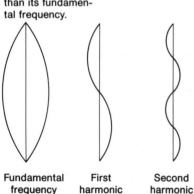

Second harmonic
First harmonic
Pure tone

(B)

Figure 17.9 The loudness of a harmonic will be less than its fundamental frequency.

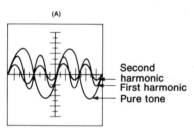

Fundamental frequency   First harmonic   Second harmonic

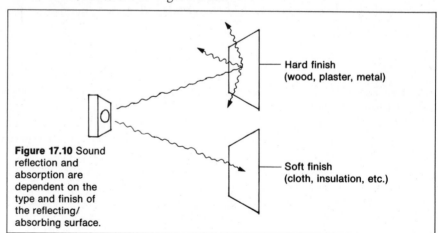

Hard finish (wood, plaster, metal)

Soft finish (cloth, insulation, etc.)

Figure 17.10 Sound reflection and absorption are dependent on the type and finish of the reflecting/absorbing surface.

CHAPTER 17: SOUND DESIGN AND TECHNOLOGY

torium is the use of a complicated and sophisticated sound system. Although the installation of very carefully engineered sound systems may alleviate the problems associated with poor acoustical design, a sound system has not been invented that will completely eliminate the need to have the shape and finish of an auditorium designed with extreme care and expertise.

SOUND PRODUCTION

In spite of what seems to be a bewildering array of equipment used to record and play back sound in the theatre (Figure 17.11), a logical, relatively straightforward set of principles guides the design of any sound system.

Basic Sound System Configuration

Every sound system works on the principles illustrated in Figure 17.12. Sound is picked up by a **transducer** such as a **microphone,** turntable, or other source, which converts it from mechanical energy (the pressure waves generated by the sound source) into electrical energy (a very small electrical signal),

(A)

(B)

Figure 17.11 An open theatrical sound booth located in the house (A) and an enclosed booth (B).

Figure 17.12 Block diagram of a monaural sound system.

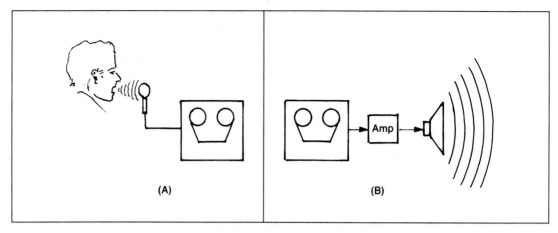

(A)   (B)

Figure 17.13 Block diagrams of (A) equalizers in a recording system and (B) a playback system.

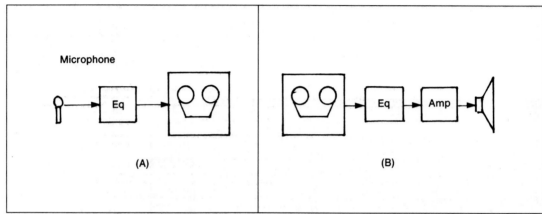

Microphone

Eq

Eq   Amp

(A)   (B)

Tape deck: A magnetic tape transport mechanism used to record an electrical signal on magnetic tape; also used to play back that signal; does not contain a playback amplifier and speaker.

Amplifier: A device used to boost the signal received from a transducer to a level that will drive a loudspeaker.

Loudspeaker: A transducer used to convert an electrical signal into mechanical energy (the movement of a vibrating membrane); converts a signal from an amplifier into audible sound.

Tone: A generic term referring to the intensity of the component frequencies contained in any particular sound.

Equalizer: An electronic device that selectively boosts or attenuates specific frequencies or ranges of frequencies.

Playback system: Devices used to play recorded sound; usually composed of a turntable, a tape deck, or both; an equalizer; an amplifier; and a speaker.

Preamplifier: A device that boosts the level of a signal, without alteration or reshaping, to the requisite input signal level of the next piece of equipment in a sound system.

as shown in Figure 17.12A. The electrical signal goes from the transducer to a **tape deck,** which records the electronic signal on recording tape.

To produce an audible recorded sound, the electrical signal is sent from the tape deck to an **amplifier,** as illustrated in Figure 17.12B. The amplifier increases (amplifies) the power of the electrical signal, so it can drive the **loudspeaker.** From the amplifier the electrical signal is sent to the loudspeaker, which converts the electrical energy back into mechanical energy. The mechanical energy (sound pressure waves) reaches our ear.

Every sound system works on these principles, but the electrical signal needs to be manipulated to control the **tone** (bass, mid-range, treble) and loudness of the sound. To accomplish this function an **equalizer** (a device that manipulates and modifies the signal) is placed in the system, as shown in Figure 17.13. Figure 17.13A shows the placement of an equalizer between the microphone and the tape recorder. The purpose of this equalizer is to modify the signal coming from the microphone to enhance the tonal quality of the sound.

Figure 17.13B shows another equalizer inserted into the **playback system** between the tape deck and the amplifier. The purpose of this equalizer is to modify the signal being fed to the amplifier, which will ultimately change the tonal quality of the sound being produced by the loudspeaker.

The basic sound systems illustrated in Figures 17.12 and 17.13 are monaural, or single-channel, systems. They mix all of the sound produced by the various sources (voices, noise, music, synthesizers, and so on) into one channel. Figure 17.14 illustrates a stereo, or two-channel, sound system. A stereo sound system is actually a paired monaural system. There are two electronically discrete (separated) sources, **preamplifiers,** tape decks, amplifiers, and

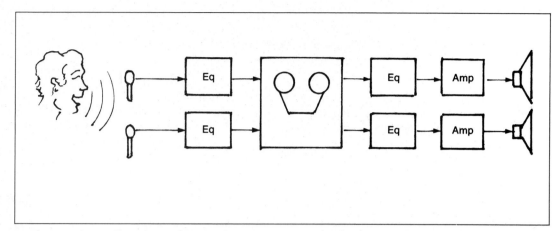

Figure 17.14 Block diagram of a stereo system.

speakers. What makes this rather confusing is that these separate elements are almost always contained in the same housing. Figure 17.15 shows a stereo tape deck and a **graphic equalizer.** Notice that each unit has a complete set of controls for the two separate channels.

Most theatrical sound systems are stereophonic or quadraphonic (four-channel), simply because such systems can produce a more lifelike quality of sound than a monaural system.

Graphic equalizer: An equalizer with individual slide controls affecting specific, usually relatively narrow, segments of the sound spectrum; so called because the position of the individual controls graphically displays a picture of the equalization of the full sound spectrum.

Figure 17.15 Stereo equipment has separate controls for each channel. A stereo tape deck (A) and an equalizer and amplifier (B).

(A)

(B)

he end product of any theatrical sound system is to produce sound that will support and enhance the mood and feeling of the production. Although it might seem appropriate to begin the planning of such a system from the point of origin of the sound (the microphone, turntable, tape deck, and so forth), actually the opposite is true. You should begin planning your system with the selection of a speaker or speaker system capable of producing the best quality sound for the money.

Once an appropriate loudspeaker or speaker system is selected, you will need to choose an amplifier that can drive those speakers efficiently and effectively. Working backward, you will next need to select equalizers and a mixer that can modify the tonal quality of the separate channels of the playback sources and can route the signal from any source to any of the amplifiers.

For planning purposes the recording system can be thought of as being separate from the playback system. In actual practice the average production company or theatre usually doesn't have the budget to purchase two separate systems, so the same equipment is usually used for both purposes.

The heart of the recording system is the tape deck. The deck (preferably two or more decks, so you can dub, or transfer, sound from one deck to the other) should be stereophonic and commercial quality—the best deck that you can possibly afford. A quality equalizer will provide the capability of modifying the tonal qualities of the signals before they are recorded. You will also need a professional-quality turntable for transferring sound effects and music from record to tape, and you will need at least two microphones to record live sounds and music.

Sound reinforcement is also an active part of many theatrical sound systems. In this case the source for the system is a microphone. Regardless of the number and type of microphones used on the production, the signal from each microphone is fed to a sound-mixing console or mixer, where the signals are equalized, balanced, and distributed to the proper amplifiers and speakers.

**Block diagram of typical theatre sound systems:
(A) record,
(B) playback,
(C) reinforcement.**

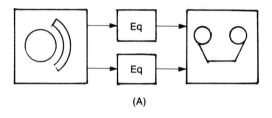

(A)

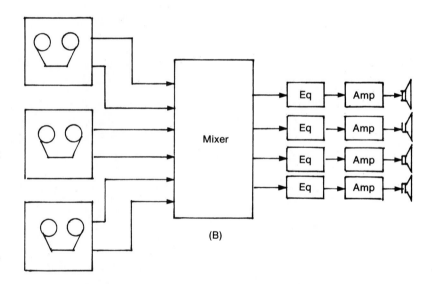

(B)

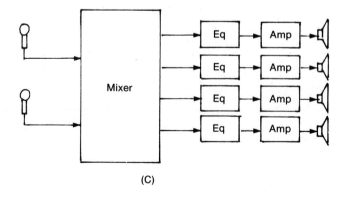

(C)

Sound System Equipment

Each piece of equipment in a sound system has a specific function, as we have seen. The functions of those elements of a sound system are described in more detail in this section.

LOUDSPEAKERS AND SPEAKER SYSTEMS The loudspeaker is a transducer that converts the electrical energy of the signal to a mechanical energy that we can hear. Figure 17.16 illustrates this principle and shows the primary parts of the speaker. The signal activates an electromagnet attached to the loudspeaker frame. The electromagnet generates a magnetic field that corresponds in intensity to the frequency and loudness of the electrical signal emitted by the amplifier. The variation in this magnetic field causes a voice coil, which is attached to the rear of a flexible paper cone, to move the cone forward and backward in a pattern that mimics the frequency and loudness dictated by the electrical signal.

Generally speaking, the quality of a cone-type loudspeaker is directly related to the power of its electromagnet, the rigidity of the speaker frame, and the flexibility of its paper cone. The power of an electromagnet is roughly determined by its weight—the heavier the magnet, the greater the power.

Speakers work most effectively and efficiently when they are designed for a relatively narrow frequency range. Speakers are generally classified as low-frequency (**woofers**), middle-frequency (**mid-range**), and high-frequency (**tweeters**).

Woofer: A low-frequency speaker, with a frequency range from 20 to approximately 150–250 Hz.

Mid-range speaker: A speaker designed to reproduce the middle range of audible frequencies—roughly 200–1,000 Hz.

Tweeter: A high-frequency speaker, generally designed to reproduce from approximately 1,000–20,000 Hz.

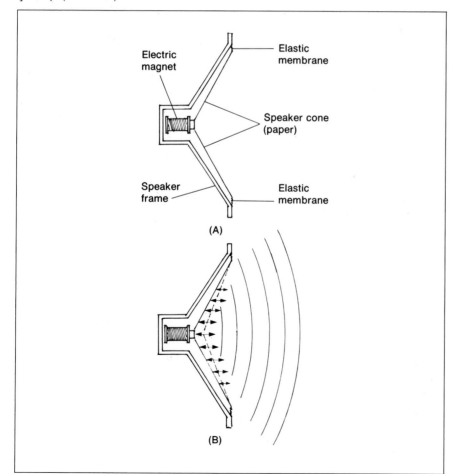

Figure 17.16 How a loudspeaker converts electrical energy to mechanical energy.

Figure 17.17 How a pressure driver works.

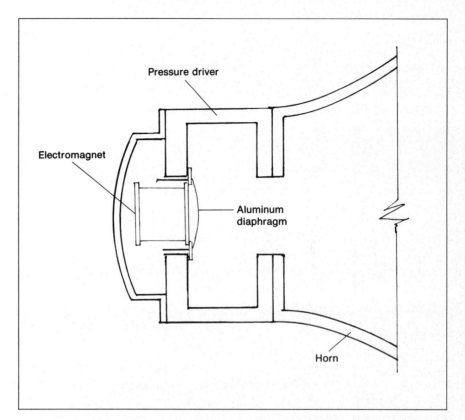

Figure 17.18
Acoustical horns.
(Courtesy of
Peavey Electronics
Corp.)

Almost all woofers are cone-type loudspeakers. Mid-range speakers and tweeters are also made using paper cones, but they are also manufactured using a **pressure driver** and **horn.** The pressure driver (also known simply as a driver), illustrated in Figure 17.17, creates sound in the same way as a paper cone speaker (a signal drives an electromagnetic voice coil, which is attached to a diaphragm that compresses air to create sound waves). The primary difference between the two is that the diaphragm in the pressure driver is made from very thin aluminum instead of paper. The aluminum is stiffer and more resilient and is capable of producing mid- and high-frequency sounds with greater intensity and clarity than a paper cone.

The pressure driver unit is used in conjunction with a horn. The horn is used to direct the sound from the driver in a particular direction and pattern. As shown in Figure 17.18, there are a number of different models of horns. The differing shapes cause the sound to be focused in specific horizontal patterns. The 60-, 90-, and 120-degree horizontal dispersion patterns are fairly standard.

SPEAKER CABINETS Speaker cabinets do more than protect the delicate paper speaker cones from damage. They form an inextricable part of the speaker mechanism, because the sound produced by any cone-type speaker is greatly affected by the shape and volume of the enclosure in which it is housed.

The design of speaker enclosures is very complex, depending on a number of interrelated variables such as the frequency range of the speaker and the volume of the cabinet. However, the operation of all speaker cabinets is based on certain common properties.

Low-, middle-, and high-frequency sounds have differing characteristics. Low-frequency sounds are fairly nondirectional and require more power to produce than mid- or high-frequency sounds. The mid-range and high-frequency sounds are more directional. Because of these characteristics most

Pressure driver: A unit housing a large magnet that vibrates a very thin metallic diaphragm to create mid-range and high-frequency sounds.

Horn: A dispersion device attached to the front of a pressure driver to direct the sound emitted by the driver into a specific pattern.

CHAPTER 17: SOUND DESIGN AND TECHNOLOGY

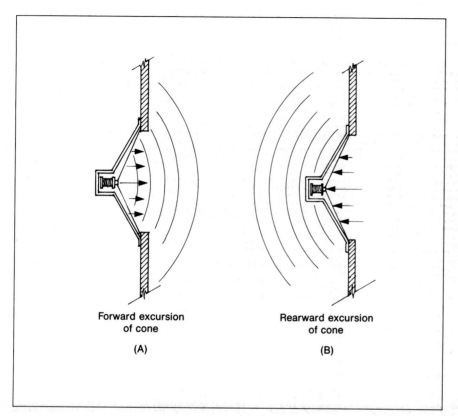

Forward excursion
of cone

(A)

Rearward excursion
of cone

(B)

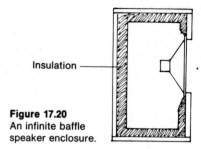

Figure 17.19
A loudspeaker
compresses air on
(A) its forward
excursion and
(B) its rearward
excursion.

Insulation

Figure 17.20
An infinite baffle
speaker enclosure.

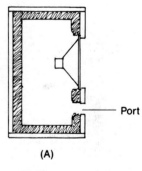

Port

(A)

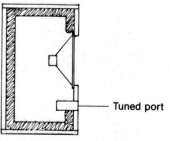

Tuned port

(B)

Figure 17.21
(A) A bass reflex
speaker enclosure.
(B) A ducted port
speaker enclosure.

speaker cabinets are designed to enhance the reproduction of the low-frequency sound spectrum.

When the cone of a woofer moves forward, as shown in Figure 17.19A, it compresses air, which produces sound waves. When the cone moves backward, as shown in Figure 17.19B, it compresses the same amount of air and produces the same amount of sound waves. If the woofer were mounted in a hole in a wall between two rooms, it would produce the same frequency, quality, and intensity of sound in both rooms. Any speaker cabinet is used to do one of two things—either absorb the sound radiating from the back of the speaker into the "room" in back of the woofer or redirect the sound radiating from the back of the woofer to reinforce the sound coming from the front of the speaker.

INFINITE BAFFLE The cabinet design that absorbs sound waves produced by the rearward excursion of the speaker cone is called an infinite baffle. It is basically an airtight box heavily lined with insulation that doesn't let any sound waves out, as shown in Figure 17.20. In practical terms it is relatively inefficient, because it doesn't let the speaker work freely, and it requires a relatively high-powered amplifier to achieve a satisfactory level of sound.

BASS REFLEX ENCLOSURE A bass reflex enclosure is a cabinet with a carefully designed hole or port in the front. This port, shown in Figure 17.21, is designed so the sound produced by the rearward excursion of the speaker cone comes out synchronized, or in phase, with the sound being produced by the forward excursion of the cone.

The bass reflex enclosure is also lined with insulation to absorb some of the low-frequency sound. Otherwise it is distinctly possible that the bass frequencies could overwhelm the mid-range and high-frequency sounds being produced by the other elements of the speaker system.

Figure 17.22
Radiation char-
acteristics of
woofers, mid-range
speakers, and
tweeters.

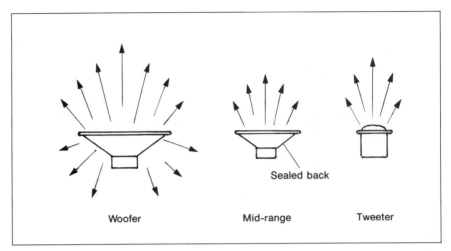

DUCTED PORT Ducted port speaker cabinets are variations of the bass reflex design. Instead of an open port, as in the bass reflex design, they have a tube of a specific length and diameter that projects into the cabinet from the face of the speaker board (the board on which the speaker is mounted). The length of this tube is "tuned" to a specific frequency range to reinforce a particular portion of the bass spectrum.

Speaker cabinets tend to be designed to reinforce the bass frequencies. This is because low-frequency sounds are omnidirectional, and unless they are focused, they spread in every direction from their source, as shown in Figure 17.22. The cabinet provides this focusing function, in addition to reinforcing the intensity of the bass. Mid-range and high-frequency sound waves tend to radiate more directionally from the front of the speaker. In general, mid-range sound waves radiate approximately 180 degrees from the face of the speaker, and the angle of radiation for high-frequency sound waves becomes narrower as the frequency increases.

The backs of most high-quality, cone-type, mid-range speakers and tweeters are sealed with a thin covering of metal to avoid any possibility of resonant interference from the vibrations of the woofer(s) when the smaller speakers are mounted in the cabinet.

CROSSOVER NETWORK Optimum sound is achieved from a speaker when it is designed for a relatively narrow frequency range. For those speakers to work most efficiently, however, they must receive only the specific frequency range for which they were designed. A crossover network, an electronic device normally mounted inside the speaker cabinet, splits the signal from the amplifier into the frequency ranges most appropriate for use by the speakers being used in the system. The woofer receives the low frequencies (approximately 20–300 Hz), the mid-range speaker is sent the middle frequencies (roughly 200–1,000 Hz), and the high frequencies (approximately 800 Hz up to inaudibility) are sent to the tweeter. There is a little overlap between the branches of the crossover network to smooth the transition of the sound as it moves from one speaker to the next within the system.

Crossovers are also designed for two-speaker systems (with a woofer and a combination mid-range and tweeter) as well as speaker systems that use three or more speakers.

POWER AMPLIFIER The power amplifier is a relatively simple beast. Its sole reason for existence is to boost the low-voltage input signal that it receives to a higher-voltage output signal capable of efficiently driving the loudspeakers.

RMS wattage rating: A system (root-mean-square) providing an accurate picture of the energy dissipation characteristics of sound equipment.

Line level: A signal voltage range of approximately .75 to 1 volt; specified as a range rather than one particular voltage because the voltage and current of the signal vary with the intensity and frequency of the sound.

Attenuate: To decrease or lessen.

There are usually only two controls associated with an amplifier—an on-off power switch and a loudness control. The amplifier pictured in Figure 17.23 has two loudness controls because there are two separate amplifiers mounted on the same chassis.

Appropriately, the power rating of the power amplifier is its most important statistic. The **RMS wattage rating** of the amplifier should match the power-loading capabilities of the speaker with which it will be used. If the speaker system can handle fifty watts of steady power, the amplifier should be rated at no more than fifty watts RMS.

It isn't uncommon to find amplifiers rated at one hundred or two hundred watts RMS in the theatre. Rock bands routinely use four-hundred-watt amplifiers to amplify each instrument and microphone in the group.

People frequently wonder why it is necessary to use amplifiers capable of generating so much power. The answer is clarity and quality of sound. A hypothetical, but realistic, example will illustrate the point. An average-sized auditorium may require twenty watts of power to play a musical selection at a reasonable listening level. If there is a momentary peak in the music that becomes twice as loud, it will take ten times the power from the amplifier to accomplish the task. The amplifier must be capable of putting out two hundred watts of power to make the music seem twice as loud. If the amplifier cannot achieve this peak, the music will become distorted and will sound fuzzy and muddy rather than clear and crisp.

PREAMPLIFIER A preamplifier, or preamp (Figure 17.24), is an electronic device that raises the output of a low-level signal so it can be read and processed, without distortion, by the next piece of equipment in the sound system. It is normally used to boost the very weak signal from the magnetic cartridge of a turntable to **line level**, which is the standard input voltage for mixers and equalizers (Figure 17.25).

EQUALIZER An equalizer, as we have seen, boosts or **attenuates** portions of the signal to affect the loudness of specific segments of the sound spectrum. The tone controls for bass and treble on a home stereo integrated amplifier are "broad-band" equalizers that affect a wide range of the bass and treble spectrums.

The equalizer pictured in Figure 17.26 has controls for boosting or attenuating a wide range of the bass and treble portions of the sound spectrum. It also has progressive filtering controls. These two controls, which can be used as a rumble filter (bass), and a scratch filter (treble), progressively filter out

Figure 17.23
A power amplifier.
(Courtesy of Crown
International.)

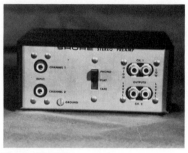

Figure 17.24 A
black box preamp-
lifier is used to
boost a weak
signal to line level.

Figure 17.25 A
block diagram of
the use of a black
box preamp.

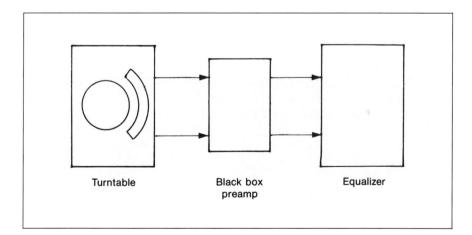

Turntable   Black box   Equalizer
                   preamp

Figure 17.26
An equalizer.

MORE ON AMPLIFIERS

power amplifier does not have the capability of shaping or modifying sound. This is confusing to many people who have home stereo units. Their "amplifiers" almost always have controls that can boost or attenuate the bass and treble spectrum in addition to controls that adjust the volume or loudness of the music.

These home stereo units are more properly called "integrated amplifiers," because they integrate the functions of the preamplifier and equalizer (the shaping of the sound spectrum—bass and treble control) and those of the power amplifier (volume or loudness) into the same piece of equipment.

In professional-quality sound systems, such as those used for theatre sound, it is more usual to provide separate pieces of equipment (preamplifiers, equalizers, and amplifiers) rather than integrated amplifiers in order to increase quality, flexibility, and usefulness.

more and more of the bass and treble spectrums. Although this style of equalizer is still used in both recording and playback, it has, to a great extent, been replaced by the graphic and parametric equalizers.

GRAPHIC EQUALIZER The equalizer pictured in Figure 17.27 is called a graphic equalizer because it graphically displays the equalization of the full sound spectrum. A specific portion of the sound spectrum is assigned to each slide control. When these controls are raised above the center position, they are boosting the specific portion of the sound spectrum that they control. When they are placed below the central position, they are attenuating the same element of the sound spectrum. When they are placed in the center of their movement range, they are not affecting the sound at all.

Figure 17.27 A graphic equalizer. (Courtesy of Ashley.)

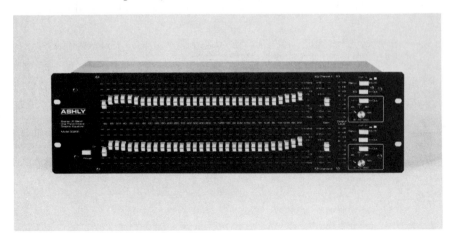

Figure 17.28
A parametric
equalizer.
(Courtesy of Orban
Associates.)

The graphic equalizer can be used during recording to help mask any scratch or rumble noises as well as enhance or shape the sound as envisioned by the sound designer. It is also used during playback of the sound into the auditorium to help balance the sound to the acoustics of the auditorium.

PARAMETRIC EQUALIZER The parametric equalizer (Figure 17.28) is similar in function to the graphic equalizer in that it boosts or attenuates specific frequencies within the sound spectrum. The primary difference is that individual frequencies or very selective custom-designed bands of frequencies can be programmed for enhancing or attenuation with this equalizer. Although it can be used very effectively during recording, the parametric equalizer is primarily used for balancing the sound during playback into the auditorium.

MIXERS The mixer (see Figure 17.29) is aptly named. It is a device that is used to mix the output from a variety of sources and route the blended signal on to other devices. With the increased use of complex sound designs, a mixer has become an almost indispensable part of the permanent sound equipment inventory of a producing theatre group.

Almost all mixers have inputs for microphones as well as line-level equipment (preamps, tape decks, and so on). These inputs are usually permanently wired into a specific control channel. In most mixers each of these channels has the capability to control not only the loudness of the signal but also the equalizing of that signal. The output from each control channel is either hard wired to a specific master control, or it can be assigned to any one of a number of master output controls through the use of buttons, as shown in Figure 17.30.

In operation, the equalized signal from any number of individual control channels is sent to a master control that reroutes the signal to whatever equipment is connected to the output for that master. This electronic capability allows the operator to create a designed mix, or blend, of almost any

Figure 17.29 A sound mixer.

Figure 17.30
A block diagram of mixer operation.

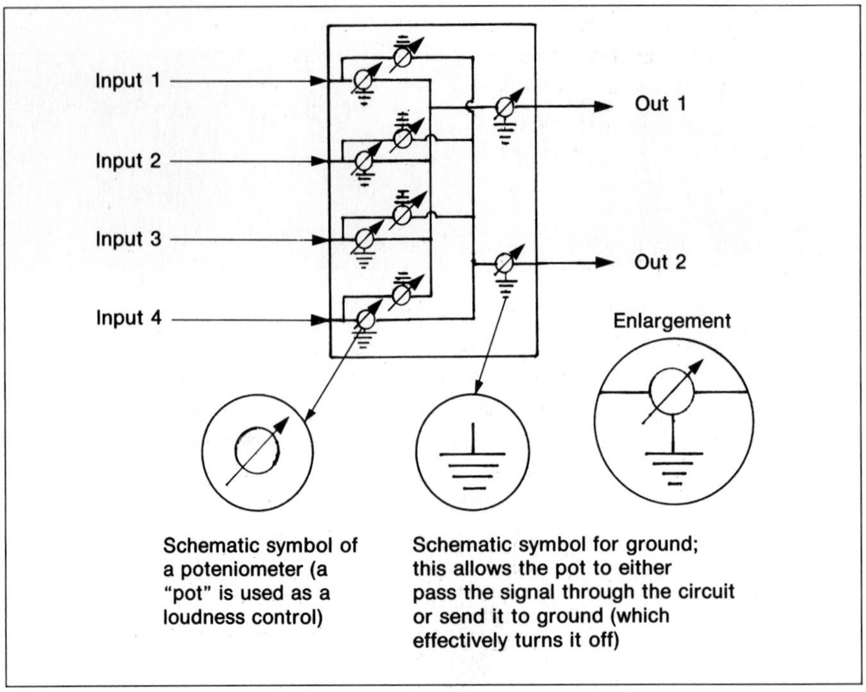

Input 1 → Out 1

Input 2

Input 3

Out 2

Input 4

Enlargement

Schematic symbol of a poteniometer (a "pot" is used as a loudness control)

Schematic symbol for ground; this allows the pot to either pass the signal through the circuit or send it to ground (which effectively turns it off)

Figure 17.31
A block diagram of how a mixer is used in recording.

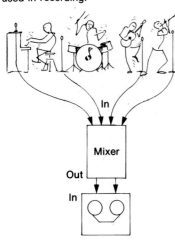

In

Mixer

Out

In

number of sources (including voices, instruments, tape decks, turntables).

In practice, the mixer is used both for recording sound and playing it back. To illustrate how the mixer can be used in recording, let's assume that the production requires a tape recording of a small band. The sound designer mikes the singer and the individual instruments in the band, as shown in Figure 17.31. Each microphone is connected to an input on the mixer. During rehearsal the sound designer sets the loudness and equalization for each of the input sources. Appropriate loudness levels of these individual sources is then sent to two master controls (so the song can be recorded in stereo), where those signals are blended. The outputs of these two masters are connected to the inputs of a stereo tape deck for recording.

The mixer can also be very useful when you need to blend a number of sources during playback. Musical comedies present interesting challenges to the sound designer, who may be asked to blend the voice of one or more lead singers, the chorus, the band or orchestra, and perhaps one or more sound effects. This type of balancing act would be all but impossible without the aid of a mixer.

The lead singers are usually fitted with a wireless (radio transmitter) microphone, the chorus voices are picked up with some general area microphones, the band is either miked or perhaps prerecorded on tape, and the effects are on tape. Each one of these sources is assigned to a control channel of the mixer, as shown in Figure 17.32. As in the previous example, the sound designer determines appropriate levels for each of these sources, and they are blended on the master control(s). In this situation the output signal of the master control(s) is sent to one or more amplifiers and loudspeakers. It is the sound designer's responsibility to ensure that the final mix of these various sources is what is needed to support the mood and feeling of the production.

PATCH BAY A sound patch bay (Figure 17.33) is similar in purpose and construction to the patch panel used in lighting. The sound patch bay is used to cross-connect between the various pieces of equipment (turntable, equaliz-

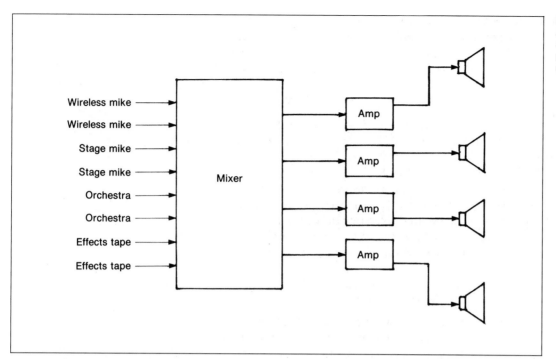

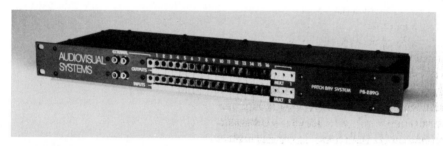

Figure 17.33
A sound patch bay. (Courtesy of Audiovisual Systems.)

ers, amplifiers, speakers, and so on). The output and input of each piece of equipment are connected to a receptacle on the patch panel. A patch cord is used to connect the output of one piece of equipment to the input of another.

TAPE DECK A tape deck transports the magnetic tape on which music and sound effects are recorded. There is a subtle distinction between a tape deck and a tape recorder. A tape deck is simply a transport mechanism for the tape; a tape recorder is a self-contained unit with a built-in amplifier and speaker so it can be used to play back the sound without the need for an external amplifier and speaker.

The tape deck has several functions, which are illustrated in Figure 17.34. The **heads,** which implant electrical data on the recording tape, are vital to the functioning of the tape deck. Top-quality decks appropriate for use in theatre sound have three or four heads. Less expensive models normally have only two heads.

Regardless of the number of heads on the tape deck, they all work in the same way. The head is basically an electromagnet made of a ring of iron, as shown in Figure 17.35. There is a small gap in the ring at the point where the recording tape contacts the tape head. (The gap isn't open; it is filled with a nonconductive metal to prevent it from snagging the tape or filling with dust.)

When an electronic signal from a microphone or other source is fed to the wire wound around the bottom of the iron ring, it creates a magnetic field

Head: A very high quality electromagnet on a tape deck or tape recorder that is used to implant, retrieve, or erase electrical data from audio tapes.

Figure 17.34
Tape deck heads.

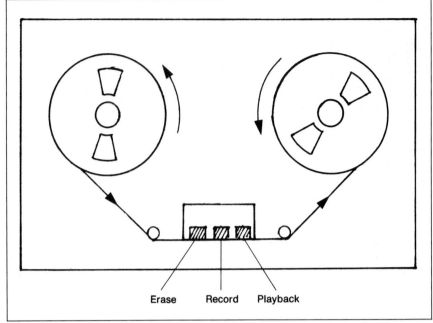

Erase   Record   Playback

Figure 17.35 How a
tape head works
(see text for
details).

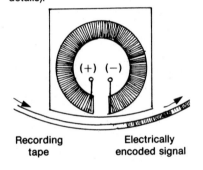

Recording   Electrically
tape   encoded signal

across the gap at the top of the ring. When the tape deck is recording, the strength of the magnetic field across the gap in the head will vary in a pattern that mimics the voltage variations of the electronic signal.

The configuration of a three-head deck is always the same. The erase head is located on the left, the record head is in the middle, and the playback head is on the right. The erase head feeds an ultrasonic (a sound frequency above the range of human hearing) signal to the tape. This effectively scrambles any previously recorded information. The record head encodes magnetic information on the tape in a pattern that mimics the electronic signal generated by the microphone or other source. The playback head is actually a reverse of the record head. The varying density of the magnetic field recorded on the tape creates a corresponding signal of varying voltage within the playback head. This signal, which is theoretically identical to the signal that was fed to record head, is then sent on to the various equalizers and amplifiers to be turned into sound waves.

If a tape deck has a fourth head (which is somewhat rare), it is dedicated to monitoring the tape.

Aside from providing the capability to erase, record, and play back the magnetically stored data, the tape deck must be capable of smoothly transporting the tape at a constant speed. Although a wide variety of tape speeds is available—$^{15}/_{16}$, 1⅞, 3¾, 7½, and 15 inches per second (IPS)—most theatrical sound designers prefer to use 7½ IPS. This speed provides a high quality of sound reproduction (approximately 20–20,000 Hz) with an acceptable level of tape consumption. A speed of 3¾ IPS can be used for background effects and low-level preshow "Muzak" tracks on which its lower frequency range (approximately 50–12,000 Hz) won't adversely affect the production. If the sound equipment is of extremely high quality and tape consumption isn't a budgetary consideration, 15 IPS is often used, because it does provide the highest level of frequency response.

Anywhere from one to three or more motors are used in various models of tape decks to transport the tape. Generally speaking, the more motors the better, simply because the individual motors can be devoted to specific functions (the various playing speeds, fast forward, rewind) rather than having one motor provide all functions through some type of gearing mechanism.

DIGITAL TAPE RECORDING

Digital recording is a new and important advance in tape recording. The principle behind it is relatively simple. In a nondigital, or analog, tape recorder the continuously varying voltage of the signal is converted into a magnetic field by the recorder head. The strength of that field varies according to the frequency, intensity, and timbre of the sound. This continuous signal is recorded onto the tape.

In a digital recorder the signal is converted into a series of individual, or discrete, numbers rather than a continuously varying magnetic field. The signal is read by an analog-to-digital converter forty-four thousand times a second. Each time that the converter analyzes the signal, it translates that information into a binary number—a series of on-off pulses. It is this binary information that is stored on the tape.

When a digital tape is played back, the process is simply reversed. The playback head reads the binary information stored on the tape. A digital-to-analog converter translates each binary number into a signal of a specific voltage and amplitude. The resulting output signal is basically continuous, because the digital-to-analog conversion happens so frequently.

The advantages of digital recording are a significant increase in the accuracy or fidelity of the recording and a reduction in background noise—tape hiss. The price of professional-quality digital recorders is quite high, but continuous technological innovations should bring it within reason in a few years.

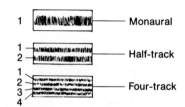

Figure 17.36
Monophonic, stereophonic, and quadraphonic tape tracks.

A variety of track configurations is used on tape decks, as shown in Figure 17.36. Generally speaking, the more tape that comes into contact with the head, the better the sound. Most professional-quality theatre sound is recorded on either full track (for monaural recording), half-track stereo (for stereo), or four-track (for quadraphonic sound).

Almost all theatre sound is recorded on one-quarter-inch reel-to-reel tape decks, because these commercial- or studio-quality decks (Figure 17.37) are readily available and the tape is relatively easy to handle and edit. High-quality cassette decks are also used, but their use is generally limited to preshow and intermission music, for which it isn't necessary either to edit the tape or have an exact cue point.

Cartridge tapes, which were originally designed for use in radio broadcasting, are occasionally used in the theatre. The cartridges use one-quarter-inch tape and are manufactured in lengths that correspond with specific time frames (fifteen, thirty, or ninety seconds, for example). These machines have

Figure 17.37
Tape decks. (Courtesy of Nakamichi and Otari.)

an automatic cuing function. Each time you record something on the cartridge, an electronic pulse is placed on the tape just ahead of the recorded material. Just before the time to play the cue the cartridge is inserted into the machine, which automatically searches for the pulse and then turns itself off. When you are ready to play the cue, you just have to push the play button, and the sound begins instantly.

Although these machines might seem to be the answer to a sound designer's prayers, they do have some drawbacks. It is very inconvenient, if not impossible, to edit the tape inside the cartridge. This means that you have to do your editing on one-quarter-inch reel-to-reel tape and then transfer the sound to the cartridge. Cartridges cannot easily be used for a rapid succession of cues, because once started the cartridge has to run for its full length before it will shut off. It is also necessary to have an individual cartridge for every cue. Although cartridge machines are not an ideal solution at this time, it is distinctly possible that as the development of these machines continues, they will become more and more useful in theatre sound.

TURNTABLE A turntable is used for playing records (Figure 17.38). The turntable platter revolves at a constant speed, and the pickup arm carries the cartridge and stylus (needle), which is the device that actually takes the sound from the record. A turntable suitable for use in a theatrical sound system should have the following characteristics:

1. It should have a heavy turntable. The weight helps to smooth out any variations in the speed at which the turntable is spinning.
2. It should have a reasonably vibration-free mounting. A sponge rubber or spring-mounted base will free the turntable from the effects of footsteps and slamming doors.
3. It should have a lightweight pickup arm. The tracking pressure (the pressure exerted by the stylus on the record) for a high-quality magnetic cartridge is extremely light, and a lightweight pickup arm makes the entire assembly easier to counterbalance.
4. It should be capable of playing at 33⅓ and 45 revolutions per minute (RPM). It is also extremely helpful if the machine has a continuously variable speed capability so the pitch and timing of various sound effects can be raised and lowered.

There is an old joke that asks how many grooves are on a record. The answer is one. The groove of a monaural record contains the sound as a series of structural variations on the sides of the groove, as shown in Figure 17.39A. These squiggles correspond with the frequency variations of the music or sound. The cartridge needle sits in the groove as the record spins on the turntable, as shown in Figure 17.39B. The variations in the groove walls force the stylus to move back and forth in a lateral pattern. The lateral movement of the stylus—which is actually a tiny metal rod that projects up into the cartridge, where it bisects the poles of a very small electromagnet (Figure 17.39C)—sets up minute voltage variations between the poles of the magnet. These voltage fluctuations are the electrical translation (signal) of the mechanical frequency pattern (music) imprinted on the walls of the record groove.

In a stereo record the conversion of the mechanical information (record groove) into an electrical signal is accomplished in the same manner. The only difference is that there are two channels on a stereo record. The informa-

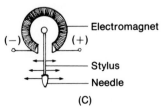

Figure 17.38
A turntable.

Figure 17.39
(A) Top and side views of record grooves; (B) stylus movement in a monaural record groove; (C) how a stylus works.

Top view

Side view showing bottom of groove

(A)

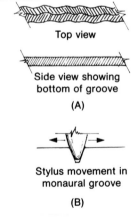

Stylus movement in monaural groove

(B)

Electromagnet

(−)   (+)

Stylus

Needle

(C)

CHAPTER 17: SOUND DESIGN AND TECHNOLOGY

tion for one channel is imprinted on the walls of the groove, and the information for the other channel is imprinted on the bottom of the groove, as shown in Figure 17.40.

Because the strength of the signal generated by the magnetic cartridge is so small, it has to be boosted by a "black box" preamp before it is sent on to the equalizer, mixer, and power amplifier(s).

MICROPHONES As noted, microphones convert mechanical sound waves into an electrical signal. Although the ideal microphone would make this conversion without altering the frequency, timbre, or dynamic range (loudness variations) of the mechanically produced sound, such a microphone, unfortunately, does not exist. There are five basic types of microphone, each making the conversion of sound waves into electrical signals with slightly different techniques and with considerable differences in quality.

CARBON MICROPHONE When the vibrations of sound waves strike the diaphragm of a carbon microphone, as shown in Figure 17.41, they exert minute pressure changes on the granules of carbon. These pressure changes cause a change in the electrical resistance of the granules. The change in resistance causes corresponding changes in a low-voltage current that is applied to the variable resistance of the carbon granules.

The carbon microphone is widely used in the mouthpiece of telephones. It is extremely rugged and has a very narrow frequency response. Carbon mikes are not really suitable for recording theatre sound unless you are trying to duplicate the sound of someone talking over a telephone.

CRYSTAL MICROPHONE Crystal microphones take advantage of the **piezoelectric** properties of certain crystalline minerals. In a crystal microphone piezoelectric crystals are sandwiched between two pieces of metal, as shown in Figure 17.42. Sound waves striking the diaphragm exert pressure on the crystals, and they produce a signal whose voltage variations mimic the pressure changes caused by the sound source.

Crystal mikes have a little better frequency response than carbon ones, and they are also extremely rugged. They are often sold with less expensive tape recorders. They are not of really high enough quality to be used for recording sound that will be used in the theatre.

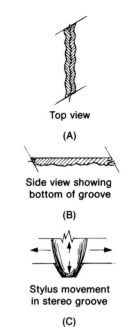

Top view

(A)

Side view showing bottom of groove

(B)

Stylus movement in stereo groove

(C)

Figure 17.40
A stereo record groove.

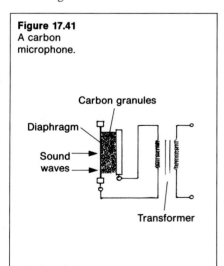

Figure 17.41
A carbon microphone.

Carbon granules

Diaphragm

Sound waves

Transformer

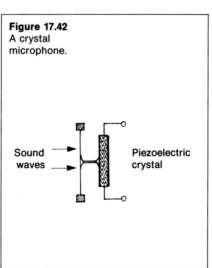

Figure 17.42
A crystal microphone.

Sound waves

Piezoelectric crystal

Piezoelectricity: Voltage produced when pressure is placed on certain crystals.

Figure 17.43
A ribbon
microphone.

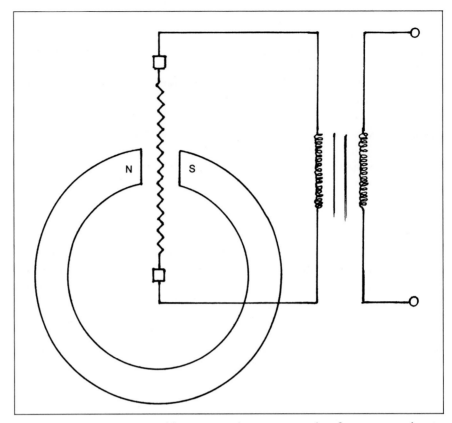

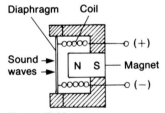

Figure 17.44
A dynamic
microphone.

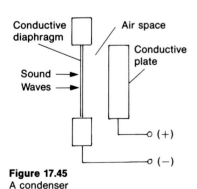

Figure 17.45
A condenser
microphone.

RIBBON MICROPHONE Ribbon microphones are made of a corrugated strip of very thin metal that is suspended between the poles of a magnet, as shown in Figure 17.43. When someone speaks into the microphone, the sound waves strike the ribbon of metal, moving it back and forth within the field of the magnet. This movement induces a small voltage between the two ends of the ribbon. The pattern of this varying voltage is an electrical duplication of mechanical pressure changes produced by the voice of the person speaking into the mike.

The ribbon microphone has a very good frequency response, but it is quite delicate. The ribbon can be easily broken just by blowing on it. High-quality ribbon mikes are frequently used in radio broadcasting, but their delicacy makes them a little too fragile to stand up to the sometimes abusive treatment they receive in the theatre.

DYNAMIC MICROPHONE Dynamic microphones create their signals by inducing a small current in a coil that is firmly attached to the diaphragm of the microphone. The coil is surrounded by a magnetic yoke, as illustrated in Figure 17.44. Pressure changes caused by the sound waves striking the diaphragm move the coil up and down within the magnetic field generated by the yoke, with the result that a current is induced in the coil. The strength of the induced current mimics the frequency and intensity of the sound source. Dynamic microphones have very good frequency response, are rugged, and are suitable for recording of theatre sound.

CONDENSER MICROPHONE The condenser mike is the most electrically complex type of microphone. The diaphragm, which is made of thin conductive material, forms one plate of a condenser, or capacitor. The other plate is placed very close to it, as shown in Figure 17.45. A constant voltage is applied across these plates. When a sound wave strikes the diaphragm, the pressure changes the space between the two plates. This causes a change in the **capacitance** of the condenser, which results in a change in the voltage applied between the two plates. The resultant variations in the voltage are an electrical reproduction of the mechanical pressure changes originated by the sound source.

The condenser microphone is probably the highest quality one used for recording sound in the theatre. It has excellent frequency response and dynamic range (sensitivity to changes in loudness). It needs a power supply, but in most cases a small battery supplies the necessary power. As with any precision instrument, the condenser microphone needs to be handled with care, but it is reasonably rugged and can stand up to the type of abuse that it will receive in theatrical work.

MICROPHONE PICKUP PATTERNS Microphones do not discriminate in what they hear. They will pick up, and convert into an electrical signal, any sound within their pickup range. Several distinct pickup patterns have been developed to assist in making microphones somewhat discriminating.

An *omnidirectional* microphone pattern extends in a spherical pattern around the mike head, as shown in Figure 17.46A. Wireless microphones (see box) frequently have omnidirectional patterns. For stage use the microphone is usually small enough to be hidden somewhere in the actor's costume. The microphone is connected to a small battery-powered transmitter that is also hidden within the costume.

Stage monitor systems, which pick up the actors' voices and send them to various remote locations around the theatre (lighting and sound booths, dressing rooms, and so on) generally use a microphone with an omnidirectional pattern so the voices and noises of the production can be picked up regardless of their location on stage.

The *bidirectional* configuration, commonly referred to as the figure 8 pattern (Figure 17.46B), easily picks up sounds in front of and behind the microphone but does not readily "hear" sounds to its side. Because of their structure, ribbon microphones, which were described in the last section, inherently possess this bidirectional property. They can, however, be designed to have other pickup patterns. This type of microphone pattern is very good for conducting interviews, for recording two instruments when the musicians are facing each other, and for similar situations.

Directional microphone patterns use two primary configurations, cardioid

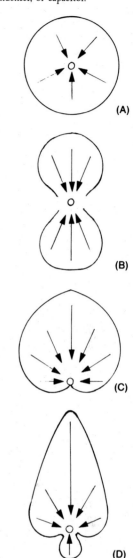

(A) Omnidirectional
(B) Bidirectional
(C) Cardioid
(D) Hypercardioid

Figure 17.46
Microphone pickup patterns.

HOW A CONDENSER, OR CAPACITOR, WORKS

Condenser is actually an obsolete word for a capacitor. A capacitor is a device that has two conductive surfaces separated by some type of insulating material, such as air. The capacitor acts as an electrical reservoir and flood gate. It will store a certain amount of electrical energy. When it reaches its capacity, it allows an alternating current to pass through it as long as the current does not reduce its "full" state. If the distance between the two conducting plates is changed, the "capacity" (more properly known as capacitance) of the capacitor is similarly changed. A greater distance between the plates increases the capacitance; less distance decreases it.

WIRELESS MICROPHONES

A wireless microphone has a significant advantage over its wired counterpart. It does not need a mike cable to connect it to the mixer. Instead, the signal is broadcast by a low-power FM radio transmitter to a receiver and subsequently fed into the mixer.

At first glance the wireless microphone may seem the answer to the sound designer's dreams. However, it does have some significant drawbacks. The batteries that power the microphone transmitter must be checked, and usually changed, for every performance. Since the signal is broadcast, the receiver is also subject to receiving other broadcast signals, as well as other types of interference. In moderate to large cities it is not unusual for wireless microphone receivers to pick up local radio stations as well as the microphones. If more than one wireless microphone is to be used, they need to transmit on different frequencies so the sound operator can monitor the individual performers. Typically, a production requires three to five leading characters to be equipped with wireless microphones. Finally, the systems are expensive. A good-quality wireless microphone, which will transmit and receive within a very narrow frequency range, costs between $1,000 and $3,000.

But even with all of these drawbacks, the wireless microphone provides an excellent method of miking a show. If the challenges outlined above can be surmounted (and they can), the wireless microphone provides probably the finest method of reinforcing the voice in the theatre. The presence attained by having the microphone placed within one foot of the actor's mouth can be matched only with a hand-held microphone; no other theatrical reinforcement system comes close.

and hypercardioid. The *cardioid* pattern, shown in Figure 17.46C, is somewhat heart shaped. It has excellent pickup characteristics directly to the front of the microphone, and the sensitivity falls off as you move to the sides. Once you move past the sides of the microphone, there is almost no pickup from the rear. The cardioid pattern is probably most useful for general theatrical applications. It is very good for recording and reinforcement, because of its characteristic rejection of noise from the side and back.

The *hypercardioid,* or supercardioid, pattern is simply a more directional adaptation of the cardioid pattern, as shown in Figure 17.46D. Although it has a stronger rejection of lateral sounds, it does have an increased sensitivity to the rear.

Any type of microphone (carbon, crystal, ribbon, dynamic, or condenser) can be designed with any pickup pattern. For theatrical purposes high-quality dynamic or condenser microphones with cardioid pickup patterns are the most useful.

As with almost every other type of equipment, a wide variety of microphones are available. A few of the more common types used in the theatre are illustrated in Figure 17.47.

It is all but impossible to determine the pickup pattern of a microphone simply by looking at it. However, every quality microphone will have the manufacturer's name and the model number indicated somewhere on the case of the microphone. When this information is known, the type and pattern of the microphone can be found by referring to the appropriate manufacturer's catalog.

CHAPTER 17: SOUND DESIGN AND TECHNOLOGY

(A)

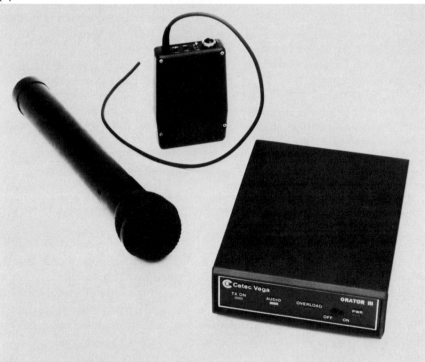

(B)

(C)

Figure 17.47
Microphones.
(A) Hand-held microphones can be held by performers or mounted on stands. (Courtesy of Electro-Voice.)
(B) Wireless microphones use a small radio transmitter and receiver to send the signal to the mixer. (Courtesy of Cetec Vega.)
(C) Pressure-zone microphones (PZM) are very small omnidirectional condenser microphones that pick up, with great clarity and presence, sounds up to ten or fifteen feet away. (Courtesy of Crown International.)

SOUND EQUIPMENT MAINTENANCE

Despite the rugged appearance of some pieces, all sound equipment is basically delicate. The proper functioning of speakers, microphones, turntables, and tape decks relies on the maintenance of physical tolerances measured in thousandths of an inch. All electronic equipment is adversely affected by dust, moisture, and smoke. For these reasons the following procedures should be followed:

1. Never smoke, eat, or drink in the sound booth or around sound (or other electronic) equipment.

2. Cover all tape decks, turntables, amplifiers, and other equipment with cloth dustcovers when they are not in use. While plastic dustcovers will protect the equipment from dust, the static electricity charges that can be generated with some types of plastics can adversely affect the equipment.

3. Store microphones on some type of padded surface in a cabinet.

4. Coil all microphone and speaker cable and hang on a peg board when not in use.

5. Inspect the connectors for all microphone and speaker cables before and after each use. Make sure that there are no loose or frayed wires and that the strain reliefs (where applicable) are in place.

6. Never blow into a microphone when trying to determine if it is "on" or "live." Blowing can damage or get moisture on the internal parts. Don't thump the mike. Speak into the microphone in a normal voice, or gently snap your fingers.

The Sound Booth

The sound booth is designed to facilitate both the recording of cues and the playback of sound effects during the production. The specific layout, or placement, of the equipment in the booth is really a matter of individual taste, but the operator should have a view of the stage when playing the sound during the production. The layout should be both logical and efficient (Figure 17.48).

Figure 17.48
A typical sound booth layout.

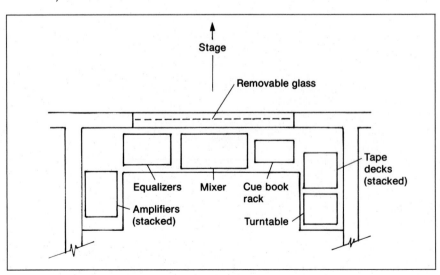

If extensive reinforcement or balancing of a variety of sources has been dictated by the sound design, the sound operator needs to be located in the auditorium rather than the sound booth (see Figure 17.11 on page 393). This configuration is required because the operator needs to hear what the audience is hearing to create a properly balanced mix of the various sources. Although this arrangement may annoy some theatre patrons, the improvement in the balance and focus of the sound mix more than compensates for the slight aesthetic annoyance of having the sound operator and his or her equipment perched in the middle of the audience space.

Rehearsal and Performance Procedures

For a very good reason, the rehearsal and performance procedures for sound are almost identical to those for lights. Both media are intangible, so you must have clear, concise instructions that tell you at what level to set each piece of equipment (preamps, mixers, equalizers, and amplifiers) for every cue in the production. In this way, the loudness level of the sound will be the same from each rehearsal or performance to the next. A sample cue sheet is shown in Figure 17.49.

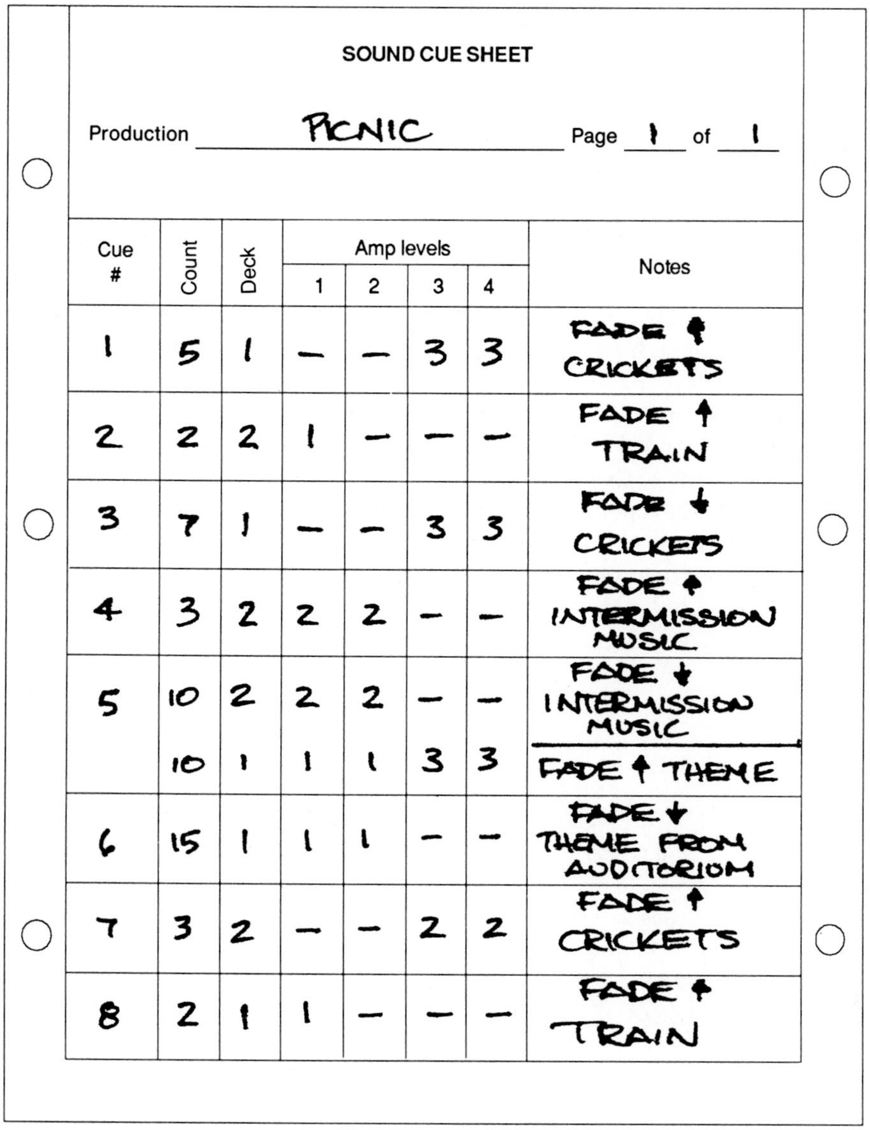

SOUND CUE SHEET

Production: PICNIC Page 1 of 1

Cue #	Count	Deck	Amp levels				Notes
			1	2	3	4	
1	5	1	—	—	3	3	FADE ↑ CRICKETS
2	2	2	1	—	—	—	FADE ↑ TRAIN
3	7	1	—	—	3	3	FADE ↓ CRICKETS
4	3	2	2	2	—	—	FADE ↑ INTERMISSION MUSIC
5	10	2	2	2	—	—	FADE ↓ INTERMISSION MUSIC
	10	1	1	1	3	3	FADE ↑ THEME
6	15	1	1	1	—	—	FADE ↓ THEME FROM AUDITORIUM
7	3	2	—	—	2	2	FADE ↑ CRICKETS
8	2	1	1	—	—	—	FADE ↓ TRAIN

Figure 17.49
A sample sound cue sheet.

The sound cue sheet provides the sound operator with an organized method of recording not only the level of each piece of equipment but also notations on whether the cue is to fade in or start at a specific level. There is also space to make notes regarding anything of importance pertaining to the cue.

Tape Layout

Sound cues are similar in many ways to lighting cues. They are most noticeable when a mistake is made. Comedians have developed entire comedy routines around sound cues that either don't happen or happen too early or too late—gunshots that come three seconds after the trigger is pulled, explosions that don't go off, clocks tolling the wrong time, and so on.

Many of these "glitches" have happened because the tape was not cued up properly. Figure 17.50 illustrates a method of editing a production tape that all but eliminates improper tape cuing.

A four- to five-foot-long piece of white or colored leader tape clearly marked with the word *head* and the name of the production is located at the beginning, or head, of the tape. The first sound cue is spliced to this piece of leader. The point on the magnetic tape at which the sound begins is placed one-half inch from the splice. The tape containing the first cue is cut about one foot after the sound of the first cue has ended. The end of the first cue is spliced to a two-foot piece of white or colored leader tape. *Cue 2* is marked toward the end of this leader tape near the splice for the second cue. The point at which the sound for the second cue begins is again located one-half inch from the splice. The pattern of leader, cue, leader, cue is repeated until either the reel is full or the cues for the show are completed. After the last cue on the tape, attach another six- to eight-foot piece of leader marked with the name of the production and the word *end* in several places. Be sure that this "tail" is long enough to allow the machine to be stopped after the last cue has ended and before the leader comes off the reel. It will make the job of rewinding the tape considerably less frustrating if you don't have to rethread the machine. Figure 17.51 provides instructions on how to splice one-quarter-inch audio tape.

Every reel of tape that is used on a production should be clearly marked with the name of the production and the tape deck on which it will be played. If more than one reel is to be used on any deck during the show, the sequence (*1 of 2, 2 of 3,* and so forth) should also be marked on those reels.

Figure 17.50
A typical tape production layout.

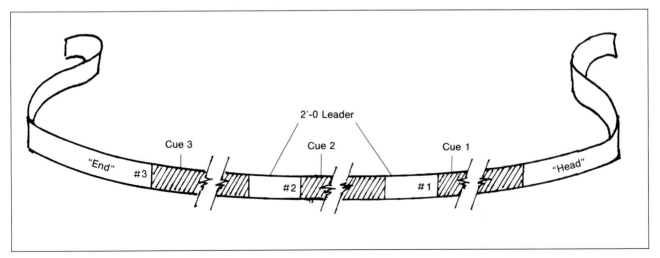

CHAPTER 17: SOUND DESIGN AND TECHNOLOGY

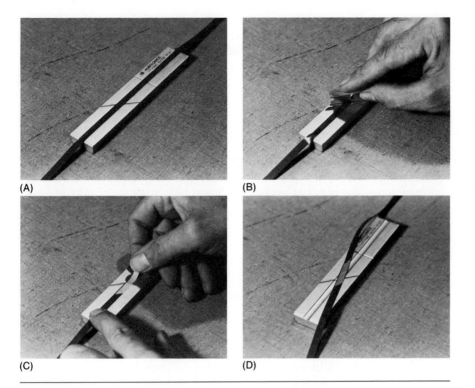

(A)　　(B)　　(C)　　(D)

Figure 17.51 Audio tape splicing techniques. (A) Place uncut tape in a splicing block (magnetic face down). (B) Cut the tape with a single-edge razor blade. Be sure the blade isn't magnetized. (C) Tape the splice with mylar splicing tape. (D) A finished splice.

PRACTICAL CONSIDERATIONS

Every time you hook up a modular sound system (one in which each component of the system is a separate unit), you need to be aware of the input and output levels of the various elements. Otherwise, you could damage or destroy one or more of the pieces of equipment.

Preamp and Power Amp Output

The electronic signal that is created by a sound source (microphone, turntable, synthesizer, and the like) is a low-voltage AC signal. Generally, this signal ranges from about 1 to 750 millivolts, depending on the intensity and frequency of the sound. This very small signal is quite susceptible to interference from almost any device in the vicinity that generates a magnetic field around it. The interference creates noises that range from clicks and hisses to a steady hum, depending on its strength and nature. If the voltage of the signal were greater, however, the effects of the interference would be lessened. Consequently, as soon as the signal is generated by the source, it is usually boosted to line level by a preamp.

Line level is the dynamic voltage range of the signal that is used between the various pieces of equipment of a typical sound system. Because the input and output signal is the same strength (line level) for the various pieces of equipment that make up the major part of any theatrical sound system, it is possible to configure the equipment in any way that suits your needs (mike to preamp to equalizer to tape deck; tape deck to mixer to equalizer to power amp; and so on).

The output of a power amplifier has a much higher voltage so it will be capable of driving its associated speaker system. Depending on the loudness of the sound, a typical power amp output signal can range between one and thirty-five volts. Because of the power amp's relatively high voltage output, its output terminal should never be patched into the input of anything other

A magnetic field is generated around any electrical wire that has current flowing through it. This includes the permanent wiring running through the walls of a theatre, an electric motor, a table lamp, or an extension cord. To minimize the effects of interference caused by these magnetic fields, you need to understand how they are generated. The field takes the form of a cylinder of varying density and size around the current-carrying wire. The size and strength of the field are dependent on the amount of current passing through the wire: the more current, the stronger and bigger it is.

If a cable carrying a sound signal is placed parallel with the offending electrical wire, a strong signal is induced in the cable. This induced signal is heard as a hum or hiss. If the cable is placed perpendicular to the wire that is generating the field, however, almost no signal is induced in the cable.

The effects of induced interference (known as inductance) can also be lessened by removing the sound cable from the vicinity of the power wire. This solution doesn't always work, because when you move the cable away from one power line, you are probably moving it closer to another.

If you have ever been in a recording studio, you may have noticed that the microphone cables look rather messy, zig-zagging across the floor. This frequently changing, apparently random pattern is created to reduce the effects of inductance from nearby power lines.

than a speaker. If you were to do so, you would probably destroy the equipment that the power amp was patched into and severely damage the amplifier as well.

Speaker Hookup Methods

A wide variety of wiring practices can be used to connect a speaker to a power amplifier. Most of these methods can be conveniently categorized as either low- or high-voltage systems.

LOW-VOLTAGE SYSTEMS Most power amps have a variety of output options, as shown in Figure 17.52A. To ensure the best quality sound from the system (and to avoid damaging the amplifier) you should always match the

Figure 17.52
(A) Output terminal board; (B) 8-ohm speaker hookup.

Impedance: Resistance in an AC circuit; the only difference between impedance and resistance is that impedance is defined as resistance to the flow of an *alternating* current.

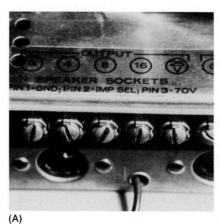

(A)

(B)

CHAPTER 17: SOUND DESIGN AND TECHNOLOGY

Two systems are used for distributing the electronic signal between the various pieces of a modular sound system, unbalanced line and balanced line.

UNBALANCED LINE

The unbalanced line method of circuiting, shown in the top figure, utilizes one insulated conductor wrapped in a braided or foil shield. This shield is protected by an outer covering of insulation. The single conductor carries the signal, and the shield is used as a combined neutral and ground connection.

BALANCED LINE

The balanced line is identical to the unbalanced line, except that it has two conductors wrapped in the shield. One of the conductors carries the signal, and the other acts as the neutral. The shield is used as a ground connection. The balanced line requires the use of two small line transformers, so called because they are connected into the line or cable. One, a step-up transformer, is used at the source; a step-down transformer is attached at the other end of the cable. The balanced line creates a circuit that is basically immune to the effects of magnetically induced interference.

There are two primary differences between the two types of lines. The balanced line (two conductors) costs more and greatly reduces magnetically induced interference.

Balanced lines are frequently employed with microphones used

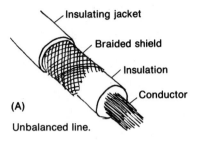

(A)
Unbalanced line.

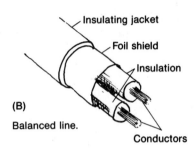

(B)
Balanced line.

to reinforce actors' voices during a production. In these cases it is almost always necessary to run the microphone cables for a long distance before they are fed into a mixer. Using a balanced line for these long cable runs keeps induced interference to a minimum.

Unbalanced lines are normally used to hook up the various pieces of equipment in the sound booth. In this type of situation the cable runs are usually short, which keeps the effects of magnetically induced interference to a relatively minimal level.

impedance of the speaker (normally four, eight, or sixteen ohms) with the output impedance of the amplifier. The most expedient method of matching impedances is to connect a speaker system of a specific impedance to the power amp speaker output of the same impedance, as shown in Figure 17.52B. However, it is frequently necessary or desirable to drive more than one speaker with a single amplifier. This can be accomplished by wiring the speakers in either a series, parallel, or combination circuit before attaching them to the output terminal of the amplifier.

Figure 17.53 Series
wiring of speakers.

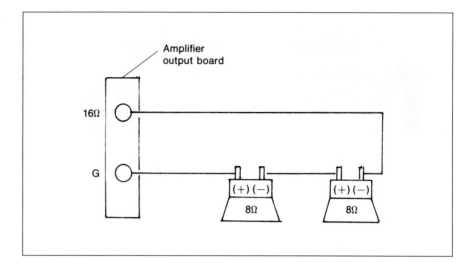

Figure 17.54
Parallel wiring of
speakers.

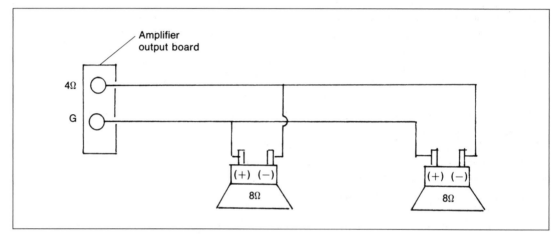

Figure 17.53 illustrates how to wire speakers in series. To determine the total load for a series circuit you simply add the impedances of all speakers in the circuit. In the illustrated example the two speakers each have an impedance of eight ohms. Adding them yields sixteen ohms, which is the total load for the speaker circuit. To achieve distortion-free sound you would connect this circuit to the sixteen-ohm connection on the speaker terminal board of the amplifier.

Loudspeakers or speaker systems can also be wired in parallel, as shown in Figure 17.54. The load for a parallel circuit is determined by the following formula:

$$\text{Circuit impedance} = \frac{\frac{S + S + S}{N}}{N},$$

where S equals the impedance of each speaker in the circuit and N equals the number of speakers in the circuit. In Figure 17.54 each of the two speakers in the circuit has an impedance of eight ohms. Inserting those figures in the formula provides the answer to the circuit impedance:

$$\frac{\frac{S + S}{N}}{N} = \frac{\frac{8 + 8}{2}}{2} = \frac{\frac{16}{2}}{2} = \frac{8}{2} = 4 \text{ ohms.}$$

CHAPTER 17: SOUND DESIGN AND TECHNOLOGY

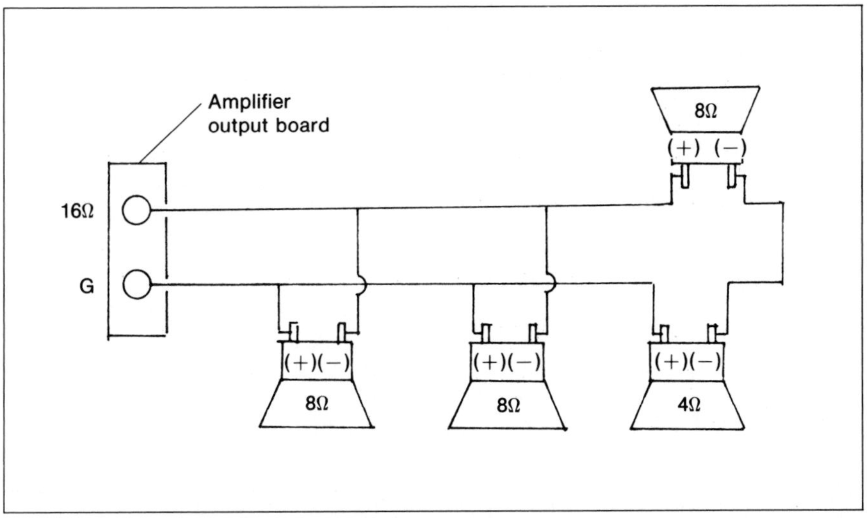

Figure 17.55
Combination wiring
in a speaker
circuit.

This circuit should be connected to the four-ohm outlet by attaching one wire to the four-ohm and the other to the ground or neutral outlet on the speaker terminal board of the amplifier.

In order to balance the impedance of the speakers to the impedance of the amplifier output, it may become necessary to use a combination circuit, as illustrated in Figure 17.55. The combination circuit combines the effects of both series and parallel circuitry. To calculate the total impedance of the circuit you first calculate the impedance of the parallel portions of the circuit. Then, treating each parallel portion of the circuit as though it were just one speaker in a series circuit, you add the impedances of the individual speakers to determine the impedance of the whole circuit.

In general, speakers that are wired in parallel have a cleaner sound than speakers wired in series. Series-wired speakers suffer a slight loss of quality, and the sound may seem somewhat muddy.

Most quality amplifiers are capable of driving speakers or speaker systems whose impedance is from one-half to double the rated output impedance of the amplifier. There will be some loss of quality, but most amplifiers are capable of driving these mismatched loads without suffering major damage. However, it is infinitely preferable to exactly match the impedance of the load with the impedance of the speaker. This solution will produce the best possible sound and will also minimize the chances of damaging the amplifier. The ideal solution to all of these challenges is to have each speaker driven by its own matched amplifier.

To avoid any loss of signal due to resistance in the wire that is used to connect the speaker to the amplifier, all connections where the speaker is less than 50 feet from the amplifier (or wall-mounted speaker outlet terminal) can usually be made with eighteen-gauge electrical wire. When the speaker is between 50 and 150 feet away from the amplifier (or wall-mounted speaker outlet), sixteen-gauge electrical wire can be used. Lamp cord (also known as zip cord) provides a perfectly adequate, reasonably low-cost alternative to the more expensive stereo hookup wire sold in sound shops.

HIGH-VOLTAGE SPEAKER SYSTEMS As previously shown in Figure 17.52A there are often additional speaker output terminals besides the traditional low-voltage four-, eight-, and sixteen-ohm outputs. In the United States these high-voltage outputs have been standardized at twenty-five and seventy volts.

High-voltage outputs have three primary advantages: (1) they provide an effective alternative solution when it is necessary to have a number of speak-

Figure 17.56 High-voltage speaker system.

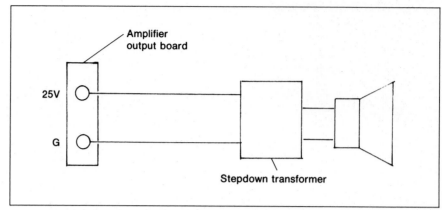

ers on the same system, (2) they transmit the signal over a long cable run with less loss of quality than a low-voltage system, and (3) they reduce the effects of inductive interference.

The high-voltage transmission system steps up the voltage of the output signal at the amplifier. When the high-voltage signal reaches the speaker cabinet, it is first passed through a step-down transformer, which decreases the voltage to a level that will not burn out the speaker (nominally 3.2 volts), as shown in Figure 17.56. If the step-down transformer is not used, the voice coil of the speaker will probably be destroyed.

Determining the proper loading of the amplifier and speakers in a high-voltage system isn't very difficult. The relatively high voltage of the signal pragmatically nullifies the effects of the impedance in the system. When connecting a speaker or speakers to the system, simply make sure that you do not exceed the output wattage of the amplifier with the total wattage of the transformer and speakers attached to the system. Since, in any system, the low-wattage speakers will not be as loud as the high-wattage speakers, the system can be designed to take advantage of this phenomenon. Figure 17.57 shows a typical stage monitor system. The dialogue is picked up by an omnidirectional mike and sent to various locations around the theatre. The higher-wattage speakers are normally located in the makeup and dressing rooms, where the ambient noise level is relatively high. The lower-wattage speakers are used in the quieter offices and box office. A multi-speaker high-voltage system can also be used to distribute sound throughout an auditorium. The higher-wattage (louder) speakers are placed on stage, and the lower-wattage (quieter) speakers are distributed in various locations about the auditorium. While this configuration blankets the auditorium with sound and gives the impression that the sound is emanating from the stage, it does not allow the loudness levels of the individual speakers to be adjusted during the run. To have effective loudness control, each speaker must be driven by its own amplifier.

The step-down transformers used with high-voltage speaker systems normally have several different input taps (terminals) that can be used to vary the wattage associated with the speakers. They also have additional taps that are used to match the impedance of the transformer to the impedance of the speaker.

The contemporary theatre is truly an exciting place to be for someone interested in sound design, simply because what were formerly regarded as "rules" for the "proper" use of sound and music in the threatre have been thrown out, to be replaced with an exciting atmosphere of experimentation and dynamic growth.

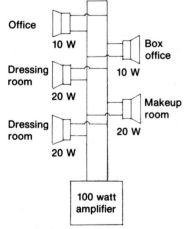

Figure 17.57 Typical application of a high-voltage speaker system.

18

Mechanical Drafting

Diagrams, free-hand drawings, and perspective sketches give a clear, general picture of what a proposed design or prop is supposed to look like, but they don't tell you how to build it. Similarly, sketches, notes, and verbal explanations describing the hanging location of the various instruments used to light a production are frequently more confusing than helpful. Fortunately, mechanical drawing provides a convenient, and efficient, solution to these challenges.

Mechanical drafting involves the use of a drafting instrument, such as a T square, triangle, compass, or template, to draw each line. The object being illustrated is **drawn to scale,** and it is shown from as many views as necessary to provide a clear understanding of the shape of the finished object. Mechanical drawings, when accompanied by **specifications,** provide a complete visual and verbal description of the object.

In theatrical drafting the scale used for the mechanical drawings needed for most scenic construction is ½ inch to 1 foot. This means that each ½ inch measured on a drawing represents 1 foot on the corresponding full-scale object. The width of the flat drawn to scale in Figure 18.1 is indicated to be 3 feet, but if you measured the drawing, you would find that the flat was only 1½ inches wide.

Mechanical drawings, and the ability to produce them, are extremely important in technical theatre. The scenic designer uses them to accurately describe every element of the setting(s) so that those elements can be built as he or she envisioned them. The technical director uses them to show how each object is to be constructed. For the lighting designer mechanical drafting provides the accurate scale "road map" that the electricians will use as a guide for hanging the lighting instruments. The sound designer uses mechanical drafting to show, in exact scale representation, the location of the equipment

Draw to scale: To produce a likeness that is a proportional reduction of an object.

Specifications: Clarifying notes that explain the building materials, textures, or special effects to be used in a design or other project.

423

Blueline: To copy drawings made on tracing vellum; the lines on the vellum are printed in blue or, sometimes, in black; also known as the diazo process.

that will be used in support of the production. The scenic technicians, electricians, and sound technicians must be able to read and understand the information contained on the mechanical drafting sheets, or plates.

DRAFTING MATERIALS AND INSTRUMENTS

The list of drafting equipment used in theatrical mechanical drawing isn't extensive. It includes a drafting board minimally twenty-four inches high by thirty-six inches wide (a larger board of approximately thirty by forty-two inches will be better if you are also going to be drawing light plots); a good T square with a shaft long enough to reach across the width of the drafting board; one eight-inch 45-45-90-degree triangle and one twelve-inch 30-60-90-degree triangle; a pencil compass; an architect's scale rule; an eraser; 2H, 3H, and 4H drafting pencils; and drafting tape.

All drafting should be done on good-quality, translucent drafting paper such as Clearprint or a brand of similar quality. Drawings made on this type of paper can be easily **bluelined** for use by other members of the production design team and the various construction shops. Cheap tracing paper tears easily when an erasure is attempted, and becomes brittle and unusable with age. Tracing paper with grids shouldn't be used, as the lines will interfere with the drawings that you will be making on the paper.

Drafting Board

The size of the drafting board is not too important provided that the board is large enough to accept the dimensions of the stage for which you will be designing drawn to a scale of $^1/_2$ inch to 1 foot. The board is usually made of white pine and may be covered with a plastic laminate. The ends of the board should be finished smoothly or, preferably, covered with a metal or plastic cap strip. The edges of the board must be absolutely straight so the head of the T square will ride evenly on them. (See Figure 18.2.)

If the face of the drafting board is not covered with a plastic laminate, it should be padded with either a sheet of heavy white paper or drafting board padding material. The padding not only makes the drawing easier to see but also prevents sharp pencil points from scoring the wooden surface of the board.

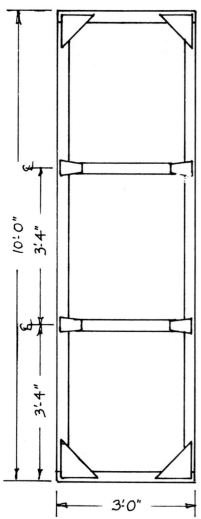

Figure 18.1 A flat drawn to scale.

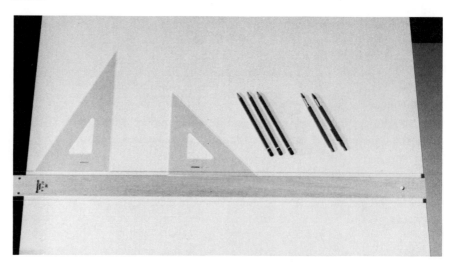

Figure 18.2 Drafting equipment.

CHAPTER 18: MECHANICAL DRAFTING

(A)

(B)

(C)

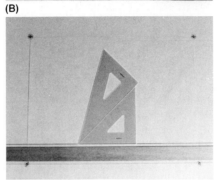

Figure 18.3 How to use a T square.

Figure 18.4 How to draw 15- and 75-degree angles.

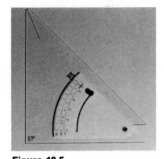

Figure 18.5 A set square.

Figure 18.6 (A) A compass and (B) a circle template.

(A)

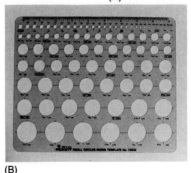

(B)

T Square

The accuracy of any mechanical drawing depends, to a great extent, on the condition of the T square. All horizontal lines are made by placing the head of the T square snuggly against the edge of the drawing board and guiding a pencil along the upper edge of the leg of the T square, as shown in Figure 18.3A. Vertical lines are drawn by placing the base of the triangle against the leg or shaft of the T square and guiding a pencil along the vertical edge of the triangle, as shown in Figure 18.3B. If the head of the T square is not firmly attached to the shaft at a true right angle, neither vertical nor horizontal lines will be accurate. Other types of equipment, such as the Mayline (Figure 18.3C), perform the same function as the T square but are considerably more expensive.

Triangles

Triangles can be purchased in many different sizes, but the eight-inch 45-45-90-degree and the twelve-inch 30-60-90-degree triangles are ideally suited for most drafting purposes. Triangles any smaller than these necessitate shifting both the T square and triangles to a new position to draw a long vertical line. By placing one triangle against another, as shown in Figure 18.4, and guiding both with the T square, angles of 15 and 75 degrees can be drawn.

The set square, shown in Figure 18.5, is an adjustable triangle with two parts joined by a plastic protractor reading from zero to forty-five degrees. A threaded bolt and thumbscrew allow the two halves of the triangle to be locked in any desired position.

Compass and Circle Template

A medium-quality compass (Figure 18.6A) is needed for drawing circles and arcs. A substitute preferred by many drafters is a circle template, shown in Figure 18.6B. When purchasing a circle template select one with a large number of circle diameters, because a template will almost invariably have every size except the one you want to use.

Architect's Scale Rule

The key to making all scaled mechanical drawings is the use of an architect's scale rule. The scales found on the rule make the process of allowing a fraction of a foot to represent a full foot practically painless.

The architect's rule (Figure 18.7) is made in two shapes, triangular and flat. The triangular rule (which is less expensive) has a standard foot measure on one edge and ten different scales, two on each of the remaining five edges: 1 foot to ³⁄₃₂, ⅛, ³⁄₁₆, ¼, ⅜, ½, ¾, 1, 1½, and 3 inches. The flat rule may be a little more convenient to use, but it only has eight scales and is more expensive.

The one-half-inch scale, as noted, is the most frequently used in theatrical drafting. This scale reads from right to left on the architect's scale shown in Figure 18.8A. At the extreme right of the rule is a one-half-inch space that has been divided into twelve spaces representing inches, with each scale inch subdivided into halves by shorter lines. Foot measurements are indicated in multiples of two; they read zero, two, four, six, and so on. Odd-numbered foot measurements, not indicated by a numeral, are found by using the marks for the one-inch scale. These marks fall midway between the numerals of the one-half-inch scale. On the one-half-inch scale the foot measurements are read to the left of the zero, and the inches are read to the right.

Figure 18.8B shows how the architect's scale rule is used to measure a line. One end of the line is placed on a full-foot mark, and the other end of the line projects into the inch breakdown of the scale foot. The length of the line is read by counting the number of feet to the right of the zero point on the scale and the number of inches to the left.

Figure 18.7
Architect's scales.

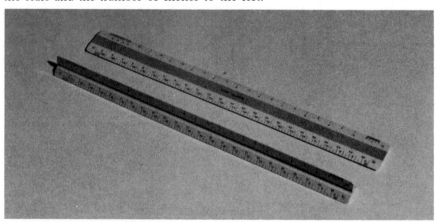

Figure 18.8 (A) A half-inch scale. (B) How to measure the scale length of a line.

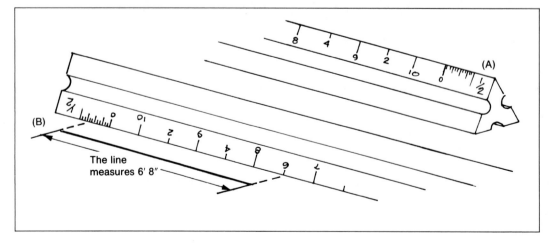

The line measures 6' 8"

Drawing Pencils

Most drafting for theatrical work is done with drafting pencils marked 2H (soft), 3H (medium), and 4H (hard). Drawing pencils (those designated by the letter *B*) leave a blacker line, but they smudge easily and quickly leave both the drafter's hands and drawing instruments covered with graphite. It is much easier to handle and manipulate a long drafting pencil than one that has been worn down to a stub. A sharp pencil is essential for accurate drafting, because only a sharp point can draw a clean, crisp line of unvarying width. The mechanical push-point drafting pencils, which use leads of diameters that correspond to the widths of the various drafting lines—approximately 2 mm for thin lines and 4 mm for thick lines—solve a lot of the problems with dull points that seem to plague neophyte drafters. However, whether you choose mechanical or wood pencils is strictly up to you; the two work equally well.

Eraser

A soft, pliable, pink eraser or a kneadable eraser (Figure 18.9) is the best choice for correcting penciled mistakes. Each removes the graphite without discoloring or damaging the paper.

Powdered eraser, contained in either a shaker can or a bag called a **pig,** can be sprinkled on the drafting paper while the drawing is being made. The movement of the T square and triangles over these particles keeps the underside of the instruments clean and prevents a graphite "shadow" from forming on the paper.

Drafting Tape

Drafting tape is used for holding the paper in place on the drafting board. Drafting tape and masking tape look alike. However, drafting tape will not leave a sticky residue on your drawings, whereas masking tape will.

To tape the paper to the board you will need to adjust it until the upper or lower edge of the paper is parallel with the T square shaft. Use two- to three-inch strips of drafting tape to hold down the four corners of the paper, as shown in Figure 18.10. Commercially available small circular taping tabs can also be used to tape the paper to the drawing board.

Pig: A loosely woven bag containing powdered eraser material.

Figure 18.9
Auxiliary drafting equipment.

Figure 18.10 (A) Use of drafting tape. (B) Taping tabs.

(A)   (B)

DRAFTING SYMBOLS AND CONVENTIONS

The information in this section has been extracted from the United States Institute for Theatre Technology's (USITT) recommendations for standard graphic language in scenic design and technical production. The concept of a standard must evolve from some logical base. In this case that base is the only inflexible rule of technical drawing—that any graphic communication must be clear, consistent, and efficient. Although the USITT recommendations do not contain specific guidelines for the spacing of objects on a plate, any graphic presentation needs to adhere to the general recommendation of clarity: do not crowd or unevenly space individual items on a plate. Equally important, all line weights, line types, symbols, conventions, and lettering should be consistent from plate to plate in a given set of drawings. This does not mean that everyone will be expected to letter in the same manner or draw arrowheads in precisely the same way. It means that each drafter should be able to establish his or her style within the guidelines of the recommended standards and conform to that style throughout the drawings for a particular

Figure 18.11
A ground plan for
1986 Arizona
Summer Arts
Festival, University
of Arizona;
designed by
K. Pistor.

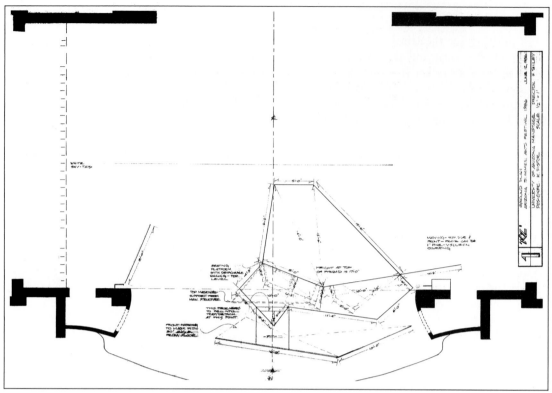

project or production. Finally, the standards and symbols used in any recommended guide should be efficient, both in ease of drawing and in ease of comprehension for the reader.

A great deal of technical theatre drafting is directly related to the ground plan. The USITT-recommended definition of a ground plan is a **horizontal offset section** with the cutting plane passing at whatever level—normally four feet above the stage floor—is required to produce the most descriptive view of the set (Figure 18.11).

Line Weights

The USITT recommends a modified two-thickness line system. This means that the vast majority of the technical drawing will be done with two specific line weights—thin (.3 mm in pencil) and thick (.5 mm in pencil), as shown in Table 18.1. The third line weight, extra thick (.9 mm in pencil), may be infrequently used for emphasis, as for a plate border, suitable section cutting plane line, and so on.

Drafting Conventions

The drawing on the ground plan of standard theatrical units such as chandeliers, shelves, fireplaces, and the like should be made using a sectional cutting plane four feet above the stage floor unless another view would be more descriptive. Using this guideline, an item such as a chandelier would be indicated by a circle utilizing a hidden line style (see Table 18.1), because it does not intersect the standard four-foot height of the cutting plane. The circle should be drawn, in scale, as the actual diameter of the chandelier at its widest point. This graphic would be placed in its appropriate location on the floor plan.

Other suspended objects such as ceiling beams or drops not in contact with the stage floor (for example, an Act II drop on an Act I floor plan)

Horizontal offset section: A section drawing with a horizontal cutting plane, which does not remain fixed but varies to provide a view of important details.

CHAPTER 18: MECHANICAL DRAFTING

Table 18.1
Drafting Conventions

Type	Style	Notes and Line Weights
Plate border		Extra thick Thick two lines
Cutting plane	A A′	Thick
Section outline		Thick
Visible outline		Thick
Hidden construction		Thin
Plaster ceiling and set line	Plaster line	Thin—note indicates type
Center line (all applications)		Thin—label ₵ on axis
Leader line	To dimension Within outline To outline	Thin
Extension and dimension lines		Thin—full arrowhead preferred
Section interior		Thin—evenly spaced at 45° angle to edge of paper or as clarity requires
Break line	Short Long	Thin—both applications
Phantom line		Thin—used when an object repeats between points. Used as alternate position line. Also used to designate location of adjacent parts

Any special lines not listed above should be noted in the legend of each sheet.

Figure 18.12
Single-stroke
gothic lettering.

Single-stroke gothic lettering.

would be drawn in the appropriate outline using the hidden line type.

Another recommended convention involves the drafting of flats on the ground plan. They should be drawn in scale thickness and should have the space darkened between the two visible lines that outline the thickness of the flat.

Lettering

Lettering should be legible, and the style should allow for easy and rapid execution. Characters that generally conform to the single-stroke gothic style shown in Figure 18.12 meet these requirements. Only upper-case letters should be used on drawings, unless lower-case letters are needed to conform to other established standards or nomenclature.

Title Block

The title block should be in the same location on all drawings of a single project. It should be located in either the lower right-hand corner of the drawing or in a strip along the bottom of the drawing. In either case, the block should include the following information:

1. name of producing organization or theatre
2. name of production, act, and scene, if appropriate
3. drawing title
4. drawing number
5. predominant scale of the drawing
6. date the drawing was drafted
7. designer of the production
8. drafter, if different from the designer
9. approval of drawing, if applicable

Dimensions

Use of the following guidelines will help to ensure that your drawings are easily understood by everyone who must read them.

1. Dimensions must be clear, consistent, and easily understood.
2. Dimensions should be oriented to read from the bottom or the right-hand side of the plate.
3. Dimensions less than one foot are given in inches without a foot notation (for example, 6″, 9½″).
4. Dimensions one foot and greater include the whole foot with a single apostrophe followed by a dash and then inches followed by a double apostrophe (for example, 7′-0½″, 18′-5¼″, 1′-3″).

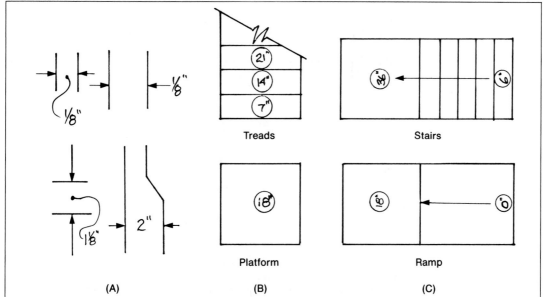

Treads   Stairs

Platform   Ramp

(A)   (B)   (C)

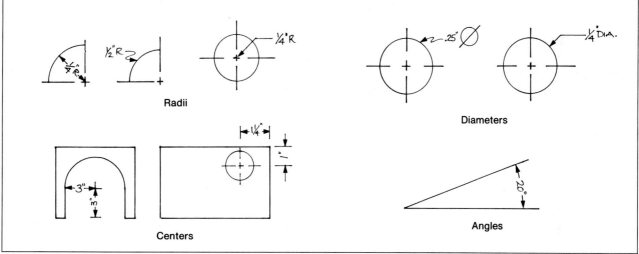

Radii

Diameters

Centers

Angles

Figure 18.14
Methods of indicating radii, diameters, centers, and angles.

5. Metric dimensions less than one meter should be noted as zero, decimal point, and portion of meter in numerals (for example, 0.25m, 0.90m). All measurements one meter and greater should be given as a whole meter number, decimal point, and portion of meter (for example, 1.5m, 2.35m).

6. Dimensions that require more space than available between extension lines are placed in proximity to the area measured, parallel with the bottom edge of the sheet, and directed to the point of reference by means of a leader line (see Table 18.1) as shown in Figure 18.13A.

7. Platform and tread heights are given in inches above the stage floor. Such heights are placed in circles at or near the centers of the platform or tread, as shown in Figure 18.13B.

8. Directions of arrows (when used to indicate elevation change on stairs, ramps, and the like) point away from the primary level of the drawing, as shown in Figure 18.13C.

9. A number of acceptable ways to indicate radii, diameters, centers, and angles are detailed in Figure 18.14.

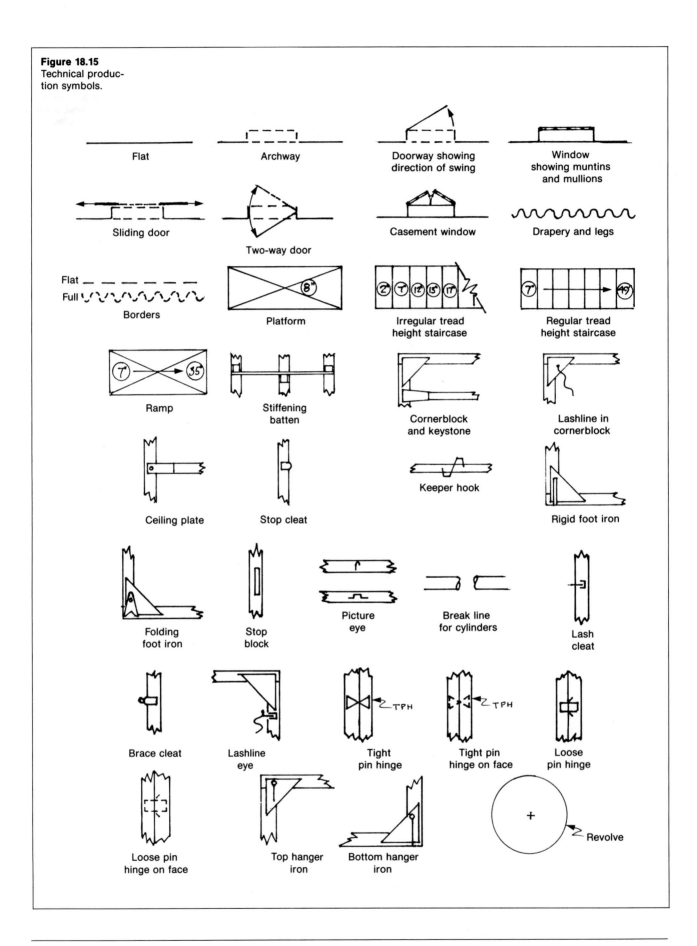

Figure 18.15
Technical production symbols.

Flat

Archway

Doorway showing direction of swing

Window showing muntins and mullions

Sliding door

Two-way door

Casement window

Drapery and legs

Flat
Full
Borders

Platform

Irregular tread height staircase

Regular tread height staircase

Ramp

Stiffening batten

Cornerblock and keystone

Lashline in cornerblock

Ceiling plate

Stop cleat

Keeper hook

Rigid foot iron

Folding foot iron

Stop block

Picture eye

Break line for cylinders

Lash cleat

Brace cleat

Lashline eye

Tight pin hinge

Tight pin hinge on face

Loose pin hinge

Loose pin hinge on face

Top hanger iron

Bottom hanger iron

Revolve

CHAPTER 18: MECHANICAL DRAFTING

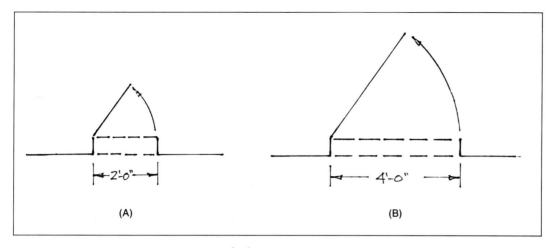

Figure 18.16 (A) A two-foot doorway and (B) a four-foot doorway. Notice that the symbol is the same, only the width varies.

Symbols

Figure 18.15 shows the standard symbols used in theatrical drafting. These symbols should be used as substitutions for drawings of the actual objects.

Objects of nonstandard size, such as doorways, windows, platforms, archways, stairs, and ramps, should be drawn in their actual scale size using the conventions indicated by the symbols for those objects. Using this principle a two-foot-wide doorway would use the convention for a doorway, but the width of the doorway would be drawn in scale to two feet, as shown in Figure 18.16A. In a similar manner a four-foot-wide doorway would use the same convention, as shown in Figure 18.16B, but the scale width of the door would measure four feet. In both cases the depth of the door casing would be drawn to its actual scale depth. Decorative detail on either the door or the door casing need not be indicated on the ground plan unless it alters the depth or width of the door or casing.

TYPES OF DRAWING

Ground Plan

The ground plan is probably the single most important mechanical drawing used in the theatre. Created by the scenic designer, it is a top view of the setting and shows the position of the set in relationship to the physical structure of the stage and auditorium.

Depending on the complexity of the production there may be one or several ground plans. If the play requires a simple single-set interior, a single plan may be able to show the three requirements of any ground plan: (1) the shape of the set, (2) the position of the set within the physical structure of the theatre, and (3) the location of the furniture and set pieces within the set. If the play is a complex multiset show, such as a musical, it may be necessary to have a separate ground plan for each set. There is no hard and fast rule that dictates the number of ground plans necessary for any given production. The guideline that should be followed is that every drawing needs to be clear, consistent, and efficient.

Ground plans are usually drawn in a scale of one-half inch to one foot. Drawings in this scale are easy to read, and the size of the paper, usually twenty-four by thirty inches, is convenient for use in the shop. If you are working in a very large, or very small, theatre, it might be appropriate to use

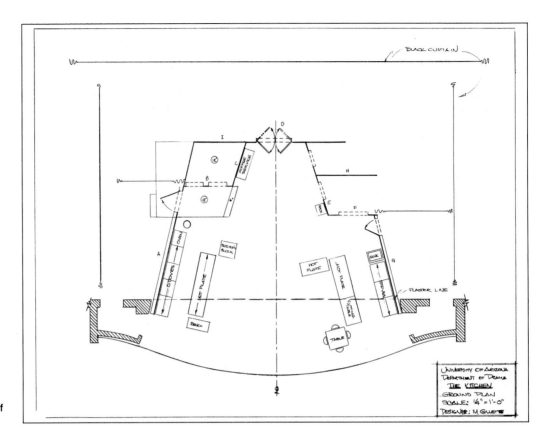

Figure 18.17
Ground plan of
The Kitchen.

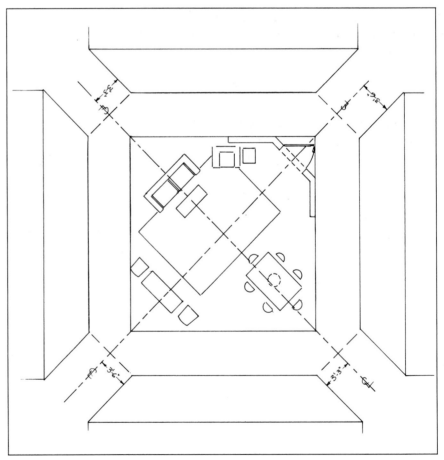

Figure 18.18 An
arena ground plan.

CHAPTER 18: MECHANICAL DRAFTING

a larger or smaller scale for the ground plan. The ground plan shown in Figure 18.17 illustrates all the pertinent data that need to be included on the ground plan for a proscenium production.

The set line is a leader line that extends, parallel with the proscenium arch, across the farthest downstage point(s) of the set. The plaster line is a leader line that extends across the opening of the proscenium arch. The fixed point from which this line normally extends is the upstage edge of the proscenium arch, although any other permanent or semipermanent physical element of the stage or its equipment, such as the edge of the false proscenium, could also be used. The center line runs perpendicularly to the set line from the midpoint, or center, of the opening of the proscenium arch. It extends from the apron to the upstage wall of the stage. The margin line is a nonfunctional, but aesthetically pleasing, line that is placed around the border of the plate approximately one-half inch from the edge of the paper.

Procedurally, it is normally advisable and convenient to draw the structure of the theatre first, then draw the scenery, and finish the plate by drawing the furniture and the margin line. If you are designing for a thrust or arena stage, you will not have a proscenium arch to serve as a reference for your set line and center line. In this case you still need to establish two reference lines that have an identifiable connection with some permanent element of the stage or auditorium space, as shown in Figure 18.18. Most designers prefer to establish two intersecting lines that cross in the relative center of the set and then extend those lines until they intersect some element of the physical structure of the theatre. It then becomes a relatively simple matter to measure from that point of intersection to an identifiable element of the theatre's structure such as a door frame or exposed water pipe. On either a proscenium, thrust, or arena stage these intersecting lines (set and center) are used as the base lines for transferring the scenic designer's ground plan from the drawings to the actual stage floor.

Sectional Drawings

A sectional drawing provides a view of an object as though it had been cut along some imaginary plane. A scenic sectional, also called a hanging plot (Figure 18.19A), shows a sectional view of the stage with the cutting plane of the section being on the center line of the stage. This drawing is used to show the relative position of the set, masking, and various lighting instruments. It is used to help determine trim heights for masking, the heights of various scenic pieces, and similar tasks. A sectional drawing frequently provides the best way of explaining a shape with irregular surfaces, as shown in Figure 18.19B.

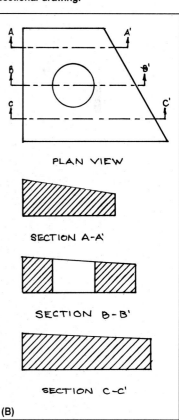

Figure 18.19
(A) Sectional drawing of a stage.
(B) An irregularly shaped object can be explained with a sectional drawing.

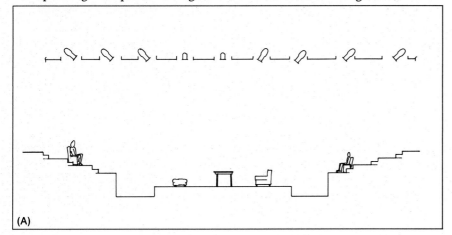

(A)

Other sectional drawings are used for a variety of purposes. The vertical and horizontal sectional drawings that are used for determining sight-line drawings are discussed in Chapter 19, *Perspective,* and the sectional drawings used in lighting design were discussed in Chapter 12, *Lighting Design.*

Front Elevations

A front elevation is a front view of the setting as it would appear if it were flattened out until it was in a single plane, and viewed as though the observer were standing exactly at right angles to it. The purpose of these drawings, usually drafted in a scale of one-half inch to one foot, is to show the location and measurements of all objects that cannot be recorded on the ground plan. As shown in Figure 18.20, the position, size, and arrangement of all structural elements such as walls, doors, and windows, as well as the location of any built-in items, are given on the front elevations. Decorative and trim features on the walls such as pictures, baseboards, chair rails, wainscoting, cornices, and so on are also indicated on the front elevations.

Rear Elevations

Rear elevations show the reverse side of objects depicted in the front elevations. This rear view allows the construction details—placement and dimensions of stiles, rails, toggles, and so forth—to be shown. Rear elevations, shown in Figure 18.21, are normally drawn in the same scale as their front-elevation counterparts. The outline of the flats for the rear elevations is very easily produced by turning the tracing paper that contains the front elevations over, covering it with another piece of tracing vellum, and tracing the outline using your T square and triangles.

Although the responsibility for producing rear elevations is one of the genuinely gray areas of theatrical production, the need for these drawings isn't. Rear elevations must be drawn when the construction crew is inexperienced or just learning how to build scenery. In the professional theatre, where the construction is done by trained theatrical carpenters, rear elevations are not normally drawn for ordinary construction items such as flats and platforms. They are made only when the object to be built is unusual enough to warrant the precise explanation that the rear elevation provides. In those instances the drawings are usually done by the scene shop foreman in consultation with the scenic designer.

In educational theatre the responsibility for the production of the rear elevations becomes fuzzier. Generally speaking, the rear elevations are the responsibility of the technical director. Due to a variety of circumstances, however, the actual drawing may be accomplished by the scenic designer or student assistant designers. Regardless of who actually draws the rear elevations, they are vital, as previously noted, to give student carpenters a precise guide for building every element of the setting. Rewards will be reaped in terms of reduced construction errors, better training techniques, lower costs, better use of time, and less-frustrated (therefore happier) students.

Detail Drawings

Many times the scale of ½ inch to 1 foot normally used in drawing the front elevations reduces the size of some of the smaller set features to the point that it is difficult, if not impossible, to include all the dimensions and notes necessary for a complete understanding of the object. In these cases a larger scale, such as 1 or 1½ inches to 1 foot, is frequently used.

If the smaller features of the set are intricately detailed, it is usually both

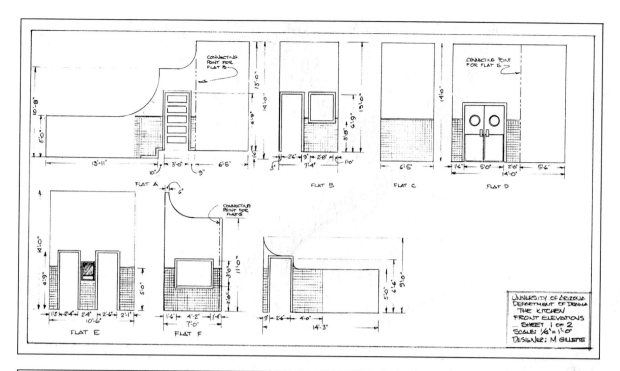

Figure 18.20 Front elevations of *The Kitchen.*

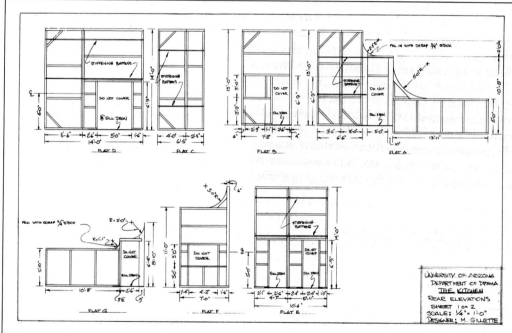

Figure 18.21 Rear elevations of *The Kitchen.*

easier and faster to draw them full scale. This would certainly be the case with the design for a turned banister or the pattern for a wallpaper design. It is much easier to construct this type of object from a life-size drawing than from one that has been proportionally reduced to a smaller scale.

Many features of a setting cannot be fully described by drawing them in top and front views alone. Three-dimensional objects normally require a third (usually side) view to supplement the other two. Objects that cannot be fully described with only a front, top, and side view, such as an elaborate fireplace or an intricately designed stained-glass window, can usually be very well described through the use of orthographic projection, isometric drawing, oblique drawing, or cabinet drawing.

Figure 18.22
Orthographic
projection.

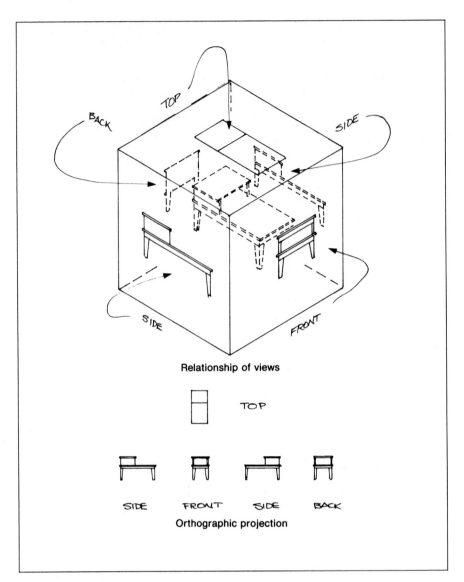

Relationship of views

TOP

SIDE　　　FRONT　　　SIDE　　　BACK

Orthographic projection

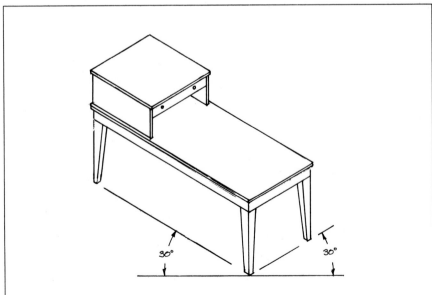

Figure 18.23
Isometric drawing.

ORTHOGRAPHIC PROJECTION Orthographic projection describes an object with a series of scale elevations showing each side of the article, as shown in Figure 18.22.

The different views of the table are each represented by a separate drawing. Notice that each drawing shows the table as if the observer were standing at right angles to that side of the table.

ISOMETRIC DRAWING Isometric drawing provides a fast and easy way of representing an object pictorially without becoming involved with perspective. These drawings are based on three lines called the isometric axes. Two of these axes, illustrated in Figure 18.23, are located at thirty degrees above the horizontal plane on either side of the third axis, which is perpendicular to the base line. Dimensions can be measured at their true length along any of the isometric axes or on lines parallel to them. Lines that are not located on or parallel to the isometric axes cannot be measured.

Since isometric drawing does not take into account the effects of foreshortening or the principles of perspective, it is inevitable that some finished drawings will appear to be distorted. This is especially true of large drawings; the larger the drawing, the more obvious the distortion becomes. Irregular shapes (those with nonsquare bases) are also difficult to draw and, if drawn, may seem to be misshapen.

OBLIQUE DRAWING Oblique drawing is actually a combination of the principles of orthographic and isometric drawing. In oblique drawing one of the faces of the object is placed at right angles to the observer's line of sight (as in orthographic projection), and the other faces subscribe to the tenets of isometric drawing, as shown in Figure 18.24.

If the most complicated surface of the object being drawn is placed in the front view, then the distortion problems encountered with isometric drawing are minimized. The remaining two sides of the object are drawn to the right or left of the front view at angles of thirty or forty-five degrees.

Although the object being drawn will probably appear to be distorted, the advantage of the oblique drawing technique is that it is possible to measure all elements of the drawing that are parallel to the vertical, horizontal, or base (thirty- or forty-five-degree) axes.

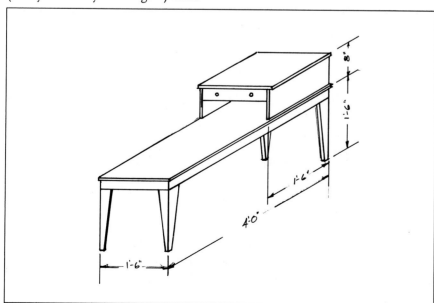

Figure 18.24
Oblique drawing.

Figure 18.25
Cabinet drawing.

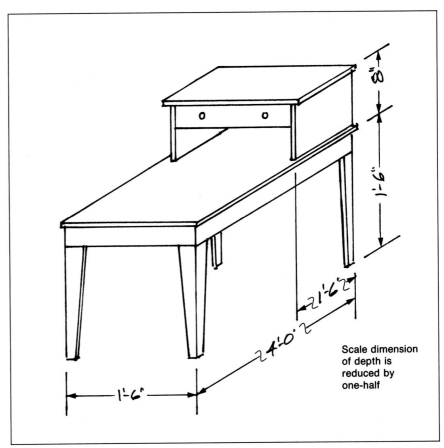

Scale dimension
of depth is
reduced by
one-half

CABINET DRAWING Cabinet drawing (Figure 18.25) and oblique drawing
are similar in every detail except one; the depth or thickness measurements of
a cabinet drawing are reduced by one-half or a similar ratio such as 1:4. This
foreshortening is done in an attempt to reduce the pictorial distortion that
occurs if the depth measurement is excessive.

Two precautions should be taken when using this drafting technique. Be
sure to write the ratio of reduction in a conspicuous place on the drawing
and to specify that the written depth dimension is its true length. The reversed **2** figure placed on either side of the dimension indicates that the
length of the dimension line is not an exact scale measurement and that the
stated figure is the correct dimension.

All mechanical drawings are created for one purpose—to provide clear,
comprehensive visual communication. The standards and guidelines that have
been suggested in this chapter are intended to help you reach that goal. But
don't follow them blindly simply because they look like rules. Remember
that it is the intended application of each drawing that dictates the appearance
of that specific plate. For example, the general guidelines suggest that elevations are usually drawn in a scale of one-half inch to one foot. But common
sense counsels that if another scale will provide a better representation of the
object, that scale should be used. In addition to thinking about the purpose of
each drawing be sure to develop good drafting habits. Keep your work area
and drafting equipment clean; use a "pig" to keep your drawings clean; practice and develop a clear and confident printing style based on single-stroke
gothic; apply consistent pressure to the pencil; and always, always keep your
pencil sharp.

19

The process of perspective drawing provides a sketch with the illusion

Perspective

of realistic depth. The form of perspective drawing that will be discussed in this chapter provides you with an accurate, and relatively simple, method of sketching stage sets from a scale ground plan.

PRINCIPLES OF PERSPECTIVE

The craft of drawing three-dimensional objects on a flat plane so they will seem to have depth is based on an understanding of **foreshortening,** the principle that receding parallel lines apparently converge into a single point, as illustrated in Figure 19.1. In this scene we seem to be looking at a desolate highway stretching into the empty flatness of west Texas. Telephone pole A seems to be closer than telephone pole B because it is taller. The portion of the road at the bottom of the picture appears to be closer to us than the road at the horizon because it is wider. The fence on the right side of the road seems to get smaller as it recedes toward its **vanishing point** (VP) on the horizon. The apparent depth in this drawing is caused by the converging of the parallel lines (the tops and bottoms of the telephone poles, the sides of the road, the

Foreshortening: Representing the lines of an object as shorter than they actually are in order to give the illusion of proper relative size.

Vanishing point: The point on the horizon to which a set of parallel lines recedes.

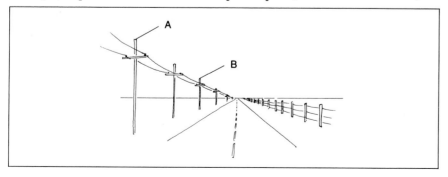

Figure 19.1 The principles of foreshortening.

Horizon line: A line in a perspective drawing representing the meeting of the earth
and the sky; normally drawn parallel to the
top or bottom edge of the paper.

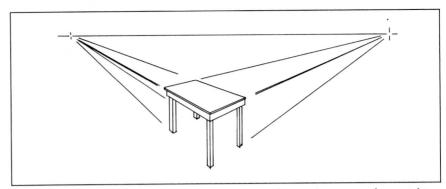

Figure 19.2 Parallel
sets of lines recede
to the same van-
ishing point.

barbed wire strung between the fence posts, and so on) to a single vanishing
point on the horizon.

The basic principles of any perspective drawing can be further illustrated
through the drawing of an everyday object such as a table (Figure 19.2).
Again, notice how all of the parallel lines recede to the same vanishing points
on the **horizon line** (HL).

To draw an accurate perspective sketch you have to know the following
basic information:

1. the distance from the observer to the object being drawn
2. the height of the observer's eye above the object being drawn
3. the size and shape of the object

Figure 19.3 illustrates the interrelationship among these three facts.

You also need to know the relative position of the object in relationship
to a vertical plane that is placed between the observer and the object, as
illustrated in Figure 19.4. You might better understand the principles of this
method of drawing if you think of this vertical plane as a transparent piece of
glass. You are sitting in the auditorium looking through this "window" at
the objects on the stage (in this case, the table illustrated in Figure 19.4B).
A perspective drawing of this table would be created if its outline were to
magically appear on this huge plate of glass, as shown in Figure 19.4C.

You don't need magic to create a perspective drawing; the following
method provides you with the ability. It enables you to draw the outline of
those objects on that vertical plane. The only significant differences are that
the vertical plane is your drawing paper, not glass, and you don't have to be
sitting in the auditorium looking at the stage to create the drawing.

Figure 19.3 To
draw in perspective
you need to know:
(A) the distance to
the object; (B) your
height above the
object; (C) the size
and shape of the
object.

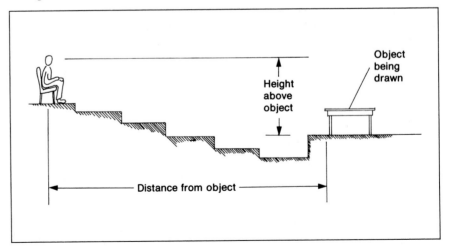

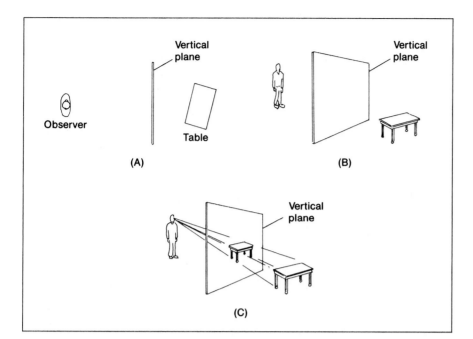

Figure 19.4
Perspective drawing is like drawing the outline of the object on a vertical pane of glass erected between you and the object you're observing.

Vertical plane

Observer

Table

(A)

Vertical plane

(B)

Vertical plane

(C)

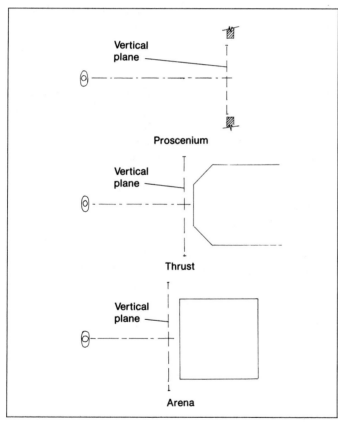

Vertical plane

Proscenium

Vertical plane

Thrust

Vertical plane

Arena

Figure 19.5 The vertical plane for the three forms of stage configuration is usually located in slightly different places.

The location of this vertical plane is the only adjustment that needs to be made when applying this method of perspective drawing to proscenium, thrust, or arena theatres. As illustrated in Figure 19.5, the vertical plane in a proscenium theatre could be placed to coincide with the proscenium arch. For a thrust theatre it would be more appropriate to locate the vertical plane just outside the auditorium end of the thrust. For an arena stage it could be erected in the aisle just beyond the edge of the stage that is closest to the observer.

Floor line: The base of the vertical plane in a perspective drawing; for a proscenium sketch, usually drawn across the stage in contact with the downstage edge of the proscenium arch; in a thrust drawing, normally placed just outside the auditorium end of the thrust; in an arena sketch, usually placed in the aisle closest to the observer.

Experience really *is* the best teacher, so the easiest way for you to develop a full understanding of drawing in perspective is to actually create a drawing in mechanical perspective. Later in this chapter we'll go step by step through several practice exercises.

Creating a Perspective Drawing

Imagine that you are sitting in a proscenium theatre looking at a flat lying on the stage floor, as shown in Figure 19.6. Your seat (observation point [OP]) is in the center of the auditorium, eighteen feet from the proscenium arch, as shown. The flat is lying in the center of the stage floor with its near corner in contact with a line (the **floor line**) that has been drawn across the stage from the downstage edge of one side of the proscenium arch to the other. The sides of the flat make a forty-five-degree angle with the floor line. In this particular seat (OP) your eyes are six feet above the stage floor, which means that the horizon line (HL) is located six feet above the stage floor. Figure 19.7A shows how this information is used to lay out the basic grid used with this perspective method, which consists of only four lines—one vertical and three horizontal.

After you lay out the basic grid and the flat, the next thing you need to do is establish the vanishing points for the various sets of parallel lines. (Remember that in perspective drawing each set of receding parallel lines converges on a specific vanishing point located on the horizon line. The only exception to this rule is lines that are parallel to the floor line—they don't converge; they stay parallel to the floor line.) The flat in Figure 19.7A provides an example of this principle. There are two sets of parallel lines: AB and DC are parallel, and AD and BC are also parallel. Each of these systems of lines (AB/DC and AD/BC) has its own vanishing point on the horizon line.

To establish the vanishing point for lines AB/DC on the perspective grid, draw a very faint guide line, parallel to lines AB/DC, from OP until it intersects the floor line, as shown in Figure 19.7B. (Notice that this guide line for lines AB/DC angles to the right from OP.) From the point of intersection between the guide line for AB/DC and the floor line, drop a vertical line until it intersects the horizon line. This point of intersection between the dropped vertical and the horizon line establishes the vanishing point for line system AB/DC. The vanishing point for lines AD/BC is found in the same way. (The only difference is that the guide line for AD/BC angles to the left from OP.) Draw a very light guide line from OP (parallel with lines AD/BC—which is the same as the angle of intersection between AD and the floor line) until it intersects the floor line. From this point of intersection drop a vertical to the horizon line. This point of contact will be the vanishing point for lines AD/BC.

Figure 19.6 Plan and section layouts for the practice exercise.

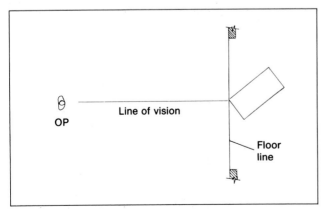

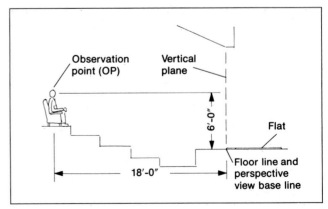

CHAPTER 19: PERSPECTIVE

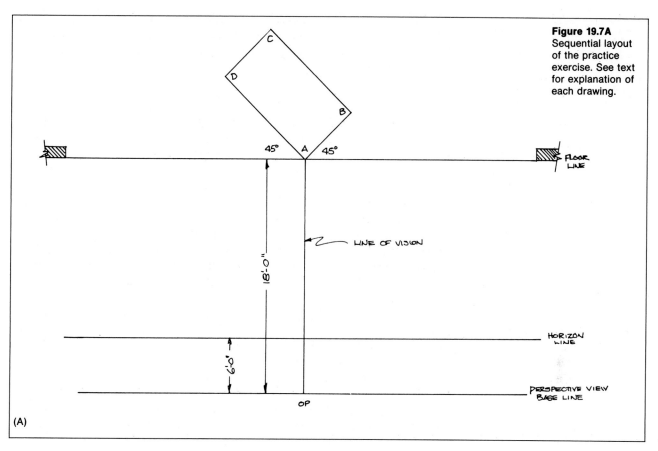

Figure 19.7A
Sequential layout
of the practice
exercise. See text
for explanation of
each drawing.

(A)

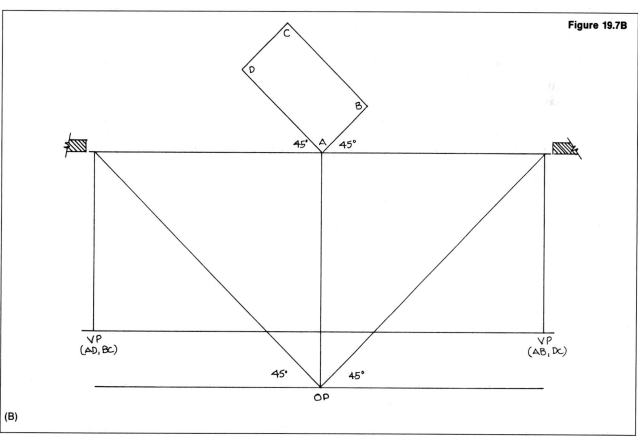

Figure 19.7B

(B)

A basic rule of this perspective method is that any point in contact with the floor line is unaffected by the laws of perspective. Pragmatically, this means that a line can be dropped (a vertical line drawn parallel to the **line of vision**) from any point on the floor line until it contacts the **perspective view base line.** The reason that any point in contact with the floor line is unaffected by the laws of perspective is because the floor line and the perspective view base line are simply different views of the same line. The floor line is a ground plan view of an imaginary line drawn across the stage at some easily identifiable location such as the upstage edge of the proscenium arch. The perspective view base line is the bottom edge of a vertical plane that is erected from the floor line.

Since point A of the flat is in contact with the floor line, a vertical line can be dropped from point A until it contacts the perspective view base line at point A′ (the prime points—A′, B′, C′, and so on—will establish the perspective view of the object), as shown in Figure 19.7C. In this particular case point A happens to be located in the center of the floor line, so the dropped vertical coincides with the line of vision and point A′ coincides with the observation point (OP).

To find the perspective view of line AB you extend a light guide line from A′ to the vanishing point for the line system AB/DC, as shown in Figure 19.7D. This gives you a perspective view of line A′B′ extended, but it doesn't show you the location of point B′.

To find the location of point B′ on line A′B′ extended, draw a light guide line between OP and corner B on the flat, as shown in Figure 19.7E. Where this guide line intersects the floor line, drop a vertical until it intersects line A′B′ extended. This is the location of point B′. (Remember that any point in contact with the floor line is unaffected by perspective, so a line parallel with the line of vision can be dropped from that point on the floor line to the perspective view base line.)

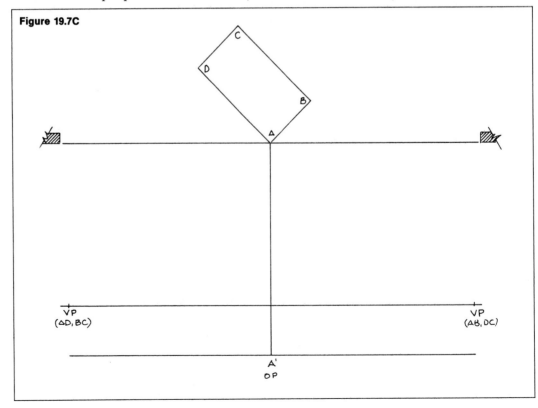

Figure 19.7C

Figure 19.7D

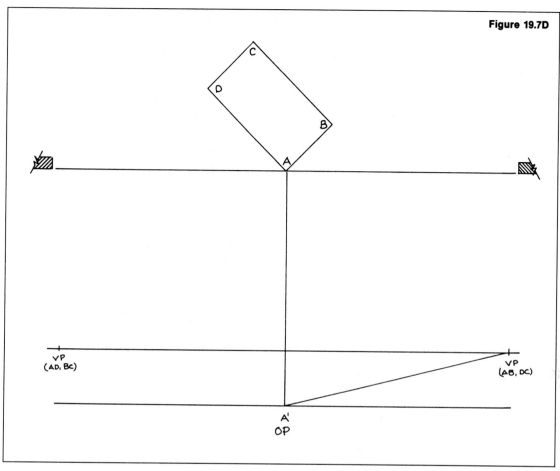

Figure 19.7E

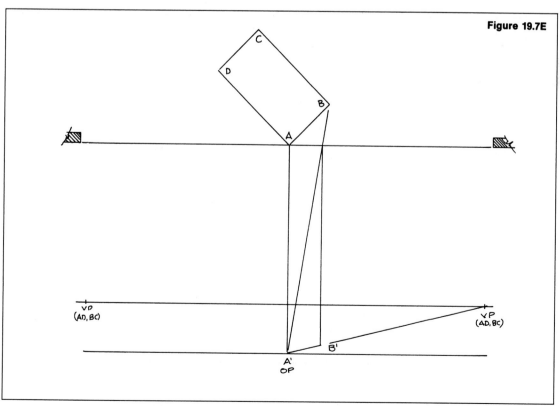

PRINCIPLES OF PERSPECTIVE

Figure 19.7F

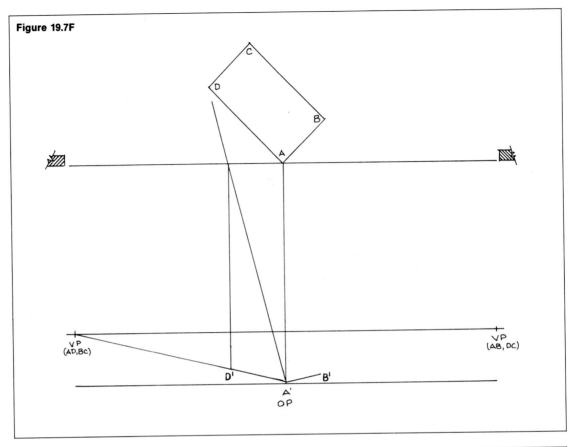

Figure 19.7G

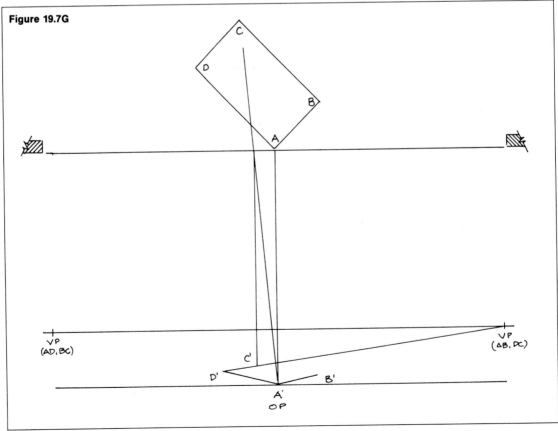

Figure 19.7H

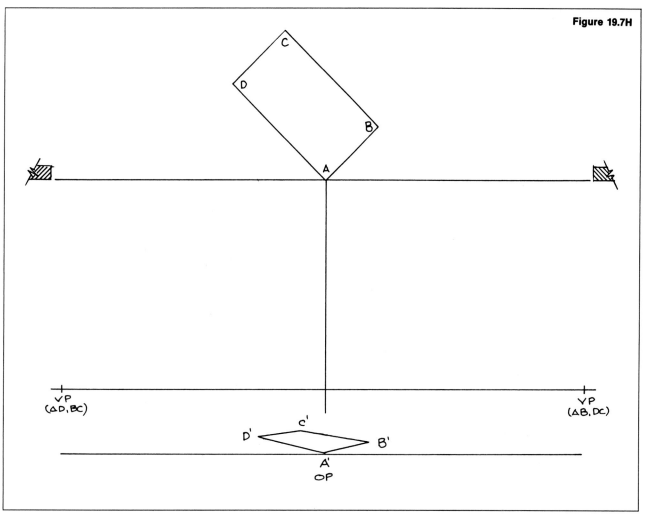

To find the perspective view of line A'D' repeat the process used to find the perspective view of line A'B', but this time use the vanishing point for the line system AD/BC. Draw a light guide line from A' to the vanishing point for line system AD/BC to form line A'D' extended, as shown in Figure 19.7F. Next draw a light guide line between OP and corner D on the flat. Where this line intersects the floor line, drop a vertical until it intersects line A'D' extended. This will be the location of point D'.

To find the perspective location of the last corner of the flat, point C', use the same process you used to find the location of B' and D'. Line D'C' is parallel to line A'B', so they have the same vanishing point (the vanishing point for line system AB/DC). To find line D'C' extended you draw a light guide line from point D' to the vanishing point for line system AB/DC, as shown in Figure 19.7G. To find the location of C' on line D'C' extended, you draw a guideline from OP to C. Where that guide line intersects the floor line, drop a vertical until it intersects line D'C' extended. This point of intersection will be the location of point C'.

To complete the perspective view of the flat you just need to play connect the dots between points B' and C', as shown in Figure 19.7H.

A Review of Perspective Procedure

Before moving on to the perspective exercises, you might want to review the procedure that is used to create these drawings.

1. All of the drawings are made on a basic grid composed of four lines, as shown in Figure 19.8A.

2. The vanishing point for any line or system of lines is determined by extending, from OP, a line parallel to the ground plan view of that particular line until it intersects the floor line, as shown in Figure 19.8B. From that point of intersection a vertical line is dropped until it intersects the horizon line. That point of intersection is the vanishing point for that line system.

3. Any point in contact with the floor line is unaffected by the laws of perspective. Therefore a line parallel to the line of vision can be dropped from that point to the perspective view base line, as shown in Figure 19.8C.

4. A perspective view of a line can be established by extending a line from the point of contact with the perspective view base line to the vanishing point for that particular line, as shown in Figure 19.8D.

5. To find the location of any point on the perspective view of a line, draw a sight line from the observation point (OP) to the ground plan view of that point, as shown in Figure 19.8E. From the point of intersection between that sight line and the floor line, drop a vertical until it intersects the extended line (A′B′ extended, and A′C′ extended).

Figure 19.8 The perspective procedure.

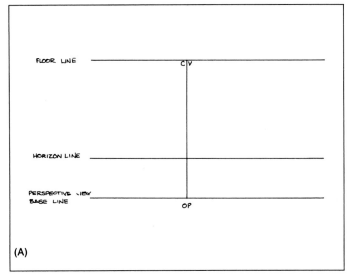

(A)

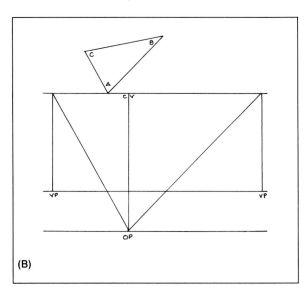

(B)

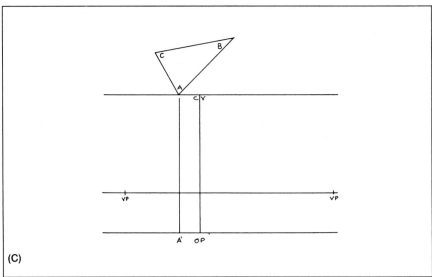

(C)

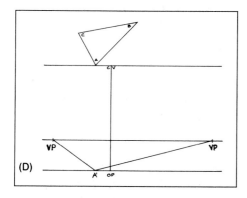

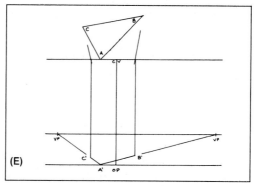

Figure 19.8D–F

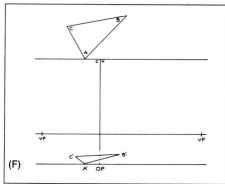

6. After all of the perspective points have been located using the techniques described above, connect those points to provide a perspective view of the object, as shown in Figure 19.8F.

WORDS OF ENCOURAGEMENT

As you wade through the frequently frustrating complexities of learning to draw in mechanical scale perspective, take heart. Every major scenic designer has had the same kind of heartburn. They all had to learn how to draw in perspective. Some of them, such as Ming Cho Lee and Jo Mielziner, received their early training in art schools. Others, such as Peter Wexler, were formally trained as architects. Increasing numbers of rising designers are choosing university educational theatre training. All of them have a common bond—learning how to draw in perspective.

Assimilating the principles of any mechanical perspective technique is difficult. But as with any craft, the more you practice, the easier it becomes.

In reality, the reason for learning any mechanical perspective technique is to train your eye. As you practice, you learn how various objects are supposed to look when they are drawn. As you become adept at using mechanical perspective you will also find that your freehand sketches will start to look better—more real. This is because you *are* training your eye. Eventually you will find that you'll be able to sketch full sets freehand in accurate perspective, and you'll only occasionally need to use the perspective method to monitor or check your work. This kind of proficiency doesn't happen overnight; it comes with practice. But if you have a passion for drawing and designing, the practice won't be work, it'll be fun.

Craft is learned through doing. This perspective method is a craft. The following nine practice exercises, which are arranged in an ascending order of difficulty, provide specific examples of a variety of common situations and challenges frequently encountered in perspective drawing.

Exercise 1

The closer your eye level (horizon line) is to the stage floor, the less you will see of the actual form of some object resting on the stage.

> **Scale:** ¼″ = 1′-0″
>
> **OP:** 36′-0″ right and 8′-0″ up[1]
>
> **Floor line:** 20′-0″ from **OP**
>
> **Horizon line:** 3′-0″ from **OP**
>
> **Perspective view base line:** extends horizontally through **OP**
>
> **Object being drawn:** an 8′-0″ square resting on the stage floor with its sides at a 45-degree angle to the floor line and the near corner (**A**) in contact with the floor line at the line of vision.

Figure 19.9
Exercise 1.

PROCEDURE No new challenges have been introduced here, so you can follow the procedure summarized in the previous section to do this exercise.

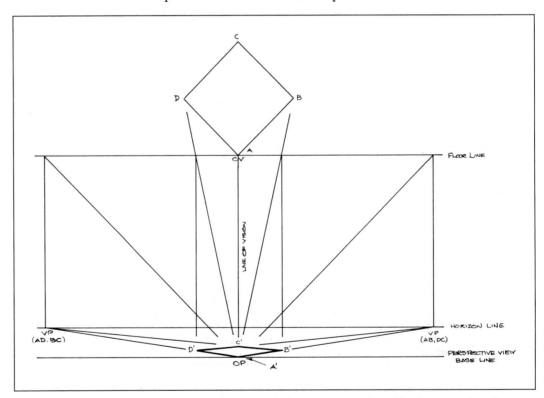

1. These dimensions are intended to help you center your drawing in the middle of a 12 × 18 sheet of paper. By measuring, in quarter-inch scale, 36′-0″ to the right of the lower left-hand corner, and 8′-0″ up from the bottom edge of the sheet of paper, the observation point (**OP**) will be placed in a position that will center the perspective exercise in the middle of the paper. These dimensions don't have a thing to do with drawing in perspective; they just help to make the whole sheet look attractive and balanced. These exercises won't fit on a sheet smaller than 10 × 14, but if you are using paper larger than 12 × 18, just center the **OP** about one-quarter or one-third of the way up from the bottom of the sheet.

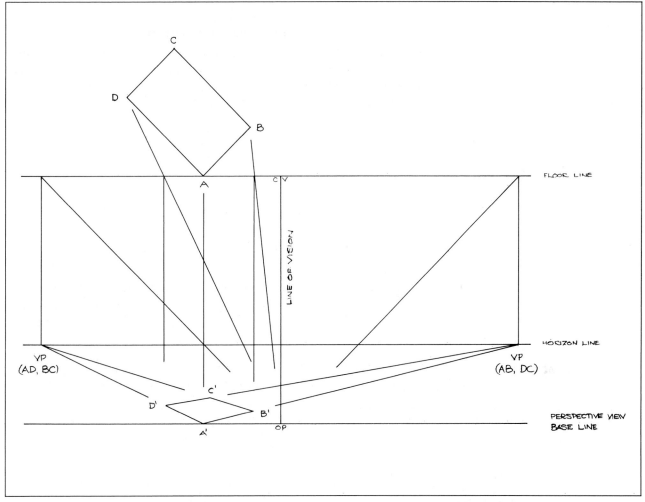

Exercise 2

Figure 19.10
Exercise 2.

The second exercise shows what to do if an object contacts the floor line in some location other than the point of intersection between the floor line and the line of vision.

Scale: ¼″ = 1′-0″

OP: 36′-0″ right and 8′-0″ up

Floor line: 22′-0″ from **OP**

Horizon line: 7′-0″ from **OP**

Perspective view base line: extends horizontally through **OP**

Object being drawn: a flat 6′-0″ by 10′-0″ with its sides at a 45-degree angle to the floor line. The near corner (**A**) is in contact with the floor line and 7′-0″ to the left of the intersection between the line of vision and the floor line.

PROCEDURE Since the corner of the flat (**A**) is in contact with the floor line, it is unaffected by the laws of perspective. A vertical can be dropped from point **A** until it intersects the perspective view base line, as shown in Figure 19.10. This point will be the perspective location of point **A′**.

After determining the location of **A′**, the rest of the exercise can be done using the procedure summarized in the previous section.

Finding the perspective of an object that has height, as well as width and length, requires an additional step in the perspective procedure.

Scale: ¼″ = 1′-0″

OP: 50′-0″ right and 8′-0″ up

Floor line: 23′-0″ from **OP**

Horizon line: 8′-0″ from **OP**

Perspective view base line: extends horizontally through **OP**

Object being drawn: a platform 8′-0″ square by 3′-6″ high is placed on the stage with its sides forming 30- and 60-degree angles with the floor line. Corner **A** is in contact with the floor line and 12′-0″ to the left of the intersection of the floor line and the line of vision.

PROCEDURE Any point in contact with the floor line is unaffected by the laws of perspective. Corner **A** of the platform is in contact with the floor line, so a vertical can be dropped to the perspective view base line to determine the perspective location of **A′**. Since this point (**A′**) is similarly unaffected by perspective, it is possible to determine the height of the platform by measuring the true vertical distance from **A′**.

Along a light vertical guide line erected from **A′** lay out, in scale, the 3′-6″ height of the platform. This distance will determine the perspective location of point **A″**, which is the top of the front corner of the platform.

Draw guide lines from both **A′** and **A″** to the vanishing point for the **AB/DC** line system. The perspective location of corner **B** of the platform will be the point where these lines (the guide lines drawn between **A′** and **A″** and the vanishing point for the **AB/DC** line system) are intersected by the vertical dropped from the point of intersection between the floor line and a sight line drawn between **OP** and **B**, as shown in Figure 19.11.

Figure 19.11
Exercise 3.

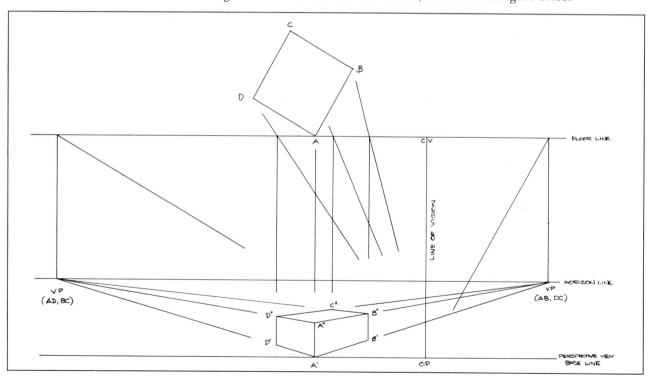

The perspective view of the other face (**A′D′/A″D″**) of the platform is determined in the same manner, except that you use the vanishing point for the line system **DA/BC**.

The perspective view of the two upstage edges of the platform (**B″C″** and **D″C″**) are determined by drawing lines between **D″** and the vanishing point for the **AB/DC** line system and between **B″** and the vanishing point for the **AD/BC** line system. Where these two lines intersect will be the location of **C″**.

Point **C″** can also be located in the conventional manner by drawing a sight line from **OP** to **C**. Where the sight line crosses the **floor line**, a vertical can be dropped until it intersects line **B″C″** extended or **D″C″** extended. This will be the location of **C″**.

Exercise 4

Drawing a perspective view of an object that is not in contact with the floor line adds one more step to the procedure but uses the same principles.

Scale: ¼″ = 1′-0″

OP: 40′-0″ right and 10′-0″ up

Floor line: 20′-0″ from **OP**

Horizon line: 8′-0″ from **OP**

Perspective view base line: extends horizontally through **OP**

Object being drawn: a small flat, 6′-0″ by 10′-0″, lying on the stage floor with its sides at a 45-degree angle to the floor line. The near corner **A** is 4′-6″ to the left of the intersection between the floor line and the line of vision and 2′-6″ upstage of it.

PROCEDURE Extend the line that forms one side of the flat (**DA**) until it intersects the floor line (**X**). Since any point in contact with the floor line is

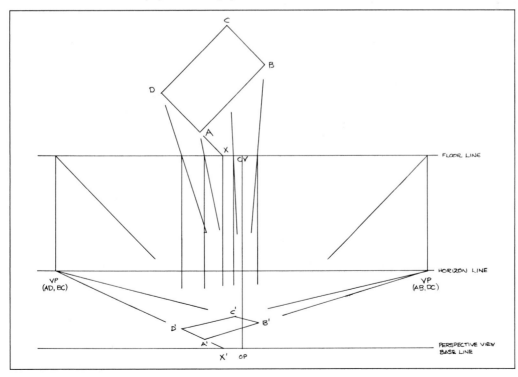

Figure 19.12
Exercise 4.

unaffected by the laws of perspective, a vertical can be dropped to the perspective view base line to determine the perspective location of point **X′**. Draw a light guide line between **X′** and the vanishing point for line system **AD/BC**. The locations of points **A′** and **D′** are determined in the usual manner. Sight lines are drawn between **OP** and points **A** and **D**. Where those sight lines cross the floor line, verticals are dropped until they intersect the guide line drawn between **X′** and the vanishing point for line system **AD/BC**.

The perspective view of the rest of the flat is determined using the same principles used in the previous exercises. Guide lines are drawn between **A′** and **D′** and the vanishing point for line system **AB/DC**. Sight lines are drawn between **OP** and points **B** and **C**. Where those sight lines cross the floor line, verticals are dropped until they intersect the guide lines drawn between **A′**, **D′** and the vanishing point for line system **AB/DC**. These points of intersection will be the location of **B′** and **C′**.

Exercise 5

Drawing a perspective view of an object whose sides are either parallel with or perpendicular to the floor line doesn't differ in principle from the procedures that have been previously established.

Scale: ¼″ = 1′-0″

OP: 36′-0″ right and 8′-0″ up

Floor line: 20′-0″ from **OP**

Horizon line: 3′-0″ from **OP**

Perspective view base line: extends horizontally through **OP**

Object being drawn: a large rectangular ceiling flat, 10′-10″ by 14′-0″, lying on the stage floor with its longer side parallel with, and 2′-0″ upstage from, the floor line. Notice that the floor line has been placed at the outer face of the proscenium arch to facilitate your creating a perspective drawing of the arch. The proscenium arch is 32′-0″ wide, 16′-0″ high, and 1′-0″ thick, as shown in Figure 19.13.

PROCEDURE Fortunately, creating a perspective drawing of objects whose sides are parallel with or perpendicular to the proscenium arch follows exactly the same procedure that has been used in the previous perspective exercises. First, find the vanishing point for the line system **AB/DC**, as shown in Figure 19.13A. From **OP** draw a line parallel to **AB** and **DC** until it intersects the floor line. From that point drop a vertical until it intersects the horizon line. You will notice that this point happens to coincide with the intersection between the horizon line and the line of vision. Any line that is perpendicular to the floor line will always have this center vanishing point (CVP).

To find the perspective location of the lines that form the sides of the ceiling piece (**AB** and **DC**), extend those lines until they intersect the floor line. From those points drop verticals until they intersect the perspective view base line (points **X** and **Y**). From **X** and **Y** draw light guide lines to the center vanishing point (vanishing point for line system **AB/DC**). You can determine the perspective location of points **A** and **B** or **D** and **C** in the usual manner and connect the dots to form a perspective view of the ceiling flat lying on the stage floor.

An alternative method: Instead of using the center vanishing point you can draw diagonal lines between the **CA** and **BD**, as shown in Figure 19.13B.

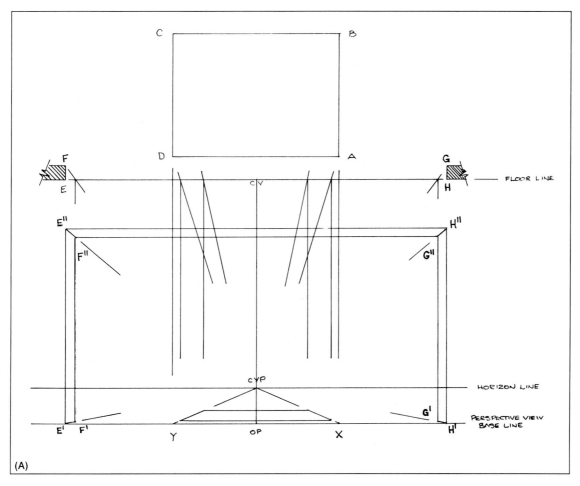

Figure 19.13
Exercise 5.

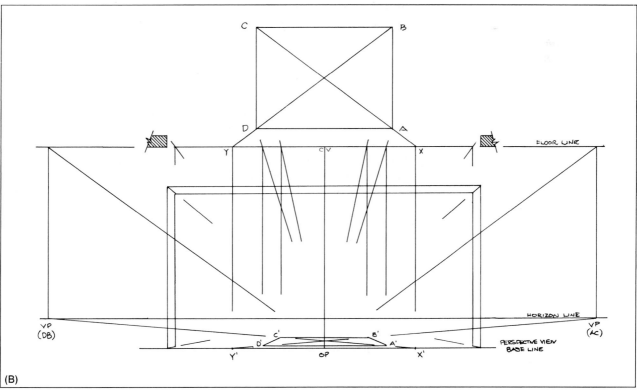

Extend those diagonals until they intersect the floor line, and then locate the vanishing point for those lines in the usual manner. The rest of the exercise can be done using the procedure as previously outlined.

Determining the perspective location of the proscenium arch is relatively easy, since the downstage edge of the arch is in contact with the floor line. From points **E** and **H** drop verticals to the perspective view base line. The vertical height of the proscenium arch can be measured from **E′** and **H′**, since those points are in contact with the perspective view base line and are consequently unaffected by the laws of perspective. Locating the top of the perspective view of the proscenium arch is done by connecting the dots between **E″** and **H″**.

The perspective view of the depth of the proscenium arch can be determined by using the methods previously described. To locate the base of the stage-right side of the arch, draw a light guide line from **E′** (the downstage edge of the proscenium arch) to the center vanishing point. To locate **F′** draw a sight line from **OP** to **F.** Where that sight line crosses the floor line, drop a vertical until it intersects the guide line drawn from **E′** to the center vanishing point. This will be the location of **F′**.

The top of the stage-right side of the proscenium arch is found by drawing a guide line from **E″** to the center vanishing point. Where this line intersects the vertical erected from **F′** will be the location of **F″**.

The other side of the proscenium arch is determined in the same manner. The top of the proscenium arch can be determined by connecting **E″** and **H″** as well as **F″** and **G″**.

Exercise 6

This exercise synthesizes all of the previous material and allows you to draw a perspective view of a full stage set.

> **Scale:** ¼″ = 1′-0″
> **OP:** 36′-0″ right and 6′-0″ up
> **Floor line:** 22′-0″ from **OP**
> **Horizon line:** 6′-0″ from **OP**
> **Perspective view base line:** extends horizontally through **OP**
> **Proscenium arch:** 16′-0″ high, 36′-0″ wide, 1′-0″ thick
> **Object being drawn:** a full stage setting, as illustrated in Figure 19.14

PROCEDURE Although the concept of drawing a full setting may, at first glance, be somewhat overwhelming, you can accomplish it by using the techniques described in this chapter. "Where do I begin?" is a logical first question. The answer isn't clear cut and absolute. Drawing the proscenium arch first provides a visual framework and reference that makes most designers feel fairly comfortable. After you've drawn the proscenium (refer to the instructions for drawing the proscenium arch detailed in Exercise 5, if you need them), start on the set. It is usually easiest to begin by drawing the set at one corner of the ground plan. Point **A,** which is the downstage end of the bottom of flat AB, provides a fairly convenient beginning place.

FLAT AB To find the location of point **A** you will need to set up the vanishing point for flat **AB.** This can be done by measuring, with a protractor, the angle of intersection between **AB** extended and the floor line, and duplicating that angle from **OP,** to lay out the vanishing point. The full

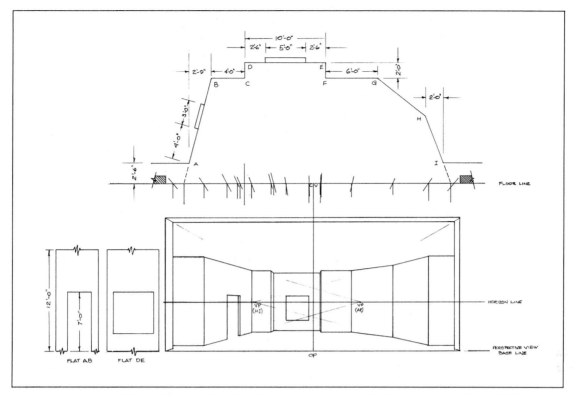

Figure 19.14
Exercise 6.

perspective view of flat **AB** can then be drawn using the techniques previously described. The sides and top of the door opening can be drawn by using the same techniques that are used to locate the sides and tops of the flat.

FLAT BC Since flat **BC** is parallel to the proscenium (and the floor line), horizontal lines can be extended from the top and bottom of the upstage end of flat **AB** to create a perspective view of the top and bottom of flat **BC**. The onstage (**C**) end of flat **BC** is determined by drawing a sight line between **OP** and **C**. Where that sight line crosses the floor line, a vertical is dropped toward the perspective view base line. Where that dropped vertical intersects the horizontal lines extending from the upstage end of the top and bottom of flat **AB** determines the location of the onstage edge of flat **BC**.

FLAT CD Because flat **CD** is perpendicular to the floor line, it will have a center vanishing point. Draw guide lines from the top and bottom edges of the onstage (**C**) end of flat **BC** to the center vanishing point to determine the perspective view of the top and bottom edges of flat **CD**. To find the upstage end of the flat draw a light sight line from **OP** to **D**. Where it crosses the floor line, drop a vertical until it intersects the guide lines that define the top and bottom edges of flat **CD**.

FLAT DE Flat **DE** is parallel to the proscenium, so you use the techniques described for flat **BC**. To create a perspective view of the window determine the height of the top and bottom edges of the window on either edge (**D** or **E**) of the flat, using the techniques described in Exercise 3. From those points extend horizontal lines across the flat. Draw light sight lines from **OP** to the edges of the ground plan view of the window. Where those sight lines cross the floor line, drop verticals until they intersect the horizontal lines that describe the top and bottom height of the window. These lines will denote the sides of the window.

FLAT EF Since **EF** is perpendicular to the proscenium, use the techniques described for flat **CD.**

FLAT FG Flat **FG** is also parallel to the proscenium, so use the techniques described for flat **BC.**

FLAT GH You can find the perspective view of flat **GH** in one of two ways: (1) either establish the vanishing point for the flat and proceed as usual, or (2) instead of working on flat **GH**, forget about it for the moment, and move on to flat **HI.** If you draw flat **HI**, using the techniques described for flat **AB,** you can find the location of flat **GH** by simply connecting the tops and bottoms of flats **FG** and **HI.**

FLAT HI As mentioned, the perspective view of flat **HI** can be found by using the techniques described for flat **AB.**

TORMENTORS The tormentors are the flats on either side of the stage connected to the downstage ends of flats **AB** and **HI** and extending behind, and parallel to, the proscenium arch. Because they are parallel to the proscenium, they can be drawn by extending horizontal lines from the tops and bottoms of the downstage ends of flats **AB** and **HI** until they intersect the sides of the proscenium arch.

Exercise 7

The drawing of furniture presents a significant challenge to many beginning scenic designers. Here is a technique that can help to visually anchor the furniture to the floor. Almost all furniture can be placed in a box, as shown in Figure 19.15. If these "furniture boxes" are placed around the furniture on the ground plan, it becomes fairly simple to draw them, in perspective, on the scenic sketch.

Scale: ¼″ = 1′-0″

OP: 36′-0″ right and 4′-0″ up

Floor line: 20′-0″ from **OP**

Horizon line: 6′-0″ from **OP**

Perspective view base line: extends horizontally through **OP**

Proscenium arch: 32′-0″ wide, 16′-0″ high, 1′-0″ thick

Objects being drawn: a very simple set with 14′-0″ walls, a 7′-0″ door, a sofa, a chair, a table, and a rug. The sofa is 6′-0″ long, 2′-6″ deep, and 3′-0″ high. The wingback chair is 3′-0″ wide, 3′-0″ deep, and 4′-0″ high. The table is 2′-0″ square and 3′-0″ high.

PROCEDURE To give yourself a visual reference you will probably draw the proscenium arch first. If you are a little hazy on the procedure for drawing the arch, refer to Exercise 5 for specific instructions.

Second, draw the walls of the set. It will probably be easiest to draw a perspective view of flat **AB** first and then flat **CD.** After these two flats have been laid out, you can connect the dots between their tops and bottoms, respectively, to create flat **BC.** Exercise 6 reviews the procedure for drawing the walls of a set.

Finally, put the "furniture boxes" on the set. The corners of the boxes coincide with the corners of the furniture that you are trying to draw. All of the furniture boxes are located on the set according to the instructions detailed in Exercises 3 and 4.

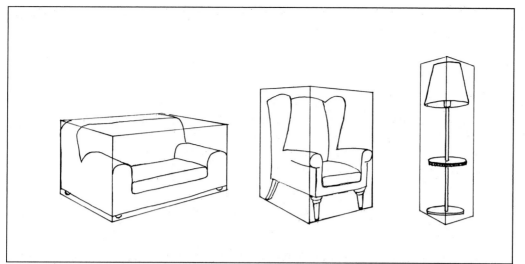

Figure 19.15
Furniture can be
sketched relatively
easily if it is placed
inside boxes.

Figure 19.16
Exercise 7.

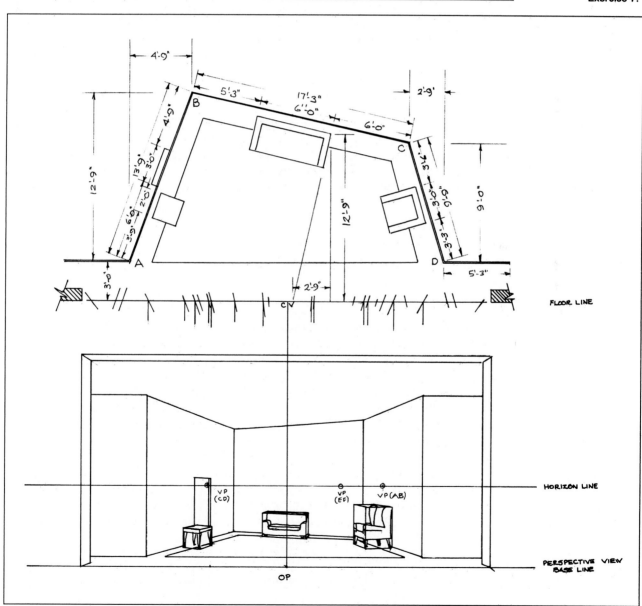

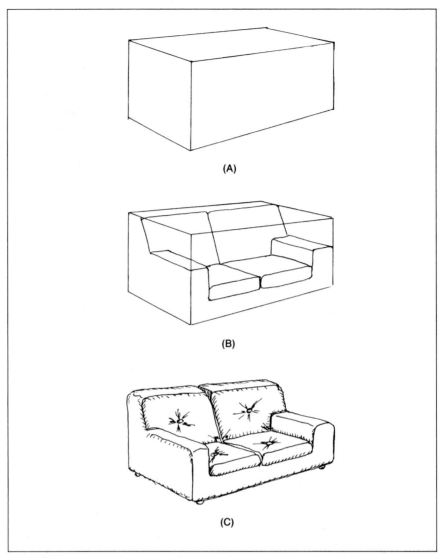

After you have drawn the furniture boxes (use light lines) on the perspective sketch, you can sketch the appropriate view of the furniture piece on each exposed face of the box, as shown in Figure 19.17.

Exercise 8

The perspective technique outlined in this chapter can also be used to create a mechanically accurate sketch of a scenic design done for an arena or thrust production. This exercise shows the procedure for creating a perspective sketch of an arena production.

Scale: ¼″ = 1′-0″

OP: 36′-0″ right and 6′-0″ above

Floor line: 15′-0″ from **OP** (Note that the floor line is placed 2′-0″ toward the audience from the edge of the stage. This placement allows you to create a drawing of the full stage.)

Horizon line: 8′-0″ from **OP**

Perspective view base line: extends horizontally through **OP**

Object being drawn: a scenic design for an arena production

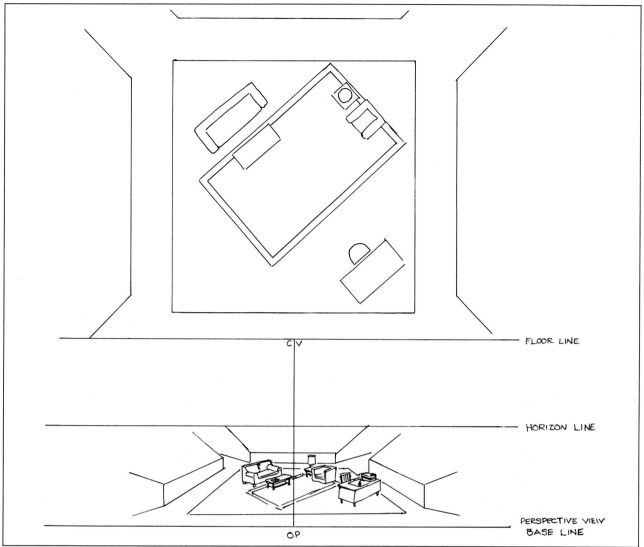

FLOOR LINE

HORIZON LINE

PERSPECTIVE VIEW
BASE LINE

C|V

OP

Figure 19.18
Exercise 8.

PROCEDURE The procedure for drawing an arena design is exactly the same as for any other production. Although most scenic designs for arena stages are noticeably devoid of any tall vertical elements such as walls and doorways, the design may contain some low walls or cutaway doors. If these elements are present, they will provide the visual framework for the design and will consequently be an appropriate beginning point for drawing the sketch. After the visual framework has been established, the furniture and other set pieces can be drawn using the furniture box technique described in Exercise 7.

Exercise 9

This exercise provides a demonstration of the perspective technique as applied to a play produced on a thrust stage.

Scale: ¼″ = 1′-0″

OP: 24′-0″ right and 14′-0″ up

Floor line: 25′-0″ from **OP** (Note that the paper has been turned 90 degrees and the floor line is located just in front of the front edge of the thrust stage. This placement allows you to achieve a full view of the stage and the set.)

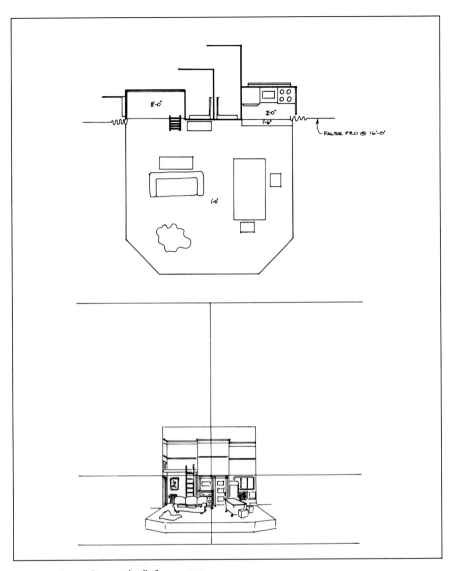

Figure 19.19
Exercise 9.

Horizon line: 7'-0" from **OP**

Perspective view base line: extends horizontally through **OP**

Object being drawn: a scenic design for a thrust production. The flats are 14'-0" tall and the doors are 6'-9".

PROCEDURE The procedure for drawing a perspective view of a design created for a thrust stage production is exactly the same as that for the other stages.

The understanding and use of the perspective method presented in this chapter should enable you to create accurate scale perspective drawings of scenic designs for proscenium, thrust, and arena productions. However, this mechanical method is just a tool to show you *how* to draw in perspective. Once you become confident in your ability to use this technique, you should wean yourself from it. Learn to sketch in reasonably accurate perspective. If you encounter a problem or if some element of your design doesn't look right, you can check its accuracy with this perspective method. But once you've learned how to use the method, try to work without it, so its necessarily mechanical processes won't inhibit the free flow of your design ideas.

20

Rendering

Theatrical rendering is another of the visual communication techniques employed by scenic and costume designers. Renderings are final color sketches that the designer creates toward the end of the design development process, after the majority of the production meetings and the presentation, and revision(s), of any thumbnail and pencil sketches. The primary purpose of theatrical rendering is to provide a color representation of the general appearance and flavor, or character, of the design.

There are literally as many styles of rendering as there are designers. Every good designer will ultimately develop a distinctive style for creating scenic or costume sketches. Rest assured, however, that no beginning designer ever just sat down and magically began to draw and paint. Personal style develops after a great deal of time, practice, and effort. Before you begin to practice you need to learn about the basic materials and techniques of sketching and rendering.

MATERIALS

Designers use a wide variety of materials to create their sketches and renderings. These materials can be roughly divided into two categories—the material being applied—paint, pastels, pencils, or markers—and paper.

Paint

Costumes and scenic sketches or renderings have traditionally been painted with transparent watercolor paints. Although this practice continues, most designers use other materials as well.

WATERCOLOR Watercolor paint is a pigment mixed with water to create a transparent paint. It is the traditional medium for theatrical rendering, because

Matte: Dull, nonreflective.

Life: Brilliance, visual depth, and sparkle.

Gloss: Highly reflective, mirrorlike.

Spine: The relative stiffness of bristles; good watercolor bristles will flex easily but will also have enough spine to remain erect when fully saturated with paint.

Figure 20.1
Watercolor pigment is available in tube, cake, and liquid forms.

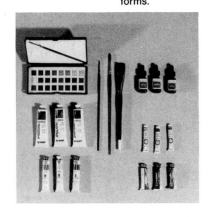

Figure 20.2
Pastels, colored pencils, and associated materials.

transparent watercolor provides the sketches with a luminescent quality that closely approximates the appearance that costumes and scenery will have under stage lights. If too much pigment is added to the mix, the watercolor becomes opaque, the dried surface of the painting will have an uneven gloss, and the luminescent quality of the rendering will be lost.

Watercolor pigments are available in three types—tube, cake, and liquid—as shown in Figure 20.1. The tube colors are emulsified pigments of approximately the consistency of well-chilled sour cream. The cake colors are manufactured in hard blocks of watercolor pigment. The liquid watercolors are packaged in small bottles of highly saturated hues.

Both tube and cake watercolors provide the same high-quality pigment, so the choice of which to use is basically a matter of personal preference. Tube colors are a little more convenient for painting a large expanse, such as a sky in a scenic rendering. Similarly, the cake colors are a little more convenient if you need only a small amount of paint to provide trim color on a costume sketch. The third type of watercolor shown in Figure 20.1, Dr. Martin's Watercolors, is a liquid of extremely strong saturation and brilliance. Because these paints are already liquid, they mix very easily and always remain transparent.

DESIGNER'S GOUACHE Designer's gouache is an opaque watercolor. It is available in tubed form in a wide range of hues similar to those of transparent watercolor. Designer's gouache closely resembles the **matte** reflective properties and colors of scene paint. When thinned sufficiently the paint becomes transparent. The primary differences between designer's gouache and transparent watercolor are that gouache has a matte finish regardless of whether it is mixed to an opaque or transparent consistency, and watercolors seem to have a little more **life.**

ACRYLIC Acrylic paint is very versatile. It can be thinned with water to the consistency of watercolor and can be used for the same purposes. When it is used as a substitute for watercolor or designer's gouache, the only significant difference is that the acrylic leaves a slightly **glossy** surface, and the watercolor and gouache finishes are matte.

BRUSHES It is a truism that you should buy the best brushes that you can possibly afford. With this proviso in mind, most artists would agree that best watercolor brushes are made from red sable. The next best alternative is the synthetic bristles made to duplicate the characteristics of sable, such as Sabline.

Red sable and high-quality synthetic bristles, such as most manufacturers' student line of brushes, carry watercolor pigment easily, have good **spine,** and cling together when wet. Brushes other than these do not have these qualities, and they will not allow you to do your best work. Consequently, you're wasting your money and your time if you buy them.

While the number and type of brushes that you purchase are matters of choice, you will need brushes of at least two sizes with which to begin. The size of artist's brushes is indicated by numbers—the higher the number, the bigger the brush. A No. 3 brush can be effectively used for most detail work, and a No. 7 can be used for laying in most washes. A No. 12 brush is very handy for creating large, smooth washes.

Pastels

There are two primary types of pastel, chalk and oil, as shown in Figure 20.2. Colored pencils are also shown, because even though they are not made of pastel, they are used in basically the same manner. Ultimately the way in which an artist uses any tool is a matter of personal choice, but each type of pastel has specific working characteristics.

CHALK PASTELS Chalk pastels are formed into square or round sticks that have approximately the same consistency as blackboard chalk. The square sticks are about 3 1/2 inches long, and the round sticks are about 6 inches. The square sticks are generally more useful for theatrical sketching, because you can draw a relatively sharp line with the edges of the stick as well as a smooth wash with the flat surfaces.

Chalk pastels are available in three hardnesses: soft, medium, and hard. The brilliance of the color is linked to its hardness—the harder the stick, the less brilliant its color. Soft- and medium-consistency chalk pastels are extremely useful for laying down a smooth background color or a graded wash (which smoothly varies in hue from top to bottom or side to side). Medium and hard pastels are useful for detail work.

OIL OR WAX PASTELS Oil or wax pastels have a slightly greasy feeling, because they are manufactured with a soft wax binder. The wax makes them very easy to blend. If you are planning to use oil pastels in conjunction with watercolors, you will need to remember to "paint first and pastel second," because the wax prevents paint from adhering to the paper.

BLENDING WITH PASTELS

Both chalk and oil pastels can be blended using either paper or felt blending stumps. The figures show some blending techniques. In addition to the commercial paper and felt blending stumps, newsprint, toilet paper, facial tissues, or your fingers can also be used.

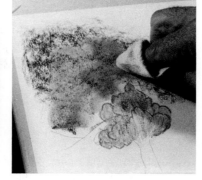

Chalk pastel blending techniques.

Colored Pencils

Watercolor pencils are also extremely versatile tools for the designer. Sharp lines of pigment can be drawn with the pencils. Then, by overlaying them with a water wash, tints of the same hue can be achieved. Regular hard-lead watercolor pencils don't work well over designer's gouache. If you are planning to draw detail work on this surface, you'll need to work with the softer-leaded pencils such as those manufactured by Prismacolor.

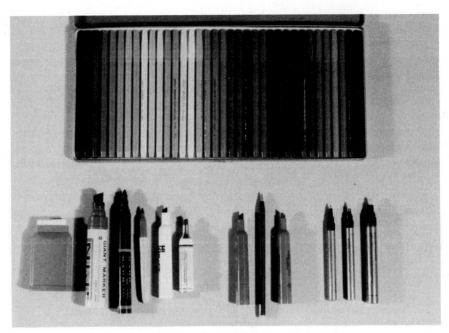

Figure 20.3
Markers.

Markers

A number of different markers and marking pens are available. The principal differences are in the shape and material of the tip and the nature and characteristics of the paint or ink contained in the marker (Figure 20.3).

The majority of these markers, such as the Magic Marker brand, contain a permanent semitransparent ink that dries very quickly and is generally available in a relatively limited range of colors. Several lines of artist's markers contain watercolor ink that is more transparent than this permanent ink. Watercolor markers are also available in a much wider range of colors. Both types of marker can be used very effectively for detail work on renderings.

Another type of marker contains a lacquer-based metallic paint. Generally available in silver, gold, bronze, and copper, these markers are very useful for applying metallic detail or highlights to renderings.

CHOOSING A WATERCOLOR PAPER

I f you are going to be rendering with watercolor, designer's gouache, or acrylic paint, you'll have a lot fewer headaches of you use watercolor board rather than watercolor paper. Although the board is more expensive, the backing prevents it from wrinkling and causing the paint to collect in little puddles.

Watercolor paper can be used, but you will need to prepare it. If you are going to be making large washes, mount the paper on some type of backing so it won't wrinkle. Thumbtack or firmly tape the paper to a smooth board, such as a drawing board or smooth-finished plywood at least three-eighths of an inch thick. After you've attached the paper, and several hours before you plan to paint, thoroughly wet the paper, and let it dry. This will "relax" the paper and let it shrink before you start to paint.

Cold-press illustration board, such as Crescent 100 or Bristol board, or a rough-surface watercolor paper or board works very well for most scenic or costume renderings in watercolor.

CHAPTER 20: RENDERING

Paper

Most scenic and costume sketches are drawn or painted on some type of watercolor paper or **illustration board.** Illustration board is simply watercolor paper that has been mounted on a stiff pressboard backing to keep it from bending or wrinkling. Other types of paper such as charcoal or velvet paper can be used for work with pastels, pencils, and markers, but they don't work well with paint.

There are three primary surface finishes for watercolor papers and illustration board. A **hot-press finish** is very slick and smooth. The **cold-press finish** has a slight texture similar to a heavy bond typing paper. **Rough-finish** paper has a very noticeable texture.

Your choice of which paper to use should be dictated by the medium in which you plan to work. The hot-press finish is good for opaque paints, pencils, and markers. The cold-press papers work well with all media. The rough-finish papers are particularly well suited for pastels and watercolor.

Matte boards (hot-press illustration board with colored surfaces) are also interesting surfaces for designer's renderings, particularly if you are planning on working with any of the opaque media such as designer's gouache, pastels, or pencil.

To determine which paper is suitable for a particular project you will need to develop an understanding of the characteristics of the various papers and their surfaces. This knowledge can be gained only by playing and experimenting with the various media on the different papers and illustration boards.

Illustration board: Watercolor paper mounted on a pressboard backing.

Hot-press finish: A slick, smooth texture achieved by pressing paper between hot rollers; this treatment leaves a thin layer of oil, which makes the paper unsuitable for use with transparent watercolor; works well with designer's gouache, acrylic, pencils, and markers.

Cold-press finish: A slight surface texture achieved by pressing paper between cold rollers; no oil residue results, so the paper can be used with transparent watercolor, designer's gouache, acrylic, markers, or pencils.

Rough finish: A pebble-grained texture achieved by cold-pressing paper with a textured roller, or by other techniques; suitable for painted and pastel renderings having little intricate detail.

RENDERING TECHNIQUES

The following suggestions will familiarize you with some of the basic techniques that are used with the various media. Try the suggested application techniques. Doodle with the paint, pencils, pastels, and markers. Have fun with them. After you've worked with each medium separately, try combining them. Whatever else, be sure that you have fun, because you will improve only with practice, and you will practice only if you're having fun.

Sketching

Scenic, costume, and property designers need to be able to make quick, clear sketches. Thumbnail drawings and pencil roughs are presented and modified during the production meetings, and almost all renderings begin with pencil sketches.

Initially, almost everyone feels intimidated by the idea of sketching. But some relatively simple hints may help you improve your ability to sketch.

A sketch does not need to, nor is it supposed to, create a photographic likeness of a person or object. Sketching creates a simplified view that shows the basic appearance and, of equal importance, the spirit or character of the object.

A major stumbling block that many people encounter when learning to sketch is that they try to draw what they think they see rather than what they actually see. Figure 20.4A shows a photograph of a table. Because people know that the top of a table is its most useful surface, they tend to draw the top of the table as the most dominant visual element, as shown in Figure 20.4B. They're not drawing what they see. If you really look at the photo of

(A)

(B)

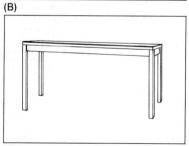

(C)

Figure 20.4 Draw what you see, not what you think you see (review the text for details).

the table, you'll see that the top is only a relatively narrow sliver in comparison with the overall size of the table. Figure 20.4C is a sketch that was made after careful observation of the photo of the table. Notice that even though the sketch doesn't show every detail, it does provide an accurate representation of the table, and it also gives you a feeling about its nature or character.

All sketches are based on three principal elements: thematic lines; line angles and intersections; and proportions. Most objects are composed of more than one thematic or predominant line, like the rocking chair shown in Figure 20.5A. The intersection of these thematic lines allows you to use a relatively easy method to accurately lay out the proportions of an object. While you're noting the angle of intersection of the thematic lines (the chair back, legs, seat, rockers, and the floor), also note the relative position where those line intersections take place. On the rocking chair, notice that the seat intersects the back just a little more than one-third of the way up the back. Also notice that the seat itself is just a little bit longer than the distance from the seat to the rockers. This "ratio technique" generally reduces a beginning artist's anxiety (which allows you to be more creative), because it depersonalizes the sketching process. You're no longer "drawing a chair," you're simply observing lines of intersection and recreating them. An accurate sketch of the rocking chair, Figure 20.5B, can be made simply by using these observations as a guide. The rest of the detailing of the sketch, Figure 20.5C, is based on the same type of observational techniques. The locations of the various solid and spindle elements of the chair are determined by observing their relative positions on the model and then, using the ratio technique, drawing them on the sketch.

Figure 20.5
Sketching techniques (see text for details).

(A)

(B)

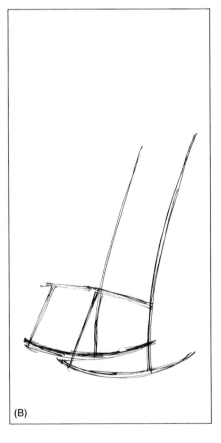

(C)

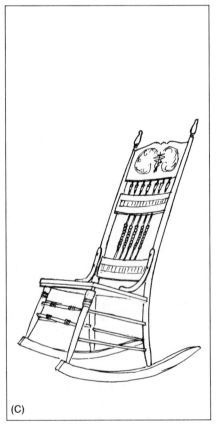

CHAPTER 20: RENDERING

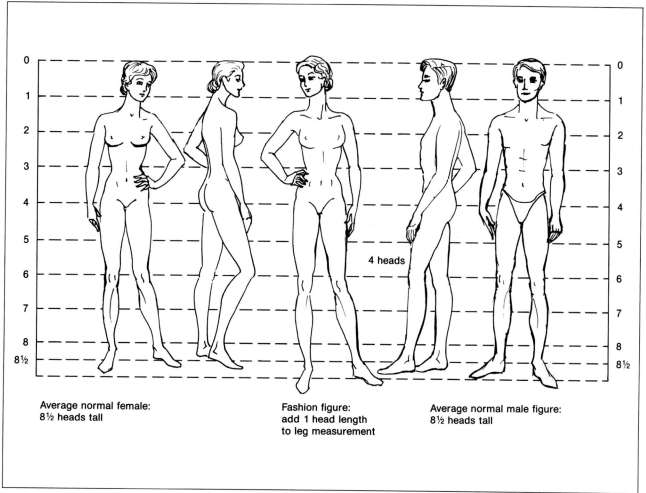

0
1
2
3
4
5
6
7
8
8½

0
1
2
3
4
5
6
7
8
8½

4 heads

Average normal female:
8½ heads tall

Fashion figure:
add 1 head length
to leg measurement

Average normal male figure:
8½ heads tall

Figure Drawing

Both costume designers and scenic designers must be able to sketch figures. The costume designer's need for this skill is obvious. For clothes to look right they must be designed to fit a particular figure. Since the costume design sketch is a picturization of that design, the costumer must be able to draw the figures that the clothes will fit. Most scenic designers like to put a human figure or two on their renderings to provide an easily identifiable visual scale for the design.

Figure 20.6 illustrates the basic proportions of the human figure. Some designers believe that it is important that a figure have a readily identifiable face. Others do not. However, almost all designers agree that a visually dynamic sketch, one in which the figure, and consequently the costume, appears to be in motion, is an important aid in representing the character of the costume. Although Figure 20.6 provides basic instructions on how to draw a naturally proportioned figure, the general guidelines in Figure 20.5—working quickly and simply and creating thematic lines—will greatly assist you in drawing figures that appear to be vital, dynamic, and alive.

Graphite Transfers

Watercolor and pastel renderings and sketches usually begin with a pencil drawing. It is fairly standard practice to draw the design on tracing vellum, since the vellum is fairly rugged and will be able to sustain a fair amount of

Figure 20.6
Proportions of
male and female
figures.

Figure 20.7
Graphite transfer technique. Cover the reverse side of the sketch with soft graphite (A). Turn the drawing over and trace the sketch (B and C) to transfer the linework to the watercolor paper or board (D).

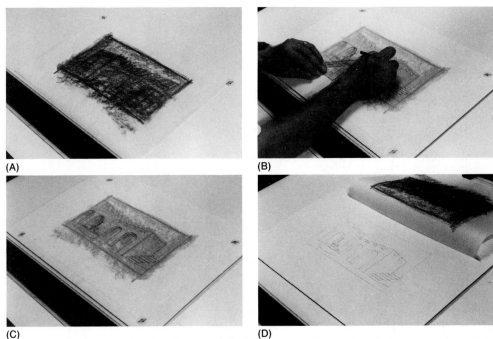

(A)

(B)

(C)

(D)

erasing as the sketch is modified. Figure 20.7 explains the process of graphite transfers. After the sketch is completed, turn the vellum over, and cover the back side of the sheet with **graphite.** (A soft stick is used for this purpose.) Tape the drawing, face up, to the illustration or watercolor board, and trace the outline of the sketch. (If you use a fine-point ballpoint pen with red ink, it will be very easy to see where you've been as you are tracing the drawing.) As you trace the outline of the sketch, you will be transferring the design to the illustration board.

You may be tempted to employ the carbon paper used for making copies in typing instead of going through the rather laborious task of "graphiting" the reverse side of the tracing vellum. If you are planning on using a transparent medium such as watercolor, try to resist this temptation, because the carbon paper graphite is very dark and will bleed through any transparent paint that you may apply to the paper. If you are planning on working with opaque media, however, the colored carbon papers typically used by costumers to transfer pattern outlines will work very nicely. Colored carbon paper is usually available at most fabric stores.

Watercolor

The **wash** can be laid down wet or dry. A wet wash is made by wetting the area to be painted with water before applying the paint, as shown in Figure 20.8. Using your brush, paint the outlined area with water, let it dry until the area has a uniformly dull finish, and then apply the paint. A wet wash conceals brush strokes a little better than a dry wash.

Since watercolor is a transparent medium, you'll need to remember that the whites and light colors are achieved by letting the paper show through. Because of this characteristic, it is normal procedure to build up a watercolor rendering from light to dark. This simply means that you paint the light areas first, then move to those of middle tone, and finish by painting the darkest details or objects. Applying each hue individually is also a normal technique in watercolor painting. After each coat has dried, additional layers can be built up over the original coat to deepen or change its hue or add texture or detail. Fine detail work can either be applied over the washes after they have dried,

Graphite: A soft carbon similar to the lead in a pencil; sticks can be purchased in most art supply stores.

Wash: The covering of a relatively large area with a smooth covering of paint; a smooth wash consists of only one color; a blended wash is created by smoothly segueing from one color to another.

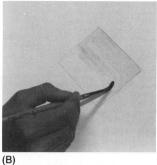
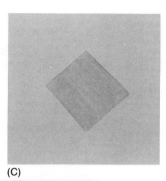

(A) (B) (C)

Figure 20.8
Applying a wet wash with watercolor. First wet the area with water (A). When the water has partially dried (the paper will have a uniform dull sheen), smoothly spread the watercolor across the area (B) to create a smooth wash of color (C).

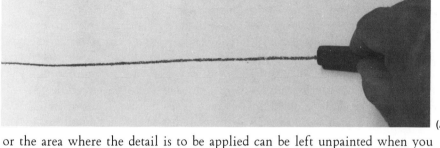

(A)

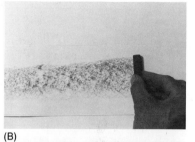

(B)

(C)

(D)

Figure 20.9 Pastel application techniques. (A) A straight line. (B) A smooth wash. Pastels can be used to lay down background washes (C). Be sure to use drafting tape to mask areas to be left "unwashed." Spray the drawing with workable fixative (D) to lock the pastel to the paper.

or the area where the detail is to be applied can be left unpainted when you are putting in the wash. Detail work can also be applied directly on top of a dried transparent wash with opaque media such as designer's gouache, acrylic, pastels, or markers.

If you have some intricate detail that will be silhouetted against a large wash area, you can "paint" the detail area with rubber cement before laying in the wash. After the wash has dried, peel off the rubber cement to expose the unpainted paper, and paint in the detail work.

Pastels

The design can be transferred to the pastel paper or illustration board using the graphite transfer technique.

Oil or wax pastels, which are very easy to blend, give a smooth, opaque finish that somewhat resembles a drawing done with crayons. Chalk pastels give a chalkier, luminescent finish. Most theatrical designers prefer working with chalk pastels, because they can be used with watercolor whereas oil pastels cannot. (The oil in the wax pastel causes the watercolor to bead up and dry in little blobs rather than a smooth wash.)

How you actually apply the pastel to the paper has a great deal to do with the finished appearance of the design. Chalk pastels will leave a definite line when applied using an edge, as shown in Figure 20.9. A smooth coverage over a large area can be accomplished by using a softer blend (soft or medium hardness) and the flat side of the pastel stick.

Once the pastel has been applied, it can be blended using felt or paper blending sticks, tissue, or your fingers. Stick pastel can also be erased (although not completely) with a kneadable or soft pink eraser.

If you don't want to get the pastel on a particular area of the drawing, mask off that space with drafting tape. Large areas can be effectively masked using paper held in place with drafting tape. Be sure not to use masking tape, which will leave a slightly gummy residue on the paper when it is removed. Additionally, the adhesive on masking tape is sufficiently strong that it can pull the finish surface layer right off the paper!

Chalk pastels are basically colored chalk. The image they leave on the

(A)

(B)

(C)

(D)

(E)

Figure 20.10 Combining media can produce interesting results. The building masked in the pastel drawing shown in Figure 20.9 is unmasked (A), and the detail is sketched in and colored with watercolor pencils (B), which are blended with a brush and water (C). After the water has dried, additional detail is sketched in with pens (D) and markers to create a drawing with an interesting appearance of depth (E).

paper is made of chalk dust and is very easy to smear. Although this characteristic is handy for blending two or more colors, a spray fixative is needed to prevent the picture from being smeared after it is finished.

A workable fixative enables you to create several layers on a pastel rendering. If you first draw and blend the background and then spray it with fixative, you can draw the foreground detail without smearing the background work. Each successive layer should be sprayed, and when the rendering is complete, it should be sprayed again. Be sure to use workable fixatives; its finish won't affect the application of additional layers of pastel.

Pencils and Markers

Colored pencils and pens as well as watercolor or oil markers can be used to good effect for both scenic and costume renderings.

The watercolor drawing pencils, which are hardened watercolor pigments, can be used to sketch in detail. The edge of the line can be softened by painting it with water, as shown in Figure 20.10.

Artist's markers are available in a full range of hues and saturations. The ink has the same transparent properties as watercolor paint, while the oil markers are generally translucent or opaque. Either type of marker can be used in a variety of ways to achieve any number of interesting effects.

Combined Media

To be able to select the appropriate visual expression for a specific design concept, a designer should feel free to use and combine a wide variety of rendering materials, styles, and techniques. The rendering for a soft, ethereal, dye-painted scrim is probably best achieved with chalk pastels, watercolors, or a combination of the two. The sketch for a costume with a sequined bodice and a long, flowing diaphanous skirt could be effectively realized with watercolor or designer's gouache and fine line markers or pen and ink. A nonrepresentational setting of abstract forms in strongly contrasting colors might best be expressed by cutting the forms from colored construction paper and pasting them to a representation of the stage space. Ultimately, the selection of which medium, or combination of media, to use for a specific rendering is the designer's choice, and those choices will be more varied if the designer is familiar with a number of media and rendering techniques.

As with any craft, your personal ability to use this information about rendering will improve only with practice. Take courses in drawing, life drawing, pastel sketching, and watercolor painting in your school's art department to help learn the many techniques and media that can be used to visually communicate your design ideas. As you become more familiar with the materials and techniques of sketching and rendering, you will discover that your ability to manipulate them is improving as well.

A

Accessory: in costuming, anything other than clothing that is worn or carried, including wigs, hats, footwear, jewelry, and similar items.

Acoustics: the sound transmission characteristics of a room, space, or material; also, the science that studies these qualities.

Acrylic: a plastic most readily identified by its trade name Plexiglas; available in rigid sheets and in liquid form (for use as a casting resin).

Acting areas: those areas of the stage on which specific scenes, or parts of scenes, are played.

Additive color mixing: the transmission of light of varying hues to the eye and the brain's interpretation of the ratio of the light mixture as a specific hue.

Adjustable arc-joint pliers: long-handled pliers with a series of jaw pivot points that provide a variety of jaw opening ranges; used for gripping square and round objects with a great deal of leverage; also known as alligator pliers.

Adjustable-end wrench: generally known by the trade name Crescent Wrench, the adjustable-end wrench has smooth jaws that adjust to fit almost any small to medium-sized nut; used to tighten bolts and nuts.

Adjustable wood clamp: a wooden clamp with two adjustable faces; the jaws can be adjusted to various angles that are useful in holding furniture frames while the glued joints are drying.

Aerial perspective: an optical phenomenon in which objects that are farther away appear less sharply in focus and less fully saturated in color.

Air caster: a nonwheeled caster that lifts objects and holds them up using high-volume, low-pressure compressed air; three to four air casters are used to raise most objects; the one-foot-diameter air caster, load rated at two thousand pounds, is the standard size used in theatrical production.

Aircraft cable: extremely strong, flexible, multistrand, twisted metal cable; eighth-inch aircraft cable is frequently used for flying heavy scenery because it has a breaking strength of approximately one ton.

Allen wrench: an L-shaped piece of steel rod with a hexagonal cross-sectional shape; used for working with Allen-head screws and bolts.

Alligator pliers: see adjustable arc-joint pliers.

Ambient: surrounding or background.

Ampere: the unit of measurement of electrical current.

Amplifier: a device used to boost the signal received from a transducer to a level that will drive a loudspeaker.

Amplitude: synonym for loudness.

Analog: in electronics, a circuit or device in which the output varies as a continuous function of the input.

Aniline dye: transparent pigment made from aniline, a poisonous derivative of benzene; characterized by brilliant hues and full saturation; a strong solution can be made by putting one teaspoon of dye into a quart of boiling water.

Animal glue: a natural glue (a by-product of the meat-packing industry) used for securing muslin to flat frames and as a binder in dry pigment and binder scene paint.

Anvil: a heavy, solid metal device with variously shaped faces; used in conjunction with a mechanic's or blacksmith's hammer for shaping metal.

Appliqué: a decorative item attached to a basic form.

Apron: the flat extension of the stage floor that projects from the proscenium arch toward the audience.

Arc: an electric current that leaps the gap between two closely placed electrodes.

Arc welder: a welder that uses an electrical arc to melt the metals being welded. The approximately one-eighth-inch-diameter electrode melts and flows into the welding zone to provide filler metal.

Arena stage: a stage completely surrounded by the audience.

Armature: a basic skeletal form that holds the covering materials in the desired shape or alignment.

Artistic director: person responsible for the major artistic decisions of a theatrical production company—hiring of production personnel, selection of season, and so on.

Asymmetrical balance: a sense of equipoise achieved through dynamic tension created by the juxtaposition of dissimilar design elements.

Atom: the smallest particle of a chemical element that retains the structural properties of that element.

Atomic theory: a generally accepted theory concerning the structure and composition of substances.

Auditorium: the seating area from which the audience observes the action of a play.

Auger bits: spiral-shaped bits designed to be used with a brace; used for drilling holes (one-fourth inch to approximately two inches in diameter) in wood.

B

Backing: flats, drops, or draperies placed on the offstage side of doors and similar openings to prevent the audience from seeing backstage.

Backsaw: a fine-toothed (twelve to fourteen teeth per inch) crosscut saw with a stiffening spine on its back; used with a miter box to make accurate miter cuts.

Balance: the arrangement of parts of a composition to create a sense of restfulness; also, to adjust the loudness and equalization levels of individual signals while mixing, to achieve an appropriate blend.

Balanced line: a sound cable in which two insulated conductors are wrapped in a braided or foil shield.

Ball peen hammer: a hammer made of hardened steel with a round ball on the back of its head; used for bending and shaping metal and seating rivets.

Band saw: a stationary power saw with a narrow continuous loop (or band) blade that passes through a table that supports the work; used for making curvilinear cuts.

Banister: the vertical member that supports the handrail of a staircase rail.

Bar clamp: similar to a pipe clamp except a notched bar is substituted for the pipe.

Barn door: an accessory for a Fresnel spotlight whose movable flippers are swung into the beam to control it.

Base coat: the first coat of the finished paint job; provides the basic color for the ensuing texture coats.

Bass reflex speaker enclosure: an insulated box with a carefully designed hole or port in front that synchronizes the phase of the rearward speaker excursion with its forward excursion to reinforce the bass frequencies.

Baste: to loosely and temporarily stitch pieces of cloth together.

Batten: a wooden dowel or metal pipe (generally $1\frac{1}{4}$ to $1\frac{1}{2}$ inches in diameter) attached to the onstage lines from a rope set or counterweight system. Scenery is attached to the batten.

Batten-clamp drop: a drop that can be quickly attached to or removed from a batten by the use of batten clamps.

Battened butt joint: two pieces of lumber butted end to end with a small piece of similar width attached directly above the joint.

Beam angle: that point where the light emitted by an instrument is diminished by 50 percent when compared with the output of the center of the beam.

Beam projector: a lensless instrument with a parabolic primary reflector and a spherical secondary reflector that creates an intense shaft of light with little diffusion.

Belt clamp: a woven nylon belt with a ratchet device to tighten the belt around the work; used to clamp irregularly shaped objects.

Belt sander: a hand-held, portable power tool that uses belts of sandpaper for rapid sanding of (primarily) wood.

Bench grinder: a stationary stand- or bench-mounted power tool consisting of an electric motor with shafts extending from either end; various grinding and buffing wheels, as well as wire brushes, can be mounted on the shafts to perform a variety of grinding, buffing, and polishing functions.

Bench sander: a stationary, stand- or bench-mounted, power tool that consists of a combination of a belt and a disk sander; used to bevel or smooth the surface or edges of wood and some plastics.

Bevel protractor: measuring device similar to the combination square except the angle of the blade is adjustable: used for marking angles between zero and ninety degrees.

Bevel set: a measuring device similar to a tri square except the angle between the blade and handle is adjustable; used for transferring angles from one piece of work to another.

Bidirectional: two directions; a microphone pickup pattern primarily receptive to the front and back.

Binder: an adhesive in paint that "glues" the pigment and fillers to the painted material after the vehicle has evaporated.

Bleeding: the characteristic of dyes and thinned paints to spread through cloth in the same way that water spreads through blotter paper.

Blocking: the actors' movements on the stage.

Block plane: a small plane with a relatively shallow (approximately fifteen to twenty degrees) blade angle; used to smooth across the grain of wood.

Blueline: to copy drawings made on tracing vellum; the lines are printed in blue or, sometimes, in black; also known as the diazo process.

Blueprint: a drawing reproduction technique in which the background is blue and the lines are white; frequently used as a misnomer for blueline.

Board foot: a unit of measurement equivalent to a piece of stock lumber that is twelve inches long, twelve inches wide, and one inch thick.

Board operators: the electricians who run the light board during rehearsals and performances.

Bobbinet: a transparent, open, hexagonal weave material; used as a glass substitute, diffusion drop, net backing for cutout drops, and similar applications.

Bodice: the upper part of a woman's dress.

Bolt cutter: heavy-duty shears with a great deal of leverage; used to cut through bolts and mild steel round stock up to one-half inch in diameter.

Book: to fold hinged flats together so they resemble a book.

Book ceiling: two large flats about the same width as the proscenium arch, stored in a booked position in the flies; when needed to create a ceiling, they are opened and lowered onto the walls of the set.

Boomerang: (1) a rolling scaffold with several levels; used for painting vertical scenery; (2) a device to hold color media in a followspot.

Borders: wide, short, framed or unframed cloth drops suspended over the stage to prevent the audience from seeing above the stage. In the Restoration theatre borders normally matched the decorative treatment on the wings and drops. In modern practice borders are frequently made of black, unpainted velour.

Bottom hanger iron: flying hardware; a metal strap iron with a D ring at the top and a hooked foot at the bottom; used at the bottom of heavy flats to support the load under compression.

Box: to pour paint back and forth between buckets to ensure a complete and uniform mix.

Box-end wrench: a wrench with a closed,

toothed head that must be fit over the head of the bolt or nut; used to tighten bolts and nuts.

Box nail: nail with a narrower shaft than a common nail, to reduce the chance of splitting the lumber.

Brace: a hand-cranked drill used for turning auger bits; used for drilling large diameter-holes in wood.

Brace cleat: bracing hardware; attached to the stile on the back of a flat to provide means for securing a stage brace to the flat.

Brocade: fabric similar to damask but lighter in weight; woven patterns achieved by weaving high-luster yarn into a matte finish background can be either raised or flat; used for making costumes, upholstery, and decorative drapery.

Bulb: the Pyrex glass or synthetic quartz container for a lamp filament and gaseous environment.

Butcher paper: a medium-weight brown paper, available in 36-inch wide rolls; also known by its trade name, Kraft paper.

Butt joint: a wood joint; two pieces of wood are square cut and fit together either end to end, end to edge, edge to edge, end to face, or edge to face.

Butt weld: a welded metal joint; the pieces being welded are joined edge to edge.

C

Cabinet drawing: a type of detail drawing that subscribes to the principles of oblique drawing except that all depth measurements are reduced by one-half or some similar ratio, such as 1:4.

Call: to tell specific crew members when to perform their cues.

Capacitance: the electrical capacity of a condenser, or capacitor.

Cardioid: a heart-shaped pickup pattern that primarily picks up sounds in front of, and slightly to the sides of, the microphone.

Carpenter's level: a two- to three-foot piece of wooden, steel, or aluminum I beam with glass tube spirit levels at either end and the middle; used to determine true horizontal and vertical.

Carpenter's rule: see folding wood rule.

Carpenter's vise: a vise for holding wood; attached to a workbench, one or both faces are covered with hardwood to prevent the vise from scratching, denting, or marring the surface of the work.

Carriage: the part of a stair unit that supports the tread and risers.

Carriage bolt: a bolt whose upper face has a rounded surface and whose underside has a slightly tapered square collar a little wider than the diameter of the bolt shaft; used to join wood to wood or wood to metal.

Cartooning: the process of transferring line work (and color blocks) from the painter's elevations to the scenery.

Casein: a natural or synthetically derived phosphoprotein—a chief component of milk.

Casein paint: a paint with a casein binder; has good covering power, is water resistant when fully dry, and can usually be thinned with a ratio of between two and four parts water to one part paint concentrate.

Casket lock: a heavy-duty hidden lock used to

hold platforms together and similar applications.

Cassette tape: audio recorder tape, also used in computer storage.

Caster: a wheel/axle device attached to platforms and the like to make them roll; casters for theatrical use should have hard rubber tires, a load rating of at least three hundred pounds, and sturdy construction.

Casting resins: any number of liquid plastics used for casting forms in molds.

Cavea: Roman term for auditorium.

C clamp: a clamp composed of a U-shaped frame with a threaded shaft; work is clamped between a pressure plate at one end of the U and the toe of the shaft; used for a wide variety of jobs, such as holding work together while parts are being assembled or while glue joints are drying.

Ceiling plate: flying hardware; a flat metal plate with an O ring in the center; attached to the primary structural members of ceiling flats to provide a means of attaching the flying lines to the ceiling.

Center line: a leader line that runs perpendicular to the set line from the mid-point or center of the opening of the proscenium arch.

Center line sectional: a sectional drawing with the cutting plane located on the center line of the stage and auditorium; used to show the height of the various elements of the stage and theatre and any pertinent set pieces.

Center punch: a pointed tool made of hard steel; used for indenting shallow holes in wood and metal.

Chalk line: a metal or plastic housing holding a long piece of twine and filled with dry scenic pigment; used for marking straight lines.

Character: the distinctive qualities, traits, and personality of a person, place, or thing. Also, the emotional quality (e.g., soft, hard, harsh, sensuous) of a line.

Chiffon: a sheer, usually translucent, cloth frequently made from rayon or silk; used for scarves and diaphanous blouses and gowns.

Chopper: see shutter.

Chroma: see saturation.

Chuck: the adjustable jawed clamp at the end of a drill that holds the drill bits.

Circuit: a conductive path through which electricity flows; also, to connect a lighting instrument to a stage circuit.

Circuit breaker: a device to protect a circuit from an overload; it has a magnetic device that trips open to break circuit continuity.

Circular saw: a portable circular bladed saw; the angle and depth of cut is variable; used to cross and angle cut as well as rip stock and plywood.

Claw hammer: a hammer with two sharply curved claws projecting from the back of its head that facilitates nail removal; used for driving nails.

Cleat: a piece of wood used to brace, block, or reinforce.

Clothesline: a small-diameter cotton rope; not used for raising or suspending loads, but the standard rope for lash lines and as the operating rope for traveling drapes (travelers).

Clout nail: a wedge-shaped nail made of soft iron used to attach cornerblocks and keystones to the frame of a flat; it is driven through the wood onto a steel backing plate, which curls the end of the nail back into the lumber.

Coated box nail: a box nail with an adhesive applied to the shaft that tightly bonds the nail to the wood.

Cobbler: one who makes shoes.

Cold chisel: a chisel made of hard steel; used for cutting or shearing mild steel and nonferrous metals.

Cold-press finish: a slight surface texture achieved by pressing paper between cold rollers; no oil residue results, so the paper can be used with transparent watercolor, designer's gouache, acrylic, markers, pencils, pastel, and so forth.

Color: a perception created in the brain by the stimulation of the retina by light waves of certain lengths; a generic term applied to all light waves contained in the visible spectrum.

Color frame: a lightweight metal holder for color media that fits in a holder at the front of a lighting instrument.

Color media: colored plastic, gel, or glass filters used to modify the color of light

Combination square: a twelve-inch steel rule with a movable handle angled at forty-five and ninety degrees; used for marking those two angles, and the rule can be used for measuring.

Commando: a lightweight cotton fabric with a short, feltlike, almost matted pile; available in two weights and widths, the heavyweight is suitable for stage drapery; the material face is generally too susceptible to wear for use as an upholstery fabric; also known as duvetyn.

Common nail: nail with a large head and thick shank; used for heavier general construction.

Complementary colors: two hues that, when combined, yield white in light or black in pigment; colors that are opposite to each other on a color wheel.

Composition: an arrangement of parts to create a whole.

Compressor: a pump that drives air into a tank; the output pressure from the tank is controlled by a valve called a regulator.

Condensing lens: a device that condenses the direct and reflected light from a source and concentrates it on the slide plane aperture of a projector.

Conduit: thin-wall metal (aluminum or steel) tubing; used as a housing for electrical wiring and decorative stage material.

Conduit bender: a tool for bending conduit.

Cones: nerve cells in the retina that are sensitive to bright light; they respond to red, blue, or green light.

Connecting strip: an electrical gutter or wireway that carries a number of stage circuits; the circuits terminate on the connecting strip in female receptacles.

Constructed sound: any sound created by editing, manipulating, or changing previously recorded sounds.

Construction calendar: a calendar that details when various technical elements of a production will be constructed.

Construction crew: those who build the set, move it into the theatre, and set it up onstage.

Construction line: in a two-line-weight system, a thick line .5 mm thick (in pencil) or .020 to .025 inch thick (in pen).

Contact cement: an adhesive for bonding nonporous surfaces together; surfaces bond as soon as they come in contact with each other.

Continental parallel: a platform made of a folding framework of nonvariable height; the top and center supports are removable; the frame folds into a more compact unit than the standard parallel.

Contrast: the juxtaposition of dissimilar elements.

Coping saw: a lightweight handsaw composed of a U-shaped frame with a narrow, fine-toothed (sixteen to eighteen teeth per inch) replaceable blade; used for making curvilinear cuts in thin plywood and lumber.

Corduroy: a cotton material whose pile ridges, called wales, alternate with a low-luster backing; available in a wide variety of wale widths and depths; heavier weights are used for upholstery, while lighter weights are used in costuming; waleless corduroy is similar to a short-nap velour, with similar uses.

Cornerblock: a triangular-shaped piece of quarter-inch plywood used to reinforce the joint between a stile and a rail of a flat.

Corner brace: a diagonal internal framing member that helps keep a flat square.

Corner plate: an L-shaped piece of one-sixteenth-inch galvanized steel, predrilled for use with flat-head wood screws; used to reinforce corners of doors, windows, and so on.

Picture hook and eye: hooks and eyes that facilitate rapid hanging and removal of decorative draperies

Corrugated fasteners: corrugated strips of metal used primarily to hold lightweight frames together.

Costume designer: person responsible for the design, visual appearance, and function of the costumes, accessories, and makeup.

Costumer: person responsible for the construction of the costumes and supervision of the costume shop.

Cotton canvas: a durable lightweight, coarse-weave material; used for covering platforms and making ground cloths.

Cotton duck: a lightweight cotton canvas; used more in costumes than scenic construction.

Cotton rep: a tough cotton fabric with a ribbed finish similar to a narrow, short-nap corduroy; good for stage draperies, costumes, and upholstery.

Counterweight arbor: a metal cradle that holds counterbalancing weights used in flying.

Crepe: a thin, crinkle-finished, soft cloth usually made from rayon, silk, or fine cotton; frequently used for women's blouses.

Crescent wrench: see adjustable-end wrench.

Crosscut saw: a handsaw with an approximately twenty-six-inch blade whose angle-sharpened teeth bend outward so the kerf is wider than the blade; designed to cut across the grain of the wood. Crosscut saws with ten to twelve teeth per inch are suitable for most scenic purposes.

Crossover network: an electronic device that splits the signal from the amplifier into frequency ranges most appropriate for use by woofers, mid-range speakers, and tweeters.

Crowbar: a round metal bar with flattened metal claws similar to those on a claw or rip hammer on one end and a tapered wedge on the other.

Cue: a directive for action, for example, a

change in the lighting.

Cure: to harden and reach full strength (in reference to glue).

Cut Awl: a portable power saw with a reciprocating blade mounted in a swiveling head; available with a variety of blades to make intricate curvilinear cuts in materials ranging from fabric to wood, paper, and plastic.

Cutoff saw: a semiportable stand-mounted circular bladed power saw that can be equipped with a wood or metal cutting blade for square and angle cutting of lumber or metal stock; can be set up for cutting either wood (wooden table without holding clamps) or metal (metal table with holding clamps); also known as a motorized miter box.

Cutout line: see silhouette.

Cutter: person who pins patterns to fabrics and cuts the material.

Cutting plane: the plane at which an object is theoretically cut to produce a sectional view.

Cyanoacrylate cement: a powerful, rapid-bonding adhesive that will bond almost anything to anything; generically known by the trade names Super Glue, Crazy Glue, and so forth.

Cyc light: a lensless instrument with an eccentric reflector used to create a smooth wash of light on a cyc or skytab from a relatively close distance.

Cyclorama: a large drop used to surround the stage.

D

Dado head: a specialty circular saw blade consisting of a set of toothed blades that sandwich a chisel-like chipper. The blades smooth-cut the outside edges of the ferf while the chipper gouges out the wood between the blades. The distance between the blades is variable; used with table and radial arm saws.

Dado joint: a wood joint made by cutting a notch or groove in the face of one piece of lumber to receive the edge of another piece of stock.

Damask: a rich-appearing cloth with raised patterns of high-luster yarn that are normally woven into the matte finish of the background cloth; used for making costumes, upholstery, and decorative drapery.

Dart: a short, tapered seam resembling a narrow "V"; used to make clothes fit more closely.

Dead hang: to suspend without means of raising or lowering.

Decibel: a unit for expressing the intensity of sounds; an increase or decrease of one decibel is just about the smallest change in loudness that the human ear can detect.

Decking: the covering surface of a structure on which people will walk.

Decorative prop: any item that is used to enhance the setting visually but is not specifically touched by an actor, such as window curtains, pictures, doilies, table lamps, bric-a-brac, and so forth.

Demi-mask: a mask, normally mounted on a stick, that covers one half the face.

Denim: a coarsely woven cotton or cotton blend twill.

Designer's cue sheet: a form used by the lighting designer to record pertinent information (dimmer levels, timing, "go" point, and so forth) about every cue in the production.

Detail drawings: drawings that describe the detail of objects. Usually drawn in a fairly large scale, normally between $\frac{3}{4}$ inch = 1 foot and $1\frac{1}{2}$ inches = 1 foot.

Diagonal cutters: pliers with beveled cutting faces on the jaw rather than flat gripping faces; used for cutting soft wire.

Diffuse: to soften the appearance of light by using a translucent filtering element to scatter the light rays.

Digital tape recording: a form of recording in which the audio information is stored on the magnetic tape as binary information rather than an analog signal.

Dimension: the relative length and width of a line.

Dimmer: an electrical device that controls the intensity of a light source connected to it.

Dimmer circuit: an electrical circuit terminating on one end at a dimmer. The other end terminates at either a patch panel or onstage. Synonymous with stage circuit when it terminates onstage.

Director: person responsible for interpreting the script, creating a viable production concept, and directing the actors.

Distress: to create a worn or aged appearance as with fabric, wood, or metal.

Double-headed nails: nails with two heads; they are driven into the wood until the lower head is flush with the surface, leaving the upper head exposed so that it can be pulled out easily; used for scaffolding or any temporary structure that needs to be dismantled quickly.

Double piano-convex lens train: two plano-convex lenses placed with their curved surfaces facing each other; creates a system that has a shorter focal length than either of its component lenses.

Double whip: a block and tackle configuration that provides a 2:1 mechanical advantage.

Douser: a mechanical dimming device used in followspots.

Dowel: a short cylinder of hardwood, usually birch.

Doweled joint: a butt joint that is internally supported by dowel pegs.

Drape: a vertical element of heavy fabric that frames the sides of a window or archway.

Draw to scale: to produce a likeness that is a proportional reduction of an object.

Dremel tool: a hand-held router similar to a dentist's drill that can be equipped with a number of bits for grinding, cutting, or carving of wood, metal, and plastic.

Dress: to place decorative props such as curtains, doilies, knickknacks, or magazines on the set to help make the environment look lived in and provide clues as to the personalities of the characters who inhabit the set. Also, to work with hair or a wig to create a specific style or look.

Dress rehearsal: a run through with all technical elements, including costumes and makeup.

Drill press: a stationary bench or stand-mounted power drill with a variety of speeds. The chuck will generally hold bits up to one-half inch in diameter.

Drop: a large expanse of cloth, usually muslin or scenic canvas, on which something (a land-scape, sky, street, room) is usually painted.

Drop box: a small connecting strip, generally containing four to eight circuits, that can be clamped to a boom or a pipe.

Dry brushing: a painting technique frequently used to create a woodgrain appearance; done by lightly charging a brush and lightly stroking it across the surface of the work.

Ducted port speaker enclosure: a speaker enclosure similar in operational theory to the bass reflex enclosure except that a tube of specific diameter and length is substituted for the open hole or port; it reinforces bass frequencies.

Dust mask: a device covering the nose and mouth that filters particulate matter from the air.

Dutchman: a five- to six-inch wide strip of cloth of the same material as the flat covering; used to hide the joints between flats in a wall unit.

Duvetyn: see commando.

E

Effects head: a motor-driven unit capable of producing relatively crude moving images with a scenic projector.

Electric: any pipe that is used to hold lighting instruments.

Electrical current: the flow or movement of electrons through a conductor.

Electrical potential: the difference in electrical charge between two bodies; measured in volts.

Electric glue pot: a thermostatically controlled pot used for melting animal glue.

Electric hand drill: a portable, hand-held power drill; some models have variable speed and reverse controls; it generally accepts bit shanks up to three-eighths of an inch in diameter.

Electricians: those who work on the stage lighting for a production.

Electrician's cue sheet: a form used by the board operator that contains the primary operating instructions for every lighting cue in the production.

Electricity: a directed flow of electrons used to create kinetic energy.

Electric screwdriver: a portable, hand-held power tool that resembles an electric hand drill; equipped with a variable-speed motor, a clutch, and a chuck that holds a screwdriver tip; used to insert and remove screws.

Electron: a negatively charged fundamental particle that orbits around the nucleus of an atom.

Electronics: the field of science and engineering concerned with the behavior and control of electrons within devices and systems, and the utilization of those systems.

Ellipsoidal reflector floodlight: a lensless instrument with a conical ellipse reflector; used for lighting cycs and drops; also known as a scoop.

Ellipsoidal reflector spotlight: a lighting instrument characterized by hard-edged light with little diffusion; designed for relatively long throws, it is manufactured with fixed and variable focal-length lenses; the light beam is shaped with internally mounted shutters.

Emery cloth: fabric whose surface has been coated with abrasive grit; used for smoothing wood, metal, and plastic.

Enamel: an oil-, lacquer-, or synthetic-based paint that has a hard surface and excellent covering power. It is usually formulated so it dries with a smooth satin or gloss finish

Epoxy: an extremely strong, waterproof plastic most frequently used in the theatre as an adhesive and casting resin.

Epoxy resin adhesive: a two-part epoxy-based adhesive available in a variety of formulations that enable the user to do gluing, filling, and painting.

Equalizer: an electronic device that selectively boosts or attenuates specific frequencies or ranges of frequencies.

F

Fader: a device, usually electronic, that effects a gradual changeover from one circuit to another; in lighting it changes the intensity of one or more dimmer circuits; in sound it changes audio circuits or channels.

False proscenium: a rigid framework covered with drapery material that is used to adjust the height and width of the proscenium arch. Sometimes unframed drapes are used to create a false proscenium.

Felt: a material made by matting together short fibers by the use of heat, water, and light pressure.

Ferrule: the metal part of a brush that binds the bristles to the handle.

Field angle: that point where the light output diminishes to 10 percent of the output of the center of the beam.

Filament: the light-producing element of a lamp; usually made of tungsten wire.

Filler: a material that creates opacity (covering power) in paint.

Filler rod: a metal piece of the same composition as material being welded; used to replace the metal lost during welding or to fill a hole or groove in the work.

Fillet weld: a welded metal joint; made when the edge of one piece is welded to the face of another; both sides of the joint should be welded.

Fill light: the light or lights that fill the shadows created by the key light.

Finish nail: a nail with a slender shaft and minute head; designed to be driven below the surface of the wood so the nail head can be hidden.

First electric: the onstage pipe for lighting instruments that is closest, from the onstage side, to the proscenium arch.

Five-quarter lumber: a specialty lumber, straight grained and free from knots, that is one and one-quarter inches thick.

Fixture: see lighting instrument.

Flange weld: a welded metal joint; similar to a butt weld, except the edges of the material are bent up; the weld is made by melting the upturned flanges.

Flannel: a lightweight, loosely woven material usually made from soft-finish wool, wool blend, or cotton thread; used for men and women's suits, trousers, and shirts.

Flat: a framework, normally made of wood or metal; usually covered with fabric, although a variety of other covering materials may be used.

Flat-head wood screw: common screw with a flat head that is beveled on the underside to easily dig into the wood; used for attaching hardware (hinges, doorknobs) and joining various wood elements together.

Flexible glue: animal glue with glycerine added.

Floor line: the base of the vertical plane in a perspective drawing. For a proscenium sketch, it is usually drawn across the stage in contact with the upstage edge of the proscenium arch; in a thrust drawing, it is normally placed just outside the auditorium end of the thrust; in an arena sketch, it is usually placed in the aisle closest to the observer.

Floor plate: bracing hardware; a block of wood with a nonskid material (foam, rubber) attached to the bottom; the foot of a stage brace is attached to the top of the floor plate, and weights (sandbags, counterweights) are piled on to keep it from moving.

Floor pocket: a connecting box, usually containing three to six circuits, whose top is mounted flush with the stage floor.

Floppy disk: a thin piece of plastic coated with metal oxide, used to record the information stored in a computer's memory.

Fluorocarbons: a family of tough, durable, low-friction, nonstick plastics best known by the trade names Teflon; used in the theatre as a bearing surface where its slippery qualities can be used to advantage.

Flush: smooth, level, even.

Flux: a chemical that reduces surface oxidation and thus aids in soldering or welding.

Fly: to raise an object or person above the stage floor with ropes or cables.

Fly cyc: a single drop, hung on a U-shaped pipe, that surrounds the stage on three sides.

Fly gallery: the elevated walkway where the pin rail is located.

Fly loft: the open space above the stage where the scenery and equipment are flown.

Focal length: the distance from the lens at which light rays converge to a point; for lenses used in stage lighting instruments, the focal length is usually measured in even inches.

Focusing: directing light from the lighting instruments to a specific area.

Folding wood rule: a six-foot wooden rule, composed of twelve segments that fold into a unit seven and half inches long; used for measuring lumber in scenic construction.

Followspot: a lighting instrument with a high-intensity, narrow beam; mounted in a stand that allows it to tilt and swivel so the beam can "follow" an actor.

Forced perspective: a process that creates apparent depth in a set by angling the horizontal line.

Foreshortening: representing the lines of an object as shorter than they actually are in order to give the illusion of proper relative size.

Form: space enclosed within a line or lines that meet or cross. Also, elements that have similar physical characteristics, such as arena theatres, thrust stages, proscenium stages, and so forth.

Found theatre spaces: structures originally designed for some other purpose that have been converted into performing spaces.

Framing square: a large steel L, typically sixteen inches on the bottom leg and twenty-four on the vertical leg; used for checking the accuracy of ninety-degree corner joints.

Free electron: an electron that has broken away from its "home" atom to float free.

Frequency: the rate at which an object vibrates; measured in hertz (cycles per second).

Fresnel lens: a type of step lens with the glass cut away from the convex face of the lens.

Fresnel spotlight: a spotlight that produces a soft, diffused light; the Fresnel lens is treated on the plano side to diffuse the light.

Front elevation: a front view of each wall segment of the set, including all detail such as windows, doors, pictures, trim, and so forth.

Front-of-house: the area in an auditorium that is relatively close to the stage.

Front projection screen: an opaque, highly reflective, usually white material used to reflect a projected image; the projector is placed on the audience side of the screen.

Full-scale drawings: scale drawings made actual size.

Functional model: a three-dimensional thumbnail sketch of a scenic design; normally built on a scale of one-quarter or one-half inch to one foot. Usually made from file folders or similar cardboard; also known as a white model.

Funnel: an accessory for a Fresnel spotlight that masks the beam to create a circular pattern; also called a snoot or top hat.

Fuse: a device to protect a circuit from an overload; it has a soft metal strip that melts, breaking circuit continuity.

G

Garbage paint: any paint left over from previous paint jobs; the various paints are mixed and neutralized to create a medium gray or brown hue; frequently used for a prime coat.

Gel: to put a color filter into a color frame and insert it in the color-frame holder of a lighting instrument.

Gesso: plaster of paris in liquid state; approximately the consistency of sour cream; dries to a hard plaster finish.

Glaze: a transparent, usually lightly tinted, slightly glossy coating.

Gloss: highly reflective, mirrorlike.

Gobo: a thin metal template inserted into an ellipsoidal reflector spotlight to create a shadow pattern of light.

Graded base coat: a base coat that gradually changes hue or value over the height or width of the painted surface.

Grand drape: the curtain that covers the opening of the proscenium arch.

Grand rag: slang synonym for grand drape.

Grand valance: a teaser or border made of the same material as the grand drape. Used in conjunction with the grand drape, it masks the scenery and equipment just upstage of the proscenium arch.

Graphic equalizer: an equalizer with individual slide controls affecting specific, usually relatively narrow, segments of the sound spectrum; so called because the position of the indi-vidual controls graphically displays a picture of the equalization of the full sound spectrum.

Graphite: a soft carbon similar to the lead in a pencil; sticks can be purchased in most art supply stores.

Grid: a network of steel I beams supporting elements of the counterweight system.

Grid transfer: transferring a design from an elevation to the scenery by use of a scale grid on the elevation and a full-scale grid on the scenery.

Grommet: a circular metal eyelet used to reinforce holes in fabric.

Grommet set: a hole punch, a small anvil, and a crimping tool; used to seat grommets.

Ground plan: a scale mechanical drawing in the form of a horizontal offset section with the cutting plane passing at whatever level, normally a height of 4 feet above the stage floor, required to produce the most descriptive view of the set.

Ground row: generally low, horizontal flats used to mask the base of cycs or drops; frequently painted to resemble rows of buildings, hedges, or similar visual elements.

Gusset: a triangular piece of material used to reinforce a corner joint.

H

Hacksaw: an adjustable frame handsaw with an extremely fine toothed (twenty to twenty-five teeth per inch) replaceable blade; used for cutting metal.

Halved joint: a wood joint made by removing half the thickness of both pieces of lumber in the area to be joined, so the thickness of the finished joint will be no greater than the stock from which it is made; also called a halved lap joint.

Hand drill: a hand-cranked device used for spinning drill bits; used for making small-diameter holes in wood.

Hand power grinder: a portable, hand-held version of the bench grinder; useful on pieces that are too heavy or awkward to be worked with the bench grinder.

Hand power sander: a slightly less powerful version of the hand power grinder; equipped with a flexible disk that provides backing for sanding discs of varying grit; used for rough sanding of wood, metal, and plastic.

Hand prop: a small item that is handled or carried by an actor.

Handrail: the part of the stair rail that is grabbed with the hand; supported by the banister and newel posts.

Hanger iron: flying hardware; a metal strap with a D ring at the top; the hanger iron is attached to the top or bottom of the back of a flat, one end of a line is attached to the D ring, and the other end is attached to a counterweight batten.

Hanging: the process of placing lighting instruments in their specified locations.

Hanging crew: those responsible for the hanging, circuiting, patching, focusing, and coloring of the lighting instruments; they are under the supervision of the master electrician.

Hanging positions: the various locations around the stage and auditorium where lighting instruments are placed.

Hang tag: the small label usually attached to the cardboard core of a bolt of fabric that indicates the percentages of various component fibers.

Hardboard: generic term for composition sheet goods such as Masonite and particle board.

Hard teaser: the horizontal element of the false proscenium; usually hung from a counterweighted batten so its height can easily be adjusted.

Harmonics: frequencies that are exact multiples of a fundamental pitch or frequency.

Harmony: a sense of blending and unity that is achieved when the various parts of a design fit together to create an orderly, congruous whole.

Head: (1) a housing that holds scenic projector lenses in fixed positions to project images of a specific size. (2) a high-quality electromagnet on a tape deck or tape recorder that is used to implant, retrieve, or erase electrical data from audio tapes.

Head block: a multisheave block with two or more pulley wheels, used to change the direction of all the ropes or cables that support the batten.

Header: a small flat that can be placed between two standard-sized flats to create a doorway or window.

Heat filter: a glass medium that removes much of the infrared spectrum from light.

Heat gun: a high-temperature air gun, visually similar to a hand-held hair dryer.

Heat welding: the use of a heat gun to fuse two pieces of plastic.

Heavy-duty hand drill: similar to the electric hand drill, but with a heavier duty motor; the chuck will generally accept bit shanks up to one-half inch in diameter.

Hinged-foot iron: bracing hardware similar to the rigid foot iron but hinged so it can fold out of the way for storage.

Hole saws: saw-toothed cylinders of hardened steel with a drill bit in the center that is used to center the saw in the work; used with a power drill to make holes from three-quarters of an inch to two inches in diameter in wood that is one and a half inches thick or less.

Homespun: a coarse, loosely woven material usually made from cotton, linen, or wool.

Honeycomb paper: a manufactured paper product with a hexagonal structure similar to a honeycomb.

Hookup sheet: a sheet containing pertinent information (hanging position, circuit, dimmer, color, lamp wattage, focusing notes) about every lighting instrument used in the production. Also known as an instrument schedule.

Horizon line: in perspective drawing a line representing the meeting of the earth and the sky; normally drawn parallel to the top or bottom edge of the paper.

Horizontal offset section: a section drawing with a horizontal cutting plane; the cutting plane does not remain fixed—it varies to provide views of important details.

Horn: a dispersion device attached to the front of a pressure driver to direct the sound emitted by the pressure driver into a specific pattern.

Hot melt glue gun: a hand-held electric tool that heats sticks of adhesive to make rapid-hold bonds on a wide range of materials, such as

wood, plastic, paper, cloth, metal, dirt, sand, and so forth.

Hot-press finish: a slick, smooth texture achieved by pressing paper between hot rollers; this treatment leaves a thin layer of oil, which makes the paper unsuitable for use with transparent watercolor. It works well with designer's gouache, acrylic, pencils, and markers.

Hot spot: an intense circle of light created when a projector lens is seen through a rear projection screen.

Hot-wire cutter: a tool for cutting foam; it consists of a wire that is heated to incandescence.

House: synonym for auditorium.

Hue: the qualities that differentiate one color from another.

Hypercardioid: a directional, narrow, elongated cardioid pickup pattern that all but eliminates pickup from anywhere except directly in front of, and for a short distance immediately behind, the microphone.

I

Illustration board: watercolor paper mounted on pressboard backing.

Image of light: a picture or concept of what the light should look like for a production.

Immersion heater: an electric heater that can be immersed in a bucket of liquid to heat it; used for heating water for starch mixtures, aniline dye, flameproofing solutions, and so forth.

Impact wrench: a power-driven tool that uses sockets to tighten or loosen bolts or nuts; may be either electric or pneumatic.

Impedance: resistance in an AC circuit; the only difference between impedance and resistance is that impedance is defined as resistance to the flow of an alternating current.

Improved stage screw: bracing hardware; an improved version of the stage screw consisting of a steel plug, threaded on the outside and inside, that is inserted into an appropriately sized hole drilled in the stage floor. The screw screws into the plug, and the plug can be removed and a piece of dowel inserted into the floor to fill the hole.

Infinite baffle speaker enclosure: an airtight, heavily insulated box that absorbs the sound waves produced by the rearward excursion speaker; it is relatively inefficient and requires a high-wattage amplifier to achieve satisfactory sound levels.

Inner above: the elevated area located directly above the inner below in the Elizabethan theatre.

Inner below: the curtained area at the upstage edge of the playing area in the Elizabethan theatre.

Instrument schedule: a form used to record all of the technical data about each instrument used in the production; also known as a hookup sheet.

Intensity: the relative loudness of a sound.

Iris: a device with movable overlapping metal plates, used with an ellipsoidal reflector spotlight to change the size of the circular pattern of light.

Irregular flat: a flat having nonsquare corners.

Isometric drawing: a scaled mechanical drawing that presents a pictorial view of an object on three axes; the primary axis is perpendicular

to the base line and the other two project from its base, in opposite directions, 30 degrees above the base line.

J

Jack: a triangular brace.

Jog: a flat less than two feet wide.

Joists: parallel beams that support flooring.

K

Kerf: the width of the cut made by a saw blade.

Keyhole saw: a handsaw with a narrow, tapering blade of ten to twelve teeth per inch; used for making curvilinear cuts in plywood and lumber.

Key light: the brightest light on a particular scene.

Keystone: a wedge or rectangular-shaped piece of quarter-inch plywood used to reinforce the joint between a stile and togglebar of a flat.

Keystoning: the linear distortion created when a projector is placed on some angle other than perpendicular to the projection surface.

L

Lacquer: refined shellac or varnish with quick-drying additives.

Lag screw: large wood screw with a hexagonal or square head; used in situations where bolts are not practical, such as attaching something to a wall or floor.

Laminate: to build up an object from several layers.

Lap joint: a wood joint made when the faces of two pieces of wood are joined.

Lap weld: a welded metal joint; made when the pieces being welded are overlapped.

Lashing: a method of joining scenery; a piece of quarter-inch cotton clothesline (lash line) is served around special hardware on adjoining flats to hold them together.

Lash-line cleat: lashing hardware secured so the pointed end projects over the inside edge of the stile.

Lash-line eye: lashing hardware with a hole through which the lash line passes, attached to the inside edge of the stile.

Lash-line hook: used for same purposes as a lash-line cleat, but has a hook instead of a point; used on extra-wide stiles or in situations that preclude the use of a lash-line cleat.

Latch keeper: see S hook.

Latex: a natural or synthetic liquid plastic with the flexible qualities of natural latex or rubber; bonds well and is flexible.

Latex cement: a milky-white flexible cement.

Latex paint: a paint with a latex binder; has fair to good covering power, may or may not be water resistant, and can be thinned very little, usually no more than one pint of water per gallon of paint.

Lathe: a stationary, stand- or bench-mounted, variable-speed power tool that rapidly spins wood so it can be carved with the use of special chisels. Can be used to turn foam.

Leader line: in a two-line-weight system, a thin line .3 mm thick (in pencil) or .010 to .0125 inch thick (in pen).

Legs: narrow, vertical stage drapes used for masking.

Lensless projector: a projector that works by projecting a shadow image without a lens, such as the Linnebach and curved-image projectors.

Life: in rendering, the qualities of brilliance, visual depth, and sparkle.

Lift jack: a jack equipped with swivel casters, used to pick up and move platforms.

Lighting area: a cylindrical space approximately eight to twelve feet in diameter and seven feet high; lighting areas are located within acting areas to facilitate creating a smooth wash of light within the acting area.

Lighting cue: generally, some type of action involving lighting; usually the raising or lowering of the intensity of one or more lighting instruments.

Lighting designer: person responsible for the appearance of the lighting during the production.

Lighting grid: a network of pipes, usually connected in a grid pattern, from which lighting instruments and other equipment can be hung.

Lighting instrument: a device that produces a controllable light; for example, an ellipsoidal reflector spotlight, a fresnel spotlight, and so forth.

Lighting key: a drawing that illustrates the plan angle and color of the various sources that are illuminating the image of light.

Lighting rehearsal: a run through, without actors, attended by the director, stage manager, lighting designer, and appropriate running crews to look at the intensity, timing, and placement of the various lighting cues.

Lighting sectional: a composite side view, drawn in scale, of the set showing the hanging position of the instruments in relationship to the physical structure of the theatre, set, and stage equipment.

Lighting template: a guide for use in drawing lighting symbols.

Light plot: a scale drawing showing the placement of the lighting instruments relative to the physical structure of the theatre and the location of the set.

Line level: a signal voltage range, approximately .75 to 1 volt; specified as a voltage range rather than one particular voltage because the voltage and current of the signal vary with the intensity and frequency of the sound.

Linen canvas: an excellent flat covering material; extremely durable, it accepts paint very well and doesn't shrink much; expensive.

Line of vision: the vertical line drawn from OP to the floor line in a perspective grid; it represents the line of sight from the observer to the vertical plane.

Liner: in makeup, any saturated color that is used as rouge, as eye shadow, or to create other areas of highlight or shadow.

Lining: painting narrow, straight lines; done with lining brushes and a straight edge.

Livery: identifiable clothing associated with a specific occupation or trade.

Load: a device that converts electrical energy into another form of energy: a lamp converts electrical energy to light and heat; an electric motor converts electricity to mechanical energy.

Load-in: the moving of scenery and associated equipment into the theatre and their positioning (setup) on the stage.

Loading platform: a walkway suspended just below the grid where the counterweights are loaded onto the arbor.

Locking pliers: generally known by the tradename Vise Grip, locking pliers are available in a wide variety of sizes and configurations; used for gripping and holding, the size of the jaw opening and amount of pressure applied by the jaws are adjustable by the screw at the base of the handle.

Locking rail: a rail that holds the rope locks for each counterweight set.

Loft block: a grooved pulley mounted on top of the grid, used to change the direction in which a rope or cable travels.

Long-nose pliers: pliers with long tapering jaws; used for holding small items and bending very light wire; also called needle-nose pliers.

Loudspeaker: a transducer used to convert an electrical signal from an amplifier into audible sound.

M

Machine bolt: bolt with a square or hexagonal head used to attach metal to metal.

Machinist's vise: a vise with toothed steel faces; used to hold and clamp metal; can be used to hold wood, but the serrated steel faces will mar the surface unless protective blocks of wood are used to sandwich the work.

Main drape: synonym for grand drape.

Mallet: a hammer with a wooden, plastic, or rubber head; the wooden and plastic mallets are generally used for driving chisels; all three can be used for shaping thin metal.

Managing director: person responsible for the business functions of a theatrical production company—fundraising, ticket sales, box office management.

Manila rope: a strong, yet flexible rope; used in the theatre for raising and suspending loads and as the operating line for counterweight systems.

Mansions: small scenic representations of the standard locations (heaven, hell, garden, palace, etc.) used in medieval plays.

Margin line: an extra-heavyweight line that forms a border for the plate one-half inch in from the edge of the paper.

Mask: to block the audience's view—generally, of backstage equipment and space.

Masonite: a registered trade name for a sheet stock made from binder-impregnated wood pulp compressed into four-by-eight-foot sheets.

Mass: the three-dimensional manifestation of form.

Master electrician: person responsible for ensuring that the lighting equipment is hung, focused, and run according to written and verbal instructions from the lighting designer.

Master seamer: person responsible for costume construction and direct supervision of costume crews.

Matte: dull, nonreflective.

Matte knife: see utility knife.

Mechanical perspective: a picture, in scale, drawn with drafting tools, that provides an illusion of depth.

Mechanic's hammer: a hammer with a heavy, relatively soft metal head; used for shaping metal.

Merrow machine: a machine that, in one operation, sews a seam, cuts both pieces of fabric about one quarter of an inch from the seam, and makes an overcast stitch on the edge of both pieces of fabric to prevent raveling.

Metal file: any file with very fine teeth; used for smoothing metal.

Microcassette tape: audio recorder tape for use in small cassettes; used in computer storage.

Microphone: a transducer used to convert sound waves into electrical energy.

Mid-range speaker: a speaker designed to reproduce the middle range of audible frequencies—roughly 200 to 1000 Hz.

MIG (metal inert gas) welder: a welder that focuses a flow of inert gas (usually carbon dioxide or argon) on the welding zone to prevent or reduce oxidation of the weld; the electrode is a thin piece of wire automatically fed through the welding handle from a spool stored in the housing of the power unit.

Mike: (*verb*) to pick up a sound with a microphone; (*noun*) microphone.

Mike: to place one or more microphones in proximity to a sound source (instrument, voice).

Mild steel: a medium-strength, easily worked ferrous metal that is easy to weld; the metal most commonly used in stage construction.

Milliner: one who constructs and styles hats.

Miter: an angle that is cut in a piece of wood or metal, usually in pairs, to form a corner.

Miter box: a guide used with a backsaw to make accurate angle cuts in wood.

Miter joint: similar to a butt joint, but the edges to be joined are angle, rather than square, cut.

Mix: to blend the electronic signals created by several sound sources.

Mixer: an electronic device used to mix the output of a variety of sources and route the blended signal(s) on to other equipment; it can be used for both recording and playback.

Model: an object that is being used as the subject of a mold casting.

Mold: a matrix used to create a form.

Molding cutter head: a heavy cylindrical arbor in which a variety of matched cutter blades or knives can be fit; used with a table or radial arm saw to cut decorative molding.

Monkey wrench: a heavyweight, smooth-jawed adjustable wrench for use on large nuts or work that is too large for an adjustable-end wrench.

Monofilament line: a single-strand, transparent, monofilament line; sold as fishing line in sporting goods stores; also known as trick line.

Mood: the feeling of a play—comic, tragic, happy, and so forth.

Mortise: a square hole; used in conjunction with a tenon to make a mortise and tenon joint.

Mortise and tenon joint: a wood joint made by fitting a tenon (square peg) into a mortise (square hole).

Mortise drill bit: a drill bit housed inside a square hollow chisel; used with a drill press to make square holes.

Motorized miter box: see cutoff saw.

Mullion: a vertical crossbar in a window.
Muntin: a horizontal crossbar in a window.
Muslin: a flat-surfaced, woven cotton fabric.

N

Nail puller: a tool with a movable jaw on one end for grasping nail heads and a movable slide hammer on the other to drive the jaws into the wood to grasp the nail; used to pull nails out.
Needle-nose pliers: see long-nose pliers.
Neutralization: subtractive color mixing; the selective absorption of light as the result of mixing complementary pigment hues; the creation of gray.
Neutron: a fundamental particle in the structure of the nucleus of an atom; possesses a neutral charge.
Newel post: the post at the bottom or top of a flight of stairs that terminates the handrail.
Nicopress tool: a plierlike tool that crimps Nicopress sleeves onto wire rope or cable to make permanent, nonremovable friction clamps.
Nonrepresentational design: a style in which the portrayed elements do not represent physically identifiable objects.
Nonspecific musical effect: any sound effect that does not reinforce a readily identifiable source such as a doorbell or telephone.
Notched joint: a wood joint made by cutting a notch from a piece of lumber; the size of the notch is determined by the width and thickness of the other piece of stock that the notch will receive.
Noxious: harmful to one's health.
Nut driver: tool similar in appearance to a screwdriver with a cylindrical socket instead of a slot or Phillips head; used for tightening small hex (six-sided) nuts.

O

Objective lens: a device used to focus a projected image on a screen or other surface.
Oblique drawing: a scaled mechanical drawing with one face of the object, drawn as an elevation, placed at right angles to the observer's line of sight; the remaining faces project from the elevation to the right or left using a 30 or 45 degree base line.
Ohm's Law: the law that states: As voltage increases, current increases; as resistance increases, current decreases.
Oil stone: an abrasive composite stone, usually with different grits on opposite faces; used for sharpening knives, chisels, and other cutting tools.
Omnidirectional: in all directions; a spherical microphone pickup pattern.
Open-end wrench: a wrench with nonadjustable U-shaped jaws on both ends; the opening between the jaws is of a specific width to grip bolts and nuts of specific diameters; used to tighten bolts and nuts.
Orchestra: the circular area on which the majority of the action of the play took place in a Greek theatre.
Orchestra pit: the space between the stage and the auditorium, usually below stage level, that holds the orchestra.
Orthographic projection: a series of eleva-

tions, drawn to scale, that show each side or face of an object.
Overlay: a garment, usually made of lace or a similar lightweight, semitransparent fabric, designed to lie on top of another garment.
Oxford cloth: a flat-surfaced cotton or cotton blend material frequently used for making shirts.
Oxidation: a chemical reaction between metal and air that forms a thin, discolored "skin" over the work that effectively prevents heat transfer. Oxidation adversely affects the strength and conductivity of both soldered and welded joints.

P

Pageant wagon: a staging convention used during the medieval period. Basically, a bare platform backed with a plain curtain mounted on a wagon. The wagon could be pulled from town to town.
Paint chip: a small rectangle of paper or thin cardboard painted in a specific hue.
Paint crew: persons responsible for painting the scenery and properties; they are under the supervision of the scenic artist.
Painter's elevations: front elevations of a set painted to show the palette and painting styles to be used on the actual set.
Pan: to rotate an object about its vertical axis.
Papier-mâché: a process of building up a form by laminating wheat-paste-soaked strips of newspaper; also available commercially in a powdered form to make a paste suitable for forming in molds.
Parametric equalizer: an equalizer in which individual frequencies or custom-designed bands of frequencies can be programmed for boost or attenuation.
Paraskenia: long, high walls that extended on either side of and parallel with the skene of the Greek theatre.
PAR can: a holder for a parabolic aluminized reflector (PAR) lamp; creates a powerful punch of light with a relatively soft edge; the PAR 64 is commonly used for concert lighting.
Particle board: a sheet stock composed of small wood chips and sawdust mixed with a glue binder and compressed into four-by-eight-foot sheets; it is quite brittle so it cannot be used as a load-bearing surface.
Patch: to connect a stage circuit to a dimmer circuit.
Patch bay: a cross-connect or patch panel for sound.
Patch panel: an interconnecting device that allows one to connect any stage circuit to any dimmer.
Pattern maker: person who makes patterns based on information contained in the costume designer's sketch, notes, and instructions.
Perspective view base line: the bottom edge of a perspective drawing.
Phillips-head screwdriver: see screwdriver.
Piano wire: extremely strong wire made from spring steel; frequently used for flying scenery because of its strength; should not be sharply bent as this significantly reduces its strength.
Picture frame stage: a configuration in which the spectators watch the action of the play

through a rectangular opening; synonym for proscenium arch stage.
Pietzoelectricity: voltage produced when pressure is placed on certain crystals.
Pig: a loosely woven bag containing powdered eraser material.
Pigment: material that imparts color to a substance such as paint or dye.
Pilot hole: see starter hole.
Pinch bar: a flattened metal bar configured like a crowbar.
Pin rail: a horizontal pipe or rail studded with belaying pins; the ropes of the rope set system are wrapped around the belaying pins to hold the batten at a specific height.
Pipe: a counterweighted batten or fixed metal pipe that holds lighting instruments.
Pipe clamp: a threaded pipe with a movable end plate and an adjustable head plate; used for clamping furniture frames and similar wide objects. A bar clamp is similar except a notched bar is substituted for the pipe.
Pipe cutter: a tool used for making clean right-angle cuts through steel tubing of half inch and larger diameters.
Pipe wrench: similar in shape to the monkey wrench, the pipe wrench has jaws that are serrated to bite into the soft metal of pipes; used for holding or twisting pipes and their associated couplings.
Pit: (1) the ground in front of the stage where the lower-class audience stood to watch the play in Elizabethan theatres. (2) In twentieth-century theatres, a commonly used abbreviation for orchestra pit.
Pitch: the characteristic tone produced by a vibrating body; the higher the frequency of vibration, the higher the pitch.
Plan angle: the ground-plan view of an object.
Plane: a knife-edged tool used to smooth or round the edges or corners of wood.
Plano-convex lens: a lens with one flat and one outward-curving face.
Plaster line: in drafting, a leader line extending across the opening of the proscenium arch.
Plate: a sheet of mechanical drawings, drawn to scale.
Platea: the open acting area in front of the mansions of the medieval stage.
Playback system: devices used to play recorded sound; usually composed of a turntable and/or tape deck, an equalizer, an amplifier, and a speaker.
Playwright: person who develops and writes the script.
Plug: a wooden insert used to replace a knothole or other imperfection in the surface layer of a sheet of plywood.
Plush: fabric similar to velveteen but with softer and longer pile; common drapery and upholstery fabric.
Plywood: a sheet stock made by laminating several layers of wood; its superior strength is created by alternating each successive layer so its grain lies at a ninety-degree angle to the layers immediately above and below it.
Pneumatic nailer: a compressed-air-powered tool similar in appearance to a pneumatic stapler but using clips of adhesive-coated nails rather than staples.
Pneumatic stapler: a compressed-air-powered stapler capable of driving staples with legs up

to one and one-half inches long; adhesive-coated staples are generally used for assembling flat frames, putting tops on platforms, and similar functions.

Polyethylene: a class of plastics that, in solid form, have a characteristically slick, waxy surface; polyethylene film is frequently used as a drop cloth and can be used as a projection surface; polyethylene foam, generally known by the trade name Ethafoam, is flexible and is available in sheets, rods, and tubes.

Polystyrene: a class of plastics with a variety of formulations useful in theatrical production; high-impact polystyrene sheeting has a hard surface and is moderately flexible, fairly strong, and somewhat brittle. It is used in vacuum forming; polystyrene foam is commonly known by the trade name Styrofoam; it is available in sheets and is frequently decorative trim.

Polyvinyl chloride: a family of plastics that are, in solid form, characteristically strong, lightweight, and rigid; PVC water pipe can be used for a variety of functional and decorative purposes; also available in sheet, rod, and other forms.

Polyvinyl glue: a white liquid adhesive that resembles white glue; has excellent adhesion to porous surfaces and good flexibility.

Pop riveter: a tool used to secure rivets in thin metal.

Position: relative placement of objects within a composition.

Power amplifier: see amplifier.

Power hacksaw: a stationary power tool for cutting metal; a horizontal reciprocating metal-cutting blade is used to cut through various types of metal stock.

Power pipe cutter: a stationary stand-mounted power tool for cutting and threading metal pipes with diameters from approximately one-half to two inches.

Preamplifier: an electronic device that boosts the level of a signal, without alteration or reshaping, to the requisite input signal level of the next piece of equipment in a sound system.

Preset sheet: a form used by the electrician to record the intensity levels for each dimmer during major shifts in the lighting.

Pressure driver: a unit housing a large magnet that vibrates a thin metallic diaphragm to create mid-range and high-frequency sounds.

Primary colors: hues that cannot be derived or blended from any other hues. In light the primaries are red, blue, and green; in pigment the primary colors are red, blue, and yellow.

Prime coat: the first layer of paint; applied to all elements of the scenery to provide a uniform base for the rest of the paint job.

Producer: person who selects the script, finds financial backing, and hires all production personnel.

Production concept: the creative interpretation of the script, which will unify the artistic vision of the production design team.

Production design team: the producer, director, and scenic, costume, lighting, and sound designers who, working together, develop the visual/aural concept for the production.

Production manager: coordinator of production scheduling and administrative/logistic details of a multishow theatrical season.

Production meeting: a conference of appro-priate production personnel to share information.

Production model: a scale model similar to a functional model but fully painted and complete with furniture and decorative props.

Production team: everyone working, in any capacity, on the production of a play.

Profile: see silhouette.

Prompt book: a copy of the script with details about each actor's blocking as well as the location, timing, and, as necessary, action, of all set, prop, light, and sound cues.

Propane torch: an open-flame torch powered by propane gas; used for heavy-duty soldering and heat shaping of thin-gauge steel.

Properties: elements such as furniture, lamps, pictures, table linens, bric-a-brac, and window draperies that provide the finished set with visual character.

Property crew: those who construct or acquire all props and run (organize, shift, store) props during rehearsals and performances.

Property master: one responsible for the design, construction, and finishing of all properties.

Proscenium: a stage configuration in which the spectators watch the action through a rectangular opening (the proscenium arch) that resembles a picture frame.

Proskenium: a columned arch that supported a porchlike projection from the upper floor of the skene in the Greek theatre.

Prosthetic device: in makeup, a device such as a false nose, beard, or other appliance that is added to the face to change the actor's appearance.

Proton: a fundamental particle in the structure of the nucleus of an atom; possesses a positive charge.

Push drill: a hand-powered drill that uses a springloaded shaft to spin the drill bit when one pushes downward on the handle; for light usage, it uses bits from one sixty-fourth to three-sixteenths of an inch in diameter; useful for making starter holes.

Push drill bits: steel bits with sharp points and straight fluted indentations running up the sides of the shaft; used with the push drill to drill narrow holes (one sixty-fourth to three-sixteenths of an inch in diameter) in wood.

Pyroxylin: Celastic is the trade name for a pyroxylin-impregnated felt material that becomes extremely limp when dipped in acetone; when the acetone evaporates the pyroxylin stiffens the felt so it will hold its molded shape.

Q

Quadraphonic: a sound system composed of four discrete sound channels.

Quality: the nature or intrinsic properties (e.g., straight, curved, jagged) of a line.

R

Radial arm saw: a circular bladed stationary power saw; the motor and blade are suspended from an arm above a table. The height and angle of the blade are adjustable. Primarily used for cross and angle cutting, this versatile saw can be used for ripping and trim molding as well.

Rail: a top or bottom framing member of a flat.

Raked stage: a stage that is higher at the back than the front.

Ratchet winch: a device used for hoisting that consists of a crank attached to a drum. One end of a rope or cable is attached to the drum, the other end to the load; by turning the crank the load can be moved; a ratchet gear prevents the drum from spinning backward.

Rat-tail file: a file with a circular cross-sectional configuration; depending on surface finish it can be used for smoothing wood; metal, or plastic; also known as a round file.

Rear elevations: Scale mechanical drawings that show the back of flats depicted on front elevations.

Rear projection screen: translucent projection material designed to transmit the image through the projection surface; the projector is placed in back of the screen.

Related colors: colors that are adjacent to each other on the color wheel.

Representational design: a style in which the portrayed elements represent some recognizable object, such as a room, a forest, or a street corner.

Resistance: the opposition to electron flow within a conductor, measured in ohms; the amount of resistance is dependent in part on the chemical makeup of the material through which the electricity is flowing.

Respirator: a mask covering the nose and mouth that filters out gases as well as particulate matter; the type of filtering medium used determines the type of gases removed from the air.

Reverberate: to reflect in a series of echoes.

Reverberation: a multiple reflection of a sound that persists for some time after the original source has decayed.

Revolve: large, circular platform that pivots on its central axis; also called turntable.

Revolving stage: generally refers to a revolve that is built into the stage floor as part of a theatre's permanent equipment.

Rhythm: the orderly and logical interrelationship of successive parts in a composition.

Rigid caster: a caster that cannot swivel or rotate.

Rigid foot iron: bracing hardware; an L-shaped piece of metal, one leg attached to the bottom of the flat, the other secured to the floor with a stage screw that is inserted through the ring at the end of the leg.

Rip bar: tool similar to a crowbar, but the nail-removing claws have more curl for better leverage.

Rip hammer: a hammer with two relatively straight claws projecting from the back of its head that can be used for prying or ripping apart previously nailed wood; used for driving nails.

Rip saw: a handsaw with an approximately twenty-six-inch blade whose chisel-sharpened teeth bend outward so the kerf is wider than the blade; designed to cut parallel with the grain of the wood. Rip saws have fewer teeth per inch than a crosscut saw.

Riser: the vertical face of a stair unit.

RMS wattage rating: a system (root-mean-square) providing an accurate picture of the energy dissipation characteristics of sound equipment.

Rods: nerve cells in the retina that are sensitive to faint light.

Rope set: a counterbalanced flying system in which ropes are used to fly the scenery. Sandbags are tied to the offstage end of the ropes to counterbalance the weight of the scenery.

Rough finish: a pebble-grained texture achieved by cold-pressing paper with a textured roller or by other techniques; suitable for painted and pastel renderings having little intricate detail; can be worked with other media as well.

Roundel: a glass color medium for use with striplights; frequently has diffusing properties.

Round file: see rat-tail file.

Round-head wood screw: screw with a head that has a flat underside and a rounded upper surface; used when having the top of the screw flush with the surface of the work is not desirable, as when attaching thin metal or fabric to a wood frame.

Router: a portable, hand-held power tool that uses a chisel-like rotating bit (25,000 RPM) to shape or carve the surface or edge of the piece of wood; primarily used for shaping decorative moldings and trim pieces.

RTV (room temperature vulcanizing) silicone rubber: a compound used to make flexible molds.

Running: controlling or operating some aspect of production.

Running block: a block and tackle system that provides a 2:1 mechanical advantage.

Running crew: those responsible for operating lighting equipment and shifting scenery and props during rehearsals and performances.

S

Saber saw: a portable power saw with a reciprocating blade; used for making curvilinear cuts in wood and plastic.

Sandpaper: paper whose surface has been coated with abrasive grit; used for smoothing wood and plastic.

Satin: a stiff, heavy fabric with a smooth, shiny finish on the front and a dull finish on the back; if patterned, the design is usually printed on rather than woven in; used for making costumes, upholstery, and decorative drapery.

Saturated polyester: a plastic used to form the fiber from which polyester fabrics such as Dacron are made; also used to form films such as Mylar.

Saturation: the relative purity of a particular hue.

Scaenae frons: an elaborately decorated facade or wall that was located at the rear of the stage in the Roman theatre. Its historical antecedent was the skene of the Greek theatre.

Scarf joint: two boards joined lengthwise by making a shallow angle cut approximately 18 inches long in the face of each board; the joint is secured by gluing and screwing or bolting.

Scene shop foreman: person responsible for supervising the crews who build and rig the scenery and some of the larger props.

Scenic artist: person responsible for the painting of the scenery and properties.

Scenic designer: person responsible for the design and function of the scenery and properties.

Scenic projector: a high-wattage instrument used for projecting large-format slides or moving images.

Scoop: see ellipsoidal reflector floodlight.

Score: to cut partially through.

Scratch awl: see scribe.

Screwdriver: a tool for inserting or driving screws; the standard screwdriver has a narrow blade for work with standard screws; the Phillips-head screwdriver has a four-flanged tip that matches the crossed slots of the Phillips-head screw.

Screw nail: nail with a threaded shaft that rotates as it is driven into wood; used for jobs that require greater holding power.

Scribe: a sharp metal tool used to mark wood, metal, and plastic; also called a scratch awl.

Scrim: a drop made from translucent or transparent material.

Scumbling: a blending of paints of several hues or values to create the appearance of texture; done with brushes.

Secondary colors: the result of mixing two primary colors.

Secrets: the name used to describe the stage machinery in medieval times.

Sectional: a drawing, usually in scale, of an object that shows what it would look like if cut straight through at a given plane.

Sectional angle: the angle of intersection between the axis of the cone of light emitted by an instrument and the working height—usually the height of an average actor's face (about five feet, six inches)—of the lighting areas.

Set line: in drafting, a leader line that extends, parallel with the proscenium arch, across the farthest downstage point(s) of the set.

Set prop: a large, movable item, not built into the set, that is used in some way by an actor, such as a sofa, floor lamp, table, and so forth.

Shade: a color of low value; usually created by mixing one or more hues with black.

Sharkstooth scrim: an open-weave material used to make transparent scrims.

Sheer: a thin gauze curtain that hangs across the opening of a window to soften the sunlight and obscure the view into a room.

Sheet-metal screw: a pan-head or hex-head screw used for joining sheets of metal.

Sheet stock: a generic term that applies to lumber products sold in sheet form, such as plywood, upson board, and Masonite.

Shell: the basic form of a costume, basted or pinned together that covers the torso, arms, and legs.

Shellac: a generally clear glossy coating made of resinous material (lac—the secretions of certain scale insects) suspended in wood alcohol; also known as spirit varnish.

Shift: to change the position of the scenery, props, or stage equipment.

Shift rehearsal: a rehearsal, without actors, where the director, scenic designer, technical director, and stage manager work with the scenery and prop crews to perfect the choreography and timing of all scenic and prop shifts.

S hook: an S-shaped piece of steel strap used to hold stiffening battens on the back of wall units that are made up of two or more flats; also called a latch keeper.

Show portal: a false proscenium that visually supports the style and color palette of a particular production.

Shutter: a lever-actuated device used to control the height of the top and bottom edges of a followspot beam; also called a chopper.

Shuttle stage: a long narrow wagon that moves back and forth across the stage, like a shuttle in a loom. Used for shifting scenery.

Sight line: a sighting extending from any seat in the house to any position on stage.

Sight-line drawing: a scale drawing (plan and section views) of sightings that extend from the extreme seats (usually the outside seats on the front and last rows of the auditorium) to any position on the stage; used to determine how much of the stage and backstage will be visible from specific auditorium seats.

Silhouette: the general outline of form; frequently used to refer to the shape of a garment, set, or prop. The quality and character of the line determines the evocative characteristics of the resultant form. Also known as a profile or cutout line.

Sill iron: a strap of mild steel attached to the bottom of a door flat to brace it where the rail has been cut out.

Single-hand welding: a technique in which one hand holds the welding handle and the other hand is not used.

Single whip: a block and tackle configuration that changes the direction of travel of the line but provides no mechanical advantage.

Size coat: a paint coat used to shrink previously unpainted scenic fabric and to fill the weave of the fabric.

Size water: a mixture of approximately one cup of hot animal glue and one tablespoon of Lysol (or one cup of white glue) per gallon of warm water; the amount of binder in the size water is dependent on the weight of the pigments being used.

Skene: originally a wall or facade to hide backstage action in Greek theatres. By the end of the fifth century B.C. the wall had evolved into a two-story building.

Skid: a low-profile substitute for a wagon; usually a piece of three-quarter-inch plywood on which some small scenic element is placed.

Skin: a top or bottom plywood covering for a platform.

Sky drop: a large drop made to be hung flat, without fullness; used to simulate the sky.

Sky tab: synonym for sky drop.

Slide plane aperture: the point in a projection system where a slide or other effect is placed.

Slide projector: a reasonably high output instrument capable of projecting standard 35mm slides.

Slip-joint pliers: common pliers with an adjustable pivot point that provides two ranges of jaw openings; used for clamping, gripping, bending, and cutting light wire.

Slipstage: a stage wagon large enough to hold an entire set.

Sloper: a muslin mock-up of a costume.

Smooth base coat: a base coat that has no texture.

Smoothing plane: a relatively large, heavy plane with a blade angle of approximately twenty-five to thirty degrees; used to smooth parallel with the grain of wood.

Socket set and ratchet handle: sockets are cylindrical wrenches used with a ratchet handle; the reversible ratchet handle allows one to tighten or loosen nuts without removing the socket from the nut; used to tighten or loosen nuts and bolts in confined spaces or where other wrenches might not fit.

Solder: a metal alloy made of lead and tin.

Soldering: the process of forming a low-strength bond in metal by flowing a molten metal over a joint area.

Soldering gun: a quick-heating, trigger-activated soldering iron that physically resembles a pistol.

Soldering iron: a device to heat solder and the item to be soldered to the point where a good bond can be made.

Soldering pencil: a low-wattage soldering iron.

Sole: the bottom plate of a plane, with a slot through which the tip of the blade projects.

Sound crew: those who record and edit sound and who set up and run any sound equipment during the production.

Sound designer: person responsible for the design, recording, and playback of all music and sound effects used in a production.

Sound mixer: an electronic device used to adjust the loudness and tone levels of several sources, such as microphones and tape decks.

Sound plot: a list describing each sound cue in the production.

Sound reinforcement system: the amplification of sound coming from the stage.

Source: the origin of electrical potential, such as a battery or 120 volt wall outlet.

Source light: the apparent source of light that is illuminating a scene or object.

Spade bits: see wood bits.

Spattering: the process of applying small drops of paint to a surface; done by spraying paint with a garden sprayer or slapping a lightly charged brush against the heel of one's hand to throw paint drops at the scenery.

Specifications: clarifying notes that explain the building materials, textures, or special effects to be used in a design or other project.

Spectrometer: a device for measuring specific wavelengths of light.

Spidering: running a cable directly from the dimmer to the instrument; also known as direct cabling.

Spindle chuck: a device used to hold wood in a lathe.

Spine: the relative stiffness of brush bristles; good watercolor bristles will flex easily but will also have enough spine to remain erect when fully saturated with paint.

Spirit: the manner and style in which a play is presented to the audience.

Spoke shave: a small plane with a wide, narrow, slightly rounded sole and a steeply angled (approximately thirty to thirty-five degrees) blade; it is pulled rather than pushed across the surface of the wood; used to soften or round sharp edges rather than to smooth flat surfaces.

Spray cone: the shape or pattern of paint emitted from the nozzle of a spray gun.

Spray gun: a pistol-like device that shoots out a cone of paint.

Stage: the area where the action of the play takes place.

Stage brace: an adjustable wooden or aluminum pole that is attached to a brace cleat on the back of a flat to hold it vertical.

Stage business: a specific action, also known as a "bit," performed by an actor during the play.

Stage circuit: an electrical circuit terminating on one end in a female receptacle in the vicinity of the stage. The other end is connected to a dimmer or a patch panel. Synonymous with dimmer circuit when it terminates at a dimmer.

Stage crew: those who shift the sets and, sometimes, props during rehearsals and performances.

Stage house: the physical structure enclosing the area above the stage and wings.

Stage manager: person who assists the director during rehearsals and manages all backstage activity once the play has opened.

Stage screw: bracing hardware; a coarse-threaded, large, hand-driven screw used to anchor a foot iron or the foot of a stage brace to the stage floor; leaves ragged holes in the stage floor.

Standard parallel: a platform made of a folding framework of nonvariable height; the top is removable and the frame folds like a giant parallelogram for storage.

Staple gun: a tool with a spring-driven piston used to drive staples; used in upholstery, in attaching muslin to flat, and so forth.

Staples: U-shaped fasteners sharpened at both ends; used to attach wire, rope, cording, chicken wire, screening, and similar materials to supporting wooden frames.

Starter hole: a small hole bored into a piece of wood to hold the tip of a screw or drill bit; also called a pilot hole.

Stencil brush: a relatively short, squat brush with a circular pattern of short, stiff bristles; the bristles are pressed onto, rather than stroked across, the work, to prevent the paint from bleeding under the edges of the stencil.

Stencil paper: stiff, water-resistant paper used for making stencils.

Step-down transformer: a transformer whose output voltage is lower than its input voltage.

Step lens: a plano-convex lens with the glass on the plano side cut away in steps that are parallel with the plano face.

Step-up transformer: a transformer whose output voltage is higher than its input voltage.

Stereo: two distinct sound channels; a stereo system is composed of two discrete monaural systems.

Stiffening batten: a length of 1 × 3 attached to a multiflat wall unit to keep it from wiggling.

Stile: the vertical side members of a flat.

Stippling: a texturing technique, similar in appearance to spattering, but leaves a heavier texture; stippling is done by touching a sponge, feather duster, or ends of a brush to the surface of the work.

Stitcher: one who sews costumes together.

Stock: regularly sized lumber that can be purchased in a lumber yard.

Stock furniture: furniture items owned by the producing organization and held in storage until they are needed for a production.

Stock set: scenery designed to visually support a generalized location (garden, city street, palace, interior) rather than a specific one.

Stop block: a small piece of scrap wood attached to the stile of a flat to prevent flats from slipping past each other when lashed together in an inside corner configuration.

Stop cleat: metal tabs used to prevent flats from slipping past each other when they are being lashed in an outside corner configuration.

Stove bolts: bolts smaller than carriage or machine bolts and with threads on the entire length of the shaft; used for attaching stage hardware, hinges, and similar items that require greater fastening strength than screws.

Stovepipe wire: soft iron wire approximately one-sixteenth of an inch in diameter and generally black; very flexible but has little tensile strength; used for tying or wiring things together; is not strong enough to be used for flying scenery.

Straight edge: a thin piece of wood, usually four to six feet long, with a handle attached in the center; used as a guide while painting straight lines.

Straps: rectangular strips of quarter-inch plywood used to reinforce butt joints on the interior support elements (toggle bars, diagonal braces) of flats; substitute for keystones.

Stream-of-consciousness questioning: asking whatever relevant questions pop into your mind in the course of a discussion.

Striplight: a long, narrow troughlike instrument with three or four circuits controlling the individual lamps; each circuit is normally equipped with a separate color; used for blending and creating color washes; also known as an x-ray.

Style: specific compositional characteristics that distinguish the appearance of one type of design from another; e.g., realism, expressionism, surrealism, and so forth.

Subtractive color mixing: the selective absorption of light by a filter or pigment.

Surform blade: a thin, disposable strip of spring steel honeycombed with sharpened protrusions projecting from its surface; the serrated blade face doesn't leave a smooth surface, so the wood generally has to be smoothed with sandpaper.

Surform tools: tools that use the Surform blade—planes, files, routing bits, and gouges.

Sweep: a wooden curvilinear form frequently used to outline an arch or irregular form in door and window flat openings.

Swivel caster: a caster that swivels or rotates around a vertical axis; the bearing plate should have a ball-bearing swivel.

Symmetrical balance: mirror-image balance; objects on the left side of a composition are identical in form and arrangement with objects on the right.

Synthesizer: a musical instrument that creates sound electronically; can be used to create a close facsimile of instrumental, vocal, or natural tones.

T

Table saw: a circular bladed stationary power saw; the blade projects upward from the underside of a table; the height and angle of the blade are adjustable; used to rip lumber, plywood, and other sheet goods.

Tack hammer: a lightweight hammer with a small magnetized head for inserting tacks and a large face for seating them; used only with tacks.

Tap and die: tools used to cut threads on pipe and rod stock; the tap is used to cut internal threads; the die cuts external threads.

Tape deck: a magnetic tape transport mechanism used to record an electrical signal on magnetic tape; also used to play back that signal; it does not contain a playback amplifier or speaker.

Tape measure: a retractable, flexible metal rule housed in a plastic or metal case; used for measuring in general stage work.

Tape recorder: a magnetic tape transport mechanism used to record and playback an electrical signal on magnetic tape; it has a built-in playback amplifier and speaker(s).

Teaser: a short, horizontal drape used for masking the flies. Synonym for *border*.

Technical director: person responsible for supervising the construction, mounting, rigging, and shifting of the scenery and properties.

Technical production: all organizational and procedural aspects of the construction, painting, and operation of scenery and properties.

Technical rehearsals: run throughs in which the sets, lights, props, and sound are integrated into the action of the play.

Tenon: a square tab projecting from a piece of stock; used in conjunction with a mortise to make a mortise and tenon joint.

Texture: the relative roughness or smoothness of the finish of an object.

Theatrical gauze: a fine mesh weave, similar to cheesecloth, but the threads are thicker and the weave is slightly tighter; 72 inches wide; used for apparition effects and applications similar to sharkstooth scrim.

Theatron: the steeply raked seating area for the audience in a Greek theatre.

Theme: the repetitive use of similar elements to create a pattern or design.

Throw distance: the distance the light travels from its hanging position to the center of its focus area.

Thrust stage: a stage projecting into, and surrounded on three sides by, the audience.

Thumbnail sketch: a small, quickly drawn rough sketch, usually done in pencil, that shows the major outline, character, and feeling of an object but doesn't show much detail.

Tie-off cleats: special cleats used in pairs approximately thirty inches above stage level to tie off the line after the flats have been lashed together.

Ties: strips of material (usually 36-inch pieces of half-inch wide cotton tape, or 36-inch shoestrings) used for tying stage drapes to battens.

Tilt: to rotate an object about its horizontal axis.

Timbre: the distinctive quality of a sound that distinguishes one voice, musical instrument, or sound from another of the same pitch and intensity.

Tin snips: scissorlike tools used for cutting thin metal.

Tint: a color of high value; usually created by mixing one or more hues with white.

Tip jack: two (or more) large interconnected jacks that are fitted with swivel casters; normally used for moving wall units.

Toggle bar: an interior horizontal framing

member of a flat.

Tone: (1) a color of middle value achieved by mixing one or more hues with black and white. (2) A generic term referring to the intensity of the component frequencies contained in any particular sound.

Tormentor: the vertical flats that form the side elements of the false proscenium.

Toxic: poisonous.

Transducer: a device that converts energy from one state into another, such as a microphone or loudspeaker.

Transformer: a device that changes voltage in an electrical system.

Travel: to move horizontally relative to the stage floor, as with a drape that opens in the middle and is pulled to the sides.

Traveler: any drapery that moves or opens horizontally; generally, travelers are composed of two sections of stage drapes covering the full width of the proscenium; the sections split in the middle, and each section retracts in an offstage direction.

Tread: the horizontal surface of a stair unit—the part on which you walk.

Trick line: see monofilament line.

Tri square: a small, rigid, hand square with a steel blade and steel, composition, or wooden handle; used as a guide for marking ninety-degree angles across narrow (under six inches) materials.

Truss: an engineered beam in which a downward force at any point on its top will be distributed over its full width by a series of interlocking triangles that channel and redirect the downward force into a horizontal force.

"Tubed" building adhesive: an adhesive product, such as Liquid Nails, packaged in a caulking tube and designed to be dispensed with a caulking gun.

Tubing cutter: a tool used for making clean right-angle cuts on steel and nonferrous metal tubing one-half inch and smaller.

Tumbler: a thin (three-fourths inch thick by one inch wide) piece of stock used as a spacer when three or more flats are going to be booked.

Turntable: see revolve.

Tutu: the short, stiff skirt frequently worn by ballerinas.

Tweed: a rough-surfaced woolen fabric in plain, twill, or herringbone weave of two or more shades of the same color; used for men's and women's suits and trousers.

Tweeter: a high-frequency speaker generally designed to reproduce from approximately 1000 to 20,000 Hz.

Twill: a weaving pattern that results in parallel diagonal lines or ribs; a flat-surfaced, durable, relatively heavy cotton fabric used for making dresses, men's suits, and work clothes.

Twist drill bits: drill bits made of mild steel, filed to a point, with spiral indentations in the shaft to carry away material being removed from the hole; used for drilling holes of approximately one-sixty-fourth to one-half inch in diameter in wood, plastic, mild to medium steel, and nonferrous metals.

Two-fer: an electrical "Y" that has female receptacles at the top of the "Y" and a male plug at the bottom leg of the "Y"; used to connect two instruments to the same circuit.

Two-handed welding: a technique in which the torch or welding handle is held in one hand and the filler rod in the other.

U

Unbalanced line: a sound cable in which a single insulated conductor is wrapped in a braided or foil shield.

Unbleached muslin: a cotton fabric commonly used to cover flats; available in a variety of widths from 72 inches to 33 feet; for scenic construction purposes it should have a thread count of 128 or 140 threads per inch.

Undercut: an indentation in a form that leaves an overhang or concave profile, such as the nostrils on a mask of a face.

Unit set: a single set in which all of the play's locations are always visible and the audience's attention is usually shifted by alternately lighting various parts of the set.

Unsaturated polyester: a liquid plastic generally used as a casting resin and as the bonding agent to create the multipurpose material known by the trade name Fiberglas.

Upson board: a sheet stock composed of a paper pulp and binder compressed into four-by-eight-foot sheets.

Urethane: a class of plastics that have a variety of formulations: flexible foam, rigid foam, and liquid casting resin. Because of toxic fumes emitted when working urethane foams, their use is not recommended.

Utility knife: a metal handle with a usually retractable replaceable blade; used for a variety of jobs including cutting cardboard and trimming fabric from the edges of flats; also called a matte knife.

V

Vacuforming: the process of shaping heated plastic, usually high-impact polystyrene, around a mold through the use of vacuum pressure.

Valance: a horizontal element at the top of a drapery arrangement that covers the curtain rod.

Valence shell: the outermost plane of orbiting electrons in the structure of an atom.

Value: the relative lightness or darkness of an object.

Vanishing point: the point on the horizon to which a set of parallel lines recedes.

Varnish: a transparent coating made of synthetic or natural resinous materials suspended in an oil (oil varnish), alcohol (spirit varnish), or synthetic (polyurethane, vinyl acrylic) vehicle.

Vehicle: the liquid medium—water, oil, lacquer, and the like—in which pigments, fillers, and binders are suspended to create a paint mixture; after the paint is applied, the vehicle evaporates.

Velour: a thick, heavy material with a deep pile; generally made of cotton or cotton/nylon blends; heavier weights are used for upholstery and draperies; lighter weights can be used in costuming.

Velum: an awning covering the cavea (auditorium) of a Roman theatre. Also known as a velarium.

Velvet: a rich, lustrous material with a soft, thick pile; frequently made of rayon with a cotton or cotton blend backing; used in dresses, coats, upholstery, and draperies.

Velveteen: fabric possessing the same general characteristics as velour but much lighter (six to eight ounces); used in upholstery and costumes.

Vinyl acrylic concentrates: highly saturated pigments with a vinyl acrylic binder.

Vinyl acrylic paint: paint made with a vinyl acrylic binder; in scene painting, thinned vinyl acrylic concentrates (two parts water to one part concentrate) are mixed with an opaque white base to create tints and are mixed with a transparent base for fully saturated hues; after curing for twenty-four hours the paint is highly water resistant; can be thinned with up to ten parts of water depending on particular application.

Void: an unfilled, empty space.

Volatility: in computers, loss of electronic data when a computer loses its power supply.

Volt: the unit of measurement of electrical potential.

W

Wafer board: a sheet stock composed of large chips of wood mixed with a binder and compressed into four-by-eight-foot sheets; stronger and cheaper than plywood; can be used for the same purposes as plywood.

Wall pocket: a connecting box similar to a floor pocket but mounted so that its face is flush with a wall.

Warp: the vertical threads in a fabric.

Wash: the covering of a relatively large area with a smooth covering of paint. A smooth wash consists of only one color; a blended wash is created by smoothly segueing from one color to another.

Watch tackle: a block and tackle system that provides a 3:1 mechanical advantage.

Weft: the horizontal threads in a fabric.

Welding: the process of making a high-strength bond in metal by heating the parts to be joined to their melting points and allowing the parts to become fused together.

Welding rod: a rod, usually coated with flux, that serves as the positive electrode in arc welding.

Wheat paste: a mixture of unrefined wheat flour and water; used for attaching dutchmen and similar low-strength gluing.

White glue: commonly known by the trade name Elmer's Glue-All, white glue is a casein or milk-based glue used extensively in scenic and property construction.

White model: see functional model.

Whiting: a white powder extender, basically low-grade chalk, used to increase the covering power of dry pigment and binder paint.

Wigmaker: one who makes, styles, and arranges wigs.

Winch-driven system: a system that uses a motorized or handpowered winch to move a cable; frequently used to move wagons or skids across the stage or to turn small revolves.

Wings: (1) tall cloth-covered frames or narrow unframed drops that are placed on either side of the stage, parallel with the proscenium arch, to prevent the audience from seeing backstage. In the Restoration theatre, wings were usually painted to match the scene on the upstage drop. (2) The off-stage space adjacent to the stage in a proscenium arch theatre.

Wire-crimping tool: specialty pliers whose jaws are designed to pressure-clamp solderless connectors to electrical wire.

Wireless microphone: a microphone system that uses a short-range FM radio transmitter and receiver instead of a cable to send the signal from the microphone to the mixer.

Wire nails: small finish or box nails with very slender shafts; used for attaching delicate decorative moldings or panels to larger scenic elements.

Wire strippers: specialty pliers used for removing insulation from electrical wires.

Wood bits: paddle-shaped bits primarily for use in drilling wood, although they can be used in some plastics; must be used in a power drill; also known as spade bits.

Wood chisel: a steel blade sharpened at a thirty-degree angle; used for gouging, paring, or smoothing wood.

Wood file: a file with medium-sized teeth; can be flat on both faces, flat on one face and curved on the other, or round; used for smoothing wood and plastic.

Wood rasp: an extremely course-toothed file; usually has one flat and one rounded face; used for rough shaping of wood.

Woofer: a low-frequency speaker with a frequency range from approximately 20 to 150–250 Hz.

Work: the object on which work is being performed.

Working sectional: a drawing showing the sectional angle for a lighting instrument; used to determine its trim height; not to be confused with a lighting sectional.

Work light: a lighting fixture, frequently a scoop, PAR, or other wide-field-angle instrument, hung over the stage to facilitate work.

Worsted: a tightly woven, smooth-surfaced fabric of wool or wool blend; used for men's and women's suits and trousers.

Wrecking bars: generic name for the class of metal tools used to pry wood apart and remove nails.

X

X-ray: see striplight.

Z

Zoom ellipse: an ellipsoidal reflector spotlight with movable lenses that allow the focal length and beam-edge sharpness to be varied.

SELECTED REFERENCES

Acoustics and Architecture

Beranek, Leo L. *Music, Acoustics and Architecture.* Robert E. Krieger Publishing, 1979.

Burris-Meyer, Harold, and Edward C. Cole. *Theatres and Auditoriums.* Reinhold, 1949.

Burris-Meyer, Harold, and Lewis Goodfriend. *Acoustics for the Architect.* Reinhold, 1957.

Mullin, Donald C. *The Development of the Playhouse.* University of California Press, 1970.

Scenic/Property Design and Construction

Arnold, Richard L. *Scene Technology.* Prentice-Hall, 1985.

Bay, Howard. *Stage Design.* Drama Book Specialists, 1974.

Baldwin, John. *Contemporary Sculpture Techniques: Welded Metal and Fiberglass.* Reinhold Publishing, 1967.

Bellman, Willard F. *Scene Design, Stage Lighting, Sound, Costume and Makeup.* Harper & Row, 1983.

Birren, Faber. *Creative Color.* Van Nostrand, Reinhold, 1961.

Bowman, Ned. *Handbook of Technical Practices for the Performing Arts.* Scenographic Media, 1975.

Bryson, Nicholas L. *Thermoplastic Scenery for the Theatre, Vol. 1: Vacuum Forming.* Drama Book Specialists, 1972.

Burris-Meyer, Harold, and Edward C. Cole. *Scenery for the Theatre.* Little, Brown, 1972.

Gillette, A. S., and J. Michael Gillette. *Stage Scenery.* Harper & Row, 1981.

Gottshall, Franklin H. *How to Design and Construct Period Furniture.* Reprinted by Bonanza Books, original copyright 1937.

Kenton, Warren. *Stage Properties and How to Make Them.* Drama Book Specialists, 1978.

Meyers, L. Donald. *The Furniture Lover's Book: Finding, Fixing, Finishing.* Sunrise Book, E. P. Dutton, 1977.

Neuman, Jay Hartley, and Lee Scott. *Plastics for the Craftsman.* Crown Publishers, 1972.

Parker, W. Oren, Harvey K. Smith, and R. Craig Wolf. *Scene Design and Stage Lighting.* Holt, Rinehart and Winston, 1985.

Payne, Darwin Reid. *Theory and Craft of the Scenographic Model, rev. ed.* Southern Illinois University Press, 1985.

Pecktal, Lynn. *Designing and Painting for the Theatre.* Holt, Rinehart and Winston, 1975.

Taylor, Douglas C. *Metalworking for the Designer and Technician.* Drama Book Specialists, 1979.

Lighting Design and Production

Bellman, Willard F. *Lighting the Stage: Art and Practice.* Harper & Row, 1974.

Gillette, J. Michael. *Designing with Light.* Mayfield Publishing, 1978.

Parker, W. Oren, Harvey K. Smith, and R. Craig Wolf. *Scene Design and Stage Lighting.* Holt, Rinehart and Winston, 1985.

Pilbrow, Richard. *Stage Lighting.* Drama Book Publishing, 1979.

Rosenthal, Jean, and Lael Wertenbaker. *The Magic of Light.* Little, Brown, 1972.

Warfel, William, and Walter A. Klappert. *Color Science for Lighting.* Yale University Press, 1981.

Costume/Makeup Design and Production

Barton, Lucy. *Historic Costume for the Stage.* Baker's Plays, 1963.

Corey, Irene. *The Mask of Reality.* Anchorage Press, 1968.

Corson, Richard. *Stage Makeup.* Prentice-Hall, 1986.

Ingham, Rosemary, and Elizabeth Covey. *The Costumer's Handbook: How to Make All Kinds of Costumes.* Prentice-Hall, 1980.

Prisk, Berneice. *Stage Costume Handbook.* Greenwood, 1979.

Russell, Douglas. *Costume History and Style.* Prentice-Hall, 1983.

Russell, Douglas. *Stage Costume Design: Theory, Technique and Style.* Prentice-Hall, 1985.

Waugh, Norah. *The Cut of Men's Clothes 1600–1900.* Theatre Arts Books, 1964.

Waugh, Norah. *The Cut of Women's Clothes 1600–1930.* Theatre Arts Books, 1968.

Sound Design and Production

Collison, David. *Stage Sound.* Drama Book Publishers, 1982.

Heil, Bob. *Practical Guide for Concert Sound.* Melco Publishing, 1976.

Drafting for the Theatre

Morgan, Harry. *Perspective Drawing for the Theatre.* Drama Book Specialists, 1979.

Sweet, Harvey, and Deborah M. Dryden. *Graphics for the Performing Arts.* Allyn, 1985.

Warfel, William. *Handbook of Stage Lighting Graphics.* Drama Book Specialists, 1974.

Periodicals

Lighting Dimensions
Theatre Crafts
Theatre Design and Technology

Reinforcement, sound, 16, 387, 396
Related colors, 232
Release agents, 257–258
Renaissance theatre, 39–40
Rendering techniques, 465–474
Renderings, 105–106
Representational design, 93
Research, 110, 357, 392
    background, 21, 98–99, 354, 357
    conceptual, 22, 110, 357, 392
Resin
    casting, 150
    polyester, 224, 226, 243, 261
Resistance, 296, 298
Resistance dimmers, 324, 325
Respirator, 150, 171, 260
Restoration theatre, 42–43, 93
Retina, 86
Reupholstery, 253–254
Reverberation, 390, 391
Reverberation time, 51
Revolve, 52, 213
Rhythm, 73–74, 81
Ribbon microphone, 410
Rigid foot iron, 166, 167
Rigid joining, 196
Rigid steel platforms, 201
Rigid wooden platforms, 200, 201
Ringers, 94
Rip bar, 129
Rip hammer, 118
Rip saw, 119, 120
Risers, 209, 210
RMS wattage rating, 401
Rocks, stage, 215, 217
Rods, 86
Rollers, 226
Roman theatre, 35–36
Romance Languages, 95
Romeo and Juliet, 78, 356
Rope, 169–170
Rope set, 53–54
Roscolux colors, 277
Rough finish, 469
Round-head wood screw, 156
Roundels, 319
Router, 140, 141
RTV silicon rubber, 257, 259
Ruch, Mark, 386–387
Running, 14
Running block, 57
Running crew, 15

S

S hook, 166, 167, 196
Saber saw, 134
Sable bristles, 466
Safety
    with counterweight systems, 56
    with dimmers, 326
    with electricity, 304
    fire, 64
    with flammable paints, 221
    with foam carving, 260

    with hammers, 118
    with lighting instruments, 322
    with power tools, 132, 134
    of ropes, 170
    in the scene shop, 178
    with tungsten-halogen lamps, 312
    with urethane plastics, 152
    in welding, 181
    with wood lathe, 262
Safety equipment, 171–172
Salt water dimmer, 325
Sandbags, 54
Sanders, 140, 141
Sandpaper, 128
Satin, 255
Saturable core dimmer, 325
Saturation, 86, 89, 90, 92
Saws, 119–120
    power, 132–134
Scaenae frons, 35, 39
Scaffolding nails, 154
Scale, 423, 440
    for detail drawings, 436
    for ground plans, 433, 435
Scale rule, 426
Scarf joint, 179
Scene painting, 219
    materials for, 219–228
    preparation for, 228–230
    techniques of, 230–240
Scene shop foreman, 14
Scenery
    budget for, 105
    construction of, 176–218
    portability of, 103
    soft, 198–200
    three-dimensional, 200–218
    two-dimensional, 186–200
Scenery shifts, 4
Scenic artist, 12
Scenic design, 12, 13, 28–30
    budgeting for, 105
    use of color in, 91–92
    considerations in, 96–105
    design process in, 110
    and lighting design, 103
    practical considerations in, 102–105
    rendering techniques for, 469–474
    rules in, 96
    texture in, 79
    visual presentations of, 105–114
    voids in, 80
Scenic designer, 12, 25, 26
Scenic models, 106–108
Scenic projectors, 343–345, 348
Schedules, 103, 105
Scheduling, 8–9, 103, 105
Scissors, 120
Scoop, 319
Scoring, 209
SCR dimmer, 326–327
Screens, projection, 346–348
Screw eyes, 161, 162
Screw heads, 155
Screw hook, 161, 162

Screw nail, 154
Screwdrivers, 128
    electric, 140, 141
Screws, 155–156
Scribe, 117
Scrim drops, 199, 200
Scrims, 64
Script, 2, 7, 11
    analysis of, 19–20
Scumbling, 235–236, 241
Seamer, master, 15
Season of year, 100, 354
Seating, 50, 65, 68
    evolution of, 43, 44
Secondary colors, 87
Secrets, 38
Section drawings, 285–288, 428
Sectional, 108
Sectional angle, 266, 286–287
Sectional drawings, 435–436
Select wood, 142
Selection, 25–26, 110, 357, 392
Selective focus, 264
Series circuit, 301
Series wiring, 420
Set, 12
Set construction. *See* Construction, scenic
Set line, 435
Set props, 247
Set square, 425
Setting, practicality of, 102–105
Sewing machines, 365
Shade, 86
Sharkstooth scrim, 64, 199
Sheers, 254
Sheet-metal screw, 156
Sheet stock, 145–148
Shell, 371
Shellac, 221, 224, 231
Shift rehearsal, 4
Shifting, 14, 174
Shoes, 374
    safety, 172
Short circuit, 297
Shutter, 320
Sight line, 111
Sight-line drawings, 111, 113, 114
Silhouette, 73, 78, 353
Silicon controlled rectifier (SCR)
    dimmer, 326–327
Silicon release agent, 258
Silicon rubber, 257, 259
Silk, 363
Sill iron, 192
Single-hand welding, 183
Sisal rope, 170
Size coat, 230–231
Size water, 220
Sizing, 230–231
Skene, 33, 35
Sketches, 105–106
Sketching, 469–470
Skids, 151, 214
Skins, 203, 205
Sky drop, 59, 62